Lecture Notes in Computer Science 4477

Commenced Publication in 1973
Founding and Former Series Editors:
Gerhard Goos, Juris Hartmanis, and Jan van Leeuwen

Joan Martí   José Miguel Benedí
Ana Maria Mendonça   Joan Serrat (Eds.)

Pattern Recognition and Image Analysis

Third Iberian Conference, IbPRIA 2007
Girona, Spain, June 6-8, 2007
Proceedings, Part I

 Springer

Volume Editors

Joan Martí
University of Girona
Campus Montilivi, s/n., 17071 Girona, Spain
E-mail: joanm@eia.udg.es

José Miguel Benedí
Polytechnical University of Valencia
Camino de Vera, s/n., 46022 Valencia, Spain
E-mail: jbenedi@dsic.upv.es

Ana Maria Mendonça
University of Porto
Rua Dr. Roberto Frias, s/n, 4200-465 Porto, Portugal
E-mail: amendon@fe.up.pt

Joan Serrat
Centre de Visió per Computador-UAB
Campus UAB, 08193 Belaterra, (Cerdanyola), Barcelona, Spain
E-mail: joan.serrat@cvc.uab.es

Library of Congress Control Number: 2007927717

CR Subject Classification (1998): I.4, I.5, I.7, I.2.7, I.2.10

LNCS Sublibrary: SL 6 – Image Processing, Computer Vision, Pattern Recognition, and Graphics

ISSN   0302-9743
ISBN-10   3-540-72846-5 Springer Berlin Heidelberg New York
ISBN-13   978-3-540-72846-7 Springer Berlin Heidelberg New York

Springer is a part of Springer Science+Business Media

springer.com

© Springer-Verlag Berlin Heidelberg 2007
Printed in Germany

Typesetting: Camera-ready by author, data conversion by Scientific Publishing Services, Chennai, India
Printed on acid-free paper   SPIN: 12070350   06/3180   5 4 3 2 1 0

Preface

We welcome you to the 3rd Iberian Conference on Pattern Recognition and Image Analysis (IbPRIA 2007), jointly promoted by AERFAI (Asociación Española de Reconocimiento de Formas y Análisis de Imágenes) and APRP (Associção Portuguesa de Reconhecimento de Padrões). This year, IbPRIA was held in Girona, Spain, June 6–8, 2007, and was hosted by the Institute of Informatics and Applications of the University of Girona. It followed the two successful previous editions hosted by the Universitat de les Illes Balears (2003) and the Institute for Systems and Robotics and the Geo-systems Center of the Instituto Superior Técnico (2005).

A record number of 328 full paper submissions from 27 countries were received. Each of these submissions was reviewed in a blind process by two reviewers. The review assignments were determined by the four General Chairs, and the final decisions were made after the Chairs meeting in Girona, giving an overall acceptance rate of 47.5%. Because of the limited size of the conference, we regret that some worthy papers were probably rejected.

In keeping with the IbPRIA tradition of having a single track of oral presentations, the number of oral papers remained in line with the previous IbPRIA editions, with a total of 48 papers. The number of poster papers was settled to 108.

We were also very honored to have as invited speakers such internationally recognized researchers as Chris Willians from the University of Edinburgh, UK, Michal Irani from The Weizmann Institute of Science, Israel and Andrew Davison from Imperial College London, UK.

For the first time, some relevant related events were scheduled in parallel to the IbPRIA main conference according to the Call for Tutorials and Workshops: Antonio Torralba from MIT, USA and Aleix Martínez from Ohio State University, USA taught relevant tutorials about object recognition and Statistical Pattern Recognition, respectively, while the "Supervised and Unsupervised Ensemble Methods and Their Applications" workshop and the first edition of the "Spanish Workshop on Biometrics" were successfully developed.

We would like to thank all the authors for submitting their papers and thus making these proceedings possible. We address special thanks to the members of the Program Committee and the additional reviewers for their great work which contributed to the high quality of these proceedings.

We are also grateful to the Local Organizing Committee for their substantial contribution of time and effort.

Finally, our thanks go to IAPR for support in sponsoring the Best Paper Prize at IbPRIA 2007.

The next edition of IbPRIA will be held in Portugal in 2009.

June 2007   Joan Martí
                                                    Ana Maria Mendonça
                                                    José Miguel Benedí
                                                    Joan Serrat

Organization

IbPRIA 2007 was organized by AERFAI (Asociación Española de Reconocimiento de Formas y Análisis de Imágenes) and APRP (Associação Portuguesa de Reconhecimento de Padrões), and as the local organizer of this edition, the Computer Vision and Robotics Group, Institute of Informatics and Applications, University of Girona (UdG).

General Conference Co-chairs

Joan Martí	University of Girona, Spain
José Miguel Benedí	Polytechnical University of Valencia, Spain
Ana Maria Mendonça	University of Porto, Portugal
Joan Serrat	Universitat Autònoma de Barcelona, Spain

Invited Speakers

Chris Williams	University of Edinburgh, UK
Michal Irani	The Weizmann Institute of Science, Israel
Andrew Davison	Imperial College London, UK

National Organizing Committee

Marc Carreras
Xavier Cufí
Jordi Freixenet
Rafael García
Xavier Lladó
Robert Martí
Marta Peracaula
Pere Ridao
Joaquim Salvi
Marcel Alofra
Elisabet Batlle
Anna Bosch
François Chung
Andrés El-Fakdi
Jordi Ferrer
Emili Hernández
Maryna Kudzinava
Arnau Oliver
Jordi Palau
Ricard Prados

Narcís Palomeras
David Raba
David Ribas
Miquel Villanueva

Program Committee

Lourdes Agapito	Queen Mary University of London, UK
Helder Araújo	University of Coimbra, Portugal
Hervé Bourlard	EPFL, Switzerland
Patrick Bouthemy	IRISA, France
Joachim Buhmann	ETH Zurich, Switzerland
Horst Bunke	University of Bern, Switzerland
Hans Burkhard	University of Freiburg, Germany
Francisco Casacuberta	Polytechnical University of Valencia, Spain
Vicent Caselles	Universitat Pompeu Fabra, Spain
Aurélio Campilho	University of Porto, Portugal
Luís Corte-Real	University of Porto, Portugal
Hervé Delinguette	INRIA, France
Pierre Dupont	Université catholique de Louvain, Belgium
Marcello Federico	ITC-irst Trento, Italy
Marco Ferreti	University of Pavia, Italy
Ana Fred	Technical University of Lisbon, Portugal
Andrew Gee	University of Cambridge, UK
Vito di Gesú	University of Palermo, Italy
Edwin R. Hancock	University of York, UK
Francisco Mario Hernández Tejera	Universidad de Las Palmas, Spain
Laurent Heutte	Université de Rouen, France
José Manuel Iñesta Quereda	Universidad de Alicante, Spain
Jorge Marques	Technical University of Lisbon, Portugal
Hermann Ney	University of Aachen, Germany
Wiro Niessen	University of Utrecht, The Netherlands
Francisco José Perales	Universitat de les Illes Balears, Spain
Nicolás Pérez de la Blanca	University of Granada, Spain
Fernando Pérez Cruz	Universidad Carlos III, Spain
Maria Petrou	Imperial College, UK
Pedro Pina	Technical University of Lisbon, Portugal
Armando Pinho	University of Aveiro, Portugal
Ioannis Pitas	University of Thessaloniki, Greece
Filiberto Pla	University Jaume I, Spain
Alberto Sanfeliu	Polytechnical University of Catalonia, Spain
Gabriella Sanniti di Baja	Istituto di Cibernetica CNR, Italy

Pierre Soille   Joint Research Centre, Italy
Karl Tombre   LORIA, France
M. Inés Torres   University of the Basque Country, Spain
Jordi Vitrià   Universitat Autònoma de Barcelona, Spain
Joachim Weickert   Saarland University, Germany
Reyer Zwiggelaar   University of Wales, Aberystwyth, UK

Reviewers

Maria José Abasolo   University of the Balearic Islands, Spain
Antonio Adán   Universidad de Castilla La Mancha, Spain
Francisco Jávier López Aligué   University of Extremadura, Spain
René Alquézar   UPC, Spain
Joachim Buhmann   ETH Zurich, Switzerland
Juan Carlos Amengual   UJI-LPI, Spain
Hans Burkhard   University of Freiburg, Germany
Ramon Baldrich   Computer Vision Center, Spain
Jorge Pereira Batista   ISR Coimbra, Portugal
Luis Baumela   UPM, Spain
Alexandre Bernardino   Instituto Superior Técnico, Portugal
Lilian Blot   University of East Anglia, UK
Imma Boada   University of Girona, Spain
Marcello Federico   ITC-irst Trento, Italy
Michael Breuss   Saarland University, Germany
Jaime Santos Cardoso   INESC Porto, Portugal
Modesto Castrillón   Universidad de Las Palmas de Gran Canaria,
                                     Spain
Miguel Velhote Correia   Instituto de Engenharia Biomédica, Portugal
Xevi Cufí   University of Girona, Spain
Jorge Alves da Silva   FEUB-INEB, Portugal
Hans du Buf   University of Algarve, Portugal
Óscar Deniz   Universidad de Las Palmas de Gran Canaria,
                                     Spain
Daniel Hernández-Sosa   Universidad de Las Palmas de Gran Canaria,
                                     Spain
Olga Duran   Imperial College, UK
Claudio Eccher   ITC-irst Trento, Italy
Arturo De la Escalera   Universidad Carlos III de Madrid, Spain
Miquel Feixas   Universitat de Girona, Spain
Francesc J. Ferri   Universitat de València, Spain
David Fofi   Le2i UMR CNRS 5158, France
Jordi Freixenet   University of Girona, Spain
Maria Frucci   Institute of Cybernetics "E. Caianiello", Italy
Cesare Furlanello   ITC-irst Trento, Italy
Miguel Ángel García   Universidad Autónoma de Madrid, Spain
Rafael García   University of Girona, Spain

Joao Silva Sequeira   Instituto Superior Técnico, Portugal
Margarida Silveira   Instituto Superior Técnico, Portugal
Joao Manuel R.S. Tavares Universidade do Porto, Portugal
Antonio Teixeira   Universidade de Aveiro, Portugal
Javier Traver   Universitat Jaume I, Spain
Maria Vanrell   Computer Vision Center, Spain
Javier Varona   Universitat de les Illes Balears, Spain
Martin Welk   Saarland University, Germany
Laurent Wendling   LORIA, France
Michele Zanin   ITC-irst Trento, Italy

Sponsoring Institutions

MEC (Ministerio de Educación y Ciencia, Spanish Government)
AGAUR (Agència de Gestió d'Ajuts Universitaris i de Recerca, Catalan
    Government)
IAPR (International Association for Pattern Recognition)
Vicerectorat de Recerca en Ciència i Tecnologia, Universitat de Girona

Table of Contents – Part I

Known Unknowns: Novelty Detection in Condition Monitoring......... 1
  John A. Quinn and Christopher K.I. Williams

Seeing the Invisible and Predicting the Unexpected.................. 7
  Michal Irani

Vision-Based SLAM in Real-Time 9
  Andrew J. Davison

Handwritten Symbol Recognition by a Boosted Blurred Shape Model
with Error Correction 13
  Alicia Fornés, Sergio Escalera, Josep LLadós, Gemma Sánchez,
  Petia Radeva, and Oriol Pujol

Bayesian Hyperspectral Image Segmentation with Discriminative Class
Learning.. 22
  Janete S. Borges, José M. Bioucas-Dias, and André R.S. Marçal

Comparison of Unsupervised Band Selection Methods for Hyperspectral
Imaging 30
  Adolfo Martínez-Usó, Filiberto Pla, Jose M. Sotoca, and
  Pedro García-Sevilla

Learning Mixture Models for Gender Classification Based on Facial
Surface Normals 39
  Jing Wu, W.A.P. Smith, and E.R. Hancock

Feature Selection Based on a New Formulation of the
Minimal-Redundancy-Maximal-Relevance Criterion 47
  Daniel Ponsa and Antonio López

Topological Histogram Reduction Towards Colour Segmentation 55
  Eduard Vazquez, Ramon Baldrich, Javier Vazquez, and
  Maria Vanrell

Dealing with Non-linearity in Shape Modelling of Articulated
Objects... 63
  Grégory Rogez, Jesús Martínez-del-Rincón, and Carlos Orrite

Human Motion Characterization Using Spatio-temporal Features....... 72
  Manuel J. Lucena, José Manuel Fuertes, and
  Nicolás Pérez de la Blanca

Fast Stochastic Context-Free Parsing: A Stochastic Version of the
Valiant Algorithm... 80
    José-Miguel Benedí and Joan-Andreu Sánchez

Supervised Segmentation Based on Texture Signatures Extracted in
the Frequency Domain... 89
    Antonella Di Lillo, Giovanni Motta, and James A. Storer

Analysis of Relevant Maxima in Distance Transform. An Application
to Fast Coarse Image Segmentation 97
    *Luis Antón-Canalís, Mario Hernández-Tejera, and
    Elena Sánchez-Nielsen*

Performance Analysis of Classifier Ensembles: Neural Networks *Versus*
Nearest Neighbor Rule.. 105
    R.M. Valdovinos and J.S. Sánchez

Robust Multiple-People Tracking Using Colour-Based Particle Filters ... 113
    Daniel Rowe, Ivan Huerta, Jordi González, and Juan J. Villanueva

Structure Restriction for Tracking Through Multiple Views and
Occlusions 121
    B. Martínez, A. Pérez, L. Ferraz, and X. Binefa

On the Detection of Regions-of-Interest in Dynamic Contrast-Enhanced
MRI 129
    David Raba, Marta Peracaula, Robert Martí, and Joan Martí

Dealing with the Perspective Distortion to Detect Overtaking Cars for
Driving Assistance 137
    S. Mota, E. Ros, J. Díaz, R. Agís, R. Rodriguez, and R. Carrillo

3D Reconstruction on MRI to Analyse Marbling and Fat Level in
Iberian Loin.. 145
    M.M. Ávila, M.L. Durán, T. Antequera, R. Palacios, and M. Luquero

Epiflow Based Stereo Fusion.................................... 153
    Hongsheng Zhang and Shahriar Negahdaripour

Automatic Segmentation of the Liver in CT Using Level Sets Without
Edges 161
    J.F. Garamendi, N. Malpica, J. Martel, and E. Schiavi

Spectral Modes of Facial Needle-Maps 169
    Roberto Fraile and Edwin R. Hancock

Classifiers for Vegetation and Forest Mapping with Low Resolution
Multiespectral Imagery 177
    *Marcos Ferreiro-Armán, Lourenço P.C. Bandeira,
    Julio Martín-Herrero, and Pedro Pina*

A Robust Audio Fingerprint's Based Identification Method............ 185
  Jérôme Lebossé, Luc Brun, and Jean-Claude Pailles

Development of a Methodology for Automated Crater Detection on
Planetary Images 193
  Lourenço P.C. Bandeira, José Saraiva, and Pedro Pina

Rao-Blackwellized Particle Filter for Human Appearance and Position
Tracking... 201
  *Jesús Martínez-del-Rincón, Carlos Orrite-Uruñuela, and
  Grégory Rogez*

Parameter System for Human Physiological Data Representation and
Analysis 209
  Olga Kurasova, Gintautas Dzemyda, and Alfonsas Vainoras

Face Recognition in Color Using Complex and Hypercomplex
Representations 217
  Mauricio Villegas and Roberto Paredes

A Semi-automatic Approach to Photo Identification of Wild
Elephants.. 225
  *Alessandro Ardovini, Luigi Cinque, Francesca Della Rocca, and
  Enver Sangineto*

Language Identification Based on Phone Decoding for Basque and
Spanish.. 233
  Víctor G. Guijarrubia and M. Inés Torres

Computer Assisted Transcription of Speech 241
  Luis Rodríguez, Francisco Casacuberta, and Enrique Vidal

Word Segments in Category-Based Language Models for Automatic
Speech Recognition 249
  Raquel Justo and M. Inés Torres

Part-of-Speech Tagging Based on Machine Translation Techniques...... 257
  Guillem Gascó i Mora and Joan Andreu Sánchez Peiró

Bilingual Text Classification 265
  Jorge Civera, Elsa Cubel, and Enrique Vidal

Robust Lane Lines Detection and Quantitative Assessment............ 274
  Antonio López, Joan Serrat, Cristina Cañero, and Felipe Lumbreras

Matrics, a Car License Plate Recognition System 282
  *Andrés Marzal, Juan Miguel Vilar, David Llorens,
  Vicente Palazón, and Javier Martín*

Automatic Labeling of Colonoscopy Video for Cancer Detection........ 290
*Fernando Vilariño, Gerard Lacey, Jiang Zhou, Hugh Mulcahy, and
Stephen Patchett*

Functional Pattern Recognition of 3D Laser Scanned Images of
Wood-Pulp Chips 298
Marcos López, José M. Matías, José A. Vilán, and Javier Taboada

Hardware Implementation of Moment Functions in a CMOS Retina:
Application to Pattern Recognition................................ 306
*Olivier Aubreton, Lew Fock Chong Lew Yan Voon,
Matthieu Nongaillard, Guy Cathebras, Cédric Lemaitre, and
Bernard Lamalle*

Decimation Estimation and Linear Model-Based Super-Resolution
Using Zoomed Observations 314
*Prakash P. Gajjar, Manjunath V. Joshi, Asim Banerjee, and
Suman Mitra*

Line Extraction from Mechanically Scanned Imaging Sonar............ 322
David Ribas, Pere Ridao, José Neira, and Juan Domingo Tardós

Road Signs Recognition by the Scale-Space Template Matching in the
Log-Polar Domain 330
Bogusław Cyganek

The Condition of Kernelizing an Algorithm and an Equivalence
Between Kernel Methods... 338
WenAn Chen and Hongbin Zhang

A Probabilistic Observation Model for Stereo Vision Systems:
Application to Particle Filter-Based Mapping and Localization 346
Francisco Angel Moreno, Jose Luis Blanco, and Javier Gonzalez

New Neighborhood Based Classification Rules for Metric Spaces and
Their Use in Ensemble Classification 354
Jose-Norberto Mazón, Luisa Micó, and Francisco Moreno-Seco

Classification of Voltage Sags Based on MPCA Models 362
Abbas Khosravi, Joaquim Melendez, and Joan Colomer

On-Line Handwriting Recognition System for Tamil Handwritten
Characters 370
Alejandro H. Toselli, Moisés Pastor, and Enrique Vidal

A New Type of Feature – Loose N-Gram Feature in Text
Categorization... 378
Xian Zhang and Xiaoyan Zhu

Variational Deconvolution of Multi-channel Images with Inequality
Constraints 386
    Martin Welk and James G. Nagy

HMM-Based Action Recognition Using Contour Histograms 394
    M. Ángeles Mendoza and Nicolás Pérez de la Blanca

Locating and Segmenting 3D Deformable Objects by Using Clusters of
Contour Fragments....................................... 402
    Manuel J. Marín-Jiménez, Nicolás Pérez de la Blanca, and
    José I. Gómez

Development of a Cascade Processing Method for Microarray Spot
Segmentation 410
    Antonis Daskalakis, Dionisis Cavouras, Panagiotis Bougioukos,
    Spiros Kostopoulos, Ioannis Kalatzis, George C. Kagadis, and
    George Nikiforidis

Haar Wavelets and Edge Orientation Histograms for On–Board
Pedestrian Detection 418
    David Gerónimo, Antonio López, Daniel Ponsa, and Angel D. Sappa

Face Recognition Using Principal Geodesic Analysis and Manifold
Learning 426
    Matthew P. Dickens, William A.P. Smith, Jing Wu, and
    Edwin R. Hancock

Optimized Associative Memories for Feature Selection 435
    Mario Aldape-Pérez, Cornelio Yáñez-Márquez, and
    Amadeo José Argüelles-Cruz

Automatic Construction of Fuzzy Rules for Modelling and Prediction
of the Central Nervous System.................................... 443
    Fernando Vázquez and Pilar Gómez

A Clustering Technique for Video Copy Detection.................... 451
    N. Guil, J.M. González-Linares, J.R. Cózar, and E.L. Zapata

Invariant Multi-scale Object Categorisation and Recognition 459
    João Rodrigues and J.M. Hans du Buf

Combination of N-grams and Stochastic Context-Free Grammars in an
Offline Handwritten Recognition System 467
    Verónica Romero, Vicente Alabau, and Jose Miguel Benedí

Phrase-Based Statistical Machine Translation Using Approximate
Matching 475
    Jesús Tomás, Jaime Lloret, and Francisco Casacuberta

Motion Segmentation from Feature Trajectories with Missing Data   483
  *Carme Juliá, Angel Sappa, Felipe Lumbreras, Joan Serrat, and
  Antonio López*

Segmentation of Rigid Motion from Non-rigid 2D Trajectories   491
  Alessio Del Bue, Xavier Lladó, and Lourdes Agapito

Hierarchical Eyelid and Face Tracking   499
  J. Orozco, J. Gonzàlez, I. Rius, and F.X. Roca

Automatic Learning of Conceptual Knowledge in Image Sequences for
Human Behavior Interpretation   507
  Pau Baiget, Carles Fernández, Xavier Roca, and Jordi Gonzàlez

A Comparative Study of Local Descriptors for Object Category
Recognition: SIFT vs HMAX   515
  *Plinio Moreno, Manuel J. Marín-Jiménez, Alexandre Bernardino,
  José Santos-Victor, and Nicolás Pérez de la Blanca*

Moment-Based Pattern Representation Using Shape and Grayscale
Features   523
  Mikhail Lange, Sergey Ganebnykh, and Andrey Lange

Parsimonious Kernel Fisher Discrimination   531
  Kitsuchart Pasupa, Robert F. Harrison, and Peter Willett

Explicit Modelling of Invariances in Bernoulli Mixtures for Binary
Images   539
  Verónica Romero, Adrià Giménez, and Alfons Juan

Computer Vision Approaches to Pedestrian Detection: Visible
Spectrum Survey   547
  David Gerónimo, Antonio López, and Angel D. Sappa

A Decision-Tree-Based Online Speaker Clustering   555
  Wei Wang, Ping Lv, QingWei Zhao, and YongHong Yan

Classification of Continuous Heart Sound Signals Using the Ergodic
Hidden Markov Model   563
  Yong-Joo Chung

A Protocol to Cipher Digital Images Based on Cat Maps and Cellular
Automata   571
  A. Martín del Rey, G. Rodríguez Sánchez, and A. de la Villa Cuenca

Perceptually-Based Functions for Coarseness Textural Feature
Representation   579
  *J. Chamorro-Martínez, E. Galán-Perales, B. Prados-Suárez, and
  J.M. Soto-Hidalgo*

Vehicle Trajectory Estimation Based on Monocular Vision   587
   Daniel Ponsa and Antonio López

A Neural Network Model for Image Change Detection Based on Fuzzy
Cognitive Maps   595
   *Gonzalo Pajares, Alfonso Sánchez-Beato, Jesús M. Cruz, and
   José J. Ruz*

Semiring Lattice Parsing Applied to CYK   603
   *Salvador España Boquera, Jorge Gorbe Moya, and
   Francisco Zamora Martínez*

Constrained Monocular Obstacle Perception with Just One Frame   611
   Lluís Pacheco, Xavier Cufí, and Javi Cobos

Author Index   621

Known Unknowns: Novelty Detection in Condition Monitoring

John A. Quinn[1,2] and Christopher K.I. Williams[1]

[1] School of Informatics
[2] Simpson Centre for Reproductive Health
University of Edinburgh, United Kingdom
{john.quinn, c.k.i.williams}@ed.ac.uk

Abstract. In time-series analysis it is often assumed that observed data can be modelled as being derived from a number of regimes of dynamics, as e.g. in a Switching Kalman Filter (SKF) [8,2]. However, it may not be possible to model all of the regimes, and in this case it can be useful to represent explicitly a 'novel' regime. We apply this idea to the Factorial Switching Kalman Filter (FSKF) by introducing an extra factor (the 'X-factor') to account for the unmodelled variation. We apply our method to physiological monitoring data from premature infants receiving intensive care, and demonstrate that the model is effective in detecting abnormal sequences of observations that are not modelled by the known regimes.

1 Introduction

In time-series analysis it is often assumed that observed data can be modelled as being derived from a number of regimes of dynamics, as e.g. in a Switching Kalman Filter (SKF) [8,2]. However, in complex, real-world data (as found e.g. in medicine, engineering or finance) it may be that there are a very large number of possible regimes, and that a model may only have knowledge of commonly occurring ones. In this case it can be useful to represent explicitly a 'novel' regime, in order to model observations that do not correspond to any of the known regimes. The inclusion of this extra regime gives a condition monitoring system two potential benefits. Firstly, it is useful to know when novel regimes are being followed, e.g. in order to raise an alarm. Secondly, the new class provides a measure of confidence for the system. That is, by confidently classifying a regime as 'none of the above' we know that there is some structure in the data which is missing in the model.

We use the Factorial Switching Kalman Filter (FSKF), an extension of the SKF, as a general framework for condition monitoring. The FSKF has a number of factors which affect the dynamics of the observations; conditional on a particular combination of factor settings, the model is equivalent to a Kalman filter. In section 2 we extend the model of Williams ct al. [9] by adding an extra factor, referred to here as the 'X-factor', representing all variation which is not normal and not similar to any of the known regimes.

J. Martí et al. (Eds.): IbPRIA 2007, Part I, LNCS 4477, pp. 1–6, 2007.

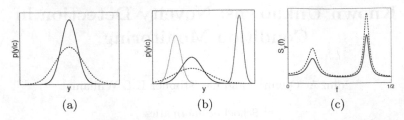

Fig. 1. (a) Class conditional likelihoods in a static 1D model, for the normal class (solid) and the X-factor (dashed). (b) Likelihoods of the normal class and X-factor in conjunction with other known, abnormal regimes (shown dotted). (c) The power spectral density of a latent AR(5) process with white observation noise (solid), and that of a corresponding X-factor process (dashed).

In section 3 we apply our method to physiological monitoring data from premature infants receiving intensive care. This data typically has a number of common regimes—artifactual and basic physiological patterns—as well as some uncommon regimes. Examples of the causes of uncommon regimes might be neurological problems or sepsis, or even the baby's reaction to a linen change or the flash of a camera, and include so many possibilities that it would be very difficult to model them all explicity. The model is shown to be successful in identifying clinically significant novelty in complex multivariate data.

2   Model Description

As a general condition monitoring framework we use the FSKF [9,3]. In this model, M discrete factor settings $f_t^{(1)} \ldots f_t^{(M)}$ affect the hidden continuous state $\mathbf{x}_t$ and the observations $\mathbf{y}_t$. The system dynamics and observation process are taken to be dependent on the variable s_t, an index which is a cross-product of the factor settings,

$$\mathbf{x}_t \sim \mathcal{N}\left(\mathbf{A}^{(s_t)}\mathbf{x}_{t-1}, \mathbf{Q}^{(s_t)}\right), \qquad \mathbf{y}_t \sim \mathcal{N}\left(\mathbf{C}^{(s_t)}\mathbf{x}_t, \mathbf{R}^{(s_t)}\right), \qquad (1)$$

so that s_t effectively 'switches' the model in and out of different dynamical regimes. Conditioned on s_t, the model is equivalent to a linear Gaussian state-space (Kalman filter). The factor settings are taken to be a priori independent and first-order Markovian.

2.1   Novel Dynamics

First imagine that we have independent, one-dimensional observations which are conditionally Gaussian, $\mathbf{y}|s \sim \mathcal{N}\left(\boldsymbol{\mu}^{(s)}, \boldsymbol{\Sigma}^{(s)}\right)$. For condition monitoring we are interested in problems where we assume that the possible settings of s represent a 'normal' mode and a number of known additional modes. We assume here that the normal regime is indexed by $s = 1$, and the additional known modes by

$s = 2, \ldots, K$. In this static case, we can construct a new model for unexpected data points by inflating the covariance of the normal mode, so that

$$\boldsymbol{\Sigma}^{(*)} = \xi \boldsymbol{\Sigma}^{(1)}, \qquad \boldsymbol{\mu}^{(*)} = \boldsymbol{\mu}^{(1)} . \tag{2}$$

where normally $\xi > 1$. This type of construction for unexpected observations is referred to as an 'X-factor'[1].

The likelihood functions for a normal class and a corresponding X-factor are shown in Figure 1(a). Clearly, data points that are far away from the normal range are more likely to be classified as belonging to the X-factor. For condition monitoring this can be used in conjunction with a number of known classes, as shown in 1(b). Here, the X-factor has the highest likelihood for regions which are far away from any known modes, as well as far away from normality.

We can generalise this approach to novelty detection by adding a new factor to a trained FSKF, with parameters based on those of the learnt normal dynamics as follows:

$$\mathbf{Q}^{(*)} = \xi \mathbf{Q}^{(1)} , \tag{3}$$

$$\left\{ \mathbf{A}^{(*)}, \mathbf{C}^{(*)}, \mathbf{R}^{(*)} \right\} = \left\{ \mathbf{A}^{(1)}, \mathbf{C}^{(1)}, \mathbf{R}^{(1)} \right\} , \tag{4}$$

where the switch setting $s_t = 1$ again represents normal dynamics, where no factor is active. To see why (3) and (4) are a dynamic generalisation of (2), consider the specific case of a hidden scalar AR(p) process,

$$x_t \sim \mathcal{N} \left(\sum_{k=1}^{p} \alpha_k x_{t-k}, \sigma_q^2 \right), \quad y_t \sim \mathcal{N}(x_t, \sigma_r^2) . \tag{5}$$

The power spectral density for the hidden process x_t at frequency f is given by

$$S_x(f) = \frac{\sigma_q^2}{\left| 1 - \sum_{k=1}^{p} \alpha_k e^{-2\pi i f k} \right|^2} , \tag{6}$$

where $-\frac{1}{2} \leq f \leq \frac{1}{2}$, assuming one observed value per unit of time. By inflating σ_q^2 (as specified in (3)) we observe that the power is increased at each frequency. The observed process has the spectrum $S_y(f) = S_x(f) + \sigma_r^2$. As the scale of $S_y(f)$ is determined by the magnitudes of the two noise variances, inflating σ_q^2 will have the effect of increasing the power at every frequency, as illustrated in Figure 1(c).

Under an AR(p) model driven by Gaussian noise, any sequence of x's (and also the y's) are jointly Gaussian. The eigenfunctions are sinusoids and the eigenvalues are given by the power spectrum. Hence inflating the system noise has created a dynamical analogue of the static construction given above.

Preliminary experiments with the data described below showed that $\xi = 2$ was a suitable setting. It is possible to learn ξ using EM, see [6].

---

[1] The notation ξ is chosen by association with the word $\xi\epsilon\nu o\varsigma$, or *xenos*, meaning 'strange'.

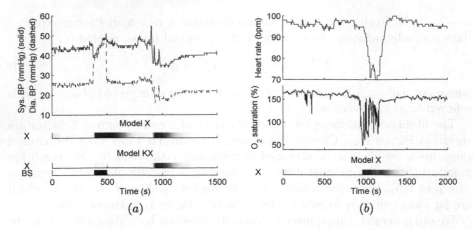

(a)   (b)

Fig. 2. Inferred durations for known factors and the X-factor. Panel (a) shows systolic and diastolic blood pressure readings containing a blood sample (BS) artifact between times 300 and 500, and physiological disturbance between times 800 and 1100. The **X** model picks up both these periods, while adding the known factors causes the artifact to be correctly reclassified. In panel (b), the X-factor picks up another significant and unusual period of variation. The minor variation around time 300 was not judged to be clinically significant, and was not picked up by the X-factor.

3   Experiments

24 hour periods of monitoring data were collected from 13 premature babies receiving intensive care in the neonatal unit at the Royal Infirmary of Edinburgh. Each period comprised of readings taken once per second: heart rate, blood pressures, core and peripheral temperatures, oxygen saturation and environmental temperature and humidity. This data was annotated by clinical experts with the times during which four common physiological and artifactual patterns occurred: bradycardia, a slowing of the heart; changes related to handling the baby; core temperature probe disconnection; blood sample artifacts; also the times in which other clinically significant patterns were apparent which were did not match any of the previous categories. FSKF models were set up with linear Gaussian state-space dynamics representing each of these patterns (for details see [6]). The thirteen data periods were split into four training cases and nine test cases. Normal dynamics were trained separately for each baby, and for this a 30 minute period for each baby was annotated as 'normal'. Approximate inference was performed in this model using the Gaussian sum method [1], to find the filtered estimates of the factor settings and hidden continuous state $p(s_t, \mathbf{x}_t | \mathbf{y}_{1:t})$. In all the following experiments, the setting $\xi = 2$ was used.

We consider three models with three different sets of factors. Model **K** contains factors representing known patterns (blood sample, bradycardia etc) only. Model **KX** contains the known factors and the X-factor. Model **X** contains one factor that switches between normality and the X-factor. Examples of the operation of these models are shown in Figure 2. In panel (a), a period of blood pressure

Table 1. Summary statistics of performance. AUC denotes area under ROC curve and EER denotes the equal error rate.

Model		X-factor	Bradycardia	Core temp.	Blood sample	Handling
K	AUC	-	0.96	0.90	0.93	0.75
	EER	-	0.06	0.20	0.18	0.32
KX	AUC	0.81	0.97	0.92	0.95	0.74
	EER	0.22	0.06	0.19	0.16	0.33

measurements contains a known artifactual pattern, caused by taking a blood sample, and a novel pattern of physiological disturbance. In model **X**, both patterns are picked up by the X-factor. Adding the known patterns causes the artifactual period to be correctly claimed by the appropriate factor. In panel (b), another period of physiological instability is picked up by the X-factor.

Quantitative results for the **K** and **KX** models are given in Table 1. Recall that the test data has annotations for each of the five factors (the four specific ones and the X-factor). We compare the inferred filtered probability of each factor to the relevant gold standard binary annotation. For each factor a ROC curve is plotted, and summary statistics of the area under curve (AUC) and equal error rate[2] (EER) are computed. Note that because of the periods of novel dynamics, model **K** has an incomplete factor set. The table shows that adding the X-factor allows these periods of novel dynamics to be classified while maintaining the accuracy of the known patterns. For the **X** model, any non-normal episode was annotated as belonging to the X-factor. An AUC of 0.73 and EER of 0.29 was obtained in this case.

3.1   Relation to Previous Work

There is a large body of work on statistical approaches to novelty detection, reviewed in [5]. In general the goal is to learn the density of training data and to raise an alarm for new data points which fall in low density areas. In a time-series context this involves modelling the next observation $p(\mathbf{y}_{t+1}|\mathbf{y}_{1:t})$ based on the earlier observations, and detecting observations that have low probability. This method is used, for example, by Ma and Perkins [4]. Such approaches define a model of normality, and look for deviations from it, e.g. by setting a threshold.

A somewhat different take is to define a broad 'outlier' distribution as well as normality, and carry out probabilistic inference to assign patterns to the normal or outlier components. For time-series data this approach was followed by Smyth [7], who considered the use of an unknown state when using a HMM for condition monitoring. This uses a similar idea to ours but in a simpler context, as in his work there is no factorial state structure and no explicit temporal model.

Acknowledgements. The authors thank Neil McIntosh and Birgit Wefers for providing expert annotation of the monitoring data. Author JQ was supported by

---

[2] We give error rates, so smaller numbers are better. Often 1 - error rate is given in EER tables.

a grant from the premature baby charity BLISS. The work was also supported in part by the IST Programme of the European Community, under the PASCAL Network of Excellence, IST-2002-506778. The title is inspired by a quotation from Donald Rumsfeld.

References

1. Alspach, D.L., Sorenson, H.W.: Nonlinear Bayesian Estimation Using Gaussian Sum Approximations. IEEE Transactions on Automatic Control 17(4), 439–448 (1972)
2. Ghahramani, Z., Hinton, G.E.: Variational Learning for Switching State-Space Models. Neural Computation 12(4), 963–996 (1998)
3. Ma, J., Deng, L.: A mixed level switching dynamic system for continuous speech recognition. Computer Speech and Language 18, 49–65 (2004)
4. Ma, J. Perkins, S.: Online Novelty Detection on Temporal Sequences. In: Proceedings of the ninth ACM SIGKDD international conference on Knowledge discovery and data mining, pp. 613–618 (2003)
5. Markou, M., Singh, S.: Novelty detection: a review - part 1: statistical approaches. Signal Processing 83, 2481–2497 (2003)
6. Quinn, J.A.: Condition Monitoring in Neonatal Intensive Care. PhD thesis, School of Informatics, University of Edinburgh (2007)
7. Smyth, P.: Markov monitoring with unknown states. IEEE Journal on Selected Areas in Communications 12(9), 1600–1612 (1994)
8. West, M., Harrison, P.J.: Bayesian Forecasting and Dynamic Models, 2nd edn. Springer, Heidelberg (1997)
9. Williams, C.K.I., Quinn, J.A., McIntosh, N.: Factorial Switching Kalman Filters for Condition Monitoring in Neonatal Intensive Care. In: Weiss, Y., Schölkopf, B., Platt, J. (eds.) Advances in Neural Information Processing Systems 18, MIT Press, Cambridge (2006)

Seeing the Invisible and Predicting the Unexpected

Michal Irani

Department of Computer Science and Applied Mathematics
The Weizmann Institute of Science
Rehovot, Israel

Analysis, interpretation and manipulation of complex visual data is something which humans do quite easily. We can easily recognize different instances of objects (like faces, bodies, flowers, etc.), in spite of the huge variations in their appearances. We have no problem determining that two actions are the same, even though they are performed by different people wearing different clothes against different backgrounds. Moreover, we humans can predict and make inferences about very complex static and dynamic visual information which we have never seen. We can infer about the appearance of unfamiliar places, objects and actions, as well as detect saliency and abnormalities in such data. Such complex visual tasks require sophisticated notions of visual similarity and dissimilarity.

In this talk I will show how such complex visual inference tasks can be performed by comparing and integrating local pieces of visual information within and across different parts of the visual data. When dealing with static objects and still imagery, the integrated pieces of data are spatial in nature, and are integrated within and across differen parts of the image. When dealing with actions and dynamic behaviors in video data, such inference is performed within a space-time setting, namely, by comparing and integrating local space-time pieces of visual data within and across space-time video volumes. *Such an "Inference by Composition" approach allows to make inferences about complex static and dynamic visual information <u>without any explicit prior examples</u>.*

I will demonstrate the power of this approach through several example problems:

1. *Detection of Complex Objects and Actions* – Different instances of the same object (e.g., different flowers, different faces, etc.) as well as different instances of the same action share distinctive patterns of local self-similarities. By *matching internal patters of local self similarities*, we can detect and retrieve complex objects in cluttered images and complex behaviors in video data. This can be done using a SINGLE example of the object or action of interest (often only a rough hand-sketch), without any learning of prior examples, without fg/bg segmentation, nor any motion estimation. This part of the talk is based on our recent work [4].
2. *Seeing the Invisible* – Prediction and completion of complex missing visual data is made possible by coherently integrating space-time visual information from other visible parts of the video data. This allows recovery of the *most probable* static and dynamic visual information (and, again, does not require any fg/bg segmentation nor any motion estimation). This part of the talk is based on our work [5,6].
3. *Predicting the Unexpected* – Detection of the "irregular" and "unexpected" in visual data is made possible by detecting those visual regions which cannot be composed

J. Martí et al. (Eds.): IbPRIA 2007, Part I, LNCS 4477, pp. 7–8, 2007.

(i.e., predicted) from other parts of the available visual data. This gives rise to detection of suspicious/salient behaviors in video, saliency/attention in images, and other applications. This part of the talk is based on our work [1,3,2].

References

1. Boiman, O., Irani, M.: Detecting irregularities in images and in video. ICCV, pp. 462–469 (2005)
2. Boiman, O., Irani, M.: Similarity by composition. Advances in Neural Information Processing Systems (NIPS) (2006)
3. Boiman, O., Irani, M.: Detecting irregularities in images and in video. International Journal of Computer Vision (IJCV) (2007)
4. Shechtman, E., Irani, M.: Matching local self-similarities across images and videos. In: CVPR (2007)
5. Wexler, Y., Shechtman, E., Irani, M.: Space-time video completion. In: CVPR (1), pp. 120–127 (2004)
6. Wexler, Y., Shechtman, E., Irani, M.: Space-time completion of video. IEEE Transactions on Pattern Analysis and Machine Intelligence (PAMI) 29(3), 463–476 (2007)

Vision-Based SLAM in Real-Time*

Andrew J. Davison

Department of Computing
Imperial College London
London SW7 2AZ
UK
http://www.doc.ic.ac.uk/~ajd/

1 Introduction

When a world-observing camera moves through a scene capturing images continuously, it is possible to analyse the images to estimate its *ego-motion*, even if
nothing is known in advance about the contents of the scene around it. The key
to solving this apparently chicken-and-egg problem is to detect and repeatedly
measure a number of salient 'features' in the environment as the camera moves.
Under the usual assumption that most of these are rigidly related in the world,
the many geometric constraints on relative camera/feature locations provided
by image measurements allow one to solve simultaneously for both the camera
motion and the 3D world positions of the features. While global optimisation
algorithms are able to achieve the most accurate solutions to this problem, the
consistent theme of my research has been to develop 'Simultaneous Localisation
and Mapping' (SLAM) algorithms using probabilistic filtering which permit sequential, *hard real-time* operation.

The sequential SLAM approach originated in the mobile robotics literature,
where real-time localisation and mapping is a requirement, and much recent
research has focused on large-scale mapping algorithms for autonomous robots
with sophisticated sensor suites. We made a breakthrough in 2003 with the
MonoSLAM algorithm [1,2] which showed that an agile, standard and low-cost
monocular camera with no additional sensory input can perform SLAM in real-
time — bringing SLAM into the 'pure vision' domain where off-line structure
from motion methods had been prevalent. MonoSLAM and other recent approaches it has inspired [3,4,5,6] enable high performance, repeatable localisation
at frame-rate of cameras which build world consistent maps as they go through
previously unknown scenes.

2 Approach

Our work has been highly focused on high frame-rate real-time performance
(typically 30Hz) as a requirement. In applications, real-time algorithms are

* The author's recent research has been supported by an EPSRC Advanced Research
Fellowship and EPSRC Grants GR/R89080/01 and GR/T24684. He is grateful to
his long-term collaborators, particularly Ian Reid, José María Montiel, Nobuyuki
Kita, Olivier Stasse, Walterio Mayol and David Murray.

J. Martí et al. (Eds.): IbPRIA 2007, Part I, LNCS 4477, pp. 9–12, 2007.

necessary only if they are to be used as part of a loop involving other components in the dynamic world — a robot that must control its next motion step, a human that needs visual feedback on his actions or another computational process which is waiting for input. In these cases, the most immediately useful information to be obtained from a moving camera in real time is where it is, rather than a fully detailed "final result" map of a scene ready for display. Although localization and mapping are intricately coupled problems and it has been proven in SLAM research that solving either requires solving both, in this work we focus on localization as the main output of interest. A map is certainly built, but it is a sparse map of landmarks optimized toward enabling localization.

Further, real-time camera tracking scenarios will often involve extended and looping motions within a restricted environment (as a humanoid performs a task, a domestic robot cleans a home, or room is viewed from different angles with graphical augmentations). Repeatable localization, in which gradual drift from ground truth does not occur, will be essential here and much more important than in cases where a moving camera continually explores new regions without returning. This is where a fully-probabilistic SLAM approach comes into its own: it will naturally construct a persistent map of scene landmarks to be referenced indefinitely in a state-based framework and permit loop closures to correct long-term drift. Forming a persistent world map means that if camera motion is restricted, the processing requirement of the algorithm is bounded and continuous real-time operation can be maintained. Further, using sequential SLAM we are able both to implement on-the-fly probabilistic estimation of the state of the moving camera and its map, and immediately benefit from this in using the running estimates to guide efficient processing. Our approach to mapping can be summarized as "a sparse map of high quality features."

The MonoSLAM algorithm has been demonstrated in several real-time room-scale localisation and mapping scenarios; most notably in augmented reality and in humanoid robot localisation [2], as illustrated in Figure 1.

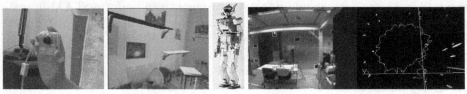

Hand-held camera   Augmented scene   HRP-2 with image, trajectory and map

Fig. 1. MonoSLAM applications: real-time augmented reality with a hand-held camera, and real-time SLAM for the full-size humanoid robot HRP-2.

3   Recent Advances

Our recent work with Montiel *et al.* [3] presented a scheme which allows the straightforward use in MonoSLAM of features at any depth — even features at 'infinity' in outdoor scenes. The key was a new 'inverse depth' feature parameterisation with good linear properties for probability propagation. Continuing in this theme, we are currently investigating further stripping away restrictions and assumptions from vision-based SLAM and to the minimum set of prior information which must be present for instant sequential operation. Key to this we believe is the development of a fully *dimensionless* parametrisation for monocular SLAM which removes scale from the estimation [7].

Another current theme is to efficiently increase the representational capability of the sparse scene maps within MonoSLAM via non-point feature models such as straight lines [8] or planar facets [9]. We hope that this direction of moving towards higher-level representations may one day lead to rapid human-like semantic scene understanding, and other authors [10] have already investigated including explicit object recognition within a MonoSLAM framework.

4   Research Prospects

A long term goal in SLAM shared by many would be to achieve a system with the following performance: a single low-cost camera attached to a portable computer would be switched on at an arbitrary location in an unknown scene, then carried off by a fast-moving robot (perhaps flying or jumping) or even a running human through an arbitrarily large domain, all the time effortlessly recovering its trajectory in real time and building a detailed, persistent map of all it has seen. There has recently been a great deal of promising work attacking the issue of building very large maps without the computational scaling problems of the basic Extended Kalman Filter approach, and highly efficient new SLAM algorithms which lie somewhere between full continuous filtering and graph-like optimisation have been proposed (e.g. [11,12]). We believe that these methods will soon be fully and fruitfully integrated with advances in 'visual odometry' techniques (e.g. [13,14]), which can highly accurately estimating the local motion of camera rigs, to result in practical large-scale vision-based mapping.

We plan to continue approaching the problem from the other direction, retaining at the current time a probabilistic filtering approach and sparse, persistent scene representation, but solving issues relating to highly dynamic 3D motion, commodity vision-only sensing, processing efficiency and relaxing platform assumptions. As one key research avenue, we will investigate the way to extract with ultimate efficiency the motion information available in an image sequence — this is the key to algorithms which will run in real-time at the very high frame-rates (perhaps 1000Hz) needed to track motions of extreme dynamics or on very limited computer processors. We believe that the key to matching features efficiently is to use an *active* strategy of only performing the image processing work which is really required — and to take advantage in particular of the fact that at high frame-rates this required work may be minimal, since motion predictions become increasingly good as inter-frame time intervals decrease. We have recently shown [15] that in real-time tracking, information theory can be used to predict the information content of individual feature measurements — the value of each in absolute bit units — and that strategies for active search can then be deduced by also considering the image processing cost of measurements.

References

1. Davison, A.J.: Real-time simultaneous localisation and mapping with a single camera. In: Proceedings of the 9th International Conference on Computer Vision, Nice (2003)
2. Davison, A.J., Molton, N.D., Reid, I.D., Stasse, O.: MonoSLAM: Real-time single camera SLAM. Accepted for publication in IEEE Transactions on Pattern Analysis and Machine Intelligence (2007)
3. Montiel, J.M.M., Civera, J., Davison, A.J.: Unified inverse depth parametrization for monocular SLAM. In: Proceedings of Robotics: Science and Systems, Philadelphia (2006)
4. Eade, E., Drummond, T.: Scalable monocular SLAM. In: Proceedings of the IEEE Conference on Computer Vision and Pattern Recognition, New York (2006)
5. Chekhlov, D., Pupilli, M., Mayol, W.W., Calway, A.: Real-time and robust monocular slam using predictive multi-resolution descriptors. In: Proceedings of the 2nd International Symposium on Visual Computing (2006)
6. Lemaire, T., Lacroix, S., Solà, J.: A practical 3D bearing-only slam algorithm. In: Proceedings of the IEEE/RSJ Conference on Intelligent Robots and Systems (2005)
7. Civera, J., Davison, A.J., Montiel, J.M.M.: Dimensionless monocular SLAM. In: Proceedings of the Iberian Conference on Pattern Recognition and Image Analysis (2007)
8. Smith, P., Reid, I., Davison, A.J.: Real-time single-camera SLAM with straight lines. In: Proceedings of the 17th British Machine Vision Conference, Edinburgh (2006)
9. Molton, N.D., Davison, A.J., Reid, I.D.: Locally planar patch features for real-time structure from motion. In: Proceedings of the 15th British Machine Vision Conference, Kingston (2004)
10. Castle, R.O., Gawley, D.J., Klein, G., Murray, D.W.: Towards simultaneous recognition, localization and mapping for hand-held and wearable cameras. In: Proc. International Conference on Robotics and Automation, Rome, April 2007 (2007)
11. Dellaert, F.: Square root SAM. In: Proceedings of Robotics: Science and Systems, Cambridge, USA (June 2005)
12. Frese, U.: Treemap: An $o(logn)$ algorithm for indoor simultaneous localization and mapping. Autonomous Robots 21(2), 103–122 (2006)
13. Nistér, D., Naroditsky, O., Bergen, J.: Visual odometry. In: Proceedings of the IEEE Conference on Computer Vision and Pattern Recognition (2004)
14. Konolige, K., Agrawal, M., Bolles, R.C., Cowan, C., Fischler, M., Gerkey, B.P.: Outdoor mapping and navigation using stereo vision. In: Proc. of the Intl. Symp. on Experimental Robotics (ISER) (July 2006)
15. Davison, A.J.: Active search for real-time vision. In: Proceedings of the 10th International Conference on Computer Vision, Beijing (2005)

Handwritten Symbol Recognition by a Boosted Blurred Shape Model with Error Correction

Alicia Fornés, Sergio Escalera, Josep LLadós, Gemma Sánchez, Petia Radeva, and Oriol Pujol

Computer Vision Center, Dept. of Computer Science, Universitat Autònoma de Barcelona, 08193, Bellaterra, Spain

Abstract. One of the major difficulties of handwriting recognition is the variability among symbols because of the different writer styles. In this paper we introduce the boosting of blurred shape models with error correction, which is a robust approach for describing and recognizing handwritten symbols tolerant to this variability. A symbol is described by a probability density function of blurred shape model that encodes the probability of pixel densities of image regions. Then, to learn the most distinctive features among symbol classes, boosting techniques are used to maximize the separability among the blurred shape models. Finally, the set of binary boosting classifiers is embedded in the framework of Error Correcting Output Codes (ECOC). Our approach has been evaluated in two benchmarking scenarios consisting of handwritten symbols. Compared with state-of-the-art descriptors, our method shows higher tolerance to the irregular deformations induced by handwritten strokes.

1 Introduction

The analysis of handwritten documents has been a subject of intensive research for the last decades. The interest devoted to this field is not only explained from the scientific point of view, but also in terms of the social benefits that convey those systems. Two examples of interesting applications are the analysis of old handwritten archive manuscripts and sketching or calligraphic interfaces. The analysis of ancient documents is a growing interest in Europe and its main concern is not only the digitization but the extraction of knowledge from ancient documents to convert them to digital libraries, so that these documents can be edited and published, contributing to the diffusion and preservation of artistic and cultural heritage. Concerning to sketching interfaces, it is a joint interest between the fields of Pattern Recognition and Human Computer Interaction, which allows computers to integrate a natural way of interaction based on handwritten strokes which are interpreted as textual annotations or graphical gestures.

Although the analysis of textual handwritten documents has an intensive activity, the analysis of hand-drawn documents with graphical alphabets is an emerging subfield. Due to the fact that architectural, cartographic and musical documents use their own alphabets of symbols (corresponding to the domain-dependent graphic notations used in these documents), the automatic interpretation of such documents requires specific processes, within the field of Graphics

J. Martí et al. (Eds.): IbPRIA 2007, Part I, LNCS 4477, pp. 13–21, 2007.

Recognition, more than the field of Cursive Script Recognition. Two major differences between the two problems can be stated. Cursive script recognition has the context information in one dimensional way, but graphical alphabets usually are bidimensional. In addition, the use of syntactical knowledge, and lexicons, is more effective in text recognition than in diagrammatic notations because of the variability of structures and alphabets of the latter.

Symbol recognition is one of the central topics of Graphics Recognition [3]. A lot of effort has been made in the last decade to develop good symbol and shape recognition methods inspired in either structural or statistic pattern recognition approaches. The presence of handwritten symbols increases the difficulty of classification: there is a high variability in writing style, with different sizes, shapes and intensities, increasing the number of touching and broken symbols. In addition, working with old documents even increases the difficulties in these stages because of paper degradation and the frequent lack of a standard notation.

Symbol recognition in document images can be seen as a particular case of Shape Recognition. Two major focus of interest can be stated: the definition of expressive and compact shape description signatures, and the formulation of robust classification methods according to such descriptors. Zhang [7] reviews the main techniques used in this field, mainly classified in contour-based descriptors (i.e. polygonal approximations, chain code, shape signature, and curvature scale space) and region-based descriptors (i.e. Zernike moments, ART, and Legendre moments [9]). A good shape descriptor should guarantee inter-class compacity and intra-class separability, even when describing noisy and distorted shapes. It has been proved that some descriptors, robust with some affine transformations and occlusions in printed symbols, are not efficient enough for handwritten symbols. Thus, the research of other descriptors for elastic and non-uniform distortions is required, coping with variations in writing style and blurring.

Concerning classification, numerous techniques (not necessary independent from each other) have been investigated based on statistical or structural approaches [3]. Elastic deformations of shapes modelled by probabilities tend to be learnt using statistical classifiers. One of the most well-known techniques in this domain is the Adaboost algorithm due to its ability for feature selection, detection, and classification problems [1]. Most classification algorithms are designed for multiclass problems. Nevertheless, this extension is normally hardly difficult. In such cases, the usual way to proceed is to reduce the complexity of the problem into a set of simpler binary classifiers and combine them. An usual way to combine these simple classifiers is the voting scheme (one-versus-one or one-versus-all grouping schemes are the most frequently applied). Dietterich et. al. [2] proposed a framework inspired in the signal processing coding and decoding techniques to benefit from error correction properties. The method is based on combining the weak classifiers as codified columns of a matrix and generate a codeword for each class. Thus, a test sample is evaluated with all the binary classifiers, and codewords are compared in the classification stage [2].

In this paper we present an approach to model and classify handwritten symbols. The method uses the context of the shape and defines a blurred region of the shape that makes the technique robust against elastic deformations (section 2). The Adaboost algorithm (section 3) is proposed to learn the descriptor features that best split classes, and the pairwise scheme (one-versus-one) with ECOC increases the classification accuracy by correcting possible weak classifiers errors. Finally, results (section 4) and the concluding remarks are exposed.

2   BSM: Blurred Shape Model

Handwritten symbol recognition is a hard task due to the high variability of symbol appearance because of the differences in writer sytles, and even also by the degradation in old documents (resolution, noise). The Blurred Shape Model (BSM) is based on the object shape parametrization, allowing the definition of spatial regions where some parts of the shape can be involved: Given a binary handwritten symbol, it is first skeletonized, and skeleton points are used as features to compute the BSM signature. The skeleton is applied to normalize the object shape in order to assign to each contour point the same importance and also to prevent different widths at some parts of the object. Then, the image is divided in a grid of $n \times n$ equal-sized subregions (where $n \times n$ identifies the blurring level allowed for the shapes). Each bin receives votes from the shape points in it and also from the shape points in the neighboring bins. Thus, each shape point contributes to a density measure of its bin and its neighboring ones. This contribution is weighted according to the distance between the point and the bin centroid of each neighbor.

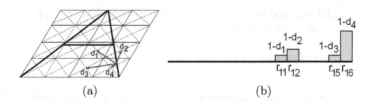

(a)   (b)

Fig. 1. (a) Shape pixel distances estimation respect to neighbor centroids. (b) Vector actualization of the region 16th, where d1+d2+d3+d4=1.

In Fig. 1, a letter shape parametrization is shown. Figure 1(a) shows the distances estimation of a shape point respect to the nearest centroids. To give the same importance to each shape point, all the distances to the neighbors centroids $\{d_1, d_2, d_3, d_4\}$ are normalized so that $d_1 + d_2 + d_3 + d_4 = 1$. The output descriptor is a vector histogram v of length $n \times n$, where each position corresponds to the amount of shape points in the context of the sub-region. The estimated normalized distances d_i for each affected sub-region r is used to actualize their corresponding vector locations adding the $1 - d_i$ values. Fig. 1 (b) shows the vector at this stage for the analyzed point of Fig. 1(a).

The resulting vector histogram, obtained by processing all feature points, is normalized in the range $[0..1]$ to obtain the probability density function (pdf)

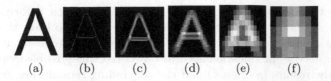

(a)   (b)   (c)   (d)   (e)   (f)

Fig. 2. (a) Input image. (b) Thinned image. (c) 64 regions blurred shape. (d) 32 regions blurred shape. (e) 16 regions blurred shape. (f) 8 regions blurred shape.

of $n \times n$ bins. In this way, the output descriptor represents a distribution of probabilities of the object shape considering spatial distortions. In Fig. 2, an input shape is processed. The symbol is filtered to obtain a thin shape, and the sequent figures correspond to the blurred parameterizations considering 64×64, 32×32, 16×16, and 8×8 sub-regions, respectively. The whole algorithm is summarized in Table 1.

Table 1. Blurred Shape Model algorithm. $|.|$ Is the Euclidean distance and $cen(r)$ is the centroid coordinates of the sub-region r.

> Given a binary image I,
>   Obtain the skeleton S of I
>   Divide I in $n \times n$ equal size sub-regions
>
>   for each point $(x, y) \in S$,
>   let be $r_{x,y} \in R$ the sub-region containing (x, y),
>
>   for $r_{x,y}$ and each $r'_{x,y} = \{r' \subset R | r'$ is neighbor of $r_{x,y}\}$
> $d_r = |cen(r), (x, y)|$
>
>   Normalize each distance d_r as:
> $d_r = \frac{d_r}{\sum_{\forall i \in r'_i} d_i}$
>   Actualize the probabilities vector v for $r_{x,y}$ and each $r'_{x,y}$
>   positions as:
> $v(r) = v(r) + (1 - d_r)$
>
>   Obtain the blurred pdf normalizing the vector v as:
> $v = \frac{v(i)}{\sum_{j=1}^{n^2} v(j)} \forall i \in [1, ..., n^2]$

3   Classification

In this section, the architecture of the classifier for the Blurred Shape Model descriptor and its benefits for handwritten symbols recognition is described. The whole process of the classification system is shown in Fig. 3.

Adaboost [1] is used to train the classifier from Blurred Shape Model descriptors. The BSM has a probabilistic parametrization on the object shape considering its possible shape distortions. Different types of objects may share local

Classes samples ⟹ BSM Description ⟹ Adaboost ⟹ ECOC ⟹ Strong classifier

Feature vectors   Binary classifiers

Fig. 3. Boosted blurred shape model with error correction scheme

features [4] (see Fig. 4(a)). For this reason, Adaboost has been chosen to boost
the BSM model in order to define a classifier based on the features that best
discriminate one classes against the others. In particular, we use the Discrete
Adaboost version [1] with 50 iterations of decision stumps. To outperform the
Adaboost behavior, we embed the Adaboost binary classifiers in the framework
of Error Correcting Output Codes.

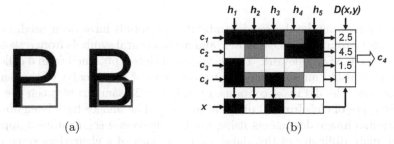

(a)   (b)

Fig. 4. (a) Discriminate features for symbols that shares features. (b) Error Correcting
Output Codes coding matrix for a 4 multiclass problem $\{c_1, ..., c_4\}$ using 5 binary
classifiers $\{h_1, ..., h_4\}$. A test sample x is tested and classified by class c_4 applying the
distance $D(x, y)$ between the test codeword and each class codeword.

The basis of the ECOC framework is to create a codeword for each of the
N_c classes. Arranging the codewords as rows of a matrix, a "coding matrix" M
is defined, where $M \in \{-1, 0, 1\}^{N_c \times n}$, being n the code length. From the point
of view of learning, M is constructed by considering n binary problems (dichotomies), each corresponding to a matrix column. Joining classes in sets, each
dichotomy defines a partition of classes (coded by +1, -1, according to their class
set membership, or 0 if the class is not considered by the dichotomy). In Fig. 4(b)
an example of a matrix M is shown. The matrix is coded using 5 dichotomies
$\{h_1, ..., h_5\}$ for a four multiclass problem (c_1, c_2, c_3, and c_4). The white regions
are coded by 1 (considered as positive for its respective dichotomy, h_i), the dark
regions by -1 (considered as negative), and the grey regions correspond to the
zero symbol (not considered classes for the current dichotomy). Applying the n
trained binary classifiers, a code is obtained for each data point in the test set.
This code is compared to the base codewords of each class defined in the matrix
M, and the data point is assigned to the class with the "closest" codeword. In
Fig. 4(b), an input test sample x is shown. This input is tested using the five
classifiers, and assigning the outputs to each codeword position (down of the
figure). Finally, the hamming distance is applied between each class codeword

and test codeword in the form $D(x,y) = \sum_{i=1}^{n} |x_i - y_i|/2$, where y is a class codeword, n is the number of classifiers, and $|.|$ is the absolute value. Finally the test input x is classified by the class at minimum distance c_4.

The ECOC framework shown increases the classification performance by the embedding of binary classifiers [2], [5]. In [8], it has been proved that the one-versus-one coding strategy outperforms the other traditional pre-defined coding strategies, and also that the Euclidean distance outperforms the traditional Hamming distance decoding. For this reason, the former strategy is used to evaluate the distance between the test sample and the class codewords. The estimation applied for each class candidate is $d(x,y) = \sqrt{\sum_{i=1}^{n}(x(i) - y(i))^2}$, where n is the code length, and x and y are the codewords for a test sample and a class.

4   Results

Two benchmarking databases of handwritten symbols have been used, namely clefs symbols from old musical scores, and architectural symbols from a sketching interface in a CAD framework. The database of clefs is obtained from a collection of modern and old musical scores (19th century) of the Archive of the Seminar of Barcelona. The database contains a total of 2128 samples between the three different types of clefs from 24 different authors. The images have been obtained from original image documents using a semi-supervised segmentation approach [6]. The main difficulty of this database is the lack of a clear class separability because of the variation of writer styles and the absence of a standard notation. In Fig. 5(a), one of the used old musical score is shown. The high variability of clefs' appearance from different authors can be observed in the segmented clefs of Fig. 5(b). The database of architectural hand-drawn symbols has 2762 total samples organized in the 14 classes shown in Fig. 6. Each class consists of an average of 200 samples drawn by 13 different authors. This database has been used to test the scalability of our method.

Fig. 5. (a) Old musical score, (b) High variability of clefs appearance: first row shows treble clefs, second row shows alto clefs and the third one shows bass clefs

Fig. 6. Architectural handwriting classes.

To better assess the performance of our approach, it is compared with ART, Zoning, and Zernike descriptors [7][10]. The compared descriptors are also introduced in the classification framework to quantify the robustness of each descriptor at the same conditions. For all the experiments, stratified ten-fold cross-validation at 95% of the confidence interval is used. The descriptors for BSM and Zoning techniques are of length 8×8, from the considered sub-regions. The parameters for ART are radial order with value 2 and angular order with value 11; and for the Zernike descriptor, 7 Zernike moments are used.

The accuracy and confidence ranges results for the old musical score clefs are shown and graphically represented in Fig.7(a) and Fig.7(b), respectively. ART and Zernique descriptors obtain the minor results, while the Zoning descriptor in the classification scheme technique offers good results. The BSM strategy is the most robust, obtaining an accuracy upon 98%.

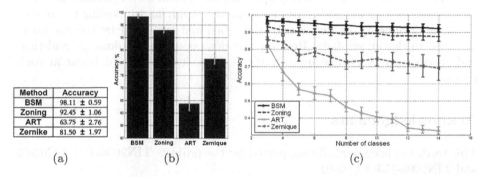

Method	Accuracy
BSM	98.11 ± 0.59
Zoning	92.45 ± 1.06
ART	63.75 ± 2.76
Zernike	81.50 ± 1.97

(a)   (b)   (c)

Fig. 7. (a) and (b) Clefs classification results. (c) Descriptors classification accuracy increasing the number of architectural symbol classes.

The architectural symbol database has been used to test the performance under an increasing number of classes. We started the classification using the first 3 classes. Iteratively, one class was added at each step and the classification is repeated. The higher number of classes, the higher confusion degree among them because of the elastic deformations inherent to hand drawn strokes, and the higher number of objects to distinguish. The results of accuracy recognition in terms of an increasing number of classes are shown in Fig. 7(c). The performance of the ART and Zernike descriptors decreases dramatically when increasing the confusion in terms of the number of classes, while Zoning obtains higher performance. Finally, the accuracy of the BSM outperforms the other descriptors results, and its confidence interval only intersects with Zoning in few cases. This behavior is quite important since the accuracy of the latter descriptors remains stable, and BSM can distinguish the 14 classes with an accuracy upon 90%. Referring the computational complexity, for a region of $n \times n$ pixels, the $k \leq n \times n$ skeleton points are considered to obtain the BSM with a cost of $O(k)$ simple operations, which is faster than the moment estimation of the ART and Zernike descriptors. Besides, the Adaboost and ECOC strategies are very suitable for real-time multi-class classification problems [1].

5   Conclusions

We have presented the boosting of blurred shape models with error correction. A blurred shape model pdf is designed for each binary object, where the shape is parameterized with a set of probabilities that define the spatial invariance to elastic deformations of handwritten symbols. Adaboost learns the discriminative vector features, and the binary classifiers are embedded in the Error Correcting Output Codes framework. The evaluation of the technique in two real hand-written problems shows the outperforming of the novel methodology in comparison with the state-of-the-art descriptors and high robustness against elastic deformations. The skeleton information can also be changed to other structure criteria in the framework, allowing the context-based blurring of different object properties.

As future work, we are currently applying the symbol-based trained classifiers for symbol spotting in hand-written documents. Applying windowing techniques to image documents, regions can be described and evaluated by the classifiers in order to detect symbols. Besides, the detection can be done in real-time and speeded up by estimating only the features learned by Adaboost at each region.

Acknowledgements

This work has been partially supported by the projects TIN2006-15694-C02-02 and TIN2006-15308-C02-01.

References

1. Friedman, J., Hastie, T., Tibshirani, R.: Additive logistic regression: a statistical view of boosting. The. Annals of Statistics 8(2), 337–374 (1998)
2. Dietterich, T., Bakiri, G.: Solving multiclass learning problems via error-correcting output codes. Artificial Intelligence Research 2, 263–286 (1995)
3. Lladós, J., Valveny, E., Sánchez, G., Martí, E.: Symbol Recognition: Current Advances and Perspectives. In: Blostein, D., Kwon, Y.-B. (eds.) GREC 2001. LNCS, vol. 2390, pp. 104–127. Springer, Heidelberg (2002)
4. Torralba, A., Murphy, K., Freeman, W.: Sharing visual features for multiclass and multiview object detection, Technical Report, Massachusetts Institute of Technology Computer Science and Artificial Intelligence (MIT AIM) (2004)
5. Escalera, S., Pujol, O., Radeva, P.: ECOC-ONE: A Novel Coding and Decoding Strategy. In: International Conference on Pattern Recognition (ICPR), Hong Kong 3, 578–581 (2006)
6. Fornés, A., Lladós, J., Sánchez, G.: Primitive segmentation in old handwritten music scores. In: Liu, W., Lladós, J. (eds.) Graphics Recognition: Ten Years Review and Future Perspectives. LNCS, vol. 3926, pp. 279–290. Springer, Heidelberg (2006)
7. Zhang, D., Lu, G.: Review of shape representation and description techniques. Pattern Recognition 37, 1–19 (2004)

8. Pujol, O., Radeva, P., Vitrià, J.: Discriminant ECOC: a heuristic method for application dependent design of error correcting output codes. In: IEEE Transaction on Pattern Analysis and Machine Intelligence 28, 1007–1012 (2006)
9. Manjunath, B., Salembier, P., Sikora, T.: Introduction to mpeg-7. In: Multimedia content description interface, John Wiley and Sons, New York, NY (2002)
10. Kim, W.: A new region-based shape descriptor, Technical report, Hanyang University and Konan Technology (1999)

Bayesian Hyperspectral Image Segmentation with Discriminative Class Learning

Janete S. Borges[1], José M. Bioucas-Dias[2], and André R. S. Marçal[1]

[1] Faculdade de Ciências, Universidade do Porto
[2] Instituto de Telecomunicações, Instituto Superior Técnico, TULisbon
jsborges@fc.up.pt, bioucas@lx.it.pt, andre.marcal@fc.up.pt

Abstract. This paper presents a new Bayesian approach to hyperspectral image segmentation that boosts the performance of the discriminative classifiers. This is achieved by combining class densities based on discriminative classifiers with a Multi-Level Logistic Markov-Gibs prior. This density favors neighbouring labels of the same class. The adopted discriminative classifier is the Fast Sparse Multinomial Regression. The discrete optimization problem one is led to is solved efficiently via graph cut tools. The effectiveness of the proposed method is evaluated, with simulated and real AVIRIS images, in two directions: 1) to improve the classification performance and 2) to decrease the size of the training sets.

1 Introduction

In recent years much research has been done in the field of image segmentation. Several methods have been used in a wide range of applications in computer vision. However, its application to high dimensional data, such as hyperspectral images, is still a delicate task, namely owing to well known difficulties in learning high dimensional densities from a limited number of training samples.

The discriminative approach to classification circumvent these difficulties by modelling directly the densities of the labels, given the features. This framework have shown success in dealing with small class distances, high dimensionality, and limited training sets. As a consequence, discriminative classifiers hold the state-of-the art in supervised hyperspectral image classification (see, *e.g.*, [1]).

Real world images tend to exhibit piecewise spatial continuity of categorical properties (*i.e.*, classes). Thus, an intuitive way of improving the performance of discriminative classifiers (and others) consists in adding contextual information in the form of spatial dependencies. This direction has been pursued in [2], introducing the concept of discriminative random fields in the computer vision applications, and in [3] and [4] using composite kernels, in hyperspectral applications.

This paper introduces a new Bayesian segmentation approach for hyperspectral images. Spatial dependencies are enforced by a Multi-Level Logistic (MLL) Markov-Gibs prior, which favours neighbouring labels of the same class. The class densities are build on the discriminative Fast Sparse Multinomial Regression (FSMLR) [5], which a fast version of the Sparse Multinomial Regression

J. Martí et al. (Eds.): IbPRIA 2007, Part I, LNCS 4477, pp. 22–29, 2007.

(SMLR) [6]. The SMLR includes a Laplacian prior to control the complexity of the learned classifier and, therefore, to achieve good generalization capabilities.

To compute an approximation to the Maximum A Posteriori probability (MAP) segmentation, we adopt the α-Expansion graph cut based algorithm proposed in [7]. This tool is computationally efficient and yields nearly optimum solutions.

The paper is organized as follows. Section 2 formulates the problem, describe briefly the FSMLR classifier, the MLL Markov Gibs prior, and the α-Expansion optimization algorithm. Section 3 presents results based on simulated and real hyperspectral datasets.

2 Formulation

A segmentation is an image of labels $\mathbf{y} = \{y_i\}_{i \in \mathcal{S}}$, where $y_i \in \mathcal{L} = \{1, 2, \ldots, K\}$. Let $\mathbf{x} = \{x_i \in \mathbb{R}^d, i \in \mathcal{S}\}$ be the observed multi-dimensional images, also known as feature image. The goal of the segmentation is to estimate $\mathbf{y}$, having observed $\mathbf{x}$. In a Bayesian framework, this estimation is done by maximizing the posterior distribution $p(\mathbf{y}|\mathbf{x}) \propto p(\mathbf{x}|\mathbf{y})p(\mathbf{y})$, where $p(\mathbf{x}|\mathbf{y})$ is the likelihood function (or the probability of feature image) and $p(\mathbf{y})$ is the prior over the classes.

In the present approach, we use the discriminative FSMLR classifier [5] to learn the class densities $p(y_i|x_i)$. The likelihood is then given by $p(x_i|y_i) = p(y_i|x_i)p(x_i)/p(y_i)$. Noting that $p(x_i)$ does not depend on the labeling $\mathbf{y}$ and assuming $p(y_i) = 1/K$, we have

$$p(\mathbf{x}|\mathbf{y}) \propto \prod_{i \in \mathcal{S}} p(y_i|x_i), \tag{1}$$

where conditional independence is understood.

In the following sections, we briefly describe the FSMLR method yielding the density $p(\mathbf{y}|\mathbf{x})$, the MLL prior $p(\mathbf{y})$, and α-Expansion optimization algorithm.

2.1 Class Density Estimation Using Fast-SMLR Method

Given the training set $\mathcal{D} = \{(x_1, y_1), \ldots, (x_n, y_n)\}$, the SMLR algorithm learns a multi-class classifier based on the multinomial logistic regression. By incorporating a Laplacian prior, this method performs simultaneously feature selection, to identify a small subset of the most relevant features, and learns the classifier itself [6]. The goal is to assign to each site $i \in \mathcal{S}$ the probability of $y_i = k$, for $k = 1, \ldots, K$. In particular, if $y_i = [y^{(1)}, \ldots, y^{(K)}]^T$ is a 1-of-K encoding of the K classes, and if $w^{(k)}$ is the feature weight vector associated with class k, then the probability of $y_i^{(k)} = 1$ given x_i is

$$P\left(y_i^{(k)} = 1|x_i, w\right) = \frac{\exp\left(w^{(k)^T} h(x_i)\right)}{\sum_{k=1}^{K} \exp\left(w^{(k)^T} h(x_i)\right)}, \tag{2}$$

where $w = [w^{(1)^T}, \ldots, w^{(K)^T}]^T$ and $h(x) = [h_1(x), \ldots, h_l(x)]^T$ is a vector of l fixed functions of the input, often termed features. Possible choices for this vector are $h(x_i) = [1, x_{i,1}, \ldots, x_{i,d}]^T$, where $x_{i,j}$ is the jth component of x_i, and $h(x) = [1, K(x, x_1), \ldots, K(x, x_n)]^T$, where $K(\cdot, \cdot)$ is some symmetric kernel function. The latter nonlinear mapping guarantees that the transformed samples are more likely to be linearly separable. Nevertheless, in this paper, we consider only the linear mapping, because it is much lighter from the computational point of view (note that the linear and the nonlinear mapping have $l = d + 1$ and $l = n + 1$, respectively, and, usually, $n \gg d$) yet it leads to competitive results.

The MAP estimate of w is

$$\hat{w}_{MAP} = \arg\max_w L(w) = \arg\max_w [l(w) + \log p(w)], \tag{3}$$

where $l(w)$ is the log-likelihood function and $p(w) \propto \exp(-\lambda \|w\|_1)$, where λ is a regularization parameter controlling the degree of sparseness of $\hat{w}_{MAP}$. The inclusion of the Laplacian prior does not allow the use of the classical IRLS method. However, the bound optimization framework [8] supplies a tool that makes it possible to perform exact MAP multinomial logistic regression, with the same cost as the original IRLS algorithm for ML estimation (see [6] for details).

In practice, the application of SMLR to large datasets is often prohibitive. A solution for this problem consists in using the Block Gauss-Seidel method [9] to solve the system used in the IRLS method. In each iteration, instead of solving the complete set of weights, only blocks corresponding to the weights belonging to the same class are solved [5], resulting in an improvement of the order of $O(K^2)$, where K is the number of classes.

2.2   The MLL Markov-Gibs Prior

The MLL prior is a MRF which models the piecewise continuous nature of the image elements, considering that adjacent pixels are likely to belong to the same class. According to the Hammersly-Clifford theorem, the prior probability of an MRF is a Gibb's distribution [10]. Thus

$$p(\mathbf{y}) = \frac{1}{Z} \exp\left(-\sum_{c \in C} V_c(\mathbf{y})\right), \tag{4}$$

where Z is a normalizing constant and the sum is over the prior potentials $V_c(\mathbf{y})$ for the set of cliques[1] C over the image, and

$$-V_c(\mathbf{y}) = \begin{cases} \alpha_{y_i} & if \ |c| = 1 \text{ (single clique)} \\ \beta_c & if \ |c| > 1 \text{ and all sites in } c \text{ have the same label} \\ -\beta_c & if \ |c| > 1 \text{ at least one site has a different label,} \end{cases} \tag{5}$$

where β_c is a nonnegative constant.

---

[1] A clique is a set of pixels that are neighbours of one another.

Let $\alpha_k = \alpha$ and $\beta_c = \frac{1}{2}\beta > 0$. This choice gives no preference to any label nor to any direction. Under this circumstances, (4) can be written as

$$p(\mathbf{y}) = \frac{1}{Z} e^{\beta n(\mathbf{y})}, \qquad (6)$$

where $n(\mathbf{y})$ denotes the number of cliques having the same label. The conditional probability is given by

$$p(y_i = k | y_{\mathcal{N}_i}) = \frac{e^{\beta n_i(k)}}{\sum_{k=1}^{K} e^{\beta n_i(k)}}, \qquad (7)$$

where $n_i(k)$ is the number of sites in the neighbourhood of site i, $\mathcal{N}_i$, having the label k.

2.3 Energy Minimization Via Graph Cuts

Using the FSMLR to learn $p(\mathbf{x}|\mathbf{y})$ and the MLL prior $p(\mathbf{y})$, the MAP segmentation is given by

$$\hat{\mathbf{y}} = \arg\max_{\mathbf{y}} p(\mathbf{x}|\mathbf{y})p(\mathbf{y})$$

$$= \arg\max_{\mathbf{y}} \sum_{i \in \mathcal{S}} \log p(x_i|y_i) + \beta n(\mathbf{y})$$

$$= \arg\min_{\mathbf{y}} \sum_{i \in \mathcal{S}} -\log p(x_i|y_i) - \beta \sum_{i,j \in c} \delta(y_i - y_j). \qquad (8)$$

Minimization (8) is a combinatorial optimization problem, where the right hand side pairwise interaction term is equivalent to a metric[2] and thus α-Expansion algorithm can be applied, yielding very good approximations to the MAP segmentation [7].

3   Results

3.1   Experimental Setup

Simulated datasets were used to test the proposed method. Images of labels were generated using a MLL distribution, with a 2nd order neighbourhood. The shape of these label images depends on a parameter (β_0) that controls the spatial continuity (β_0 represents the β in (6)). This parameter takes values between 1 and 2, with increments of 0.2. Figure 1 shows four examples of these label images with 4 classes, for $\beta_0 = 1$, $\beta_0 = 1.4$, $\beta_0 = 1.6$ and $\beta_0 = 2.0$. Images with 4 and 10 classes were generated, for each value of β_0, resulting in a total of 12 different label images. The feature images were obtained by adding zero-mean Gaussian independent noise with standard deviation σ to a source matrix of

---

[2] A metric is obtained by adding β to terms $-\beta\delta(y_i - y_j)$.

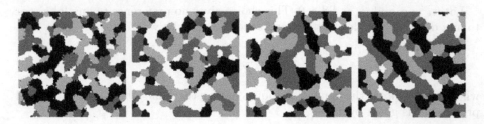

Fig. 1. Image labels with four classes generated by a MLL distribution with $\beta_0 = 1$, $\beta_0 = 1.4$, $\beta_0 = 1.6$ and $\beta_0 = 2$ (from left to right, respectively)

mineral signatures. This source matrix is provided by a Matlab data file [11], and was extracted from the USGS spectral library. Each signature is evaluated in 221 spectral bands, resulting in a dataset of dimension $120 \times 120 \times 221$ (120×120 is the spatial size of the simulated images). Datasets with added noise standard deviation of 0.01, 0.1 and 1 were generated. The variation of the parameters β and σ was made to evaluate the response of the proposed method to the spatial continuity of label images and to the amount of noise present in the feature data. To evaluate the method performance depending on the size of the training sets, tests were made using 10%, 30%, 50%, 70% and 90% of the training set.

Datasets with the characteristics described above were simulated 10 times for each set of parameters, in order to better evaluate the segmentation results.

3.2   Results on Simulated Data

The ratio of the correct classified pixels over the total number of pixels, termed overall accuracy (OA), was computed for each dataset. The regularization parameter is $\beta = 1.5$.

Graphics with the overall accuracies as function of β_0 are presented in Figures 2(a) and 2(b), for 4 and 10 classes, respectively. Lines corresponds to the overall accuracies for the MRF segmentation and dotted lines for the FSMLR classification. For each method, results for different training set size are also presented. The graphics are displayed for different values of feature noise: $\sigma = 0.01, 0.1$ and 1. In some plots, the overall accuracy of the FSMLR classifier (dotted lines) are nearly 100%, and the lines are thus not visible in those plots.

In the case of $K = 4$ (Fig.2(a)) and for larger values of β_0 and $\sigma = 0.01$ or 0.1, the results from FSMLR classifier and MRF segmentation are similar. When the noise increases, the MRF outperforms the FSMLR by over 5%. As expected for values of low values of β_0, the performance of the MRF segmentation is slightly worse. However, our method clearly outperforms the FSMLR classification when the noise is high ($\sigma = 1$). The different sizes used for the training set do not seems to affect the results, except for the case of $\sigma = 1$, where the use of a smaller training set degrades the performance of the FSMLR.

In the case of $K = 10$ (Fig.2(b)), the results for $\sigma = 0.01$ and $\sigma = 0.1$ are very similar for both methods. For $\sigma = 0.1$, it is nevertheless possible to see a small improvement of the accuracy achieved with MRF segmentation. Once again,

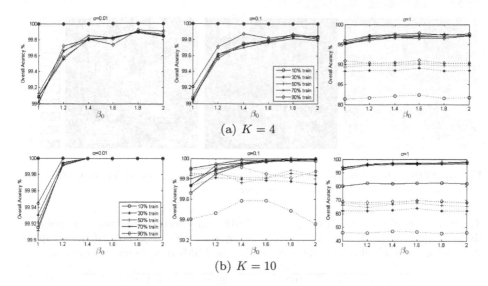

(a) $K = 4$

(b) $K = 10$

Fig. 2. Overall accuracies as function of spatial continuity (β_0) of the label images. Lines represent the MRF segmentation results and dotted lines the FSMLR classification results.

when higher noise in the feature image is considered ($\sigma = 1$), MRF segmentation clearly outperforms FSMLR classifier, by over 30%.

3.3   Results on Real Data

We applied the proposed MAP segmentation to an AVIRIS spectrometer image, the Indian Pines 92 from Northern Indiana, taken on June 12, 1992 [12]. The ground truth data image consists of 145 x 145 pixels of the AVIRIS image in 220 contiguous spectral bands. Experiments were carried out without 20 noisy bands. Due to the insufficient number of training samples, seven classes were discarded, leaving a dataset with 9 classes distributed by 9345 elements. This dataset was randomly partitioned into a set of 4757 training samples and 4588 validation samples. The spatial distribution of the class labels is presented in Figure 3. Each of the nine land cover classes is represented in one of nine grey levels. The black areas are the areas with unknown classes.

The results presented in this section are the overall accuracy measured in the independent (validation) dataset with 4588 samples. Experiments were evaluated using 10%, 20% and the complete training set. As in the previous section, we use a linear mapping h in the FSMLR. Parameter β was learned in a supervised fashion leading to $\beta = 1.5$ and $\beta = 4$, when the complete and subsets of the training set were used, respectively.

The results of overall accuracy from FSMLR classification and segmentation with MRF are presented in Table 3.3. From these results we observe that, regardless the size of the training set used to learn the density function, the MRF segmentation with a linear mapping h outperforms all other methods compared. The

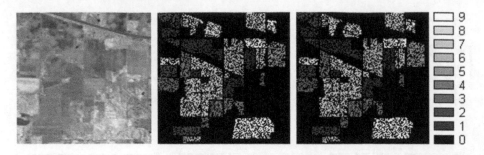

Fig. 3. AVIRIS image used for testing. Left: original image band 50 (near infrared); Centre: training areas; Right: validation areas

Table 1. Overall accuracy of the proposed MRF segmentation with linear mapping h, the SVM [1], the LDA, and the FSMLR, using 10%, 20% and 100% of the complete training set. The number of bands selected by the FSMLR is shown in brackets.

	10%	20%	100%
MRF (no. of bands)	**88.40%** (24)	**89.56%** (39)	**95.51%** (37)
SVM [1]	82.70%	86.70%	94.44%
FSMLR	75.57%	79.69%	85.77%
LDA	69.40%	78.40%	82.08%

gains with respect to the FSMLR and the linear discriminant analysis (LDA) are larger than 10%. Based on this results, we foresee that the proposed approach using kernel functions h will achieve much better performance than that of SVD [1].

4   Conclusions

A new segmentation technique for hyperspectral images was introduced. The procedure uses a sparse method for the estimation of feature densities, and includes statistical spatial information using a MLL Markov-Gibs based prior. The α-Expansion optimization tool is used to estimate the optimal segmentation.

Experiments were done using simulated datasets and an AVIRIS image. When compared with the support vector machines (SVM), the sparse multinomial logistic regression (SMLR), and the linear discriminant analysis (LDA), the proposed segmentation approach outperformed them all.

We believe that there is clearly room for improvement, namely by adopting kernel functions in the multinomial regression and by implementing accurate supervised learning of the model parameters.

Acknowledgments. The first author would like to thank the Fundação para a Ciência e a Tecnologia (FCT) for the financial support (PhD grant SFRH/BD/ 17191/2004). The authors acknowledge Vladimir Kolmogorov for the max-ow/ min-cut C++ code made available on the web. See [13] for more details; and David Landgrebe for providing the AVIRIS data.

This work was supported by the Fundacão para a Ciência e Tecnologia, under the project PDCTE/CPS/49967/2003,and by the Instituto de Telecomunicaões under the project IT/LA/325/2005, and by CICGE under POCI 2010 programme.

References

1. Camps-Valls, G., Bruzzone, L.: Kernel-based methods for hyperspectral image classification. IEEE Transactions on Geoscience and Remote Sensing 43(6), 1351–1362 (2005)
2. Kumar, S., Hebert, M.: Discriminative Random Fields. International Journal of Computer Vision 68(2), 179–202 (2006)
3. Camps-Valls, G., Gomez-Chova, L., Muñoz-Marí, J., Vila-Francés, J., Calpe-Maravilla, J.: Composite kernels for hyperspectral image classification. IEEE Geoscience and Remote Sensing Letters 3(1), 93–97 (2006)
4. Plaza, A., Benediktsson, J., Boardman, J., Brazile, J., Bruzzone, L., Camps-Valls, G., Chanussot, J., Fauvel, M., Gamba, P., Gualtieri, A., Tilton, J., Trianni, G.: Advanced Processing of Hyperspectral Images. IEEE IGARSS Proceedings, vol. IV, pp. 1974–1979 (2006)
5. Borges, J.S., Bioucas-Dias, J., Marçal, A.R.S.: Fast Sparse Multinomial Regression Applied to Hyperspectral Data. In: Campilho, A., Kamel, M. (eds.) ICIAR 2006. LNCS, vol. 4142, pp. 700–709. Springer, Heidelberg (2006)
6. Krishnapuram, B., Carin, L., Figueiredo, M.A.T., Hartemink, A.J.: Sparse Multinomial Logistic Regression: Fast Algorithms and Generalization Bounds. IEEE Transactions on Pattern Analysis and Machine Intelligence 27(6), 957–968 (2005)
7. Boykov, Y., Veksler, O., Zabih, R.: Fast Approximate Energy Minimization via Graph Cuts. In: IEEE Transactions on Pattern Analysis and Machine Intelligence, vol. 23(11), pp. 1222–1239. IEEE Computer Society Press, Los Alamitos (2001)
8. Hunter, D., Lange, K.: A Tutorial on MM algorithms. The American Statistician 58, 30–37 (2004)
9. Quarteroni, A., Sacco, R., Saleri, F.: Numerical Mathematics. TAM Series, vol. 37. Springer, Heidelberg (2000)
10. Geman, S., Geman, D.: Stochastic relaxation, Gibbs distribution, and the Bayesian restoration of images. IEEE Transactions on Pattern Analysis and Machine Intelligence 6, 721–741 (1984)
11. The MathWorks : MATLAB The Language of Technical Computing - Using MATLAB : version 6. The Math Works, Inc. (2000)
12. Landgrebe, D.A.: NW Indiana's Indian Pine. Available at http://dynamo.ecn.purdue.edu/~biehl/MultiSpec/ (1992)
13. Boykov, Y., Kolmogorov, V.: An experimental comparison of mincut/max-flow algorithms for energy minimization in vision. IEEE Transactions on Pattern Analysis and Machine Intelligence 26(9), 1124–1137 (2004)

Comparison of Unsupervised Band Selection Methods for Hyperspectral Imaging*

Adolfo Martínez-Usó, Filiberto Pla, Jose M. Sotoca, and Pedro García-Sevilla

Dept. Lenguajes y Sistemas Informáticos, Jaume I University
Campus Riu Sec s/n 12071 Castellón, Spain
{auso,pla,sotoca,pgarcia}@uji.es
http://www.vision.uji.es

Abstract. Different methods have been proposed in order to deal with the huge amount of information that hyperspectral applications involve. This paper presents a comparison of some of the methods proposed for band selection. A relevant and recent set of methods have been selected that cover the main tendencies in this field. Moreover, a variant of an existing method is also introduced in this work. The comparison criterion used is based on pixel classification tasks.

1 Introduction

The benefits of hyperspectral imaging in several disciplines is producing many emerging applications. Multi or hyperspectral sensors acquire data from a range of wavelengths in the spectrum and, unquestionably, they have produced an important improvement of the results obtained from just one/three bands in some demanding application fields like remote sensing, medical imaging, product quality inspection, fine arts, etc.

A very focused topic on hyperspectral imaging is the reduction of the amount of input data, which sometimes can be huge and hard to deal with. Obviously, it is essential to perform this task without losing classification accuracy in a significant way. This reduction could be done in two different ways: feature extraction [10,8] or feature selection [1]. In feature extraction we would obtain a new and reduced data set representing the transformed initial information, whereas in feature selection we would have a subset of relevant data from the original information.

In this paper, we present a comparison of several unsupervised methods for reducing the initial amount of information acquired by a multispectral camera by means of the next feature (band) selection methods:

1. WaLuMI: _Ward's Linkage strategy using Mutual Information_ [11] (Sect. 2.1).
2. WaLuDi: _Ward's Linkage strategy using Divergence_, a novel technique presented in this paper (Sect. 2.2).
3. CBS methods: _Constrained Band Selection_ [5] (Sect. 2.3).
4. MVPCA: _Maximum Variance Principal Component Analysis_ [4,5] (Sect. 2.4).
5. ID: _Information Divergence_ [5] (Sect. 2.5).

---

* This work has been partly supported by projects ESP2005-07724-C05-05 from Spanish CICYT.

J. Martí et al. (Eds.): IbPRIA 2007, Part I, LNCS 4477, pp. 30–38, 2007.

The methods have been chosen for their relevance and with the intention of covering as many tendencies as possible in this field. In the case of WaLuDi, which is new, it applies a different measure into the same hierarchical strategy employed by WaLuMI. It has been introduced in order to measure how important the strategy becomes. Thus, attending to the different tendencies covered, we can still do the following classification:

- Methods based on information theory. The use of information measures, like Mutual Information, provide a methodology to find generalised correlations among image bands. Thus, WaLuMi technique [11] exploits this concept for band selection. On the other hand, the here proposed WaLuDi uses a divergence measure that has been frequently used in order to compare different probability distributions.
- Methods based on CBS. Due to the effectiveness that *Constrained Energy Minimisation* (CEM) has shown in hyperspectral target detection, Chang *et al.* [5] have recently published several methods based on this concept in order to perform a new approach to band selection.
- Methods based on eigenanalysis and decorrelation of the input data. They have been widely used in the literature and, therefore, they always provide an interesting reference point in any comparison [4,5].

In section 3, we will show some experimental results using the sets of bands selected by these methods. The final relevance of each method is tested by means of the classification accuracy achieved by the different bands selected.

It was considered useful and necessary to perform this study between the results obtained from information theoretic criteria-based methods and CBS-based methods due to the successful results they achieved with regard to other methods in previous comparisons which are already published [4,5,11]. However, it is always interesting not to lose some perspective on other unsupervised and well-known dimensionality reduction methods of the literature. In this way, the MVPCA and ID methods can be the most relevant ones, and they have been added to this comparison.

Section 4 will conclude with some remarks and a summary about this work.

2 Description of the Methods

2.1 WaLuMI

The methodology of the algorithm presented in [11] can be summarised as follows. A similarity space is defined among bands, where a dissimilarity measure is defined based on the mutual information between a pair of bands. From the initial set of bands that form a multispectral image, the process starts with a hierarchical clustering in the defined dissimilarity space, until reaching the K number of clusters of bands desired. In order to progressively construct a hierarchical family of derived clusters the method uses a linkage strategy with an inter-cluster distance as the objective function to optimise. Finally, a band representing each final cluster is chosen, which are considered the K most relevant bands. The K selected bands from the final K clusters will have a significant degree of independence, and therefore, provide an adequate reduced representation that will provide satisfactory classification results.

2.2 WaLuDi

From information theory [6,12], the Kullback-Leibler divergence can be considered as a kind of a distance between two probability densities, though it is not a real distance measure because it is not symmetric. Thus, a modified version of the Kullback-Leibler divergence is used, which is symmetric and can be used to measure the discrepancy between any two probability distributions. In this sense, it can be also used to measure the similarity between two bands, representing each band by a probability distribution.

Assume that p_l and p_k are the probability distributions associated to the lth and kth bands of a multispectral image. This divergence measure is used as a criterion to know how far the distributions are. Thus, it can be expressed in the discrete domain as follows

$$D(p_l, p_k) = \sum_i p_{l_i} log(\frac{p_{l_i}}{p_{k_i}}) + \sum_i p_{k_i} log(\frac{p_{k_i}}{p_{l_i}}).$$

It is important to stress again that this method follows the same strategy as WaLuMI, that is, a hierarchical clustering process based on the Ward's linkage method, which eventually chooses an instance from each cluster. However, the distance matrix has been changed in order to use D to calculate differences between images. In fact, this measure is also used by Chang *et al.* in [4] to measure the overlapped information contained in any pair of images as a band-decorrelation algorithm.

2.3 LCMV-CBS

In [5], it was developed an approach called *constrained band selection* (CBS), which is different from the variance-based methods or information theoretic criteria-based methods. This approach constrains linearly a band while minimising the correlation or dependency of this particular band from the other bands in a hyperspectral image. CBS methods include four solutions to an optimisation problem, two based on correlation and two based on dependency.

The CBS presented in [5] derives from the *linearly constrained minimum variance* (LCMV) and the *constrained energy minimisation* (CEM) approaches [2]. Thus, it is important to point out that there are two ways to implement these processes. On one hand, the implementation based on CEM involves a huge computational cost, and the alternative approach LCMV [2,7,3] reduces substantially this complexity. The experimental results show that LCMV-CBS and CEM-CBS perform very similarly [5] and the sizes of the images used in this comparison make infeasible the use of the CEM-CBS implementation. Therefore, LCMV-CBS will be the alternative presented in our comparison. In addition, from the four LCMV-CBS methods, *Band Correlation Minimisation* (BCM), *Band Dependence Minimisation* (BDM), *Band Correlation Constraint* (BCC) and *Band Dependence Constraint* (BDC), the BCM/BDM and BCC/BDC alternatives have been joined together due to the similar results they produced (their results were also joined in this way in [5]).

2.4 MVPCA

This section presents a joint band-prioritisation and band-decorrelation approach to band selection which was already used in [4] for hyperspectral image classification and in the comparison of band selection methods published in [5]. The band prioriti-sation was based on an eigenanalysis, decomposing a matrix into an eigenform ma-trix from which a loading factors matrix could be constructed and used to prioritise bands. The loading factors determined the priority of each band and ranked all bands in accordance with their associated priorities. Thus, bands are sorted from high to low variance.

2.5   Information Divergence (ID)

This ID method is related to [5], where the probability distribution associated to each band of the multispectral image is compared with a Gaussian probability distribution. As in section 2.2, let us assume that p_l is the probability distribution associated to the lth band of a multispectral image. Now, we introduce the second probability distribution g_l as a Gaussian distribution with the mean and variance determined by the same lth band. Hence, taking into account probability distributions p_l and g_l and according to the divergence measure introduced in section 2.2, high values in D involve a large deviation from a Gaussian distribution. In this sense, authors in [5] measure the non-Gaussianity and sort the bands according to the decreasing order of ID, that is, from non-Gaussian bands to Gaussian ones.

3   Experiments and Results

To test the described approaches, three different databases of multispectral images were used in the experimental results:

1. The $92AV3C$ source of data corresponds to a spectral image (145 X 145 pixels, 220 bands, 17 classes) acquired with the AVIRIS data set and collected in June 1992 over the Indian Pine Test site in Northwestern Indiana (http:/dynamo.ecn.purdue. edu /~biehl/MultiSpec). As described in [9], several bands should be discarded from this database due to the effect of the atmospheric-absorption. In our case, 177 bands were used, discarding the lower signal-noise ratio bands.
2. $DAISEX'99$ project provides useful aerial images about the study of the variabil-ity in the reflectance of different natural surfaces. This source of data corresponds to a spectral image (700 X 670 pixels, 6 classes) acquired with the 128-bands HyMap spectrometer during the DAISEX-99 campaign (http:/io.uv.es/projects/daisex/). In this case, 126 bands were used, discarding the lower signal-noise ratio bands.
3. Spectrograph RetigaEx (Opto-knowledged Systems Inc., Canada) was used to cre-ate a database of multispectral images of oranges with different defects on their surface. From this database, the VIS collection ranges from 400 nm to 720 nm in the visible spectrum with a spectral resolution of 10 nm (676 X 516 pixels, 33 bands, 4 classes). Thus, the image selected in our experiment belongs to the defect *rot* and no band was discarded in this case.

Figure 1 shows some instances of these databases presented as RGB compositions.
In order to assess the performance of the method, a Nearest Neighbour (NN) classi-fier was used to classify individual pixels into the different classes. The performance

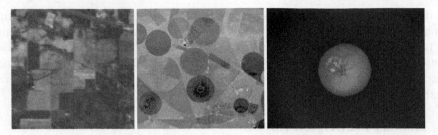

Fig. 1. RGB compositions. First for AVIRIS (92AV3C), second for HyMap spectrometer and third for the Orange image from VIS collection.

of the NN classifier was considered as the validation criterion to compare the significance of the subsets of selected image bands obtained, since there are a significant number of samples. Moreover, in order to increase the statistical significance of the results, classification rates that correspond to the average classification accuracy obtained by the NN classifier over five random partitions are worked out. The samples in each partition were randomly assigned to the training and test set with equal sizes as follows: HyMap = 37520 pixels, 92AV3C = 2102 pixels, VIS = 34882 pixels. The proposed set up satisfies that the sum of the elements from the different partitions

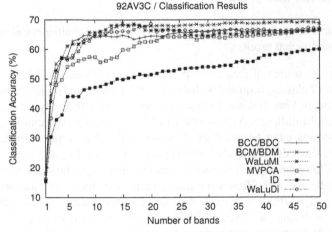

	WaLuMI	WaLuDi	BCC/BDC	BCM/BDM	MVPCA	ID
rank 1	11	5	5	39	0	0
rank 2	15	30	19	8	2	0
rank 3	8	12	10	2	5	0
rank 4	16	3	16	1	7	0
rank 5	0	0	0	0	36	0
rank 6	0	0	0	0	0	50
Average %	63.8216	63.8284	63.3756	65.5876	60.4798	51.3690

Fig. 2. Graphical results for 92AV3C DB. Ranking position out of 50.

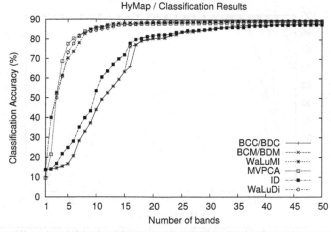

	WaLuMI	WaLuDi	BCC/BDC	BCM/BDM	MVPCA	ID
rank 1	34	38	1	1	13	1
rank 2	13	7	0	0	17	0
rank 3	3	5	0	0	19	0
rank 4	0	0	25	25	0	42
rank 5	0	0	23	24	0	0
rank 6	0	0	1	0	1	7
Average %	83.9308	84.0740	69.5802	69.7912	83.5454	72.0358

Fig. 3. Graphical results for DAISEX'99 DB. Ranking position out of 50.

constitutes the entire original set and the a priori probabilities for each partition are preserved, as well as the statistical independence between training and test sets of every partition.

Using these databases, the described methods were applied in order to obtain a ranking of relevance of the spectral bands. Figures 2, 3 and 4 present graphs with the classification rates related to the subset of K bands selected by each method.

Tables in figures 2, 3 and 4 present the same results as the graphs but, in order to provide an alternative way of interpreting results, these tables summarise the classification rates as a ranking. The first six rows of the tables show how many times each method ranked in each position. Although we have enough precision to assign a different rank to each method, we have rounded the classification rate to the nearest unit and have discarded the decimal figures. This fact involves that several methods can be ranked at the same position[1]. Hence, taking into account all possible values of K (30 or 50 depending on the database used), *rank 1* shows how many times each method won according to the classification rate, *rank 2* shows how many times each method ranked second and so on. On the other hand, the last row of the tables (*average %*) shows the

---

[1] The sum of the ranking of the table rows does not have to be equal to the number of bands considered in x axe in Figures 2, 3 and 4. However, the sum of the ranking columns fulfils this condition since it represents the times that each method has been in each position.

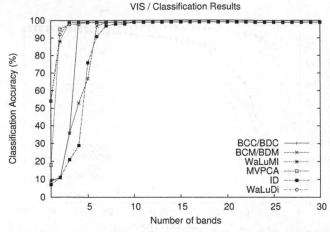

Fig. 4. Graphical results for VIS DB. Ranking position out of 30.

	WaLuMI	WaLuDi	BCC/BDC	BCM/BDM	MVPCA	ID
rank 1	29	27	8	5	26	13
rank 2	0	3	2	1	2	0
rank 3	1	5	0	0	2	0
rank 4	0	0	13	13	0	11
rank 5	0	0	7	9	0	1
rank 6	0	0	0	2	0	5
Average %	97.6790	97.8240	91.4332	88.8165	96.6725	87.4105

classification accuracy average from 1 to 30/50 bands (where we can consider that all the methods reach the plate).

From this comparison several interesting points arise:

1. WaLuMI and WaLuDi methods generally obtained equal or better performance with respect to the rest of methods in all databases. Therefore, regarding to the band selection problem, where there exists high correlation among different features (image bands), the principle of looking for non-correlated bands from the different regions of the spectrum by reducing the mutual information or a divergence measure between two bands, have proved to be effective measures to obtain subsets of bands that also provide results with satisfactory classification accuracy.

2. It is worth remarking how important the methodology used is to achieve the final set of selected bands. Note that only WaLuMI and WaLuDi methods involve a measure among the bands into a global strategy of clustering. Thus, Mutual Information and Divergence measures are not only an adequate correlation or dependence measures, but the clustering strategy applied acquires a special relevance. In fact, the robustness proved by these methods in all databases demonstrates that the effectiveness of the final set of clusters comes from the clustering method adopted. The better these clusters, more robust the final K selected bands become.

3. LCMV-CBS methods, and particularly the BCM/BDM method, provided the best behaviour in 92AV3C image. However, these methods lacked of consistency when HyMap or VIS databases were used because they achieved worse results.
4. MVPCA has generally achieved a good performance (see *average %* row in all databases). Although it achieves few times the best classification rates, its main characteristic is the robustness demonstrated in all databases.
5. ID method was the weaker one, its classification rates are quite poor. This measure of non-Gaussianity seems to be unsuitable to perform a band selection process.

4 Conclusions

Several methods for removing redundant information in hyperspectral imagery have been compared. The classification rates achieved by these methods show how WaLuMI and WaLuDi methods present a more consistent and steadier behaviour with respect to the other methods. On the other hand, LCMV-CBS methods have shown a lack of consistency due to the different results they achieved depending on the input database. In addition, we have also tested classical methods from the dimensionality reduction literature. Thus, it is remarkable how the MVPCA has also obtained a consistent behaviour, whereas ID has always been quite behind all the methods.

We are currently extending this comparison to other databases and other classification techniques. These conclusions have to be considered as a preliminary result that need to be contrasted with more databases of multispectral images. However, the present work seems to point out that measures among the bands integrated in a clustering process work better than other type of approaches.

Acknowledgements

We would like to deeply thank Prof. Chein-I Chang and specially Ms Su Wang, both from RSSIPL, for their help in the implementation of the CBS methods.

References

1. Bruzzonne, L., Roli, F., Serpico, S.B.: An extension to multiclass cases of the jeffreys-matusita distance. IEEE Trans on GRS 33, 1318–1321 (1995)
2. Chang, C.-I.: Hyperspectral Imaging: Techniques for Spectral Detection and Classification. Plenum, New York (2003)
3. Chang, C.I.: Target signature-constrained mixed pixel classification for hyperspectral imagery. IEEE Trans on GRS 40(5), 1065–1081 (2002)
4. Chang, C.I., Du, Q., Sun, T.L., Althouse, M.L.G.: A joint band prioritization and band-decorrelation approach to band selection for hyperspectral image classification. IEEE Trans on GRS 7(6), 2631–2641 (November 1999)
5. Chang, C.I., Wang, S.: Constrained band selection for hyperspectral imagery. IEEE Trans on GRS 44(6), 1575–1585 (2006)
6. Cover, T.M., Thomas, J.A.: Elements of Information Theory. Wiley, Chichester (1991)
7. Frost III, O.L.: An algorithm for linearly constrained adaptive array processing. In: Proc. IEEE 60(8), 926–935 (1972)

8. Jimenez, L., Landgrebe, D.: Supervised classification in high dimensional space: Geometrical, statistical, and asymptotical properties of multivariate data. IEEE Transactions on System, Man, and Cybernetics 28, Part C(1), 39–54 (1998)
9. Jimenez, L.O., Landgrebe, A.: Hyperspectral data analysis and supervised feature reduction via projection pursuit. IEEE Trans on GRS 37(6), 2653–2667 (1999)
10. Kumar, S., Ghosh, J., Crawford, M.M.: Best basis feature extraction algorithms for classification of hyperspectral data. IEEE Trans on GRS 39(7), 1368–1379 (2001)
11. Martinez-Uso, A., Pla, F., Sotoca, J.M., Garcia-Sevilla, P.: Clustering-based multispectral band selection using mutual information. ICPR, pp. 760–763 (2006)
12. Webb, A. (ed.): Statistical Pattern Recognition, 2nd edn. Wiley, Chichester (2002)

Learning Mixture Models for Gender Classification Based on Facial Surface Normals

Jing Wu, W.A.P. Smith, and E.R. Hancock

Department of Computer Science, The University of York, York, YO10 5DD, UK
{jwu,wsmith,erh}@cs.york.ac.uk

Abstract. The aim in this paper is to show how to discriminate gender using a parameterized representation of fields of facial surface normals (needle-maps). We make use of principle geodesic analysis (PGA) to parameterize the facial needle-maps. Using feature selection, we determine the selected feature set which gives the best result in distinguishing gender. Using the EM algorithm we distinguish gender by fitting a two component mixture model to the vectors of selected features. Results on real-world data reveal that the method gives accurate gender discrimination results.

1 Introduction

Humans are remarkably accurate determining the gender of a subject based on the appearance of the face alone. In fact, an accuracy as good as 96% can be achieved with the hair concealed, facial hair removed and no makeup [1]. Experiments by Bruce etc. showed that the gender of the face is conveyed by several cues including: (i) superficial and/or local features, (ii) configural relationships between features, and (iii) the 3-D structure of the face [2]. In [1], Burton etc. attempt to discover a gender discriminator by explicit measurements on the feature points of frontal facial views and profile views. However, their method requires manually labeled 14 landmark points. As a result it is unsuitable for automatic gender classification.

In this paper, we present a statistical framework for gender discrimination that does not require explicit landmark measurements. The method makes use of a representation of facial shape based on a parameterisation of fields of facial needle-maps. The needle-map is a 2.5-D shape representation which is mid-way between the 2D intensity image and the 3D surface height function [3]. The representation can be acquired from 2D intensity images using shape-from-shading [4] and is invariant to illumination. To parameterize the facial needle-maps we make use of principle geodesic analysis (PGA) [5], [6]. PGA is a generalization of principle components analysis (PCA), and is better suited to the analysis of directional data than PCA. Our aim is to distinguish the genders of a sample of subjects by fitting a two-component mixture model to the distribution of the selected PGA parameters.

The standard method to learn the mixture models is the expectation - maximization (EM) algorithm [7], [8], [9], [10]. However, applying the EM algorithm

J. Martí et al. (Eds.): IbPRIA 2007, Part I, LNCS 4477, pp. 39–46, 2007.

directly to high dimensional facial needle-maps yields two problems. The first is the analysis of the distribution of needle-maps cannot be effected in a linear way, because a linear combination of unit vectors (normals) is not itself a unit vector. The second problem is that the covariance over the full dimensions of the data is too large to be computationally tractable. The first of these problems is overcomed if we use PGA parameters (feature vectors) to represent the facial needle-maps since the parameter vectors reside in a vector space. To overcome the problem of dimensionality, we select a d out of the full dimensional feature set to discriminate gender. Experimental results show that the mixture model learnt by our method has a correct gender classification rate of 95.5%.

The outline of the paper is as follows. Section 2 reviews the principal geodesic analysis. Section 3 explores the selected feature set used for gender classification. In Section 4, a description of the learning phase and the classification method is given. Experiments are presented in Section 5. Finally, Section 6 concludes the paper and offers directions for future investigation.

2   Principle Geodesic Analysis

The surface normal $n \in R^3$ may be considered as a point lying on a spherical manifold $n \in S^2$, therefore, we turn to the intrinsic mean and PGA proposed by Fletcher et al. [5] to analyze the variations of the surface normals.

If $u \in T_n S^2$ is a vector on the tangent plane to S^2 at n and $u \neq 0$, the exponential map, denoted Exp_n, of u is the point, denoted $Exp_n(u)$, on S^2 along the geodesic in the direction of u at distance $\| u \|$ from n. This is illustrated in Fig. 1. The log map, denoted Log_n is the inverse of the exponential map.

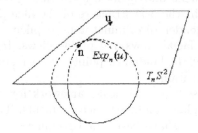

Fig. 1. The exponential map

The intrinsic mean is defined as $\mu = \arg\min_{n \in S^2} \sum_{i=1}^{N} d(n, n_i)$, where $d(n, n_i) = \arccos(n \cdot n_i)$ is the arc length. For a spherical manifold, the intrinsic mean can be found using the gradient descent method of Pennec [6]. Accordingly, the current estimate $\mu^{(t)}$ is updated as follows: $\mu^{(t+1)} = Exp_{\mu^{(t)}} (\frac{1}{N} \sum_{i=1}^{N} Log_{\mu^{(t)}} (n_i))$.

In PGA each principle axis is a geodesic curve. In the spherical case this corresponds to a great circle. For a geodesic G passing through the intrinsic mean μ, π_G may be approximated linearly in the tangent plane $T_\mu S^2$: $Log_\mu(\pi_G(n_1)) \approx$

$\sum_{i=1}^{K} V^i \cdot \text{Log}_\mu(n_1)$, where $V_1, \dots V_K$ is an orthonormal basis for $T_\mu S^2$, which are the principal eigenvectors of the covariance matrix of the long vectors $U = [u^1|\dots|u^K]$. $u^k = [u_1^k, \dots, u_N^k]^T$ is the log mapped long vector of the kth sample data, in our experiment, the kth training needle-map.

We use the numerically efficient snap-shot method of Sirovich [11] to compute the eigenvectors of L. And, in our experiments, we retain the 10 leading eigenvectors of L as the columns of the eigenvector matrix (projection matrix) $\Phi = (e_1|e_2|\dots|e_{10})$. Given a long vector $u = [u_1, \dots, u_N]^T$, we can get the corresponding vector of parameters (feature vector) $b = \Phi^T u$. Given a feature vector $b = [b_1, \dots b_S]^T$, we can generate a needle-map using: $n_p = \text{Exp}_{\mu_p}((\Phi b)_p)$.

3   Feature Selection

As stated in [12], the classification of patterns as performed by humans is based on a very few of the most important attributes. Therefore, we select the most significant features from the PGA parameters for gender discrimination.

To measure the class separability of each feature, we use the criterion function introduced in [12]: $J(\xi) = \frac{|S_w + S_b|}{|S_w|} = \prod_{k=1}^{d}(1 + \lambda_k)$, where S_w and S_b are the between and within class scatter matrices, λ_k, $k = 1 \dots d$ are the eigenvalues of matrix $S_w^{-1} S_b$. The values of J for the first 10 features are shown in Table 1.

Table 1. J values on the first 10 feature components

	B(1)	B(2)	B(3)	B(4)	B(5)	B(6)	B(7)	B(8)	B(9)	B(10)
J	1.6231	1.0681	1.0024	1.0073	1.1644	1.1532	1.0010	1.0026	1.0243	1.0084

Two search algorithms introduced in [12] are explored to select a subset of d out of the 10 features to construct the selected feature set. Best Features is the simplest search algorithm. The selected feature set is formed by the features with the d highest J values. Sequential Forward Selection is a bottom up search procedure. The selected feature set is initialized to be empty. At each time, one feature is selected to be added to the selected feature set so that the new enlarged set of selected features has a maximum J value. In our application, for d from 1 to 10, the two search algorithms have the same results shown in Table 2.

In our empirical selection, we examine the distribution for the first 10 components of the PGA parameter vectors for the 200 data samples in our experiments. Here the first 100 are females, and the last 100 are males (see Fig. 2). By

Table 2. Best Features and Sequential Forward Selection

d	1	2	3	4	5	6	7	8	9	10
J_4	1.6231	2.1057	2.9234	3.5933	3.9282	4.0619	4.1859	4.2311	4.2737	4.2914
Ftrs	1	1,5	1,5,6	1,5,6,2	1,5,6,2,9	1,5,6,2,9, 10	1,5,6,2,9, 10,4	1,5,6,2,9, 10,4,8	1,5,6,2,9, 10,4,8,3	1,5,6,2,9, 10,4,8,3,7

inspection, the 1st, 5th and 6th components have the most significant difference between genders. Figure 3 shows the mean face and its variations along the directions of the 1st, 5th and 6th principal geodesic directions. The 3 feature components do convey some gender information. Turning attention to the 1st component, as λ_1 increases, the face becomes larger and more solid, and, the cheeks thinner. In the case of the 5th component, as λ_5 decreases, the face becomes wider and the eyes deepen. All these are masculine characteristics. In the case of the 6th component, as λ_6 increases, there is also a more masculine appearance. Fig. 2 and Fig. 3 indicate that our empirical selection is consistent with the results of the search algorithms when $d = 3$. However, when d increases, the significance for gender classification of the feature components other than the 1st, 5th, 6th features are not intuitively obvious. In section 5, we will do experiments to evaluate the performance of the different selected feature sets and select the most significant one to be used as the selected feature vectors in gender classification using EM algorithm.

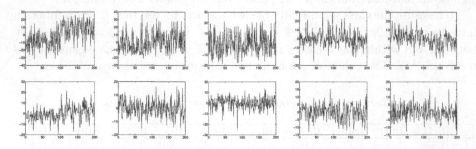

Fig. 2. Plots of the first 10 feature components. From left to right, the first line is B(1), B(2), B(3), B(4), B(5) the second line is B(6), B(7), B(8), B(9), B(10). X axis ranging from 1 to 200 stand for the 200 faces, the first 100 are females, the second 100 are males. Y axis is the value of the feature components.

4   Learning Gaussian Mixture Models

We use the EM algorithm to fit a two component mixture model to vectors of selected features.

In Initialization step, the method outlined in [9] is used. For 2-component Gaussian mixture models, we set $\alpha_1^{(0)} = \alpha_2^{(0)} = \frac{1}{2}$, $\mu_{b1}^{(0)} = \mu_b + \varepsilon_1$, $\mu_{b2}^{(0)} = \mu_b + \varepsilon_2$, and $\Sigma_{b1}^{(0)} = \Sigma_{b2}^{(0)} = det(\Sigma_b)^{1/d}I_d$. Here α_1, α_2 is the a priori probability of each class, μ_b is the overall mean of the selected feature vectors, Σ_b is the overall covariance matrix of the selected feature vectors, ε_1 and ε_2 are two small random vectors of the same dimension of the selected feature vectors.

In E – Step the a posteriori class membership probability is updated by applying the Bayes law to the Gaussian class-conditional density:

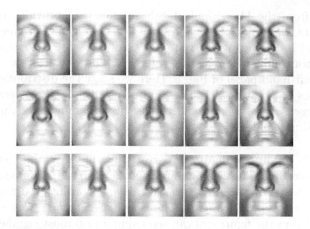

Fig. 3. The mean face and its variances along the 1st, 5th and 6th feature components. The lines are according to the features (from top to bottom): 1st, 5th, 6th features. The columns are according to the variances (from left to right): λ=-30, λ=-20, λ=0 (the mean face), λ=20, and λ=30.

$p(B_j|\mu_{bc}^{(t)}, \Sigma_{bc}^{(t)}) = \frac{1}{\sqrt{(2\pi)^d|\Sigma_{bc}^{(t)}|}} \exp[-\frac{1}{2}(B_j - \mu_{bc}^{(t)})^T \times (\Sigma_{bc}^{(t)})^{-1} \times (B_j - \mu_{bc}^{(t)})]$. Here, B_j donates the selected feature vector of the jth sample data. At iteration t+1, the a posteriori probability is updated as follows:

$$W_c^{(j,t)} \equiv P(j \in c|B_j, \mu_{bc}^{(t)}, \Sigma_{bc}^{(t)}) = \frac{\alpha_c^{(t)}p(B_j|\mu_{bc}^{(t)}, \Sigma_{bc}^{(t)})}{\sum_{i=1}^2 \alpha_i^{(t)}p(B_j|\mu_{bi}^{(t)}, \Sigma_{bi}^{(t)})}. \tag{1}$$

In M – Step the parameters for each class are updated to maximize the expected log-likelihood function. At iteration t+1, the revised estimates of the parameters are: $\alpha_c^{(t+1)} = \frac{1}{n}\sum_{j=1}^n W_c^{(j,t)}$, $\mu_{bc}^{(t+1)} = \frac{\sum_{j=1}^n W_c^{(j,t)}B_j}{\sum_{j=1}^n W_c^{(j,t)}}$, and $\Sigma_{bc}^{(t+1)} = \frac{\sum_{j=1}^n W_c^{(j,t)}(B_j - \mu_{bc}^{(t+1)})(B_j - \mu_{bc}^{(t+1)})^T}{\sum_{j=1}^n W_c^{(j,t)}}$.

After the mixture model of genders has been learnt, we use the a posteriori class probability to classify faces to one of the genders. Given the needle-map n of a test face, first get its selected feature vector b through PGA and feature selection. Then compute the a posteriori probabilities W_f and W_m through formula (1), using the acquired mean vectors μ_{bf}, μ_{bm} and the covariance matrixes Σ_{bf}, Σ_{bm}. If $W_f > W_m$, then the face is classified as female. Otherwise, the face is classified as male.

5   Experiments

In this section, we evaluate the performance of the method for discriminating gender on the basis of the learnt two-component mixture model for the distribution of shape-features. The data consists of 200 facial needle-maps with known ground truth from the Max Plank database [13], [14], provided by the Max-Planck Institute for Biological Cybernetics in Tuebingen, Germany. There are 100 females and 100 males. We first apply PGA to the data to extract the shape parameter vectors and perform feature selection. The visualization of the data is shown in the left-hand panel of Fig. 5. Here we show the distribution of the 1st and 5th features as a scatter plot. The data is relatively well clustered according to gender. There is some overlap and this is due to feminine looking males and masculine looking females.

Experiment 1. We first evaluate the performance of the method using different set of selected features. The 200 data are used to learn the 2-component mixture model. The accuracy of the gender classification according to different selected feature vectors are shown in Fig. 4. The selected feature vectors are indicated from Table 2. From the figure, we can see using 5 or 6 most significant features achieves the highest classification rate. Less or more features both deteriorate the accuracy. The result is consistent with the statement in [12] that humans classification of patterns is based on a very few of the most important attributes. In the following experiments, we use the 1st, 5th, 6th, 2nd, and 9th features to form the selected feature vectors for gender classification.

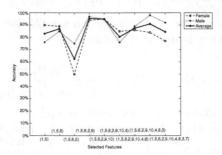

Fig. 4. Classification rates of different selected feature vectors

Experiment 2. We use the 200 data for unsupervised learning. Figure 5 shows the learning steps and the final classification of the data. After convergence of the EM algorithm on the 5-component selected feature vectors, the data are reasonably well clustered according to gender. The correct classification rate reaches 94% for females, and 97% for males, which is comparable to the humans 96% accuracy on gender classification as stated in [1]. From Fig. 5, around 4.5% of the errors are due to the misclassification of the data in the overlap region.

Experiment 3. We randomly selected 40 needle-maps from the 200 available for use as test data. The remaining 160 are used as training data. First, we obtain the 5-component selected feature vectors of the training and test data using the intrinsic mean and projection matrix obtained from the full sample of 200 data. Then we get the mixture model from the training data. We visualize the models

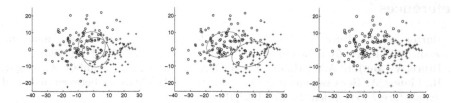

Fig. 5. Learning and classification results visualized on 1st and 5th features. From left to right, are the results of EM initialization, on convergence, and result of classification.

in the left-hand panel of Fig. 6. The classification rate is evaluated by fitting the mixture models to the test data. The result is shown in the right-hand panel of Fig. 6 and compared with the original test data shown in the middle of Fig. 6. The classification rate for females is 90% and for males 95%. This is a good result showing that our method has good generalization.

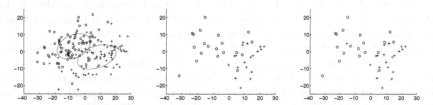

Fig. 6. Training and Testing result visualized on 1st and 5th features. The left is the learnt models on the training data. In the middle is the original testing data. The right is the classification on the testing data.

6   Conclusion

In this paper, we apply feature selection and EM algorithm to PGA shape parameters of the facial needle-maps to perform gender classification. We explore the performances of different feature sets for gender discrimination, and use the EM algorithm to cluster the selected features. Experimental results show that using the selected feature vectors, facial needle-maps can be well clustered according to gender. Moreover, it demonstrates that it is feasible to construct a 2-component Gaussian mixture models from the facial needle-maps to classify the gender.

However, there are still some problems that require further investigation. First, feature selection is based on the simplest search algorithms. And the consistency of the best selected feature set with the empirical selection need further investigation. Second, we will try more reliable EM initialization methods, such as short runs of EM [10], split and merge EM [9]. Third, our current experiments are based on the ground truth needle-maps extracted from range images. In the future, we will apply our method to needle-maps recovered from facial images using SFS.

References

1. Burton, A.M., Bruce, V., Dench, N.: What's the difference between men and women? Evidence from facial measurement. Perception 22, 153–176 (1993)
2. Bruce, V., Burton, A.M., Hanna, E., Healey, P., Mason, O., Coombes, A., Fright, R., Linney, A.: Sex discrimination: how do we tell the difference between male and female faces? Perception 22, 131–152 (1993)
3. Marr, D.: Vision. W.H. Freeman, San Francisco (1982)
4. Smith, W.A.P., Hancock, E.R.: Recovering Facial Shape and Albedo using a Statistical Model of Surface Normal Direction. Tenth IEEE International Conference on Computer Vision 1, 588–595 (2005)
5. Fletcher, P.T., Joshi, S., Lu, C., Pizer, S.M.: Principal geodesic analysis for the study of nonlinear statistics of shape. IEEE Transactions on Medical Imaging 23, 995–1005 (2004)
6. Pennec, X.: Probabilities and statistics on riemannian manifolds: A geometric approach. Technical Report RR-5093, INRIA (2004)
7. Figueiredo, M.A.T., Jain, A.K.: Unsupervised Learning of Finite Mixture Models. IEEE Transactions on Pattern Analysis and Machine Intelligence, vol. 24(3) (2002)
8. Figueiredo, M.A.T., Leitao, J.M.N., Jain, A.K.: On Fitting Mixture Models. In: Hancok, E., Pellilo, M. (eds.) Engergy Minimization Methods in Computer Vision and Pattern Recognition, pp. 54–69. Springer, Heidelberg (1999)
9. Ueda, N., Nakano, R., Ghabramani, Z., Hinton, G.E.: SMEM Algorithm for Mixture Models. Neural Computation 12(9), 2109–2128 (2000)
10. Biernacki, C., Celeux, G., Govaert, G.: Choosing starting values for the EM algorithm for getting the highest likelihood in multivariate Gaussian mixture models. Computational Statistics & Data Analysis 41(3-4), 561–575 (2003)
11. Sirovich, L.: Turbulence and the dynamics of coherent structures. Quart. Applied Mathematics XLV(3), 561–590 (1987)
12. Devijver, P., Kittler, J.: Pattern Recognition: A Statistical Approach. PrenticeHall, Englewood Cliffs (1982)
13. Troje, N., Bulthoff, H.H.: Face recognition under varying poses: The role of texture and shape. Vision Research 36, 1761–1771 (1996)
14. Blanz, V., Vetter, T.: A Morphable Model for the Synthesis of 3D Faces. SIGGRAPH'99 Conference Proceedings, pp. 187–194 (1999)

Feature Selection Based on a New Formulation of the Minimal-Redundancy-Maximal-Relevance Criterion

Daniel Ponsa and Antonio López

Centre de Visió per Computador, Universitat Autònoma de Barcelona
Edifici O, 08193 Bellaterra, Barcelona, Spain
{daniel,antonio}@cvc.uab.es
www.cvc.uab.es/adas

Abstract. This paper proposes an incremental method for feature selection, aimed at identifying attributes in a dataset that allow to buid *good* classifiers at low computational cost. The basis of the approach is the minimal-redundancy-maximal-relevance (mRMR) framework, which attempts to select features relevant for a given classification task, avoiding redundancy among them. Relevance and redundancy have been popularly defined in terms of information theory concepts. In this paper a modification of the mRMR framework is proposed, based on a more proper quantification of the redundancy among features. Experimental work on discrete–valued datasets shows that classifiers built using features selected by the proposed method are more accurate than the ones obtained using original mRMR features.

1 Introduction

In the last years, many research efforts in areas like machine learning, clustering and data mining have focused on problems that require the management of big volumes of data. Applications like multimedia indexing, text classification or gene expression array analysis demand these disciplines to work in domains with tens or hundreds of thousands of variables, while domains hardly surpassed the hundred of variables just few years ago. Elements in datasets are described by a huge number of variables, and selecting a relevant subset of them upon which to focus attention is still an open problem. This is the task carried out by variable or feature selection algorithms[1]. The objective pursued when selecting features may depend on the final application, being common purposes:

- removing useless features (noise or distracters) in order to save computing time and data storage;
- improving the performance of a predictor (a classifier or a regressor) learned from the dataset, since the risk of over-fitting decreases if the domain of the problem has lower dimensionality;

---

[1] In this paper we use equivalently the terms variables and features to denote the attributes of elements in a dataset.

J. Martí et al. (Eds.): IbPRIA 2007, Part I, LNCS 4477, pp. 47–54, 2007.
© Springer-Verlag Berlin Heidelberg 2007

– making the understanding of the process that has generated the dataset
easier (reverse engineering).

For an excellent introduction on feature selection algorithms, the reader is
referred to [1], where different contributions in this field are compiled.

The topic of this paper is feature selection for pattern classification. Given a
labeled dataset of N samples $\{(\mathbf{x}_i, l_i)\}_{i=1}^{N}$, where $\mathbf{x}_i = \{x_{ij}\}_{j=1}^{M}$ is a vector of
M features, and l_i the target classification label, the feature selection problem
consists in finding, from the observation space $\mathbb{R}^M$, a subspace of at most $m \ll M$
features $\mathbb{R}^m$ from where to train a classifier characterizing l. The difficulty of
this task is that the number of possible subspaces in $\mathbb{R}^M$ of dimension less or
equal to m is $\sum_{i=1}^{m} \binom{M}{m}$, and examining all of them exhaustively can not be done
in practice. To deal with this problem, different algorithms have been proposed,
based on suboptimal strategies to explore the space of solutions (greedy search,
best–first, genetic algorithms, etc.). These methods require a criterion to evaluate
the inspected subsets and guide the search. Two different philosophies can be
distinguished depending on the nature of this criterion, namely *wrapping* and
filtering.

Wrappers [2] use the learning machine of interest (the one to be used in the
final classifier) to score subsets according to their predictive power, selecting in
that way features tailored to a particular algorithm. On the other hand, filters
evaluate subsets by criteria independent of the chosen predictor. In general,
filters have a lower computational cost than wrappers, and are commonly used
to preprocess datasets before training classifiers, or before starting a wrapping
process.

This paper proposes a filtering method based on the *minimal-redundancy-
maximal-relevance* (mRMR) proposal in [3]. The aim of the mRMR approach is
to select a subset of features well–suited for a given classification task, by taking
into account the relevance (ability) of features to identify the classification label,
as well as the redundancy among them. These concepts are defined in terms of
the Mutual Information between features. This paper proposes a modification of
the (mRMR) proposal, based on an alternative formulation of the redundancy
among features. The significance of this modification is evaluated experimentally,
by comparing the performance of classifiers in two different problems, when
features selected by the original mRMR method or the ones selected by the
proposed method are used.

This paper is organized as follows. Section 2 reviews information theory concepts necessary to understand the mRMR criterion, which is presented in section 3. Then, section 4 proposes modifications on the mRMR criterion, to make a
more coherent formulation of the concept of redundancy among features. Section
5 quantifies the benefits of the proposed method, by comparing experimentally
the accuracy of classifiers trained with features selected by the presented proposal, against the accuracy of classifiers trained with original mRMR features.
The paper ends by drawing some conclusions.

2 Information Theory Concepts

Consider a discrete[2] random variable x, taking values in the set of N symbols $\{s_i\}_{i=1}^N$. Let $P(s_k)$ be the probability of $x = s_k$, then, the (Shannon's) information obtained when we are informed that $x = s_k$ is computed from the expression

$$I(x) = \log\left(\frac{1}{P(x)}\right) = -\log(P(x)) \ . \tag{1}$$

Thus, the information received by observing $x = s_k$ is bigger the less likely s_k is. If the basis 2 is used for the logarithm, the information in x is measured in bits. For example, if x is a binary variable with states $\{s_1, s_2\}$ of equal probability (i.e. $P(s_1) = P(s_2) = 0.5$), a bit of information is obtained when the state of x is observed. On the other hand, if $P(s_1) = 1$, then the observation of the value of x does not really provide information, since it is already known that its value will be s_1. Equation (1) quantifies the information obtained when a *concrete* value of x is observed. The information that the variable x can provide corresponds to the average of the information provided by the different values it may take. This corresponds to the expectation of the information $E[I(x)]$, which is computed by

$$H(x) = \sum_{i=1}^N P(s_i)I(s_i) = -\sum_{i=1}^N P(s_i)\log(P(s_i)) \ . \tag{2}$$

By $H(x)$ is denoted the *Shannon's entropy* of x, and it is a measure of its uncertainty. Using this same concept, one can compute the uncertainty about x when the state of a second discrete random variable $y = s_j$ is known. Similarly to expression (2), the *conditional entropy* of x given $y = s_j$ is computed by

$$H(x|s_j) = -\sum_{i=1}^N P(s_i|s_j)\log(P(s_i|s_j)) \ .$$

The conditional entropy of x for any value of y corresponds to the weighted average (with respect to $P(y)$ probabilities) of the entropies $H(x|s_j)$. Therefore, it corresponds to

$$H(x|y) = -\sum_{j=1}^N P(s_j)\sum_{i=1}^N P(s_i|s_j)\log(P(s_i|s_j)) \ .$$

$H(x|y)$ measures the uncertainty in x once variable y is known. Combining $H(x|y)$ and $H(x)$, one can quantify the information about x provided by y, what has been termed as the *mutual information* between x and y. This is done with the expression

$$MI(x, y) = H(x) - H(x|y) \ .$$

---

[2] Continuous variables imply equivalent expressions, replacing summatories by integrals, and probabilities by density functions.

That is to say, if from the uncertainty of x one subtracts the uncertainty of x once y is known, this provides the information (in bits) that variable y provides about x. MI is widely used as a measure to determine the dependency of variables. It can be shown that MI can also be computed by

$$MI(x,y) = \sum_{i=1}^{N} \sum_{j=1}^{N} P(s_i, s_j) \log \frac{P(s_i, s_j)}{P(s_i)P(s_j)} \ .$$

Next section describes a proposal to use this concept in order to select a proper subset of features for classification tasks.

3   mRMR Criterion

Many filter approaches to feature selection are based on first ranking features according to a scoring function, to then defining a subset of them from the m ones of highest score. For classification tasks, this scoring function has to identify features with the highest relevance to the class label l. One common approach to quantify this relevance is the mutual information between features and the class label $MI(x, l)$.

The major weakness of this scheme is that, in order to obtain a good classification performance, selecting the m best features does not imply that the best subset of m features is actually selected. Indeed, the combination of two *good* features does not imply improving the classification performance, if both have a very similar behavior in determining l. Thus, it seems reasonable to avoid the *redundancy* among selected features. The work in [3] proposes to do that with the heuristic *minimal–redundancy–maximal–relevance* framework, where the redundancy between two features x and y is determined by $MI(x, y)$. The task of feature selection is posed as selecting from the complete set of features S, a subset S_m of m features that maximizes

$$\frac{1}{m} \sum_{x_i \in S_m} MI(x_i, l) - \frac{1}{\binom{m}{2}} \sum_{x_i, x_j \in S_m} MI(x_i, x_j) \ . \tag{3}$$

This expression takes into account the relevance of features with the class label while penalizing redundancy among them. Since the search space of subsets of m elements in $\mathbb{R}^M$ is too big to be explored in practice, the paper proposes to determine S_m incrementally by means of a forward search algorithm. Having a subset S_{m-1} of $m-1$ features, the feature $x_i \in \{S - S_{m-1}\}$ that determines a subset $\{x_i, S_{m-1}\}$ maximizing (3) is added. It can be shown that this nested subset strategy is equivalent to iteratively optimize the following condition:

$$\max_{x_i \in S - S_{m-1}} \left(MI(x_i, l) - \frac{1}{m-1} \sum_{x_j \in S_{m-1}} MI(x_j, x_i) \right) \ . \tag{4}$$

Experiments in [3] show that for subsets of more than 20 features, the S_m obtained with this method achieves more accurate classification performances than the subset obtained by maximizing the $MI(S_m, l)$ value[3] , while the required computation cost is significantly lower.

4   A Reformulation of the mRMR Criterion

The criterion presented in the previous section is based on an heuristic formulation of how a subset of *good* features for classification purposes should be. It should contain features that provide maximal information of the classification label l, while providing minimal information of the rest of the features in the set. These two concepts are considered in (4) by quantifying this information in bits. However, we found that in order to quantify the redundancy among features, this is not a proper way to proceed. Let's consider an example where $MI(x, y) = 0.5$. This half a bit of information may correspond to different redundancy situations of x and y. For instance, if the uncertainty (information) in x is equal to 0.5 (i.e., its entropy is $H(x) = 0.5$), then $MI(x, y) = 0.5$ tells that y provides at least the same information than x. This means that if a feature subset S_m already contains y, adding the feature x is completely redundant. On the other hand, if $H(x) > 0.5$ and $H(y) > 0.5$, then the redundancy among both variables is *weaker*. By using expression (4) to select features, these two situations are considered identical. In order to represent the concept of redundancy more properly, this paper proposes the use of the coefficient of uncertainty [4]. Given two variables x and y, the term

$$R(x, y) = \frac{MI(x, y)}{H(y)} , \qquad (5)$$

quantifies the redundancy of y with respect to x with a value between $[0, 1]$, with 1 being a situation of complete redundancy. It measures the ratio of information of y already provided by x. Note that this definition of redundancy is non–symmetric (i.e., $R(x, y)$ may not be equal to $R(y, x)$), which is consistent with reality. The fact that the value of x can completely determine the value of y does not mean that the same occurs in the opposite direction. Examples are feature relationships like $y = |x|$, or $y = x^2$. In these cases, adding x in a set that contains y is not completely redundant (some new information is added to the data set), while the opposite assignment is uninformative. By using the redundancy factor in (5), now a new incremental feature selection algorithm is proposed, based on maximizing at each iteration the condition

$$\max_{x_i \in X - S_{m-1}} \left(MI(x_i, l) - \frac{1}{m - 1} \sum_{x_j \in S_{m-1}} R(x_j, x_i) \right) .$$

---

[3] That is, the mutual information between the whole subset of variables and the classification label l.

5   Experiments

In order to test the proposed feature selection algorithm, the experiments on discrete data proposed in [3] have been reproduced, using the Multiple Features dataset of handwritten digits (HDR) and the Arrhythmia dataset (ARR). Both datasets, available at the UCI repository [5], describe its elements by a relatively big number of continuous features. In the experiments, features have been discretized as proposed in [3]. Table 1 details dataset characteristics.

Table 1. Datasets used in the experiments

Dataset	Acronym	Discretization	# Classes	# Examples/class	# Features
Multi-Feature	HDR	-1 if $x_i \le \mu$ 1 otherwise	10	200 per class	649
Arrhythmia	ARR	-1 if $x_i < \mu - \sigma$ 1 if $x_i > \mu + \sigma$ 0 otherwise	2	237 and 183	278

Performance of the mRMR and the proposed method is evaluated by a 10-fold cross validation procedure (Figure 1). From each dataset, 10 pairs of training/testing sets are generated. Then, the feature selection algorithm is applied in each training set, generating a sequence of 50 nested subsets $S_1 \subset S_2 \subset \ldots \subset S_{50}$ maintaining the features selected to solve the classification task. For a given subset S_i, a linear Support Vector Machine (SVM) is trained using the training portion of the dataset, and then its accuracy is quantified by the classification error rate on the testing portion. To train and test classifiers, the SVM implementation in the LIBSVM package [6] has been used, using default parameters.

The feature selection methods implemented require the availability of the probability terms $P(x)$ and $P(x, y)$ for features in the dataset. These terms

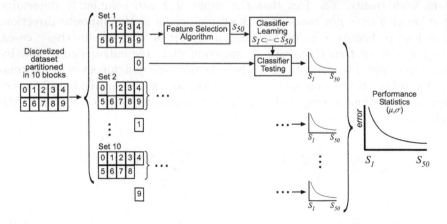

Fig. 1. 10–fold Cross-Validation process

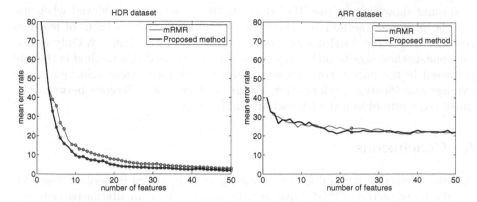

Fig. 2. Mean error rate of the classifiers learned using the mRMR approach, and the proposed method, for the HDR and ARR datasets. Circles on plotted lines highlight cases where the difference in performance is statistically significant ($\alpha = 0.05$).

have been simply estimated by counting the relative frequency of the categorical symbols of each feature in the dataset. For instance, $P(x = 1)$ is determined by the number of examples in the dataset having $x = 1$, divided by the total number of examples.

Figure 2 shows, for each dataset, the mean classification error rate of the classifiers learned using features selected by the two methods considered. For each subset of features S_i, an statistical test has been applied to determine whether the classifiers obtained with the proposed method really outperform the mRMR ones. This has been done using the 10-Fold Cross-Validated Paired t test described in [7]. For the cases in which methods have a statistical significant difference in their performance, plots have been highlighted with a circle.

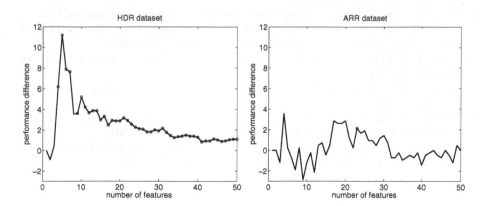

Fig. 3. Difference between the mean error rates obtained with each method. Positive values correspond to improvements provided by the proposed method. Circles on plotted lines highlight statistically significant differences ($\alpha = 0.05$).

Results show that in the HDR dataset, the performance achieved when using the proposed method is clearly better for most of the subsets of features considered. For the ARR dataset, both methods perform similarly. Only in one case one method significantly outperforms the other, and this method is the one proposed in the paper. For a clearer view of the improvement achieved in the average classification performance, Figure 3 shows the difference between the mean error rate obtained with each method.

6   Conclusions

A feature selection method for classification tasks has been presented. The proposal is based on the mRMR framework [3], an introduces an alternative criterion to quantify the redundancy among features. This criterion leads to a feature selection algorithm better suited for classification purposes than the original mRMR proposal. This has been certified in experiments done, measuring the performance of SVM classifiers when trained using the features selected by our proposal and the ones by [3]. Results show that with the features selected by the proposed method, classifiers perform at least as well, and in many cases statistically significantly better, than using the original mRMR selected features.

Acknowledgments. This research has been partially funded by Spanish MEC project TRA2004-06702/AUT.

References

1. Guyon, I., Elisseeff, A.: An introduction to variable and feature selection. Journal of Machine Learning Research (3), 1157–1182 (2003)
2. Kohavi, R., John, G.H.: Wrappers for feature subset selection. Artificial Intelligence 97(1–2), 273–324 (1997)
3. Peng, H., Long, F., Ding, C.: Feature selection based on mutual information: Criteria of max–dependency, max–relevance, and min–redundancy. IEEE Transactions on Pattern Analysis and Machine Intelligence 27(8), 1226–1238 (2005)
4. Press, W.H., Flannery, B., Teukolsky, S.A., Vetterling, W.T.: Numerical recipes in c. Cambridge (1988)
5. Newman, D.J., Hettich, S., Blake, C., Merz, C.: UCI repository of machine learning databases (1998)
6. Chang, C.C., Lin, C.J.: LIBSVM: a library for support vector machines. Software available at http://www.csie.ntu.edu.tw/~cjlin/libsvm. (2001)
7. Dieterich, T.G.: Approximate statistical test for comparing supervised classification learning algorithms. Neural Computation 10(7), 1895–1923 (1998)

Topological Histogram Reduction Towards Colour Segmentation

Eduard Vazquez, Ramon Baldrich, Javier Vazquez, and Maria Vanrell

Computer Vision Center, Dept. Ciències de la Computació. Edifici O, Universitat Autònoma de Bacelona. 08193 Bellaterra (Barcelona), Spain

Abstract. One main process in Computer Vision is image segmentation as a tool to other visual tasks. Although there are many approaches to grey scale image segmentation, nowadays most of the digital images are colour images. This paper introduces a new method for colour image segmentation. We focus our work on a topological study of colour distribution, e.g., image histogram. We argue that this point of view bring us the possibility to find dominant colours by preserving the spatial coherence of the histogram. To achieve it, we find and extract ridges of the colour distribution and assign a unique colour at every ridge as a representative colour of an interest region. This method seems to be not affected by shadows in a wide range of tested images.

1 Introduction

Image segmentation is a useful tool, as a prior step, on quite computer vision tasks and, in this sense, an accurate and fast segmentation is required to work on real problems. On natural segmentation tasks, colour is a visual cue which humans use to differentiate between several objects on real world. Moreover, some methods reinforce this cue with the spatial coherence to distinguish between objects of an image. This paper proposes a method for colour image segmentation without the spatial coherence and its viability in real image segmentation. Although we are focused on the above conditions, the method can be extended to introduce spatial information.

On existing literature we can find some different methods focused on colour segmentation. A survey of these methods can be read on [1] and [2]. We are interested on the segmentation process as a topological analysis of the colour distribution. In this sense the existing method that best suit this model is the mean shift algorithm [3,4]. It is focused on finding regions with high density and join different local maxima by detecting saddle points. But, whereas mean shift works under a statistical point of view by finding the modes of a density function, we propose to find meaningful information under a topological point of view by taking a colour histogram as a 3-dimensional landscape. To achieve this topological segmentation, we propose a two step algorithm. First we apply a creaseness algorithm to enhance interest regions and discard regions of a low interest and, second, we propose an algorithm to find meaningful ridges from the relevant information in the creaseness values of the colour distribution. These

J. Martí et al. (Eds.): IbPRIA 2007, Part I, LNCS 4477, pp. 55–62, 2007.

ridges will represent the most representative colours, or dominant colours present in the image.

The paper is organized as follows: section 2 introduces the method and justifies the ridge concept; section 3 introduces our two-steps algorithm;. Section 4 shows some results, discussing the parameters in the operator, and conclusions and further work can be found on section 5.

2   Method Outline

A grey-scale NxM image can be understood as an NxM landscape using grey values as height. What we propose is to extend this idea at our 3-dimensional space (colour histogram). The height value is explained, in our case, by the number of occurrences of every colour in the image, whereas red, green and blue in RGB space or hue, saturation and lightness on HSL, and so on, are the spatial position of each colour in the landscape. Theoretically, a surface with an homogeneous RGB colour should have just one RGB coordinate in its histogram. The problem resides in incident light and on the own acquisition devices which cause an elongated cloud (from shadows to saturation) in the RGB cube. What we expect is to extract the most representative colour inside this cloud, ideally, the original RGB value. We argue that inside this cloud exists a unique path with maximum height, e.g., a ridge, which summarizes the whole cloud and keeps the most representative colour.

The main idea of this ridge extraction is that ridges join different local maxima, e.g., local maxima which can be conceptually considered to belong to the same topological structure, and this idea avoids a possible over-segmentation and introduces the idea of spatial distribution coherence. Figures 1a and 1b illustrates with an ideal example this concept of distribution coherence that we include to achieve a good reduction of the RGB histogram. Figures 1c and 1d show a simplified 2D example (just showing normalized Red and Green channels) with a real image. In figure 1d we can guess a peak for every dominant colour in figure 1c. In other words, there exist, inside the histogram distribution, an intrinsic low-dimensional structure which summarizes the distribution preserving the spatial relationships between meaningful data. To find this structure we need, first, to spurn non representative data and, second, achieve a measurement that allow us to detect these possible highest paths without gaps due to local irregularities. In this sense, mean shift procedure has its own method for saddle point detection but has, as a main drawback, a high computational cost because it requires multiple initializations and some prior knowledge is needed to reduce the number of executions [5]. We propose to work on the topological definition of ridge.

3   Topological Reduction of a Colour Distribution

As we told, we need to find a method to avoid the drawbacks related to acquisition conditions. In this sense, the operator proposed in [6], named *Multilocal*

Fig. 1. Different possible shape interpretations for m_1 and m_2. Without p_1, p_2 and p_3, is not possible to distinguish between (a) and (b); (c) a real image and (d) its normalized Red-Green histogram, in spite of we really work with RGB histogram, but it is, obviously, impossible to show a 4-Dimensional space.

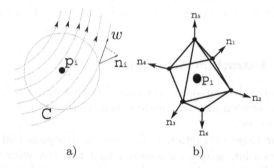

Fig. 2. (a) Geometry involved in the definition of $k(p)$. A boundary C given by a neighbourhood of size σ_1. Divergence will be the dot product between vectors $\bar{w}$ and n.(b) Boundary C for a 3D ($d = 3$) regular grid according to the six nearest neighbours ($r = 6$).

Creassenes Based on the Level-Set Extrinsic Curvatures Based on the Image Structural Tensor Field (MLSEC-ST), in the following $\gamma(D, \sigma_1, \sigma_d)$, gives us a useful tool. The creaseness analysis associates to every point the likelihood to be a ridge point and it is not affected by local irregularities. This operator assigns, to every point p, a creaseness value $k(p)$, by means of divergence calculation $Div(\overline{w}_p)$ between normalized gradient vector $\overline{w}_p$ and unit normal vectors $n_1, ..., n_r$ of the neighbourhood points. Multilocality, e.g., the fact because this operator is not affected by local irregularities, is achieved by computing divergence , not just on a point p, but taking into account gradient vectors of a neighbourhood of size σ_i. Figure 2a shows a graphical example. We define the creaseness operator on a d-dimensional space with r-connectivity neighbourhood (see figure 2b) as:

$$k(p) = -Div(\overline{w}_p) = -\frac{d}{r} \sum_{k=1}^{r} \overline{w}_k^t(\sigma_i) \cdot n_k \tag{1}$$

Finally to improve results, the Structural Tensor (ST) study allows us to get a coarse measure of the degree of anisotropy to assign low creaseness values at zones of low interest like flat regions. ST performs an eigensystem calculation of gradient vectors on the neighbourhood with a Gaussian kernel of standard deviation σ_d and, as a result, enhances dominant directions of landscape. Then we can summarize first step of our algorithm as follows:

$$C(D) = \gamma(D, \sigma_1, \sigma_d). \tag{2}$$

Where D is a given distribution; in this case, D is the image histogram.

Once we apply the creaseness operator, we have enhanced the meaningful information of D, without gaps due to local irregularities, on a new distribution C. This information can be collected by a ridge extraction procedure as a good descriptor of D and its spatial structure. In this sense, if we directly extract ridges on D, local irregularities will break ridges and it will cause different interpretations where, if we maintain spatial coherence, there should be only one.

3.1   The Ridge Extraction Algorithm

A good ridge characterization on a gray-scale image domain is introduced in [7] and a comparison between main algorithms is introduced in [8] where the use of $\gamma(D, \sigma_1, \sigma_d)$ is proposed.

Our method for ridge extraction is focused on a topological point of view. If we want to cross a landscape, we consider that the way with lowest cost is a ridge. When we walk across a ridge, we observe that mountain falls on both sides. In other words, a ridge occurs where there is a local maximum in one direction or, symmetrically, when a zero crossing on the gradient image occurs. It can be translated, in discrete domain, as follows: x is a ridge point if is higher than all its neighbours except one point x' which is, in fact, a neighbour belonging to the ridge. Hence, in a 3-dimensional r, g, b space with 26-connectivity neighbourhood, we define $R(C) = \{r_1, ..., r_n\}$, the collection of ridge points, as:

$$R(C) = \{x \in C \mid \mu(x, C) < 2\} \tag{3}$$

$$\mu(x, C) = \sharp \{y \in neighbourhood(x) \mid C(y) \geq C(x)\} \tag{4}$$

This ridge operator is defined and discussed in [9]. But due to discrete domain, this approach has some drawbacks as figure 3a illustrates. The main problem is that ridges are broken and it entail an over-segmented image.

We propose a new definition of ridge operator on the discrete domain, by beginning in points which are not affected by discretization, e.g., local maxima (figure 3b). Hence, as initialization step, we find local maxima on C, $\lambda(C)$ as follows:

$$\lambda(C) = \{x \in C \mid \mu(x, C) = 0\} \tag{5}$$

Then, we just have to follow ridges starting on $\lambda(C)$ points to avoid discretization problems. It means that we follow a ridge from a local maximum until its

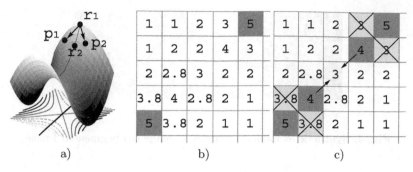

a) b) c)

Fig. 3. (a) an example of discretization: r_1 and r_2 are ridge points. Theoretically r_2 should be higher than all neighbours except r_1, but the discreatization process takes p_1 and p_2 as points higher than r_2. (b),(c) A synthetic 2D creaseness image: (b) Local maxima found in gray, e.g., $\lambda(C)$. (c) Second step: Applying $\mathcal{R}(C)$ points labeled with 4 become ridge points. The next step should be to go to light grey squares labeled with 3.8, but we do not take these into account because belong to Ω. Then, we achieve a straight ridge. On the next step just the central point of the square can be a ridge point.

ending. Let $neigh(x) = \{n_1, ..., n_{26}\}$ be the neighbourhood of a point x. We also define $\Omega(x, n_j) = \{\omega_1, ..., \omega_r\}$,$j = 1..26$, as the set containing common neighbours between x and one of its neighbours n_j; having $r = 16$ if $dist(x, n_j) = 1$, $r = 10$ if $dist(x, n_j) = \sqrt{2}$ and $r = 6$ if $dist(x, n_j) = \sqrt{3}$. Where $dist(x, n_j)$ is the euclidean distance. Notice that neither x nor n_j are included in Ω. Then, we define the ridge points in a creaseness image C, as:

$$\lambda_z(C) = \lambda_{z-1}(C) \bigcup \{n \in neigh(l) \mid l \in \lambda_{z-1}(C), \mu'(l, n) = 0\} (C) \qquad (6)$$

$$\mu'(x, n_j) = \sharp \{y \in \Omega(x, n_j) \mid C(y) \geq C(n_j)\} \qquad (7)$$

Then, we add iteratively new points to $\lambda(C)$. This process stops, in the pth step, when ridge arrives on a flat region, achieving a new image with as many ridges as mountains in C. Hence:

$$\mathcal{R}(C) = \lambda_p(C) \qquad (8)$$

Once we find a new ridge point n_j, we will not to take into account points belonging to $\Omega(x, n_j)$ as a possible ridge points on a further steps, in order to avoid discretization problems and achieve a ridge of width equal to 1 as figure 3b and 3c illustrates.

As we told before, every ridge r_j summarizes its mountain, lets said, M_j. In a final step, we assign to every point x belonging to M_j the average colour of r_j. It implies that we must know the borders of M_j. At present, we do an approximation by making a rgb cube partition with a Voronoi calculus from ridges.

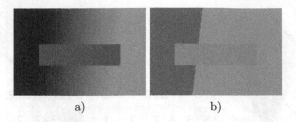

a)   b)

Fig. 4. Synthetic example: (a) Original image (b) Segmented Image

4   Experimental Results

With our topological colour segmentation we have achieve promising results. Prior experimental results demonstrate that our operator is not affected by shadows in a wide range of digital images. Furthermore, whole process works at quasi-real time since it is able to process seven images per second on a standard PC.

When we deal with colour distributions we must choose a correct colour representation between all well-known colour spaces. The most used colour space is the RGB (red, green, blue) space, basically due to acquisition and display devices which usually work with this three chromatic coordinates. Some other possibilities would be perceptual colour spaces as CIELUV or CIELAB, [10] and other device dependent spaces such as HSL or NRGB [11]. Since our topological distribution reduction is a generic operator and is not focused on a concrete colour space, we do not care on which space we perform its behavior analysis. As for experimental use, we test it on RGB, CIELAB and normalized RGB spaces. Figure 4 shows an example with a synthetic RGB image.

In order to evaluate the possibilities of our method, we used real indoor and outdoor images, what allows us to better appreciate how exactly ridges are found, because histogram of a synthetic image is not enough illustrative. Figue 5 shows an example of the whole procedure. First, we take an RGB image (figure 5a) and its histogram (figure 5b). Ridges found, and final partition of RGB cube, can be seen on figure 5c. We can observe that ridges maintain the structure of the original colour distribution. Finally, figure 5d shows the segmented image.

Figure 6a and 6b illustrates an example with a CIELAB image. The main problem is that perceptual colour spaces require a calibrated image for a good conversion from another space. Thus, to convert non calibrated images to a perceptual colour space will imply some errors, and its viability should be evaluated. What does not mean that RGB is the best representation for colour segmentation. Actually, RGB has two important shortcomings. First, the nonlinearity, second, a high correlation between its components, and third, is not a perceptually uniform space, e.g., relative distances between colours do not reflect the perceptual differences. HSV is a linear transformation from RGB, thus, inherits its drawbacks. Finally, figures 6c and 6d show an example with normalized RGB which tries to avoid the effects related to incident light.

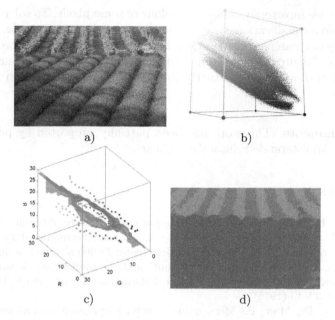

Fig. 5. Real image example:(a)Original outdoor image.(b) RGB histogram of a). (c) Ridges found and RGB cube final partition. (d) Image segmented.

Fig. 6. Real image example: (a)Original outdoor CIELAB image and (b) its segmentation. (c)NRGB image and (d) its segmentation.

On these experiments the behavior of σ_i and σ_d has been checked, It seems that results are robust against slight changes of σ_1 and σ_d. In fact, results of figures 4 and 5 have the same σ_i and σ_d values.

5   Conclusions

Our topological colour segmentation method attain good results on a wide range of images even without using spatial coherence and is conceptually easy and computationally efficient.

Nevertheless there are some things that must be improved. First, the RGB cube partitioning is, right now, just an approximation of the best solution because delimitation between mountains is not correctly found. It means that, in some images, we incorrectly assign the colour of some pixels. To solve this problem we can do a classification of every coordinate of the histogram or, at least, a further study of creaseness distribution, to find where exactly the borders of any mountain are. Finally, we must study other colour spaces and the characteristics of the segmentation, or what exactly implies to do a segmentation in each of these spaces.

Acknowledgments. This work has been partially supported by project TIN 2004-02970 (Ministerio de Educación y Ciencia).

References

1. Lucchese, L., Mitra, S.: Color image segmentation: A state-of-the-art survey
2. Llahí, J.V.: Color constancy and image segmentation techniques for applications to mobile robotics, Ph.D. dissertation, Universitat Politécnica de Catalunya (2005)
3. Fukunaga, K., Hostetler, L.D.: The estimation of the gradient of a density function, with applications in pattern recognition. Information Theory, IEEE Transactions on 121(1), 32–40 (1975)
4. Comaniciu, D., Meer, P.: Mean shift: A robust approach toward feature space analysis. IEEE Trans. Pattern Anal. Mach. Intell. 24(5), 603–619 (2002)
5. Comaniciu, D., Ramesh, V., Bue, A.D.: Multivariate saddle point detection for statistical clustering. In: Heyden, A., Sparr, G., Nielsen, M., Johansen, P. (eds.) ECCV 2002. LNCS, vol. 2350, pp. 561–576. Springer, Heidelberg (2002)
6. López, A.M., Lloret, D., Serrat, J., Villanueva, J.J.: Multilocal creaseness based on the level-set extrinsic curvature. Computer Vision and Image Understanding: CVIU 77(2), 111–144 (2000)
7. Wang, L., Pavlidis, T.: Direct gray-scale extraction of features for character recognition. IEEE Trans. Pattern Anal. Mach. Intell. 15(10), 1053–1067 (1993)
8. López, A.M., Lumbreras, F., Serrat, J., Villanueva, J.J.: Evaluation of methods for ridge and valley detection. IEEE Trans. Pattern Anal. Mach. Intell. 21(4), 327–335 (1999)
9. Vazquez, E., Baldrich, R., Tous, F., Vanrell, M.: n-dimensional distribution reduction preserving its structure. In: Artificial Intelligence Research and Development I, 167–175 (2006)
10. Fairchild, M.D.: Color Appearance Models. Addison-Wesley, London, UK (1998)
11. Tkalcic, J.T.M.: Colour spaces - perceptual, historical and applicational background, In: Zajc, M.T.B. (eds.) Eurocon 2003 Proceedings, IEEE Region, vol. 8 (2003)

Dealing with Non-linearity in Shape Modelling of Articulated Objects*

Grégory Rogez**, Jesús Martínez-del-Rincón***, and Carlos Orrite

CVLab, Aragon Institute for Engineering Research, University of Zaragoza, Spain
{grogez, jesmar, corrite}@unizar.es
http://www.cv.i3a.unizar.es

Abstract. We address the problem of non-linearity in 2D Shape modelling of a particular articulated object: the human body. This issue is partially resolved by applying a different Point Distribution Model (PDM) depending on the viewpoint. The remaining non-linearity is solved by using Gaussian Mixture Models (GMM). A dynamic-based clustering is proposed and carried out in the Pose Eigenspace. A fundamental question when clustering is to determine the optimal number of clusters. From our point of view, the main aspect to be evaluated is the mean gaussianity. This partitioning is then used to fit a GMM to each one of the view-based PDM, derived from a database of Silhouettes and Skeletons. Dynamic correspondences are then obtained between gaussian models of the 4 mixtures. Finally, we compare this approach with other two methods we previously developed to cope with non-linearity: Nearest Neighbor (NN) Classifier and Independent Component Analysis (ICA).

1 Introduction

Thanks to the structural knowledge, people are able to deduce the pose of an articulated object (e.g. a person) from a simple binary silhouette. Following this statement, our idea was to construct a human model encapsulating within a point distribution model (PDM) [1] body silhouette information given by the 2D Shape (landmarks located along the contour) and the structural information given by the 2D Skeleton joints. In that way, the 2D pose could be inferred from the silhouette. Due to the high non-linearity of the feature space, mainly caused by the rotational deformations inherent to the articulated structure of the human body, we consider in this work the necessity to use non-linear statistical models. They have been previously proposed by Bowden [2] that demonstrated how the 3D structure of an object can be reconstructed from a single view of its outline.

In a previous work[3], we presented a first version of the model. The problem of non-linear principal component analysis was partially resolved by applying a different PDM depending on previous pose estimation (4 views were considered:

---

* Work supported by spanish grant TIC2003-08382-C05-05 (MCyT) and FEDER.
** Funded by FPU grant AP2003-2257 from Spanish Ministry of Education.
*** Supported by Spanish Ministry of Education under FPI grant BES-2004-3741.

J. Martí et al. (Eds.): IbPRIA 2007, Part I, LNCS 4477, pp. 63–71, 2007.

frontal, lateral, diagonal and back views) and the same procedure will be followed in this work. Additionally, results were obtained from measurement by selecting the closest shape from the training set by means of a Nearest Neighbour (NN) classifier. However, to cope with the remaining non-linearity, we consider in this work the use of Gaussian Mixture Models (GMM). A dynamic-based clustering is considered by partitioning the 3D pose space. The 4 view-based GMM are then built in their respective Shape space using this same labelling. Dynamic correspondences are then obtained between gaussian models of the 4 mixtures. In [4], we proposed to use Independent Component Analysis (ICA) to cope with the problem of non-linearity in human shape modelling. Results obtained with our GMM will be compared with results from ICA and NN modelling.

In Sect. 2, we introduce the training database construction. In Sect. 3, we detail the construction of our view-based GMM. Some results are presented in Sect. 4 and some conclusions are finally drawn in Sect. 5.

2   Human Shapes and Skeletons Training Database

Our goal is to construct a statistical model which represents a human body and the possible ways in which it can deform. Point distribution models (PDM) are used to associate silhouettes (shapes) and their corresponding skeletal structures.

Training Database construction. The generation of our 2D deformable model follows a procedure similar to [5]. CMU MoBo database [6] is considered for the training stage: good training Shapes are extracted manually trying to get accurate and detailed approximations of human contours. Simultaneously, we extract 13 fundamental points corresponding to a stick model: head centre, shoulders, elbows, wrists, hips, knees and ankles. The Skeleton vectors are then defined as $\mathbf{k}_i = [x_{k1}, ..., x_{k13}, y_{k1}, ..., y_{k13}]^\top$. Two gait cycles (low and high speed) and 4 viewpoints (frontal, lateral, diagonal and back views) are considered for each one of the 15 selected subjects. By this manual process we generated a very precise database but without shape-to-shape landmarks correspondences.

Shapes Normalization. The good results obtained by a PDM depend critically on the way the data set has been normalized and on the correspondences that have been established between its members [7]. Human silhouette is a very difficult case since people can take a large number of different poses that affect the contour appearance. A big difficulty relies on establishing correspondences between landmarks and normalizing all the possible human shapes with the same number of points. We propose to use a large number of points for defining all the contours and "superpose" those points that are not useful (see Fig.1).

We apply a rectangular grid with horizontal lines equally spaced to the contours database. This idea appears as a solution to the global verticality of the shapes and the global horizontality of the motion. The intersections between contours and grid are then considered. The Shapes are then divided into 3 different zones delimited by three fixed points: the higher point of the head (FP1) and the intersections with a line located at 1/3 of the height (FP2 and

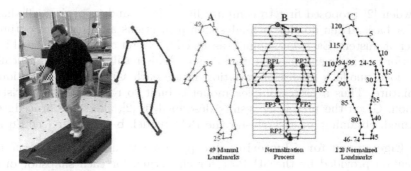

Fig. 1. From *left* to *right*: MoBo Image, 2D Skeleton and Shape normalization: hand-labelled landmarks (A), rectangular grid (B), 120 normalized landmarks (C), part of them grouped at "repository points": 24-26 at RP2, 46-74 at RP3 and 94-99 at RP1

FP3). A number of landmarks is thus assigned to each segment and a repository point (RP) is selected to concentrate all the points that have not been used. In this paper, all the training Shapes are made of 120 normalized landmarks, $\mathbf{s}_i = [x_{s1}, ..., x_{s120}, y_{s1}, ..., y_{s120}]^\top$.

PCA Model. Shapes and Skeletons are then concatenated into Shape-Skeleton vectors $\mathbf{v}_i = [\mathbf{s}_i^\top \ \mathbf{k}_i^\top]^\top$. This training set is aligned using Procrustes analysis (each view being aligned independently) and Principal Component Analysis (PCA) is applied [1] for dimensionality reduction generating 4 models so that:

$$\mathbf{v} \simeq \bar{\mathbf{v}} + \mathbf{Pb} \tag{1}$$

where $\bar{\mathbf{v}}$ is mean Shape-Skeleton vector, $\mathbf{P}$ is the matrix of Eigenvectors and $\mathbf{b}$ is the projection of $\mathbf{v}$ in the Eigenspace i.e. a vector of weights $\mathbf{b} = [b_1, b_2...b_n]^\top$. The main problem relies on the inherent non linearity of the data we assume to be Gaussian when applying PCA. This leads to a wrong description of the data set and drives us to search for new approaches.

3   View-Based Shape-Skeleton Gaussian Mixture Models

Related previous works. Many researchers have proposed approaches to non-linear PDM [1,2]. The use of Gaussian Mixture Model (GMM) was proposed by Cootes and Taylor [1]. They suggested modelling non-linear data sets using a GMM fitted to the data using the Expectation Maximisation (EM) algorithm. This provides a more reliable model since the feature space is limited by the bounds of each Gaussian that appear to be more precise local constraints.

$$p_{mix}(\mathbf{b}) = \sum_{j=1}^{m} \omega_j \, \mathcal{N}(\mathbf{b} : \bar{\mathbf{b}}_j, \mathbf{S}_j) \tag{2}$$

where $\mathcal{N}(\mathbf{b} : \bar{\mathbf{b}}, \mathbf{S})$ is the p.d.f. of a gaussian with mean $\bar{\mathbf{b}}$ and covariance $\mathbf{S}$.

Bowden [2] proposed first to compute linear PCA and to project all shapes on PCA basis. Then do cluster analysis on projections and select an optimum number of clusters. Each data point is assigned to cluster and separate local PCA are performed independently on each cluster. This results in the identification of the local model's modes of variation inside each Gaussian distribution of the mixture. Thus a more complex model is built to represent the statistical variation. Given the promising results described in [2], the same procedure is performed, obtaining for each cluster the PCA model: $\mathbf{b} \simeq \bar{\mathbf{b}} + \boldsymbol{\Phi}\mathbf{r}$ (see Eq.1).

Pose Eigenspace for Clustering. We proposed to use only the structural information provided by the 3D Pose for clustering: for each snapshot of the training set, the 3D Skeleton is built from the corresponding 2D poses $\mathbf{k}_i$ of the 4 views. The resulting set of 3D Poses is reduced by PCA obtaining the Pose Eigenspace (Fig.2a) that will be considered to obtain a dynamic-based clustering.

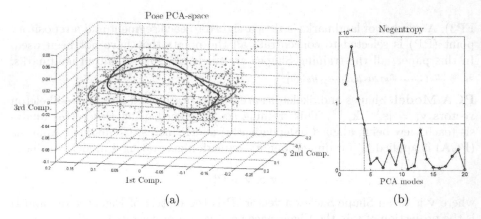

(a)   (b)

Fig. 2. (a) Low and high speed gait cycles represented on the 3 first modes of the Pose Eigenspace. (b) Negentropy of the 20 first modes of the Pose Eigenspace.

Principal components selection. The non-linearity of the training set is mainly localized in the first components of the PCA that capture the dynamics, as shown in Fig.2a. These components are really influent during the partitioning step while the last ones, more linear, only model local variations (details) and do not provide so much information for clustering. We propose to select only the first non-linear components to perform the clustering of the data in a lower dimensional space. For components selection, we need to measure the non-gaussianity of the data on each component. We thus exploit Negentropy, the classic information theory's measure of non-Gaussianity, whose value is zero for Gaussian distribution. Fig.2b shows how the Negentropy converges to 0 when considering lower modes. This convergence is achieved at the 4th mode. According to this analysis, the 3 first components will be considered for clustering.

Determining the number of clusters. K-means algorithm is used fairly frequently as a result of its ease of implementation but it is extremely sensitive to the initial seeds. We run the algorithm N times and cluster the NxK resulting points. For each case (k=2...N), a GMM is fitted to the Pose Eigenspace using the Expectation Maximisation (EM) and a local PCA's is applied on each cluster. Since we want to model local modes of variation inside each Gaussian distribution of the mixture, one of the aspects that should be evaluated when determining the optimal number of cluster is the global gaussianity of the GMM. All the points of the training set are then projected onto the corresponding local PCA space and the Negentropy is computed for each cluster. In Fig.3a, we can

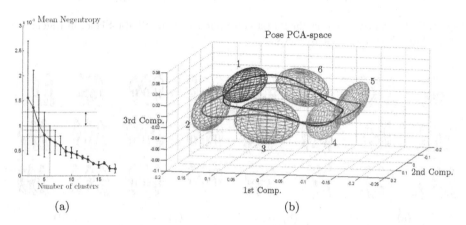

(a)   (b)

Fig. 3. (a) Negentropy of the GMM (mean & st.dev.) vs. number of clusters. (b) GMM (k=6) represented in the Pose Eigenspace together with low and high speed gait cycles.

observe the evolutions of the mean Negentropy for k varying from 2 to 18. The curve decreases and converges logically to 0. We consider that a good compromise between number of clusters and gaussianity is reached at k=6. Fig.3b shows the GMM obtained, represented in the Pose Eigenspace. This graphical representations shows the accuracy of GMM only by simple visual criteria: comparing with Fig. 2, we can observe how well the GMM limits the feature space.

GMMs construction. We now fit a view-based GMM in the 4 Shape-Skeleton Eigenspaces using the structure-based clustering obtained before. In Fig.4, we can observe how the GMMs limit the feature spaces: the clustering imposes a particular location of the gaussians that consequently treat some unseen data as valid (interpolating). Fig.5 shows how both Shape and Skeleton deform linearly in each one of the cluster of the view-based GMM. Dynamic correspondences are obtained between gaussian models of the 4 mixtures, each cluster corresponding to one of 6 basic gait phases.

Model fitting. When given a new shape, we treat the structural parameters as missing variables in a SS-vector. The corresponding $\mathbf{b}^*$ is then computed from Eq.1 and the nearest cluster, defined by Eigenvectors $\mathbf{\Phi} = [\Phi_1, \Phi_2, ...\Phi_t]$ and Eigenvalues λ_i, is selected. Thus the closest allowable SS-vector from the model

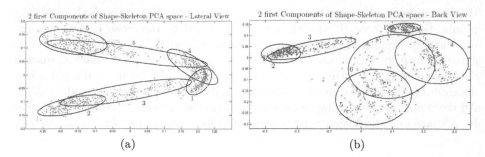

(a)   (b)

Fig. 4. GMM represented on the 2 first components of the Shape-Skeleton Eigenspace
for the lateral(a) and back(b) views

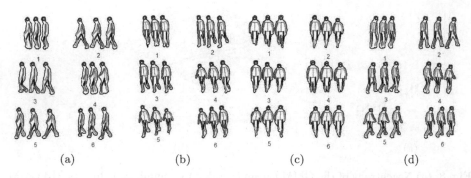

(a)   (b)   (c)   (d)

Fig. 5. Principal modes of variation of the 6 corresponding gaussian models for the 4
view-based GMMs: lateral(a), diagonal(b), frontal(c) and back(d) views

is constructed by finding $\mathbf{r}$ so that:

$$\mathbf{r} = \Phi^{-1}(\mathbf{b}^* - \bar{\mathbf{b}}) \quad \text{and} \quad -\beta\sqrt{\lambda_i} \le r_i \le \beta\sqrt{\lambda_i}. \tag{3}$$

This leads to a model-based estimation of both Shape and Skeleton (cf Fig.6).

4   Results

The first approach we followed to cope with the non-linearity of the Eigenspace
was to select the closest allowable shape from the training set by means of a
Nearest Neighbor (NN) classifier[3]. This technique always warranties a valid
contour but is imperfect because it can not generate new shapes absent from the
training data. Moreover, the computational cost makes this approach infeasible
with a very large database. In [4] we proposed to use Independent Component
Analysis (ICA) for human shape modelling. The dynamic-based GMM developed
in this paper will be compared to both methods.

For the evaluation of our models, we select from the Caviar database [8] 4
gait sequences whose viewpoints correspond more or less to our 4 training views

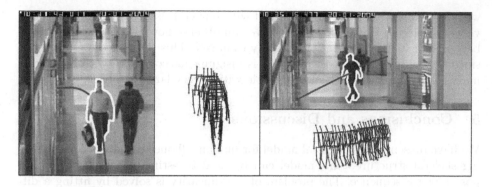

Fig. 6. Selected Caviar sequences for testing frontal (*left*) and diagonal (*right*) views-based GMM. For each of the 2 sequences, we show a frame with fitted shape and the 2D poses automatically generated when applying the SS-model along the sequence.

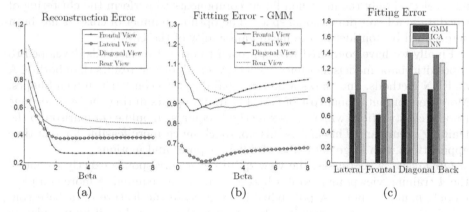

Fig. 7. Reconstruction Error(a) & Fitting Error(b) obtained applying our GMM on the 4 Caviar sequences. (c) Comparative results for the NN, ICA and GMM.

(cf Fig.6). On the one hand, groundtruth data are constructed by manually extracting the silhouettes of selected people appearing in the scene and on the other hand, human blobs are calculated by motion detection. Errors will be calculated as Euclidean distances between groundtruth and estimated Shapes.

Two kinds of errors can be estimated: Reconstruction and Fitting Errors. The first one is calculated by projecting and reconstructing a groundtruth Shape with the model: this error characterizes the ability of the model to generate new silhouettes. The Reconstruction Error decreases and converges logically for the 4 models when augmenting parameter β from Eq.3 (see Fig.7a). The Fitting Error is calculated by correcting the Shape extracted from the human blob with the model: this error characterizes the ability of the model to correct bad shapes. On Fig.7b, we can observe how the Reconstruction Error decreases until a minimum value and then starts increasing for the 4 models when augmenting β. This allows us to determine the optimal value of β for every View-based GMM. On Fig.7c, we compare the Fitting Error obtained with our GMMs, NN and ICA for the 4 views (4 selected Caviar sequences). We can observe how GMM performs much better than ICA and better or similarly than NN. This is an encouraging result since the computational cost of GMM is insignificant compared with NN and it makes this approach much more feasible with a very large database.

5   Conclusions and Discussions

We have presented a statistical model for human silhouette and the corresponding skeletal structure. This model can be used to estimate human shape and pose along a sequence. The problem of non-linearity is solved by fitting a different Gaussian Mixture Model (GMM) to several training views. Since Shape variations of articulated objects are closely linked to the Pose evolution along time, we have clustered the total training set using only the structural information projected in the Pose Eigenspace. In order to simplify the problem, we have selected only the most non-linear components to perform the clustering of the data in a lower dimensional space. The optimal number of clusters has been determined by considering the mean gaussianity of the GMM.

Finally we have compared this approach to other two methods developed to cope with shape models non-linearity: GMM exhibits best results than both ICA and NN methods, and shows a better capability to reconstruct unseen Shapes. Moreover computational cost of GMM mainly appears during the off-line stage (model construction) while the NN method requires an online comparison to the training exemplars. This makes this approach much more feasible for real-time applications with large databases of different poses and motions.

Obviously, in real cases, the view quite never corresponds exactly to one of the 4 training viewpoints. So if a better accuracy is required, a more complete model should be built. A possibility is to increase the feature data base considering other camera viewpoints. In a future, these models will be included in a global multi-view 2D models framework. The dynamical correspondences we have established between view-based GMM will be taken into account to manage the eventual viewpoint changes along sequences. Another important improvement we are currently working on is the use of the skeletal temporal dynamic to reduce the allowable deformations of the silhouette in consecutive frames.

References

1. Cootes, T., Taylor, C.: A mixture model for representing shape variation. British Machine Vision Association, Essex, UK, pp. 110–119 (1997)
2. Bowden, R., Mitchell, T., Sarhadi, M.: Non-linear statistical models for the 3d reconstruction of human pose and motion from monocular image sequences. Image and Vision Computing 18, 729–737 (2000)
3. Orrite, C., Martínez, J., Herrero, E., Rogez, G.: 2D silhouette and 3D skeletal models for human detection and tracking. In: ICPR, Cambridge, UK, pp. 244–247 (2004)
4. Rogez, G., Orrite, C., Martínez, J.: Human figure segmentation using independent component analysis. In: IbPRIA, Estoril, Portugal, pp. 300–307 (2005)

5. Koschan, A., Kang, S., Paik, J., Abidi, B., Abidi, M.: Colour active shape models for tracking non-rigid objects. Pattern Recognition Letters, pp. 1751–1765 (2003)
6. Gross, R., Shi, J.: The cmu motion of body (mobo) database, Robotics Institute, Carnegie Mellon University, Pittsburgh, PA (2001)
7. Davies, R., Twining, C., Allen, P.D., Cootes, T., Taylor, C.J.: Building optimal 2d statistical shape models. Image Vision Comput 21, 13–14 (2003)
8. (EC funded CAVIAR project IST 2001 37540)

Human Motion Characterization Using Spatio-temporal Features

Manuel J. Lucena[1], José Manuel Fuertes[1], and Nicolás Pérez de la Blanca[2]

[1] University of Jaén (Spain)
[2] University of Granada (Spain)

Abstract. Local space-time features can be used to detect and characterize motion events in video. Such features are valid for recognizing motion patterns, by defining a vocabulary of *primitive features*, and representing each video sequence by means of a histogram, in terms of such vocabulary. In this paper, we propose a supervised vocabulary computation technique which is based on the prior classification of the training events into classes, where each class corresponds to a human action. We will compare the performance of our method with the global approach to show that not only does our method obtain better results but it is also computationally less expensive.

1 Introduction

Human motion characterization has been a highly active research area in recent years [1,2,3]. Some approaches are based on local space-time features [4,5], which have been proven useful to provide semantic meaning of video events by providing a compact and abstract representation of patterns. For the purpose of classification, each feature is labeled according to a event vocabulary, in order to obtain a histogram with appearance frequencies for each feature class [6,7].

The main goal of this article is to present a grouping strategy for detected events according to the human actions considered in the video sequence database. This technique will increase the precision of the classification. The starting point for our work is the extension carried out by Laptev towards the spatio-temporal domain [8,9] of the so-called *interest points*, representing important local variations on the image intensity [4,10,11].

Each human motion defines characteristic changes in speed and/or appearence associated to body parts. On the images, those changes mean strong variations in the grey-level patterns along the temporal axis [12,13,14], giving rise to the aforementioned spatio-temporal events.

This work is organized as follows. In Section 2 we describe the spatio-temporal feature detection process. We discuss our vocabulary computation technique in Section 3. In Section 4 we describe the classification method. The experiments are showed in Section 5. Finally, we discuss the results and present our conclusions in Section 6.

J. Martí et al. (Eds.): IbPRIA 2007, Part I, LNCS 4477, pp. 72–79, 2007.

2 Motion Events

In order to represent motion events, we use the local spatio-temporal features defined by Laptev in [15], which extend the Harris operator [10] into the spatio-temporal domain. These features correspond to non-constant motion of 2D image structures and are computed as follows: given an image sequence $f(x, y, t)$ and its scale-space representation $L(\cdot, \sigma^2, \tau^2) = f * g(\cdot, \sigma^2, \tau^2)$, with a Gaussian convolution kernel, we compute the second-moment matrix using spatio-temporal image gradients $\nabla L = (L_x, L_y, L_t)^T$ within a Gaussian neighborhood of each point:

$$\mu(\cdot; \sigma^2, \tau^2) = g(\cdot; s\sigma^2, s\tau^2) * (\nabla L(\nabla L)^T). \tag{1}$$

The position of the detected features are the local maxima of

$$H = \det(\mu) - k \operatorname{trace}^3(\mu) \tag{2}$$

over (x, y, t).

In order to enable invariance with respect to camera motion, the neighborhood of each local feature is warped using estimated velocity values [16]. Each feature is then represented using spatio-temporal jets:

$$l = (L_x, L_y, L_t, L_{xx}, L_{xy}, \dots, L_{tttt}) \tag{3}$$

computed at the center of its neighborhood, using normalized derivatives. The use of the previously detected scale parameters (σ^2, τ^2) when computing the local jets provides invariance with respect to the size of the moving pattern. In our work, we have computed N-jets of order four (**4jets**), containing 34 coefficients.

3 Representation of Motion Patterns

Given a training set of image sequences (where each sequence depicts a single action), we use the K-means clustering algorithm on the set of feature descriptors (3) computed in each sequence to obtain a vocabulary of n primitive events h_i. The number of features of every class h_i present in a sequence defines a feature histogram $H = (m_{h_1}, \dots, m_{h_n})$. We will use these histograms to characterize each sequence.

Instead of applying the K-means algorithm on the entire training set (global cluster computation)[6], we propose that a separate set of primitive events be obtained for each of the m different actions present in our database (*class-based cluster computation*).

Let us suppose that we have two partially overlapping clusters C_1 and C_2, with n_1, n_2 samples, centered at points x_1 and x_2, with $n_1 >> n_2$. It is well known that K-means will favor the one with more samples, giving a biased estimation of x_2 towards x_1. Similar types of distortion occur when the mean sample-centroid distance is significantly different for C_1 and C_2. If we can separate the samples corresponding to C_1 and C_2, and apply K-means independently, the cluster center estimation will be closer to the real values.

In order to test such an idea, we have sampled two isotropic two-dimensional Gaussian probability distributions, D_1 and D_2, with standard deviations σ_1 and σ_2, varying the center of the first. Using two additional distributions, D_3 and D_4, centered on far enough positions so as not to interfere with D_1 and D_2, we have applied the K-means algorithm in two ways:

1. globally to the four sets of samples, obtaining the set $G = \{g_1, g_2, g_3, g_4\}$ of estimated centroids;
2. grouping the samples into two classes, $A = D_1, D_3$ and $B = D_2, D_4$, then applying K-means to each class, obtaining $P_a = \{p_1, p_3\}$ and $P_b = \{p_2, p_4\}$.

Finally, we classified every point and assigned the nearest centroid to each one using G and P, respectively, and we then measured the correct-matching rate for the samples of D_1 and D_2 in both cases. We repeated this experiment with a different number of samples and values of σ_1 for D_1 and obtained the results shown in Figure 1.

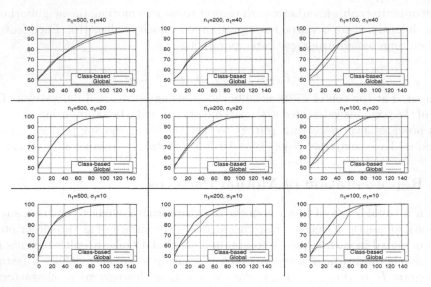

Fig. 1. Comparison between global and class-based K-means computation of clusters (see Section 3). The second cluster, D_2, has $n_2 = 500$ samples, and $\sigma_2 = 20$ in all the experiments. The vertical axis represents the correct labeling rate (%), and the horizontal axis represents the distance between D_1 and D_2. Results are averaged over 100 repetitions.

As we can see, the separate application of K-means performs better when the value of σ and/or the number of samples differ significantly between the two clusters. Moreover, when two centroids belonging to different classes are very close, we can consider that the same primitive event is present in both classes and simply merge the two clusters.

Since we take advantage of the fact that our training sequecenes are labeled, we can consider our technique a supervised one. Nevertheless, the described method does not suppose any computational overhead, compared to the unsupervised, global vocabulary computation method.

In order to compute a vocabulary of n primitive events, our technique proceeds in two steps: first, we divide the whole training set into m subsets, corresponding to the sequences that contain a particular action, and apply K-means to obtain n/m clusters per class:

$$H = (h_1^1, h_2^1, \ldots, h_{n/m}^1, h_1^2, \ldots, h_{n/m}^m) \tag{4}$$

where h_i^j corresponds to the i-th primitive event of the action j. Secondly, we merge every two clusters that satisfy these two conditions: a) they belong to two different classes; and b) the distance between their centroids is smaller than a given threshold λ.

This yields a vocabulary of primitive events, which we can employ to compute the feature histograms used to characterize motion patterns. Due to the large number of samples in the training set and the fact that computational cost of K-means depends on that number, the learning phase is significantly faster than with the global method, and also gives better results, as we will see in the experimental section of this work.

4 Classification

In order to compare two histograms, s_1 and s_2, computed from the events detected in two sequences, we considered the following dissimilarity measures:

- The χ^2 measure:

$$\chi^2(s_1, s_2) = \sum_i \frac{(s_1(i) - s_2(i))^2}{s_1(i) + s_2(i)} \tag{5}$$

- The Euclidean distance:

$$E(s_1, s_2) = \sum_i (s_1(i) - s_2(i))^2 \tag{6}$$

In the experiments shown in this work, we employed the χ^2 measure, which provided better results.

For the purpose of recognizing the action performed in a test sequence given a training set T, we need a classification scheme. We have chosen the nearest neighbor classifier (NNC), which assigns to the test sequence the class of the most similar training sequence, because of its simplicity.

5 Experiments

In this section, we will evaluate the performance of class-based histograms, and compare them with the global method. We have used two different video databases:

First, the *KTH database* [6], contains a total of 2391 sequences, comprising six types of human actions (walking, jogging, running, boxing, hand waving, hand clapping) performed by 25 different people.

Secondly, the *Campus database*, is our own database (Figure 2). It currently contains 270 sequences, in which 10 different identified individuals and an unknown number of unidentified people perform 11 different actions. In our experiments, we have only used the subset of the 186 sequences containing actions which are common to the KTH database. The sequences have been captured in 4 different settings: one inside with a homogeneous background, and three outside with complex backgrounds, with a static camera with a 25fps frame rate.

Fig. 2. *Campus* Database image samples

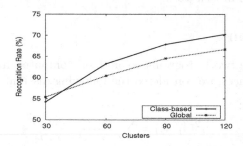

Fig. 3. Comparison between global and class-based histograms. Recognition rate obtained with the KTH sequence database, using 20 people as training set and the rest as test set for each experiment. Classification is carried out using 30, 60, 90 and 120 clusters, a distance of χ^2 for the NNC classification algorithm, and a value of $\lambda = 5$ for class-based histograms.

5.1   KTH Database

The first batch of experiments uses elements from the KTH database both as training and test set. We randomly selected a number of sequences (corresponding to 20 people), compute their histograms, and classified the remaining sequences. The results, shown in Figure 3, are averaged over 30 repetitions.

As we can see, except in the case of 30 clusters and a training set of 5 people, the results are consistently better for *class-based* histograms. In fact, this method obtains a 70.3% success rate for 120 clusters, unlike the 66.6% obtained by the global method with the same number of clusters.

5.2   *Campus* Database

For this experiment, we have used the entire KTH database as training set, and the *Campus* database as test set. In this case, due to the lower computational resources needed, we have obtained 180 clusters for both characterization methods. The results are depicted in Figure 4, and Table 1.

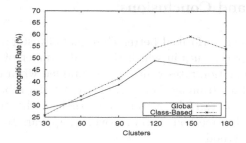

Fig. 4. Comparison between global and class-based histograms, using the KTH database as training set, and the *Campus* database as test set. Classification is carried out using 30, 60, 90, 120, 150 and 180 clusters, a distance of χ^2 for the NNC classification algorithm, and a value of $\lambda = 5$ for class-based histograms.

As expected, the recognition rates are lower than in the first experiment, but still acceptable. The best rate for global histograms is 48.9% with 120 clusters, and 59.1% for class-based histograms with 150 clusters. Higher numbers of clusters for both methods give lower rates, and this suggests that overfitting starts to occur.

It is possible to observe in Table 1 how the global method classifies more than 20% of *hand waving* and *hand clapping* events as *walking*, and this makes it

Table 1. A: Confusion matrix obtained with global histograms of 120 bins, using the KTH database as training set, and the *Campus* database as test set. B: Confusion matrix obtained with class-based histograms of 150 bins, using the KTH database as training set, and the *Campus* database as test set.

A	Walking	Running	Jogging	Boxing	Handcl.	Handw.
Walking	50.0	16.7	22.2	0.0	0.0	11.1
Running	10.0	60.0	23.3	3.3	0.0	3.3
Jogging	23.3	20.0	53.3	0.0	0.0	3.3
Boxing	3.3	13.3	0.0	60.0	13.3	10.0
Handclapping	20.0	6.7	0.0	10.0	53.3	10.0
Handwaving	23.3	3.3	0.0	10.0	46.7	16.7

B	Walking	Running	Jogging	Boxing	Handcl.	Handw.
Walking	63.9	8.3	16.7	0.0	5.6	5.6
Running	3.3	63.3	23.3	10.0	0.0	0.0
Jogging	6.7	20.0	73.3	0.0	0.0	0.0
Boxing	0.0	0.0	3.3	66.7	23.3	6.7
Handclapping	13.3	3.3	0.0	13.3	30.0	40.0
Handwaving	3.3	3.3	0.0	13.3	23.3	56.7

difficult to distinguish between *hand* and *feet* events. If we only consider this distinction, global histograms provide a success rate of 84.9%, unlike the 91.9% given by class-based histograms. Another interesting fact is that the global method completely fails to completely classify *handwaving* events, while class-based histograms fail (although to a lesser degree) to classify *handclapping*.

6 Discussion and Conclusions

Class-based histograms performed better than global histograms in all our experiments, except for the ones in which the total number of clusters was very small. The high recognition rates which were obtained when different sequence databases were used for training and testing suggest the robustness of the histogram as a motion pattern descriptor. Nevertheless, the optimal number of clusters, over which the method starts to overfit, appears to be slightly larger for the class-based method.

The training phase for the supervised, class-based method is significantly faster than for the global, unsupervised method, while the rest of the process remains the same. Due to the large number of events present in a typical training set –about 140000 in KTH database–, the computation of the centroids takes much less time when we divide the aforementioned set into classes. In our experiments, the global computation of 180 clusters takes an average of eight times more time than the class-based computation of the same number of clusters.

It should be stressed, as pointed out in [16], that certain actions in the KTH database are extremely similar (e.g. *running* and *jogging*) and this accounts for the high level of confusion between them. In fact, there are people *running* whose visually most similar action is the *jogging* action of another person.

We can conclude that class-based histograms can be used to characterize motion patterns, and provide high recognition rates which are comparable to other relative approaches. We have evaluated the behavior of the method with a public database using cross-validation. We have also trained with the same database and tested with our own database and we have found that performance loss is acceptable.

As future work, we plan to increase the size of the *Campus* database, and make it publicly available. We will also test the inclusion of information about the spatio-temporal location of the detected events, and replace NNC with a more sophisticated classification scheme (e.g. Support Vector Machines or AdaBoost) in order to further improve recognition rates.

References

1. Buxton, H.: Learning and understanding dynamic scene activity: A review. Image and Vision Computing 21(1), 125–136 (2003)
2. Hu, W., Tan, T., Wang, L., Maybank, S.: A survey on visual surveillance of object motion and behaviors. Transaction on Systems, Man and Cybernetics 34(3), 334–352 (2004)

3. Moeslund, T., Hilton, A., Krüger, V.: A survey of advances in vision-based human motion capture and analysis. Computer Vision and Image Understanding 104, 90–126 (2006)
4. Lindeberg, T.: Feature detection with automatic scale selection. International Journal of Computer Vision 30(2), 77–116 (1998)
5. Nagel, H., Gehrke, A.: Spatiotemporal adaptative filtering for estimation and segmentation of optical flow fields. In: Proceedings of the Fifth European Conference on Computer Vision (1998)
6. Schüldt, C., Laptev, I., Caputo, B.: Recognizing human actions: A local SVM approach. In: Proceedings of ICPR. Vol. 3, pp. 32–36, Cambridge, UK (2004)
7. Dollár, P., Rabaud, V., Cottrell, G., Belongie, S.: Behavior Recognition via Sparse Spatio-Temporal Features. In: Proc. VS-PETS. pp. 65–72 (2005)
8. Laptev, I., Lindeberg, T.: Velocity adaptation of spatio-temporal receptive fields for direct recognition of activities: an experimental study. Image and Vision Computing 22, 105–116 (2004)
9. Laptev, I.: On space-time interest points. International Journal of Computer Vision 64(2/3), 107–123 (2005)
10. Harris, C., Stephens, M.: A combined corner and edge detector. In: Proceedings of The Fourth Alvey Vision Conference, Manchester, UK. pp. 147–151 (1988)
11. Schmid, C., Mohr, R., Bauckhage, C.: Evaluation of interest point detectors. International Journal of Computer Vision 19(5), 151–172 (2000)
12. Koenderink, J.: Scale-time. Biological Cybernetics 58, 159–162 (1988)
13. Florack, L.: Image Structure. Kluwer Academic Publishers, Dordrecht (1997)
14. Zelnik-Manor, L., Irani, M.: Event-based analysis of video. In: Proc. Computer Vision and Pattern Recognition (2001)
15. Laptev, I., Lindeberg, T.: Space-time interest points. In: Proc. ICCV. pp. 432–439 (2003)
16. Laptev, I., Lindeberg, T.: Velocity adaptation of space-time interest points. In: Proc. ICPR. vol. 1., Cambridge, UK. pp. 52–56 (2004)

Fast Stochastic Context-Free Parsing: A Stochastic Version of the Valiant Algorithm

José-Miguel Benedí and Joan-Andreu Sánchez

Universidad Politécnica de Valencia
46022 Valencia (Spain)
{jbenedi,jandreu}@dsic.upv.es

Abstract. In this work, we present a fast stochastic context-free parsing algorithm that is based on a stochastic version of the Valiant algorithm. First, the problem of computing the string probability is reduced to a transitive closure problem. Then, the closure problem is reduced to a matrix multiplication problem of matrices of a special type. Afterwards, some fast algorithm can be used to solve the matrix multiplication problem. Preliminary experiments show that, in practice, an important time savings can be obtained.

1 Introduction

Stochastic Context-Free Grammars (SCFGs) are an important specification formalism that are frequently used in Syntactic Pattern Recognition. SCFGs have been widely used to characterize the probabilistic modeling of language in Computational Linguistics [1,2], Speech Recognition and Understanding [3], and Biological Sequence Analysis [4]. The main advantages of this formalism are: the capability to model the long-term dependencies that can be established between the different parts of a sentence, and the possibility of incorporating the stochastic information to allow for an adequate modeling of the variability phenomena that are always present in complex problems. However, a notable obstacle to using these models is the time complexity of both the stochastic parsing algorithms and the algorithms that are used for the probabilistic estimation of the models from a training corpus.

Most of the stochastic parsing algorithms are based either on the Earley algorithm, for SCFGs in general format [1], or on the Cocke-Younger-Kasami (CYK) algorithm, for SCFGs in Chomsky Normal Form (CNF) [3]. Both algorithms are based on a Dynamic Programming scheme and have a time complexity $O(gn^3)$, where n is the length of the string and g is the size of the grammar. One of the well-known algorithms for computing the probability of a string given a SCFG in CNF is the inside algorithm [5].

There are theoretical works that attempt to improve the time complexity of the parsing algorithms for context-free grammars. In [6], a version of the CYK algorithm was proposed whose time complexity is $O(M(n))$, where $M(n)$ is the time complexity of the product of two boolean matrices of dimension n. The close relation between context-free parsing and boolean matrix multiplication is demonstrated in [7]. A version of the Valiant algorithm that is based on the computation of shortest paths is presented in [8].

J. Martí et al. (Eds.): IbPRIA 2007, Part I, LNCS 4477, pp. 80–88, 2007.

There are a lot of interesting works in the literature for matrix multiplication [9,10]. The classical method is the well-known Strassen algorithm [9]. This algorithm has a time complexity $O(n^{2.8})$. Another method is the Coppersmith & Winograd algorithm, which has a time complexity $O(n^{2.38})$ [10]. Although this algorithm is asymptotically faster, it involves such huge hidden constants that it is not practical.

In this work, we present a fast stochastic context-free parsing algorithm that is based on a stochastic version of the Valiant algorithm. The parsing problem is reduced to a multiplication problem of matrices of a special type. Fast algorithms can be used for this matrix multiplication problem. However, the constant that is associated to fast matrix multiplication algorithms is large. Moreover, in the case of parsing algorithms that are based on matrix multiplication, the size of the grammar is another factor that also affects the time complexity of the algorithm. In real tasks, the grammar can have thousands of rules.

In the following section, some preliminary concepts are introduced. In Section 3, we will reduce the computation of the probability of a string to the transitive closure of matrices. In Section 4, we will reduce the transitive closure to a matrix product. In Section 5, preliminary experiments are reported.

2   Preliminaries

First, we introduce the notation for SCFGs. Then, we present the preliminary definitions that constitute the formal framework used in this work.

A *Context-Free Grammar* (CFG) G is a four-tuple (N, Σ, S, P), where N is a finite set of non-terminals, Σ is a finite set of terminals $(N \cap \Sigma = \emptyset)$, $S \in N$ is the initial non-terminal, and P is a finite set of rules: $A \to \alpha$, $A \in N$, $\alpha \in (N \cup \Sigma)^+$ (without loss of generality, we only consider grammars with no empty rules). A CFG in Chomsky Normal Form (CNF) is a CFG in which the rules are of the form $A \to BC$ or $A \to a$ $(A, B, C \in N$ and $a \in \Sigma)$. A *left-derivation* of $x \in \Sigma^+$ in G is a sequence of rules $d_x = (q_1, q_2, \ldots, q_m)$, $m \geq 1$, such that: $(S \overset{q_1}{\Rightarrow} \alpha_1 \overset{q_2}{\Rightarrow} \alpha_2 \overset{q_3}{\Rightarrow} \ldots \overset{q_m}{\Rightarrow} x)$, where $\alpha_i \in (N \cup \Sigma)^+, 1 \leq i \leq m-1$ and q_i rewrites the left-most non-terminal of α_{i-1}. The *language generated* by G is defined as $L(G) = \{x \in \Sigma^+ \mid S \overset{*}{\Rightarrow} x\}$.

A *Stochastic Context-Free Grammar* (SCFG) is defined as a pair (G, p), where G is a CFG and $p : P \to]0, 1]$ is a probability function of rule application such that $\forall A \in N : \sum_{i=1}^{n_A} p(A \to \alpha_i) = 1$, where n_A is the number of rules associated to A.

Let G_s be a SCFG. Then, we define the *probability of the derivation* d_x of the string x, $\mathrm{Pr}_{G_s}(x, d_x)$ as the product of the probability application function of all the rules used in the derivation d_x. Given that for some $x \in L(G)$ there can be more than one derivation, we also define the *probability* of the string x as: $\mathrm{Pr}_{G_s}(x) = \sum_{\forall d_x} \mathrm{Pr}_{G_s}(x, d_x)$.

The probability of generating a string, given G_s, can be computed from the well-known inside algorithm [5]. The inside algorithm is the stochastic version of the classical parsing algorithm of Cocke-Kasami-Younger.

In the following sections, we will present the inside algorithm in terms of the matrix product. To do this, the following concepts must be introduced.

Definition 1. *Given a SCFG G_s, we define a* stochastic non-terminal symbol vector *(SNTV) related to this SCFG as a vector C with $|N|$ components, where each* *component is associated with a non-terminal symbol such that* $0 \leq C[A] \leq 1, \forall A \in N$. *A special SNTV* $\overline{0}$ *can be defined:* $\overline{0}[A] = 0, \forall A \in N$.

We define a binary operation $\oplus$ on arbitrary SNTVs, a and b as follows:

$$(a \oplus b)[A] = a[A] + b[A] \quad \forall A \in N$$

It can be seen that this operation is associative, commutative, and $a + \overline{0} = \overline{0} + a = a$. Note that this operation is not always an inner operation. However, we will see later that depending in the context of use, it can be an inner operation.

We also define another binary operation $\odot$ on arbitrary SNTVs, a and b as follows:

$$(a \odot b)[A] = \sum_{B,C \in N} \Pr(A \to BC)a[B]b[C] \quad \forall A \in N \qquad (1)$$

This is an inner operation because $0 \leq a[B], b[C] \leq 1, \forall B, C \in N$, and $\sum_{B,C \in N} \Pr(A \to BC) = 1$. Note that $a \odot \overline{0} = \overline{0} \odot a = \overline{0}$. This operation is neither associative nor commutative. However, operation $\odot$ distributes over operation $\oplus$.

Definition 2. *A SNTV matrix is a square matrix in which each element is a SNTV.*

Given two $n \times n$ square SNTV matrices, U and V, their sum is defined as:

$$(u + v)_{i,j} = u_{i,j} \oplus v_{i,j} \quad 1 \leq i, j \leq n$$

and the product is defined as:

$$(u\,v)_{i,j} = \sum_{k=1}^{n} u_{i,k} \odot v_{k,j} \quad 1 \leq i, j \leq n$$

where the sum is defined in terms of operation $\oplus$. We will see later that the conditions in which these operations are used guarantee that both of them are inner operations. The sum of SNTV matrices is associative and commutative and has unit element. The product is neither associative nor commutative. However, the product distributes over the sum.

From the previous definitions and following a notation very close to [11], the inside algorithm can expressed in terms of a $(n + 1) \times (n + 1)$ SNTV matrix t, such that:

$$t_{i,j}[A] = \Pr_{G_s}(A \overset{*}{\Rightarrow} x_{i+1} \ldots x_j)$$

Initializing $t_{i,j} = \overline{0}, \; 0 \leq i, j \leq n$, and $\forall A \in N$:

$t_{i,i+1}[A] = \Pr(A \to x_{i+1}) \quad 0 \leq i < n,$

$$t_{i,i+j}[A] = \sum_{B,C \in N} \Pr(A \to BC) \sum_{k=1}^{j-1} t_{i,i+k}[B] t_{i+k,i+j}[C] \quad 2 \leq j \leq n, 0 \leq i \leq n - j$$

and therefore,

$$t_{i,i+j} = \sum_{k=1}^{j-1} t_{i,i+k} \odot t_{i+k,i+j} \qquad (2)$$

In this way, $\Pr_{G_s}(x) = t_{0,n}[S]$.

Note that in expression (2), the sum is defined in terms of $\oplus$. It can be observed that by definition, $t_{i,j}[A] \leq 1$, and because the combinations of probabilities are always bounded by one then the $\oplus$ operation is only used as an inner operation.

3 Reducing the Inside Probability to the Transitive Closure

Following a presentation that is similar to the one in [12], we now explain how the SNTV matrix t can be computed by means of square SNTV matrix operations.

Definition 3. *Given a SCFG G_s and a string $x_1 \cdots x_n \in \Sigma^*$, we define E as a square SNTV matrix with dimension $n + 1$ such that $\forall A \in N$:*

$$e_{i,i+1}[A] = \Pr(A \to x_{i+1}) \qquad\qquad 0 \leq i \leq n - 1,$$
$$e_{i,j} = \bar{0} \qquad\qquad\qquad\qquad \text{otherwise.}$$

From this definition, E^2 can be computed in the following way:

$$e_{i,j}^{(2)} = \sum_{k=0}^{n} e_{i,k} \odot e_{k,j} \ , \quad 0 \leq i,j \leq n - 2$$

Given that $e_{i,k} = \bar{0}$ if $k \neq i + 1$ and, consequently, $e_{k,j} = \bar{0}$ if $j \neq i + 2$, then the only element that is different from zero in row i is:

$$e_{i,j}^{(2)} = e_{i,i+1} \odot e_{i+1,i+2}$$

Therefore, $e_{i,i+2}^{(2)} \neq \bar{0}, 0 \leq i < n - 2$, and $e_{i,j}^{(2)} = \bar{0}$, otherwise.

For E^3: $E^3 = E^2 E + E E^2$, given that the product between square SNTV matrices is not commutative. Thus:

$$e_{i,j}^{(3)} = \sum_{k=0}^{n} e_{i,k}^{(2)} \odot e_{k,j} + \sum_{k=0}^{n} e_{i,k} \odot e_{k,j}^{(2)} = e_{i,i+2}^{(2)} \odot e_{i+2,i+3} + e_{i,i+1} \odot e_{i+1,i+3}^{(2)}$$

Therefore, $e_{i,i+3}^{(3)} \neq \bar{0}, 0 \leq i < n - 3$, and $e_{i,j}^{(3)} = \bar{0}$, otherwise.

This result can be easily extended for l, $1 \leq l \leq n$:

$$e_{i,i+l}^{(l)} \neq \bar{0} \qquad\qquad\qquad 0 \leq i \leq n - l \ .$$

Lemma 1. *The positive closure of a square SNTV matrix E is defined as:* $E^+ = \sum_{i=1}^{n} E^i$.

From the result of the previous definition, it can be seen that, for $l = n$, the only no null value in E^n is $e_{0,0+n}^{(n)}$ and, for $l > n$, all values of E^l are null.

Theorem 1. *Let G_s be a SCFG and let $x \in \Sigma^+$ be a string. Let E^+ be the positive closure of matrix E which was defined previously. Then $E^+ = E^n = t$, and $e_{i,i+l}^{(l)} = t_{i,l}, 1 \leq l \leq n, 0 \leq i \leq n - l.$*

The demonstration is by induction on l. For $l = 1$, by definition of E and t:

$$e_{i,i+1}[A] = \Pr(A \to x_{i+1}) = t_{i,i+1}[A] \qquad 0 \leq i \leq n - 1, \forall A \in N.$$

Suppose that for j, $1 < j < l$, then: $e_{i,i+j}^{(j)}[A] = t_{i,i+j}[A]$ By expression (2) in the definition of t:

$$t_{i,i+j}[A] = \sum_{B,C \in N} \Pr(A \to BC) \sum_{k=1}^{j-1} t_{i,i+k}[B] t_{i+k,i+j}[C] = \sum_{k=1}^{j-1} t_{i,i+k} \odot t_{i+k,i+j}$$

For l:

$$e_{i,i+l}^{(l)} = \sum_{j=1}^{l-1} e_{i,i+j}^{(j)} e_{i+j,i+l}^{(l-j)} = \sum_{j=1}^{l-1} t_{i,i+j} t_{i+j,i+l} = t_{i,i+l}$$

$\square$

Corollary 1. *Let G_s be a SCFG and let $x \in \Sigma^+$ be a string. Then $\Pr_{G_s}(x) = t_{0,n}[S] = e_{0,0+n}^{(n)}$.*

4   Reducing the Transitive Closure to a Matrix Multiplication

In this section, we describe how to compute the positive closure of a square SNTV matrix E by reducing the computation to the multiplication of a square SNTV matrix. Following Valiant's work [6] and taking into account the properties of the operation for square SNTV matrices defined in Section 2, the following lemma is proposed:

Lemma 2. *Let E be a $(n \times n)$ SNTV matrix, and suppose that, for some $r > n/2$, the transitive closure of the partitions $[1 \le i, j \le r]$ and $[n - r < i, j \le n]$ is known. Then the closure of E can be computed by*

(i) performing a single matrix multiplication, and
(ii) finding the closure of a $2(n - r) \times 2(n - r)$ upper triangular matrix for which the closure of the partitions $[1 \le i, j \le n - r]$ and $[n - r < i, j \le 2(n - r)]$ is known.

The demonstration of the lemma is similar to the one that is presented in [6]. The lemma shows that the only part of E^+ that needs to be calculated is the top-right partition. Figure 1 shows in bold the parts of the upper triangular matrix E of the lemma that are known. The parts of E in the squares are multiplied in step (i) of the lemma, and an $(n - r) \times (n - r)$ matrix C is obtained. This gives a partial computation of the closure of $e_{i,j}$, $1 \le i \le n - r$, $r < j \le n$. The computation is completed in step (ii), which is explained below.

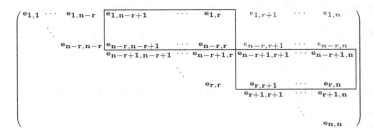

Fig. 1. Upper triangular matrix E

Let D be the $2(n-r) \times 2(n-r)$ matrix obtained from E by replacing its top-right part by C, and eliminating all the ith rows and columns for $n - r < i \le r$. In the step (ii), the closure of D is computed and the top-right partition of E^+ is obtained.

Theorem 2. *Let $M(n)$ be the time complexity of a matrix multiplication algorithm that is well behaved in the sense that there is a constant $\gamma \ge 2$ such that for all m, $2^\gamma \cdot M(2^m) \le M(2^{m+1})$. Then, there is a transitive closure algorithm of complexity $T(n)$ such that $T(n) \le M(n) \cdot f(n)$, where $f(n)$ is a constant function if $\gamma > 2$, and $f(n) = O(\log n)$ in any case.*

The demonstration of this theorem can be seen in [6].

Note that the elements of the matrices are SNTVs, and the matrix product is stated in terms of operation (1). Therefore, the size of the grammar affects the time complexity of the most inner operation of the matrix product. A fast matrix multiplication algorithm that decreased the number of operations could lead to important improvement in real tasks. In the following section, we explore this idea.

5 Experiments

In this section, we describe the experiments that were carried out to test the stochastic parsing algorithm described in the previous section. Two different experiments were carried out. In the first experiment, we tested the parsing algorithm with synthetic tasks. In the second experiment, we tested the parsing algorithm with a SCFG obtained from the UPenn treebank corpus.

For these experiments, we implemented both the classical version of the inside algorithm and the new version of the parsing algorithm that is based on matrix multiplication. Note that both algorithms produce exactly the same results, that is, the probability of the input string (see Corollary 1). We chose a simple fast matrix multiplication algorithm, since the emphasis of this experiment was on the reduction of the parsing problem to the matrix multiplication problem. In these experiments, we used the classical version of the Strassen algorithm [9]. In all the experiments, we measured the time complexity for both algorithms. The memory consumption of the matrix multiplication based parsing algorithm increased a logarithmic factor, depending on the size of the input string, with respect to the classical algorithm.

All the software was implemented in C language and the gcc compiler (version 3.3.5) was used. All experiments were carried out on a personal computer with an Intel Pentium 4 processor of 3.0GHz, with 1.0 GB of RAM and with a Linux 2.6.12 operating system.

5.1 Experiments with Synthetic Tasks

In this first experiment, we considered a very simple task. We parsed strings of increasing length with only one terminal symbol, given that the number of terminal symbols is not relevant for the parsing algorithm. We parsed the strings with grammars of increasing size. We used ergodic grammars with different numbers rules. Note that since the probabilities of the rules are not relevant for the parsing algorithm, they were randomly generated. In all the experiments, we measured the time in the number of seconds that were necessary to parse each string. Figure 2 shows the ratio between the time needed by the classical algorithm and the fast algorithm for strings of different length with grammars of increasing size. Note that in all cases the ratio was between two and three. The ratio decreased for small strings and large grammars due to the amount of overhead. However, the ratio kept over two for large grammars and large strings.

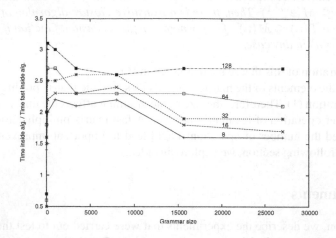

Fig. 2. Ratio between the time needed by the classical algorithm and the fast algorithm for strings of different length (8, 16, 32, 64, 128) with grammars of increasing size

5.2   Experiments with a Real Task

In this section, we describe the experiment that was carried out with a real task. The corpus used in the experiment was the UPenn Treebank corpus [13]. This corpus was automatically labeled, analyzed, and manually checked as described in [13]. There are two kinds of labeling: a POStag labeling and a syntactic labeling that is represented by brackets. The POStag vocabulary is composed of 45 labels. For this experiment, we used only the tagged part of the corpus.

We constructed an initial ergodic SCFG with the maximum number of rules that can be composed with 45 terminal symbols (the POStag set) and 35 non-terminal symbols. Therefore, the initial grammar had 44,450 rules. We trained this ergodic SCFG with the *inside-outside* algorithm [5]. After the estimation process, most of the rules disappeared due to underflow issues, and the final estimated grammar had 35 non-terminal symbols, 45 terminal symbols, and 1,741 rules.

Then, we parsed a string of the corpus of size 2^n for $n \geq 2$ with this SCFG. The results obtained in this experiment are shown in Figure 3.

Note that this figure corresponds to one point in the x-axis of the Figure 2. This figure shows that in this experiment the fast parsing algorithm parsed the strings in less time than the classical parsing algorithms. For strings with length near the average length (24 words in this corpus) the fast algorithm was twice quicker than the classical algorithm. This result shows that the fast parsing algorithm can be used in real problems.

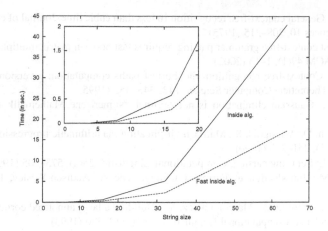

Fig. 3. Results obtained from the SCFG estimated with the UPenn Treebank corpus. The SCFG had 1,741 rules.

6   Conclusions

In this work, a stochastic version of the Valiant parsing algorithm has been presented. It has been shown that, in real tasks, the new algorithm notably improves the parsing time with respect to the classical inside algorithm. For future work, we intend to study the improvement of the time complexity of the estimation algorithms for SCFGs. In addition, we plan to use other fast matrix multiplication algorithms.

Acknowledgment

This work has been partially supported by the EC (FEDER) and Spanish MEC under contract (TIN2006-15694-C02-01) and by the UPV with the ILETA project.

References

1. Stolcke, A.: An efficient probabilistic context-free parsing algorithm that computes prefix probabilities. Computational Linguistics 21(2), 165–200 (1995)
2. Benedí, J., Sánchez, J.: Estimation of stochastic context-free grammars and their use as language models. Computer Speech and Language 19(3), 249–274 (2005)
3. Ney, H.: Stochastic grammars and pattern recognition. In: Laface, P., Mori, R.D. (eds.) Speech Recognition and Understanding. Recent Advances, pp. 319–344. Springer, Heidelberg (1992)
4. Sakakibara, Y., Brown, M., Hughey, R., Mian, I., Sjölander, K., Underwood, R., Haussle, D.: The application of stochastic context-free grammars to folding, aligning and modeling homologous rna. Computer and Information Science UCSC-CRL-94-14, Univ. of California, Santa Cruz, Ca (1993)
5. Baker, J.: Trainable grammars for speech recognition. In: Klatt, Wolf. (eds.) Speech Communications for the 97th Meeting of the Acoustical Society of America, Acoustical Society of America (1979) 31–35

6. Valiant, L.: General context-free recognition in less than cubic time. Journal of computer and system sciences 10, 308–315 (1975)
7. Lee, L.: Fast context-free grammar parsing requires fast boolean matrix multiplication. Journal of the ACM 49(1), 1–15 (2002)
8. Rytter, W.: Context-free recognition via shortest paths computation: a version of valiant's algorithm. Theoretical Computer Science 143, 343–352 (1995)
9. Strassen, V.: Gaussian elimination is not optimal. Numerische Mathematik 13, 354–356 (1969)
10. Coppersmith, D., Winograd, S.: Matrix multiplication via arithmetic progressions. J. Symb. Comput. 9(3), 251–280 (1990)
11. Goodman, J.: Semiring parsing. Computational Linguistics 25(4), 573–605 (1999)
12. Harrison, M.: Introduction to Formal Language Theory. Addison-Wesley, London, UK (1978)
13. Marcus, M., Santorini, B., Marcinkiewicz, M.: Building a large annotated corpus of english: the penn treebank. Computational Linguistics 19(2), 313–330 (1993)

Supervised Segmentation Based on Texture Signatures Extracted in the Frequency Domain

Antonella Di Lillo[1], Giovanni Motta[2], and James A. Storer[1]

[1] Brandeis University, Waltham, MA 02453
{dilant,storer}@cs.brandeis.edu
[2] Bitfone Corp., Laguna Niguel, CA 92677
gmotta@bitfone.com

Abstract. Texture identification can be a key component in Content Based Image Recognition systems. Although formal definitions of texture vary in the literature, it is commonly accepted that textures are naturally extracted and recognized as such by the human visual system, and that this analysis is performed in the frequency domain. The method presented here employs a discrete Fourier transform in the polar space to extract features, which are then classified with a vector quantizer for supervised segmentation of images into texture regions. Experiments are conducted on a standard database of test problems that show this method compares favorably with the state-of-the-art and improves over previously proposed frequency-based methods.

1 Introduction

The extraction of metadata based on the identification of textures can be used as an important tool to improve performance of a Content Based Image Retrieval (CBIR) system. For CBIR, the general problem is identifying images in a database of similar content, given a sample image. Manual annotation of image data is often unfeasible (because of the amount of data involved) and unreliable (since it may be impossible to predict which characteristics of the image are relevant to the search). Methods to automatically extract information from images have been developed in the past, in order to produce metadata annotation for CBIR. Most of these methods are based on statistical distributions of the gray-scale value or the color value of single pixels. These methods have achieved good performance in many circumstances, but the main drawback is that the same gray-scale and color distribution may be identical for a number of different spatial arrangements of pixels.

Here we focus our attention on the extraction of metadata based on the identification of textures.

Despite many mathematical models that have been proposed in an attempt to converge on a unified definition of texture, vision researchers have still not produced a universally accepted formal definition. While there is no agreement on a formal definition of texture, it is commonly accepted that textures are naturally extracted and recognized as such by the human visual system, and that relevant features are extracted in the frequency domain, independently of their illumination and the presence of noise. Furthermore, human experiments have revealed that the visual cortex contains orientation and scale band-pass filters that are used for vision analysis.

J. Martí et al. (Eds.): IbPRIA 2007, Part I, LNCS 4477, pp. 89–96, 2007.

Inspired by the human visual system, we classify textured images using a feature extractor operating in the frequency domain in combination with vector quantization (VQ). Section 2 outlines previous work to which we will compare our results. Section 3 describes the proposed method. Section 4 presents experiments on a standard texture database, which includes image problems that show our method to compare favorably with past approaches.

2 Previous Work

Based on the defining property of texture such as uniformity, density, coarseness, roughness, regularity, linearity, directionality, direction, frequency, and phase, a wide variety of feature extraction techniques have been proposed. Tuceryan and Jain [1] identify four major feature extraction methods in texture analysis: statistical, geometric, model-based, and signal processing based.

Many feature extractors based on the Fourier transform with feature reduction have been studied [2], and recently several authors have proposed the use of VQ in classification [3, 4]. Unfortunately, direct comparison with these proposals is often impossible because there is no agreement on the experimental setting. Despite over 30 years of research, there have been no widely accepted benchmarks for texture analysis. The Brodatz album [5] has been the most widely deployed texture image database, but even limiting image selection to this set gives no guarantee of comparable experimental results. This is because the particular images selected, the digitization and preprocessing, and the division into training and testing sets greatly impacts the outcome of the texture classification. As such, we compare our work with that of Randen and Husøy [6] and Mäenpää, Pietikäinen, and Ojala [7], who used the same test suite, which is now part of *Outex* [8] a framework for empirical evaluation of texture analysis algorithms.

Randen and Husøy [6] focused attention on different filter methods using the same system setup for each. The filters that have been compared are: Laws filter masks, Ring and Wedge filters, Dyadic Gabor filter bank, Wavelet transform, Discrete Cosine Transform, Quadrature Mirror filters, and the Tree-Structured Gabor filter bank. They also added to the comparison the co-occurrence and the autoregressive methods. The conclusion of their study was that there was no single method that performed the best for all the images, and that a low feature vector dimensionality, maximized feature separation, and in some cases, a simpler classifier was highly preferable.

These results were improved by Mäenpää, Pietikäinen, and Ojala [7] with the use of Local Binary Pattern texture operator (LBP) introduced by Ojala, Pietikäinen, and Harwood [9]. LBP is a statistical feature extractor that has been used in different classification and segmentation problems. It works by computing a 256-bin histogram over a window region, and measuring the dissimilarity among them with the log-likelihood. LBP preserves information regarding the texture's spatial distribution, and it is invariant to all monotonic gray scale transformations. The collection of textural features at different scales is also addressed in [7]; using a multi-scale version of LBP (MP-LBP) that combines histograms collected at various resolutions.

3 Proposed Method

In this work, we classify textured images with a *supervised segmentation* approach. Texture features are extracted in the frequency domain and classified with a vector quantizer. In supervised segmentation, the classifier is trained on texture samples and then tested on images, which in our case are the composition of different textures.

3.1 Training

Training aims at extracting significant and discriminating features from a set of training images. The features extracted characterize the textural properties of the training samples. The basis for the classification consists of a set of d features extracted from n training images, which are formed by textures belonging to c different classes. Feature extraction is therefore the process of mapping the measurement space of the raw data to a feature space. Performance of the feature extractor will greatly influence the correct classification rate.

The first step (Fig.1) is the placement of a *wsize×wsize* window W centered on each pixel (x_i, y_i) of a textured image belonging to the training set. Large images are randomly sampled in order to reduce memory and computational burden.

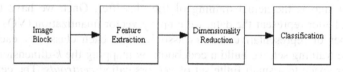

Fig. 1. Block diagram of method

The second step consists of extracting the features by weighing the image block W by a 2-dimensional Hamming window before the application of a 2D Fourier transform (FT). The magnitude of the Fourier coefficients is further transformed into polar coordinates:

$$FP_W(r,\theta) = \left| \int_{-\infty}^{\infty} \int_{-\infty}^{\infty} W(x,y) e^{-ir(x\cos\theta + y\sin\theta)} dx dy \right|. \tag{1}$$

The use of a frequency-domain method is consistent with the findings of researchers in biological vision. Many researchers [10, 11, 12, 13, 14, 15], have all provided a great deal of information about the early stages of processing that occurs in the retina, the lateral geniculate nucleus and the visual cortex. Furthermore, through both psychophysical and neurophysiologic experiments, they have established the existence of spatial frequency channels.

Mapping the magnitude of the FT in polar coordinates improves the precision of the classifier on the test problems. We speculate that this is due to an improved directionality of the system. Note that although the FT and polar mapping can be combined in a way that extracts features invariant to translation and rotation, the way polar coordinates are being used here has experimentally proved to be slightly better than this more traditional combination of transforms.

The third step is dimensionality reduction. For n training images of dimension $M{\times}N$, this process generates $n{\times}(M - wsize){\times}(N - wsize)$ features of dimension $wsize^2$. This large set of features is highly correlated. Reducing the dimensions of this set is convenient for two reasons. First, a small number of features can alleviate the curse of dimensionality. This means that as we increase the number of discriminating features past an optimal number we will decrease the performance of the classification system. Second, having a small number of features lightens the computational burden and the resulting classifier will be faster and will use less memory. It is therefore convenient to perform some type of dimensionality reduction and use an alternative and smaller set of features, derived from the initial ones, for the classification.

Our system uses Principal Component Analysis (PCA), a method commonly used for data reduction. PCA is based on the idea of performing an orthonormal transformation and retaining only significant eigenvectors of the whole dataset, called *principal components*. Each eigenvector is associated with a variance represented by the corresponding eigenvalue. The magnitude of an eigenvalue ranks the corresponding feature and allows the selection of the most important components. Selecting the most important principal components compacts the feature vectors without loss of information. After the PCA, the original feature space of dimension d has been reduced to a subspace of dimension k. In our system, dimensionality reduction is performed independently on each class.

The final step is the actual training of the classifier. Once we have the feature vectors that better represent the data, we employ vector quantization (VQ) to select a small number of representative vectors associated to each class. For each textured image in the training set, we build a codebook by mapping the k-dimensional vectors in the vector space to a small finite set of vectors called *centroids*. The centroids are determined so that they minimize the mean squared error from all the input vectors and capture the representative features of each texture.

3.2 Testing

During testing we analyzed the performance of our classification system by counting the number of pixels correctly classified.

The classifier is applied to a number of unknown test images (also called *problems*). The segmentation of the problem is done on a pixel-by-pixel basis. A window of size $wsize{\times}wsize$ is centered on each pixel of the problem image and the features are extracted with the method described in the training phase. The feature vector is transformed with the result of the PCA, the most important features are selected and the resulting vector, compared to all centroids. The class associated with the closest centroid is the one assigned to the pixel. Since adjacent pixels are likely to belong to the same texture, the classification rate can be improved with a post-processing filter. The simplest method uses a smoothing (low-pass) filter, which preserves the edges of the segmented areas. The filter introduced by Kuwahara, Hachimura, Eiho, and Kinoshita [16], is an example of such edge-preserving filter.

The Kuwahara filter divides a square neighborhood of each pixel into four overlapping quadrants each containing the central pixel (Fig. 2). Mean and variance are computed on the pixel values in each quadrant; then the value of the central pixel is replaced by the mean of the quadrant having smallest variance.

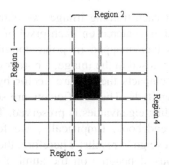

Fig. 2. Overlapping quadrants in a Kuwahara filter

We aim at filtering segmentation maps consisting of codebook indices, not natural images for which Kuwahara filter has been designed. Indices do not have a physical meaning, so determining mean and variance of the quadrants is not appropriate. It is possible however to use the same strategy of the Kuwahara filter and instead compute the histogram and the entropy of the indices of each quadrant. Our *Kuwahara-like filter* will replace the central index with the index having highest frequency in the quadrant that has smallest entropy.

4 Experimental Results and Conclusions

We have compared our results to those of Randen and Husøy [6] and Mäenpää, Pietikäinen, and Ojala [7], on the same test suite used in their work. The test images are taken from three different texture databases: the Brodatz album [5], the MIT Vision and Modeling Texture databases [17], and the MeasTex Image Texture database [18]. The classification is complicated by the fact that source images are taken from three different databases, so different equipment has been used to digitize them, and the conditions under which there were acquired are different. The source images are all gray-scale, and have equalized histograms (i.e., similar luminosity). The problem set has images of size *256×512* (2 textures), *256×256* (5 textures), *256×640* (*10* textures with simple borders), and *512×512* (*16* textures with complex borders). To each texture in a problem corresponds a *256×256* training image. Training and testing are done on different portions of the same texture, so that unbiased error estimates are attained.

Texture segmentation identifies regions of uniform texture. Segmentation quality depends largely on the size of the window W used in both the training and the testing stage. In the training stage, we want to find relationships among pixels that belong to a similar texture, and therefore a large window with more information is desirable. In the testing stage, the opposite is true; a small window is more desirable, since the main goal is to find a precise localization of boundary edges between adjacent regions. For simplicity, we have tested our method on windows having radius of *20* pixels (*wsize = 41*), as suggested in [7].

In the training phase, for each training image, we extract the features from a 2-dimensional Hamming window centered on each pixel of the image. The magnitude of the Fourier transform is then mapped in polar coordinates. To ensure that the window is always entirely enclosed in the image, a border of size *20* is excluded from the processing. The PCA compacts the feature vector by reducing its dimensions, typically by an order of magnitude. The coefficients are selected so that *90%* of the magnitude of the corresponding eigenvalues is preserved. The last step of the training phase determines the VQ codebook. Empirically, we found that *4* centroids per texture are sufficient to achieve good results. Therefore, the total size of the codebook ranges from *8* to *64* centroids, depending on the number of textures in the problem image. Mean squared error is used to find the best match between a feature vector and a centroid in the codebook. Filtering improves the consistency of the segmentation.

Fig. 3 shows examples of how our algorithm classifies regions for problems containing 2, 5, 10, and 16 textures. The top row shows the problem, the middle row shows the ground truth (the perfect classification), and the bottom row, the classification achieved by our method.

Table 1 reports the percentage of problem pixels correctly classified (classification rate), and compares our results with that of Randen and Husøy [6] and Mäenpää, Pietikäinen, and Ojala [7] (Basic LBP and multi-scale variations). On average, our method improves by *7.2%* over Randen and Husøy (which are also using spatial filtering) and by *1.2%* over Basic LBP (which is a time-domain statistical method). Our algorithm offers some advantages over the previous methods. Unlike Randen and Husøy, our method employs a single feature extraction method for all problems, and it is much simpler than their sophisticated filterings. The classification rate of our method is also roughly comparable to Multi-Predicate LBP, a more complex method that combines features collected at multiple resolutions. The modest gain achieved by the multi-predicate approach, also compatible with our method, does not seem to justify the increased complexity. In addition, our algorithm is robust to variations in the rotational angle of the texture (due to the use of polar coordinates), which is not an issue in the test problems used here. The polar mapping typically accounts for about *4.5%* of the performance, on average, over the FT itself because it provides a more precise characterization of textures exhibiting a quasi-random pattern. This resilience to rotational variance and a more precise characterization of textures appears to allow for better performance on natural images. For example, one image in Fig. 4 shows a scene of mountains by the ocean on the left, two user-selected texture samples are shown in the middle, and the segmentation of the image is on the right.

Table 1. Experimental results: percentage of problem pixels correct classified

	P1	P2	P3	P4	P5	P6	P7	P8	P9	P10	P11	P12	Avg
Textures	5	5	5	5	5	16	16	10	10	2	2	2	
Randen-Husøy	92.80	81.10	79.40	83.20	82.80	65.30	58.30	67.70	72.20	99.30	99.80	97.50	81.62
Basic LBP	93.80	81.90	87.90	90.00	89.10	83.20	79.20	77.20	80.80	99.70	99.00	90.10	87.66
MP-LBP(1,3)	93.30	85.70	89.80	90.90	92.00	84.70	79.30	81.90	78.60	99.60	99.20	94.70	89.14
MP-LBP(1,5)	92.70	85.50	86.30	89.50	90.60	84.50	76.70	79.70	76.70	99.40	99.30	93.20	87.84
MP-LBP(1,2,3)	93.00	86.40	88.90	91.20	91.70	84.50	78.10	82.40	76.80	99.60	99.20	94.70	88.88
Our method	96.54	83.39	89.77	91.37	91.48	81.48	74.77	80.89	80.41	99.60	98.47	97.89	88.84

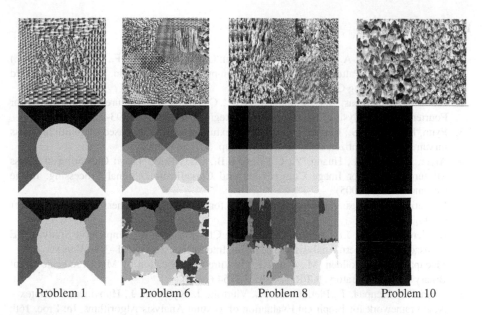

Problem 1   Problem 6   Problem 8   Problem 10

Fig. 3. Problem image (top), ground truth (middle) and results of the segmentation (bottom) for four problems of the test set

Fig. 4. Problem image (left), sample textures (center) and segmented scene (right)

References

1. Tuceryan, M., Jain, A.K.: Texture Analysis. In: Chen, C.H., Pau, L.F., Wang, P.S.P. (eds.) The Handbook of Pattern Recognition and Computer Vision, 2nd edn. pp. 207–248. World Scientific Publishing Co, Singapore (1998)
2. Clark, A.A., Thomas, B.T., Campbell, N.W., Greenway, P.: Texture Deconvolution for Fourier-Based Analysis of Non-Rectangular Regions. BMVC, pp. 193–202 (1999)
3. Pyun, K., Won, C.S., Lim, J., Gray, R.M.: Texture classification based on multiple Gauss mixture vector quantizer. In: Proc. of ICME, pp. 501–504 (2002)
4. Aiyer, A., Pyun, K., Huang, Y., O'Brien, D.B., Gray, R.M.: Lloyd Clustering of Gauss Mixture Models for Image Compression and Classification. Signal Processing: Image Communication (2005)
5. Brodatz, P.: Textures: A Photographic Album for Artists and Designers. New York, Dover (1996)
6. Randen, T., Husøy, J.H.: Filtering for Texture Classification: A Comparative Study. IEEE Transaction on Pattern Analysis and Machine Intelligence 21(4), 291–310 (1999)
7. Mäenpää, T., Pietikäinen, M., Ojala, T.: Texture Classification by Multi-Predicate Local Binary Pattern Operators. ICPR, pp. 3951–3954 (2000)
8. Ojala, T., Mäenpää, T., Pietikäinen, M., Viertola, J., Kyllönen, J., Huovinen, S.: Outex – New Framework for Empirical Evaluation of Texture Analysis Algorithms. In: Proc. 16th Int. Conf. on Pattern Recognition, pp. 701–706 (2002)
9. Ojala, T., Pietikäinen, M., Harwood, D.: A Comparative Study of Texture Measures with Classification Based on Feature Distributions. Pattern Recognition 29, 51–59 (1996)
10. Blakemore, C.B., Campbell, F.W.: On the existence of neurons in the human visual system selectivity sensitive to the orientation and size of retinal images. Journal of Physiology 203, 237–260 (1969)
11. Campbell, F.W., Cleland, B.G., Cooper, G.F., Enroth-Cugell, C.: The angular selectivity of visual cortical cells to moving gratings. J. Physiol. 198, 237–250 (1968)
12. Campbell, F.W., Nachmias, J., Jukes, J.: Spatial frequency discrimination in human vision. J. Opt. Soc. Am. 60, 555–559 (1970)
13. Maffei, L., Fiorentini, A.: The visual cortex as a spatial frequency analyzer. Vision Res. 13, 1255–1267 (1973)
14. Maffei, L., Fiorentini, A.: Spatial frequency rows in the striate visual cortex. Vision Res. 17, 257–264 (1977)
15. de Valois, R.L., Albrecht, D.G., Thorell, L.G.: Spatial frequency selectivity of cells in macaque visual cortex. Vision Res. 22, 545–559 (1982)
16. Kuwahara, M., Hachimura, K., Eiho, S., Kinoshita, M.: Digital Processing of Biomedical Images, pp. 187–203. Plenum Press, New York NY (1976)
17. MeasTxt: http://www.cssip.elec.uq.edu.au/~guy/meastex/meastex.html(1998)
18. MIT Vision and Modeling Group: http://www.media.mit.edu/vismod (1998)

Analysis of Relevant Maxima in Distance Transform. An Application to Fast Coarse Image Segmentation

Luis Antón-Canalís[1], Mario Hernández-Tejera[1], and Elena Sánchez-Nielsen[2]

[1] Institute for Intelligent Systems and Numerical Applications in Engineering - IUSIANI. University of Las Palmas de Gran Canaria (ULPGC). Campus Universitario de Tafira, Las Palmas, Spain
{lanton,mhernandez}@iusiani.ulpgc.es
[2] Departamento de Estadística, Investigación Operativa y Computación, 38271 University of La Laguna, S/C Tenerife, Spain
enielsen@ull.es

Abstract. The Distance Transform is a powerful tool that has been used in many computer vision tasks. In this paper, the use of relevant maxima in distance transform's medial axis is proposed as a method for fast image data reduction. These disc-shaped maxima include morphological information from the object they belong to, and because maxima are located inside homogeneous regions, they also sum up chromatic information from the pixels they represent. Thus, maxima can be used instead of single pixels in algorithms which compute relations among pixels, effectively reducing computation times. As an example, a fast method for color image segmentation is proposed, which can also be used for textured zones detection. Comparisons with mean shift segmentation algorithm are shown.

1 Introduction

Digital image comprehension is a difficult and subjective issue in computer vision. Scene understanding has to deal with enormous amounts of information supplied by still images or video sequences. It is compulsory to simplify this information in order to manage, classify and extract conclusions from the world shown in an image. In this paper we present a tool that can be used to reduce information while maintaining spatial relations, chromatic information and local descriptors, consisting on the extraction of Distance Transform's medial axis representative maxima.

An application of these maxima to real time image color segmentation is proposed. Classic color segmentation methods usually require computations on every pixel in order to cluster them properly [18]. However, many authors point to mean shift segmentation as the current best segmentation method [6], although it is computationally expensive and not suitable for real time applications. Due to the drastic reduction of the amount of information made possible

J. Martí et al. (Eds.): IbPRIA 2007, Part I, LNCS 4477, pp. 97–104, 2007.

through relevant maxima in distance transform, a membership propagation function will be able to perform a solid segmentation quickly enough to be used in video sequences.

Section 2 will review the Distance Transform and its applications. Section 3 will explain representative maxima extraction in detail. Section 4 will show the application of maxima in image segmentation, comparing results with the well-known mean shift color segmentation algorithm. Finally, Section 5 will present conclusions and future work.

2   The Distance Transform

The Distance Transform (DT) [12] or distance map of a digital image assigns to each image point a value which represents the minimum distance to some locus of points (usually object boundaries). DT commonly operates on thresholded images or binary edge images obtained with an edge detector. The resulting image can be considered a topological representation of the original image where object boundaries become valleys (lower values) separated by hills (higher values). The crest of these hills, known as medial axis, can be obtained by a process called skeletonization. They represent objects' skeletal remnants, and largely preserve their morphologies discarding most foreground pixels and thus reducing the amount of data. Although the application of the original DT concept (label each point with the distance to the closest object pixel) would be computationally expensive, there is a large amount of optimizations [17] that allow a real time computation.

DT images have been extensively used in computer vision, with applications in image comparison, both in their medial axis representation for object comparison [7] and in their original form, speeding up the calculation of Champfer [4] and Hausdorff [9] distances; in path planning, where each pixel represents the distance to the closest obstacle [5]; in active contour modeling, interpreting its inverted values as an attraction force field towards boundaries [19]; and medial axis can be used as seeds for the watershed algorithm [15], among other uses.

Some DT implementations improve the original concept in different ways. The Feature Distance Transform [14] stores not only a distance but also the object pixel from which it is measured. The Salience Distance Transform [16] is calculated from a non-binarized edge image, obtained after non-maxima suppression on a gradient magnitude image, and thus avoiding the binarization step. Finally, some works claim to obtain a Distance Transform directly from grayscale images [1]. In this paper, the original DT will be applied to binary edge images obtained from a modified version of the Canny algorithm [11]. From DT's medial axis, representative maxima are extracted and presented as a concise simplification of the morphology of the objects in the image, as seen in Fig. 1. These maxima do not represent objects' skeletons any more, but their actual shape and color, and contain a local descriptor based in Local Binary Patterns [13]. A direct application of these maxima is a convincing fast segmentation of the original image.

Fig. 1. A 250x322 RGB color image simplified to 804 relevant maxima in DT medial axis. Maxima with $r < 2$ are discarded.

3   Medial Axis' Representative Maxima Extraction

The first step in medial axis' representative maxima extraction is the application of an edge detector. As monochrome edge detection may not be sufficient for certain scenes where pixels with different hues may share similar intensities, a straightforward approach to color edge detection is used. Image gradient is extracted independently in each channel of RGB images and then fused using the information from the channel where the maximum gradient magnitude is found for each pixel. Once the horizontal and vertical gradient is obtained, a variation of the Canny edge detector [3] is applied in order to binarize edges. This method uses an adaptive dynamic threshold operation on the thin gradient image with expanded dynamic range, instead of classical hysteresis. This results in more stable edges in video sequences, where no blinking edges appear between consecutive frames.

A fast implementation of the DT based on the checkboard distance [8] supplied by the OpenCV libraries [10] is then applied on the resulting edge image. Then, local maxima in 4-neighborhoods are located and thus the medial axis are extracted, as seen in Fig. 2

Every point **p** that shapes extracted medial axis has a value r which represents the distance to the closest boundary pixel. A point and a radius define a circle. We propose that a subset of these circles is able to simplify the information contained in a digital image while preserving morphological, chromatic and local information, dramatically reducing the amount of points needed to describe an image. The subset of circles must be selected in order to maximize the coverage of the image while minimizing circle superposition (thus minimizing the number of circles). Therefore, all medial axis' points are sorted according to decreasing radius values, and then analyzed starting from the bigger one. Only those circles which center is not placed inside an already analyzed circle are selected for the final subset.

Fig. 2. Edges are extracted from a given image. Then the chessboard distance transform is obtained and local maxima are extracted, obtaining the medial axis (right image).

Selected circles become the relevant maxima, defined by the 4-uple $<\mathbf{p}, \mathbf{r}, \mathbf{c}, \mathbf{d}>$. $\mathbf{p}$ is the maximum position, r is its radius (value in the original DT image), $\mathbf{c}$ is the average color (CIELuv) in the area within a square centered on $\mathbf{p}$ with sides $r/4$ and $\mathbf{d}$ is a local descriptor which will be explained later. It is easily understood that within a circle centered on $\mathbf{p}$ with radius r no edges are found, so they will share chromatic attributes. This way, a single circle comprises πr^2 pixels, maximizing the simplification of an image without strong morphological dissimilarities. An image sized $Width \cdot Height$ pixels where M maxima are found with an average radius μ_r is *reduced* $M \cdot \pi \mu_r^2$ times, meaning that the total amount of pixels may be represented by much smaller amount of maxima.

3.1   Local Descriptor

A local descriptor based on Local Binary Patterns [13] is used to describe the *crest* shape of the DT image on each maximum. It is important to store this shape because maxima sharing similar crest shapes may be related together. The descriptor $\mathbf{d}$ of a maximum contains information of the crests directions in the vicinity of the maxima's center $\mathbf{p}$. Points are sampled around maxima each α angles in a radius $r/2$. Fig. 3 shows some examples. The descriptor $\mathbf{d}$ will store crest information in a binary array with size $360/\alpha$, where each bit represents the presence or absence of a crest in a bin of α angles, starting from $0°$ anti-clockwise. Two maxima will share similar crests if their descriptor include at least one mark in opposite positions or in adjacent opposite positions (thus allowing small turns). A single coincidence relates two maxima, as they may be laying in the same crest. Fig. 3 shows some examples.

4   Image Segmentation

The reduction of an image sized thousands of pixels to only a few hundred relevant maxima that still conserve morphological and chromatic information

Fig. 3. Main crests found in example maxima. Points are sampled each 30° at a distance of $r/2$ pixels. Black lines show approximated crest directions. With 12 bins, opposites are checked 6 bins to the right, circularly. Two coincidences are found considering also adjacent cells, corresponding to top-right maxima's north-west crest and south crest with bottom-right maxima's south crest and north crest.

Top-right maxima	0 0 1 0 0 1 0 0 0 1 0 0
Bottom-right maxima	0 0 0 1 0 0 1 0 0 1 0 0

results very useful for many different applications. A consequence of this drastic simplification is that it is much faster to calculate relations among pixels grouped in relevant maxima, because there is no need to check each and every pixel in an image. Color segmentation is a direct application of this advantage.

When working with relevant maxima it is possible to achieve fast color segmentation due to a much smaller amount of information. We implemented a naive segmentation method based on group membership propagation using the Euclidean distance in the perceptually linear CIELuv color space, ignoring maxima descriptors. Basically, groups are created extracting one unlabeled maximum from a sorted maxima list each time and recursively propagating its label to all contacting non-labeled maxima which color difference with the group is less than a given threshold, as the following pseudocode summarizes:

```
M <- Sorted decreasing unlabeled maxima list
L <- Empty maxima list
ID = 0
While M not empty
    m <- First non-labeled maximum extracted from M
    Label m with ID
    Increment ID
    Insert m into L
    While L not empty
        u <- First maximum extracted from L
        For all non-labeled v in contact with u in M
            If D(u, m) < T
                Label v with u's label
                Insert v in L
```

Where $D(u, m)$ means the Euclidean Distance in CIELuv and T is a threshold obtained from the averaged standard deviation of the RGB channels. The higher

Fig. 4. Three examples of segmentation using relevant maxima. First column shows the original image. Middle column shows results for mean shift as described in [6]. Last column shows early segmentation using relevant maxima, representing each maximum with a rectangle filled by its group color.

the standard deviation, the higher the contrast between colors in the image:

$$D(u, v) = \sqrt{(\triangle L)^2 + (\triangle)u^2 + (\triangle v)^2}$$
$$T = 0.5 \cdot (\sigma_R + \sigma_G + \sigma_B)/3.0$$

Some segmentation results are shown in Fig. 4. Compared to mean shift results, this early segmentation using relevant maxima returns a coarse segmentation. Naturally, being a per-pixel operation, mean shift conserves fine details that are removed by our proposal. But depending on the application, it may not be necessary such amount of details. However, it creates a smaller amount of segments: 68 for the first image, 86 for the second image and 118 for the third image, while the mean shift algorithm creates 156, 170 and 445 groups respectively with a range bandwith of 7 and a space bandwith of 6.5. Our proposal is ten times faster than the mean shift algorithm. With $200x180 images$ from Fig. 4 it takes $125ms$, $78ms$ and $156ms$, while the mean shift algorithm needs $920ms$, $760ms$ and $1600ms$.

Furthermore, high frequency areas where color segmentation is not useful are easily identified as those zones not covered my large groups. Thus, another application of our segmentation method is a fast division of an image into

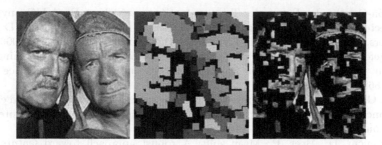

Fig. 5. Left: Original image. Center: Homogeneous regions detected using relevant maxima. Small groups were removed. Right: Textured patches.

textured/non textured segments, which may result useful for salient region detection, as shown in Fig.5

5   Conclusions and Future Work

Relevant Maxima in Distance Transform constitute a powerful mechanism for image data reduction, being specially useful in those situations where relations among image pixels have to be computed, like clustering or region growing. Because each maximum represents many pixels sharing chromatic attributes, operations on these maxima are equivalent to operating on all enclosed pixels in parallel. As an example, an application for coarse color segmentation is presented, suitable for applications where fine details are not relevant or may be detected in later stages of the interpretation process. Although an early and naive segmentation method is used, results are fast and convincing.

Future work will be aimed towards avoiding the binarization step, applying DT directly to grayscale images [1] or non-binary edges [16]. Maxima clustering will include the use of maxima descriptors and the application of the mean shift algorithm on the maxima space. Applications to salient region detection will be considered, studying maxima behavior in different scales.

Acknowledgments. This work has been supported by the Spanish Government under project TIN2004-07087 and a research scholarship for Luis Antón-Canalís with reference code BES-2005-8272.

References

1. Arlandis, J., Perez-Cortes, J.C.: The continuos distance transformation: a generalization of distance transformation for continuos-valued images. Proceedings of the VIII SNRFAI, vol. 1 pp. 195–202. Spain (1999)
2. Gooch, A.A., Olsen, S.C., Tumblin, J., Gooch, B.: Color2Gray: Salience-Preserving Color Removal. ACM Transactions on Graphics, vol. 24(3), pp. 634–639, Proceedings of ACM SIGGRAPH (2005)

3. Antón-Canalís, L., Hernández-Tejera, M., Sánchez-Nielsen, E.: AddCanny: Edge Detector for Video Processing. In: Blanc-Talon, J., Philips, W., Popescu, D., Scheunders, P. (eds.) ACIVS 2006. LNCS, vol. 4179, Springer, Heidelberg (2006)
4. Borgefors, G.: Hierarchical chamfer matching: A parametric edge matching algorithm. IEEE Transactions on Pattern Analysis and Machine Intelligence 10(6), 849–865 (1988)
5. Cho, G.S., Ryeun, J.: Mobile robot path planning by circular scan code and circular distance transform method. In: Proc. of International Conference on Intelligent Computing (ICIC), pp. 1102–1107 (2006)
6. Comaniciu, D., Meer, P.: Mean shift: A robust approach toward feature space analysis. IEEE Trans. Pattern Anal. Machine Intell 24, 603–619 (2002)
7. Fernández-Vidal, S., Bardinet, E., Malandain, G., Damas, S., De la Blanca Capilla, N.P.: Object Representation and Comparison Inferred from Its Medial Axis. In: International Conference on Pattern Recognition (ICPR 2000), vol. 1, pp. 1712–1715, Barcelone, Espagne (2000)
8. Borgefors, G.: Distance Transformations in Digital Images. Computer Vision, Graphics and Image Processing 34, 344–371 (1986)
9. Huttenlocher, D., Klanderman, G., Rucklidge, W.: Comparing images using the hausdorff distance. IEEE Transactions on Pattern Analysis and Machine Intelligence 15(9), 850–863 (1993)
10. Intel's Open Source Computer Vision Library. http://www.intel.com/technology/computing/opencv
11. Canny, J.: A Computational approach to Edge Detection. IEEE Transactions on Pattern Analysis and Machine Intelligence, vol. 8(6) (1986)
12. Paglieroni, D.W.: Distance Transforms. Computer Vision, Graphics and Image Processing: Graphical Models and Image Processing 54, 56–74 (1992)
13. Pietikäinen, M.: Image analysis with local binary patterns. In: Kalviainen, H., Parkkinen, J., Kaarna, A. (eds.) SCIA 2005. LNCS, vol. 3540, pp. 115–118. Springer, Heidelberg (2005)
14. Strzodka, R., Telea, A.: Generalized Distance Transforms and skeletons in graphics hardware. In: Proceedings of EG/IEEE TCVG Symposium on Visualization (VisSym '04), pp. 221–230 (2004)
15. Roerdink, Meijster.: The Watershed Transform: Definitions, Algorithms and Parallelization Strategies. In: FUNDINF: Fundamenta Informatica, vol. 41, IOS Press, Amsterdam (2000)
16. Rosin, P.L., West, G.A.W.: Salience distance transforms. CVGIP: Graphical Models and Image Processing 57(6), 483–521 (1995)
17. Shih, F.Y., Wu, Y.-T.: The efficient algorithms for achieving Euclidean distance transformation. IEEE Transactions on Image Processing 13(8), 1078–1091 (2004)
18. Weeks, A.R., Hague, G.E.: Color segmentation in the HSI color space using the K-means algorithm. Proc. of Conference on Nonlinear Image Processing, vol. VIII, pp.143–154 (1997)
19. Yang, R., Mirmehdi, M., Xie, X.: A Charged Active Contour Based on Electrostatics. In: Blanc-Talon, J., Philips, W., Popescu, D., Scheunders, P. (eds.) ACIVS 2006. LNCS, vol. 4179, pp. 173–184. Springer, Heidelberg (2006)

Performance Analysis of Classifier Ensembles: Neural Networks *Versus* Nearest Neighbor Rule

R.M. Valdovinos[1] and J.S. Sánchez[2]

[1] Lab. Reconocimiento de Patrones, Instituto Tecnológico de Toluca
Av. Tecnológico s/n, 52140 Metepec (México)
li_rmvr@hotmail.com
[2] Dept. Llenguatges i Sistemes Informàtics, Universitat Jaume I
Av. Sos Baynat s/n, E-12071 Castelló de la Plana (Spain)
sanchez@uji.es

Abstract. We here compare the performance (predictive accuracy and processing time) of different neural network ensembles with that of nearest neighbor classifier ensembles. Concerning the connectionist models, the multilayer perceptron and the modular neural network are employed. Experiments on several real-problem data sets demonstrate a certain superiority of the nearest-neighbor-based schemes, in terms of both accuracy and computing time. When comparing the neural network ensembles, one can observe a better behavior of the multilayer perceptron than that of the modular networks.

1 Introduction

The combination of classifiers (ensemble of classifiers) is now a well-established research line in Pattern Recognition and other related areas. The fundamental idea presents a number of advantages when compared to the use of individual classifiers [10, 15]: the correlated errors of the individual components can be eliminated when considering the total of the decisions, the training patterns cannot often provide enough information to select the best classifier and finally, the individual space search may not contain the objective function.

Let $\mathcal{D} = \{D_1, \ldots, D_h\}$ be a set of h classifiers. Each classifier D_i $(i = 1, \ldots, h)$ gets as input a feature vector $x \in \Re^n$, and assigns it to one of the c problem classes. The output of an ensemble of classifiers is an h-dimensional vector $[D_1(\mathbf{x}), \ldots, D_h(\mathbf{x})]^T$ containing the decisions of each of the h individual classifiers. For combining the individual decisions, the most popular (and simplest) method is the majority voting rule, although there exist other more complex schemes (e.g., average, minority, medium, product of votes) [15, 2].

To ensure the success of the combining systems, two fundamental conditions are considered: the ratio of error in the individual components and the level of diversity in the individual decisions [10]. Two classifiers are said to be diverse if their decisions are different when classifying a same input pattern, that is, if the individual classifiers do not always agree. No benefit arises from combining the predictions of a set of classifiers that frequently coincide in the classifications (strongly correlated classifiers). Although measuring diversity is not straightforward [16], this diversity in combining classifiers

J. Martí et al. (Eds.): IbPRIA 2007, Part I, LNCS 4477, pp. 105–112, 2007.
© Springer-Verlag Berlin Heidelberg 2007

has been sought through different ways: by manipulating the training patterns (training each classifier on different subsets of the training sample) [7], by using different decision rules, or by incorporating random noise into the feature values or into some parameters of the learning model considered [18], among others.

In the present paper, the performance (in terms of overall predictive accuracy and processing time) of nearest neighbor classifier ensembles and artificial neural network ensembles are comparatively analyzed. This type of evaluation has several precedents in the literature, although all they pursue different goals. For example, Brown and Wyatt [8] carried out a detailed analysis of neural network ensembles and the impact of negative correlated learning on classification performance.

For the neural networks, we here focus on two different models: the multilayer feedforward perceptron and the modular neural network. Diversity and independence are achieved by using two resampling methods: the well-known Bagging scheme [7] and the random selection without replacement [3]. Both are applied by performing a way of class-dependant (or stratified) resampling [20], that is, resampling is done separately over the training instances of each class, thus obtaining the same class distribution in each subsample as that of the original training set.

2 Theoretical Background of the Ensembles

This section provides the main characteristics of the ensembles that will be analyzed in the present work. We describe the particular topology of the neural networks and the basis of the nearest neighbor classifier.

2.1 The Multilayer Perceptron Ensemble

The Multilayer Perceptron (MP) neural network is one of the most popular connectionist models for classification purposes. It organizes the representation of knowledge in the hidden layers and has a very high power of generalization. The typical topology consists of three sequential layers: input, hidden and output [11, 13].

Currently, there does not exist empirical evidence on the optimal number of neurons in the hidden layer. For the ensemble of multilayer perceptrons proposed in this study, all the networks have n input units and c output units corresponding to the number of input features (or attributes) and data classes, respectively. Also, each network has only one hidden layer with two different structures, here called MP1 and MP2. In the former, the amount of neurons in the hidden layer is set to $(n + 1)$ [17] whereas in the latter, it is set to 2. The initial values of the connection weights are randomly picked out in the range $[-0.5, 0.5]$.

The networks will be here trained by using the backpropagation algorithm with a sigmoidal activation function for both the hidden and output layers. The backpropagation algorithm is simple and easy to compute. It often converges rapidly to a local minimum, but it may not find a global minimum and in some cases, it may not converge at all. To overcome this problem, a momentum term can be added to the minimization function, and a variable learning rate can be applied. In our experiments, the learning rate and momentum will be set to 0.9 and 0.7, respectively, whereas the number of training iterations will be 5000.

2.2 The Modular Neural Network Ensemble

The second neural model used in this paper is the modular neural network (also known as Mixture of Experts, ME) [14]. This is based on the human nervous system, in which each cerebral region has a specific function but at the same time, the regions are interconnected to each other. A modular network solves a complex computational task by dividing it into a number of simpler subtasks and then combining their individual solutions. Thus, a modular neural network consists of several *expert neural networks* (modules), where each expert is optimized to perform a particular task of an overall complex operation. An integrating unit, called *gating network*, is used to select or combine the outputs of the modules in order to form the final output of the network. In the more basic implementation, all the modules are of a same type [4, 12], but different schemes could be used.

There exist several implementations of the modular neural networks, although the main difference among them refers to the nature of the gating network. In some cases, this corresponds to a single neuron evaluating the performance of the other expert modules [12]. Others are based on a network trained with a data set different from the one used for training the expert networks [4]. In this work, all modules (both the experts and the gating network) will be trained with a unique data set [14] (see Fig. 1).

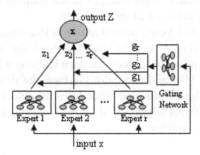

Fig. 1. Representation of the modular neural network architecture. Each module is a feedforward network and receives the same input vector. The final output of the system is the sum of $z_j g_j$.

All modules, including the gating network, have n input units, that is, the number of features. The number of output neurons in the expert networks is equal to the number of classes c, whereas in the gating network it is equal to the number of experts, say r. The learning process is based on the stochastic gradient algorithm, being the objective function defined as follows:

$$-\ln \left(\sum_{j=1}^{r} g_j \cdot \exp \left(-\frac{1}{2} ||s - z_j||^2 \right) \right) \tag{1}$$

where s is the output desired for input x, $z_j = x w_j$ is the output vector of the j'th expert network, $g_j = \frac{\exp(u_j)}{\sum_i \exp(u_j)}$ is the normalized output of the gating network, u_i is the total weighted input received by output unit j of the gating network, and g_j can be viewed as the probability of selecting expert j for a particular case.

The configuration of the ensembles used in this paper is as follows. Each individual component in the ensemble corresponds to a modular neural network, each one with the same structure: five expert networks and one gating network. As in the case of the multilayer perceptron, the decisions of the base classifiers in the ensemble will be finally combined by simple majority voting.

2.3 The Nearest Neighbor Classifier Ensemble

The Nearest Neighbor (NN) rule [9] constitutes one of the most studied learning algorithms in Pattern Recognition. Interest in this method is mainly due to its conceptual and implementational simplicity along with an asymptotic error rate conveniently bounded in terms of the optimal Bayes error. In its classical manifestation, given a set of N previously labelled instances (or training sample), this classifier assigns any input pattern to the class indicated by the label of the closest example in the training set.

Earlier reported results stimulated research into and applications of ensembles of classification models like neural networks and decision trees, while they discouraged the use of ensembles of NN classifiers. Experiments with Bagging did not show a difference in performance in the built ensemble as compared to the single NN classifier trained with the original learning set. These results led to the conclusion that the NN classifier is a very stable model: small changes in the training sample do not produce serious perturbations in the behavior of the classifier.

Nevertheless, in the last few years, several attempts to create ensembles of NN classifiers have been reported. Bay [5] searches to break down the stability by constructing different nearest neighbor individual classifiers, each learning with a randomly selected subset of features. Skalak [19] and Alpaydin [1] base the destabilization of the NN classifier upon the application of different procedures for reducing the training set size. This approach has the additional advantage of allowing a decrease in the computational burden inherent to the NN classifiers.

3   Resampling Methods

In this work, two different methods for designing the training sample are used: Bagging [6] and random selection without replacement [3]. These are here implemented by means of the class-dependent strategy [20], which consists of picking instances up in a way that the initial class distributions are preserved in each of the h subsamples generated. The rationale behind this strategy is to reduce the possibly high computational complexity (computing time and storage loads) of the base classifiers induced by each of the subsamples.

Briefly, in a class-dependent Bagging ensemble, each base classifier is trained on a set of N/h training examples randomly drawn, by replacement, from the original training set (of size N). Such a set is called a bootstrap replicate of the original training sample. By this technique, many examples may appear multiple times, while others may be left out. This negative effect can be overcome by using the random selection without replacement method, in which each example can be selected only once.

4 Experiments and Results

The results here reported correspond to the experiments over eight real-problem data sets taken from the UCI Machine Learning Database Repository (http://www.ics. uci.edu/~mlearn), whose main characteristics are summarized in Table 1. For each data set, 5-fold cross-validation was used to estimate the average predictive accuracy and processing time: 80% of the patterns for training and 20% for the test set.

Table 1. A brief summary of the UCI databases

	No. Classes	No. Features	No. Patterns
Cancer	2	9	685
Pima	2	8	770
Iris	3	4	150
Vehicle	4	18	848
Phoneme	2	5	5406
Waveform	3	21	5001
Segment	7	19	2212
Satimage	6	36	6437

In all experiments, the ensembles consist of nine individual classifiers. For each ensemble, the corresponding training samples have been designed by using the class-dependent Bagging and random selection without replacement techniques, as described in Sect. 3. Four different configurations for the base classifiers have been tested: NN, MP1, MP2, and ME. The results (predictive accuracy and processing time) for each single classifier (i.e., with no combination) has also been included as a baseline. The experiments have been carried out using a personal computer with Intel Centrino 1.3 GHz and 512 MB of RAM.

From results in Table 2, some initial comments can be drawn. Firstly, for all data sets there exists at least one ensemble whose classification accuracy is higher than that obtained when using the single classifier (training sample). On the other hand, while the NN ensembles show a favorable and uniform behavior on all data sets, accuracy of the neural network ensembles can strongly differ from one problem to another depending on each particular database. For example, the MP1 ensemble is better than the respective single classifier for the Phoneme database, but it clearly gives poorer results in the case of Vehicle and Satimage.

When comparing the overall predictive accuracies of the ensembles, in most cases the NN-based solutions provide better results than the neural networks. The most significant gains are in Iris, Vehicle, Phoneme, and Satimage; in these cases, the NN ensemble is about 12% superior to the best connectionist model (MP2). Concerning the neural network ensembles, one can observe that the multilayer perceptrons generally yield better results than the ME. Also, note that the behavior here discussed seems to be independent of the resampling method used, that is, both random selection without replacement and Bagging give very similar accuracy rates in all data sets.

Table 2. Overall classification accuracies (second row of each database corresponds to standard deviations)

	Single				Random w/o replacement				Bagging			
	NN	MP1	MP2	ME	NN	MP1	MP2	ME	NN	MP1	MP2	ME
Cancer	95.6	94.6	97.1	88.4	96.2	96.3	96.6	87.1	96.4	95.6	96.6	86.5
	0.025	0.023	0.021	0.038	0.029	0.025	0.021	0.047	0.028	0.034	0.017	0.042
Pima	65.9	71.1	75.2	66.5	72.8	72.2	72.7	66.1	72.7	72.2	73.1	67.8
	0.052	0.027	0.012	0.025	0.049	0.031	0.017	0.023	0.012	0.035	0.016	0.024
Iris	96.0	94.7	94.7	80.7	98.0	95.3	96.0	78.0	94.0	97.3	97.3	80.0
	0.015	0.022	0.028	0.076	0.018	0.038	0.037	0.077	0.044	0.015	0.028	0.067
Vehicle	64.2	57.5	46.7	36.4	61.4	44.1	51.3	42.2	60.6	47.3	43.0	43.5
	0.018	0.019	0.021	0.025	0.019	0.103	0.106	0.040	0.023	0.033	0.048	0.038
Phoneme	76.1	68.7	69.7	67.9	75.0	71.7	70.9	67.7	75.0	72.6	70.9	68.1
	0.080	0.066	0.031	0.036	0.099	0.067	0.025	0.042	0.094	0.057	0.038	0.042
Waveform	78.0	80.7	82.0	77.2	82.7	83.6	83.6	79.2	83.2	83.6	84.1	80.2
	0.029	0.015	0.020	0.028	0.018	0.017	0.008	0.038	0.014	0.010	0.014	0.033
Segment	94.8	94.1	73.3	78.2	87.6	93.8	80.1	76.9	87.7	93.5	81.4	74.5
	0.014	0.017	0.020	0.019	0.026	0.018	0.022	0.024	0.021	0.015	0.016	0.018
Satimage	83.6	70.4	70.4	34.9	82.9	42.9	70.5	58.9	82.9	44.1	71.9	48.9
	0.116	0.112	0.105	0.048	0.145	0.160	0.095	0.053	0.143	0.273	0.080	0.075

The Satimage database constitutes a very particular case, in which differences are especially important. The accuracy obtained by the MP2 ensemble is 28% higher than that given by MP1, whereas the average predictive accuracy of the ME ensemble is 24% higher than that of the single classifier. Analogously, the NN ensemble presents an accuracy 40% higher than MP1, 24% higher than ME, and about 12% higher than the MP2 ensemble.

Apart from accuracy, the time required for training a classification system is another important factor to take into account when analyzing the performance. This is particularly interesting in the case of neural network ensembles because for several models, training may suppose a very important time consuming process. Thus, a certain trade-off between predictive accuracy and processing time should be achieved to decide which classifier ensemble has to be used. Correspondingly, Table 3 reports the processing times, relative to training and classification phases.

The significant differences in processing time between the three ensembles and the single neural networks result evident (see Table 3). For example, in the case of the Iris data, time required by the single MP1 is one minute, whereas the corresponding ensembles (Bagging and random selection without replacement) need only 10 seconds for training and classification. Focusing on the neural network ensembles, it is clear enough that, as expected, the MP2 configuration is faster than MP1 and ME. In fact, remind that the MP1 structure consists of $(n + 1)$ neurons in the hidden layer, while the MP2 scheme is formed by only two neurons. Similarly, each individual component in the ME ensemble corresponds to a modular neural network, each one consisting of five expert networks and one gating network. Obviously, these differences in the structures imply considerable differences in computational cost. In the case of NN, we did not

Table 3. Processing times for the different learning schemes (in minutes)

	Single				Random w/o replacement				Bagging			
	NN	MP1	MP2	ME	NN	MP1	MP2	ME	NN	MP1	MP2	ME
Cancer	0.1	4.5	5.2	11.3	0.1	0.4	0.3	9.5	0.1	0.3	0.4	9.2
Pima	0.1	8.5	3.6	9.8	0.9	5.7	4.1	9.6	0.1	6.8	3.9	9.8
Iris	0.0	1.0	0.4	2.3	0.0	0.1	0.1	1.8	0.0	0.1	0.1	1.8
Waveform	4.5	437.9	65.1	174.5	4.2	167.3	44.8	133.0	4.2	131.2	41.1	127.2
Vehicle	0.3	60.5	10.7	0.3	0.3	36.3	7.4	0.3	0.3	32.4	7.0	0.3
Satimage	8.3	134.4	134.5	593.2	10.4	913.9	88.3	420.6	10.5	829.4	82.4	409.0
Phoneme	1.7	60.5	21.3	66.8	1.0	39.4	22.6	57.4	1.0	41.9	23.7	59.0
Segment	1.1	210.9	35.0	1.4	1.6	81.8	24.4	2.1	1.7	63.1	23.0	2.1

find significant differences between times required by the ensembles and the single classifier. This is due to the resampling method described in Sect. 3, since the ensemble and the single classifier process the same amount of patterns.

5 Concluding Remarks and Further Extensions

Design of ensembles with NN classifiers, multilayer perceptrons and modular neural networks has been here analyzed. All ensembles consist of nine individual classifiers. In the case of perceptrons, the number of neurons in the hidden layer has been determined according to two criteria. In the first case, this has been set to $(n+1)$, while in the second configuration it has been set to 2. For the modular architecture, we have employed five expert networks and one gating network.

The experimental results allow to compare these ensemble models, in terms of processing time and predictive accuracy. From this, it has been possible to corroborate that in general, an ensemble of classifiers clearly outperforms the single classifier. Also, when comparing the four ensembles, it has been empirically demonstrated that the employment of a NN classifier results in the best performance: higher accuracy and lower computational cost.

Focusing on the results given by the three neural network ensembles, in most cases the MP2 configurations consume much less processing time than the other two schemes. It is due to the fact that the MP2 schemes are formed by only two neurons in the hidden layer, thus allowing considerable savings in computing time. Also, it is important to remind the classification results obtained with the three ensembles. From these results, it seems possible to conclude that in general, the MP2 ensemble provides a well-balanced trade-off between time requirements and predictive accuracy, becoming somewhat superior to MP1 and ME.

Future work is primarily addressed to improve the performance when using ensembles of neural networks. Within this context, other architectures, different parameters, and possible regularization/cross-validation mechanisms have to be analyzed in the future. Also, it should be further investigated the relationship between the individual classifiers and the resampling methods in order to determine the "optimal" scenario.

Acknowledgements. This work has partially been supported by grants 10007-2006-01 (ref. 51626) and SEP-2003-C02-44225 from the Mexican CONACYT, and DPI2006-15542 from the Spanish CICYT.

References

1. Alpaydin, E.: Voting over multiple condensed nearest neighbors. Artificial Intelligence Ressearch 11, 115–132 (1997)
2. Bahler, D., Navarro, L.: Methods for combining heterogeneous sets of classifiers, In: Proc. 17th Natl. Conf. on Artificial Intelligence, Workshop on New Research Problems for Machine Learning (2000)
3. Barandela, R., Valdovinos, R.M., Sánchez, J.S.: New applications of ensembles of classifiers. Pattern Analysis and Applications 6, 245–256 (2003)
4. Bauckhage, C., Thurau, C.: Towards a fair'n square aimbot — Using mixture of experts to learn context aware weapon handling, In: Proc. GAME-ON. Ghent, Belgium, pp. 20–24 (2004)
5. Bay, S.: Combining nearest neighbor classifiers through multiple feature subsets, In: Proc. 15th Intl. Conf. on Machine Learning. Madison, WI, pp. 37–45 (1998)
6. Breiman, L.: Bagging predictors. Machine Learning 24, 123–140 (1996)
7. Breiman, L.: Arcing classifiers. Annals of Statistics 26, 801–823 (1998)
8. Brown, G., Wyatt, J.: Negative correlation learning and the ambiguity family of ensemble methods, In: Proc. Intl. Workshop on Multiple Classifier Systems. Guilford, UK, pp. 266–275 (2003)
9. Dasarathy, B.V. (ed.): Nearest Neighbor Norms: NN Pattern Classification Techniques. IEEE Computer Society Press, Los Alamos, CA (1991)
10. Dietterich, G.T.: Machine learning research: four current directions. AI Magazine 18, 97–136 (1997)
11. Funahashi, K.: On the approximate realization of continuous mapping by neural networks. Neural Networks 2, 183–192 (1989)
12. Hartono, P., Hashimoto, S.: Ensemble of linear perceptrons with confidence level output, In: Proc. 4th Intl. Conf. on Hybrid Intelligent Systems. Kitakyushu, Japan, pp. 186–191 (2004)
13. Hornik, K., Stinchcombe, M., White, H.: Multilayer feedforward networks are universal approximators. Neural Networks 2, 359–366 (1989)
14. Jacobs, R., Jordan, M., Hinton, G.: Adaptive mixture of local experts. Neural Computation 3, 79–87 (1991)
15. Kuncheva, L.I.: Using measures of similarity and inclusion for multiple classifier fusion by decision templates. Fuzzy Sets and Systems 122, 401–407 (2001)
16. Kuncheva, L.I., Whitaker, C.J.: Measures of diversity in classifier ensembles. Machine Learning 51, 181–207 (2003)
17. Pao, Y.H.: Adaptive Pattern Recognition and Neural Networks. Addison-Wesley, Reading, MA, London, UK (1989)
18. Raviv, Y., Intrator, N.: Bootstrapping with noise: an effective regularization technique. Connection Science 8, 356–372 (1996)
19. Skalak, D.B.: Prototype Selection for Composite Nearest Neighbor Classification. Ph.D. Thesis, University of Massachusetts (1996)
20. Valdovinos, R.M., Sánchez, J.S.: Class-dependant resampling for medical applications, In: Proc. 4th Intl. Conf. on Machine Learning and Applications. Los Angeles, CA, pp. 351–356 (2005)

Robust Multiple-People Tracking Using Colour-Based Particle Filters

Daniel Rowe[1], Ivan Huerta[1], Jordi Gonzàlez[2], and Juan J. Villanueva[1]

[1] Computer Vision Centre, Universitat Autònoma de Barcelona, Spain
[2] Institut de Robòtica i Informàtica Industrial, UPC, Barcelona, Spain

Abstract. Robust and accurate people tracking is a key task in many promising computer-vision applications. One must deal with non-rigid targets in open-world scenarios, whose shape and appearance evolve over time. Targets may interact, causing partial or complete occlusions. This paper improves tracking by means of particle filtering, where occlusions are handled considering the target's predicted trajectories. Model drift is tackled by careful updating, based on the history of likelihood measures. A colour-based likelihood, computed from histogram similarity, is used. Experiments are carried out using sequences from the CAVIAR database.

1 Introduction

Robust and accurate people tracking is a key task in many promising computer-vision applications, such as smart video surveillance or human-computer interfaces [6,4,1]. The interest in multiple-people tracking is also prompted by the challenge of emulating the amazing capabilities of natural systems to detect motion and keep lock on several moving objects simultaneously.

However, serious difficulties should be expected. The system must deal with non-rigid targets, often highly articulated and elastic, who may wear loose-fitting clothes. In open-world applications, neither the number of targets, nor their appearance or shape can be specified in advance. Considerable foreground diversity should be taken into account. Further, both observed shape and appearance evolve over time depending on the point of view, or on the local illumination and background, specially if these are uncontrolled. Finally, as the targets interact, they may group and split, causing occlusions, and changing the observed appearance and shape. This paper enhances tracking by means of particle filtering (PF). A preliminary work was published in [11]. The main contributions of the presented approach are the following:

- it copes with clutter distracters by adopting a colour-based likelihood computed from histogram similarity. Colour information relative to the target surroundings is used to tune the colour histograms.
- It deals with multiple targets simultaneously, paying special attention to the *sampling impoverishment* phenomenon. The systems scales well with the number of targets, avoiding the curse of dimensionality common to PF.

J. Martí et al. (Eds.): IbPRIA 2007, Part I, LNCS 4477, pp. 113–120, 2007.

- Model drift is precluded by careful updating, based on likelihood measures, thereby ensuring proper tracking despite noisy measures, estimate errors, occlusions, and changes in illumination conditions and camera viewpoint.
- Occlusions are handled considering the predicted trajectories of all targets within the scene and the history of likelihood measurements.

The remainder of this paper is organised as follows. Section 2 covers the probabilistic framework and related approaches. A colour-based particle filter for multiple-target tracking is proposed in Section 3. Section 4 shows some experimental results, and section 5 summarises the conclusions.

2   Probabilistic Tracking Framework

The computation of the state $\mathbf{s}_t$ given all evidence to date $\mathbf{e}_{1:t}$ is called *filtering*. The posterior pdf $p\left(\mathbf{s}_t \mid \mathbf{e}_{1:t}\right)$ can be calculated through *recursive estimation*:

$$p\left(\mathbf{s}_t \mid \mathbf{e}_{1:t}\right) \propto \underbrace{p\left(\mathbf{e}_t \mid \mathbf{s}_t\right)}_{\substack{\text{likelihood} \\ \text{updating}}} \int \underbrace{p\left(\mathbf{s}_t \mid \mathbf{s}_{t-1}\right)}_{\text{trans. model}} \underbrace{p\left(\mathbf{s}_{t-1} \mid \mathbf{e}_{1:t-1}\right)}_{\text{previous post.}} d\mathbf{s}_{t-1}. \tag{1}$$

The pdf is projected forward according to the transition model, making a prediction. It is then updated in agreement with the new evidence, $\mathbf{e}_t$. When non-Gaussian, non-linear distributions are involved, this problem is overcome by simulating N i.i.d. random samples from the posterior pdf, $\left\{\mathbf{s}_t^i; i = 1 : N\right\}$. This leads to the *particle filter approach*. This works as follows: the posterior pdf at time $t-1$, $p\left(\mathbf{s}_{t-1} \mid \mathbf{e}_{1:t-1}\right)$, is represented by a weighted set of samples, $\left\{\hat{\mathbf{s}}_{t-1}^i, \overline{\pi}_{t-1}^i; i = 1 : N\right\}$. The set is re-sampled using normalised weights $\overline{\pi}_{t-1}^i$ as probabilities. The temporal prior $\left\{\hat{\mathbf{s}}_t^i\right\}$ is obtained by applying the transition model $p\left(\mathbf{s}_t \mid \mathbf{s}_{t-1}\right)$ to each sample. The likelihood $p\left(\mathbf{e}_t \mid \mathbf{s}_t\right)$ is represented by weights π_t^i, which are then normalised. Expectations are approximated as:

$$\mathbb{E}_{p\left(\mathbf{s}_t \mid \mathbf{e}_{1:t}\right)}\left(\mathbf{s}_t\right) \simeq \sum_{i=1}^{N} \overline{\pi}_t^i \hat{\mathbf{s}}_t^i. \tag{2}$$

Although SIR methods have been widely used in recent years, they have important drawbacks [7]. *Sampling impoverishment* is one of the main ones: samples are spread around several *modes* pointing out hypotheses in the state space, but most of them may be spurious. Unfortunately, there is a non-negligible probability of losing modes, a low probability of recovering them and the remaining modes could be all spurious. Different approaches have been taken in order to overcome these and other issues. Nummiaro et al. [9] use a PF based on colour-histogram cues. However, no multiple-target tracking is considered, which implies that no scene event such as target grouping or occlusion can be analysed. Perez et al. [10] propose also a PF based on a colour-histogram likelihood. They introduce interesting extensions in multiple-part modelling, incorporation of background information, and multiple-target tracking. Nevertheless, it requires an extremely large number of samples, since one sample contains information about the state of all targets, dramatically increasing the state dimensionality. Further, no appearance model updating is performed, what usually leads to target loss in dynamic scenes. Deutscher et al. [3] present an interesting approach called *annealing particle filter* which aims to reduce the required number of samples. However, pruning hypotheses with lower likelihood could be undesirable in a cluttered environment. Contour tracking have also been explored [8], although this may be inappropriate if used as the only cue in crowded scenarios because of multiple occlusions. BraMBLe [5] is an appealing approach to multiple-blob tracking which models both background and foreground using Mixtures of Gaussians (MoG). However, no model update is performed, there is a common foreground model for all targets, and suffers for the curse of dimensionality, since it tackles multiple-target tracking combining information about all targets in every sample. Therefore, even though a great number of improvements have been introduced in recent years, there is still much ground to cover.

3   A Multi-target Colour-Based PF

The motion of the central point of an elliptical region is modelled using first-order dynamics in image coordinates. The l-labelled target's state is defined as $\mathbf{s}_t^l = \left(\mathbf{x}_t^l, \mathbf{u}_t^l, \mathbf{w}_t^l, \mathbf{q}_t^l, \rho_t^l, \lambda_t^l\right)^T$, where components are the ellipse position, velocity, both axes, the appearance model, the occlusion status, and the expected target likelihood. A label l associates a specific appearance model to the corresponding samples, allowing multiple-target tracking. Given the high dimensionality of images, a feature extraction process is mandatory. In this approach, evidences $\mathbf{e}_t$ are given by colour histograms computed at each predicted location and size.

After the initialisation, no sample is generated using detection, since it would mask tracking misbehaviours. Thus, just tracking performances are tested by means of propagating hypotheses and weighting them according to evidence. Clearly, by incorporing detection, the general performance will be enhanced, providing the system with error-recovery capabilities.

3.1   Transition Model

The position, speed, and size of each sample are predicted according to:

$$\hat{\mathbf{x}}_t^{i,l} = \mathbf{x}_{t-1}^{i,l} + \mathbf{u}_{t-1}^{i,l}\Delta t + \xi_{\mathbf{x}}^i,$$
$$\hat{\mathbf{u}}_t^{i,l} = \mathbf{u}_{t-1}^l + \xi_{\mathbf{u}}^i,$$
$$\hat{\mathbf{w}}_t^{i,l} = \mathbf{w}_{t-1}^{i,l} + \xi_{\mathbf{w}}^i. \tag{3}$$

The random vectors $\xi_{\mathbf{x}}^i, \xi_{\mathbf{u}}^i, \xi_{\mathbf{w}}^i$, sampled from WAGN processes, provide the system with a diversity of hypotheses. Sample likelihoods depend on sample position and size, but not on their speeds. Thus, if speeds were propagated considering the previous speed, they would be in quasi open loop[1]. Thus, their values

---

[1] There would still be a weak relation, since speeds are used to predict positions, and position errors can be measured, but a considerable delay would be introduced.

could become completely different from the true values within a few frames, and an important proportion of samples would be wasted. In order to avoid this phenomenon, the estimated target speed $\mathbf{u}_{t-1}^l$ at time $t-1$ is fed back into the prediction of $\hat{\mathbf{x}}_t^{i,l}$.

3.2 Likelihood Function

The likelihood function computes the pdf of image features given the state. The target appearance can be represented by means of colour histograms. Histograms are broadly used to represented human appearance, since they are claimed to be less sensitive than colour templates to rotations in depth, the camera point of view, non-rigid targets, and partial occlusions. Thus, the $l-$model is given by:

$$\mathbf{q}^l = \left\{ q_k^l; k = 1 : K \right\},\qquad(4)$$

where K is the number of bins, and the probability of each feature is:

$$q_k^l = C^l \sum_{a=1}^M \delta\left(b\left(\mathbf{x}_a\right) - k\right),\qquad(5)$$

where C^l is a normalisation constant required to ensure that $\sum_{k=1}^K q_k^l = 1$, δ the Kronecker delta, $\{\mathbf{x}_a; a = 1 : M\}$ the pixel locations, and $b\left(\mathbf{x}_a\right)$ a function that associates the given pixel to its corresponding histogram bin. The target distribution at the predicted position $\hat{\mathbf{x}}_t^{i,l}$ and ellipse size $\hat{\mathbf{w}}_t^{i,l}$, is given by $\mathbf{p}_i^l$, which is calculated in the same way as the model. The similarity between two histograms can be computed using the following metric [2,9]:

$$d_B = \sqrt{1 - \rho\left(\mathbf{p}, \mathbf{q}\right)},\qquad(6)$$

where $\rho\left(\mathbf{p}, \mathbf{q}\right) = \sum_{k=1}^K \sqrt{p_k q_k}$. is the *Bhattacharyya coefficient*. Therefore, similar histograms have a high Bhattacharyya coefficient, which should correspond to high sample weights. The computed metric can be mapped using a Gaussian distribution [9], and samples are thus weighted according to:

$$\pi_t^{i,l} = p\left(\mathbf{e}_t \mid \hat{\mathbf{s}}_t^{i,l}\right) = \mathcal{N}\left(d_B; \mu, \sigma^2\right).\qquad(7)$$

So far no background information has been used. However, tracking success depends on how distinguishable the target is from a local environment. Thus, foreground features present also in its surroundings should be less important for target localisation. Here, an approach similar to [2] is adopted by using a *centre-surround* model to compute the background histogram $\mathbf{r}^l$ according to the outer region which encloses the target. Hence, the background histogram is used to compute a weight for each bin:

$$\omega_k = \left\{ \min\left(\frac{r_k^*}{r_k}\right); k = 1 : K \right\},\qquad(8)$$

where r_k^* is the minimum non-zero value. Thus, these weights are then applied to both model and target histograms to diminish the importance of those bins which represent the local background.

3.3 Weight Normalisation

In a multiple-target tracking scenario, those targets whose samples exhibit lower likelihood are more likely to be lost, since the probability of propagating one mode is proportional to the cumulative weights of its samples. In order to avoid one target absorbing other target samples, genetic drift must be prevented. Thus, a memory term, which takes into account the number of targets being tracked, is included. Weights are normalised according to:

$$\bar{\pi}_t^{i,l} = \frac{\pi_t^{i,l}}{\displaystyle\sum_{i=1,j=l}^{N} \pi_t^{i,j}} \frac{1}{L}, \tag{9}$$

where L is the number of tracked targets. Each weight is normalised according to the total weight of the target's samples. Thus, all targets have the same probability of being propagated, since the addition of the weights of each target samples sums $\frac{1}{L}$. This allows multiple-target tracking using a single PF, despite the differences between their likelihoods and the genetic drift phenomenon.

3.4 State Estimation

The l-target estimates are computed according to:

$$\mathbf{x}_t^l = (1 - \alpha_{\mathbf{x}}) \left(\mathbf{x}_{t-1}^l + \mathbf{u}_{t-1}^l \Delta_t \right) + \alpha_{\mathbf{x}} \left(L \sum_{i=1}^{N} \bar{\pi}_t^{i,l} \hat{\mathbf{x}}_t^{i,l} \right),$$

$$\mathbf{u}_t^l = (1 - \alpha_{\mathbf{u}}) \mathbf{u}_{t-1}^l + \alpha_{\mathbf{u}} \left(\frac{\mathbf{x}_t^l - \mathbf{x}_{t-1}^l}{\Delta_t} \right),$$

$$\mathbf{w}_t^l = (1 - \alpha_{\mathbf{w}}) \mathbf{w}_{t-1}^l + \alpha_{\mathbf{w}} \left(L \sum_{i=1}^{N} \bar{\pi}_t^{i,l} \hat{\mathbf{w}}_t^{i,l} \right), \tag{10}$$

where $\alpha_{\mathbf{x}}, \alpha_{\mathbf{u}}, \alpha_{\mathbf{w}} \in [0, 1]$ denote the adaptation rates. Target speeds are not estimated according to sample speeds and their weights, since significant errors would be introduced: samples are chosen only because of sample weights, which do not directly depend on the current speed. This fact could imply a significant amount of jitter and many samples would be wasted. Therefore, target speeds are computed from successive position estimates. Further, both position and speed estimates are enhanced by regularising them according to their histories.

The target appearance must also be updated. However, this is a sensitive task which may lead to the well-known *model drift* phenomenon. Thus, models are then only updated when two conditions hold: (i) the target is not occluded and (ii) the likelihood of the estimated target's state suggests that the estimate is sufficiently reliable. In this case, they are updated using an adaptive filter:

$$\mathbf{q}_t^l = (1 - \alpha_{\mathbf{q}}) \mathbf{q}_{t-1}^l + \alpha_{\mathbf{q}} \mathbf{p}_t^l, \tag{11}$$

where $\alpha_{\mathbf{q}} \in [0, 1]$ is the learning rate. In order to determine when the estimate is reliable, the likelihood of the current estimate is computed, $p\left(\mathbf{e}_t \mid \mathbf{s}_t^l\right)$.

The appearance is then updated when this value is higher than an indicator of the expected likelihood value, calculated following an adaptive rule:

$$\lambda_t^l = (1 - \alpha_l) \lambda_{t-1}^l + \alpha_l p \left(\mathbf{e}_t \mid \mathbf{s}_t^l \right). \tag{12}$$

3.5 Occlusion Handling

Although the appearance model is not updated during occlusions, these still constitute a main cause of catastrophic failures. Partial occlusions may cause inaccurate size updating, according to the area that can be seen. In case of complete occlusions, sample likelihoods are meaningless, and the re-sampling phase randomly propagate them, quickly losing the target.

Hence, proper handling of occlusions is crucial. The state binary variable ρ_t^l tracks the occlusion status. Occlusions are predicted according to the learned dynamics. When the predicted occlusion is significant, and the target likelihood is lower than the expected one given by λ_t^l, the target state changes into occluded. Then, the following changes are introduced: (i) the adaptation rates are set to zero: neither the size, nor the velocity or the indicator itself is updated, and the position is just propagated; (ii) those samples belonging to the occluded target are not re-sampled. As a result, samples are spread around the target because of the uncertainty predictions terms. The other targets' samples are re-sampled, but are not assigned to the occluded target since otherwise this one would monopolise the whole sample set. When the occlusion is no longer predicted or a sample likelihood exceeds the value previous to the occlusion, ρ_t^l turns into 0, which immediately implies pruning those samples with lower weights. Furthermore, all estimates are again updated.

4   Experimental Results

The performance of the algorithm has been tested using the CAVIAR database[2]. In the sequence *OneLeaveShopReenter1cor* (Caviar database, 389 frames at 25 fps, 384 x 288 pixels), two targets are tracked simultaneously, despite their being articulated and elastic objects whose dynamics are highly non-linear, and that move through an environment which locally mimics the target colour appearance. The first target performs a rotation and heads towards the second one, eventually occluding it. The background colour distribution is so similar to the target ones that it constitutes a source of clutter. Furthermore, several oriented lighting sources are present, dramatically affecting the target appearance. Significant speed and size changes can also be observed.

The tracker performance is shown in Fig. 1. Both targets' appearance models are updated when reliable measures are obtained, see Fig. 1.(a). Poor localisations and occlusions are correctly detected, thereby avoiding re-sampling of samples of the occluded target and erroneous dynamic and appearance models updating, see Fig. 1.(b), (c). The tracker successfully recovers from occlusion, see

---

[2] http://homepages.inf.ed.ac.uk/rbf/CAVIAR

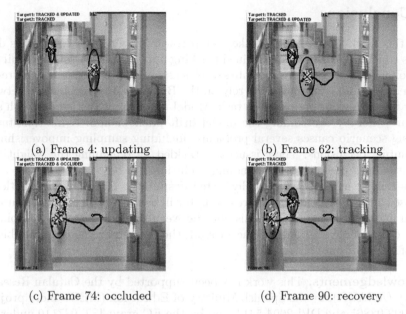

(a) Frame 4: updating   (b) Frame 62: tracking

(c) Frame 74: occluded   (d) Frame 90: recovery

Fig. 1. Each target's estimated position is denoted by an ellipse and tagged accordingly; milestones are placed on the target trajectory every 25 frames; each predicted sample is drawn using a dark dot, whereas re-sampled particles are drawn in a light ones

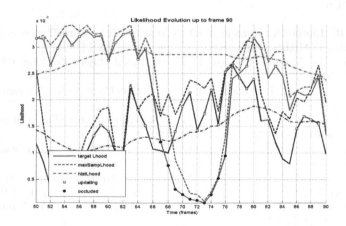

Fig. 2. Likelihood evolution

Fig. 1.(d). The maximum sample and target likelihoods, and the likelihood indicator is shown in Fig. 2. The tracker deals with multiple-target tracking whose dynamics are highly non-linear, despite using a simple constant speed approach. They move through an environment which mimics the target appearances. Furthermore, their trajectories intersect causing a severe partial occlusion. It copes with sizeable appearance and shape changes.

5   Conclusions

With this work we attempt to take a step towards solving the numerous difficulties which appear in unconstrained tracking applications. A robust likelihood function is used to properly evaluate samples associated to targets which present a high appearance variability. We rely on the Bhattacharyya coefficient between colour histograms to perform this task. Model updating is carried out with special care, thereby overcoming the model drift phenomenon. A multiple-target tracking scenario causes several problems, including sampling impoverishment and mutual occlusions. These issues are tackled by redefining the weight normalisation and predicting and handling occlusions.

The tracker has been successfully tested despite the fact that no detection is ever used after initialisation. Future research will be focused on careful feature selection in order to maximise the distance between the histograms corresponding to the different targets and the background, thereby enhancing the disambiguation of targets from clutter.

Acknowledgements. This work has been supported by the Catalan Research Agency (AGAUR), by the Spanish Ministry of Education (MEC) under projects TIC2003-08865 and DPI-2004-5414, and by the EC grant IST-027110 under the HERMES project.

References

1. Collins, R., Lipton, A., Kanade, T.: A System for Video Surveillance and Monitoring. In: 8th ITMRRS, Pittsburgh, USA, pp. 1–15. ANS (1999)
2. Comaniciu, D., Ramesh, V., Meer, P.: Kernel-based Object Tracking. PAMI 25(5), 564–577 (2003)
3. Deutscher, J., Reid, I.: Articulated Body Motion Capture by Stochastic Search. IJCV 61(2), 185–205 (2005)
4. Haritaoglu, I., Harwood, D., Davis, L.: W4: real-time surveillance of people and their activities. PAMI 22(8), 809–830 (2000)
5. Isard, M., MacCormick, J.: BraMBLe: A Bayesian Multiple-Blob Tracker. In: 8th ICCV, Vancouver, Canada, vol. 2, pp. 34–41. IEEE, (2001)
6. Kahn, R., Swain, M., Prokopowicz, P., Firby, R.: Gesture Recognition Using the Perseus Architecture. In: CVPR, San Francisco, USA, pp. 734–741. IEEE, (1996)
7. King, O., Forsyth, D.: How Does CONDENSATION Behave with a Finite Number of Samples? 6th ECCV, Ireland 1, 695–709 (2000)
8. MacCormick, J., Blake, A.: A Probabilistic Exclusion Principle for Tracking Multiple Objects. IJCV 39(1), 57–71 (2000)
9. Nummiaro, K., Koller-Meier, E., Van Gool, L.: An Adaptive Color-Based Particle Filter. IVC 21(1), 99–110 (2003)
10. Pérez, P., Hue, C., Vermaak, J., Gangnet, M.: Color-based Probabilistic Tracking. 7th ECCV, Copenhaguen, Denmark. LNCS, pp. 661–675. Springer, Heidelberg (2002)
11. Rowe, D., Rius, I., González, J., Villanueva, J.J.: Improving Tracking by Handling Occlusions. 3rd ICAPR, UK. LNCS, vol. 2, pp. 384–393. Springer, Heidelberg (2005)

Structure Restriction for Tracking Through Multiple Views and Occlusions

B. Martínez, A. Pérez, L. Ferraz, and X. Binefa

Universitat Autónoma de Barcelona,
Computer Science Department,
08193 Bellaterra, Barcelona, Spain
{brais, adria, luis.ferraz, xavier.binefa}@cs.uab.es

Abstract. The last advances on multiple kernel tracking consider the kernels as estimators of target features. The state space of the target is defined by the individual state space of these features.

The aim of this work is to construct an algorithm robust against three dimensional rotations and partial occlusions. For this purpose, we take as the state space the two dimensional position of the features and an indicator of occlusions. We extract the three dimensional structure of the target from the first tracked frames and estimate the projection of this structure on each frame. By using this information, we are able to predict the position of a feature even when the kernel provides a wrong estimation, for example during an occlusion. The experimental results showed a good performance correcting errors and in presence of partial occlusions.

1 Introduction

Some of the most important advances on the tracking topic came from the kernel tracking approach. Since the Mean Shift algorithm [2] was presented several years ago, this approach gained popularity on the computer vision community. This algorithm takes advantage of its computational speed and simplicity and its robustness under small changes on the target due to scale changes, variations on the illumination or rotations out of the image plane.

As a first step for improving the Mean Shift algorithm, some authors tried to approximate other parameters apart from the kernel position. For example, the scale change problem was treated at [1], [7] or rotations in [9]. At the same time, other works [7] showed the theoretical basis of this algorithm and proved its convergence properties.

This line of research led to the possibility of estimating almost any parameter defining the target aspect [4]. This excellent work presents a tracking algorithm based on a representation generated by multiple kernels and a Newton-like minimization of any variable defining the kernels. The dimensionality of the restrictions generated by the derivatives of the set of kernels opened the possibility of minimizing several variables at the same time.

J. Martí et al. (Eds.): IbPRIA 2007, Part I, LNCS 4477, pp. 121–128, 2007.

This work changed the topic from "how to obtain information" into "what to do with this information". Translated into the tracking problem, it became possible to track a set of kernels/features and minimize a set of variables, but it is not clear at all what information can we extract by using this technical possibilities.

A promising point of view was presented on [8], where the authors present a tracking algorithm for articulated movements, as a pedestrian walk. Here an object is defined as a set of features with a certain relation between them, modeled as a Markov Network. This article gives a new light onto the problem since a target tracking is defined as tracking a set of features and the probability for a target state is defined depending on the individual states of the features. As the main drawback, this approach avoids the aim of generality, limiting its applicability because of the training stage needed. Following this problem definition, the main question is how to define the probability of the target state depending on the features.

The work by Fan [3] is an advance on the same line. Since two features from a three dimensional object can be projected in different frames with different relative positions, a new measure is defined in order to enable this flexible relative position between features. This work is quite more general, although it still needs previous information, unavailable in an unrestricted problem. Another drawback comes from the measure itself. Since the variation of the distance is penalized it may happen a situation of convergence where each kernel is not placed upon its correct position. This can lead to inexact estimations and eventually produce the lost of the target if we use model actualization.

The main problem of the unconstrained approximation of the relations between kernels comes from the nature of the data, a two dimensional projection of a three dimensional set of features. The real movement of the features correspond to a common three dimensional movement, while the two dimensional projection seems to be anarchic. Our intention is to use the structure to have an estimation of non observable features and, jointly, to restrict the position of the kernels in order to avoid convergence to clutter. To do so, we use the position and an indicator of occlusion as the state space of the features. The multiple kernel tracking gives a lecture of the state of the features. It is also important to have an estimation in order to handle lecture errors and to track consistently under occlusions.

On section two we describe the two step multiple kernel tracking and on section three we expose the main contribution of this paper, the structure restriction. On section four, experiments showing the performance correcting tracking errors and handling occlusions are presented.

2   Two-Step Kernel Tracking

2.1   Multiple Kernel Tracking

As stated on the introduction, the multiple kernel tracking method is based on a representation by a weighted histogram whose weights are defined by several kernels. This representation allows the estimation of the target parameters (f.ex. position, scale or illumination) by a Newton-like minimization.

Speaking more formally, a kernel is a smooth positive definite function that weights the contribution of every pixel x_j to the histogram p depending on to the variables defining the kernel, say θ, as its centre or its scale:

$$p_i(\theta) = \frac{1}{C} \sum_{j=1}^{n} K(x_j - \theta)\delta(b(x_j), i) \tag{1}$$

where K is the kernel function, b assigns the point x_j to its bin, δ is the Kronecker function (its value is 1 if the two parameters are equal and 0 otherwise) and C is a normalization factor.

A multiple kernel histogram comes from vertically stacking several single kernel histograms in a single column.

This representation enables the minimization of any variable defining the kernel. Since a kernel is smooth (differentiable) and a histogram is a sum of kernel values, it is differentiable as well. The Newton-like minimization relies on the first order Taylor approximation of the histogram. Even though it is possible to use many metrics, as the Bathacharyya one, used at the Mean Shift algorithm, on this point we follow [4] and choose the SSD metric (sum of square differences) for comparing histograms. So the problem is stated as finding the value of:

$$\min_\theta O(\theta) = \min_\theta \|q - p(\theta)\|^2 \tag{2}$$

where q is a histogram model, extracted on the first frame.
Applying the Taylor approximation to this formula:

$$\left\| \sqrt{q} - \sqrt{p(\theta)} - \frac{1}{2}d(p)^{-\frac{1}{2}}\frac{\delta K}{\delta \theta}\Delta\theta \right\|^2 \tag{3}$$

There exists a closed form minimization of 3 in terms of $\Delta\theta$:

$$\Delta\theta = 2\left(\left(d(p)^{-\frac{1}{2}}\frac{\delta K}{\delta \theta}\right)^t d(p)^{-\frac{1}{2}}\frac{\delta K}{\delta \theta}\right)^{-1}\left(d(p)^{-\frac{1}{2}}\frac{\delta K}{\delta \theta}\right)^t\left(\sqrt{q} - \sqrt{p(\theta)}\right) \tag{4}$$

Although the minimization is calculated by means of a closed formula, an approximation is involved in this calculation, so it is needed an iterative process. As an advantage, the convergence is significantly faster than the one provided by the Mean Shift algorithm, as shown in [4].

2.2   Two Step Tracking

The two step tracking gives an estimation of the state space of the features. The position of the features is estimated directly by the minimization routine. Occlusions are detected by comparing the similarity with respect to the model. On this section we will give an outline of this algorithm.

The multiple kernel structure gives a strong representation of a target and constitutes the basis for a robust tracking algorithm. But this structure is rigid and, therefore, not suited to handle sequences with changes on the relative positions of the kernels. There are several situations, apart from articulated movements, that require a flexible structure. For example, both rotation and displacement of the target out of the image plane or sequences with a mobile camera.

In order to take profit from the robustness provided by the rigid structure and, at the same time, allow each kernel to be placed on its correct position (flexible structure) it is possible to define a tracking in two steps [6].

The first step consists on a convergence stage using the estimation provided by the set of kernels with rigid structure. On the second step, departing from the convergence point of the first step, it is performed a convergence procedure for each single kernel. Since the first approximation is exact except from the slight change introduced by the projective transformation, each kernel is placed very close to the right position. Therefore, the second step is still robust and adapts the kernel positions to the projective part of the transformation between frames.

If we call θ the parameters of the rigid structure and θ_i are the parameters of every single kernel K_i, the histogram p depends on the global parameters θ and on the individual ones θ_i. Then the two steps consist on:

$$1. \quad \theta^{new} = \theta + \Delta\theta = \theta + \min_{\Delta\theta} \| \sqrt{q} - \sqrt{p(\theta + \Delta\theta, \theta_i)} \|^2 \tag{5}$$

$$2. \quad for \quad i = 1, \ldots, n; \quad \theta_i^{new} = \theta^{new} + \min_{\Delta\theta_i} \| \sqrt{q} - \sqrt{p(\theta^{new}, \theta_i + \Delta\theta_i)} \|^2 \tag{6}$$

By using this strategy we are able to track targets under severe aspect changes.

The two step tracking places each kernel over its corresponding feature. The SSD metric allows the comparison of the actual aspect of the feature with respect to the model. It is possible to use this information to detect partial occlusions (or in some cases just convergence to the clutter), since a feature vanishing produces a sudden decrease on the similarity with respect to the model. Occlusions are effectively detected by comparing the similarity with respect to a weighted media of the previous similarity values, where the most recent similarities have higher weights.

The results are shown in figure 1. This sequence presents a big aspect change due to a rotation out of image plane, aspect similar to the background and by the end of the sequence, an occlusion.

3   Structure Restriction

The objective of this section consists on having available a prediction of the position of a feature for every frame. There exist two main drawbacks of the multiple kernel tracking. First of all, the possibility of convergence to the clutter, together with the impossibility of recovering the position of a missed feature. On second place, the inability in order to handle non-observable features. A prediction of the feature position becomes very useful in order to solve these limitations.

Fig. 1. Output of the two step kernel tracking. These images show the tracking of a helicopter, modeled as the cabin, body and motor. The green spots show the positions of kernels while the red one indicates occlusion.

For this purpose, we calculate a three dimensional structure, say P, and the projection T^j that takes the three dimensional point P_i into the corresponding two dimensional feature position on frame j, p_i^j.

$$p_i^j = T^j P_i \quad \text{for i} = 1 \dots n \text{ and for j} = 1 \dots m \tag{7}$$

One of the most important points is the fact that it is possible to calculate the projection T^j with just three visible features (the tracking must be performed over at least four features). It is possible therefore to calculate the projection in presence of occlusions or incorrect estimations.

For calculating the estimation of the position of the point i, it is just necessary to use the rest of the visible points in order to compute the projection for this frame, T^j. The estimation of the point i is the image of the three dimensional point through T^j.

The procedure can be sumarized as:

1. With the first frames compute the 3 dimensional structure P
2. With $\{p_i / p_i$ is not occluded$\}$ compute T^j
3. $\tilde{p}_i = T^j P_i$ is the prediction of p_i

There exist several tactics in order to calculate the three dimensional structure and the projections. On this paper we use the work presented on [5] because of its capability of handling non observable data.

To summarize, we have a state space of the objective. This state space is modeled depending on the state of the features. This state is measured by means of the two step multiple kernel tracking. After the first frames it is possible to compute the three dimensional structure P. With at least three points visible on a frame we are able to compute the estimated position of a point depending on the rest of the visible points.

4   Experimental Results

In this section we will describe a set of applications. These applications consists on the position recovery after a detected or undetected convergence to the clutter and the recovery of the kernel position after an occlusion (or prediction during the occlusion).

Some situations can lead converge to the clutter of one kernel. For example, on the sequence presented on figure 2, the histogram produced by the window on the back of the pedestrian is almost exact to the model. If the kernel converges to this mode, it will always converge to the same mode, since the real one is becomes too far. Thus, a reposition strategy is needed. It is done by calculating its position by means of the structure defined on the previous frames and the transformation without considering the lost kernel.

Fig. 2. The top left image shows the model, composed by four kernels. The top right shows a convergence to the clutter undetected (the similarity is still very high). After some frames, the distance to the rest of the kernels is too big and therefore the error is detected. The bottom left image shows the recovery. The tracking continues without further problems (bottom right image).

On the grey sequence presented on figure 3, a car is tracked by a non fixed camera. The tracking fails because of the misplacement of the feature corresponding to the front wheel. The reposition of a kernel using a rigid structure would lead to the loose of the mode, since the projective change on the image transforms the relative positions between the kernels.

Fig. 3. The kernel placed on the frontal wheel is prone to converge to a very similar part of the image. If the misplacement is produced by a lasting effect, as a sparkle, the correction is affected by the projective transformation.

Fig. 4. The first image shows the initial position of the kernels. The occlusion begins on the second image. During the occlusion, the head turns left and therefore the relative position of the features change. When the occlusion ends it is shown the incorrect estimation made by a fixed structure. The restriction given by the three dimensional structure places the kernel on its right position, even while the feature is occluded. The tracking is recovered correctly when the occlusion ends.

If the problem of convergence happens on just one frame, the error introduced by a fixed structure is negligible. But the error can produce misplacement during a certain number of frames. This situation requires, thus, a projective approximation. The situation is different from the first example, since there exist no evidence of a tracking failure.

The experiment exposed hereafter shows the robustness over a sequence presenting a large partial occlusion. In order to calculate the structure P, the head is tracked briefly. It is needed that this small fragment of the sequence presents at least a slight projective transformation to estimate correctly the structure, avoiding the singularity of estimating a structure on a plane.

During the occlusion, the head turn applies a projective transformation over the head aspect. The position estimated by mantaining a fixed distance to another visible feature is not accurate. When the occlusion ends, the misplacement of the kernel may produce a fail on the tracking. On the contrary, the position estimated by using the three dimensional structure is accurate and when the feature becomes visible the kernel is correctly placed, resulting on the recovery of the tracking of the occluded feature.

It is important to notice that the end of an occlusion is detected comparing the estimated position with the model. When the similarity becomes very high again it is considered that the occlusion has ended. If we misplace the feature, even when the occlusion is over we are testing the similarity with a wrong region of the image. In consequence, the occlusion end won't be detected.

Acknowledgments. This work was partially funded with Cicyt grant n TIC2003-06075.

References

1. Collins, R.: Mean-Shift Blob Tracking Through Scale Space. In: Computer Vision and Pattern Recognition (CVPR'03). pp. 234–240 (2003)
2. Comaniciu, D., Ramesh, V., Meer, P.: Real-Time Tracking of Non-Rigid Objects Using Mean Shift. In: Computer Vision and Pattern Recognition (CVPR'00), pp. 142–151 (2000)
3. Fan, Z., Wu, Y., Yang, M.: Multiple Collaborative Kernel Tracking. In: IEEE Conference on Computer Vision and Pattern Recognition, vol. 2, pp. 502–509 (2005)
4. Hager, G., Dewan, M., Stewart, C.: Multiple Kernel Tracking with ssd. In Computer Vision and Pattern Recognition (CVPR'04), pp. 790–797 (2004)
5. Jacobs, D.W.: Linear Fitting with Missing Data for Structure-from-Motion. In: Computer Vision and Image Understanding, vol. 82(1), pp. 57–81 (2001)
6. Martínez, B., Ferraz, L., Binefa, X.: Multiple Kernel Two-Step Tracking- In: International Conference on Image Processing (2006)
7. Ramesh, V., Comaniciu, V., Meer, P.: Kernel-Based Object Tracking. In: Transactions on Pattern Analysis and Machine Intelligence, vol. 25(5), pp. 564–577 (2003)
8. Wu, Y., Hua, G., Yu, T.: Tracking Articulated Body by Dynamic Markov network. In: International Conference on Computer Vision, pp. 1094–1101 (2003)
9. Zhang, H., Huang, Z., Huang, W., Li, L.: Kernel-Based Method for Tracking Objects with Rotation and Translation. In: International Conference on Pattern Recognition, vol. 02, pp. 728–731 (2004)

On the Detection of Regions-of-Interest in Dynamic Contrast-Enhanced MRI

David Raba, Marta Peracaula, Robert Martí, and Joan Martí

Institut d'Informàtica i Aplicacions
Campus Montilivi 17071 Ed. P-IV, University of Girona
{draba,martapb,marly,joanm}@eia.udg.es

Abstract. Multivariate imaging technologies such as Dynamic Contrast-Enhanced Magnetic Resonance Imaging (DCE-MRI) have recently gained an important attention as it improves tumour detection. Modelling of contrast media uptake and washout kinetic parameters which are closely related to physiological and anatomical features helps to diagnose and detect a possible cancer. One issue that does not generally receive much attention is the process of detecting regions of interest (ROIs). An automatic region-of-interest (ROI) selection method is presented to avoid the time consuming and subjective task of manual ROI selection, which significantly affects reproducibility and accuracy of measurements.

1 Background

Among the different types of cancer, breast cancer has one of the largest incidences in the women population and is one of the most common causes of death in occidental countries. X-ray imaging is the most common modality used for the detection of breast cancer. Although in general it provides sufficient information, in some cases it is not conclusive and additional modalities which provide complementary information need to be used, such as magnetic resonance (MRI) and ultrasound (US) images.

DCE-MRI is based on capturing tissue magnetic properties during a short time period when a contrast enhancement agent has been injected to the

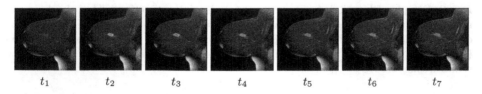

t_1 t_2 t_3 t_4 t_5 t_6 t_7

Fig. 1. Sample of temporal study with MR mammography, where t_1 is the pre-contrast selected slice from whole study and t_2-t_7 are the six post-contrast slices. While parenchyma tissue remains unaffected by the contrast agent, the intensity of the suspicious regions shows an enhancement.

J. Martí et al. (Eds.): IbPRIA 2007, Part I, LNCS 4477, pp. 129–136, 2007.

patient. The increase in intensity throughout the DCE-MRI sequence is a non-linear function of the uptake of a contrast agent (typically Gadolinium DTPA). Several studies point out DCE-MRI as a valuable tool to discriminate between benign and malign breast lesions [6,10]. Normal and abnormal tissue will respond differently to the amount of contrast uptake as it is shown in Figure 1. This contrast differences allows a better visualisation of many different types of tissue abnormalities and disease processes.

A common study for DCE-MRI data consists in looking for breast areas with rapid and strong enhancement of the intensity signal (enhanced by the contrast agent), followed by a quick descent. In terms of contrast uptake-washout behaviour, commonly used approaches for selecting the ROI under evaluation consist of manually outlining the suspicious area. This ROI is within the area of highest contrast agent uptake. Since manually choosing this ROI is more likely to be affected by subjective decisions, it is commonly accepted that inter-observer and intra-observer variability should be minimised hence, reducing reproducibility errors [6]. The kinetic curve is formed by calculating the average enhancement over a ROI at all time steps, where the enhancement is defined as the percentage of signal intensity increase relative to the pre-contrast signal intensity as proposed in the study by Kuhl *et al.* [7] (see Figure 2).

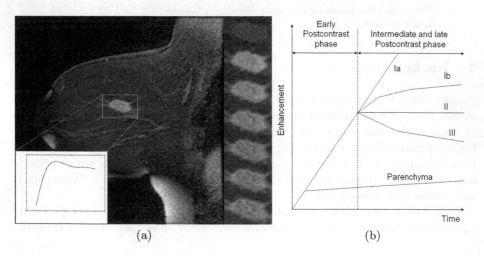

(a)   (b)

Fig. 2. Sample of kinetic behaviour where (a) shows the kinetic profile behaviour on manually selected ROI along seven time steps and (b) the typical signal enhancement curves [7] that classify the different profiles as benign tissue (Ia-Ib), suspicious tissue (II), malign tissue (III), and parenchyma response. All curves start with pre-contrast signal within the ROI.

Efforts done in DCE-MRI data analysis include two main strategies, one of them is based on conventional pattern recognition techniques [2] by studying the shape of the extracted profile looking for patterns on the shape using artificial neural networks, support vector machines, or other classification approaches. On the other hand, the uptake-washout behaviour of abnormal tissue can also be studied by using pharmacokinetic models which try to describe the time varying distribution of contrast agent during the exchange between blood plasma and extracellular space compartments [1]. In addition the mixture of both strategies has also obtained good results [8]. Mainly these works aim to distinguish between malign or benign ROI, not focusing on obtaining valid ROIs from the whole volume, whereas the goal of our work is to develop an automatic method to detect suspicious regions in DCE-MRI. This localisation of ROI candidates is performed depending on the kinetic and morphological parameters of the kinetic profile.

Briefly outlining the structure of the paper, Section 2 presents our method while Section 3 shows evaluation results. The paper ends with conclusions and further work.

2   Materials and Methods

We have evaluated three subjects with DCE-MRI study (GE, Signa LX $1.5T$, both breasts, fat saturation, coronal, $512x320$ matrix, $1.5mm$ slice thickness). One pre- and six post-contrast one minute series were obtained. In DCE-MRI, the injection of a contrast agent has the property of enhancing highly vascularised regions which is characteristic of malignant regions. In those studies, the patient movement is common as MR acquisition is a relatively long procedure (about 10 minutes). Hence, image registration is a key processing step to improve diagnosing results, correcting slight movements of the patient during the imaging process. Registration has generally been applied to dynamic sequences corresponding a pre-contrast volume to a volume after a contrast agent has been injected. Acquired volumes were automatically registered using $CADStream^{TM}$ software.

The method consists of four steps: optimal enhancement localisation, breast tissue segmentation, feature extraction and kinetic curve model identification which are detailed in next sections.

2.1   Optimal Enhancement Localisation

Even within a well manually outlined ROI, the shape of kinetic curve extracted from different points within the same ROI presents a high inhomogeneity [2], thereby looking for ROIs with desirable kinetic behaviour (rapid enhancement and posterior washout curve) within the volume obtains a considerable amount of false positives (FP). In order to minimise the number of FP, we propose a novel method to drive the search of ROIs.

An exploration consists of seven volumes (V_i with $i \in (1..7)$), one pre-contrast and six post-contrast acquisitions. We propose the use of a maximum intensity projection (MIP) using the seven volumes to produce a Key-volume that captures the essential enhancement of the whole DCE-MRI exploration. Thus, within the Key-volume each Key-slice $S_{i,j}$ is calculated as the maximum intensity value along the projecting ray trough the stack of images using the j-th slice taken from each V_i volume.

Once the Key-volume has been obtained, next step consists of segmenting the key-volume to obtain: (1) a breast segmentation into background and breast volume and (2) a set of regions of interest within the breast. For this task, an unsupervised image segmentation is desirable avoiding the tedious and error prone task of manually segmenting the images. Next section presents our proposal in this direction.

2.2   Breast Tissue Segmentation

Certainly, a global segmentation is required since MR breast images show not only breast regions, but also the chest area and non-homogeneous background. Thus, the MR volume is split into breast and non-breast regions. The algorithm used is based on simple morphological filters (two openings and one dilation filtering). Next, a threshold is used to extract the breast region from the background. The value of this threshold is determined using the minimum value between the first two most important peaks, which are the peaks of the background and the breast tissue. Subsequently, a Connected Component Labeling algorithm is used in order to recover the largest area, merging the smaller regions that belong to the breast. The chest area has also been extracted from the image by using the profile segmentation of MRI slice between the two breasts, in order to remove the artifacts from the hearth and other areas not related to the breast.

Once the breast profile is detected, a step forward is to identify the different breast tissue regions. Our internal tissue segmentation approach is based on the Expectation-Maximization algorithm (EM) on a mixture of Gaussians [4]. The EM approach allows to assign each pattern to belong to a specific cluster in a Gaussian Mixture model. In this probabilistic model, each pattern is characterised by a set of mixtures of Gaussian:

$$p(x_i; M) = \sum_{m=1}^{M} \pi_m g_m(x_i) \tag{1}$$

where g_m is a Gaussian distribution and π_m a prior distribution ($\sum_m \pi_m = 1$) and m is the number of mixtures, the different tissue types in our case. The model parameters and cluster membership are determined by maximizing the log-likelihood estimator:

$$l(M) = \sum_i log(p(x_i; M)) \tag{2}$$

This second step is efficiently done using the Expectation Maximization algorithm [4]. Segmentation process is carried out using 3D intensity data from the previously obtained Key-volume.

2.3   Feature Extraction

In order to detect candidate valid ROI we focus on detecting quickly and strongly enhanced regions. These valid ROIs are conceived as possible malignant regions. Therefore, each region obtained after the segmentation step, represents a

ROI candidate. Nevertheless, we have to deal with wide range of regions sizes. Thereby, assuming that the possible lesion is a candidate ROI and that small regions are more susceptible to be a lesion, a uniform number of samples is obtained for each segmented region. Hence, N points randomly uniformly sampled, without replacement, are selected as seeds from the values in each region. A kinetic curve is obtained by averaging over a $w \times w$ window around the seed.

Additionally, five features are extracted from each kinetic curve to depict *maximum contrast enhancement* (F_{n1}), *time to peak* (F_{n2}), *uptake rate* (F_{n3}), *washout rate* (F_{n4}) [2] and *curve angles* (F_{n5}). The intensity signal of each sample is represented by S_t at time step $t(1, 2..., T)$, S^* represents the maximum of the T signal intensity values and p is the time point of S^*. Thus,

$$S^* = \max_{t=1,2,...T} S_t, \qquad p = \arg \max_{t=1,2,...T} S_t, \tag{3}$$

and the four features are defined as,

$$F_{n1} = (S^* - S_1)/S_1, \quad F_{n2} = p, \quad F_{n3} = \frac{F_{n1}}{F_{n2}}, \quad F_{n3} = \frac{F_{n1}}{F_{n2}} \tag{4}$$

$$F_{n4} = \begin{cases} \frac{S^* - S_T}{S_1(T-p)} & if\, p \neq T, \\ 0 & if\, p = T. \end{cases}, \quad F_{n5} = \arctan(S_{t+1}, S_t), \ t(1, 2..., T-1) \tag{5}$$

2.4   Kinetic Curve Model Identification

With the feature extraction process a set of features including the uptake profiles are obtained, which should be grouped into three main behaviours: parenchyma, benign or suspicious/malignant. In order to cluster this data we have used a partitional clustering algorithm such as K-Means. It aims to minimise the total within-cluster dispersion, namely

$$e^2(K) = \sum_{k=1}^{K} \sum_{i \in C_k} ||x_i - c_k||^2 \tag{6}$$

where c_k is the centroid of cluster C_k. K-means clustering is applied by using the set of automatically extracted profiles. An unweighted city-block distance metric is used to evaluate the distance between two profiles. Defined on $\mathbb{R}^n$, it is

$$d(a, b) = \sum_{i=1}^{n} |b_i - a_i| \tag{7}$$

where a and b are vectors in $\mathbb{R}^n$ with $a = (a_1, ..., a_n)$ and $a = (b_1, ..., b_n)$.

Once the profiles are clustered, we calculate a distance (Eq. 7) within the cluster to assign a probability of belonging to that class. An expert radiologist labels each cluster as being normal, benign or malign. As a result, we obtain for each region a classification into normal, benign or malign and the profile membership probability to its class. Thus, regions with higher probabilities within the suspicious class will be reported as final ROIs.

3 Evaluation and Results

The evaluation of the automatic and manual ROI detection is presented using confusion matrices [5] and a leave-one-out scheme over a k-Nearest Neighbours classifier algorithm. In the leave-one-out methodology, each ROI is classified using a model trained with the rest of ROIs, and this procedure is repeated until all ROIs have been used as a query image.

The k-Nearest Neighbours classifier [5] (kNN) consists of classifying a non-classified vector into the k most similar vectors found in the training set. Because kNN is based on distances between sample points in feature space, features need to be re-scaled to avoid that some features are weighted much more than others biasing the results. Hence, all features have been normalised to unit variance and zero mean. For the kNN classifier, the membership value of a class is different from zero if there is at least one neighbour (of k possible neighbours) belonging to this class. The membership value for each class will be the sum of the inverse Euclidean distances among each neighbour of the class and the pattern. A final unit normalisation between all the membership values is required.

To evaluate our approach we have used a DCE-MRI from three patients. Parenchyma, benign and suspicious/malign tissue types are present in this images and manually sampled by an expert providing a total of 106 samples. Program execution is done using the following parameters: Key-volume segmentation into four classes and automatic sample labeling using K-Means with K value fixed depending on the desired number of classes. Additionally, each confusion matrix include the kappa (κ) coefficient [3]. This is used as a means of estimating agreement in categorical data, and is computed as:

$$\kappa = \frac{P(D) - P(E)}{1 - P(E)} \tag{8}$$

where $P(D)$ is the proportion of times the model values was equal to the actual value (the diagonal terms) and $P(E)$ is the expected proportion by chance. A κ coefficient equal to one means a statistically perfect model whereas a value equal to zero means every model value was different from the actual value. Table 1 shows a commonly used interpretation of the various κ.

Table 2(b-d) shows classification results for the proposed method, (A-kNN) the k-Means profile clustering and the subsequent classification into three and two classes. Comparison with manual profile labelling (M-kNN) is also provided (Table 2(a-b)) in order to evaluate the benefits of using an automatic clustering such as k-Means.

In order to compare classification results between normal and automatic clustered profiles, we must take the possible clustering disagreement into account. That is, different ROIs have different labels and therefore classification could have been using slightly different data. Nevertheless, the labelling agreement has been quantified as being around 77%, which is fairly acceptable. Moreover this error is gathered between parenchyma and normal classes, remaining the suspicious class quite unaffected. Keeping this issue in mind classification results can

Table 1. Common interpretation of the various *kappa* values

Agreement	Poor	Slight	Fair	Moderate	Substantial	Almost Perfect
κ	< 0	$[0, 0.20]$	$[0.21, 0.40]$	$[0.41, 0.60]$	$[0.61, 0.80]$	$[0.81, 1.00]$

be compared drawing interesting conclusions. Although more data would be desirable, classification results using automatic clustering seem to have a positive impact in reducing the number of False positives (classification says is suspicious when is not) while keeping similar True positive values. This is specially evident for the two-class classification problem. For instance, slightly better result are obtained with automatically labeled data (A-kNN) in comparison with manually labeled data ($\kappa = 0.93$ vs $\kappa = 0.89$) which can be due to its automatically clustered origin. Although these results seem to be promising, further improvements and testing on larger database will show the feasibility of our approach for providing robust ROI detection.

Table 2. Confusion matrices of the kNN classifier. While (a) show results obtained using manually labelled data ($\kappa = 0.91$) and (b) automatically labeled data ($\kappa = 0.90$) taking into account three classes, (c) presents the results using a simplification into two classes (Parenchyma-Normal vs Suspicious, using manually labelled data ($\kappa = 0.89$) and (d) automatically labelled ($\kappa = 0.93$).

M-kNN 3 classes

Truth		Parenchyma	Normal	Suspicious
	Parenchyma	47	1	2
	Normal	1	36	1
	Suspicious	0	1	17

(a)

A-kNN 3 classes

Truth		Parenchyma	Normal	Suspicious
	Parenchyma	44	2	0
	Normal	1	42	0
	Suspicious	0	3	14

(b)

M-kNN 2 classes

Truth		Non Suspicious	Suspicious
	Non Suspicious	84	4
	Suspicious	0	18

(c)

A-kNN 2 classes

Truth		Non Suspicious	Suspicious
	Non Suspicious	87	1
	Suspicious	1	17

(d)

4   Conclusions

An automatic method to detect suspicious area in Dynamic Contrast Enhancement MRI data have been presented in this paper. Besides, a set of discriminant features have been tested using a kNN classifier obtaining satisfactory results compared to manually labelled data. Although the present work has been based on a reduced set of cases, promising results have been obtained. However, this needs to be tested clinically far more thoroughly than we have been able to do to date. The fact that the training of the system is based on direct-image data, not depending on an signal modelling step means that the method can be adapted to other imaging protocols and different imaging location like prostate, liver or brain imaging.

Acknowledgments. Thanks to Dr. Joan Carles Vilanova who has provided the image sources. This work has been supported by Spanish CICYT project (TIN2006-08035).

References

1. Armitage, P., Behrenbruch, C., Brady, M., Moore, N.: Extracting and visualizing physiological parameters using dynamic contrast-enhanced magnetic resonance imaging of the breast. Medical Image Analysis 9, 315–329 (2006)
2. Chen, W., Giger, L., Bick, U., Newstead, G.M.: Automatic identification and classification of characteristic kinetic curves of breast lesions on DCE-MRI. Med. Phys. 33(8), 2878–2887 (2006)
3. Cohen, J.: A coefficient of agreement for nominal scales. Educational and Psicological Measurement 20, 27–46 (1960)
4. Dempster, A.P., Laird, N.M., Rubin, D.B.: Maximum likelihood from incomplete data via the EM algorithm. Journal of the Royal Statistical Society, Series B. 39(1), 1–38 (1977)
5. Duda, R.O., Hart, P.E., Stork, D.G.: Pattern Classification, 2nd edn. John Wiley & Sons, New York (2001)
6. Galbraith, S., BChir, M.: Antivascular cancer treatments: Imaging biomarkers in pharmaceutical drug development. B. Journal of Radiology 76, 83–86 (2003)
7. Kuhl, C.K., Mielcareck, P., Klaschik, S., Leutner, C., Wardelmann, E., Gieseke, J., Schild, H.H.: Dynamic breast MR imaging: Are signal intensity time course data useful for differential diagnosis of enhancing lesion? Radiology 211, 101–110 (1999)
8. Lucht, R.E.A., Knopp, M.V., Brix, G.: Classification of signal-time curves from dynamic MR mammography by neural networks. Magnetic Resonance Imaging 19(1), 51–57 (2000)
9. Padhani, A.R.: Dynamic Contrast-Enhanced MRI in Clinical Oncology: Current Status and Future Directions. Journal of MRI 16, 407–422 (2002)
10. Szabó, B.K., Aspelin, P., Wiberg, M.K., Boné, B.: Dynamic Mr Imaging Of The Breast: Analysis of kinetic and morphologic diagnostic criteria. Acta Radiologica 44(8), 379–386 (2003)

Dealing with the Perspective Distortion to Detect Overtaking Cars for Driving Assistance

S. Mota[1], E. Ros[2], J. Díaz[2], R. Agís[2], R. Rodriguez[2], and R. Carrillo[2]

[1] Department of Computer Sciences and Numerical Analysis, University of Córdoba,
Campus de Rabanales s/n, Edificio Albert Einstein, 14071, Córdoba, Spain
[2] Department of Computer Architecture and Technology, University of Granada, Periodista
Daniel Saucedo Aranda s/n, 18071 Granada, Spain
smota@uco.es,
{eros,jdiaz,ragis,rrodriguez,rcarrillo}@atc.ugr.es

Abstract. The driver's loss of attention is an important problem in which are spent considerable research efforts in different areas such as psychology, automobile technology, computer vision and driving assistance. We use here a simple algorithm based on rigid-body and motion detection. This scheme efficiently segments moving objects using the visual field of the driver's rear-view mirror. The overtaking scene in the rear-view mirror is distorted due to perspective, making it difficult to detect the overtaking car. Thus we propose two alternative methods to deal with this problem and compare the results in different overtaking sequences.

1 Introduction

Biological systems represent high efficient computing schemes. In particular, visual motion detection is complex and accurate system. It is expected that in 10 years, vehicles will incorporate devices based in computer vision applied to driving assistance. The long-medium term goal is to implement devices based on vertebrates' visual systems, because of their amazing efficiency in analysing dynamic scenes. However, current vision models require high computational resources. Therefore a system for driving assistance working in real time might be simpler if designed specifically for this task.

As an option it can be used motion detection scheme based on insects motion detection systems, which is a good example of a simple visual motion detection model. Reichardt described a correlation model of motion detection based on elementary motion detectors (EMDs) that emulate the behaviour of early visual stages in insects [1].

In this work, we use an algorithm which in its initial stage is a motion-detection algorithm (based on EMDs) and in a second stage includes rigid-body-motion (RBM) rules to filter noisy patterns.

We apply this approach to overtaking scenarios, which is one of the most dangerous situations in driving because the rear-view mirror is sometimes not watched by the driver or is momentarily useless because of the blind spot. The whole algorithm detects the moving vehicle behind and determines whether it is approaching

J. Martí et al. (Eds.): IbPRIA 2007, Part I, LNCS 4477, pp. 137–144, 2007.

or not; thus the proposed system also helps the driver when he does not give attention therefore the system may be considered a self-contained alarm device for dangerous moments and situations. There are commercial devices that work as driving assistance but the comparison against them it is not easy because there is no available information about the algorithms they follow.

We have used some sequences taken with a camera fixed onto the driver's rear-view mirror. This view is complex, not only because everything is moving in scene (due to the ego-motion of the camera), besides the scene is distorted by the perspective (the scene converges to a vanishing point at the left-hand side of the image). This is a result from the projection of a 3D scene onto a 2D surface. Due to this effect an overtaking vehicle, although moving at a constant speed, seems to accelerate as it approaches, and as the overtaking car approaches the camera it is increasing in size, which adds an expanding motion to the translational one.

Therefore we need to devise a way of reducing the distortion effect in order to enhance the segmentation capabilities of a vision system based on EMD detectors. We have addressed the problem by checking out two different approaches: velocity channels and space-variant mapping.

The test sequences were taken with a high-dynamic-range (HDR) camera and a CCD camera, 288 x 384 pixels per frame, in different weather and illumination conditions. We show the results of four sequences.

The approach described in this paper is implemented with digital real-time hardware on an FPGA platform. Therefore the system has been designed taking into account feasibly applicable primitives.

2 Motion Detection Algorithm

It is known that the detection and analysis of motion are achieved by neural operations in biological systems, starting with registration of local motion signals, at low level processing stages, within restricted regions of the visual field, and continuing with the integration of those local motion features into global descriptions of the direction, speed and object motion, in higher level processing stages.

This bottom-up strategy is adopted in the proposed system. The algorithm uses the motion information to solve the segmentation problem.

Firstly the system extracts the structure of the scene that is mainly embodied in highly contrasted features (edges), as biological systems do using specific cells (local contrast on-centre-off-surround and vice versa) [2, 3, 4]. Neurophysiology experiments have suggested that the edges of an object are the most important cues to extracting scene structure [5]. We chose the Sobel gradient detector [6] because it is able to provide acceptable real-time outputs to our motion-detection elements. Furthermore, we only extract vertical edges since the dominant scene movements are sidewards. Note that the horizontal velocity component is enough to determine the approaching trajectory and estimate the time to contact or, at least, the relative velocity with respect to our vehicle. The output of this pre-processing stage is a sparse map composed of pixels of intensity different from zero when an edge is detected and zero otherwise.

As a consequence of the edges extraction, we reduce the number of points to be processed, thereby reducing the computational requirements.

The next point is to detect moving objects through a multiplicative correlation detectors (Elementary Motion Detectors – EMD) described by Reichardt [1], that emulate the dynamics of early visual stages in insects. Both processes take place at low level processing stage.

In a simple Reichardt detector (EMD) [1] a stimulus (an edge) reaches the two detector inputs sequentially. The EMD introduces a delay to compensate for the lag in arrival at each detector input and the output of both channels will thus be simultaneous if the delay is correct. Hence the two inputs will be perfectly correlated and the detector response will be strong if the velocity is well tuned to the characteristics of the EMD. If the input pattern velocity and cell delay are different the detector does not respond significantly. A precise velocity tuning adjustment of the delays in the Reichardt detector is very important. A single EMD provides information about features moving at a single velocity. Therefore we have used a multi-velocity detector composed of a group of single EMDs tuned to different velocities. Among all the elements in the same spatial region the EMD that maximizes the correlation wins.

The EMDs produce a diffuse cloud of points. We apply rigid-body motion (RBM) rules to segment the vehicle. In mid-level neural layer, that follows a competitive scheme, the system filters the moving features; in other words, segment the moving objects using velocity information to define a rigid body [7, 8]. The neural structure presented here can take full advantage of population coding for a specific application such as the segmentation of independent moving objects. The main goal of the proposed scheme is the improvement RBM detection by the constructive integration of local information into global patterns. If we neglect possible rotations, not present in the application, all points of a rigid body share the same speed and direction; isolated points inside a rigid body that move at other speed (amplitude or motion direction) are considered noise. Therefore, if we detect a population of pixels labelled with the same speed, and all of them are in a limited area of the image, they are good candidates of a segmented rigid body (overtaking vehicle).

To apply RBM rules we split the image in regions (windows) of fixed size and apply a competition scheme. The competitive structures are composed of the accumulation of the responses of all the cells (EMDs) in each of these windows. The mechanism neglect or reset all the EMD responses that do not belong to a population of active cells in the same window. After this filtering stage, in each x-y window only points that represent the activity of a population of EMDs with a significant response are passed on to the next stage. And they represent rigid bodies approaching to the camera (overtaking car) or going away. The system has been tested on real overtaking sequences in a full speed range (where the approaching speed is between 1-30 m/s) [9].

3 Evaluation Algorithm

The evaluation of a segmentation scheme with real images is not straightforward since the pixels are not labelled according to the object they belong to. In an overtaking scenario the motion structure of the approaching vehicle contrasts highly with the landmarks moving in the opposite direction due to the ego-motion of the host car. Therefore, in each image, we will label the motion features moving rightward as belonging to the overtaking vehicle and discard the rest.

The accuracy of the segmentation will depend on the relative size of the overtaking car. We have distinguished different cases depending on the size of the car (due to the distance from the host vehicle). The considered car sizes, estimated in area (S) as the number of pixels contained in the rectangle, are: A ($315 < S \le 450$), B ($450 < S \le 875$), C ($875 < S \le 2220$), D ($2220 < S \le 6000$) and E ($S > 6000$).

Fig. 1. Images from the sequence and manual segmentation

In a first stage, we define the segmentation rate as the ratio between the well classified features in an object and the total number of moving features segmented that belong to this object. Figure 2 shows the results of segmentation rate. They are always above 85% when rigid body motion filtering is applied.

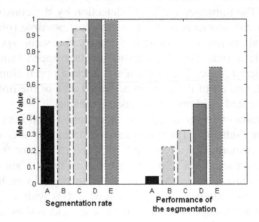

Fig. 2. Segmentation rate and Performance of the segmentation for different car sizes

In a second stage we will calculate the performance of the segmentation as the ratio between the features moving right inside the marked rectangle surrounding the car (correctly labelled features) and all the features detected with rightward motion in the scene.

Figure 2 shows the Segmentation rate and the Performance of the segmentation, each bar represent the mean of the parameter value for each car size. The results suggest we can use a simple tracking model based on the computation of a center of mass of all the features moving rightward in the filtered output. When car is bigger enough (C, D or E sizes) it is segmented quite well, although noisy patterns can miscalculate the position of the overtaking car.

We are going to use this global centre of mass to compare two methods that deal with the perspective distortion problem.

4 The Perspective Distortion Problem: Velocity-Channels Response and Space-Variant Mapping Methods

Because of perspective distortion, however, it is difficult to apply the RBM rules to segment the overtaking vehicle; in this case, points in the distant part of a rigid body seem to move more slowly than closer points and both parts accelerate from frame to frame at different ranges. Therefore it will be necessary to consider different velocities to synchronize both parts of a rigid body.

To reduce the effect of perspective distortion and segment the overtaking car we have used two different methods, velocity-channels response and space-variant mapping.

We need to cluster the velocities of the pixels into a range of velocities. We introduce a new concept, the velocity channels (VC) that allow us to apply the RBM rule. With the VC method, we accumulate the single velocities into small velocities ranges (Vi-n, Vi, Vi+n) which we call velocity channels [7, 8]. We need to accumulate features moving at different speeds because the front and rear of the overtaking car seem to move at slightly different speeds (the backside of the vehicle is far and it seems to move slowly, therefore slow velocity detectors will respond to it, while the front of the vehicle is closer and it seems to move faster). These velocity channel works as dynamic filter band pass, only survive the points of the saliency map produced around the local maximum of the velocity channel plot, others are neglected. The maximum corresponds to points were a rigid body motion induces coherent feature motion.

This solution deal with the problem of which points belong to the rigid body therefore does not solve the problem of acceleration.

With the space-variant-mapping (SVM) method we resample the original image. The Inverse Perspective Mapping [10, 11] is an affine coordinate transformation that aims at reversing the process of projection of a 3-D scene onto a 2-D surface. It is possible to compensate the effect of perspective by remapping the image so that the parallel lines and equal distances in a real scene are remapped to parallel lines and equal distances in the processed image. Practically, in our application, this means expanding the left-hand side of the image (corresponding to the part of the scene furthest from the camera) and contracting the right-hand side (corresponding to the part of the scene closest to the camera). The interpolation method used here is the truncated Taylor expansion, known as local Jet [10]. At the remapped output the mean speed of the car is more constant along the sequence and each point that belongs to the rigid body moves approximately at the same speed.

The difference between the two strategies is that with the VC approach we need to accumulate features moving at different speeds in order to synchronize the front and rear of a car. In the SVM approach this is not necessary; the effect is compensated through the remapping scheme and the acceleration problem is solved.

5 Results

After applying VC or SVM to reduce perspective distortion, and temporal-coherency rules to reduce any noisy flashing patterns that might appear, all the points at the output stage are considered as belonging to the overtaking car. Now we calculate the centre of mass of these filtered features moving rightwards. If the detection has been done correctly this point should be on the overtaking vehicle. We can calculate it for each frame in the sequence. In this way we track the overtaking car throughout the sequence.

We used different sequences to test the whole algorithm. Table 1 summarizes some of these results. The first and the fourth sequences were taken with a CCD camera on a sunny day. In the first sequence the overtaking car approaches from the distance and in the fourth appears into our line of vision suddenly from our lane. The second and third sequences are HDR ones. The second one corresponds to a cloudy day with some mist and the other was taken in twilight conditions. These two sequences show overtaking processes by far-away cars with their lights on.

To evaluate the approaches described in section 4 we have manually marked the overtaking car with a rectangle in every frame throughout the sequence. We then calculate the distance between the centre of mass of the output points and the centre of the rectangle; this distance is normalized by dividing it by the size of the x-semi-axis of the rectangle in each frame. This ratio is what we call the *Quality Measurement* (QM). If the value of QM is less than 1 we are detecting the overtaking vehicle accurately. If QM is higher than 1 on the other hand, noise patterns are dominant and lead to wrong estimations.

In the first sequence (see Table 1), when using the velocity-channels method if the overtaking vehicle is small (i.e. far away) or becomes visible through the driver's window (and we begin to lose it in the rear-view mirror) the detection contains errors because there are few points belonging to the car and the noise features shift the centre of mass. Consequently the cross marker lays outside the rectangle before frame 138 and after frame 174 (Fig 3a). But from a medium distance the vehicle is big enough and detection is made properly. In fact accurate detection occurs when the overtaking vehicle begins to be dangerously close. Figure 3b shows QM throughout the sequence when the space-variant mapping method is adopted. In this case tracking is accurate from frame 89 to the end of the sequence. Table 1 shows that tracking process is done properly from a vehicle size of 10660 pixels with the VC method and 3216 pixels with the SVM method. This size is only approximate, taken as it is from the size of the confidence rectangle used to calculate QM. The data in the next column represents the number of features detected moving rightwards, on which the estimation is based.

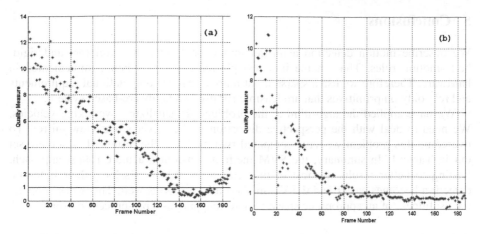

Fig. 3. Quality measurement plot of the first sequence adopting (**a**) velocity-channels method; (**b**) space-variant-mapping method

Table 1 summarizes the results for the two methods applied to four different sequences from a collection of test sequences.

In the HDR sequences the cars have their lights on. The best detected features belong to the overtaking car lights and allow an early success in the tracking task with either method. SVM constitutes a good method for medium distances in all weather conditions, even when the cars have no lights on to facilitate their detection.

Table 1. Results of the two methods applied to four different sequences

Sequence Frame	Method used	1st. Frame in successful tracking	Vehicle Size (pixels)	Features detected	Best results
	VC	139	10660	83	
	SVM	89	3216	15	√
	VC	1	899	8	√
	SVM	1	899	10	√
	VC	1	1813	22	√
	SVM	1	1813	10	√
	VC	36	32469	30	
	SVM	23	14385	17	√

5 Conclusions

We describe motion detection algorithm based on Reichardt correlators and rigid-body-motion rules. The scheme is a test platform which is being implemented in hardware. Therefore we use a sparse input map to reduce computational requirements and rely only on primitives that are feasible for use in a hardware-based system.

We have applied the algorithm to the problem of visualizing overtaking vehicles. We need to deal with the perspective distortion in the driver's rear-view mirror. To overcome this problem we have compared two methods, the results of which are set out in Table 1. In summary, the SVM method constitutes a more robust approach, leading to better results in most of the sequences. When cars have their lights on detection becomes easier and the VC method also performs well. This work supports the usefulness of an appropriate space-variant mapping as a pre-processing stage.

Acknowledgments. This work was supported by the Spanish National Project DEPROVI (DPI2004-07032), by the EU grant DRIVSCO (IST-016276-2).

References

1. Reichardt, W.: Autocorrelation, a principle for the evaluation of sensory information by central nervous system, in Sensory Communication, Rosenblith, W.A. (ed.), pp. 303–317 (1961)
2. Hubel, D., Wiesel, T.: Receptive fields, binocular interaction and functional architecture in the cat's visual cortex. Journal of Physiology (London) 160, 106–154 (1962)
3. Petkov, N., Kruizinga, P.: Computational models of visual neurons specialized in the detection of periodic and a periodic oriented visual stimuli: Bar and grating cells. Biological Cybernetics 76(2), 83–96 (1997)
4. Dresp, B., Grossberg, S.: Contour integration across polarities and spatial gaps: From local contrast to global grouping. Vision Research 37, 913–924 (1997)
5. Marr, D.: Vision. W. H. Freeman and Company, New York (1982)
6. Gonzalez, R., Woods, R.: Digital Image Processing. Addison-Wesley, London, UK (1992)
7. Mota, S., Ros, E., Ortigosa, E.M., Pelayo, F.J.: Bio-Inspired Motion Detection for Blind Spot Overtaking Monitor. International Journal of Robotics and Automation 19(4), 190–196 (2004)
8. Mota, S., Ros, E., Díaz, J., Ortigosa, E.M., Prieto, A.: Motion-driven segmentation by competitive neural processing. Neural Processing Letters 22(2), 125–177 (2005)
9. Mota, S., Ros, E., Diaz, J., Agís, R., de Toro, F.: Bio-inspired motion-based object segmentation. In: Campilho, A., Kamel, M. (eds.) ICIAR 2006. LNCS, vol. 4141, pp. 196–205. Springer, Heidelberg (2006)
10. Mallot, H.A., Bulthoff, H.H., Little, J.J., Bohrer, S.: Inverse perspective mapping simplifies optical flow computation and obstacle detection. Biol. Cybern. 64, 177–185 (1991)
11. Tan, S., Dale, J., Johnston, A.: Effects of Inverse Perspective Mapping on Optic Flow. In: ECOVISION Workshop, Isle of Skye, Scotland, UK (2004)

3D Reconstruction on MRI to Analyse Marbling and Fat Level in Iberian Loin

M.M. Ávila[1], M.L. Durán[1], T. Antequera[2], R. Palacios[3], and M. Luquero[1]

[1] University of Extremadura, Computer Science Dept.
Escuela Politécnica, Av. Universidad s/n, 10071 Cáceres, Spain
mmavila@unex.es, mlduran@unex.es
[2] University of Extremadura, Food Technology.
Facultad Veterinaria, Av. Universidad s/n, 10071 Cáceres, Spain
tantero@unex.es
[3] "Infanta Cristina" University Hospital, Radiology Service, Badajoz, Spain
ramon.palacios@ses.juntaex.es

Abstract. Dry-cured Iberian pig products are some of the most valuables meat products in Spain. Visually discernible features of fat and lean, such as marbling, have an effect on the acceptability of these products. Marbling properties include the amount and spatial distribution of intramuscular fat streaks. Thresholding techniques are the simplest and most widely used for image segmentation, but pay no attention to all spatial information on the images. In this paper we propose another method to evaluate fat level in loin and make a three-dimensional visualization with only the isolated fat in order to give knowledge about fat distribution, and about width of fat streaks, helping the experts in food science to analyze marbling. In order for fat isolation we apply a method based on a pyramidal decomposition of images combined with region-growing techniques. 3D reconstruction is obtained by marching cubes algorithm.

1 Introduction

1.1 Computer Vision and MRI on Food Science

The use of several image processing and pattern recognition techniques has been applied to images in the field of Food Technology. It has become more frequent in the last few years in an attempt to find alternatives to the traditional, and generally destructive, methodologies to predict meat quality. First approaches have studied different characteristics on beef, bovine and pig meat using images taken by a CCD camera [29] [31] [16] [14] [2]. Duran et al. [11] classifies different types of raw Iberian ham using statistical texture analysis. Cernadas et al. [7] developed a method to recognize marbling in dry-cured Iberian ham.

On the other hand, Magnetic Resonance Imaging (MRI) is widely used in medical diagnosis and surgeries for looking inside bodies at the tissue composition [24]. Non-invasive and non-destructive capabilities are decisive advantages of MRI. It provides

J. Martí et al. (Eds.): IbPRIA 2007, Part I, LNCS 4477, pp. 145–152, 2007.

a discrete three-dimensional (3D) data set consisting of two-dimensional (2D) slices from the object. MRI provides important digital information regarding muscle, bone or other soft tissue, which combined with advances in digital image processing, has led to significant progress in the case of medical diagnosis and surgery [10]. Food science has shown little interest in MRI, which has remained essentially confined to research activities despite many potential applications: process optimization of animal production (animal diet, genetic type), consumer satisfaction, etc. A few MRI applications have been published showing muscle characterization. Bonny et al. [4] and Laurent et al. [15] characterize bovine muscle structure. Cernadas et al. [8] apply texture analysis to MRI to classify raw loins from Iberian pigs. Caro et al. [6] use active contours to recognize muscles using MRI of Iberian ham obtained in different ripening process steps to quantify their volume decreases.

1.2 Fat Isolation by Segmentation

Different studies have proved that juiciness and acceptance of the meat is mainly influenced by its fat content, either in calf [20], pig [5] or lamb [30] meat. This work is centered on Iberian pork. Its meat is mainly used to produce dry-cured products, in particular, cured loins and hams. The special features of the Iberian pig meat (high intramuscular fat content, fatty acid composition, antioxidative status...) together with the prolonged ripening process produce dry-cured products with a quite special flavor that makes it one of the most valuable meat products for its high quality.

Visually discernible features of fat and lean, such as marbling, have an effect on the acceptability and palatability of ripened Iberian pieces. The amount and spatial distribution of intramuscular fat streaks has an effect on the sensorial attributes of the loin and may be used to characterize and classify it. Marbling score determination has traditionally been performed by panels of trained human graders, using descriptive analysis methods [25]. Nevertheless, the development of an objective methodology, able to determine these attributes from the visual appearance of a cut slice, has long been awaited by Iberian industries.

In relation with the fat content in Iberian pig loin, chemical analysis is the most frequently used method to determine the intramuscular fat (IMF) level [1] [26]. But, this technique is expensive, destructive and tedious.

The feasibility of alternative techniques to determine IMF level using Computer Vision techniques has been studied in [12] [13] [21]. Thresholding techniques are the simplest and most widely used methods to automatically segment images. They are based on the assumption that all pixels whose gray value lies within a certain range belong to one class. Thresholds for that range are automatically established from the image features. Nevertheless, such methods pay no attention to all the spatial information of the image and do not manage acceptably with noisy images.

The behavior of well-known standard thresholding techniques to evaluate fat content in commercial slices of dry-cured Iberian ham has been proved in our previous works [12] [13]. Otsu, Pun, Tsai and multi-level Otsu [27] [23] produced rather low correlation with chemical analysis. But Kapur, Johansen & Bille and Kittler methods showed extremely poor correlation.

These methods were applied to achieve automatic segmentation of ham images in two classes (fat and lean) in order to evaluate their IMF level. Contextual information of the images was incorporated to the proved methods by pre-processing the original images with a rule-based spatial algorithm at different scales and then applying general thresholding techniques to the resultant images. More intuitive pre-processing techniques like median filters and morphological operators have also been tested.

The above methods have proven to achieve poor results when they are used to recognise curvilinear structures. This is because some of the image features are overlooked for the segmentation process. Several methods have been used to avoid this drawback.

In order to prevent that happening, a pyramidal decomposition has been carried out [3]. In such a way, all the important features of the images are taken into account. The line operator in different equidistant orientations has been used to accurately detect curvilinear structures [22]. The obtained results are refined by using a region growing approach, based on the Otsu segmentation method.

In this paper approaches for two tasks are developed: firstly a segmentation method in order to evaluate IMF level and secondly to obtain a 3D reconstruction with only the isolated fat streaks in order to provide the experts a comprehensive information about the spatial distribution of marbling. With the purpose of isolate the fat we apply a method based on a pyramidal decomposition of images combined with region-growing techniques. The 3D reconstruction is obtained by a marching cubes algorithm.

2 Materials

The present research is based on a set of images obtained from 27 Iberian pig loins that has been the dataset for a PhD. thesis developed in the Food Science Dep. at the University of Extremadura [18]. In this thesis, besides other experiments, each pig's *longissimus dorsi* was analyzed in order to obtain intramuscular fat level, lipid fraction, and other fatty acids, ...

There is a database of images formed by MRIs of Iberian loin. The images have been acquired using an MR scanner facilitated by the "Infanta Cristina" Hospital in Badajoz (Spain). The MRI data set is obtained from sequences of T1 images with a FOV (*field-of view*) of 120x85 mm and a slice thickness of 2 mm, i.e. a voxel resolution of 0.23x0.20x2 mm. The total number of MRIs used in this work is 15 for each loin. So, the total number of images is 405 for this database. 15 loins were scanned raw, while 12 were scanned after ripening.

Intramuscular fat levels were chemically obtained for all loins. In the experiments, these chemical results were later compared with the Computer Vision results (IMF level computationally obtained), analyzing the linear correlation between these two data sets in order to validate our computational results.

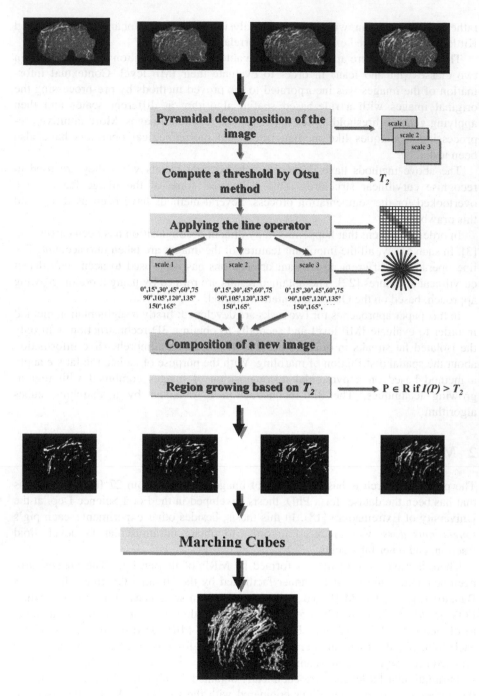

Fig. 1. Applied Methodology

3 Methods

Applied methodology is showed in the figure 1. To isolate IMF may be deemed as an object recognition task. In order to detect these curvilinear structures, fat streaks, a linear operator is applied in three scales by using a pyramidal decomposition. Twelve equidistant angular orientations are chosen (0°, 15°, 30°, 45°, 60°, 75°, 90°, 105°, 120°, 135°, 150°, 165°) yielding a scale-orientation vector.

The values of the vectors in each of the scales are mixed in a normalised image. This new image is used to measure the probability that a pixel may be labelled as fat. In this way, a set of seeds is obtained. This image offers a coarse representation of the IMF of the loin.

This set of seeds is adjusted by using a region growing method. This approach, based on the Otsu segmentation method [19], accurately detects marbling in the original image.

Dealing with pyramidal decomposition, both the original image and a pre-processed one are used in our experiment. The pre-processing methods lead to noise free images. The Rule-based algorithm [12] [13] is used as pre-processing approach, using a 3x3 and 7x7 kernels.

Images obtained by this procedure of segmentation are used to achieve the object reconstruction. Two algorithms have been tested to reconstruct a three-dimensional image of fat inside the muscle: the marching cubes and the ray casting algorithms [17] [28]. Three-dimensional surfaces are constructed from multiple 2D slices of MR and help experts to understand the complex anatomy present in the slices. Marching cubes creates triangle models of constant density surfaces from 3D medical data, using a divide-and-conquer approach to generate inter-slice connectivity. The algorithm processes the 3D data in scan-line order and calculates triangle vertices using linear interpolation. Then finding the gradient of the original data, normalizes it, and use it as a basis for shading the models. This algorithm reconstructs object surfaces without taking into account their content. The ray casting algorithm presents higher complexity in 3D reconstructions both surface and content objects. For that reason, the marching cubes algorithm has been selected in our experiments.

The image segmentation method (based on pyramidal decomposition refined with growing regions) has been proved on the dataset of images. The IMF has been computed by Computer Vision methods (non destructive methods) and by means of chemical analysis (destructive methods). Both sets of results have been compared to check the viability of our Computer Vision methods.

4 Results and Discussion

Table 1 show the Pearson correlation of IMF content obtained by the automatic Computer Vision methods and the chemical analysis for Iberian loin. Pearson correlation value mathematically varies between −1 and 1, where a higher value indicates a better estimation of chemical IMF content of the muscles by the computational methods.

According to the results shown in table 1, it is significant that, for the obtained results could be considered as satisfactory, according to the Pearson statistical correlation coefficients [9].

Table 1. Pearson's coefficient (R) for the region growing method to evaluate IMF content both raw and dry-cured Iberian loin

Pre-processing technique	Kernel size	Otsu region growing (raw loin)	Otsu region growing (dry-cured loin)
-	-	**0.71**	**0.34**
Rule-based	3	**0.83**	**0.31**
Algorithm	7	**0.78**	**0.37**

The results in figure 2 show the correlation between the Computer Vision results (Y axis) and the chemical data (X axis) only for the highlighted values of the previous tables. Both chemical and Computer Vision results are certainly comparable for the method that preprocess images using the Rule-based Algorithm and for the method with no preprocessing stage. They appear as fill figures in the graphic, close to the tendency lines.

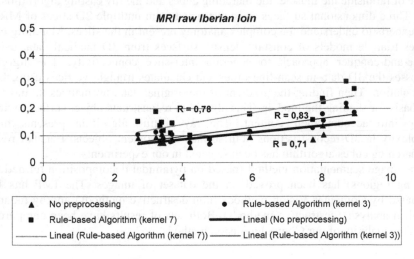

Fig. 2. Pearson's coefficients (R) for MRI raw Iberian Loin. Chemical results on X axis and Computer Vision results on Y axis.

Correlation values are higher in raw loins; which is an advantage for the evaluation of meat in industry: if we have information about IMF level and distribution, the ripening can be modified accordingly. The quality characterization of meat in the industry is frequently applied on raw meat.

5 Conclusions

A method to detect curvilinear structures with high contour accuracy has been applied on MRI. Its straightforward application to recognize marbling in Iberian loin has been evaluated.

The future line in this work is to adapt this methodology in order to be able to make a segmentation after 3D reconstruction, Since the algorithm is explicitly adjustable, we believe this is possible applying multidirectional vectors in 3D directions.

Acknowledgments

The authors wish to acknowledge and thank the support of the "Infanta Cristina" University Hospital and the "Hermanos Alonso Roa" company from Villar del Rey (Badajoz) to our study. In addition, this research has been funded by the Junta de Extremadura (Regional Government Board) under the IPR98A03P, 2PR01C025 and 3PR05B027 labeled projects.

References

1. Antequera, T., López-Bote, C.J., Córdoba, J.J., García, C., Asensio, M.A., Ventanas, J., Díaz, Y.: Lipid oxidative changes in the processing of Iberian pig hams. Food Chem 45, 105 (1992)
2. Basset, O., Buquet, B., Abouelkaram, S., Delachartre, P., Culioli, J.: Application of texture analysis for the classification of bovine meat. Food Chemistry 69, 437–445 (2000)
3. Bister, M., Cornelis, J.: A critical view of pyramid segmentation algorithms. Pattern Recognition Letters 11, 605–617 (1990)
4. Bonny, J.M., Laurent, W., Labas, R., Taylor, R., Berge, P., Renou, J.P.: Magenetic resonance imaging of connictive tissue: a non-destructive method for characterising muscle structure. Journal of the Science of Food and Agriculture 81, 337–341 (2000)
5. Cameron, N.D., Warris, P.D., Forte, J.S., Enser, M.B.: Comparison of Duroc and British Landrace Pigs for Meat and Eating Quality. Meat Science 27, 227 (1990)
6. Caro, A., Rodriguez, P.G., Cernadas, E., Duran, M.L., Muriel, E., Villa, D.: Applying active contours to muscle recognition in Iberian ham MRI. Int. Conf. Signal Processing, Pattern Recognition and Applications pp. 62–66 (2001)
7. Cernadas, E., Duran, M.L., Antequera, T.: Recognizing marbling in dry-cured iberian ham by multiscale analysis. Pattern Recognition Letters, vol. 7 (2002)
8. Cernadas, E., Antequera, T., Rodriguez, P.G., Duran, M.L., Gallardo, G., Villa, D.: Magnetic resonance imaging to classify loin from Iberian pig. A chapter in the book Magnetic resonance imaging in food science. A view to the future. In: Webb, G.A., Belton, P.S., Gil, A.M., Delgadillo, I. (eds.). Royal Society of Chemistry (2001) 239–245
9. Colton, T.: Statistical in Medicine. Little Brown and Co., Boston – USA (1974)
10. Duncan, J.S., Ayache, N.: Medical Image Analysis: Progress over Two Decades and the Challenges Ahead. IEEE Trans. on Pattern Analysis Machine Intelligence 22(1), 85–105 (2000)

11. Duran, M.L., Cernadas, E., Caro, A., Antequera, T.: Classification of different types of Iberian ham using texture analysis. REVC (EJCV) Electronic Journal of Computer Vision 1, 5 (2001)
12. Durán, M.L., Cernadas, E., Plaza, A., Sánchez, J.M., Antequera, T.: Comparative Study of Segmentation Techniques to Evaluate Fat-Level in Iberian Ham. VIII NSPRIA, Bilbao, Spain, pp. 45–46 (1999)
13. Durán, M.L., Cernadas, E., Plaza, A., Sánchez, J.M., Rodríguez, F., Petrón, M.J.: Could Machine Vision Replace Chemical Procedure to Evaluate Fat Content in Iberian Pig Meat?. An Experimental Study, 3rd Int. Conf. on Computer Vision, Pattern Recognition, and Image Processing, pp. 256–259 (2000)
14. Gerrard, D.E., Gao, X., Tan, J.: Beef Marbling and Color Score Determination by Image Processing. Journal of Food Science 61(1), 145 (1996)
15. Laurent, W., Bonny, J.M., Renou, J.P.: Muscle characterisation by NMR imaging and spectroscopic techniques. Food Chemistry 69, 419–426 (2000)
16. Li, J., Tan, J., Martz, F.A., Heymann, H.: Image texture features as indicators of beef tenderness. Meat Science 53, 17–22 (1999)
17. Lorensen, W., Cline, H.E.: Marching cubes: a high resolution 3D surface reconstruction algorithm, vol. 21(4). ACM Computer Graphics, New York (1987)
18. Muriel, E.: PhD Dissertation, Universidad de Extremadura (2001)
19. Otsu, N.: A Threshold Selection Method from Gray-Level Histograms. IEEE Trans. Systems, Man, and Cybernetics, vol. SMC-9(1) (1979)
20. Penfield, M.P., Costello, C.A., McNeil, M.A., Rienmannn, M.J.: Effects of Fat Level and Cooking Methods on Physical and Sensory Characteristics of Reestructure Beef Streaks. Journal Food Qual. 11, 349 (1989)
21. Petrón, M.J.: Estudio Comparativo de la Fracción Lipídica de Jamón Fresco en Diferentes Tipos de Cerdo Ibérico. PostGraduate Project, Universidad de Extremadura (1998)
22. Plaza, A., Cernadas, E., Durán, M.L., Rodríguez, P.G., Petrón, M.J.: Multi-scale detection of curvilinear structures with high contour accuracy. 5th Iberoamerican Symposium on Pattern Recognition. Lisbon, Portugal, pp. 405–412 (2000)
23. Ritter, Wilson: Handbook of Computer Vision in Image Algebra. CRC Press, Boca Raton, USA (1996)
24. Robb, R.A.: Three-Dimensional Biomedical Imaging. CRC Press, Boca Raton, USA (1985)
25. Ruiz, J., Ventanas, J., Cava, R., Timón, M.L., García, C.: Sensory characteristics of Iberian Ham: Influence of Processing Time and Slice Location. Food Research International 31(1), 53–58 (1998)
26. Ruiz, J.: Estudio de parámetros sensoriales y físico-químicos implicados en la calidad del jamón Ibérico. PhD Dissertation, Universidad de Extremadura (1996)
27. Sahoo, P.K., Soltani, S., Wong, A.K.C.: A Survey of Thresholding Techniques. CVGIP 41, 233–260 (1988)
28. Schroeder, W., Martin, K., Lorensen, B.: The Visualization Toolkit. An Object-Oriented Approach to 3D Graphics. Ed. Kitware (2002)
29. Shiramita, K., Miyajima, T., Takiyama, R.: Determination of Meat Quality by Texture Analysis. Pattern Recognition Letters 19, 1319–1324 (1998)
30. Touraine, B., Vigneror, P., Touraille, C., Prud'hom, M.: Influence des onditions d'elevage sur les characteristiques des carcasses et de la viande d'agneaux Merino d'Arles. Bulletin Technique de l'elevage Ovin 4, 29 (1984)
31. Yoshikawa, F., Toraichi, K., Wada, K., Ostu, N., Nakai, H., Mitsumoto, M., Katagishi, K.: On a grading system for beef marbling. Pattern Recognation Letters 21, 1037–1050 (2000)

Epiflow Based Stereo Fusion

Hongsheng Zhang[1] and Shahriar Negahdaripour[2]

[1] Mako Surgical Corp., Ft. Lauderdale FL 33317, USA
[2] University of Miami, Coral Gables, FL 33124, USA

Abstract. 3-D reconstruction from images sequences has been the center topic of computer vision. Real-time applications call for causal processing of stereo sequences, as they are acquired, covering different regions of the scene. The first step is to compute the current stereo disparity, and recursive map building often requires fusing with the previous estimate. In this paper, the epiflow framework [1], originally proposed for establishing matches among stereo feature pairs is generalized to devise an iterative causal algorithm for stereo disparity map fusion. In the context of disparity fusion, quadruplet correspondence of the epiflow tracking algorithm becomes reminiscent of the "closest point" of the 3-D ICP algorithm. Unlike ICP, the 2-D epiflow framework permits incorporating both photometric and geometrical constraints, estimation of the stereo rig motion as supplementary information, as well as identifying local inconsistencies between the two disparity maps. Experiments with real data validate the proposed approach, and improved converge compared to the ICP algorithm.

1 Introduction

Disparity fusion calls for the computation of the 3-D transformation between two disparity maps, and can be addressed by the iterative closest point (ICP) algorithm [3,9,4]. The ICP algorithm identifies the closest point in 3-D Euclidean space by geometric proximity search. Alternatively, we address the problem by the application of the epiflow algorithm, originally proposed for the matching of stereo feature correspondences by enforcing the epipolar geometry over stereo sequences. In this respect, one may draw an analogy between the concept of "closest point" in 3-D Euclidean space and the quadruplet matches of the projections of a scene feature onto two stereo pairs, acquired under the motion of a stereo rig. While the ICP algorithm merely employs geometric algorithm, the epiflow algorithm is built upon both geometric and photometric constraints. The epiflow-based disparity fusion also offers the additional advantage of improved convergence rate. Instead of searching for the "closest point" between two large point populations, epiflow-based fusion is more efficient by employing image-based optical-flow like local computations.

J. Martí et al. (Eds.): IbPRIA 2007, Part I, LNCS 4477, pp. 153–160, 2007.

2 Review of Epiflow

Let (I_1^L, I_1^R) and (I_2^L, I_2^R) be two stereo pairs. Given some initial stereo feature matches (p_1^L, p_1^R), the problem is locating the matches (p_2^L, p_2^R) in the second pair such that the quadruplet $(p_1^L, p_1^R, p_2^L, p_2^R)$ represents the projections of the same 3D point onto the two stereo views. Let $(\hat{p}_2^L, \hat{p}_2^R)$ denote an "admissible estimate", ideally in the vicinity of the true match (p_2^L, p_2^R). The epiflow constraint is expressed as $f(d^L, d^R) = \tilde{d}^{L\top} F_{st} \tilde{\hat{p}}_2^R + \tilde{\hat{p}}_2^{L\top} F_{st} \tilde{d}^R + \tilde{d}^{L\top} F_{st} \tilde{d}^R = 0$ where F^{st} is the fundamental matrix, $\tilde{d}^i = [d^\top 0]^\top$ $(i = L, R)$. $d^L = p_2^L - \hat{p}_2^L = [dx^L, dy^L]$, $d^R = p_2^R - \hat{p}_2^R = [dx^R, dy^R]$. This nonlinear constraint reveals that d^L and d^R are not independent; an admissible estimate $(\hat{p}_2^L, \hat{p}_2^R)$ must "flow" in a way inscribed by the stereo epipolar constraint to remain admissible. In other words, we must satisfy this so-called *epiflow constraint*, in calculating the motion $d = \{d^L, d^R\}$ from any admissible estimate $(\hat{p}_2^L, \hat{p}_2^R)$ to another, including the true solution (p_2^L, p_2^R). For horizontally rectified stereo, we arrive at a very simple expression for this constraint. $f(d^L, d^R) = dy^L - dy^R = 0$. Since the initial estimate $(\hat{p}_2^L, \hat{p}_2^R)$ lies on horizontal epipolar lines, any correction dy should be applied equally to both the left and right matching points. The question becomes how to apply this geometric constraint in order to solve our spatio-temporal motion stereo matching problem. Then tracking of stereo matches may be accomplished by enforcing 3 optical flow constraint equations on the motion vectors $d = (d_L, d_R)$
$$I_1^L(p_1^L) = I_2^L(\hat{p}_2^L + d^L) \quad I_1^R(p_1^R) = I_2^R(\hat{p}_2^R + d^R) \quad I_2^L(p_2^L + d^L) = I_2^R(\hat{p}_2^R + d^R)$$
subject to the epiflow constraint.

3 Stereo Fusion

Incremental fusion of disparity maps corresponding to distinct poses of the stereo rig is treated as the generalization of the quadruplet tracking problem within the epiflow framework (see fig. 1(a)). Without loss of generality, assume that the stereo rig is horizontally rectified.

Let d^{L,t_i} denote the left-based stereo disparity map at time t_i. This allows us to match a left-image point (x_i^L, y_i^L) to $(x_i^L + d^{L,t_i}, y_i^L)$ in the right image, in some stereo view at time t_i. The 3D points X^{t_i} in the (left-camera) reference frame can then be computed from stereo matches by triangulation.

Let $(\hat{R}, \hat{t})$ denote the estimated ego-motion of the stereo rig from time t_1 to t_2. This can be determined based on the quadruplet matches established by the application of the epiflow sparse stereo feature tracking. For each matching pair (x_1^L, y_1^L) and $(x_1^L + d^{L,t_1}, y_1^L)$, we can locate the corresponding points $(\hat{x}^L \hat{y}_2^L)$ and $(\hat{x}_2^L + d_p^{L,t_2}, \hat{y}_2^L)$ at time t_2 by motion-guided prediction. Here, d_p^{L,t_2} denotes the left-based disparity predicted from the estimated motion $(\hat{R}, \hat{t})$, in contrast to the horizontal disparity d^{L,t_2} that is estimated independently from the second stereo views at t_2. Let $D_p^{L,t_2} = d^{L,t_2} - d_p^{L,t_2}$ represent the "difference field". Ideally, D_p^{L,t_2} is zero. However, it is not the case in practice due to inaccuracy of the estimated motion $(\hat{R}, \hat{t})$, and noisy measurement $d^L(t_1)$ and $d^L(t_2)$.

Starting with $(\hat{x}_2^L, \hat{y}_2^L)$ and $(\hat{x}_2^L + d_p^{L,t_2}, \hat{y}_2^L)$ as the initial matches of (x_1^L, y_1^L) to $(x_1^L + d^{L,t_1}, y_1^L)$, we apply the epiflow algorithm to compute the optimal matches (x_2^L, y_2^L) and $(x_2^L + d_{eqt}^{L,t_2}, y_2^L)$; here, d_{eqt}^{L,t_2} denotes the refined left-based disparity at time t_2 determined by the epiflow algorithm. Finally, bad correspondences from occlusions and other error sources are inevitable, and thus can be removed by introducing a D_{thresh}. Where the two maps overlap, we define the difference field of the epiflow-based disparity

$$D_{eqt}^{L,t_2} = d^{L,t_2} - d_{eqt}^{L,t_2}$$

and reject a quadruplet match if $\left| D_{eqt}^{L,t_2} \right| > D_{thresh}$. With improvement in the solution, we have $\varepsilon\{D_{eqt}^{L,t_2}\} \leq \varepsilon\{D_p^{L,t_2}\}$, where $\varepsilon\{.\}$ is the expectation operation.

3.1   Iterative Refinement

As the earlier results suggest, two estimated dense disparity maps d^{L,t_1} and d^{L,t_2} are independent. While the epiflow-based algorithm to fuse the two maps allows for local improvement, we seek further refinement by incorporating a strategy that provides global consistency between the two maps. Recall that the difference field D_p^{L,t_2} is the discrepancy between the estimated disparity map d^{L,t_2} and d_p^{L,t_1}; the latter being the disparity d^{L,t_1} at time t_1 that is projected to the coordinate system of the left camera at time t_2 by the estimated ego-motion $(\hat{R}, \hat{t})$. Thus, treating d^{L,t_1} and d^{L,t_2} as fixed observations, D_p^{L,t_2} is a function of the ego-motion (R, t). If our disparity measurements are perfect, we must have $D_p^{L,t_2} = 0$ for the exact ego-motion (R, t). In practice, we compute a non-zero difference field D_p^{L,t_2} for independent noisy measurements d^{L,t_1} and d^{L,t_2}, even if apply the perfect motion (R, t). However, it is reasonable to expect a zero-mean difference field D_p^{L,t_2}, if the errors in the disparity observations are zero-mean (which is normally the case). In contrast, an erroneous estimate $(\hat{R}, \hat{t})$ leads to a difference field D_p^{L,t_2}, which is biased to some degree depending on the 3-D scene structure and the ego-motion error.

Fig. 1 provides an example. The stereo disparity map at time t_1 is given in (b). In (c), the motion-predicted stereo disparity at t_2 (left) is compared with the stereo disparity computed independently at time t_2 (right). The difference field has been depicted in (d), and (e) gives the corresponding histogram. The peak nearly at 2 clearly represents the bias between the two stereo disparity maps, mainly from the inaccurate estimate of the stereo rig ego-motion. This suggests the possibility of improvement in the estimation of the motion and hence the fused disparity.

It is noted that the distribution/variance of the difference field D_p^{L,t_2} is not a relevant measure of the motion estimation accuracy, but rather how well the two disparity maps agree (which depends on the errors in computing the two disparity maps). Taken the two disparity maps as given, the peak position counts as the indicator on the accuracy of the motion estimate! Thus, we utilize the peak

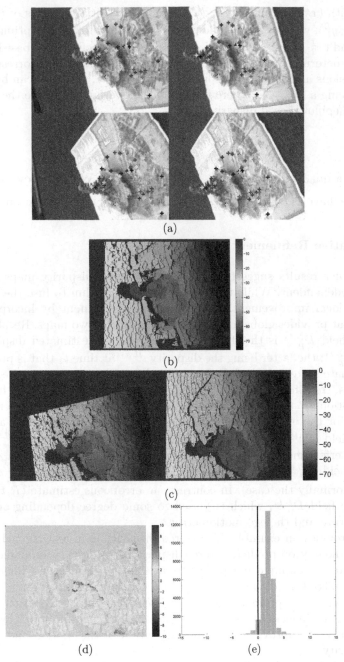

Fig. 1. Epiflow-based stereo fusion. (a) Two stereo pairs at t_1 and t_2, one on each row. The sparse feature quadruplets used to estimate ego-motion are marked by colored crosses (b) Disparity map $d^{L,t_1}(x,y)$ at t_1; (c) motion-predicted disparity map d_p^{L,t_2} (left) and measured disparity d^{L,t_2} at t_2 (right); (d) disparity difference field D^{L,t_2}, and (e) corresponding histogram.

position P in the distribution of the difference field D_p^{L,t_2} as the statistical measure to improve the accuracy in the motion (R,t) for stereo fusion. Computing P is the classical detection of local maxima/mode problem in the simplest 1-D case. Mean shift algorithm is shown to be a mode-seeking process on a surface constructed with a "shadow" kernel [7,8,5].

More formally, let P computed by mean shift algorithm denote the mode position, as explained above. P is a function of the ego-motion (R,t), for two given stereo disparity maps d^{L,t_1} and d^{L,t_2}. We estimate the ego-motion (R,t) that minimizes $|P|$:

$$\{\hat{R},\hat{t}\} = \arg\{\min|P(R,t)|\} \tag{3.1}$$

The analytical relationship between the distribution peak P and ego-motion (R,t) is difficult to derive. It becomes expensive computationally to directly apply to the above criteria a nonlinear multi-dimensional optimization algorithm, such as downhill simplex, conjugate gradient [6]. We instead propose the recursive application of the epiflow-based stereo fusion algorithm:

1. Set $k = 0$, given initial motion estimate $(\hat{R},\hat{t})^0$;
2. Register d^{L,t_1} to $(d_p^{L,t_2})^k$ with $(\hat{R},\hat{t})^k$ and compute the difference field D_p^{L,t_2};
3. Determine the peak P^k of the distribution D_p^{L,t_2};
4. If $|P^k| < P_D$ (pre-determined threshold) or $|P^k| > |P^{k-1}|$, go to step (9);
5. Apply the epiflow based algorithm to estimate $(d_{eqt}^{L,t_2})^k$;
6. Compute the difference field $(D_{eqt}^{L,t_2})^k = d^{L,t_2} - (d_{eqt}^{L,t_2})^k$, and apply the test "$|D_{eqt}^{L,t_2}| > D_{thresh}$?" to remove the outliers;
7. Estimate the motion $(\hat{R},\hat{t})^k$ from d^{L,t_1} and $(d_{eqt}^{L,t_2})^k$;
8. Increment iteration index, $k = k + 1$. Go to step (2);
9. Disparity fusion by consistency check $|(D_p^{L,t_2})^k| \le \lambda_c$.

While we may establish an analytical proof of convergence, it can be qualitatively argued and experimentally verified that convergence is often rapid within no more than a couple of iterations.

4   Experiment

We apply the iterative disparity fusion algorithm of section 3.1 to "coral reef" data. First, sparse quadruplet matches have been established by the epiflow-based feature tracking algorithm. These are used as seeds for the computation of dense disparity maps by the application of progressive stereo method [11,12,10,2]. Using the epiflow-based method, it only takes 1 iteration to bring the histogram peak of the difference field to around zero. Application of ICP algorithms [3,4] requires 10 iterations. In fig. 2(a-f), we have depicted the difference field D_p^{L,t_2} after iterations 1, 5, and 10 of stereo fusion by utilizing the epiflow-based method. In contrast, application of the ICP-based method leads to the results in (a'-f'). The improvement of the stereo fusion is clear in fig.3. Two stereo reconstructions, shown in yellow and blue, correspond to the 2 disparity maps, projected to the coordinate from of the second view by the initial

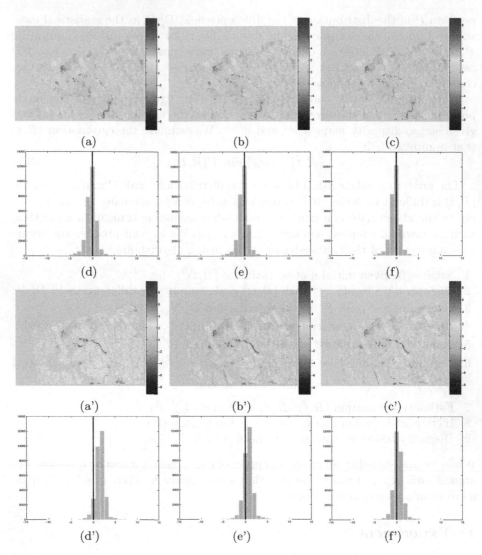

Fig. 2. Improved stereo fusion by epiflow-based method yields more consistent disparities by stereo fusion/alignment after 1, 5, and 10 iterations. (a-c) Calculated disparity difference D^{L,t_2} after various iterations and (d-f) corresponding histograms. (a'-f') Same as above previous figure for ICP-based method.

motion estimate. Improved ego-motion estimation by the iterative refinement method registers and aligns the two together better. Our iterative stereo fusion algorithm has been successfully applied to additional five underwater data sets as in fig.3(d).

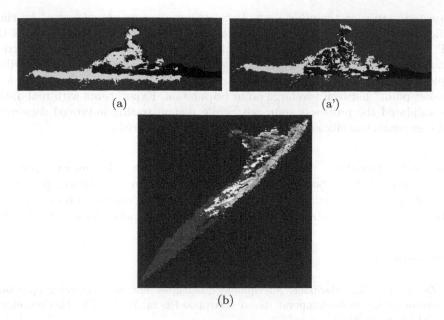

(a)   (a')

(b)

Fig. 3. Disparity fusion with improved ego-motion estimation for Coral Data. Superimposed disparity maps shown in black and gray (a) before and (a') after 1 iteration of epiflow-based fusion. (c) Final reconstruction based on proposed disparity fusion. Marked in red are voxels failing consistency check $\left|(D_p^{L,t_2})^k\right| \leq \lambda_c = 1.5$.

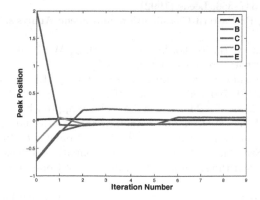

Fig. 4. Experiments on additional five underwater data, D_p^{L,t_2} histogram mode (detected by mean shift algorithm) for 10 iterations of iterative stereo fusion

5   Summary

Fusion of overlapping stereo disparity maps has been solved by the application of an epiflow-based recursive refinement algorithm. Global inconsistency of the two maps is resolved by minimizing the peak of the distribution of one map and the projected map from the other view. Local inconsistencies are addressed by the epiflow algorithm. Our method is reminiscent of the "closest point" of the 3-D ICP algorithm. However, our method enforces both geometric and photometric constraints, with faster convergence properties. In particular, an optical flow like implementation improves the computation efficiency by avoiding the search for "closest point" between two large point population. Experiments with real data has validated the proposed approach, while demonstrating improved converge and computational efficiency compared to the ICP algorithm.

Acknowledgments. This paper describes research under project NA040AR4600039 supported by NOAA under Ocean exploration program. Views and Opinions, findings, conclusions or recommendations expressed by the authors are not to be interpreted as being shared and (or) endorsed by NOAA.

References

1. Zhang, H., Negahdaripour, S.: Epiflow quadruplet matching:enforcing epipolar geometry for spatio-temporal stereo correspondences. In: WACV, Breckenridge, CO (January 2005)
2. Zhang, H., Negahdaripour, S.: Fast and robust progressive stereo reconstruction via symmetry guided fusion. In: Proc. Oceans '05 Europe, Brest,France (June 2005)
3. Besl, P.J., McKay, N.: A method for registration of 3D shapes. IEEE Trans. Pattern Anal. Mach. Intell 14(2), 239–256 (1992)
4. Zhang, Z.: On local matching of free-form curves. In: Proc. British Machine Vision Conference, pp. 347–356, Leeds (1992)
5. Duda, R., Hart, P.: Pattern Classification and Scene Analysis. Wiley, Chichester (1973)
6. Press, W., Flannery, B., Teukolsky, S., Vetterling, W.: Numerical Recipes in C. Cambridge University Press, Cambridge (1988)
7. Cheng, Y.: Mean shift, mode seeking, and clustering. IEEE Trans. Pattern Anal. Machine Intell 17(8), 790–799 (August 1995)
8. Comaniciu, D., Meer, P.: Mean shift: A robust approach toward feature space analysis. IEEE Trans. Pattern Anal. Machine Intell 24(5), 603–619 (2002)
9. Fitzgibbon, A.: Robust registration of 2D and 3D point sets. In: BMVC (2001)
10. Scharstein, D., Szeliski, R.: A taxonomy and evaluation of dense two-frame stereo correspondence algorithms. International Journal of Computer Vision 47(1), 7–42 (2002)
11. Chen, Q., Medioni, G.: A volumetric stereo matching method: Application to image-based modeling. In: Proceedings of the IEEE Conference on Computer Vision and Pattern Recognition, vol. 1, pp. 29–34, Colorado (June 1999)
12. Lhuillier, M., Quan, L.: Match propagation for image-based modeling and rendering. IEEE Trans. Pattern Anal. Mach. Intell. 24(8), 1140–1146 (2002)

Automatic Segmentation of the Liver in CT Using Level Sets Without Edges

J.F. Garamendi[1], N. Malpica[1], J. Martel[2], and E. Schiavi[1]

[1] Universidad Rey Juan Carlos, Móstoles, Madrid (Spain)
{juanfrancisco.garamendi, norberto.malpica, emanuele.schiavi}@urjc.es
[2] Fundación Hóspital de Alcorcón, Alcorcón, Madrid (Spain)
JMartel@fhalcorcon.es

Abstract. Liver volumetry is a required step for the planning of liver surgery and resection. It is generally based on Computerized tomography images, and segmentation of the liver is the most important step of the process. We propose an automatic segmentation algorithm based on a geometric level set method which provides an accurate segmentation of the liver, and requires no a priori information. We show results on different datasets, with and without a contrast agent. The segmentation is compared to manual delineation by a radiologist with good results.

1 Introduction

The planning of liver surgery requires accurate volumetric measures of the organ. Planning is generally based on computerized tomography (CT) and more recently on Magnetic Resonance Imaging (MRI). The main step for volumetry is the segmentation of the organ, which is generally carried out manually using a software platform. Manual delineation of the liver is time-consuming and can lack repeatability among users. The automatic segmentation of the liver is especially difficult due to several structural reasons:

- Hounsfield units corresponding to the liver are the same as those of neighbouring organs, so the use of simple gray level segmentation methods give inaccurate results.
- The shape and size of the liver can vary a lot between patients, making it difficult to impose a priori conditions or models.

Several semiautomatic methods have been proposed and tested, based mainly on the interactive editing of the dataset by the user. Some methods use the segmentation of other structures in the image as a reference for the liver [4]. Soler et al. use a statistical shape model, trained from previous scans, which is deformed onto the new image [3]. Pan et al. proposed a method based on level sets with a new dynamic force [2]. The model must be stopped by the user and interactively corrected. Recently, level set methods have evolved from being edge-based to including statistical information about the region to segment [1]. We have developed a variation of the Chan-Vese method for the automatic segmentation of the liver, which needs no a priori shape or size information and stops automatically.

J. Martí et al. (Eds.): IbPRIA 2007, Part I, LNCS 4477, pp. 161–168, 2007.

This paper is organized as follow, in section 2 the algorithm is described in detail. Section 3 shows some results on clinical datasets. We end with conclusions in section 4.

2   Material and Methods

2.1   Preprocessing

The original CT data is encoded in twelve bits, so we have 4096 gray levels. A supervised preprocessing step is necessarily applied in order to select a gray level window around the liver. The preprocessing step consists of a windowing dependent on the mean μ and the standard deviation σ calculated from a selected region of the liver, using function (1) or (2). The proper choice of the windowing function, (1) or (2), must be done by the user clicking on the image. Let us denote by I_0 the new image processed by using expression 1 or expression 2:

$$I_0(x,y) = \begin{cases} \mu - 3\sigma & \text{if} & I(x,y) < \mu - 3\sigma \\ I(x,y) & \text{if} & |I - \mu| \leqslant 3\sigma \\ \mu - 3\sigma & \text{if} & I(x,y) > \mu + 3\sigma \end{cases} \quad (1)$$

$$I_0(x,y) = \begin{cases} \mu + 3\sigma & \text{if} & I(x,y) < \mu - 3\sigma \\ I(x,y) & \text{if} & |I - \mu| \leqslant 3\sigma \\ \mu + 3\sigma & \text{if} & I(x,y) > \mu + 3\sigma \end{cases} \quad (2)$$

Bottom row of figure 1 shows the effect of the preprocessing using differents μ and σ, obtained from the regions shown in the top row.

2.2   Segmentation Model

Chan-Vese Algorithm. Let $\Omega \subset \mathbb{R}^2$ be an open, bounded domain (usually a rectangle) where $(x, y) \in \Omega$ denotes pixel location and $I_0(x, y)$ is a function representing the intensity image values. The Chan-Vese model for binary segmentation is based on the minimization of an energy functional expressed in terms of a level set formulation. Let $\omega \subset \Omega$ (eventually not connected) open, a positive measured sub-region of the original domain. If the curve C represents the boundary of such a segmentation ω then, in the level set formulation, the (free) moving boundary C is the zero level set of a Lipschitz function $\phi : \Omega \to \mathbb{R}$, that is: $C = \{(x, y) \in \Omega : \phi(x, y) = 0\}$, $C = \delta\omega$ where $\omega = \{(x, y) \in \Omega : \phi(x, y) > 0\}$, $\Omega \backslash \overline{\omega} = \{(x, y) \in \Omega : \phi(x, y) < 0\}$. The level set function ϕ can be characterized as a minimum of the following energy functional:

$$E_{cv}(e_{in}, e_{out}, \phi) = \mu \int_\Omega |\nabla H(\phi)| dx dy + \nu \int_\Omega H(\phi) dx dy$$

$$+ \lambda_{in} \int_\Omega H(\phi) e_{in} dx dy$$

$$+ \lambda_{out} \int_\Omega (1 - H(\phi)) e_{out} dx dy \quad (3)$$

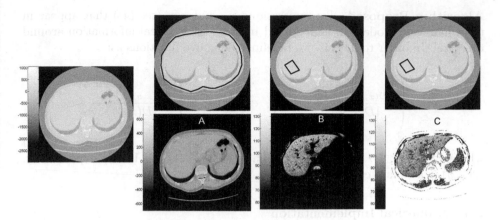

Fig. 1. The effect of preprocessing. Left, original slice. Top row, region of interest used for calculate μ and σ, below, the slice preprocessed according with expression 1 (images A and B) and expression 2 (image C). The color bar at left of each image shows the value of Hounsfield Units in the image.

where μ, ν, λ_{in} and λ_{out} are parameters which can be considered as weight factors which control the trade off between smoothness (μ, ν) and the fidelity data terms (λ_{in}, λ_{out}). The Heaviside function $H(x)$, $H(x) = 1$ if $x \geq 0$ and $H(x) = 0$ otherwise, allows to express the length of C and the area of ω respectively by

$$|C| = Length(\phi = 0) = \int_{\Omega} |\nabla H(\phi)| dxdy, \quad |\omega| = Area(\phi \geqslant 0) = \int_{\Omega} H(\phi) dxdy$$

The functions e_{in}, e_{out} are defined as

$$e_{in}(x, y) = |I_0(x, y) - c_{in}|^2, \qquad e_{out}(x, y) = |I_0(x, y) - c_{out}|^2 \qquad (4)$$

where c_{in} and c_{out} are

$$c_{in}(\phi) = \frac{\int_{\Omega} I_0 H(\phi) dxdy}{\int_{\Omega} H(\phi) dxdy}, \quad c_{out}(\phi) = \frac{\int_{\Omega} I_0 (1 - H(\phi)) dxdy}{\int_{\Omega} (1 - H(\phi)) dxdy} \qquad (5)$$

and represent the mean value inside the segmentation (c_{in}) and the mean value outside the segmentation (c_{out}).

Following the calculus of variations, the minimum of the energy E_{cv} corresponds to a solution of the Euler-Lagrange equations:

$$0 = \delta_{\epsilon}(\phi) \left[\mu \nabla \cdot \left(\frac{\nabla \phi}{|\nabla \phi|} \right) - \nu - \lambda_{in} e_{in} + \lambda_{out} e_{out} \right], \quad a.e. \ (x, y) \in \Omega \qquad (6)$$

where $\delta_{\epsilon}(x)$ is a regularized version of the Dirac delta function [1]. As usual, the equation is complemented with homogeneous Neumann boundary conditions.

Algorithm Proposed. The expressions e_{in} and e_{out} (see (4)) that appear in the Chan-Vese model can be modified in order to use local information around the pixel. In order to do this, we redefine the above functions as:

$$
e_{in}(x,y) = \left(\frac{\int_{D(x,y)} I_0 dsdr}{|D(x,y)|} - c_{in} \right)^2 \quad e_{out}(x,y) = \left(\frac{\int_{D(x,y)} I_0 dsdr}{|D(x,y)|} - c_{out} \right)^2
\tag{7}
$$

where $D(x,y) \subset \Omega$ is a domain around the pixel (x,y). In the experiments, $D(x,y)$ is a square centered in (x,y).

2.3 Numerical Implementation

As usual, instead of solving the elliptic equation (6) directly, we solve the associated parabolic equation:

$$
\frac{\partial \phi}{\partial t} = \delta_\epsilon(\phi) \left[\mu \nabla \cdot \left(\frac{\nabla \phi}{|\nabla \phi|} \right) - \nu - \lambda_{in} e_{in} + \lambda_{out} e_{out} \right]
\tag{8}
$$

The derivatives are implemented with a finite difference scheme, D_d^+ is the forward difference in the direction d and D_d^- is the backward difference in the direction d. The parabolic equation (8) is solved by an explicit gradient descent method:

$$
\frac{\phi^{n+1} - \phi^n}{\Delta t} = \delta_\epsilon(\phi) \left[\mu D_x^- \left(\frac{D_x^+ \phi^n}{\sqrt{(D_x^+ \phi^n)^2 + (D_y^+ \phi^n)^2 + \epsilon_1}} \right) + \right.
$$

$$
\left. + \mu D_y^- \left(\frac{D_y^+ \phi^n}{\sqrt{(D_x^+ \phi^n)^2 + (D_y^+ \phi^n)^2 + \epsilon_1}} \right) - \nu - \lambda_{in} e_{in} + \lambda_{out} e_{out} \right]
\tag{9}
$$

where e_{in} and e_{out} are computed by using (7) and $0 < \epsilon_1 \ll 1$ is a small parameter avoiding degeneracy in the elliptic equation.

2.4 Complete Algorithm

The global procedure for liver segmentation is implemented using a multistage approach, consisting of three tightly interleaved stages:

- *Preprocessing step:* In this stage the expert selects a Region-of-Interest (ROI) inside the liver and the image is preprocessed according with section 2.1. The value c_{in} is fixed to the mean of the ROI to guide the segmentation to the liver.
- *Segmentation step:* Equation (8) with e_{in} and e_{out} from (7) is solved using the scheme proposed in [1]:

- Initialize ϕ^0 as the ROI selected by the user at the preprocessing step. Set $n = 0$.
- Compute $c_{out}(\phi^n)$ by (5).
- Solve the PDE in ϕ from (8) to obtain ϕ^{n+1}.
- Reinitialize ϕ locally to the signed distance function to the curve.
- Check whether the solution is stationary. If not, n=n+1, recalculate c_{out} and repeat.

— *Postprocessing step:* Small bubbles are automatically removed. Only the biggest object of the segmentation (the liver) is preserved.

2.5 Data Adquisition

The test materials are a set of multi-phase CT images of human abdomen. The images were acquired at the Alcorcon Hospital in Madrid, which were collected at three phases before and after contrast agents were injected. They are called the pre-contrast, early and portal images respectively. In the first series the dimensions are (512x512x40) in the pre-contrast phase and (512x512x38) in the early and portal phase. In the second series the dimensions are (512x512x50) ,

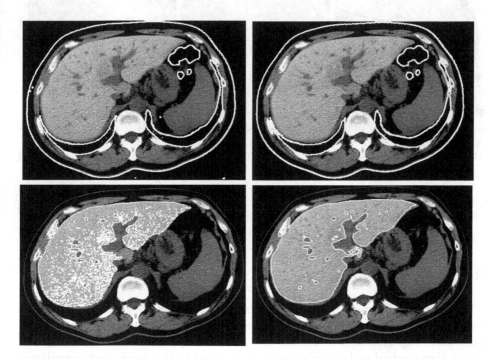

Fig. 2. The effect of preprocessing in the segmentation. At the top row, the image segmented is Fig. 1-A (without preprocessing step) with Chan-Vese algorithm (top left) and with our modification (top right). At the bottom row, the image segmented is Fig. 1-B (with preprocessin step) with Chan-Vese algorithm (bottom left) and with our modification (bottom right). all images are displayed within the range from -141 to 284 HU.

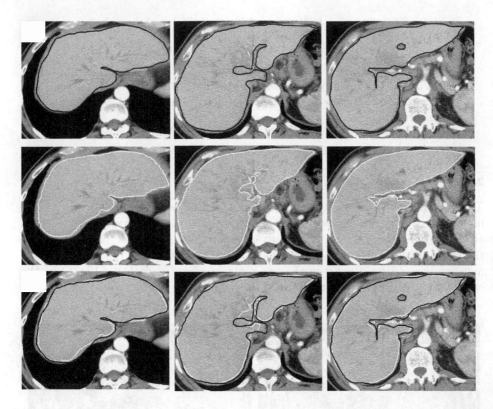

Fig. 3. In black, manual segmentation and examples of segmentation result in white over images in portal phase. Paremeters are $\mu = 10^{-1} \cdot max(I_0)^2$, $\nu = 0$, $\lambda_{in} = 0.6$, $\lambda_{out} = 1$, and $\Delta t = 0.1$, $\epsilon = 1$. All images are displayed within the range from -110 to 190 H.U.

(512x512x48) and (512x512x46) in pre-contrast, early an portal phase respectively and the dimensions of the third series are (512x512x46) in the three phases. Spatial resolution is (0.74x0.74) mm and slice thickness is 5 mm in all studies.

3   Experimental Results

The algorithm has been tested on the series explained in section 2.5 to take into account different signal to noise ratios and differents shapes of the liver. A first set of experiments was carried out to evaluate the diferences between the Chan-Vese method and the modification proposed in this work, and to evaluate the effect of the windowing in the method. Figure 2 shows the segmentation results over the same slice with the Chan-Vese algorithm (left column) and our modification (right column) using differents windowing preprocess.

Figure 3 shows four slices of the liver and the manual segmentation and the semi-automatic segmentation. The first row is a manual segmentation done by

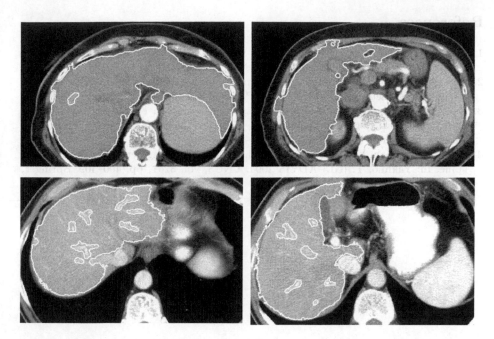

Fig. 4. Segmentation result over images in portal phase. At the left, two slices of a liver hipertrofied and at the right two slices of a cutted liver. Paremeters are $\mu = 10^{-1} \cdot max(I_0)^2$, $\nu = 0$, $\lambda_{in} = 15$, $\lambda_{out} = 1$, and $\Delta t = \epsilon = 1$. All images are displayed within the range from -110 to190 H.U.

an expert. The middle row shows the result obtained with our algorithm and the bottom row shows both segmentations on the same image. Parameters in the experiments are $\mu = 10^{-1} \cdot max(I_0)^2$, $\nu = 0$, $\lambda_{in} = 0.6$, $\lambda_{out} = 1$, and $\Delta t = 0.1$, $\epsilon = 1$.

In order to test the algorithm with 'non standard' livers, we use a CT of two patients, one with the liver bigger than normal and the other with the liver previously rejected. Figure 4 shows two slices of this CT. Parameters are $\mu = 10^{-1} \cdot max(I_0)^2$, $\nu = 0$, $\lambda_{in} = 15$, $\lambda_{out} = 1$, and $\Delta t = \epsilon = 1$.

4   Conclusions

We have proposed a new method for liver segmentation in CT images which requires no a priori information. The method is based on the Chan-Vese model, with a previous adaptive gray level windowing.. The algorithm stops automatically and is robust with respect to the initial contour. The method has been applied to clinical datasets with good results and has been tested on data sets with different liver shapes and sizes. Segmentation of the liver in different phases of contrast administration has also been achieved. Further clinical validation of the algorithm is warranted.

References

1. Chan, T.F., Vese, L.A.: Active Contours Without Edges. In: IEEE Transactions on Image Processing, vol. 10(2), IEEE, NJ, New York (2001)
2. Pan, S., Dawant, B.: Automatic 3D segmentation of the liver from abdominal CT images: a level set approach. In: Proc. SPIE Medical Imaging 4322, 128–138 (2001)
3. Soler, L., Delingette, H., Malandain, G., Montaganat, J. et al.: Fully automatic anatomical, pathological and functional segmentation from CT scans for hepatic surgery. Computer Aided Surgery 6, 131–142 (2001)
4. Seo, K., Ludeman, L.C., Park, S., Park, J.: Efficient liver segmentation based on the spine. In: Yakhno, T. (ed.) ADVIS 2004. LNCS, vol. 3261, pp. 400–409. Springer, Heidelberg (2004)

Spectral Modes of Facial Needle-Maps

Roberto Fraile[1] and Edwin R. Hancock[2]

[1] University of Leeds, UK
[2] University of York, UK

Abstract. This paper presents a method to decompose a field of surface normals (needle-map). A diffusion process is used to model the flow of height information induced by a field of surface normals. The diffusion kernel can be decomposed into eigenmodes, each corresponding to approximately independent modes of variation of the flow. The surface normals can then be diffused using a modified kernel with the same eigenmodes but different coefficients. When used as part of a surface integration process, this procedure allows choosing the trade-off between local and global influence of each eigenmode in the modified field of surface normals. This graph-spectral method is illustrated with surface normals extracted from a face. Experiments are carried with local affinity functions that convey both the intrinsic and extrinsic geometry of the surface, and an information-theoretic definition of affinity.

1 Introduction

Surface shape can be represented and analysed in a number of ways. The most straightforward methods make direct use of surface height information. However, the field of surface normals or "Gauss map" of a surface is a potentially richer source of information concerning the differential geometry of the surface [3]. Moreover, needle-maps are sometimes more easily extracted from 2D images of scenes, through processes such as shape-from-shading, shape-from-texture or photometric stereo [1,18,20]. Height information may be recovered for the field of surface normals through a process of integration [1,5]. Figure 1 illustrates the process of surface integration from surface normals.

However, the Gauss map also conveys information that can be used to analyse complex variations in surface shape. For instance, Smith and Hancock [16,15] have recently shown how statistical variations of facial shape can be conveniently captured through principal geodesic analysis of the Gauss map. There, variations in surface normal direction for a training sample data are analysed by projecting the Gauss map into a tangent space using the exponential map. The modes of variation are captured by performing principal components analysis on the resulting Cartesian data. Unfortunately, this approach requires large numbers of hand-aligned needle-maps, and this data is sometimes difficult to obtain.

In the 2D shape analysis literature an alternative to constructing shape models using PCA is to deform a shape using its vibrational modes. This is the approach

J. Martí et al. (Eds.): IbPRIA 2007, Part I, LNCS 4477, pp. 169–176, 2007.

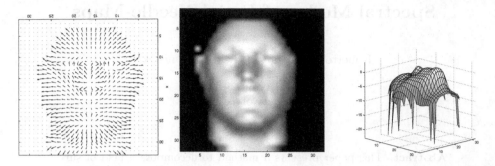

Fig. 1. A field of surface normals as projected arrows (left), its optical rendering under frontal illumination (middle), and the reconstructed surface (right)

adopted by Sclaroff and Pentland [13], who analyse shape-modes by solving the equations of motion for damped elastic boundary vibration.

Our aim in this research is to explore the application of similar ideas to the Gauss map of a surface, and to explore the influence of each mode on the integrated surface. However, rather than analysing shape modes using the equations of damped vibrational motion, we draw on ideas from spectral graph theory.

In spectral graph theory a set of data are abstracted using a weighted graph in which the nodes represent objects and the edge weights the pairwise affinity of the objects. The aim is to characterise the weighted graph using the eigenvalues and eigenvectors of the wighted adjacency matrix of the closely related Laplacian (the degree matrix minus the adjacency weight matrix). In computer vision, graph spectral methods have been used for image segmentation and perceptual grouping [12,14]. Robles-Kelly [10,11] has used graph spectral method for patch-wise surface integration. Fraile [4] has extended this work to develop global surface recovery methods using integration trees that span the entire surface. The spanning trees are found by applying Prim's algorithm to the affinity weights. Noise is modelled as a diffusion process [17] on the trees, and this process is governed by the heat equation. As a result, surface normal directions can be smoothed by averaging over the tree using the heat kernel as a weighting function. The heat kernel is found by exponentiating the Laplacian eigensystem with diffusion time t, and the degree of smoothing can be controlled by varying t.

Here we aim to build on this work to construct a modal shape representation. Our starting point is the observation that the heat kernel can be decomposed into eigenmodes [2] each of which is found by taking the self outer product of a Laplacian eigenvector. By modifying the relative weighting of the eigenmodes, we modify the kernel decomposition of the Gauss map, and this in turn modifies the shape of the surface recovered through integration. The eigenmodes of a face are used to illustrate this decomposition, and provide an insight into the relative complexity of the eigenmodes, and their suitability for a sparse representation of the shape.

2   Surface Integration

In this section we present a graph-spectral method for surface integration, i.e. the recovery of surface height from a field of surfaced normals. Given two adjacent locations i and j, and their surface normals $\mathbf{n}_i$ and $\mathbf{n}_j$, it is possible to estimate the height difference by applying the trapezium rule. We represent the field of surface normals using an matrix A which assigns a number between 0 and 1 to each pair of adjacent surface normals i and j. We represent the arrangement of surface normals by a weighted graph. Consider the graph $G = (E, V, A)$ with vertex-set V the surface normal locations and edge-set E representing the adjacency relations between surface normal locations (typically the 4-neighbours). Here we use the *Gauss* affinity function and assign

$$A_{ij} = e^{-\|\mathbf{n}_i - \mathbf{n}_j\|^2}$$

where $\mathbf{n}_i$ and $\mathbf{n}_j$ are the normals at locations i and j. This function measures distance of the normals as euclidean unit vectors.

The integration path is chosen to be the spanning tree T that maximises the total affinity weight A over the weighted graph G. Here we compute the spanning tree using the method outlined in [6].

The surface can then be reconstructed by integration along the edges of T, applying the trapezium rule to the surface normals. This optimisation procedure is independent of the affinity function, and the problem of obtaining adequate height estimates is reduced to defining an appropriate affinity function. Figure 2 illustrates the notion of integration tree.

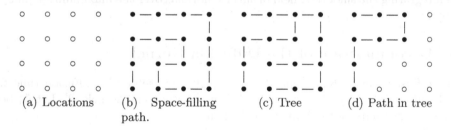

(a) Locations   (b) Space-filling path.   (c) Tree   (d) Path in tree

Fig. 2. Paths defined over the set of locations. Each location is labeled with a 3D surface normal vector. The surface is integrated over a path using the trapezium rule.

The practical use of such a path-based integration method is limited by the quality of the surface normals. The field of surface normals are potentially noisy and require smoothing. Here we use a diffusion process over the spanning tree to effect smoothing [7,19]. Let $\hat{L}$ be the normalised Laplacian associated to A, $\hat{L} = D^{-\frac{1}{2}} L D^{\frac{1}{2}}$, where $L = D - A$ and D is the diagonal matrix such that $D_{ii} = \sum_j A_{ij}$. The matrix $\hat{L}$ can be seen as a discrete approximation of the continuous Laplacian operator in the following diffusion equation [7]

$$\partial_t H = -\hat{L} H \tag{1}$$

The solution $H(t)$ can be calculated by matrix exponentiation

$$H(t) = e^{-t\hat{L}}$$

Each entry (i, j) of the matrix $H(t)$ can be interpreted as the probability of a random walk joining locations i and j, after t steps, given the transition probability A. Note that the size of both A and $H(t)$ is $|V| \times |V|$.

The heat kernel is given by the spectrum of the Laplacian matrix. Let $\Lambda = diag(\lambda_1, \lambda_2, ..., \lambda_{|V|})$ be the diagonal matrix with the ordered Laplacian eigenvalues as elements and let $\Phi = (\phi_1|\phi_2|.....|\phi_{|V|})$ be the eigenvector matrix with the corresponding eigenvectors as columns. The spectral decomposition of the Laplacian matrix is $\mathcal{L} = \Phi\Lambda\Phi^T$. The heat kernel is

$$H_t = \exp[-\mathcal{L}t] = \Phi\exp[-\Lambda t]\Phi^T$$

The presence of a path in G of high affinity between two nodes i and j increases the probability $H(t)_{ij}$. We use $H(t)$ as a weight-function to control smoothing of the surface normals over the integration tree. This is a generalisation of a simple average of neighbouring surface normals, and is similar to subjecting the surface normals to a process of anisotropic diffusion [8].

The updated normals corresponding to a diffusion time t, $N(t) = \{\mathbf{n}(t)_i\}_{i \in V}$, are defined as a weighted sum of the surface normals:

$$\mathbf{n}(t)_i = \sum_j H(t)_{ij}\mathbf{n}_j \qquad (2)$$

where the indexes i and j visit all locations. The reconstructed surface is found be integrating the smoothed field of surface normals over the maximum spanning tree T.

3   Decomposition of the Diffusion Kernel

The diffusion kernel $K(t)$ depends on a single parameter, the diffusion time t, and can be decomposed as a weighted sum of orthogonal kernels [2]. Let ϕ_s be the sth eigenvector of the Laplacian $\mathcal{L}$, then

$$H(t)_{ij} = \sum_s e^{-t\lambda_s}\phi_s\phi_s^T$$

Note that the sth eigenmode of the heat kernel is $E_s = \phi_s\phi_s^T$. We can use the eigemodes as a set of basis states over the locations of the pixel lattice. The eigenvectors are orthonormal, therefore

$$\Phi^T\Phi = \sum_{s=1}^{|V|} \phi_s^T\phi_s = I.$$

This will allow us to illustrate the kernels E_s and their truncated sums $\sum_{r=1}^{s} E_r$ by looking at their effect on the input needle-map, since, in the limit $s = |V|$, the kernel is the identity.

4   Experiments

Two affinity functions have been chosen to illustrate the eigenvalues, *Gauss* and *Logstar* [4]. The spatial resolution has been set to 32×32 for practical reasons. The surface normals are given in double precision floating point numbers. Each of the figures show the value for increasing s.

Figure 3 shows the field of normals modified by eigenmode E_s, with s between 1 and 64, when computing using the *Gauss* affinity function. Compare with Figure 4 which is the field modified by the sum $\sum_{r=1}^{s} E_s$ of the first s eigenmodes. For comparison, Figure 5 shows the field of normals modified by eigenmode E_s, computed using the *Logstar* affinity, which is defined as

$$A_{ij} = \text{length}(\text{encode}(\text{floor}(10 \cdot (\mathbf{n}_i - \mathbf{n}_j))))$$

using the logstar code [9], which maps short integers into short binary strings. The *Logstar* affinity is intended to approximate the minimum description length of the surface normal $\mathbf{n}_j$ given $\mathbf{n}_i$.

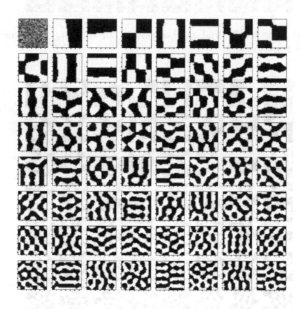

Fig. 3. First 64 eigenmodes using the Gauss affinity function

It is useful to consider the eigenmodes as incrementally modeling the shape. Thus, the first few eigenmodes produce a vertical symmetry, and further eigenmodes add more localised detail.

The apparent complexity of the eigenmodes increases in all cases. The field is effectively divided in two by each eigenmode (in the plots this is denoted by black and white pixels). The topological order of this segmentation seems to increase monotonically. Note that some consecutive eigenmodes for the *Gauss* affinity are rotated pairs.

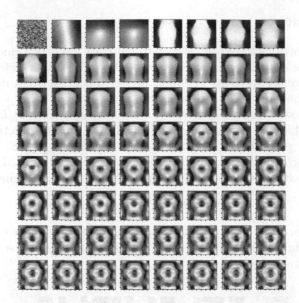

Fig. 4. Truncated sums of the first n eigenmodes, for $n = 1, \ldots, 64$ eigenvalues using the Gauss affinity function

Fig. 5. First 64 eigenmodes using the Logstar affinity function

The first few eigenmodes do not appear very complex and therefore might be amenable to a sparse representation themselves. Therefore the first few eigenvalues and eigenmodes might are suitable for a sparse representation of the vector field and the surface.

5 Conclusion

We have presented a method to decompose a field of surface normals into eigen-modes, with applications to surface reconstruction from normals. The eigen-modes and their truncated sums have been illustrated, with the purpose of examining the structure of the shape represented by a field of surface normals. The decompositions under different affinity functions have been illustrated and compared.

References

1. Agrawal, A., Chellappa, R.: An algebraic approach to surface reconstruction from gradient fields. In: Proceedings of ICCV 2005, pp. 23–114 (2005)
2. Chung, F.R.K.: Spectral Graph Theory. AMS (1997)
3. Do Carmo, M.: Differential Geometry of Curves and Surfaces. Prentice-Hall, Englewood Cliffs, New Jersey (1976)
4. Fraile, R., Hancock, E.R.: Combinatorial surface integration. In: International Conference on Pattern Recognition, vol. I, pp. 59–62 (2006)
5. Frankot, R.T., Chellappa, R.: A method for enforcing integrability in shape from shading algorithms. IEEE Trans. Pattern Analysis and Machine Intelligence 10(4), 439–451 (July 1988)
6. Gibbons, A.: Algorithmic Graph Theory. Cambridge University Press, Cambridge (1985)
7. Kondor, R.I., Lafferty, J.: Diffusion kernels on graphs and other discrete structures. ICML 2002 (2002)
8. Perona, P., Malik, J.: Scale space and edge detection using anisotropic diffusion. IEEE Transactions on Pattern Analysis and Machine Intelligence 12(7), 629–639 (1990)
9. Rissanen, J.: A universal prior for integers and estimation by minimum description length. Annals of Statistics 11(2), 416–431 (June 1983)
10. Robles-Kelly, A., Hancock, E.R.: A graph-spectral approach to shape-from-shading. IEEE Transactions on Image Processing 13(7), 912–926 (July 2004)
11. Robles-Kelly, A.: Graph-spectral methods for Computer Vision. PhD thesis, The University of York (September 2003)
12. Sarkar, S., Boyer, K.L.: Quantitative measures of change based on feature organization: Eigenvalues and eigenvectors. Computer Vision and Image Understanding 71(1), 110–136 (1998)
13. Sclaroff, S., Pentland, A.: Modal matching for correspondence and recognition. IEEE PAMI 17(6), 545–561 (1995)
14. Shi, J., Malik, J.: Normalized cuts and image segmentation. IEEE Transactions on Pattern Analysis and Machine Intelligence 22(8), 888–905 (2000)
15. Smith, W.A.P., Hancock, E.R.: Recovering facial shape using a statistical model of surface normal direction. IEEE Trans. Pattern Analysis and Machine Intelligence 28(12), 1914–1930 (2006)
16. Smith, W.A.P., Hancock, E.R.: Face recognition using 2.5D shape information. In: CVPR, pp. 1407–1414. IEEE Computer Society, Los Alamitos (2006)

17. Widder, D.V.: The Heat Equation. Academic Press, London (1975)
18. Worthington, P.L., Hancock, E.R.: New constraints on data-closeness and needle map consistency for shape-from-shading. PAMI 21(12), 1250–1267 (December 1999)
19. Zhang, F., Qiu, H., Hancock, E.: Evolving spanning trees using the heat equation. In: Int. Conf. on Computer Analysis of Images and Patterns (2005)
20. Zhang, R., Tsai, P.-S., Cryer, J.E., Shah, M.: Shape-from-shading: a survey. IEEE Transactions on Pattern Analysis and Machine Intelligence 21(8), 690–706 (1999)

Classifiers for Vegetation and Forest Mapping with Low Resolution Multiespectral Imagery

Marcos Ferreiro-Armán[1], Lourenço P.C. Bandeira[2], Julio Martín-Herrero[1], and Pedro Pina[2]

[1] Dep. de Teoría do Sinal e Comunicacións, ETSET, Universidade de Vigo, Spain
[2] CERENA, Insituto Superior Técnico, Lisboa, Portugal

Abstract. This paper deals with the evaluation of the performance of a set of classifiers on multispectral imagery with low dimensionality and low spatial and spectral resolutions. The original Landsat TM images and other 4 transformed sets are classified by 5 supervised and 2 unsupervised methods. The results for 7 land cover classes are compared and the performances of the methods for each set of input data are discussed.

1 Introduction

The classification of multivalued images is a fundamental step on remote sensing since it is the core transformation for converting satellite data into usable thematic maps. Since their commercial availability in the early 1970s, several approaches have been tested to produce maps with a high thematic quality in a variety of application domains. The reasons for using different approaches resides on the attempt to get the highest performances, which depend, among several other aspects, on the adequation of the method to the purposes of the problem under study or on the type, quality and quantity of data available. The great diversity of the Earth's surface provides beautiful but complex pictures of its structures/processes not always correctly represented due to restrictions in spatial, spectral and temporal resolutions of the sensor under use. In addition, the processes where human expertise is involved (ground truth construction, with class labeling and contour delineation) also carry some uncertainty and may be the source of some errors. But, paradoxically, the use of more complete and sophisticathed classification methods has not improved the results over a 15-year period (1989-2003), like a recent survey demonstrates [1], where a great majority of methods are applied, but other more recent approaches were still left unattended. Thus, we decided to test some of the methods that are less frequently used in the classification of remotely sended images, and to evaluate their performances on a well known hard data set (low dimensionality, low spatial and spectral resolutions and a constrained number of land cover classes).

J. Martí et al. (Eds.): IbPRIA 2007, Part I, LNCS 4477, pp. 177–184, 2007.

2   Original and Transformed Data Sets

The initial data set used consists of geometrically corrected Landsat 5 TM images of October 1997 of a rural region in the centre of Portugal of about 39×36 km^2 (1289×1205 pixels) [2]. It has 6 bands (blue, green, red, NIR-near infra-red 0.76-0.90 μm, MIR-mid-infrared 1.55-1.75 μm and mid-infrared 2.08-2.35 μm) with a spatial resolution of 30 m/pixel. The high correlation between each pair of bands suggested the combination of the original bands. We have obtained 4 additional datasets using the transformations:

- **Tasselled Cap Transform (TCT).** Initially introduced to deal with Landsat 4 MSS images to obtain a new coordinate axis system with a precise physical meaning [3]. Later, it was extended to Landsat 5 TM images where the new axes give origin to 3 components [4]: brightness (weighted mean of all the bands), greenness (contrast between the bands in the visible and NIR regions), and wetness (difference between MIR bands and the other ones).
- **Principal Component Analysis (PCA).** PCA [5] is the classical eigenvector decomposition of the covariance matrix of the data. The data is projected into a new subspace (the principal axes), where the axes are ordered by the amount of variance.
- **Independent Component Analysis (ICA).** ICA [6] is a linear transform which attempts to make linear mixtures of random variables as statistically independent as possible. The goal of ICA is to estimate in an unsupervised way these components. The underlying assumption is the statistically independent components with non Gaussian distributions (actually, it can be shown that no more than one component can be Gaussian).
- **Linear Discriminant Analysis (LDA).** LDA [7] handles the case of unequal within-class frequencies. It maximizes the ratio of between-class variance to the within-class variance, thereby offering maximal separability.

3   Classification Methods

The 7 classification methods under scrutiny can be divided into: Unsupervised (Self Organizing Maps and Fuzzy Clustering) and Supervised (k-Nearest Neighbours, Multilayer Perceptron, Radial Basis Function Neural Networks, Supervised Self Organizing Maps, and Support Vector Machines). Two of the methods, Fuzzy Clustering and Supervised SOM, perform soft classification.

Self Organizing Maps (SOM). Kohonen's SOM are artificial neural networks that use unsupervised algorithms to configure a topological representation of the input space [8],[9]. They can be used as a data visualization technique to reduce the dimensions of data. SOMs produce topology-preserving low dimensional (usually two or three) representations of higher dimensional data, called maps, where each sample is assigned to a node in an ordered array.

Fuzzy Clustering (FC). FC algorithms are unsupervised techniques that partition a data set into overlapping groups based on similarity within groups and dissimilarity amongst groups. Instead of partitioning the data into a specified number of mutually exclusive subsets, as in hard clustering, FC methods allow objects to belong to several clusters simultaneously, with different degrees of membership [10]. These algorithms determine a fuzzy partition of the data into C clusters by computing a partition matrix U and the C-tuple of corresponding cluster prototypes $V = \{v_1, \ldots, v_C\}$. The elements $u_{ik} \in [0,1]$ of U represent the membership of data object x_k in cluster i. One of the most common clustering algorithms is that by Gustafson-Kessel (GK) [11] (and variations thereof). The algorithm, extended from the standard fuzzy c-means algorithm by Gustafson and Kessel, employes an adaptive distance norm in order to detect clusters of different geometrical shapes in one data set. In this way, each cluster has its own fuzzy covariance matrix F_i,

$$F_i = \frac{\sum_{k=1}^{N}(\mu_{ik})^m(x_k - v_i)(x_k - v_i)^T}{\sum_{k=1}^{N}(\mu_{ik})^m} \tag{1}$$

where $m \in [1, \infty[$ is the weighting exponent which determines the fuzziness of the resulting clusters.

k-Nearest Neighbours (kNN). The k-nearest neighbours (k-NN) classification rule [12] is a technique for non-parametric supervised pattern classification. Given the knowledge of N prototype (feature vectors) and their correct classification into several classes, it assigns an unclassified pattern to the class that is most heavily represented among its k nearest neighbours in the pattern space.

Multilayer Perceptron (MLP). MLPs [13] are the most popular artificial neural networks (ANN). MLPs can be regarded as models of biological neural structures, where the basic constituent is an idealized neuron (also known as neurode, node, or just unit) whose behaviour follows in a simplified manner our understanding on how real neurons work. A neuron has N input lines and a single output. Each input signal is weighted with the weight of the corresponding input line. The neuron combines the weighted inputs by adding them and determines the output with reference to a threshold value and an activation function, characteristic of the neuron. In mathematical terms, a neuron can be described by the following pair of equations:

$$u = \sum_{i=1}^{N} w_i x_i, \quad y = f(u - \theta). \tag{2}$$

where $x_1, x_2, \ldots, x_N$ are the input signals, $w_1, w_2, \ldots, w_N$ are the synaptic weights, u is the activation potential of the neuron, θ is the threshold, y is the output signal of the neuron, and $f()$ is the activation function. In the standard model, units are arranged in layers, and each unit in a layer has all its inputs connected to the units of a preceding layer (or to the inputs from the external world in the case of the units in the first layer, the input layer) with full connectivity, but it does not have any connections to units in the same layer to which it belongs. There are an input layer, multiple intermediate layers and an output layer. Intermediate layers are called hidden layers. These MLPs are usually trained using gradient descent algorithms such as the backpropagation algorithm [14], [15], [16]. We used an MLP with 1 hidden layer and 20 nodes (MLP-20n) and another with 2 hidden layers with 10 and 20 nodes (MLP-20,10n).

Radial Basis Function Neural Networks (RBF). RBF emerged in the late 80's [17]. However, their roots are entrenched in classical pattern recognition techniques [18]. RBFs are organized in a two layered network, where each hidden unit implements a radial activation function. The output units implement a weighted sum of hidden unit outputs. Due to nonlinear approximation properties, RBF networks are able to model complex mappings, which MLPs can only model by means of multiple intermediary layers [19]. A common form of basis function is the Gaussian,

$$\phi_j(\mathbf{x}) = exp\left(-\frac{1}{2}(\mathbf{x} - \mu_j)^T \Sigma_j^{-1}(\mathbf{x} - \mu_j)\right) \tag{3}$$

where μ_j determines the centre of function ϕ_j, and Σ_j controls its shape.

Supervised Self Organizing Maps (S-SOM). A typical way to perform classification using SOMs is that, after training, each node in the map is assigned the class of the nearest sample in the training set. Then, any new sample vector is classified as belonging to the class of the nearest node in the map. However, a soft classification scheme has been proposed recently, called Supervised Self Organizing Map (S-SOM) [20], which takes advantage of the topology preservation property of SOMs: Neighbour nodes in a trained SOM represent neighbour samples in the feature space, and samples far apart in the feature space are represented by nodes far apart in the map. This property is not exploited in the classical provedure (except in an indirect way). S-SOM constructs smooth surfaces on the map which determine the degree of membership of each node (and its representees) to each class. Using these membership degrees, membership probabilities for each node are computed, which give the probability of that node belonging to each class. The result of a classification with S-SOM is the assignation to each new sample of the membership probabilities of the corresponding nearest node map. If a hard classification is wanted, then the soft classification can be "hardened" by a MAP criterion on the probability vectors. In this case, the probability intensity of the winning class can be interpreted as a confidence measure.

Support Vector Machines (SVM). SVMs are kernel methods that use an implicit transformation to a higher dimensional space in order to achieve good separability by means of a linear classifier in the new space [21]. The hyperplane used for separation in the higher dimensional space is chosen such that the so-called margin (the distance to the closest samples in each class) is maximized. The samples determining the margin are called the support vectors. Different transformation kernels, such as Gaussian, polynomial, linear, and sigmoidal, yield different classifiers (SVM-gk, SVM-pk, SVM-lk, SVM-sk).

4   Results and Discussion

The target study area is a rural region in the centre of Portugal where seven land-cover classes were previously defined [2]: 3 tree forest classes (OLI-olive, COR-cork oak and PEU-mixed pine-eucalyptus trees), two types of soil (BAR-bare and MIX-mixed), one type of low vegetation (VEG-agricultural fields) and also WAT-water. Due to the high mixture degree of pine and eucalyptus trees in the ground it was decided to keep both types within the same class.

Aerial photographs geometrically corrected (true colour ortophotomaps with a spatial resolution of 1 m/pixel) were also available and were used to help identify the different land cover classes in the construction of ground truth images. The total number of pixels for the 7 classes on the ground-truth map is 17570, which were randomly divided into sets of equal size (8785 pixels each, with the same proportion within each class), one for training, the other for testing. The size in pixels of each training/test class is: 840 (VEG), 1214 (BAR), 210 (WAT), 629 (OLI), 3954 (PEU), 1136 (SOB) and 802 (MIX), corresponding to the a priori probabilities observed in the scene. A detail of the study region with the respective classification is presented in Fig. 1.

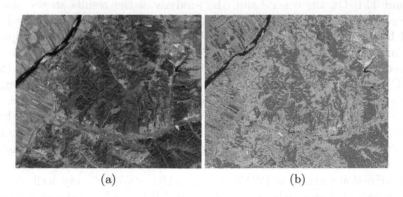

(a)   (b)

Fig. 1. (a) Detail of target region (Band 5 of Landsat 5 TM); (b) Classified image with SVM-gk method on PCA data set

The performance of each method is evaluated with the data contained in a confusion matrix (CM), which contains information about the real and the classified data. From the CM the overall accuracy (OA) of the classification can be computed, which is the overall percentage of correctly classified pixels, and also by a more significant measure, the *kappa* index (κ) [22], a measure of how far from chance are the classification results.

Table 1. Classification rates obtained on the test set

Methods	TM		TCT		PCA		LDA		ICA	
	κ	OA	κ	OA	κ	OA	κ	OA	κ	OA
Unsupervised										
SOM	.720	79.5	.683	76.5	.733	80.3	.744	81.1	.687	76.8
FC	.580	64.8	.670	75.2	.684	76.1	.695	77.2	.657	74.0
Supervised										
1-NN	.738	80.6	.762	82.4	.757	82.1	.759	82.2	.754	81.8
10-NN	.785	84.2	.796	85.0	.799	85.3	.797	85.1	.786	84.3
MLP-20n	.776	83.7	.786	84.3	.797	85.1	.787	84.4	.780	84.0
MLP-20,10n	.770	83.2	.785	84.3	.801	85.4	.785	84.3	.783	84.1
RBF	.756	82.3	.772	83.4	.796	85.0	.778	83.8	.767	83.0
S-SOM	.754	82.1	.786	84.3	.787	84.4	.790	84.7	.760	82.5
SVM-gk	**.797**	**85.2**	**.803**	**85.6**	**.804**	**85.7**	**.803**	**85.6**	**.798**	**85.2**
SVM-lk	.785	84.3	.795	85.0	.788	84.5	.795	85.0	.794	84.9
SVM-pk	.794	84.9	.802	85.5	.803	85.6	**.803**	**85.6**	**.798**	**85.2**
SVM-sk	.778	83.8	.725	79.8	.767	82.9	.756	82.1	.727	79.9
Average	.753	81.5	.764	82.6	.776	83.5	.774	83.41	.757	82.14

Each one of the 5 test sets (TM, TCT, PCA, ICA and LDA) was classified 12 times. The OA and κ values obtained are presented in Table 1. From the perspective of the data sets used in the classification, the ones with a better mean value for the 12 methods are PCA, LDA and TCT, and at the lower end, ICA and TM. On the other hand, the analysis of the results shows that the supervised approaches gives always better results than the unsupervised ones for all five input data sets. It is possible to rank the methods into 3 groups, according to their κ values: the best (SVM-gk, SVM-pk, 10-NN, SVM-lk), the intermediate (MLP-20n,MLP-20,10n, RBF, 1-NN, SVM-sk) and the worst (SOM and FC). Moreover, the κ mean values obtained fall in the top of the interval of the average κ reported in [1] of 0.6557 with a standard deviation of 0.1980. A more detailed analysis, at class level, is naturally highly desirable to better understand what errors are being committed/ommitted. The classification rates per individual class (in percentage) obtained for the PCA data set are presented in Table 2. There are 3 classes always extremely well classified no matter what the classification method is (WAT, PEU, BAR, >95%), 1 very well classified (VEG, $\approx$>85%), 2 averagely classified (COR, MIX, >65%) and one very badly classified (OLI, $\approx$16%). This behaviour is easily explained by the low spatial resolution (1 pixel is 900 m^2 on the ground): while WAT, PEU and BAR ocuppy large regions, olives, for instance, are trees that present a typical spatial pattern arranged along lines and rows with standard distances between adjacent trees, whose canopies rarely touch each other, producing a high mixture with bare or mixed soil. The same applies for cork-oak trees but with less importance, since the canopies of these trees are larger and the mixture with other classes is lower. Thus, the confusion occurs mainly between OLI and COR and MIX with a direct

Table 2. Classification rates (%) by class on the PCA test set

Methods	VEG	BAR	WAT	OLI	PEU	COR	MIX
Unsupervised							
SOM	88	93	99	27	96	50	55
FC	78	90	100	22	87	39	70
Supervised							
1-NN	87	93	99	35	96	56	61
10-NN	88	96	100	31	98	64	71
MLP-20n	86	95	100	10	98	74	77
MLP-20n,10n	87	94	100	11	98	75	77
RBF	86	96	100	8	98	76	74
S-SOM	86	98	100	15	98	67	69
SVM-gk	86	96	100	14	99	71	79
SVM-gk	87	96	100	0	98	77	71
SVM-gk	86	96	100	13	99	71	79
SVM-gk	84	95	99	12	98	72	57
Average	85.8	94.8	99.8	16.5	96.9	66.0	70.0

relation between these classes: when the rate of one class is higher in a method, it produces a decrease on the other two classes.

5 Conclusions

Being aware of the influence of the characteristics of the surface under study (type, number and spatial arrangement of cover classes) and/or of the characteristics of the sensor used (spatial, spectral and temporal resolutions), the analysis of the results obtained hints at an advantage in working with a transformed data rather than with the data in its original form, even if with low significance differences, and in using a supervised approach rather than an unsupervised one for classification.

Overall, a clear limit appears for the performance of the methods due to the selection of the classes and their representation in the terrain, what we could call the mismatch between the definition of the pure classes and the real arrangement of the landscape elements on the terrain. This mismatch is mainly determined by the spatial resolution of the sensor. Here, the results of the soft methods (FC and S-SOM) have to be placed within context: It is precisely the soft methods the ones with the potential to overcome the mixing problem, by assigning degrees of membership to each pixel (when interpreted as degrees of abundance within pixel). Further analysis taking into account in situ mixing measures is required for a complete evaluation of the soft methods. In the meanwhile, we have just shown the potential of pattern recognition methods, some of them not yet broadly used in remote sensing, for the hard task at hand.

Acknowledgments. This work has been partially funded by EFDR funds through the Interreg IIIb - Atlantic area program within the project PIMHAI.

References

1. Wilkinson, G.G.: Results and implications of a study of fifteen years of satellite image classification experiments. IEEE Trans. Geosc. Rem. Sens. 43(3), 433–440 (2005)
2. Barata, T., Pina, P.: A morphological approach for feature space partitioning. IEEE Geosc. Rem. Sens. Lett. 3(1), 173–177 (2006)
3. Kauth, R.J., Thomas, G.S.: The tasselled cap. A graphic description of the spectral-temporal development of agricultural crops as seen by Landsat. Proc. Symp. Mach. Proc. Remotely Sensed Data, pp. 41–51, Purdue (1976)
4. Crist, E.P., Cicone, R.C.: Application of the tasselled cap concept to simulated Thematic Mapper data Photogram. Eng. & Remote Sensing 50, 343–352 (1984)
5. Hotelling, H.: Analysis of a complex of statistical variables into principal components. J. Educ. Psychol. 24, 417–441, 498–520 (1933)
6. Comon, P.: Independent Component Analysis - a new concept? Signal Processing 36, 287–314 (1994)
7. Fisher, R.A.: The use of multiple measures in taxonomic problems. Annals of Eugenics 7, 179–188 (1936)
8. Kohonen, T.: Self-organizing map. Springer, Heidelberg (1997)
9. Kohonen, T.: Self-organization and associative memory. Springer, Heidelberg (1988)
10. Babuska, R.: Fuzzy modelling for control. Kluwer Acad. Pub, Norwell (1998)
11. Gustafson, D.E., Kessel, W.C.: Fuzzy clustering with a fuzzy covariance matrix. In: Proc. IEEE CDC, San Diego, pp. 761–766 (1979)
12. Fix, E., Hodges, J.L.: Discriminatory analysis, non-parametric discrimination. Technical report, USAF School of Aviation Medicine, Randolf Field,Tex. Project 21-49-004, Rept. 4, Contract AF41(128)-31 (1951)
13. Rosenblatt, F.: Principles of Neurodynamics. Spartan, New York (1962)
14. Werbos, P.J.: Beyond regression: New tools for prediction and analysis in the behavorial sciences. Master's thesis, Harvard University (1974)
15. Parker, D.B.: Learning logic. Invention report s81-64, file 1. Technical report, Office of Technology Licensing, Stanford University, Stanford (1982)
16. Rumelhart, D.E., Hinton, G.E., Williams, R.J.: Learning internal representations by error propagation. In: Rumelhart, D.E., McClelland, J.L. (eds.) Parallel Distributed Processing: Explorations in the Microstructure of Cognition, vol. 1, MIT Press, Cambridge (1986)
17. Broomhead, D.S, Lowe, D.: Multivariate functional interpolation and adaptive networks. Complex Systems 2, 321–355 (1988)
18. Tou, J.T., González, R.C.: Pattern Recognition. Addison Wesley, Reading, London, UK (1974)
19. Haykin, S.: Neural Networks: A Comprehensive Foundation. Prentice-Hall, Upper Saddle River (1994)
20. Martín-Herrero, J., Ferreiro-Armán, M., Alba-Castro, J.L.: Grading Textured Surfaces with Automated Soft Clustering in a Supervised SOM, pp. 323–330. Springer, Heidelberg (2004)
21. Vapnik, V.N.: The Nature of Statistical Learning Theory. Springer, Heidelberg, NY (1995)
22. Landis, J.R., Koch, G.G.: The measurement of observer agreement for categorical data. Biometrics 33, 159–174 (1977)

A Robust Audio Fingerprint's Based Identification Method

Jérôme Lebossé[1], Luc Brun[2], and Jean-Claude Pailles[1]

[1] France Telecom R&D
[2] University of Caen

Abstract. An Audio fingerprint is a small digest of an audio file computed from its main perceptual properties. Like human fingerprints, audio fingerprints allow to identify an audio file among a set of candidates without retrieving any other characteristics. We propose in this paper a fingerprint extraction algorithm based on a new audio segmentation method. A new scoring function based on q-grams is used to determine if an input signal is a derivated version of a fingerprint stored in the database. A rule based on this scoring function allows to either recover the original input file or to decide that no fingerprint belonging to the database corresponds to the signal. The proposed method is robust against compression and time shifting alterations of audio files.

1 Introduction

Audio fingerprint [5,1,2] aims at defining a small signature from a content based on its perceptual properties. This fingerprint allows to identify an audio file from a short sample, so the fingerprint should be composed of elementary keys (called sub-fingerprints) based on small parts of the signal computed continuously along the signal. In order to correctly identify fingerprint methods have to be robust against alterations (compression, cuts,...). Two audio files, one defined from the other using such alterations, are called *co-derivatives* [4]. Furthermore, the computational cost of a fingerprint system should thus be low and the size of the fingerprint should thus be small in order to be intergrated into a mobile device.

The first step of a fingerprint algorithm consists in extracting a sequence of intervals from the signal. The usual method [5,1] consists on decomposing the signal into a sequence of overlapping intervals called frames but is sensitive to time-shifting (Section4). This drawback is attenuated but not overcomed by the use of overlapping frames. On the other hand, onsets detection [3] methods try to find particular positions within the signal but doesn't insure sufficient intervals detected in a short sample to allow identification. The second step consists on associating to each interval a value (sub-fingerprint) which characterises it. Haitsma [5] uses a decomposition of the spectrum of each frame into bands and defines a 32 bits sub-fingerprint from the sign of the energy bands differences. Then, the recognition task consists on comparing an input fingerprint to a fingerprints database and deciding if it is considered, or not, as a co-derivative of

J. Martí et al. (Eds.): IbPRIA 2007, Part I, LNCS 4477, pp. 185–192, 2007.

one stored. Hoad [4] uses an approximate string matching technique which computes the similarity between two strings as the minimum of operations needed to transform one string into an other.

In this paper, we first describe our fingerprint construction scheme in Section 2. The proposed recognition scheme is described in Section 3. The robustness and efficiency of these two steps are then shown by experiments in Section 4.

2   A Robust Fingerprint Extraction Method

The basic idea of our method is to combine the respective advantages of Enframing and Onset methods by selecting a small time intervals within a larger one. The small interval allows the detection of characteristic parts of the signal whereas the larger interval insures a minimum selection rate of intervals.This process could be decomposed into two steps (Figure 1). First, an interval, called the Observation Interval (I_o) typically equal to few hundredths of seconds is set at the beginning of the waveform. Then, the waveform inside I_o is divided into shorter overlapping sub-intervals of a few millisecond, called Energy Intervals (I_e). The energy of each I_e interval is computed by taking the mean of the samples amplitude within the interval. The interval I_e with a maximal energy (I_{emax}) within I_o is then selected. Given an I_{emax} interval, the begining of the next I_o interval is set to the end of I_{emax} (Figure1). The distance between the centers of two I_{emax} intervals lies thus between I_{emax} and I_o-I_{emax}.

Given a sequence of detected I_{emax} intervals, sub-fingerprint values should be computed in order to build the fingerprint. We first explored [6] a construction scheme which associates to each I_{emax} interval a sub fingerprint value using an improved method of the one of Haitsma [5]. However, such a fingerprint construction scheme implies the sequential application of the segmentation and sub-fingerprint computation processes. The number of common sub-fingerprints between two co-derivative signals is thus equal to the number of sub-fingerprints which have been detected and then computed without any error. As shown by our experiments (Section 4) this additional step computation decreases significantly

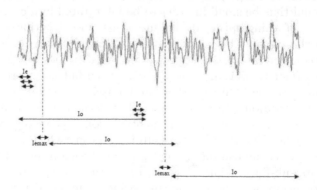

Fig. 1. Audio Segmentation Method

the number of common sub-fingerprints between two co-derivatives signals. We thus use an approach similar to the one of Hoad [4] and define the sequence of sub-fingerprint values as the gap (in ms) between two following I_{emax} intervals. The performance of our fingerprint extraction algorithm is thus the one of our segmentation step. Moreover, using the values of I_o and I_e chosen in our experiments (Section 4), each sub-fingerprint may be stored on 14 bits instead of the 32 bits required by the method of Haitsma.

3   Fingerprint Recognition

Approximate string matching appears to be a natural distance between co-derivative contents fingerprints when sub-fingerprints may be added or removed. However, the time required to compare an input signal with all the fingerprints of the database is unacceptable for database sizes used within the fingerprint recognition framework. One common solution consists to filter the database using q-grams. The computation of common q-grams between two strings is indeed more efficient than the string matching requiring editing operation. As shown below the probability that two strings share n_q q-grams decreases drastically for $n_q > 0$ when the size of the alphabet on which the fingerprints are built is large. Since the number of sub-fingerprints used within our method (i.e. the size of our alphabet) is equal to 2^{14}, we use this last property in order to avoid the computation of string edit distances. The basic idea of our fingerprint recognition method consists on computing a score proportional to the amount of information brought by the existence of common q grams between two fingerprints.

More formally, given an alphabet of size s, let us consider random fingerprints generated by drawning independently the sub-fingerprints with an uniform distribution $\frac{1}{s}$. Given two fingerprints, we denote by X_q the random variable corresponding to the number of common q grams between two fingerprints and n_q one realisation of X_q. Let us define $Q(n_{min}, \ldots, n_{max}) = p(X_{min} = n_{min} \ldots \& X_{max} = n_{max})$ the probability that the event $X_{min} = n_{min} \& \ldots \& X_{max} = n_{max}$ occurs between the two fingerprints. The symbol min denotes the minimal length of q grams considered by the score function while max is the longuest common q-grams of the two fingerprints. Our aim is to define a score function which is in $\mathcal{O}(-\log_2(Q(n_{min}, \ldots, n_{max}))$.

Let us first consider the simpler case where only one length of q grams is considered. Nicodème [7] has shown that the law of probability of X_q may be efficiently approximated by an urn and balls model where each of the s^q urns is associated to one q gram. Given two fingerprints of size n and m one thrown n white balls and m black balls, the number of common q-grams X_q between two fingerprints may be modeled as the number of urns containing simultaneously white and black balls. In the same article, Nicodème shows that the total variation distance[1] between the Poisson law of X_q and a gaussian law is always bounded. Moreover, the law of X_q converges to a gaussian when the Poisson law

---

[1] The total variation distance between two positive integer random variables of respective probability functions f_n and g_n is the sum $\sum_n |f_n - g_n|$

modeling parameters X_q tends to infinity. We can thus approximate the law of X_q using the Gaussian law with μ the mean and σ the standard deviation of X_q.:

$$p(X_q = n_q) = \frac{1}{\sqrt{2\pi}\sigma} e^{-\frac{(n_q-\mu)^2}{2\sigma^2}} \qquad (1)$$

If a uniform probability is used to model the distribution of q grams, we deduce from [7] after some calculus that:

$$\begin{cases} \mu = nmp + \mathcal{O}(p^2) \\ \sigma = nmp + \mathcal{O}(p^2) \end{cases} \qquad (2)$$

where $p = \frac{1}{s^q}$. Since, in our application $s = 2^{14}$ and n_q is an integer, the parameter μ may be neglected in equation 1. As mentioned previously in this section, the probability $p(X_q = n_q)$ decreases drastically when s becomes large and $n_q > 0$.

Let us now consider q-grams of length i and j with $i > j$ between two fingerprints. Each i-gram induces $i-j+1$ j-grams between the two fingerprints. Therefore, the existence of n_i i-grams between the two fingerprints induces $n_i(i-j+1)$ j-grams between these fingerprints. Given, the number n_j of j-grams we consider that the event relative to the apparition of the $n_j - n_i(i-j+1)$ remaining j-gram is independent of the event having produced the n_i i-gram. We have thus:

$$\forall i > j \quad p(X_j = n_j | X_i = n_i) = p(X_j = n_j - n_i(i-j+1)) \qquad (3)$$

This last relation is only an approximation of the real case where the different q-grams are not independent. However, this approach is consistent with the model used by Nicodème where the different q-grams are considered as independent. Using equation 3, if we iterate the Bayes relationship $max - min$ times on $Q(n_{min}, \ldots, n_{max})$ we obtain:

$$Q(n_{min}, \ldots, n_{max}) = \Pi_{i=min}^{max} p(X_i = u_i)$$

with $u_{max} = n_{max}, u_{max-1} = n_{max-1} - 2u_{max}$, $u_i = n_i - \sum_{j=i+1}^{max} \alpha_{i,j} u_i$ and $\alpha_{i,j} = i - j + 1$.

The expression $-\log_2(Q(n_{min}, \ldots, n_{max}))$ may thus be written as:

$$-\sum_{i=min}^{max} \log_2(p(X_i = u_i)) = \frac{1}{2}\log_2(e) \sum_{i=min}^{max} \frac{u_i^2}{\sigma_i^2} + \frac{1}{2} \sum_{i=min}^{max} \log_2(2\pi\sigma_i)$$

where σ_i denotes the standard deviation of X_i. Note that the mean of X_i (equation 2) is neglected in the above equation.

Since the second term of the above equation is independent of $(n_i)_{i \in \{min, \ldots, max\}}$ and that we are only searching for an asymptotic approximation of $-\log_2(Q(n_{min}, \ldots, n_{max}))$ we define our score $S(n_{min}, \ldots, n_{max})$ between two fingerprints as :

$$S(n_{min}, \ldots, n_{max}) = \sum_{i=min}^{max} \frac{u_i^2}{\sigma_i^2} = \frac{1}{(mn)^2} \sum_{i=min}^{max} u_i^2 s^{2i} \qquad (4)$$

where each σ_i has been replaced by its first order term $nm\frac{1}{s^i}$ (equation 2).

Since $u_i << s$, if we forget the factor $\frac{1}{mn}$, our scoring function may be understood as the value of the number $(0, \ldots, 0, u_{min}, \ldots, u_{max})$ in base s^2. Equation 4, provides us a measure of the similarity between two fingerprints which allows to weight the information concerning the number of q-grams of different length. However, for a practical implentation, due to the large value of $s = 2^{14}$, equation 4 may return values which exceed the storage capacities. We therefore consider a practical implementation of $S(n_{min}, \ldots, n_{max})$ defined as:

$$S_{prat}(n_{min}, \ldots, n_{max}) = \frac{1}{(mn)^2} \sum_{i=min}^{max} u_i^2 b^i \tag{5}$$

where $b < s$ is defined from our experiments (section 4) in order to not induce overflow errors while being as large as possible to remain valid the basic idea of computing the value of the number $(0, \ldots, 0, n_{min}, \ldots, n_{max})$ on a large base.

4   Experiments

Our database contains more than 300 songs of approximately 4 minutes each. All songs were subjected to an MP3 encoding/decoding at various rates and shifted by adding silence of various lengths at the beginning of each song. The size of the intervals I_e and I_o being set to 1 and 100 milliseconds, the minimum and maximum detection rates of $I_e max$ intervals during one second are respectively equals to 10 and 1000 (Section 2). The mean detection rate measured by exeepriments on the whole database is equal to 21.9 with a standard deviation of 3.5. Since each sub-fingerprint is stored on 14 bits, the size required by our method to store one minute of signal is equal to $21.9 * (14/8) * 60 = 2.3$ Kilo Bytes. On the other hand, the method of Haitsma required 20.5 kb. Then, confirmed by experiments, the size of the fingerprints used by our method is thus approximately 9 times lower than the ones of Haitsma.

4.1   Fingerprint Extraction Evaluation

In order to evaluate the performances of our algorithm, let us denote by T_i the set of intervals used to compute the sub-fingerprints of a signal s_i. Defining the set $SV_i \subset SI_i$ of intervals having a same location and a same sub-fingerprint value within s_i and its co-derivative version and N the number of audio files of the database, the recognition rate is defined by :

$$RR = \frac{1}{N} \sum_{i=1}^{N} \frac{|SV_i|}{|T_i|} \tag{6}$$

All the original wav audio files of our database are thus encoded using 705 $Kbps$. In our experiments, all these audio files have been encoded at the 48, 64, 96, 128, 192 and 256 $Kbps$ compression bite rates.

The top level curve of Figure 2 ($\cdots$) represents the recognition rates obtained by our method against various compression rates and thus allows to evaluate the

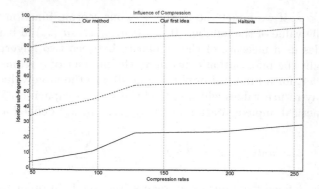

Fig. 2. Common values rates when comparing an audio file with its compressed version (at 48, 64, 96, 128, 192 and 256 Kbps)

robustness of our segmentation process. The second (- -) curve of Figure 2 represents the recognition rate obtained by our first idea of fingerprint construction scheme combined with our segmentation method (Section 2). The last curve of Figure 2 (—) shows the recognition rate obtained by the method of Haitsma (equation 6). As shown by Figure 2, the best ratio obtained by the method of Haitsma is equal to 30% for an encoding at $256Kbps$. This ratio decreases to 5% for an encoding at $48Kbps$. The best performance obtained by the method of Haitsma is thus largely lower than the worse one obtained by our method(-*-).

The greater robustness of our method against compression compared to the one of Haitsma may be explained by the following reasons : the segmentation process is done on the signal important peaks which are less sensible to the degradations induced by compression than other parts of the signal with few information. Furthermore, as explained in Section 3, the sequence of values defined by the gap between two I_{emax} intervals avoid the recognition rate decrease when using our first idea based on an improved version of the Haitsma algorithm.

We also add a silence of 1, 2, 3, 5 and 6.25 ms at the beginning of each signal to evaluate the influence of time shifting on our fingerprint extraction algorithm. We note that the number of detected I_{emax} intervals remains constant at 99% for any shift value and even for higher time-shift (10, 25 and 50 ms). This 1% error is generated by the influence of the shift operation on the position of the interval on which the two fingerprints become synchronised. On the other hand, the total recognition rates of the method of Haitsma decreases strongly when the first shift is introduced (to 71%) and then keeps on decreasing approximatly linearly until a rate of 33% for a shift of $6.25ms$.

4.2   Fingerprint Recognition

For experiments, 5 seconds digests has been taken randomly in each audio content of the database and then compressed at 128 kbps. Then, the fingerprint of each compressed digest has been computed to be identified. To evaluate the relevance of using q-grams, the Figure 3 below shows the mean length and number of q-grams shared between each query fingerprints and all those of the database.

The first line (1st) of the Figure 3 represents the mean number of shared q-grams of length q between our queries and the associated original fingerprint within the database. The second and third lines (2nd and 3rd) represent the mean number of common q-grams between our queries and the database fingerprints ranked second and third using our scoring function (Section 3). These fingerprints correspond for each query to the most similar false positives according to our scoring function. Figure3 shows that the number of q-grams of the false positives is significantly lower than the one obtained by the original fingerprint. Moreover, the length of commmon q-grams does not exceed 8 with false positives while the original fingerprint share usually much longer q-grams with the query.

Q-grams length	4	5	6	7	8	9	10
1st	13	3.65	1.54	1.15	0.81	0.55	0.46
2nd	9.2	2.19	0.17	0.03	0	0	0
3rd	5.5	0.96	0.09	0	0	0	0

Fig. 3. Mean number of common q-grams between a compressed fingerprint and the first three fingerprints of our database ranked decreasingly according to our scoring function

Figure 4 shows statistics obtained by our scoring function (Section 3) on the whole database using our queries. As mentioned, the length of our alphabet $s = 2^{14}$ may induce overflow errors. So, for our experiments, we use $b = 5$ in equation 5. The value of $q_{m}in$ has been set to 3 in these experiments. The first to fourth candidated in Table 4 correspond to the first 4 database fingerprints ranked decreasingly according to the score. In all our experiments, the original fingerprints is the one with the highest score. Therefore the score of the second fingerprint corresponds to the score that would be obtained if the fingerprint associated to the query was removed from the database. The ratio represented in the last three columns correspond to the ratio of the score respectively obtained by the first and the second candidate, the second and the third and the third and the fourth. For each column, the min, max and mean value are computed.

As shown by Figure 4, the minimal score obtained by an original content is lower than the maximal score obtained by a wrong candidate. Therefore a basic threshold on the score is not sufficient to decide if a query belongs to the database. However, in all our experiments the fingerprint associated to the query obtains a much higher score than the second fingerprint while the second to fourth fingerprints obtain roughly equivalent scores. This result is illustrated by the minimal ratio 1st/2nd on Table 4 which should be compared to the ratios of the two last columns. Therefore a combination of the threshold on the scores and the ratio allows to select the best candidate within the database and to decide if it's a co-derivative from the input. For example, a threshold on the

Scores	Candidates			Ratio	
	1st	2nd	3rd	1st/2nd	2nd/3rd
Min	28750	3125	625	199.8	1
Mean	1832.10^6	3475	1877	1113.10^6	1.48
Max	4294.10^6	188750	162500	4294.10^6	23

Fig. 4. Statistics of our scoring function computed over the database

minimal scores of 25000 and a threshold on the minimal ratio of 150 allows us to perform the good decision for all the queries of the database.

5 Conclusions

We have presented in this paper a new audio fingerprint extraction method based on an audio segmentation algorithm associated with a new scoring function based on q-grams. The segmentation algorithm determines important peaks within the signal while insuring a relatively constant detection rate. The sub-fingerprints are thus defined by the gap between two successive detected intervals. The scoring function is based on the number and lenght of common q-grams between two fingerprints. In all our experiments, the co-derivative fingerprint of the input is always ranked first and the rule designed from our scoring function allows us to decide if no database's fingerprint may be considered as a co-derivative of the input. In future work we plan to improve the indexation scheme of our database according to the use of q-grams performed by our scoring function.

References

1. Burges, J.P.C., Jana, S.: Distorsion discriminant analysis for audio fingerprinting. IEEE Transactions on Speech and Audio Processing 11(3), 165–174 (2003)
2. Doets, P., Gisbert, M., Lagendijk, R.: On the comparison of audio fingerprints for extracting quality parameters of compressed audio. In: Proc. of SPIE (February 2006)
3. Hainsworth, S., Macleod, M.: Onset detection in musical audio signals. In: Proc. of the International Computer Music Conference, Singapore (September 2003)
4. Hoad, T.C.: Video Representations for Effective Retrieval From Large Collections. PhD thesis, RMIT University, Melbourne, Australia (2004)
5. Kalker, T., Haitsma, J.: A highly robust audio fingerprinting system. In: Proceedings of ISMIR'2002, pp. 144–148 (2002)
6. Lebossé, J., Brun, L., Pailles, J.C.: Fingerprint audio robuste pour la gestion de droits. In: Actes de CORESA 2006, Caen (November 2006)
7. Nicodeme, P.: Q-grams analysis and urn models. In: Proceedings of Discrete Random Walks DRW, pp. 243–258 (2003)

Development of a Methodology for Automated Crater Detection on Planetary Images

Lourenço P.C. Bandeira, José Saraiva, and Pedro Pina

CERENA - Instituto Superior Técnico, Lisboa, Portugal

Abstract. This paper presents a methodology for the automated detection of impact craters on images of planetary surfaces. This modular approach includes a phase of candidate selection, followed by template matching and finally the analysis of a probability volume that allows for the identification of craters on the image. It is applied to a set of images of the surface of the planet Mars, with results that are very promising, in face of future improvements in the methodology.

1 Introduction

The continuing exploration of the Solar System by automated probes leads to the acquisition of large numbers of images of the surfaces of planets and satellites. The amount of information contained in these images grows at a faster rate than the availability of human operators to analyze them and to extract from them the relevant data for the characterization of the planetary body under scrutiny. When it comes to understanding the geological history of a planet, the study of impact craters (their density, patterns and morphology) assumes a capital importance. These features come in all sizes, but their numbers generally increase as we probe smaller dimensions (as a result of the availability of images with better spacial resolution). Plus, their identification by human operators is a time-consuming endeavor, time that could be applied to the analysis and interpretation of data, if the detection of craters (their location and dimension) was achieved through a trustworthy automated procedure. The creation of such an automated method for impact crater detection in images of planetary surfaces is a goal that has been pursued by several teams in recent years. The size of the challenge posed by this problem can be evaluated by the fact that, as yet, there is no reliable methodology that can be applied to all situations and produce an acceptable result (that is, one that fits inside the margin of error associated to human analysis of images). Among the different approaches worthy of mention, some have used template matching [1], [2], [3], [4], others employed texture analysis [5], [6], one applied the Hough transform [7] and another developed genetic algorithms for the identification of craters [8]. Still other works were more concerned with specific situations, such as modeling small bodies of the Solar System [9] or developing navigational systems [10] for automated probes. However, the results presented were far from being good enough to convince the planetary science community to adopt any of these approaches.

J. Martí et al. (Eds.): IbPRIA 2007, Part I, LNCS 4477, pp. 193–200, 2007.
© Springer-Verlag Berlin Heidelberg 2007

2   Methodology

An automated procedure for the identification of impact craters is proposed in this paper. It follows a sequential approach, intended to deal with the problems involved, step by step. Thus, there is a first phase in which the areas that correspond to crater rims are identified in a gray level image, while most of the noise present is eliminated. The binary image of these candidate areas is then submitted to a template matching procedure, using the Fast Fourier Transform (FFT), which leads to the construction of a probability volume, a three-dimensional matrix that can be analyzed to determine the location, dimension and associated probability to the impact craters present in a given image. This approach associates a number of techniques in the field of image processing, and is thought to conduce to results that can be acceptable for the purpose of planetary mapping. The final goal of the methodology is to constitute, after thorough development and testing, a tool capable of general application, in any area of a planet or satellite that is captured in image, whatever the geomorphological setting, the sensor and the conditions of illumination.

In this paper, in the context of its development, the methodology is applied and tested on a set of 38 images of the surface of the planet Mars, covering a non-contiguous surface area of a little more than 500 000 km^2. These images were all obtained by the MOC camera, on board the Mars Global Surveyor probe; all of them are wide-angle images, presenting a spatial resolution of around 250 meters per pixel. At this stage in the development of the methodology it was decided that it should be applied to areas with common characteristics; hence, the images were chosen from three regions (Fig. 1) that were classified in [11] as "Hprg - Ridged plains material"; this is the basal rock-stratigraphic unit of the Hesperian System, it closely resembles lunar maria (presenting a similar crater density), and it is interpreted as volcanic flows. The selection was conducted with the help of MIMS [12]. There are a number of well-defined constraints on the use of the methodology; for instance, there is no search for craters whose radius is smaller than 5 pixels.

2.1   Candidate Selection

Impact craters are features that show a roughly circular shape. Their contours are topographically marked by elevated rims, which produce shadows; the length of these is a function of the (generally low) angle of illumination chosen for image acquisition, and of a host of other factors, such as the occurrence of a number of processes that degrade the original shape of impact craters. Thus, the shadows are far from regular, and can even, in extreme cases, be absent; this does not constitute a problem for a human analyst, who will readily identify most impact craters on gray-level images of planetary surfaces. However, for a machine running an algorithm, the presence of a coupled pair of shadows (one on the inner flank of the crater, the other, 180 degrees away, on the outer flank) on

Fig. 1. Location of the three areas from which the images used in this paper were selected. Credits of global map: MOLA science team.

an image can be taken as signaling the probable presence of a crater. If shadows are thus taken as indicators of probable craters, all areas that can be equated with shadows produced by rims should be separated from the rest of the image, and enhanced, so that the template matching procedure is applied to the most promising areas of the image, saving computational time. This rationale led to the adoption of a pre-processing step in the methodology, following the lines presented in [13]. This involves the scanning of the image by a 3 × 3 matrix; though this looks simple, it carries out, in fact, a local analysis of the texture of the image that achieves excellent results, considering the problem that it is designed to answer. It may look at first glance like an edge detection procedure, but it must be stressed that its aim is to point out (identify and enhance) the best candidates for the application of the following step in the methodology, and not to directly locate the edges of craters. In fact, the most common of edge detection operators (such as Canny, Sobel, and others) do not achieve good results for the purpose in view, under the automated conditions which are fundamental for an effective use of the methodology. What this means is that the traditional methods need to be fine tuned to each image to be fully effective, and such an approach is in direct opposition to the major goal of the methodology: to identify impact craters with no human intervention from the moment the original image is fed into the machine. The advantages of the automated approach deserve to be numbered: it does not require human intervention; it is fast, and does not require a global analysis of the image to be effective; it keeps all crater candidates in the binary image it produces, even those that are below the stated limit of detection; and, not the least important, it greatly reduces the noise in the image. Thus, it fulfills its aim, and provides a binary image that can be used in the next phase of the methodology. An example can be seen on Fig. 2.

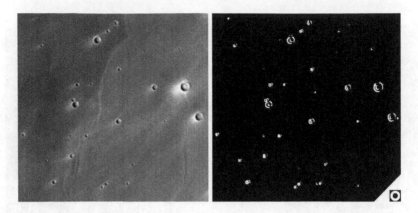

Fig. 2. Example of candidate selection on the MOC wide angle image M07-05420 (NASA/JPL/MSSS). Inset is a crater model for use as template (following section).

2.2   Template Matching

In this case, the classic problem in scene analysis can be stated as follows: there is the need to locate a given feature, an impact crater, in a binary scene image that was obtained in a previous phase of the application of the methodology. To begin with, a simplified binary model of the wanted feature is created to serve as template for the search; this should of course be a circular shape, but it must incorporate a thickness that can deal with the irregularity of the natural shapes of impact craters. Hence, the binary template employed in this phase of the methodology presents a white crown surrounded by a square of black background, such as can be seen in the inset of Fig. 2. This is cross-correlated with the scene image, and a measure of similarity between the pair is computed, as in [14]. The FFT was adopted for that purpose [15]; this is a method which works in the frequency domain, and is widely employed, being much less demanding in computational resources than, for instance, the Hough Transform. The correlations between the scene image and a series of templates are computed; the radii of the templates start at the already mentioned inferior limit of 5 pixels, and go to a chosen maximum (in this paper, 100 pixels). The resulting values must be comparable, or independent of the radius of the corresponding template. To achieve this, they are normalized between 0 and 1; this is easily accomplished by dividing the correlation value by the number of white pixels in the template, which is a function of the radius of the crown. Each of the resulting values can be taken as the probability that a given pixel is the centre of a crater with a radius r. Thus, to each pixel of the image is associated a number n of probability values that correspond to the range in radii considered. All this information is collected in a three-dimensional matrix or probability volume, $P(u, v|r)$, consisting of n planes, each containing $u \times v$ elements (the number of pixels in the scene image), such as can be seen in Fig. 3.

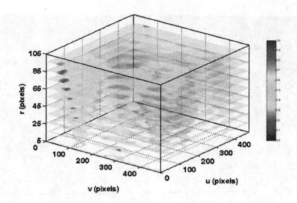

Fig. 3. Perspective view of an example of probability volume, showing several planes corresponding to different radii

2.3   Crater Detection

The identification of impact craters on an image is achieved through the analysis of the probability volume created as a result of the template matching procedure followed in the previous phase. A crater has a characteristic shape that produces an identifiable signature in the volume of data; thus, the internal structure of the volume can be probed to locate the most likely locations of craters. The first step consists in the identification of the regional maxima [16], considering the three-dimensional connectivity, in which each pixel is surrounded by six neighbors; this is followed by a culling phase in which all maxima that are below a certain threshold t_1 (in this paper, 30%) are considered to be too weak to correspond to a crater and, thus, eliminated. After this, a two-dimensional object is built around each of the surviving maxima, incorporating all the pixels whose value is at least 60% of the maximum under consideration. A binary image is thus obtained for each value of radius (plane of the volume) that shows at least one maximum. Next, a mathematical morphology operator, namely an area opening [16], is applied to these binary images. Its purpose is to remove the connected components whose area is smaller than a given proportion of r, which are taken to be too small to be markers of craters. After this, the roundness of the remaining objects is analyzed. For this purpose, a classic circularity index, $CI = 4\pi Area/Perimeter^2$, is employed. Again, there is the need to eliminate those objects whose roundness is below a given threshold, as they do not correspond to regions where craters are likely to exist. At the end of this treatment, the point with coordinates (u, v) where the maximum is located within each surviving object is considered to be the centre of a crater with radius r and an associated probability p. This probability can be thought of as the confidence level of the detection made. The process is applied to all the planes of the volume in which maxima occur; the end result is an image where craters of different dimension are plotted.

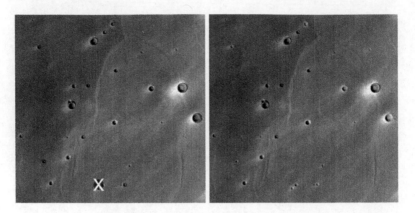

Fig. 4. Crater detection on image M07-05420 for probability thresholds of 30% (on the left) and 70% (on the right). False detections are indicated by an X.

3   Results

One way to quantitatively assess the results of the methodology is to compare the numbers of impact craters that are detected on the chosen set of images, both by the automated methodology and by visual inspection. In Fig. 4, the automated detection of craters in image MOC M07-05420 is illustrated. A total of 23 impact craters, with a radius larger than 5 pixels, were visually detected (VD) in this image. The figure clearly shows how the results obtained depend on the probability level that is chosen. Thus, on the left, for a probability level of 30% there are 18 true detections (TD), which means that 5 craters are missed; this represents a 78.3% success rate. There is one false detection (FD), representing 5.3% of all the detected craters. On the right, a higher probability level, 70%, eliminates the false detection but there are only 11 true detections, bringing the success rate down to 47.8%.

For a global analysis there are two indicators that can be computed:

$$TDR_p = \frac{TD_p}{VD} \cdot 100 \, . \tag{1}$$

$$FDR_p = \frac{FD_p}{TD_p + FD_p} \cdot 100 \, . \tag{2}$$

where TDR_p and FDR_p are, respectively, the true detection rate and the false detection rate, for a given probability, p. These were plotted for the complete set of images in Fig. 5, showing how the number of detections evolves with the variation of the associated degree of confidence. At a 30% probability threshold (PT), 84.2% of a total of 431 impact craters visually detected on the whole set of images were correctly identified. However, at this low level of confidence, the false detection rate is also at its peak, 19.0%. Though both rates fall with increasing probability, the FDR has a sharper decrease, illustrated by the fact that at a PT of 40% the TDR is still at 79.4% while the FDR is already a mere 7.3%. Obviously, a certain PT must be chosen in order to present a definite detection result for an image. This choice should be made according to the trade-off between TD and FD that the operator is prepared to accept in view of his objectives.

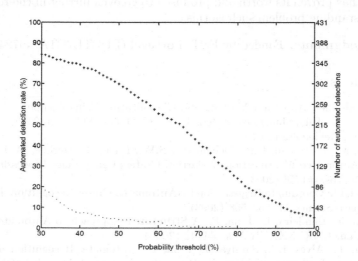

Fig. 5. Graphic illustrating the evolution of the rates for both true detections (+) and false detections (.) with increasing values of the probability threshold

4 Future Work

There are a number of intermediate steps that need to be thoroughly tested and optimized, so that they are unaffected by the characteristics of the image. The need for further testing, with images obtained by diverse sensors and with different spatial resolution, is also easy to recognize. The introduction of a verification phase, in which the marked craters will be locally assessed by a mathematical morphology operator, is planned. This should lead to the elimination of most false detections, thus allowing, in turn, for the survival of more candidates through the process of crater detection by analysis of the probability volume. In this manner, the risk of missing any true craters will be minimized. The methodology will then be able to withstand testing in larger and more geomorphologically diversified settings, from Mars and other planetary bodies of the Solar System.

5 Conclusions

The purpose of the methodology presented in this paper is the creation of a tool for automated detection of impact craters in images of planetary surfaces, whatever their origin and spatial resolution. The methodology is still in development, and the successive versions have produced results that have been steadily improving in quantitative terms. Currently, our approach is producing one of the highest crater recognition rates (84.2%) and simultaneously one of the lowest false dections rate (19.0%) when compared to the similar published studies. Thus, it can be concluded that the approach followed, including diverse techniques from the field of image processing, and applying them in a well-designed sequence, has proven its worth and promises to go even further in the resolution of a long-standing problem such as this.

Acknowledgments. Funded by FCT, Portugal (PDCTE/CTA/49724/03).

References

1. Flores-Méndez, A.: Crater Marking and Classification Using Computer Vision. In: Sanfeliu, A., Ruiz-Shulcloper, J. (eds.) CIARP 2003. LNCS, vol. 2905, pp. 79–86. Springer, Heidelberg (2003)
2. Magee, M., Chapman, C.R., Dellenback, S.W., Enke, B., Merline, W.J., Rigney, M.P.: Automated Identification of Martian Craters Using Image Processing. LPSC XXXIV Abs. #1756 (2003)
3. Michael, G.: Coordinate Registration by Automated Crater Recognition. Planetary and Space Science 51, 563–568 (2003)
4. Saraiva, J., Bandeira, L., Pina, P.: A Structured Approach to Automated Crater Detection. LPSC XXXVII Abs. #1142 (2006)
5. Barata, T., Alves, E.I., Saraiva, J., Pina, P.: Automatic Recognition of Impact Craters on the Surface of Mars. In: Campilho, A., Kamel, M. (eds.) ICIAR 2004. LNCS, vol. 3212, pp. 489–496. Springer, Heidelberg (2004)
6. Kim, J.R., Muller, J.-P., van Gasselt, S., Morley, J.G., Neukum, G.: Automated Crater Detection, A New Tool for Mars Cartography and Chronology. Photogrammetric Engineering and Remote Sensing 71, 1205–1217 (2005)
7. Vinogradova, T., Burl, M., Mjolness, E.: Training of a Crater Detection Algorithm for Mars Crater Imagery. In: Proc. IEEE Aerospace Conference, vol. 7, pp. 3201–3211 (2002)
8. Plesko, C., Werner, S.C., Brumby, S.P., Asphaug, E.A., Neukum, G.: A Statistical Analysis of Automated Crater Counts in MOC and HRSC Data. LPSC XXXVII, Abs. #2012 (2006)
9. Leroy, B., Medioni, G.G., Johnson, E., Matthies, L.: Crater Detection for Autonomous Landing on Asteroids. Image and Vision Computing 19, 787–792 (2001)
10. Cheng, Y., Johnson, A.E., Matthies, L., Olson, C.F.: Optical Landmark Detection for Spacecraft Navigation. In: Proc. 13th AAS/AIAA Space Flight Mech. Meet (2003)
11. Scott, D.H., Carr, M.H.: Atlas of Mars (1:25000000). USGS, Denver (1978)
12. Alves, E.I., Vaz, D.: MIMS – A relational database of imagery on Mars. Computers & Geosciences, in press (2007)
13. Bandeira, L., Saraiva, J., Pina, P.: Enhancing Impact Crater Rims to Increase Recognition Rates. In: Proc. Int. Conf. Computer Vision Theory and Applications (2006)
14. Aggarwal, J.K., Davis, L.S., Martin, W.N.: Correspondence Process in Dynamic Scene Analysis. In: Proc. IEEE, vol. 69, pp. 562–572 (1981)
15. Frigo, M., Johnson, S.G.: FFTW: An Adaptive Software Architecture for the FFT. In: Proc. Int. Conf. Acoustics, Speech, and Signal Processing, vol. 3, pp. 1381–1384 (1998)
16. Soille, P.: Morphological image analysis. In: Principles and applications, Springer, Heidelberg (2003)

Rao-Blackwellized Particle Filter for Human Appearance and Position Tracking

Jesús Martínez-del-Rincón, Carlos Orrite-Uruñuela, and Grégory Rogez

CVLab, Aragon Institute for Engineering Research, University of Zaragoza, Spain

Abstract. In human motion analysis, the joint estimation of appearance, body pose and location parameters is not always tractable due to its huge computational cost. In this paper, we propose a Rao-Blackwellized Particle Filter for addressing the problem of human pose estimation and tracking. The advantage of the proposed approach is that Rao-Blackwellization allows the state variables to be splitted into two sets, being one of them analytically calculated from the posterior probability of the remaining ones. This procedure reduces the dimensionality of the Particle Filter, thus requiring fewer particles to achieve a similar tracking performance. In this manner, location and size over the image are obtained stochastically using colour and motion clues, whereas body pose is solved analytically applying learned human Point Distribution Models.

1 Introduction

Articulated body models have produced successful results for human body tracking [1,2,3,4]. These models represent the human body using a set of articulated sticks or patches, providing a useful tool for higher-order processes such as character animation or human gait analysis. Constraints and relationships between articulations and limbs can be modelled as geometrical equations, which involves a huge number of degrees of freedom. This gives an insight into the difficulty of using such an articulated model: the high dimensionality of the configuration space and the exponentially increasing computational cost that implies.

Full-body articulated modelling and tracking (either deterministic or stochastic) by unconstrained search through the complete space, are not viable because of the excessive computational complexity. Nevertheless, it is possible to tackle the problem by introducing prior assumptions about dynamics or view restrictions. Particle Filter has been shown to be a robust and powerful stochastic algorithm. Many modifications have been developed to reduce the dimensionality of the search space [5].

In contrast with stochastic methods, deterministic body models based on learning techniques relate automatically image observations with body poses, avoiding exhaustive space searches due to the knowledge of dependences and constraints of the human body. On the other hand, deterministic methods require some assumptions such as image location, viewpoint estimation, dynamic knowledge, to name a few. By contrast, these pre-requisites (or needed prior information) are known in stochastic methods.

J. Martí et al. (Eds.): IbPRIA 2007, Part I, LNCS 4477, pp. 201–208, 2007.

The combination between learning techniques with stochastic methods makes feasible the dimensionality reduction limiting the prior probability as well as providing the prior information needed to make effective the learning methods. In this paper, Rao-Blackwellized particle filter is proposed as overall framework for integrating both stochastic and analytic techniques. Furthermore, Point Distribution Models (PDMs) are applied for obtaining analytic solutions to the articulated body model parameters. These models are able to estimate 2D body pose whatever the viewpoint.

1.1 Related Work

There is a large amount of publications on human body tracking. Most of them can be divided into two main groups, depending on the type of techniques used: geometric models [1,2], in which techniques of dimensionality reduction are applied, and learned models [3,4], based on learning relationships between image observations and body pose in order to map non-linear and multivalued spaces.

Rao-Blackwellized particle filter (RBPF) has been applied in other state estimation problems to reduce dimensionality. It has been used in applications so different as SLAM [6], non-linear regression [6], multi-target tracking, or appearance and position estimation [7,8,14].

Our paper contributes proposing a framework in which learning models are combined with non-linear non-gaussian tracking algorithms. While Bayesian filter allows modelling of multimodalities of the distribution, analytic solutions reduce the dimensionality of the problem. The pose variables are solved applying a set of view dependent Gaussian Mixture Models (GMMs), as in [9,14], and each motion state is modelled by means of PDMs [10,11]. RBPF combines the advantages of stochastic and deterministic methods in a unique framework.

2   Rao-Blackwellization

Particle filters can be inefficient sampling in high-dimensional spaces. However, the state can be separated into tractable subspaces in some cases. If some of these subspaces can be analytically calculated, the size of the space over which PF samples will be drastically reduced. The technique which allows marginalizing out some of the variables is called Rao-Blackwellization [12]. In particle filtering, Rao-Blackwellization refers to integrating out part of the state analytically. In this manner, fewer samples (particles) are needed for obtaining the same level of performance. This is due to the fact that part of the posterior over the state is calculated exactly, instead of using a more expensive and noisy sample set.

2.1 Rao-Blackwellized Particle Filter

Let us consider a state space model where y_t are hidden variables which respond to a set of observed variables z_t. We assume z_t as a Markov process of initial distribution $p(y_0)$ and transition equation $p(y_t|y_{t-1})$. Observations are assumed to be conditionally independent given the process y_t of marginal distribution $p(z_t|y_t)$. The aim is to estimate the joint posterior distribution $p(y_{0:t}|z_{1:t})$ or some of its characteristics such as the filtering density $p(y_t|z_{1:t})$. The pdf can be written in the recursive way

$$p(y_{0:t}|z_{1:t}) = \frac{p(z_t|y_t)p(y_t|y_{t-1})p(y_{0:t-1}|z_{1:t-1})}{p(z_t|z_{1:t-1})}, \tag{1}$$

where $p(z_t|z_{1:t-1})$ is a proportionality constant.

In multi-dimensional spaces, obtained integrals are not always tractable. However, if the hidden variables had a structure, we could divide the state y_t into two groups, r_t and s_t such that $p(y_t|y_{t-1}) = p(s_t|r_{t-1:t}, s_{t-1})p(r_t|r_{t-1})$. In such case, we can marginalize out $s_{0:t}$ from the posterior, reducing the dimensionality problem. Following the chain rule, the posterior is decomposed as follows

$$p(r_{0:t}, s_{0:t}|z_{1:t}) = p(s_{0:t}|z_{1:t}, r_{0:t})p(r_{0:t}|z_{1:t}), \tag{2}$$

where the marginal posterior distribution $p(r_{0:t}|z_{1:t})$ satisfies the alternative recursion, and

$$p(r_{0:t}|z_{1:t}) \propto p(z_t|r_t)p(r_t|r_{t-1})p(r_{0:t-1}|z_{1:t-1}). \tag{3}$$

2.2   Human Pose RBPF

As mentioned before, human body tracking requires information about the local pose of the subject as well the global location of the target in the image. In order to support multiple hypotheses for the tracking problem, a particle filter approach can be easily adapted: the state space can be extended with body pose parameters. In this way, the state $y_t = [s_t, r_t] = [x_t, \alpha_t, l_t]$ consists of two parts: the location part $r_t = l_t$ which models the target position, and the body pose variables s_t, composed of the global orientation of the body relative to the camera α_t and its local pose coefficients x_t. We divide the body pose parameters into two sets due to the fact that x_t are obtaining applying a view-dependant model which requires orientation knowledge. Assuming that the camera axis is approximatively parallel to the ground, at shoulder level, the global orientation α_t can be formulated with a single parameter: the person orientation with respect to the camera, which can be simplified as the direction of motion in the image.

In a RBPF, the posterior can be written by the chain rule of probability as

$$p(x_t, \alpha_t, l_t|z_t) = p(x_t, \alpha_t|l_t, z_t) \cdot p(l_t|z_t). \tag{4}$$

Given this formulation, we have divided the problem into two parts (Fig.1(a)), $p(x_t, \alpha_t|l_t, z_t)$ which can be solved analytically using a learned parametrical model explained in Section 3.1, and $p(l_t|z_t)$ which does not exhibit an obvious analytic solution, but can be handled by a PF because of its low dimensionality.

In contrast with previous works [14,6] where only stochastic weights were used for resampling, we compute the final importance weights including the quality

---

Algorithm 1: For each time step t, starting from the distribution $\{l^i_{t-1}, \Pi^i_{t-1}, w^i_{t-1}(x_{t-1}, \alpha_{t-1})\}^N_{i=1}$, the posterior probability $p(l_t, x_t, \alpha_t | z_t)$ is recursively approximated as a set of N weighted hybrid particle set $\{l^i_t, \Pi^i_t, w^i_t(x_t, \alpha_t)\}^N_{i=1}$

---

1. Sequential importance sampling state
   - For $i = 1, ...N$, sample

$$\hat{l}^i_t \sim q(l_t | l^i_{t-1}, z^t)$$

   - For $i = 1, ...N$, calculate the importance weights

$$\pi^i_t \propto \pi^i_{t-1} \frac{p(z_t | l^i_t) p(l^i_t | l^i_{t-1})}{q(l^i_t | l^i_{t-1}, z_t)}$$

2. Analytic step
   - For $i = 1, ...N$, calculate the posterior density $w^i_t(x_t, \alpha_t) = p(x_t, \alpha_t | z_{0:t}, \hat{l}^i_{0:t})$ on the subspace coefficients x_t, α_t using the analytical solution. We denote as $z^i_{0:t}$ the image descriptor computed at sampled location $\hat{l}^i_t$

$$w^i_t(x_t, \alpha_t) = p(x_t, \alpha_t | z^i_{0:t}) \propto p(z^i_t | x_t, \alpha_t) p(x_t, \alpha_t | z^i_{0:t-1}) = L^i_t \cdot p(x_t, \alpha_t | z^i_{0:t-1})$$

   - For $i = 1, ...N$, reweigh the samples

$$\Pi^i_t = p(z_t | \hat{l}^i_t, x_t, \alpha_t) = \pi^i_t \cdot L^i_t$$

3. Selection step
   - Multiply/suppress samples $\hat{l}^i_t$ with high/low normalized importance weights $\tilde{\Pi}^i_t = \frac{\Pi^i_t}{\sum^N_{i=1} \Pi^i_t}$, respectively, to obtain N samples l^i_t.

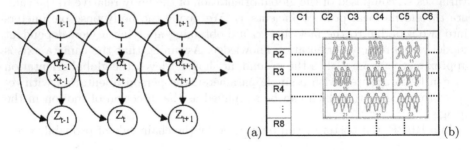

(a)   (b)

Fig. 1. (a) Graphical structure of the Rao-Blackwellized particle filter obtained by partitioning the search space into 2 parts. (b) Human pose model. Columns show the states of the gait cycle and rows the 8 discretized viewpoints.

of the analytic estimation. Thus, we guarantee a correct resampling not only in the dimensions of the stochastic parameters, but also in remaining dimensions of the space.

3   Implementation Issues

3.1   Human Modelling

As analytic model, we apply a probabilistic 2D model for pedestrian motion analysis in monocular sequences [11,13]. We have discretized the viewpoint and constructed a global framework, composed of 8 dynamical view-based models that can respond robustly to any change of direction during the sequence using the parameter α_t.

Each human model encapsulates within a Point Distribution Model (PDM) $x_t = [co_t^1, ..., co_t^{200}, sk_t^1, ...sk_t^{26}]$ the information of the full body silhouette (given by the 2D Shape made of a series of landmarks $co_t^{n_1}$ located along the human contour) and the structural information $sk_t^{n_2}$ (given by the corresponding 2D stick figure, also called Skeleton).

The method is based on learning dynamical models. Correspondences between several different views of the same walking sequences have been established. A clustering in the global Shape-Skeleton feature space where all the views considered are projected together is performed. The different clusters correspond in terms of dynamics or view-point. For each cluster, a series of local motion models is learnt by clustering the stick figure subspace. Gaussian Mixture Models (GMM) are used to cope with the problem of non-linearity of the model as proposed in various papers [9]. GMM are fitted to the total Shape-Skeleton training data using the Expectation Maximization (EM) algorithm.

In this manner, the pdf of pose for a certain view can be expressed as

$$p(x_t, \alpha_t) = \frac{1}{C+R} \sum_{c=1}^{C} p(c) \sum_{r=1}^{R} p(r) N(\mu_{r,c}, \sigma_{r,c}), \tag{5}$$

being $\mu_{r,c}$ and $\sigma_{r,c}$ the parameters of the Gaussian components, and $p(c) \cdot p(r)$ the weights estimated by the EM algorithm during the learning stage.

Temporal and spatial constraints are considered to build a Probabilistic Transition Matrix (PTM) [11] (Fig.1(b)). Temporal constraints enable a frame to frame prediction $p(C_t^i | C_{t-1}^j)$ (corresponding to the probability of being in cluster i at time t conditional on being in cluster j at time $t-1$) of the most probable local models from the GMM that have to be considered. Spatial constraints select the adequate model to be applied $p(R_t^k | R_{1:t-1}^{m_{1:t-1}})$. A more detailed explanation of this model is given in [13].

Once the model has been generated (off-line), it can be applied (on-line) to real sequences. Given an input human blob provided by the Rao-Blackwellized particle filter, Shape and Skeleton estimated in previous frames, and the point of view, the model is fitted for inferring both body shape and posture. This model fitting is applied following the classical PDM methodology [11], but introducing the constraints: the prediction of the most probable models from the GMM can be estimated by means of the PTM. It allows a substantial reduction in computational cost since only few models have to be considered.

$$p(x_t, \alpha_t | x_{t-1}, \alpha_{t-1}) = p(C_t^i | C_{t-1}^j) p(R_t^k | R_{1:t-1}^{m_{1:t-1}}) p(x_t, \alpha_t). \tag{6}$$

3.2   Image Tracking

In our case, the state $l_t = [x, y, v^x, v^y, s^x, s^y]$ characterizes the image object configuration. (x, y) specifies the translation position of the object in the image plane, (v^x, v^y) the velocity of the target and (s^x, s^y) the width and height scales. In order to estimate the velocities of the target, and predict the new location in next frames, we use a first order dynamic model (constant velocity).

An adequate likelihood function must be applied to track the targets. To weigh each particle, we have combine multiple visual clues: colour and movement.

$$p(z_t|l_t) = p_{col}(z_t|l_t) \cdot p_{mov}(z_t|l_t). \tag{7}$$

Colour is a discriminative cue which differentiates between object and background, but also between objects:

$$p_{col}(z_t|l_t) \propto \sum_{l_t} \exp\left(-\frac{(z_{l_t}^{col} - \mu_{c_F})\Sigma_{c_F}^{-1}(z_{l_t}^{col} - \mu_{c_F})^\top}{\min_{c_{Bk}}\left((z_{l_t}^{col} - \mu_{c_{Bk}})\Sigma_{c_{Bk}}^{-1}(z_{l_t}^{col} - \mu_{c_{Bk}})^\top\right)}\right), \tag{8}$$

where μ_{c_F}, Σ_{c_F} are the components of a colour mixture model of the target and $\mu_{c_{Bk}}, \Sigma_{c_{Bk}}$ are the components of a colour mixture model of the background.

Movement can not distinguish between objects, but it improves the tracking eliminating background areas with the same colours than the objects.

$$p_{mov}(z_t|l_t) \propto \sum_{l_t} \exp((z_{l_t}^{col} - M_{l_t}^{Bk})^\alpha) - 1, \tag{9}$$

where $M_{l_t}^{Bk}$ is the background model and α is an ad-hoc parameter ($\alpha = 4$).

4   Experimental Results

The algorithm has been evaluated with different testing sequences that illustrate common situations which may occur in the analysis of pedestrian motion: straight line walking, direction and scale changes, etc. The process starts with a manual initialization: indicating the location, the angle and the adequate model in the first frame. The automatization of this stage is out of the scope of this project, pending for future work.

To evaluate the results, we have extracted three different kinds of statistics: the temporal motion continuity of the model (the column of the PTM corresponding to the estimated model), the mean square error (in cm) between skeleton joints obtained in each frame and a ground truth skeleton extracted manually (pose error) and the tracking error of the bounding box (in pixels). The pose error has been normalized with respect to the real target height, thus obtaining an error independent of the scale in the image.

As illustrated in Fig.2, results for a pedestrian crossing the scene without any change in the viewpoint are excellent. In the walk-circle sequence (Fig.3), results are globally very satisfactory. However, the model fails when the system must

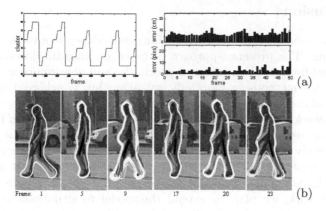

Fig. 2. (a) Pose error in centimeters and tracking error in pixels (right), and temporal clusters (left). (b) Particles obtained for the Straight line walking sequence.

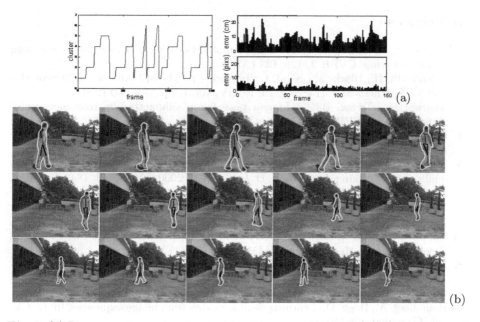

Fig. 3. (a) Pose error in centimeters and tracking error in pixels (right) and temporal clusters (left) (b) Contour and skeleton obtained for the Walk-circle sequence from www.nada.kth.se/hedvig/data.html

apply the back model because of the high sensitivity of this particular model to shadows and fragmented blobs (the difference between states in this view consists in the few pixels which compose the feet) and the viewpoint differences with the training set. However, the system is able to recuperate the dynamic behaviour of the input motion when the image measurement is improved.

5   Conclusions

In this paper we have proposed a system for view-independent monocular human body tracking. The present approach is based on Rao-Blackwellized particle filter as global framework to integrate stochastic and deterministic tracking. By combining both methods, a more efficient algorithm is achieved with a lower computational cost.

We have developed an algorithm capable of solving the location in the image using PF, and using this information to estimate analytically the body pose. The human body model applied has been constructed as a PDM with temporal and spatial constraints. The system has been evaluated on real sequences of pedestrians. Experimental results have been reported with satisfactory outcomes.

As future work, we plan to extend the model to situations with multiple people and occlusions, where multimodality can really demonstrate its utility. Furthermore, we will include a more complete set of actions and motions into the analytical model. Finally, we will deal with the automatic initialization.

References

1. Deutscher, J., Blake, A., Reid, I.: Articulated body motion capture by annealed particle filtering. CVPR 2, 126–133 (2000)
2. Sidenbladh, H., Black, M., Sigal, L.: Implicit Probabilistic Models of Human Motion for Synthesis and Tracking. In: ECCV, vol. 1, pp. 784–800 (2002)
3. Agarwal, A., Triggs, B.: 3d human pose forom silhouettes by relevance vector regression. In: CVPR (2004)
4. Elgammal, A., Lee, C.S.: Inferring 3d body pose from silhouettes using activity manifold learning, In: CVPR (2004).
5. MacCormick, J., Isard, M.: Partitioned sampling, articulated objects, and interface-quality hand tracking. In: Vernon, D. (ed.) ECCV 2000. LNCS, vol. 1843, Springer, Heidelberg (2000)
6. Doucet, A., de Freitas, N., Murphy, K., Russell, S.: Rao-Blackwellised Particle Filtering for Dynamic Bayesian Networks. In: UAI (2000)
7. Ba, S.O., Odobez, J.M.: A Rao-BLackwellized Mixed State Particle Filter for Head Pose Tracking in Meetings. In: MMMP (2005)
8. Khan, Z., Balch, T., Dellaert, F.: A Rao-Blackwellized Particle Filter for Eigen-Tracking. In: CVPR 2, 980–986 (2004)
9. Cootes, T., Taylor, C.: A mixture model for representing shape variation (1997)
10. Baumberg, A., Hogg, D.: Learning flexible models from image sequences. In: ECCV, vol. 1, pp. 299–308 (1994)
11. Bowden, R., Mitchell, T.A., Sarhadi, M.: Non-linear Statistical Models for the 3D Reconstruction of Human Pose and Motion from Monocular Image Sequences. In: Image and Vision Computing, vol. 18(9), pp. 729–737 (2000)
12. Casella, G., Robert, C.P.: Rao-Blackwellisation of sampling schemes. In Biometrika, vol. 83(1), pp. 81–94 (1996)
13. Rogez, G., Orrite, C., Martínez, J., Herrero, E.: Probabilistic Spatio-Temporal 2D-Model for Pedestrian Motion Analysis in Monocular Sequences. In: AMDO (2006)
14. Jaeggli, T., Koller-Meier, E., Van Gool, L.: Monocular Tracking with a Mixture of View-Dependent Learned Models. In: AMDO (2006)

Parameter System for Human Physiological Data Representation and Analysis

Olga Kurasova[1], Gintautas Dzemyda[1], and Alfonsas Vainoras[2]

[1] Institute of Mathematics and Informatics, Akademijos St. 4, LT 08663, Vilnius
{Kurasova, Dzemyda}@ktl.mii.lt
[2] Kaunas Medical University, M. Jankaus St. 2, LT 50275, Kaunas, Lithuania
alfavain@kmu.lt

Abstract. In this paper, two systems of physiological parameters that describe the human functional state are analysed. Some physiological features are measured on sportsmen and ischemic heart-diseased men by changing the physical load, and the system of parameters is developed. One parameter system is based on the so-called fractal dimensions, and the other one is based on the parameters of curves that approximate the change of feature values in time. The application of classification and visualization methods and neural networks allowed us to optimise the number of parameters. The results may be generalised to the large number of problems in biomedicine and bioinformatics.

1 Introduction

The analysis of medical data is a topical and important problem. Various data mining methods and software for decision support in medicine are developed [11], [13]. If some human physiological features are measured at certain time moments, some time series are obtained. Usually, all the measured human physiological features are important, therefore it is necessary to analyse them as a whole. Such an integral analysis is a task difficult enough for a doctor. In order to simplify this task, it is necessary to find some set of integral estimates that would be comprehensible more easily. It is necessary to seek the ways to develop a parameter system $x_1, x_2, \ldots, x_n$ for multidimensional data $X^1, X^2, \ldots, X^m$ corresponding to the patients. $X^i = (x_1^i, x_2^i, \ldots, x_n^i)$, $i = 1, \ldots, m$, where m is the number of patients, n is the number of parameters. Each vector (patient) X^i is assigned to a class by doctors, e.g. healthy or sick with some disease. Supervised learning classifiers are trained by using the data set $X^1, X^2, \ldots, X^m$. According to the classifiers, a new patient is assigned to one of the known classes [7].

Another way of analysis is based on the data vectors dimension reduction and mapping onto a plane for visual decisions [10]. Parameter number reduction technique [8] based on correlation matrix analysis and mapping of parameters onto a plane have been applied in this paper, too.

The research was supported by the Lithuanian State Science and Studies Foundation.

J. Martí et al. (Eds.): IbPRIA 2007, Part I, LNCS 4477, pp. 209–216, 2007.

2   Description of Parameter Systems

The analysed physiological data set consists of two groups: sportsmen (163 items) and ischemic heart-diseased men (61 items). The following physiological features that describe the human functional state are measured: heart rate (HR), interval in the electrocardiogram from point J to the end T of the wave (JT), systolic blood pressure (SBP), and diastolic blood pressure (DBP). A provocative incremental bicycle ergometry stress test is performed. The values of the features are obtained as follows: (1) before the test, four features are measured, the initial power of load is 50W; (2) during the test, the power is increased by 50W every minute, before increasing the power, four features are measured; (3) the test is finished when either a patient is unable to continue it or a doctor notices great changes in the heart action and orders to terminate the test; (4) afterwards, the recovery of an organism follows, the same features are measured every minute again during the recovery. Thus, during the test, a set of values of four features is obtained. Furthermore, the number of values for each patient is different, because it depends on the maximum power in Watts, sustained by the patient. In Fig. 1, the dynamics of heart rate (HR) is presented.

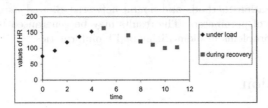

Fig. 1. The dynamics of heart rate (HR)

Such a change in the feature values in time reflects the action of the human heart. All the four physiological features (HR, JT, SBP, DBP) are important. With a view to simplify their analysis, it is necessary to find some integral estimates of these time series. Some strategies may be used. One of them is based on the calculation of fractal dimensions [1], [2]. The set of the obtained numeric data on each feature is interpolated by a cubic spline. Thus, we get a graph for each of the four features. Fractal dimensions (capacity, information, correlation) are computed for these graphs in the following way. Let us analyse a regular grid (ε is the size of a grid cell), superimposed on the graphs; the number n_i of "occupied" pixels is counted for each grid cell; it is divided by the total number N of pixels, thus, we evaluate a proportion $P_i(\varepsilon) = n_i/N$. The information function is $I \equiv -\sum_{i=1}^{N_\varepsilon} P_i(\varepsilon) \log[P_i(\varepsilon)]$, where N_ε is the number of "occupied" cells; the information dimension is $d_{\inf} \equiv -\lim_{\varepsilon \to 0} \frac{I}{\log(\varepsilon)} = \lim_{\varepsilon \to 0} \sum_{i=1}^{N_\varepsilon} \frac{P_i(\varepsilon) \log[P_i(\varepsilon)]}{\log(\varepsilon)}$; if $I = \log N_\varepsilon$, the capacity dimension is obtained, if $I = \log \sum_i (P_i(\varepsilon))^2$, the correlation dimension is obtained. Thus, the total number of the parameters is 12: four parameters for each fractal dimension.

Table 1. Average values of R^2

features	under load			during recovery		
	log.	exp.	pol.	log.	exp.	pol.
HR	0.9329	0.9424	0.9869	0.8593	0.7157	0.9276
SBP	0.8712	0.9339	0.9722	0.8811	0.8523	0.9219
DBP	0.5228	0.5449	0.7963	0.4850	0.4705	0.6876
JT	0.9312	0.9479	0.9788	0.8866	0.8134	0.9437

In this paper, we develop a parameter system taking into account the parameters of the function that approximates the time series of the human physiological features. The ideas of the strategy are given in [3]. In this paper, we develop this strategy, analyse it in more detail, and compare it with the first one. Three types of approximation functions were examined: exponential, logarithmical, and second order polynomial functions. The average of the square of the correlation coefficient R^2 is used to measure the effectiveness of the least-squares smoothing. As we see in Table 1, the feature values are approximated most accurately by the second order polynomial function. Namely this approximation function was used in further investigations in this paper.

Exponential and logarithmical functions are not suitable again due to the fact that the number of the approximating points is not large and there is no clearly observed limit of time series. A leading coefficient a of a second order polynomial (parabola) shows how a curve is curved as compared with a line. We can write $y = ax^2 + bx + c = a(x + b/2a)^2 + (c - b^2/4a)$, where a is a leading coefficient, (d, e) are the coordinates of a parabola vertex ($d = -b/2a$, $e = c - b^2/4a$). The parameters of the new system are as follows: x_1 is the maximum power in Watts; x_2 is the leading coefficient of the second order polynomial, approximating the values of HR, under load; x_3 is the value of the parameter HR in the initial state; x_4 is the value of the parameter HR, reached at the maximum power; x_5 is the leading coefficient of the second order polynomial, approximating the values of HR, during recovery; x_6, x_7, x_8, x_9 are the respective parameters of SBP; $x_{10}, x_{11}, x_{12}, x_{13}$ are the respective parameters of DBP; $x_{14}, x_{15}, x_{16}, x_{17}$ are the respective parameters of JT. The coordinates (d, e) of the parabola vertex are rejected, because they are not significant for describing a change in the human physiological features. These parameters $x_1, x_2, \ldots, x_{17}$ are calculated for all patients. The multidimensional vectors $X^i = (x_1^i, x_2^i, \ldots, x_n^i)$, $i = 1, \ldots, m$, are formed, $m = 224$, $n = 17$.

3 Results of Visualization and Classification

In this paper, four classification methods are used for pattern recognition: Naïve Bayes (NB) [14], k nearest neighbourhood (kNN) method [7], classification tree (CT) [4], and support vector machine (SVM) [5]. Three criteria to evaluate the classification quality are used: general accuracy (GA), specificity, and sensitivity. They are calculated using a cross-validation strategy, when the number of folds is equal to 10, i.e. a test set consists of 10% of the train set. The system "Orange" [6] is used for the experiments.

Three dimension reduction methods are used: Sammon's mapping [15], the self-organizing map (SOM) [12], and integrated combination of the SOM and Sammon's mapping [9]. The method of the visual analysis of correlation matrices [8] is also based on the same integrated mapping.

Classification statistics when the vectors, consisting of the parameters of fractal dimensions (for each fractal dimension separately) are presented in Table 2. Data on sportsmen and ischemic heart-diseased men are analysed. When the medical data are analysed, the main measure of the classification quality is the sensitivity: the higher the sensitivity, the less real cases of diseases are undetected. The classification quality may be evaluated by the number of misclassified persons among sportsmen and ischemic heart-diseased men, too. However, the sensitivity remains the main criterion in our research, because it represents the classification quality of new data that were not used for training. The higher sensitivity is obtained when the vectors, consisting of the parameters of capacity dimension, are classified using a support vector machine (SVM). In this case, 9 sportsmen are assigned to ischemics, and 11 ischemics are assigned to sportsmen.

In Fig. 2a, the projections of the vectors, consisting of the parameters of capacity dimension ($n = 4$), obtained by Sammon's mapping, are presented: filled rhombi indicate the vectors that correspond to the sportsmen, and are assigned to them by the SVM; filled squares indicate the vectors that correspond to the ischemics, and are assigned to them by the SVM; unfilled rhombi indicate the vectors that correspond to the ischemics, but are assigned to sportsmen by the SVM; unfilled squares indicate the vectors that correspond to the sportsmen, but are assigned to the ischemics by the SVM. As we see in Fig. 2a, the data of both groups are overlapping enough. The misclassified points, corresponding to the sportsmen (unfilled squares), "escape" from their group, they mix up among the points, corresponding to the ischemics. Doctors have to doubt if these sportsmen do not posses some symptoms of the ischemic heart-disease. Projections of the vectors, consisting of the new parameter system ($n = 17$) are presented in Fig. 2b. As we see in Fig. 2b, the visual overlapping of two groups is lesser as compared with Fig. 2a.

Table 2. Classification statistics when the vectors consisting of the parameters of fractal dimensions (information, correlation, and capacity) are classified

classi-fier	information			correlation			capacity		
	GA	Spec.	Sens.	GA	Spec.	Sens.	GA	Spec.	Sens.
NB	0.8215	0.8696	0.6984	0.7972	0.8491	0.6667	0.8332	0.8679	0.7460
kNN	0.8792	0.9441	0.7143	0.7791	0.8365	0.6349	0.8872	0.9371	0.7619
CT	0.8711	0.9193	0.7460	0.8340	0.8742	0.7302	0.8648	0.9434	0.6667
SVM	0.9065	0.9689	0.7460	0.8332	0.9308	0.5873	0.8917	0.9371	0.7778

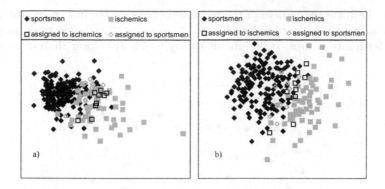

Fig. 2. Projections of the vectors consisting of the parameters of the capacity dimension $(n = 4)$ (a); the new parameter system $(n = 17)$ (b)

These data have been classified using the same classifiers. Although the accuracy is better not much (Table 3) as compared with Table 2, classification results would be as precise as possible because medical data are analysed. The best sensitivity is obtained using the Naïve Bayes classifier. As we see in Fig. 2b, if the misclassified points were eliminated from the analysed data set, the visual overlapping of the groups would be inconsiderable.

Table 3. Classification statistics when the vectors consisting of the new parameter system $(n = 17)$ are classified

classifier	GA	Spec.	Sens.
NB	0.9152	0.9441	0.8413
kNN	0.8840	0.9503	0.7143
CT	0.8887	0.9503	0.7302
SVM	0.9241	0.9627	0.8254

4   Investigation of the New Parameter System

When 17-dimensional vectors of the new parameter system are projected into a two-dimensional space, distortions are inevitable. It is reasonable to investigate this parameter system: possibly, some parameters may be eliminated. The correlation matrix $R = \{r_{x_i x_j}, \ i, j = 1, \ldots, n\}$ of the parameters has been calculated by analysing the vectors that compose the analysed data set $X^1, X^2, \ldots, X^m$. The system of the vectors $Y^1, Y^2, \ldots, Y^n$, which corresponds to the set of parameters $x_1, x_2, \ldots, x_n$ (in this case, $n = 17$), is obtained from this correlation matrix using the method, proposed in [8]. The set of vectors $Y^1, Y^2, \ldots, Y^{17}$ may be mapped onto a plane. This leads to the possible visual observation of a layout of parameters $x_1, x_2, \ldots, x_{17}$ on the plane. In Fig. 3a, the projections of seventeen 17-dimensional vectors are presented. Here the numbers indicate the indices of the parameters. As we see in Fig. 3a, the points, corresponding to the parameters $x_1, x_2, \ldots, x_{17}$, are distributed uniformly, they do not form any groups. It is difficult to say which are closer than others.

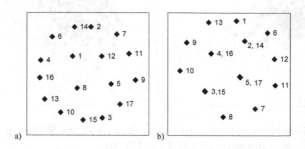

Fig. 3. Distributions of the parameters on the plane, obtained by Sammon's mapping (a); by combining the SOM and Sammon's mapping (b)

Distribution of the multidimensional vectors $Y^1, Y^2, \ldots, Y^{17}$, corresponding to the parameters $x_1, x_2, \ldots, x_{17}$ in the SOM table $[7 \times 7]$ are presented in Table 4. We see some groups of parameters. It is expedient to observe visually how much the vectors of the neighbouring cells of the table are close in the n-dimensional space. For this purpose, the integrated combination of the SOM and Sammon's mapping [9] has been used. In Fig. 3b, projections of the SOM $[7 \times 7]$ vectors-winners onto a plane are presented. We may conclude that "strong" pairs of the parameters are (x_2, x_{14}), (x_3, x_{15}), (x_4, x_{16}), and (x_5, x_{17}), though the parameters x_3 and x_{15}, x_5 and x_{17} do not fall into one cell (Table 4), however, the vectors-winners, corresponding to them, are very close each to the other (see Fig. 3b).

As shown in Section 2, the parameters $x_2 - x_5$ are parameters of HR, and the parameters $x_{14} - x_{17}$ are that of JT. We can state that there exists a high correlation between the respective HR and JT parameters. Thus, one parameter group may be eliminated from the parameter system. The pending problem becomes simpler, because the dimensionality of the analysed data decreases from 17 to 13. It is possible to analyse the vectors, consisting either of the parameters

Table 4. The SOM table $[7 \times 7]$

4, 16		15	3		5	17
8						10
		9		13		
7						6
		12				
11				1		2, 14

Table 5. Classification statistics when the vectors consisting of the parameters either without JT or without HR are classified

classifier	without JT			without HR		
	GA	Spec.	Sens.	GA	Spec.	Sens.
NB	0.9152	0.9503	0.8254	**0.9415**	0.9627	0.8889
kNN	0.8881	0.9379	0.7619	0.8666	0.9376	0.6825
CT	0.8978	0.9503	0.7619	0.8978	0.9503	0.7619
SVM	0.9113	0.9627	0.7778	0.9283	0.9689	0.8254

$x_1, x_2, \ldots, x_{13}$ (without JT parameters) or of the parameters $x_1, x_6, x_7 \ldots, x_{17}$ (without HR parameters).

When the vectors, consisting of the parameters either without JT or without HR, are classified, the classification accuracy is presented in Table 5. The highest sensitivity is obtained when the vectors consisting of the parameters without HR are classified: NB assigns 6 sportsmen to ischemics and 5 ischemics to sportsmen. When the vectors consisting of the parameters without JT are classified, NB assigns 10 sportsmen to ischemics and 8 ischemics to sportsmen. In medicine, the relation between HR and JT interval is well known (Bazett formula). HR reflects the function of regulatory systems better, when the JT interval is closer related to myocardium metabolic features. Having in mind this result is more important than regulation, it could be reasonable to refuse the HR parameter.

5   Conclusions

In this paper, the system of parameters based on the parameters of curves that approximate change of feature values in time, that can be used for description of the human functional state has been developed and analysed. The system can be used to observe and classify two groups of patients: sportsmen and ischemic heart-diseased men. The experiments showed that dynamics of the heart rate, JT interval, systolic blood pressure, and diastolic blood pressure might be successfully approximated by second order polynomials. The parameters of the polynomials make a basis for the multidimensional vectors that describe the human functional state.

The application of classification and visualization methods allowed us to optimise the number of parameters: four parameters were successfully eliminated and the set of parameters was simplified without loss of the classification accuracy. The experiments showed that the developed system can be an alternative to the fractal dimension parameter system, because the better classification accuracy may be expected. Although the improvement is better not much, the analysis results would be as precise as possible because medical data are analysed. The further research on comparison of the parameter systems should be extended to other data sets. The results may be generalised to the large number of problems in biomedicine and bioinformatics.

References

1. Bernataviciene, J., Berskiene, K., Aseriskyte, D., Dzemyda, G., Vainoras, A.: Analysis of Biomedical Informativity of the Fractal Dimensions. In: Proceedings of IX-th International Conference Biomedical Engineering, pp. 27–31 (2005)
2. Bernataviciene, J., Dzemyda, G., Kurasova, O., Vainoras, A.: Integration of Classification and Visualization for Diagnosis Decisions. International Journal of Information Technology and Intelligent Computing 1(1), 57–68 (2006)
3. Bernataviciene, J., Dzemyda, G., Kurasova, O., Marcinkevicius, V.: Decision Support for Preliminary Medical Diagnosis Integrating the Data Mining Methods. In: Pranevicius, H., Vaarmann, O., Zavadskas, E. (eds.) Proceedings of 5th International Conference Simulation and optimisation in business and industry, pp. 155–160 (2006)
4. Breiman, L., Friedman, J., Olshen, R., Stone, C.: Classification and Regression Trees. Chapman and Hall, New York (1984)
5. Cristianini, N., Shawe–Taylor, J.: Support Vector and Kernel Methods. In: Berthold, M., Hand, D.J. (eds.) Intelligent Data Analysis: An Introduction, pp. 169–197. Springer, Heidelberg (2003)
6. Demsar, J., Zupan, B., Leban, G.: Orange: From Experimental Machine Learning to Interactive Data Mining, White Paper, Faculty of Computer and Information Science, University of Ljubljana, http://www.ailab.si/orange (2004)
7. Dunham, M.H.: Data Mining Introductory and Advanced Topics. In: Pearson Education, Inc. Prentice Hall, Englewood Cliffs (2003)
8. Dzemyda, G.: Visualization of a Set of Parameters Characterized by Their Correlation Matrix. Computational Statistics and Data Analysis 36(10), 15–30 (2001)
9. Dzemyda, G., Kurasova, O.: Heuristic Approach for Minimizing the Projection Error in the Integrated Mapping. European Journ. of Operat. Research 171(3), 859–878 (2006)
10. Grinstein, G.G., Hoffman, P.E., Picket, R.M.: Benchmark Development for the Evaluation of Visualization for Data Mining. In: Fayyad, U., Grinstein, G.G., Wierse, A. (eds.) Information Visualization in Data Mining and Knowledge Discovery, pp. 129–176. Morgan Kaufmann Publishers, San Francisco (2002)
11. Jegelevicius, D., Lukosevicius, A., Paunksnis, A., Barzdziukas, V.: Application of Data Mining Technique for Diagnosis of Posterior Uveal Melanoma. Informatica 13(4), 455–464 (2002)
12. Kohonen, T.: Self-Organizing Maps. 3rd edn. Springer Series in Information Sciences, vol. 30. Springer, Heidelberg (2001)
13. Lavrac, N., Keravnou, E., Zupan, B. (eds.): Intelligent Data Analysis in Medicine and Pharmacology. Springer, Heidelberg (1997)
14. Ramoni, M., Sebastiani, P.: Bayesian Methods. In: Berthold, M., Hand, D.J. (eds.) Intelligent Data Analysis: An Introduction, pp. 131–168. Springer, Heidelberg (2003)
15. Sammon, J.W.: A nonlinear mapping for data structure analysis. IEEE Transactions on Computers 18, 401–409 (1969)

Face Recognition in Color Using Complex and Hypercomplex Representations*

Mauricio Villegas and Roberto Paredes

Instituto Tecnológico de Informática
Universidad Politécnica de Valencia
Camino de Vera s/n, Edif. 8G Acc. B 46022 Valencia (Spain)
{mvillegas,rparedes}@iti.upv.es

Abstract. Color has plenty of discriminative information that can be used to improve the performance of face recognition algorithms, although it is difficult to use it because of its high variability. In this paper we investigate the use of the quaternion representation of a color image for face recognition. We also propose a new representation for color images based on complex numbers. These two color representation methods are compared with the traditional grayscale and RGB representations using an eigenfaces based algorithm for identity verification. The experimental results show that the proposed method gives a very significant improvement when compared to using only the illuminance information.

1 Introduction

Humans have a high performance for recognizing faces even when they are in grayscale. However resent research on face recognition by humans indicates that color information is very important in certain circumstances, for example when images have an extremely low resolution [1].

The use of color introduces new sources of variability that makes the problem harder and more expensive to resolve. But despite these problems, if humans recognize faces better when they are in color, then there is no doubt that the color contains very useful information that can help improve the accuracies of current systems [1,2,3].

The main topic that we want to address in this paper is how to represent the color images in order to take advantage of all the information it holds. Moreover we are going to apply light normalization techniques to the proposed color representations in order to avoid the effect of illumination and color variability.

This paper is organized as follows: Section 2 discusses color image representations in general, describes the two representation methods being compared and two baseline techniques. Section 3 describes the normalization methods used in the experiments. Section 4 presents the algorithm used in the experiments and the adaptations to the new color representations. Section 5 shows the results of

* Work supported by the Spanish Project DPI2004-08279-C02-02 and the Generalitat Valenciana - Consellería d'Empresa, Universitat i Ciència under an FPI scholarship.

J. Martí et al. (Eds.): IbPRIA 2007, Part I, LNCS 4477, pp. 217–224, 2007.
© Springer-Verlag Berlin Heidelberg 2007

the experiments carried out. Finally section 6 draws the conclusions and directions for future research.

2   Representing Color Images

There are many ways in which a color image can be represented mathematically. The straightforward representation is to link the three color components so the dimensionality of the feature vector is three times the dimensionality of the grayscale version. We will use this representation and the grayscale representation as baselines in our experiments.

In this paper we compare two methods for representing color images. The first one using quaternion numbers, and a proposed one using complex numbers. The benefit of these representations is that they use the color information while the pixel structure is preserved.

2.1   Quaternion Representation of Images

The quaternions can be seen as a generalization of complex numbers to four dimensions [4]. Any quaternion can be written using four real numbers as

$$q = q_r + q_i \mathbf{i} + q_j \mathbf{j} + q_k \mathbf{k} \tag{1}$$

where $q_r, q_i, q_j, q_k \in \mathbb{R}$ and $\mathbf{i}$, $\mathbf{j}$, $\mathbf{k}$ are three different imaginary units related by

$$\mathbf{i}^2 = \mathbf{j}^2 = \mathbf{k}^2 = \mathbf{ijk} = -1 \tag{2}$$

The set of quaternion numbers is commonly denoted by $\mathbb{H}$ named after the person that proposed them W. R. Hamilton [4]. For the quaternions most of the algebraic properties are the same as for real or complex numbers. A particular property that distinguishes them from real or complex numbers is that multiplication is not commutative. For a more detailed review of the quaternion properties refer to [5].

The quaternions have been proposed for modelling color images [6] which has been successfully applied in digital image processing [7,8,9], although it has not been used for image recognition. This approach represents each pixel of an image using a single quaternion, the real part is set to zero and the three color components are assigned to the imaginary parts. The resulting representation is a quaternion vector of dimension the same as the number of pixels in the image.

The fact that the algebraic properties of the quaternion are similar to the real numbers and has a mathematical background, makes them very attractive to be used for representing color. In fact, most of the algorithms that exist for grayscale images can be easily generalized to the quaternion domain.

2.2   Complex Representation of Images

There is major drawback when representing color images as quaternions and using the generalized algorithms from the grayscale version. The problem is that the algorithms tend to be more computationally expensive. For example a single multiplication of two scalars in the quaternion domain in general requires sixteen distinct multiplications. It is understandable that the algorithms used for color images could be more expensive than the ones used for grayscale images. Although it would be desirable to find algorithms that can be used for color images without increasing considerably their cost.

In this section we propose to represent color images as a complex valued vector, where each pixel is represented by a single complex number. This representation also makes possible to generalize the grayscale algorithms to color, while having a lower cost than the quaternion representation. Because a complex number is composed of only two values, we need to find a way to represent the color components using two numbers. To do this we are going to define a new color space, the PCA color space.

It is complicated to define a two component color space that can be used for image recognition in general. But if we consider a specific problem, for example in this case the images are only from human faces, a better color space can be defined. It is known that the possible colors of faces lie on a well defined region of the color space [10]. If we use a dimensionality reduction technique such as Principal Component Analysis (PCA), we are capable of reducing the three color components to two while making sure that we retain most of the original color information. The first and second principal components are assigned to the real and imaginary parts respectively, and the third principal component is ignored.

This PCA color space depends on the task being considered and it needs to be calculated using the training data.

3   Illumination Normalization

In a face recognition system one of the most difficult properties to achieve is illumination invariance. This means the performance of the system must not be affected by the amount of lighting conditions. One possibility to reduce this variability is to process the image prior to the recognition stage aiming to obtain a representation invariant to the illumination conditions. In the face recognition context this is commonly called illumination normalization, for color images this is also called color constancy.

Several illumination normalization techniques exist [11,12,13]. A very simple one that gives good results is to locally make the mean of the image to zero and the variance to one [14]. Here we propose to extend this algorithm to color images by normalizing each component of the color space independently. Normalizing an image I globally for each color component c would be

$$\hat{I}_c = \frac{I_c - \mu_c}{\sigma_c} \tag{3}$$

where μ_c and σ_c is the mean and the standard deviation of the color component c respectively.

The local normalization is analogous to the global one, the difference is that the normalization function is applied locally. By applying a function locally we mean the following. A region of the image of size $w \times w$, is selected and the normalization function is applied to it. This process is repeated by moving the selection window pixel by pixel all over the image. Because the windows overlap, the final pixel value is the average of all the results for that particular pixel.

4   Face Verification Algorithm

In a face verification system a person claims a certain identity and a decision is taken whether it is or it is not the true identity. Features are extracted from the person's face image and are compared with the the model of the claimed identity. The client is accepted or rejected depending on a threshold.

The objective of the chosen algorithm is to assess if the representations described previously are adequate to be used in face verification and if they give a considerable improvement when compared to using the baseline representations. To do this we are going to define a simple algorithm that works analogously in the real domain for grayscale and linked color components images, and in the complex and quaternion domains for color images.

4.1   Eigenfaces

When images are represented by a single vector, as in our case, the original dimensionality of the feature vectors is very high. For this reason most of the recognition algorithms use some sort of dimensionality reduction technique before the classifier. A very popular technique is Principal Component Analysis (PCA), which in the context of face recognition it is known as eigenfaces [15]. Eigenfaces has become a general baseline for face recognition, therefore it is the one that we used. For the classifier we used the nearest neighbor using the Euclidean distance.

Because we are representing the images using complex and quaternion vectors, we also need PCA in these domains. PCA has already been generalized to quaternion vectors [8]. For complex vectors the generalization can be seen as a special case of quaternion PCA.

At the moment there is no mathematical software that has full support for quaternions. So in order to do a singular value decomposition of a quaternion matrix, which is needed for doing PCA, we have to use an isomorphism. This isomorphism is explained in [16].

5   Experiments

The corpora used in the experiments are the frontal datasets of the XM2VTS database [17], referred to as CDS001 and CDS006. Each dataset corresponds to one of the two shots taken at each of the sessions. Four session where taken distributed over a period of four months. In total there are eight images for each of the 295 subjects. The faces where manually cropped and resized to 24×24 pixels using the eye coordinates that are publicly available.

Verification on the XM2VTS database is evaluated using the Lausanne protocol [18]. This protocol specifies two experimentation configurations that state which images are to be used as training, evaluation and test. The protocol also specifies the measurements to be used so that the performance of different algorithms can be compared. Apart from the training, evaluation and test sets specified on the protocol configuration I, we generated nine more randomized sets. With these sets, the experiments where repeated ten times in order to make the results more reliable.

5.1 The Eigenfaces

Figure 1 shows the mean face and the first seven eigenfaces for each representation method without illumination normalization. The most interesting thing to note is that for all the methods the eigenfaces are quite similar. The eigenfaces can be seen as directions of maximum variability of the data. If these directions do not change by introducing color information, this indicates that there is a correlation between the global structure of the face and the color content. This result can be observed by considering that the race of a person not only indicates a particular skin color, but also a particular facial structure.

5.2 Verification Results

Figure 2 shows some graphs of the total error rates (see [18] for details) for the evaluation set with respect to the degrees of freedom. By degrees of freedom it is meant the amount of real numbers used to represent the feature vector. D' principal components produces D', $D'/2$ or $D'/4$ numbers for real, complex and quaternion vectors respectively. We have plotted the graphs this way because for the same degrees of freedom all of the methods have approximately the same verification computational cost. Three different graphs are obtained according to the three different preprocessing techniques: none, global and local normalization.

When there is no normalization the color representations give lower error rates although analyzing the confidence intervals it can be seen that they are not statistically better than gray. Using global normalization the color methods are considerably better than gray. The two methods rgb and cplx reach a minimum at 64 degrees of freedom, for quat the behavior is somewhat different, the minimum is located at 256 degrees of freedom.

For local normalization, the curves show the results taking the best normalization window size w for each method. Although we expected a general improvement in all of the methods [14], for gray the errors only decrease slightly and for rgb and quat the errors even increase. In contrast the errors for cplx improve considerably.

The final graph shows the best result for each of the methods. The optimum parameters for each method were: for gray $d = 64$ and local normalization $w = 22$, for rgb $d = 64$ and global normalization, for cplx $d = 64$ and local

gray

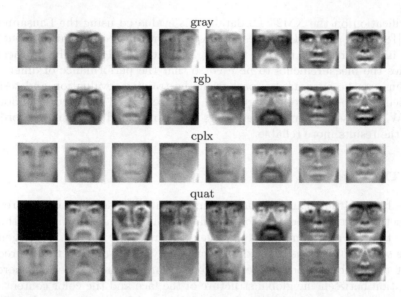

rgb

cplx

quat

Fig. 1. The mean face (left column) and the first eigenfaces (columns 2 to 8) ordered in decreasing eigenvalue for each representation method. For quat the first row is the real part and the second row are the imaginary parts represented as a color image.

Table 1. Error rates for the evaluation and test sets for each representation method, the 95% confidence intervals and the relative improvement with respect to gray

Method	Evaluation Set			Test Set		
	TER	95% conf. int.	Improvement	TER	95% conf. int.	Improvement
gray	19.0	18.4–19.7		17.3	16.4–18.1	
rgb	17.0	16.4–17.7	10.5%	16.3	15.4–17.3	5.3%
cplx	**14.1**	13.4–14.2	**26.2%**	**12.9**	12.1–13.7	**25.2%**
quat	17.0	16.4–17.7	10.5%	16.5	15.7–17.3	4.4%

normalization $w = 14$, and for quat $d = 256$ and global normalization. Only cplx gives a significant improvement with respect to gray and rgb.

Table 1 shows the error rates for each method with the optimum parameters, for both the evaluation and test sets. The relative improvement of the color representations with respect to gray is also presented.

The relative improvement obtained using the complex representation is quite significant. This suggest that the color can be used effectively as a discriminative feature in face recognition. The same improvement is seen in both the evaluation and the test set so the representation also had the characteristic of generalizing well to new data. The results obtained using the quaternion representation are disappointing, comparing with rgb, there is practically no improvement for the evaluation set and for the test it is actually worse.

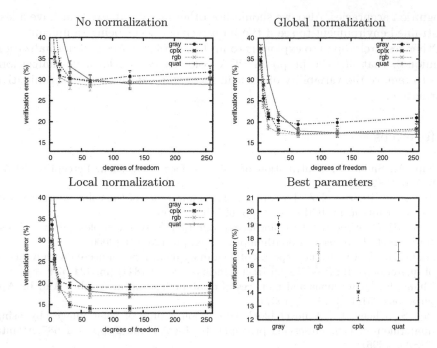

Fig. 2. The first three graphs are for the total error rates for the evaluation set [18] with respect to the degrees of freedom for the different preprocessing schemes. The last graph are the error rates for the preprocessing parameters that give the best result in each method. Error bars indicate the 95% confidence intervals.

6   Conclusions and Future Work

In this paper we studied two possible ways of representing color images for the purpose of being used in face recognition. These where tested using the XM2VTS database for face verification.

The first one is based on the quaternion model of a color image, which has been successfully used in digital image processing. It was seen that although it could improve the system performance, it requires parameters that make the algorithm very expensive.

The results from the second representation, using complex numbers, show a significant improvement. This suggests that color is an important discriminative feature that can be used to improve considerably the accuracy of a system when compared to using only the illuminance information. Although this representation gives a big improvement, it is not conclusive on whether the gain is due to the actual representation or to the color space and illumination normalization methods used.

As future research, we are going to use the same ideas presented here to extend other grayscale algorithms to color, so that we can achieve competitive recognition accuracies. Also, we should use other face databases that have a less constrained environment to see if the improvement keeps being significant.

Other research topics to explore is to find new color spaces and normalization techniques, that like the proposed PCA color space and local normalization, aims to remove the variability of color in faces while keeping the discriminative information.

References

1. Yip, A., Sinha, P.: Contribution of color to face recognition. Perception 31(5), 995–1003 (2002)
2. Torres, L., Reutter, J.Y., Lorente, L.: The importance of the color information in face recognition. In: ICIP, vol. 3, pp. 627–631 (1999)
3. Jones III, C., Abbott, A.L.: Color face recognition by hypercomplex gabor analysis. In: FG2006, University of Southampton, UK, pp. 126–131 (2006)
4. Hamilton, W.R.: On a new species of imaginary quantities connected with a theory of quaternions. In: Proc. Royal Irish Academy. vol. 2(1844) pp. 424–434
5. Zhang, F.: Quaternions and matrices of quaternions. Linear Algebra And Its Applications 251(1-3), 21–57 (1997)
6. Pei, S., Cheng, C.: A novel block truncation coding of color images by using quaternion-moment preserving principle. In: ISCAS. vol. 2, pp. 684–687 Atlanta (USA) (1996)
7. Sangwine, S., Ell, T.: Hypercomplex fourier transforms of color images. In: ICIP. Vol. 1, Thessaloniki (Greece), pp. 137–140 (2001)
8. Bihan, N.L., Sangwine, S.J.: Quaternion principal component analysis of color images. In: ICIP. Barcelona (Spain), vol. 1, pp. 809–812 (2003)
9. Chang, J.-H., Pei, S.-C., Ding, J.J.: 2d quaternion fourier spectral analysis and its applications. In: ISCAS. Vancouver (Canada), vol. 3, pp. 241–244 (2004)
10. Li, S.Z., Jain, A.K.: 6. In: Handbook of Face Recognition. Springer (2005)
11. Gross, R., Brajovic, V.: An image preprocessing algorithm for illumination invariant face recognition. In: AVBPA, Springer, Berlin Heidelberg New York (2003)
12. Lee, K., Ho, J., Kriegman, D.: Nine points of light: Acquiring subspaces for face recognition under variable lighting. In: CVPR. vol. 1, pp. 519–526 (2001)
13. Zhang, L., Samaras, D.: Face recognition under variable lighting using harmonic image exemplars. In: CVPR. vol.1. pp. 19–25 (2003)
14. Villegas, M., Paredes, R.: Comparison of illumination normalization methods for face recognition. In: COST 275, University of Hertfordshire, UK, pp. 27–30 (2005)
15. Turk, M., Pentland, A.: Face recognition using eigenfaces. In: CVPR, Hawaii, pp. 586–591 (1991)
16. Bihan, N.L., Mars, J.: Subspace method for vector-sensor wave separation based on quaternion algebra. In: EUSIPCO, Toulouse (France) (2002)
17. XM2VTS: http://www.ee.surrey.ac.uk/Reseach/VSSP/xm2vtsdb (CDS00{1,6})
18. Luettin, J., Maître, G.: Evaluation protocol for the extended M2VTS database (XM2VTSDB). IDIAP-COM 05, IDIAP (1998)

A Semi-automatic Approach to Photo Identification of Wild Elephants

Alessandro Ardovini[1], Luigi Cinque[1], Francesca Della Rocca[2],
and Enver Sangineto[1]

[1] Computer Science Department, University of Rome "La Sapienza", via Salaria 113,
00198 Rome, Italy
[2] Department of Animal and Human Biology, University of Rome "La Sapienza",
viale dell'Università 32, 00185 Rome, Italy

Abstract. Zoologists studying elephant populations in wild environments need to recognize different individuals from photos taken in different periods of time. Individuals can be distinguished by the shape of the nicks on their ears. Nevertheless, shape comparison is not trivial due to a highly cluttered background. We propose a method for partially, non-connected curve matching able to compare photos of elephant ears.

1 Introduction

We present in this paper a photo identification system for elephant recognition. Elephant conservation and study need to trace the movements of wild individuals of a given population during time. Currently one of the most common, non-invasive and cheap technique is (human-made) photo identification. Elephants are distinguished using some biological features, such as the characteristic shape of the nicks present in their ears (e.g., see Figure 1 (a)). We propose a semi-automatic elephant identification system based on a partially defined match between the set of curves representing the nicks of a query photo and the set of curves of the nick of each database photo.

For a computer vision point of view, the problem is not trivial because of the usually highly cluttered images representing the interesting shapes. The final result of a common edge detection applied on typically available (low-resolution) images is composed of a non-connected set of nick curves which must be matched with the shapes of the nicks in the database (e.g., see Figure 1 (c)).

A similar problem is dealt with in [1], where the authors use the characteristic shape of the dorsal fin for dolphin identification. The dorsal fin curve is represented by means of an attributed string and a string matching procedure is used in order to estimate the similarity between two curves. Nevertheless, representing a real curve by means of a string is an unstable operation in which minor noise can produce very different strings to deal with. Analogously, in [4] the characteristics curves of dolphin fins, sea lion flippers and grey whale flukes are used to respectively recognize individuals of the three cetaccan species. Also in this case the assumption is a one-to-one curve matching. Both the mentioned systems need a human intervention in the image segmentation phase.

J. Martí et al. (Eds.): IbPRIA 2007, Part I, LNCS 4477, pp. 225–232, 2007.

Fig. 1. (a) Elephant photos. Top row: the nicks are marked in yellow. Sometimes elephant identification using the nick shape is a non-trivial task also for human beings (e.g., bottom row). (b) The two human-input points used for the ear reference system. (c) The edge map of Figure 1 (b).

The problem of matching multiple curves in a cluttered background image is rarely dealt with in computer vision literature, since the most of the existing curve matching approaches implicitly or explicitly assume to compare a pair of isolated curves rather than two sets of curves. Some examples of curve matching methods are: *curvature scale space* [6], *Fourier descriptors* [3] and *shape signature*-based approaches [1], which assume to deal with isolated silhouettes upon a uniform background (which is clearly not our case). *Active contour* methods [5] can deal with non-uniform backgrounds but their iterative energy minimization process can easily be trapped in false local minima in images with a complex background like the ones representing elephants in an uncontrolled environment (e.g., see Figure 1 (c)).

In our system the problem of reliably matching multiple curves in a cluttered background is partially alleviated using human input information. The human operator approximately selects the nicks' positions using the mouse. Then, the system produces a set of model-image rigid transformation hypotheses which refine the segmentation-detection process looking for the transformation which minimizes the dissimilarity between the compared nicks. Each transformation hypothesis is evaluated by taking into account both the position of the nicks with respect to the whole ear and the nicks' shapes.

2   Extraction of the Nick Curvature

In this section we show the different phases of the semi-automatic segmentation process performed on each image when it is either off-line stored in the system's repository or used as on-line query.

First of all, the user is requested to input some reference points in order to approximately define the elephant's head position, orientation and scale. With the assumption that the ground direction is given by the bottom of the image, only two points are sufficient to define a similarity-invariant reference system for the whole head and to automatically select the right/left profile. In fact the user is asked for clicking on the eye's central position (**a**) and on a second point (**b**) on the ear's boarder which is the farthest from the ear attachment (Figure 1 (b)). When either **a** or **b** are not visible due to occlusions or other reasons, the user can click on an approximate estimation of their positions (e.g., Figure 1 (b)). Since the definition of **b** is a bit arbitrary and since different users can select different points **a** and **b** for the same image, the spatial information so obtained can only be approximately used in order to estimate the nicks' positions with respect to the whole ear (see Section 2).

Once **a** and **b** have been selected, the system performs an edge detection (Figure 1 (c)) using the standard Canny edge detector [2] whose binarization threshold can possibly be varied by the user by means of a slider bar provided by the system's interface. Let us call I' the edge map of the image I. I' is shown to the user who is then requested to input the initial (**e**) and the final (**f**) endpoint for each nick (see Figures 2 (b) and (c)). The order in which **e** and **f** are inserted is not important. Once a pair of endpoints for every nick has been input, the system automatically computes the shortest path in I' between **e** and **f**. If **e** and **f** are not connected or the computed path is not the desired one, the user can add/delete points on I' using a suitable GUI. This is the only time-consuming human intervention requested by our system, which is only occasionally necessary for few points per nick. However this manual operation takes few dozens of seconds per nick.

The path between **e** and **f** gives the set of edge points defining the shape of the nick curve (Figure 2 (d)), which is subsampled using a fixed number (n) of points (currently, $n = 25$). Moreover, the endpoints e_i and f_i of a given nick P_i of I are normalized with respect to a symmetric-invariant reference system defined using the reference points a_I and b_I of I. Let $x = b_I - a_I$, and $d = \|x\|_2$. Moreover, let $v_1 = \frac{1}{d}x$ (see Figure 1 (b)); and v_2 be an unitary vector centered in a_I and orthogonal to v_1 whose direction is fixed swapping a $\pi/2$ angle clockwise from x for the right ear and counterclockwise for the left ear If e' is an endpoint selected by the user, the normalized nick endpoint **e** is then given by:

$$\mathbf{e} = \frac{1}{d} \begin{pmatrix} \mathbf{v}_1^T(\mathbf{e}' - \mathbf{a}_I) \\ \mathbf{v}_2^T(\mathbf{e}' - \mathbf{a}_I) \end{pmatrix} \tag{1}$$

and the same is for **f**. The reference system defined by v_1 and v_2, centered in a_I and with unit of length d is invariant with respect to symmetric transformations of the head appearance.

Finally, if the image is used as query (Q), we indicate with $Q_1, ...Q_N$ its nicks, being each Q_j ($1 \leq j \leq N$) associated with the endpoints g_j and h_j, obtained using Equation (1) and the corresponding reference points a_Q and b_Q.

3   Curve Sequence Matching

Given a database image I with $P_1, ...P_M$ nicks and a query image Q with $Q_1, ...Q_N$ nicks, the problem is to find a portion of I and a portion of Q which are similar, i.e., contain the same nicks. Even if both I and Q represent the same elephant's ear E, we can have $N \neq M$. In fact, a portion of E can be partially occluded either in I or in Q due to possible trees or other elephants. Moreover the lobe and other parts of the ear are sometimes folded and non visible.

We assume in the following that, if both Q and I represent the same ear E of the same elephant, then there is a unique portion V of E which is visible in both I and Q. This is a very common situation in photos taken by zoologists for (human) elephant identification and leads to searching for a unique sequence V of nicks belonging to both Q and I (see Figure 2 (a)).

The aim of the global matching phase is to compare $Q_1, ... Q_N$ with $P_1, ... P_M$ looking for two subsets of k nicks $Q_j, Q_{j+1}, ... Q_{j+k-1}$ and $P_i, P_{i+1}, ... P_{i+k-1}$ with similar positions with respect to the ear's reference points, respectively $\mathbf{a}_I$, $\mathbf{b}_I$ and $\mathbf{a}_Q$, $\mathbf{b}_Q$ (see Section 2). While in this step we are interested only in comparing the *positions* of $Q_j, Q_{j+1}, ... Q_{j+k-1}$ and $P_i, P_{i+1}, ... P_{i+k-1}$, in Section 4 we show how the system compares the *shapes* of the two nick sets.

Note that if $M \leq N$ then V is delimited by either P_1 or P_M (see Figure 2 (a)). Vice versa, if $M > N$ then V is delimited by either Q_1 or Q_N. The algorithm for the case in which $M \leq N$ is described below, while the case $M > N$ is dealt with analogously by exchanging $Q_1, ... Q_N$ with $P_1, ... P_M$.

Global Matching $(Q_1, ... Q_N, P_1, ... P_M)$
1   $\mu := \infty$.
    *** Case P_1 is matched with Q_j $(j \in [1, N])$ ***
2   For each $j \in [1, N]$, do:
3      $k := \min\{M, N - j + 1\}$. *** This is the size of V ***
4   If $CheckPosition(P_1, ... P_k, Q_j, ..., Q_{j+k-1}, k)$, then:
5         $d := Shape\ Difference\ (P_1, ... P_k, Q_j, ..., Q_{j+k-1}, k)$.
6   If $\mu > d$ then $\mu := d$.
    *** Case P_1 cannot be matched with any Q_j ***
7   For each $j \in [1, M - 1]$, do:
8   If $CheckPosition(P_{M-j+1}, ..., P_M, Q_1, ..., Q_j, j)$, then:
9         $d := Shape\ Difference\ (P_{M-j+1}, ..., P_M, Q_1, ..., Q_j, j)$.
10   If $\mu > d$ then $\mu := d$.
11 Return μ.

Referring to Figure 2 (a), the case in which P_1 can be matched with any Q_j is dealt with by the above algorithm in Steps 2-6, with, either $k = M$ or $k = N - j + 1$, depending on whether P_M belongs to V or not. Steps 7-10 deal with the case in which P_1 does not belong to V. The function $CheckPosition()$ is responsible to check the position consistency of the current ordered subsequence of matched nicks. This is done using the corresponding normalized endpoints (see Section 2) and verifying that, for each couple (P_l, Q_l), $l \in [1, k]$, the distances $\|\mathbf{e}_l - \mathbf{g}_l\|_2$ and $\|\mathbf{f}_l - \mathbf{h}_l\|_2$ are both lower than a given threshold (empirically fixed).

Once all the possible subsequence matches have been analyzed, the minimum computed dissimilarity value (μ) is returned in Step 11. This is the value which will be used to rank the current photo I with respect to the other database images. The resulting decreasing order sequence of database photos is finally shown to the user. Figure 3 shows the first three images ranked by the system in correspondence of the query shown in Figure 1 (b).

4   Shape Comparison

Given a query (Q_i) and an image (P_i) nick, the shape difference of the corresponding curves can be estimated by subsampling Q_i and P_i using the same number of points (n) and then computing the squared Euclidean distance between pairs of corresponding points $(\mathbf{q}_j, \mathbf{p}_j)$, such that: $\mathbf{q}_j \in Q_i$ and $\mathbf{p}_j \in P_i$ $(1 \le j \le n)$. However, before to compare Q_i and P_i, the two curves have to be aligned, i.e., they must be represented in a symmetric-invariant reference system in order to take into account for possible viewpoint changes. Nevertheless, since the shape comparison of two curves must be *carefully* estimated, we cannot use the reference points $\mathbf{a}_I$, $\mathbf{b}_I$, $\mathbf{a}_Q$ and $\mathbf{b}_Q$ for this purpose (see Sections 2 and 3). Rather, we use the nick-specific endpoints $\mathbf{e}_i$, $\mathbf{f}_i$, $\mathbf{g}_i$ and $\mathbf{h}_i$. Moreover, we have to take into account that a user can select slightly different endpoints for the same nick in different photos of the same animal. For this reason we compare the nick defined by the endpoints $\mathbf{e}$ and $\mathbf{f}$ with the nick defined by a pair of endpoints chosen *in the proximity of* $\mathbf{g}$ and $\mathbf{h}$.

If $\mathbf{g}_i$ and $\mathbf{h}_i$ are the endpoints of Q_i and Q' is the edge map of Q, then the neighborhoods $N(\mathbf{g}_i)$, $N(\mathbf{h}_i)$, respectively of $\mathbf{g}_i$ and $\mathbf{h}_i$ are defined using:

$$N(\mathbf{x}) = \{\mathbf{p}' \in Q' : \|\mathbf{x} - \mathbf{p}'\|_2 \le \lambda, \text{and } \mathbf{x} \text{ and } \mathbf{p}' \text{ are connected}\}, \qquad (2)$$

where λ is a distance threshold. We omit the algorithm for the effective construction of $N(\mathbf{g}_i)$ and $N(\mathbf{h}_i)$ since it is a trivial visit of the connected edge point set of Q' starting from, respectively, $\mathbf{g}_i$ and $\mathbf{h}_i$.

The below algorithm *Shape Difference* shows how $N(\mathbf{g}_i)$ and $N(\mathbf{h}_i)$ are used in order to hypothesize a set of symmetry transformations able to align P_i with the nick Q_i. The transformation hypotheses depend on different choices of the endpoints respectively in the set $N(\mathbf{g}_i)$ and $N(\mathbf{h}_i)$. The algorithm is based on the well known geometric observation that, given two pairs of points $\mathbf{q}_1 = (x_1, y_1)^T$, $\mathbf{q}_2 = (x_2, y_2)^T$ and $\mathbf{p}_1 = (x'_1, y'_1)^T$, $\mathbf{p}_2 = (x'_2, y'_2)^T$, there is a unique (up to a reflection) symmetric 2D transformation T such that $\mathbf{p}_1 = T(\mathbf{q}_1)$ and $\mathbf{p}_2 = T(\mathbf{q}_2)$. We represent T by means of a vector of four parameters: $T = (t_x, t_y, \theta, s)^T$, where t_x and t_y are the translation offsets, θ is the rotation and s the scale parameter. The parameters of T are given by the following quadruple:

$$\langle s = \|\mathbf{q}\|_2/\|\mathbf{p}\|_2, \theta = \arccos \frac{\mathbf{q}^T \mathbf{p}}{\|\mathbf{q}\|_2 \cdot \|\mathbf{p}\|_2}, \\ t_x = x'_1 - s \cdot (x_1 \cdot \cos\theta - y_1 \cdot \sin\theta), t_y = y'_1 - s \cdot (x_1 \cdot \sin\theta + y_1 \cdot \cos\theta) \rangle, \qquad (3)$$

where $\mathbf{q} = \mathbf{q}_2 - \mathbf{q}_1$ and $\mathbf{p} = \mathbf{p}_2 - \mathbf{p}_1$. The details of the algorithm are:

Shape Difference $(P_1, ... P_k, Q_1, ..., Q_k, k)$

1 $d := 0$.
2 For each $i \in [1, k]$, do:
3      $d_k := \infty$.
4   For each $(\mathbf{q}_w, \mathbf{q}_z) \in N(\mathbf{g}_i) \times N(\mathbf{h}_i)$, do:
5   Compute T using Equation (3) and the points $\mathbf{q}_w, \mathbf{q}_z, \mathbf{e}_i, \mathbf{f}_i$.
6   Let $Q_i^{(\mathbf{q}_w, \mathbf{q}_z)}$ be the shortest path between $\mathbf{q}_w$ and $\mathbf{q}_z$.
            Suppose: $P_i = \{\mathbf{p}_1, ..., \mathbf{p}_n\}$ and $Q_i^{(\mathbf{q}_w, \mathbf{q}_z)} = \{\mathbf{q}_1, ..., \mathbf{q}_n\}$.
7          $d^{(\mathbf{q}_w, \mathbf{q}_z)} := \sum_{j=1}^{n} \|\mathbf{p}_j - T(\mathbf{q}_j)\|_2^2$.
8   If $d_k > d^{(\mathbf{q}_w, \mathbf{q}_z)}$ then $d_k := d^{(\mathbf{q}_w, \mathbf{q}_z)}$.
9      $d := d + d_k$.
10 Return d/k.

In Step 6 $Q_i^{(\mathbf{q}_w, \mathbf{q}_z)}$ is subsampled using the same number (n) of points used to represent all the image nicks (e.g., P_i), see Section 2. For this reason we can directly compare the j-th point $(\mathbf{q}_j)$ of $Q_i^{(\mathbf{q}_w, \mathbf{q}_z)}$ with the j-th point $(\mathbf{p}_j)$ of P_i. This is done in Step 7 where the value of difference between P_i and $T(Q_i^{(\mathbf{q}_w, \mathbf{q}_z)})$ is stored in $d^{(\mathbf{q}_w, \mathbf{q}_z)}$. In the same step, the point $T(\mathbf{q}_j) = (x', y')^T$ obtained applying T to the point $\mathbf{q}_j = (x, y)^T$ is computed using:

$$x' = t_x + s \cdot (x \cdot \cos \theta - y \cdot \sin \theta), \tag{4}$$

$$y' = t_y + s \cdot (x \cdot \sin \theta + y \cdot \cos \theta). \tag{5}$$

Since we want that the difference between P_i and Q_i is given by the best possible alignment between the two nicks, the whole process is iterated for every pair of possible endpoints $(\mathbf{q}_w, \mathbf{q}_z) \in N(\mathbf{g}_i) \times N(\mathbf{h}_i)$ and the minimum value of $d^{(\mathbf{q}_w, \mathbf{q}_z)}$ is taken as the shape dissimilarity value between P_i and Q_i. Figure 2 (d) shows a graphical representation of the shape dissimilarity between the nick extracted from the query image of Figure 2 (b) and a nick of a database image corresponding to the same individual as the query (Figure 2 (c)).

5   Results

For testing purposes we have used an elephant photo database provided by the Department of Animal and Human Biology of the University of Rome "La Sapienza", which represents individuals of the elephant population of Zakouma Ciad National Park [7]. The database used for testing is composed of 332 images of 268 different individuals. Each individual is represented by one or more photos, respectively showing either the left or the right ear, and each ear of the image repository contains from one to four nicks. Other 200 different photos of the same individuals of the database have been randomly selected and used as queries. The photo used as queries have not been included into the system's database.

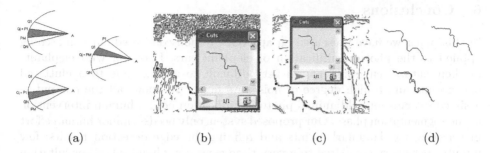

(a)	(b)	(c)	(d)

Fig. 2. (a) Matching of two nick sequences. The common subsequence V is marked in gray. (b) The nick extracted from the image of Figure 1 (c), used as query. (c) The nick extracted from the image of Figure 3 (a). (d) The difference between the two nicks once overlapped on a same reference system.

(a)	(b)	(c)

Fig. 3. The first three individuals ranked by the system with respect to the query of Figure 1 (b). The first image corresponds to the same individual of the query.

Experiments have been performed by zoologist researchers not involved in the system's implementation. Table 1 shows the results of their trials. The second row shows the number of queries for which the corresponding correct individual of the database has been ranked in the i-th position. The last column refers to those queries for which no match has been found. They all have been wrongly rejected by the *Global Matching* algorithm. The last row of Table 1 shows the *Cumulative Matching Characteristic* (CMC), defined as the probability $CMC(r)$ that, for a given query, the correct corresponding individual of the database is classified by the system in the first r positions.

Table 1. Number of queries ranked by the system in the first 10 positions

Position	1	2	3	4	5	6	7	8	9	10	N.C.
Query ♯	92	32	5	13	4	16	0	1	4	3	24
CMC	0.46	0.62	0.64	0.71	0.73	0.81	0.81	0.81	0.83	0.85	-

6   Conclusions

In this paper we have presented an approach to non-connected curve matching applied to the photo identification of elephant ears. Photo of wild elephants in their natural environment are very difficult to analyze due to a cluttered background and a high degree of noise. As far as we know, all the computer-assisted systems for wild animal photo identification need a human intervention in the segmentation phase. Our proposed system only needs a minor human effort in selecting few landmark points and refining the edge detection results: few minutes per query compared to a very time consuming hand-made consultation of a photo database. The requested human operations are conceptually simple and do not need domain-specific experience, while the transformation hypothesis generation using the neighborhoods of the user selected endpoints relax the need of a precise human intervention. Our experimental results show a very high CMC score with respect to other animal photo identification systems.

Acknowledgments. We want to thank Luciana Massaro, Dafne Petriccione and Sabrina Rossi for their precious help in testing the system.

References

1. Araabi, B.N., Kehtarnavaz, N.: A string matching computer-assisted system for dolphin photoidentification. Biomedical Engineering 28, 1269–1279 (2000)
2. Canny, J.: A computational approach to edge detection. IEEE Trans. on PAMI 8(6), 679–698 (1986)
3. Folkers, A., Samet, H.: Content-based image retrieval using Fourier descriptors on a logo database. In: ICPR '02, vol. 3, pp. 521–524 (2002)
4. Gope, C., Kehtarnavaz, N., Hillman, G., Wursig, B.: An affine invariant curve matching method for photo-identification of marine mammals. Pattern Recognition, 38, 125–132 (2005)
5. Kass, M., Witkin, A., Terzopoulos, D.: Snakes: Active contour models. International Journal of Computer Vision 1, 321–331 (1988)
6. Mokhtarian, F., Abbasi, S.: Shape similarity retrieval under affine transforms. Pattern Recognition 35(1), 31–41 (2002)
7. Petriccione, D., Ardovini, A., Cinque, L., Della Rocca, F., Massaro, L., Ortolani, A., Sangineto, E.: Computer-aided wild elephant identification. In: 11th Congress of the Int. Society for Behavior Ecology, p. 264 (2006)

Language Identification Based on Phone Decoding for Basque and Spanish*

Víctor G. Guijarrubia and M. Inés Torres

Departamento de Electricidad y Electrónica
Universidad del País Vasco, Apartado 644, 48080 Bilbao, Spain
{vgga,manes}@we.lc.ehu.es

Abstract. This paper presents some experiments in language identification for Spanish and Basque, both official languages in the Basque
Country in the North of Spain. We focus on four methods based on
phone decoding, some of which make use of phonotactic knowledge. We
run also a comparison between the use of a generic and a task-specific
phonotactic model. Despite initial poor performances, significant accuracies are achieved when better phonotactic knowledge is used. The use of
a task-specific phonotactic model performs slightly better, but it is only
useful when using less expensive methods. Finally, we present a temporal
evolution of the accuracies. Results show that 5-6 seconds are enough to
achieve similar percentage of correctly classified utterances.

1 Introduction

Language identification (LID) is a classical pattern recognition problem strongly
related to multilingual speech recognition and dialogue systems. It has typically
been addressed using different tactics, like those exploiting prosodic cues [1,2]
as rhythm or intonation. Nevertheless, most of them are based on speech recognition approximations: phone decoding approaches [3,4,5], which rely on phone
sequences; Gaussian mixture models [3,4] treating only the acoustic; and large
vocabulary continuous speech recognition approaches [6,7], which deal with full
lexical sequences.

The final goal of a LID systems is to identify the language being used by an
unknown speaker. Typically 6-9 languages are included in those LID systems.
However, for multilingual communities high performances are required, but only
for the languages in use, typically two or three.

The aim of this paper is to apply phone decoding techniques to Spanish-
Basque identification. Basque is a minority language which is the joint official
language along with Spanish for a community of 2,5 million people living in the
Basque Country in the North of Spain. Basque is more and more present in con-
temporary life, so interest in developing bilingual industrial applications related
to human language technologies has increased. However, speech recognition and
understanding systems need a robust Spanish-Basque language identification.

---

* This work was partially supported by the CICYT project TIN2005-08660-C04-03 and
by the University of the Basque Country under grant 9/UPV 00224.310-15900/2004.

The differences between Spanish and Basque fall on the lexical units and morphosyntactic structure. From a phonetic point of view, the set of Basque phones is not very different from the Spanish one. The two languages share the same vowel triangle (only five vowels). Nevertheless, Basque includes larger sets of fricative and affricate sounds. Thus, language identification using phone-based systems is presumably a difficult pattern recognition task.

The rest of the paper is organised as follows: Section 2 describes each of the methods used in this study, Section 3 contains information about the speech databases used in the experiments, Section 4 presents the results obtained using the different LID approaches, and Section 5 discusses the conclusions of the work.

2   Language Identification Methods

In order to perform the proposed language identification task, four phone decoding approaches were applied. These techniques rely on acoustic phonetic decoders, which find the best phone sequence associated to a speech signal. In our case, these decoders are based on the Viterbi algorithm, which finds the most likely path, given a input, through a probabilistic network. In the case of an acoustic phonetic decoder, this network is composed of the combination of all the acoustic models, usually Hidden Markov Models (HMMs) associated to a previously defined set of phones of the language. Thus, given a set of acoustic models Λ^l associated to a language l and an input sequence of acoustic observations $O = o_1 \ldots o_T$, a Viterbi decoder finds the best sequence of states $Q = q_1 \ldots q_T$ through the network of models,

$$Q = \arg\max_{q_1 \ldots q_T} P(q_1 \ldots q_T, o_1 \ldots o_T | \Lambda_l) \qquad (1)$$

The path Q determines a sequence of phones $X^l = X_1 \ldots X_N$, based on the previously defined set of HMMs associated to the phone set in language l.

The following subsections describe each of the techniques individually.

2.1   Parallel Acoustic Phonetic Decoding (PD)

For each language being studied, an unconstrained phone decoder is applied and the language which gives the most probable acoustic sequence is chosen as the identified language, so no phonotactic knowledge is being used. Thus, the identified language is obtained as

$$L = \arg\max_l P(O|X_l) \qquad (2)$$

2.2   Phone Decoder Scored by a Phonotactic Model (PD+PhM)

For every language being studied, an unconstrained acoustic decoder is applied, resulting in a sequence of decoding units for each language. A language-dependent phonotactic model is then employed to assign a score to each of the sequences for that language. The language of the utterance is selected to be that with the highest score; that is, the language for which

$$L = \arg\max_{l} P(X_l|Ph^l) \tag{3}$$

where Ph^l represents the phonotactic model for language l. Typically, these phonotactic models are modelled using *n-grams*.

2.3 Single Phone Decoder Scored by a Phonotactic Model (SPD+PhM)

This is a simplification of the PD+PhM method. Instead of performing one decoding per language, only one decoding is performed. For the other language, the decoded phone sequence is mapped and thus, the PD+PhM method can be applied. The idea behind this technique is to reduce the cost of the process and make the LID system faster.

2.4 Phone Decoder Constrained by a Phonotactic Model (PDPhM)

This method is similar to the first one. However, in this case the phone decoding is constrained by a phonotactic model.

The decoder is now similar to a speech recognition system. In this case, our goal is to find the a sequence of phones instead of a sequence of uttered words. Thus, the best sequence of phones X^l that fits the input sequence of acoustic observations O is found using the Bayes' rule

$$P(X^l|O) = P(O|X^l)P(X^l)/P(O) \tag{4}$$

$P(O|X^l)$ is the probability of the acoustic sequence given the phone string and is computed using the HMMs. $P(X^l)$ is the *a priori* probability of the phone sequence and is computed using a phonotactic model. In the same way, $P(O)$ represents the *a priori* probability of the acoustic sequence and is typically not computed, because is the same for all the possible lexical strings obtained from one decoding. However, when comparing the output of different recognisers, this probability should also be considered. In this work, we used an acoustic normalisation, referred as an acoustic confidence measure, in a similar way that presented in [8]. This normalisation reported improvements in other LID applications [9]. The acoustic likelihood of each of the decoded phone is normalised by the likelihood of the best unconstrained phone sequence in that period of time.

Finally, the hypothesised language is assumed to be the one for which

$$L = \arg\max_{l} P(X^l|O) \tag{5}$$

3   Speech Corpora

Experiments reported in this paper were performed using several speech databases.

To train the basic acoustic models for Basque, a phonetically balanced database called EHU-DB16 [10] was used. This database is composed of 9394 sentences uttered by 25 speakers and contains around 340000 phones. For Spanish, the phonetic corpus of the Albayzin database [11] was used. It consists of 4800 sentences uttered by 29 speakers and it is also phonetically balanced.

The evaluation set consisted of a weather forecast database recorded for both Spanish and Basque [12]. This database contains 500 different pair of sentences uttered by 36 bilingual speakers. The 500 pairs were divided into blocks of 50 sentences each and every speaker uttered the sentences in one of these blocks. A total of around 3 hours for Spanish and 3.5 for Basque were recorded, resulting in more than 8000 words for each language. Note that both languages share the same task, the same speakers and the same recording conditions in this evaluation set.

4   Experimental Results

4.1   Experimental Conditions

To perform the different experiments, the databases were parametrised into 12 Mel-frequency cepstral coefficients with delta and acceleration coefficients, energy and delta-energy. Thus, four acoustic representations were defined. The length of the analysis window was 25 ms and the window shift, 10 ms.

Each phone-like unit was modelled by a typical left to right non-skipping self-loop three state HMM, with 32 Gaussian mixtures per state and acoustic representation. A total of 35 context-independent phones were used for Basque and 24 for Spanish.

For the PD+PhM, SPD+PhM and PDPhM techniques a phonotactic model is needed to score the recognised phone sequence. In these experiments, instead of n-gram models, a *k-testable in the strict sense* (k-TTS) model [13] was used, since the k-TTS models keep the syntactic constraint of the language. Different k values were tested: from $k = 2$ to $k = 5$.

Two phonotactic models were considered for the proposed techniques: a generic and a task-specific model. Our goal in this case was to analyse whether a task adaptation is really required or not.

For the generic approach, for each of the languages, several text corpus were used to train a generic phonotactic model. For the task-specific modelling, a text corpus specific for the task of the database was used to train the different models. All the sentences in this text corpus are different from the sentences used in the evaluation database.

4.2   Results of the Experiments

In order to carry out Spanish-Basque identification experiments, a complete utterance was presented to the LID system and the different approaches of Section 2 were applied.

PD Method. Table 1 shows the percentage of correctly identified utterances.

Table 1. Percentage of correctly classified sentences when using the PD approach

Spanish	Basque
45.82	82.66

Poor performance is achieved using this technique, since both languages are acoustically similar. As suggested in [6], the channel conditions could also be affecting the results and be benefiting the Basque identification, since the recording conditions for the test database and the Basque database EHU-DB16 are more similar.

PD+PhM Method. Table 2 shows the results obtained. For these results, a recognised-string length normalisation is used, since this approximation yielded to the best results.

Table 2. Percentage of correctly classified sentences when using the PD+PhM approach. Results for different k values and generic and task-specific phonotactic models are given.

	Generic PM		Task-specific PM	
	Spanish	Basque	Spanish	Basque
k=2	97.00	74.06	99.11	69.44
k=3	95.88	92.94	99.39	89.50
k=4	95.38	95.67	99.28	93.67
k=5	96.11	95.94	99.11	95.39

As could be expected, the use of phonotactic constraint yields to a great improvement. The use of better language models increase the overall performance, since more accurate information is being used. The use of task-specific language models performs, in general, slightly better. However, it does not outperform the results obtained with generic language models.

SPD+PhM Method. Table 3 shows the classification accuracies in this case. As reported before, for this technique, in addition to the generic - task-specific phonotactic model comparison, we ran a comparison between Basque decoder and Spanish decoder.

When using the Basque decoder, the Spanish sequence is obtained mapping the decoded phone sequence. When using the Spanish decoder, a new Basque phonotactic model is used, trained on a corpus previously mapped from Basque to Spanish.

The SPD+PhM method does not perform well in overall when using the Basque decoder. Poor results are achieved for Spanish, even if it performs perfectly for Basque. This is probably because Basque is used for the phone decoding

Table 3. Percentage of correctly classified sentences when using the SPD+PhM approach. Results for different k values, generic and task-specific phonotactic models and Basque and Spanish decoder are given.

	Basque acoustic decoder				Spanish acoustic decoder			
	Generic PM		Task-specific PM		Generic PM		Task-specific PM	
	Spanish	Basque	Spanish	Basque	Spanish	Basque	Spanish	Basque
k=2	56.95	96.94	90.26	90.94	81.75	99.16	97.71	84.00
k=3	67.13	99.00	96.49	97.38	85.09	98.88	98.88	90.61
k=4	74.02	99.22	96.10	98.16	88.70	97.94	98.99	92.05
k=5	67.13	99.00	95.99	98.50	91.49	96.61	98.77	93.11

in this approach. When using the Spanish decoder, better results are achieved, but not as good as PD+PhM.

In this case, the use of a task-specific model helps more than for the PD+PhM method. Better overall results are achieved, comparable to those obtained for the PD+PhM technique.

PDPhM Method. Table 4 shows the accuracies for this method. In these experiments, in addition to the acoustic normalisation discussed in section 2.4, a recognised-string length normalisation was also applied.

Integrating the phonotactic knowledge in the decoding process and using the acoustic normalisation gives a better estimate of the score of the recognised phone sequence. As a result of this, a better identification of each utterance is obtained, resulting in accuracies of 99% with $k = 4$ or higher. In this case, the use of a task-specific phonotactic model performs slightly better, but without outperforming the LID system based on a generic phonotactic model.

Table 4. Percentage of correctly classified sentences when using the PDPhM approach and applying the acoustic normalisation

	Generic PM		Task-specific PM	
	Spanish	Basque	Spanish	Basque
k=2	99.28	72.89	99.72	81.17
k=3	99.89	93.89	99.89	96.44
k=4	99.89	98.33	99.89	99.11
k=5	99.89	99.11	99.89	99.61

4.3   Studying the Temporal Evolution

Another aspect in which we wanted to focus on was the temporal evolution of the accuracies. Our main goal is to incorporate the LID system into a speech recognition or dialogue system. For this purpose, a fast language identification is required. Thus, only speech fragments from two to six seconds were presented to the LID system.

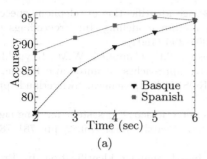 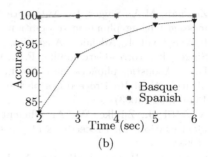

(a)   (b)

Fig. 1. Temporal evolution of the accuracies when using the (a)PD+PhM and (b)PDPhM method. Only results for generic phonotactic models with $k = 4$ are presented. Squares are used for Spanish and triangles for Basque.

Figure 1 shows the LID system accuracies when the PD+PhM and PDPhM methods are used for speech segments of two to six seconds. In both cases we used the generic phonotactic models with $k = 4$.

The figures show that 5-6 seconds of speech signal are enough to achieve accuracies similar to those presented in the 4.2 subsection. Note that the LID system tends to classify short utterance as Spanish, producing more errors for Basque. However, with some time it recovers from these mistakes and at the end, the results are similar for both languages.

5   Concluding Remarks

Several LID systems for Spanish-Basque identification were presented. Results confirm that the Spanish-Basque identification is a difficult task when relying on acoustic scores only. Nevertheless, the use of a phonotactic model to re-score the sequences of phones results in a great improvement. Accuracies of 99% are obtained when integrating the phonotactic knowledge in the decoding process.

The use of task-specific phonotactic model does not outperform the generic phonotactic model in general. However, when using less computational expensive LID systems like SPD+PhM, the inclusion of this kind of knowledge helps the LID system obtain accuracies similar to those for better techniques.

The temporal study shows that approximately 5-6 seconds are enough to achieve similar accuracies to those achieved using the full utterance.

References

1. Itakahashi, S., Du, L.: Language identification based on speech fundamental frequency. In: Proceedings of the EUROSPEECH. vol. 2, Madrid, Spain, pp. 1359–1362 (1995)
2. Mary, L., Rao, K.S., Yegnanarayana, B.: Neural network classifiers for language identification using phonotactic and prosodic features. In: Proceedings of International Conference on Intelligent Sensing and Information Processing, Chennai, India, pp. 404–408 (2005)

3. Zissman, M.A., Singer, E.: Automatic language identification of telephone speech messages using phoneme recognition and n-gram modelling. In: Proceedings of ICASSP. vol. 1., Adelaide, Australia, pp. 305–308 (1994)
4. Singer, E., Torres-Carrasquillo, P.A., Gleason, T.P., Campbell, W.M., Reynolds, D.A.: Acoustic, phonetic and discriminative approaches to automatic language identification. In: Proceedings of the EUROSPEECH, Geneva, Switzerland, pp. 1349–1352 (2003)
5. Navrátil, J., Zühlke, W.: An efficient phonotactic-acoustic system for language identification. In: Proceedings of the ICASSP. Seattle, USA, vol. 2, pp. 781–784 (1998)
6. Schultz, T., Rogina, I., Waibel, A.: Lvcsr-based language identification. In: Proceedings of the ICASSP, Atlanta, USA, pp. 781–784 (1996)
7. Metze, F., Kemp, T., Schaaf, T., Schultz, T., Soltau, H.: Confidence measure based language identification. In: Proceedings of the ICASSP, Istanbul, Turkey (2000)
8. Young, S.R.: Detecting misrecognitions and out-of-vocabulary words. In: Proceedings of the ICASSP. Adelaide, Australia, vol. 2, pp. 21–24 (1994)
9. Hieronymus, J.L., Kadambe, S.: Spoken language identification using large vocabulary speech recognition. In: Proceedings of International Conference of Spoken Language Processing, Philadelphia, USA pp. 1780–1783 (1996)
10. Guijarrubia, V., Torres, I., RodrÃ-guez, L.: Evaluation of a spoken phonetic database in basque language. In: Proceedings of the 4th International Conference on Language Resources and Evaluation. Lisbon, vol. 6, pp. 2127–2130 (2004)
11. Moreno, A., Poch, D., Bonafonte, A., Lleida, E., Llisterri, J., MariÃo, J.B., Nadeu, C.: Albayzin speech database: Design of the phonetic corpus. In: Proceedings of the EUROSPEECH, Lisbon (1993)
12. Pérez, A., Torres, I., Casacuberta, F., Guijarrubia, V.: A Spanish-Basque weather forecast corpus for probabilistic speech translation. In: 5th SALTMIL Workshop on Minority Languages, Genoa, Italy, pp. 99–101 (2006)
13. Torres, I., Varona, A.: k-tss language model in a speech recognition system. Computer Speech and Language 15(2), 127–149 (2001)

Computer Assisted Transcription of Speech*

Luis Rodríguez[1], Francisco Casacuberta[2], and Enrique Vidal[2]

[1] Departamento de Sistemas Informáticos. Universidad de Castilla La Mancha
[2] Departamento de Sistemas Informáticos y Computación. Universidad Politécnica de Valencia

Abstract. Speech recognition systems have proved their usefulness in very different tasks. Nevertheless, the present state-of-the-art of the speech technologies does not make it possible to achieve perfect transcriptions in most of the cases. Owing to this fact, human intervention is necessary to check and correct the results of such systems. We present a novel approach that faces this problem by combining the efficiency of the automatic speech recognition systems with the accuracy of the human transcriptor. The result of this process is a cost-effective perfect transcription of the input signal.

1 Introduction

Speech recognition systems are far from being perfect. Complex tasks with large vocabularies, noisy environments, spontaneous speech, etc. result in a significant number of errors in transcriptions. When high quality transcriptions are needed, a human transcriptor is required to verify and correct the (imperfect) system's transcriptions.

This process is usually performed *off-line*. First, the system returns a full transcription of the input audio signal. Next, the human transcriptor reads it sequentially (while listening to the original audio signal) and corrects the possible mistakes made by the system. This solution is rather uncomfortable and inefficient for the human corrector.

An interactive *on-line* scenario can allow for a more efficient approach. Here, the automatic speech recognition system (ASR) and the human transcriptor cooperate to generate the final transcription of the input signal. The rationale behind this approximation is to combine the accuracy provided by the human transcriptor with the efficiency of the ASR. This approach is called "Computer Assisted Transcription of Speech" (CATS) in this article and it is based on the interactive approach previously applied to Computer Assisted Translation (CAT) ([4], [3]) .

Experiments with the proposed CATS approach suggest that the interactive paradigm not only can be more confortable for the human transcriptor but can also reduce the overall effort needed.

---

* This work has been partially supported by the Spanish project iDoc TIN2006-15694-C02-01.

J. Martí et al. (Eds.): IbPRIA 2007, Part I, LNCS 4477, pp. 241–248, 2007.

The organization of the article is as follows: First, the CATS framework is introduced in section 2 and formalized in section 2.1. An initial implementation is described in section 2.3. The experiments and results are comented in section 3. Finally, some conclusions are presented in the final section.

2   Foundations of CATS

This section overviews our approach to CATS. As illustrated in figure 1, the process starts when the ASR system proposes a full *transcription* $\hat{s}$ (or a set with N-best transcriptions) of a suitable segment of the *input signal* x. Then, the human transcriptor (named *user* from now on) reads this transcription until he or she finds a mistake; i.e, he or she validates a prefix $\hat{s}_p$ of the transcription which is error-free. Now, the user can enter a word (or words), c, to *correct* the erroneous text that follows the validated prefix. This action produces a new *prefix* p (the previously validated prefix, $\hat{s}_p$, followed by c). Then, the ASR system takes into account the new prefix to suggest a suitable continuation (or a set of best possible continuations) to this prefix (i.e., a new $\hat{s}$), thereby starting a new cycle. This process is repeated until a correct, full transcription t of x is accepted by the user.

A key point on this interactive process is that, at each user-system iteration, the system can take advantage of the prefix validated so far to attempt an improved prediction.

	(**x**)	〜〜〜〜〜 (waveform)
ITER-0	(p)	( )
ITER-1	($\hat{s}$)	(*Nine extra soul are planned half beam discovered these years*)
	($\hat{s}_p$)	(**Nine**)
	(**c**)	(extrasolar)
	(p)	(Nine extrasolar)
ITER-2	($\hat{s}$)	(*planets have been discovered these years*)
	($\hat{s}_p$)	(**planets have been discovered**)
	(**c**)	(this)
	(p)	(Nine extrasolar planets have been discovered this)
FINAL	($\hat{s}$)	(*year*)
	(**c**)	(#)
	($p \equiv t$)	(**Nine** <u>extrasolar</u> **planets have been discovered** <u>this</u> **year**)

Fig. 1. Example of CATS. See the text for details.

Recently, a similar approach has been sucessfully applied in computer assisted translation (CAT) [4], [3], where experiments have shown that this kind of systems can save significant amounts of human effort.

2.1   Formal Framework for CATS

Traditionally, speech recognition is stated as the problem of searching for a sequence of words, $\hat{w}$, that with maximum probability has produced a given utterance, x:

$$\hat{w} = \underset{w}{\operatorname{argmax}} \, Pr(w \mid x)$$

$$= \underset{w}{\operatorname{argmax}} \, Pr(x \mid w) \cdot Pr(w) \tag{1}$$

$Pr(x \mid w)$ is approximated by acoustic models (usually hidden Markov models [6], [8]) and $Pr(w)$ is approximated by a language model (usually n-grams [6]).

In the CATS framework, in addition to the given utterance x, a *prefix* p of the transcription (validated and/or corrected by the user) is available and the ASR should try to complete this prefix by searching for a most likely *suffix* $\hat{s}$ as:

$$\hat{s} = \underset{s}{\operatorname{argmax}} \, Pr(s \mid x, p)$$

$$= \underset{s}{\operatorname{argmax}} \, Pr(x \mid s, p) \cdot Pr(s \mid p) \tag{2}$$

Equation (2) is very similar to (1), being w the concatenation of p and s. The main difference is that p is given. Therefore, the search must be performed over all possible suffixes s of p and the language model probability $Pr(s \mid p)$ must account for the words that can be uttered *after the prefix* p.

In order to solve equation (2), the signal x can be considered split into two fragments, x_1^b and x_{b+1}^m, where m is the length of x. By further considering the boundary point b as a hidden variable in (2), we can write:

$$\hat{s} = \underset{s}{\operatorname{argmax}} \sum_{0 \leq b \leq m} \Pr(x, b \mid s, p) \cdot \Pr(s \mid p) \tag{3}$$

We can now make the *naïve* (but realistic) assumption that the probability of x_1^b given p does not depend on the suffix and the probability of x_{b+1}^m given s does not depend on the prefix, to rewrite (3) as:

$$\hat{s} \approx \underset{s}{\operatorname{argmax}} \sum_{0 \leq b \leq m} \Pr(x_1^b \mid p) \cdot \Pr(x_{b+1}^m \mid s) \cdot \Pr(s \mid p) \tag{4}$$

Finally, the sum over all the possible segmentations can be approximated by the dominating term, leading to:

$$\hat{s} \approx \underset{s}{\operatorname{argmax}} \max_{0 \leq b \leq m} \Pr(x_1^b \mid p) \cdot \Pr(x_{b+1}^m \mid s) \cdot \Pr(s \mid p) \tag{5}$$

This optimization problem entails finding an optimal boundary point, $\hat{b}$, associated with the optimal suffix decoding, $\hat{s}$. That is, the signal x is actually split into two segments, $x_p = x_1^{\hat{b}}$ and $x_s = x_{\hat{b}+1}^m$. The first one corresponds to the *prefix* and the second to the *suffix*. Therefore, the search for the best suffix that completes a prefix p can be performed just over segments of the signal corresponding to the possible suffixes and, on the other hand, we can take advantage of the information coming from the prefix to tune the language model constraints modelled by $Pr(s \mid p)$. This is discussed in the next subsections.

2.2 Adapting the Language Model

Perhaps the simplest way to deal with $Pr(s \mid p)$ is to adapt an *n-gram* language model to cope with the consolidated prefix. Given that a conventional *n-gram* models the probability $P(\omega)$ (where ω is the concatenation of p and s, i.e the whole sentence), it is necessary to modify this model to take into account the conditional probability $Pr(s \mid p)$.

Let $p = \omega_1^k$ be a consolidated prefix and $s = \omega_{k+1}^l$ be a possible suffix. We can compute $Pr(s|p)$ as it is shown in equation 6.

$$
\begin{aligned}
Pr(s \mid p) &= Pr(p, s)/Pr(p) \\
&\approx \frac{\prod_{i=1}^l Pr(\omega_i \mid \omega_{i-n+1}^{i-1})}{\prod_{i=1}^k Pr(\omega_i \mid \omega_{i-n+1}^{i-1})} \\
&= \prod_{i=k+1}^l Pr(\omega_i \mid \omega_{i-n+1}^{i-1})
\end{aligned}
\tag{6}
$$

Moreover, for the terms from $k + 1$ to $k + n - 1$ of this factorization, we have additional information coming from the already known words w_{k-n+2}^k, leading to:

$$
\begin{aligned}
P(s \mid p) &\approx \prod_{i=k+1}^{k+n-1} Pr(w_i \mid w_{i-n+1}^{i-1}) \cdot \\
&\quad \prod_{i=k+n}^l Pr(w_i \mid w_{i-n+1}^{i-1})
\end{aligned}
\tag{7}
$$

The first term accounts for the probability of the $n - 1$ words of the suffix, whose probability is conditioned by words from the validated prefix, and the second one is the usual n-gram probability for the rest of the words in the suffix.

2.3 Searching

In this section, a possible implementation of a CATS decoder is described. In the first iteration of the CATS process, p is empty. Therefore, the decoder has to generate a full transcription of x as shown in equation (1). Afterwards, the user-validated prefix p has to be used to generate a suitable continuation s in the following iterations of the interactive-transcription process.

A simple possibility would be to perform the decoding in two steps: first, the validated prefix p could be used to segment the signal x into x_p and x_s and, then, x_s could be decoded by using a "suffix language model" (SLM) as in (7). The problem here is that the signal can not be optimally segmented into x_p and x_s if only the information of the prefix p is considered.

A better approach is to explicitly rely on equation (5) to implement a decoding process in one step, as in classical speech recognition. The decoder should be forced to *match* the previously validated prefix p and then continue searching for a suffix $\hat{s}$ according to the constraints (7). This can be achieved by building a special language model which can be seen as the "concatenation" of a *linear* model which strictly accounts for the succesive words in p and the SLM (7). An example of this language model is shown in Figure 2

Owing to the finite-state nature of this special language model, the search involved in equation (5) can be efficiently carried out using the well known *Viterbi* algorithm [10]. Apart from the optimal suffix decoding, $\hat{s}$, a correspondingly optimal segmentation of the speech signal is then obtained as a byproduct.

3   Experimental Results

To assess the CATS approximation proposed in this paper, different experiments were carried out.

3.1   Corpora

Two different corpora have been used. The first one is the *EuTrans* Corpus [1], composed of sentences describing conversations between a tourist and a hotel recepctionist. The second is the *Albayzin geographic corpus* [5], consisting of oral queries to a geographic database. The main features of both corpora are presented in table 1.

3.2   Error Measures

Two kind of measures has been adopted. On the one hand, the *well known* word error rate (WER) has been used. On the other hand, the word stroke ratio (WSR) ([4], [3]), a measure borrowed from CAT has been employed. This measure is computed by using a reference transcription of the speech segments considered. After a first CATS hypothesys, the longest common prefix between this hypothesys and the reference is obtained and the first unmatching word from the hypothesis is replaced by the corresponding reference word. This process is iterated until a full match with the reference is achieved. The WSR is the number of required corrections divided by the overall number of reference words.

The comparison between WER and WSR would give us an idea about the amount of effort required by a CATS user with respect to the effort needed by using a classical speech recognition system followed by a post-editing.

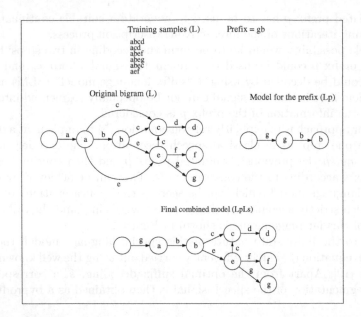

Fig. 2. Example of a CATS language model. Given the training set of the figure, a $n - gram$ (L) for this training set is built first. Then, a *linear* model (L_p) which accounts for the prefix gb is constructed. Finally, these two models are combined into a single model $(L_p L_s)$ as shown.

Table 1. Features of the Eutrans and Albayzin corpora

	Eutrans	Albayzin
Test sentences	336	4403
Speakers	20	89
Running words	3340	47822
Training vocabulary size	684	1271
Test-set perplexity (3-grams)	7.4	8.5

3.3   Experiments

The experiments have been performed using the ATROS (*Automatically Trainable Recognizer Of Speech*) system [7]. In all these experiments monophone HMMs were used. Speech preprocess and feature extraction consisted in speech boundary detection, followed by the computation the first ten MEL cepstral coefficients plus the energy, along with the corresponding first and second derivatives [7]. Lexical entries were (automatically) built into deterministic automata from the word-to-phoneme transcription of each entry [7]. Finally, as discussed in section 2.2 two different kinds of language models have been used. On the one hand, a special language model is used to force the system to recognize the prefix. On the other hand, a general *n-gram* language model is combined with the previous one as explained in section 2.3 in order to search for the suffix in each iteration of the CATS process. This language model is a *3-gram* language model, trained using the SRLIM [9] toolkit.

3.4 Results

As previously mentioned, the difference between WER and WSR results presented in Table 2 is an estimation of the reduction in human effort achieved by using CATS with respect to the post-editing classic ASR output. From these results, it can be concluded that, in the EuTrans task, the CATS approach can save about 19 % of the overall effort, in terms of word-level corrections. In the case of the Albayzin Geographic corpus, the reduction achieved is about 14 %.

Table 2. Results obtained with the Eutrans and the Albayzin corpora

	Eutrans	Albayzin
WER	11.4	11.6
WSR	9.3	10.1
% Improvement	≈ 19	≈ 14

It is important to notice that WER results in table 2 do not correspond to those reported in [2] because of the different test sets used.

4 Conclusions

A new approach to the production of perfect transcriptions of speech has been presented. This approach combines the efficiency of an automatic speech recognition system with the accuracy of a human transcriptor. A simple implementation of this system has been described and some experiments have been carried out. The results are very promising even with this simple approximation. Future work in this field will focus on developping better prefix-constrained language models.

In this first approach to the problem, experiments involving real users have not been considered, mainly due to the lack of experimental flexibility. In further developments, human transcriptors should be employed in order to properly assess the practical feasibility of the framework here presented.

In addition to this, the CATS approach could be applied to different tasks apart from pure speech transcription. Specifically, in fields like speech tagging, topic detection in speech, etc.

References

1. Amengual, J.C., Benedí, J.M., Casacuberta, F., Castano, A., Castellanos, A., Jiménez, V., Lloréns, D., Marzal, A., Pastor, M., Prat, F., Vidal, E., Vilar, J.M.: The EuTrans-I Speech Translation System. Machine Translation 15, 75–103 (2000)
2. Castro, M.J., Llorens, D., Sánchez, J.A., Casacuberta, F., Aibar, P., Segarra, E.: A fast version of the atros system. In: European Conference on Speech Communication and Technology. EUROSPEECH'99, Budapest, pp. 1299–1302 (September 1999)

3. Civera, J., Vilar, J.M., Cubel, E., Lagarda, A.L., Casacuberta, F., Vidal, E., Picó, D., González, J.: A syntactic pattern recognition approach to computer assisted translation. In: Fred, A., Caelli, T., Campilho, A., Duin, R.P.W., de Ridder, D. (eds.) Advances in Statistical, Structural and Syntactical Pattern Recognition – Joint IAPR Imternational workshops on Syntactical and Structural Pattern Recognition (SSPR 2004) and Statistical Pattern Recognition (SPR 2004). LNCS, Springer, Heidelberg (August 2004)
4. Cubel, E., Civera, J., Vilar, J.M., Lagarda, A.L., Barrachina, S., Vidal, E., Casacuberta, F., Picó, D., González, J., Rodríguez, L.: Finite-state models for computer assisted translation. In: Proceedings of the 16th European Conference on Artificial Intelligence (ECAI04), Valencia, Spain, pp. 586–590 (2004)
5. Díaz-Verdejo, J.E., Peinado, A.M., Rubio, A.J., Segarra, E., Prieto, N., Casacuberta, F.: Albayzin: A task oriented spanish speech corpus. In: Proceedings of First Intern. Conf. on Language Resources and Evaluation (LREC-98), vol. 1, pp. 497–501 (1998)
6. Jelinek, F.: Statistical Methods for Speech Recognition. The MIT Press, Cambridge, Massachusetts, USA (1998)
7. Llorens, D., Casacuberta, F., Segarra, E., Sánchez, J.A., Aibar, P.: Acoustical and syntactical modeling in ATROS system. In: Proceedings of International Conference on Acoustic, Speech and Signal Processing (ICASSP99), pp. 641–644, Phoenix, Arizona, USA (March 1999)
8. Rabiner, L.: A tutorial on hidden Markov models and selected applications in speech recoginition. In: Proceedings of the IEEE, vol. 77, pp. 257–286 (1989)
9. Stolcke, A.: SRILM - an extensible language modeling toolkit. In: Proceedings of the International Conference on Spoken Language Processing (ICSLP02), Denver, Colorado, USA, pp. 901–904 (September 2002)
10. Viterbi, A.J.: Error bounds for convolutional codes and an asymptotically optimum decoding algorithm. IEEE Trans. on Information Theory 13(2), 260–269 (1967)

Word Segments in Category-Based Language Models for Automatic Speech Recognition

Raquel Justo and M. Inés Torres

Departamento de Electricidad y Electrónica
Universidad del País Vasco
E-48080 Leioa Spain
webjublr@lg.ehu.es, manes@we.lc.ehu.es

Abstract. The aim of this work is to integrate segments of words into a category-based Language Model. Two proposals of this kind of models are presented. On the other hand an interpolation of a category-based model with a classical word-based Language Model is studied as well. The models were integrated into an ASR system and evaluated in terms of WER. Experiments on a spontaneous dialogue corpus in Spanish are reported. These experiments show that integrating word segments in a category-based Language Model, a better performance of the model can be achieved.

1 Introduction

Nowadays statistical Language Models (LM) are used in the Automatic Speech Recognition (ASR) systems. Large amounts of training data are required to get a robust estimation of the parameters of such models. However, there are a lot of ASR system applications where there is not a great deal of training material available. One of the ways to deal with the sparsness of data is to cluster the vocabulary of the application into a smaller number of categories [1]. Replacing words by the category they belong to entails significant reduction in the number of parameters to be estimated, thus, smaller training corpora can be used.

Nevertheless, the reduction in the number of parameters leads to a coarser model that is going to be less accurate in predicting the next word. As can be seen in previous works [1] a category-based language model only captures the relations between groups of words and "forgets" about the relations between particular words. This fact involves worst performance of the LM.

To avoid the lost of information associated with the use of a category-based LM, interpolated models are used. The interpolation of word-based and category-based LM-s, for instance, can take advantage of the two different information sources, providing better performances of the LM. Many authors [2] have defined an interpolated LM as a linear combination of a word-based and a category-based LM.

In this work, another way of combine the mentioned information sources is proposed. A LM based on categories consisting of word segments. Such a model could be understood as a classical category-based LM, but in this case, categories

J. Martí et al. (Eds.): IbPRIA 2007, Part I, LNCS 4477, pp. 249–256, 2007.

consist of segments of words instead of being formed by isolated words. In this way, a specific word-based LM can be generated for each category. Therefore, the information about the relations among the words, that take part in the segments of a category, will be taken into account and the whole information related to particular words is not going to be lost.

We propose, in this work, the integration of word segments in a category-based LM. Two approaches for this kind of models are presented. A linear combination of one of these models and a classical word-based LM is studied as well. These models were included into an ASR module in a dialogue system application. Dialogue systems are one of the most interesting applications in the field of speech technologies. The description of this kind of systems can be found in [3,4,5]. The aim of dialogue systems is to speak naturally with users, but natural human language is based on a large amount of prior knowledge that a system cannot use. Because of this fact, the use of an appropriate LM that is adapted to the application and capable of capturing the structure of the sentences uttered by speakers is very important.

The task consists of telephone queries about long-distance train schedules, destinations and prices uttered by potential users of the system. Experiments on a spontaneous dialogue corpus in Spanish were carried out. These experiments show that integrating word segments in a category-based LM, a better performance of the model can be achieved.

2   Word Segments in Category-Based Language Models

2.1   LM Based on Categories Consisting of Word Sequences, M_{sw}

Let $C = \{c_i\}$ be a previously defined set of categories selected using any classification criteria (statistical, linguistic,...). Each category consists of a set of segments that has been previously defined as well. Each segment in a category is formed by a sequence of several words. Our goal is to estimate the probability of a sequence of N words $\bar{w} = w_1, w_2, \ldots, w_N$ according to a LM based on categories consisting of segments. If this sequence is categorized, using any set of categories consisting of segment of words, the corresponding category sequence is written as $\bar{c} = c_1, c_2, \ldots, c_T$ where $T \leq N$. On the other hand, we are going to consider the representation of a sequence of N words in terms of a segmentation of M subsequences, as follows:

$$\bar{w} = w_1, \ldots, w_N = w_{a_0=1}^{a1}, \ldots, w_{a_{M-1}+1}^{a_M=N} . \tag{1}$$

where $w_{a_{i-1}+1}^{a_i} = w_{a_{i-1}+1}, \ldots, w_{a_i}$.

Let us define a segmentation, s, as a vector of M indexes, $s = (a_1, \ldots, a_M)$ that satisfy: $i < j \Rightarrow a_i < a_j$ and $S(\bar{w})$ as the set of all possible segmentations of a $\bar{w}$ sequence of words.

In this work, we are going to take into account only the segmentations compatible with the possible sequences of categories given a previously defined set of categories C. It means that we are going to only consider the segmentations of the following form:

$$\bar{w} = w_1, \ldots, w_N = w_{a_0=1}^{a_1}, \ldots, w_{a_{T-1}+1}^{a_T=N} .$$ (2)

where $w_{a_{i-1}+1}^{a_i}$ must be a segment belonging to a c_i category.

The way the segmentation of a sequence of words is done can be understood as a hidden variable, s. In this way, a first approach of a LM based on categories formed by segments could be represented by Equation 3:

$$P_{M_{sw}}(\bar{w}) = \sum_{\forall \bar{c} \in C} \sum_{\forall s \in S_{\bar{c}}(\bar{w})} P(\bar{w}, \bar{c}, s) = \sum_{\forall \bar{c} \in C} \sum_{\forall s \in S_{\bar{c}}(\bar{w})} P(\bar{w}, s|\bar{c})P(\bar{c}) =$$
$$= \sum_{\forall \bar{c} \in C} \sum_{\forall s \in S_{\bar{c}}(\bar{w})} P(\bar{w}|s, \bar{c})P(s|\bar{c})P(\bar{c}) .$$ (3)

being C the set of all the possible category sequences given a predetermined set of categories C and $S_{\bar{c}}(\bar{w})$ is the set of all possible segmentations of a sequence of words given a specific sequence of categories.

It is well known that the probability of a sequence of categories, $p(\bar{c})$, can be calculated as a product of the probabilities of each category conditioned to the history of the previous categories, so we are not going to extend here.

The term $P(s|\bar{c})$, in the equation above, could be estimated using different approaches. For this work, let us assume that all segmentations have the same probability, so $P(s|\bar{c}) = \alpha$ and Equation 3 can be rewritten as follows:

$$P_{M_{sw}}(\bar{w}) = \alpha \sum_{\forall \bar{c} \in C} \sum_{\forall s \in S_{\bar{c}}(\bar{w})} P(\bar{w}|s, \bar{c})P(\bar{c}) .$$ (4)

On the other hand, regarding to segments, we consider zero order models. Thus, given a sequence of categories $\bar{c}$ and a segmentation s, the probability of a segment that belongs to a category c_i, only depends on this c_i category but not on the previous ones, so:

$$P(\bar{w}|s, \bar{c}) = \prod_{i=1}^{T} P(w_{a_{i-1}+1}^{a_i}|c_i) .$$ (5)

Summing up, Equation 4 can be written as the following equation:

$$P_{M_{sw}}(\bar{w}) = \alpha \sum_{\forall \bar{c} \in C} \sum_{\forall s \in S_{\bar{c}}(\bar{w})} \prod_{i=1}^{T} P(w_{a_{i-1}+1}^{a_i}|c_i) \prod_{i=1}^{T} P(c_i|c_1^{i-1}) .$$ (6)

The probability distributions that take part in the previous equation can be estimated in the following way:

1. Estimating $P(c_i|c_1^{i-1})$

   A K-TSS model [6] has been used to estimate the conditional probability of a c_i category given the previous sequence of categories c_1^{i-1}, as Equation 7 shows. This model has been generated using a categorized corpus:

$$P(c_i|c_1^{i-1}) \simeq P(c_i|c_{i-k_a+1}^{i-1}) .$$ (7)

2. Estimating $P(w_{a_{i-1}+1}^{a_i}|c_i)$

   This term is the probability of a sequence of words , that must be a segment, given the category of this segment. To estimate this kind of probabilities K-TSS models have been used again, one for each category:

$$P(w_{a_{i-1}+1}^{a_i}|c_i) \simeq \prod_{j=a_{i-1}+1}^{a_i} P(w_j|w_{j-k_b+1}^{j-1}, c_i) \ . \tag{8}$$

Finally, the probability of a sequence of words could be given by Equation 9:

$$P_{M_{sw}}(\bar{w}) \simeq \alpha \sum_{\forall \bar{c} \in \mathcal{C}} \sum_{\forall s \in \mathcal{S}_{\bar{c}}(\bar{w})} \prod_{i=1}^{T} \left[\left[\prod_{j=a_{i-1}+1}^{a_i} P(w_j|w_{j-k_b+1}^{j-1}, c_i) \right] P(c_i|c_{i-k_a+1}^{i-1}) \right] \ . \tag{9}$$

2.2   LM Based on Categories Consisting of Lexical Units M_{sl}

In a second approach a LM based on categories consisting of lexical units has been considered. In this case, each segment $w_{a_{i-1}+1}^{a_i}$ in the corpus could be considered a new lexical unit that cannot be divided into different words. Let us denote each lexical unit by l_i where $l_i = w_{a_{i-1}+1}^{a_i}$ and $l_i \in \{\Sigma\}|$ $\{\Sigma\}$ is the set of all the possible segments previously defined. Assuming again that only segmentations compatible with the possible category sequences are considered, for a given sequence of categories, $c_1, \dots, c_T$, the possible sequences of lexical units can be represented as $\bar{l} = l_1, \dots, l_T = w_{a_0=1}^{a_1}, \dots, w_{a_{T-1}+1}^{a_T}$. Let us notice that each segmentation of a sequence of words is represented, in this approach, by a different sequence of lexical units $\bar{l}$.

Equation 10 stands for the probability of a sequence of lexical units. As a lexical unit involves a specific segmentation, in this case we do not consider the segmentation as a hidden variable:

$$P_{M_{sl}}(\bar{l}) = \sum_{\forall \bar{c} \in \mathcal{C}} P(\bar{l}|\bar{c})P(\bar{c}) \ . \tag{10}$$

being $\mathcal{C}$ the set of all the possible category sequences given a predetermined set of categories. The second term of the equation, $P(\bar{c})$, is estimated as describes Equation 7 in the previous approach.

The first term of the equation is the probability of a sequence of lexical units given a sequence of categories. Assuming again zero order models, this probability is calculated as:

$$p(\bar{l}|\bar{c}) = \prod_{i=1}^{T} P(l_i|c_i) \ . \tag{11}$$

and using the maximum likelihood criterion $P(l_i|c_i) \simeq \frac{N(l_i,c_i)}{\sum_{l'} N(l',c_i)}$ where $N(\cdot)$ is the number of times the event in brackets has been seen in the corpus.

The probability of a sequence of lexical units could be given by Equation 12:

$$P_{M_{sl}}(\bar{l}) \simeq \sum_{\forall \bar{c} \in \mathcal{C}} \prod_{i=1}^{T} \left[P(l_i|c_i)P(c_i|c_{i-k_a+1}^{i-1}) \right] . \tag{12}$$

2.3   Integration of a M_w and a M_{sw} Model

Finally, a hybrid model has been defined as a linear combination of a word-based LM and a LM based on categories consisting of word segments. Using such a model the probability of a word sequence is given by Equation 13.

$$P_{M_h}(\bar{w}) = \lambda P_{M_w}(\bar{w}) + (\lambda - 1)P_{M_{sw}}(\bar{w}) . \tag{13}$$

In the above equation, the term $P_{M_w}(\bar{w})$ is the probability of a word sequence using a classical word-based language model and in this work, a K-TSS model has been used to estimate this probability, as Equation 14 shows.

$$P_{M_w}(\bar{w}) = \prod_{i=1}^{T} P(w_i|w_1^{i-1}) \simeq \prod_{i=1}^{T} P(w_{i-k_w+1}^{i-1}) . \tag{14}$$

The second term of Equation 13, $P_{M_{sw}}(\bar{w})$ has been obtained using the first approach of a LM based on categories consisting of word segments and has been estimated using Equation 9.

3   Word Segments and Categories

Firstly, a set of linguistic categories has been defined. In this work the selected categories are independent on the task and consist of word segments with the same linguistic function. This set of categories and the segments belonging to them has been provided by *ametzagaiña*[1]. We provided them with the corpus described below and they automatically obtained categories and segments using a rule based method. Furthermore, they provided us with the segmented and categorized corpus. There are 57 different categories. It must be noticed that the classes are not homogeneous with regard to the number of segments of each class. It is due to the nature of the categories, as can be seen in the example below.

- **IZ (1198 segments):** el_próximo_viernes, un_billete_de_ida_y_vuelta, ...
- **LO-asi-como (1 segment):** así_como.
- **LO-que (13 segments):** el_que, los_que, un_euromed_que,...

4   Task and Corpus

The task consists of a human-machine dialogue corpus in Spanish. In this corpus [7], speakers ask for information about long-distance train schedules, destinations

---

[1] Ametzagaiña group. http://www.ametza.com

Table 1. Features of the corpus

CORPUS			
no. speakers	225	no. total words	89841
no. dialogues	900	category vocabulary	57
no. training sentences	8606	no. total categories	55043
no. test sentences	1379	segment vocabulary	3900
word vocabulary	938	no. total segments	55043

and prices by telephone. The dialogues were acquired using the Wizard of Oz technique. This task has high difficulty due to spontaneous speech and the shortage of the data, therefore it is suitable to study the improvements associated to modifications in the LM. The features of this corpus are detailed in Table 1.

5   Experiments

The LM-s proposed in this work were integrated into an ASR system and then evaluated in terms of Word Error Rate (WER). The ASR system looks for the best sequence of uttered words given a sequence of acoustic observations, using the Viterbi Algorithm. Thus, the decoder finds the best sequence of states through a probabilistic network, combining categories, segments, words and acoustic models.

Three series of experiments were carried out for the proposed evaluations:

– **LM based on categories consisting of word sequences**
  Firstly, a LM based on categories consisting of word segments, M_{sw}, was integrated into the ASR system, according to Equation 9. Using this LM two experiments were carried out with a value of $k_a = 3$ (see Equation 7) in both cases. One of them with a value of $k_b = 2$ (see Equation 8) and the other one with a value of $k_b = 3$ for all the categories, except for those whose segments were not long enough to generate a $k_b = 3$ k-TSS model.

– **LM based on categories consisting of lexical units**
  The second LM described in section 2, M_{sl} was integrated into the ASR system, according to Equation 12. Although the best sequence of lexical units (connected words) is obtained using this model, a sequence of lexical units can easily be transcribed into a sequence of words. Experiments were carried out with a value of $k_a = 3$

– **Integration of a word-based LM and a category-based LM**
  The M_{sw} LM was interpolated with a word-based k-TSS LM, where $k_w = 3$ (see Equation 14), and then integrated into an ASR system according to Equation 13. The experiments were carried out with a value of $k_a = 3$ and $k_b = 2$. The weight of each model in the linear combination is given by λ and in this experiment a value of $\lambda = 0.7$ was selected.

Described LM-s were previously evaluated in terms of Perplexity (PP), thus, the difficulty of the task can be estimated for these models.

Table 2. Results of PP for the described LM-s

PP		
M_w (words)	M_{sl} (lexical units)	M_{sw} (categories)
14.59	76.91	6.4

In these preliminary experiments the PP was measured over the labeled categorized test corpus. Once the test set was labeled with the sequence of classes corresponding to each sequence of words, the PP was measured over the categories as if they were words. Then, the PP was measured in the same way but using lexical units instead of categories. It must be taken into account that these values cannot be compared with each other because they measure the PP over different tokens: words, lexical units and categories. Table 3 shows the WER values obtained through the three series of experiments carried out.

Regarding to the M_{sw} model (a LM based on categories consisting of word sequences) and the two experiments described above, the results obtained with a value of $k_b = 2, 3$ shows an improvement of a 3.1% with respect to those obtained with a value of $k_b = 2$. This means that this kind of LM take advantage of the relations among the words that take part in a segment, giving better results when more information is considered (for $k_b = 3$). Nevertheless, it must be said that this model gives worst results of WER than the word-based LM. It could be due to the linguistic categorization employed. For comparison purposes, let us note experiments carried out over the same task, reported in [8]. It can be seen that Linguistic categorization provides worst results than statistical classes. In addition, the categories employed are not homogenous regarding to the number of segments in each class, as we mentioned in the section 3. Modifying this aspect of the categorization, better results could be obtained. Moreover, better results may be achieved using a new approach of the model with less restrictive assumptions.

Considering the experiments carried out with the M_{sl} model (a LM based on categories consisting of lexical units) a significant reduction in the value of WER is observed compared to the previous model. An improvement of a 13.17% is achieved with respect to the best value obtained with the M_{sw} model. In spite of this, the results for the M_w are slightly better and this could be because of the kind of categorization, as we have already explained.

Table 3. WER results for the proposed LM-s and a reference word-based LM

WER (%)		
M_w	k $=3$	19.92
M_{sw}	$k_a = 3$, $k_b = 2$	25.85
	$k_a = 3$, $k_b = 2, 3$	25.08
M_{sl}	$k = 3$	21.75
$M_{sw} + M_w$	$k_w = 3$	19.59
	$k_a = 3$, $k_b = 2$	

Finally, the best results are obtained for the hybrid model, i.e. linear combination of M_{sw} and M_w. This model improves the results obtained with the word-based LM, M_w, in a 1.67%.

6   Concluding Remarks and Future Work

The experiments show that integrating word segments in a category-based LM, a better performance of the model can be achieved. Furthermore, better results of WER are obtained, compared to a word-based LM, when a linear combination of models is used. In spite of this, the model proposed as a first approach is slightly coarse and less restrictive assumptions must be studied in future works.

On the other hand, the kind of categorization is also very important. So it could be interesting for future work to study new categories, using other classification criteria.

Acknowledgments. We would like to thank *Ametzagaiña group* and Josu Landa, in particular, for providing us with the categorization and segmentation of the corpus. On the other hand, this work has been partially supported by the CICYT project TIN2005-08660-C04-03 and by the Universidad del País Vasco under grant 9/UPV 00224.310-15900/2004.

References

1. Niesler, T.R., Woodland, P.C.: variable-length category-based n-gram language model. In: IEEE ICASSP-96, Atlanta, GA, vol. I, pp. 164–167. IEEE, Nagoya, Japan (1996)
2. Benedí, J., Sánchez, J.: Estimation of stochastic context-free grammars and their use as language models. Computer Speech and Language 19(3), 249–274 (2005)
3. Zue, V., Seneff, S., Glass, J., Polifroni, J., Pao, C., Hazen, T., Hetherington, L.: Jupiter: A telephone-based conversational interface for weather information. In: IEEE Trans. on Speech and Audio Proc. 8(1), 85–96 (2000)
4. Lamel, L., Rosset, S., Gauvin, J., Bennacef, S., Prouts, G.: The limsi arise system. In: IEEE 4th Workshop on Interactive Voice Technology for Telecommunications Applications. pp. 209–214 (1998)
5. Seneff, S., Polifroni, J.: Dialogue management in the mercury flight reservation system. In: ANLP-NAACL 2000 Satellite Workshop. pp. 1–6 (2000)
6. Torres, I., Varona, A.: k-TSS language models in speech recognition systems. Computer Speech and Language 15(2), 127–149 (2001)
7. DIHANA project: Dialogue System for Information Access Using Spontaneous Speech in Different Environments. Comisión Interministerial de Ciencia y Tecnología TIC2002-04103-C03-03 http://www.dihana.upv.es (2005)
8. Justo, R., Torres, M.I.: Category-based language model in a spanish spoken dialogue system. In: XXII Congreso de la SEPLN. pp. 19–24 (2006)

Part-of-Speech Tagging Based on Machine Translation Techniques

Guillem Gascó i Mora and Joan Andreu Sánchez Peiró

Departament de Sistemes Informàtics i Computació
Universitat Politència de València
Camí de Vera s/n, 46022 València (Spain)
{ggasco,jandreu}@dsic.upv.es

Abstract. In this paper, a new approach to the Part-of-Speech (PoS) tagging problem is proposed. The PoS tagging problem can be viewed as a special translation process where the source language is the set of strings being considered and the target language is the sequence of POS tags. In this work, we have used phrase-based machine translation technology to tackle the PoS tagging problem. Experiments on the Penn Treebank WSJ task were carried out and very good results were obtained.

1 Introduction

Most Natural Language Processing (NLP) systems have to deal with the problem of ambiguity. Ambiguity increases the number of possible interpretations of natural language, and hence, the number of possible translations of a sentence. Part-of-Speech tagging can help identify the correct meaning (or translation) of a word in a sentence.

Part-of-Speech tagging is a well studied task. Many different approaches have been proposed to solve this problem [1,2,3,4]. A POS tagger can be considered as a translator between two "special" languages: the language that has to be tagged and a language formed by the PoS tags. Therefore, when we tag a sentence, we are translating that sentence into its corresponding tags. This idea has led us to use machine translation techniques to tackle the tagging process. Machine translation techniques are also used in [5] to tackle a different problem: Natural Language Understanding.

There are several different machine translation approaches. Currently, the best reported translation results are those acquired using phrase-based systems [6]. These systems use phrases to carry out the translation process. The phrases convey contextual information that can be very useful in the PoS tagging problem. Thus, we consider this sort of information to be useful in the PoS tagging process.

Section 2 introduces the Part-of-Speech tagging problem. In section 3, we explain the phrase-based machine translation procedure. Section 4 presents the application of these techniques to the PoS tagging problem. Finally, in section 5, experimental results are reported for the PennTreebank WSJ task.

J. Martí et al. (Eds.): IbPRIA 2007, Part I, LNCS 4477, pp. 257–264, 2007.

2   Part-of-Speech Tagging

Part-of-Speech tagging is the process of assigning a syntactic class marker to each word in a text. In a certain tagged sentence, every word has one, and only one, tag assigned to it. Nevertheless, more than one tag can be assigned to a single word depending on its context. The input of a tagging algorithm is a string of words, and the output is the most appropriate syntactic tag for each word.

The first approaches that were proposed for this task used handwritten linguistic rules to assign a tag to a word [1,7,8]. The main problem with these approaches is the high cost associated with obtaining the rules. Inductive approaches were later proposed to solve this problem. For example, a rule-based system that automatically learned rules from a tagged corpus was presented in [2]. Nevertheless, the best results reported are those from stochastic inductive approaches. The most relevant of these use Hidden Markov Models [9,10,3] and Maximum Entropy Models [4]. Although these approaches have obtained very good results, a further improvement is still possible.

One important factor in POS tagger performance is its behaviour with out-of-vocabulary (OOV) words, especially when training and test sets belong to different fields. An OOV word is a word that does not appear in the training set.

The kind of information that is useful when tagging an OOV word depends on the language being tagged. OOV words in English tend to be proper nouns. In other languages, like Mandarin Chinese or German, most of the OOV words are nouns or verbs. Previous approaches to the problem of tagging OOV words use different morphological features like prefixes, suffixes[1], capitalization, or hyphenation.

3   Phrase-Based Machine Translation

The main advantage of phrase-based machine translation over single-word-based approaches is that they take contextual information into account. The translation of one word usually depends heavily on its context. The basic idea of phrase-based translation is to segment a sentence into phrases, translate them individually, and compose the target sentence from these phrase translations.

The phrase translation model is based on the noisy channel model. Using Bayes rule, we reformulate the probability for translating a foreign sentence f into a target language sentence t as

$$\operatorname*{argmax}_{t} p(t|f) = \operatorname*{argmax}_{t} p(f|t)p(t) . \tag{1}$$

Then, we have a translation model $p(f|t)$ and a separate language model $p(t)$.

The sentence f is segmented into a sequence of N phrases. Each of these phrases, f_n, is translated into a target language phrase t_n. Phrase translation is modeled by a probability distribution $\phi(f_n|t_n)$. The output phrases can be

---

[1] For inflectional languages like English or German derivational and inflectional affixes tend to be a strong indicator of word classes.

reordered. This reordering is modeled by a relative distortion probability distribution $d(a_i - b_{i-1})$, where a_i denotes the start position of the foreign phrase that was translated into the ith target language phrase and b_{i-1} denotes the end position of the foreign phrase translated into the $(i\text{-}1)$th target language phrase. A ω factor is introduced to calibrate the output length. In summary, the best target language output sentence t_{best}, given a source language input sentence, is

$$t_{best} = \operatorname*{argmax}_t (\prod_{n=1}^{N} \phi(f_n|t_n)d(a_i - b_{i-1})p(t)\omega^{|t|}) . \tag{2}$$

Obtaining a phrase probability translation table from a bilingual corpus is an important stage of phrase-based machine translation systems. This table maps source phrases to target language phrases. One of the greatest difficulties in translation is the possible reordering of words from different languages. Hence, a phrase alignment is needed to obtain good translation tables. There are several methods available for extracting the phrase probability translation table [11]. The most widely used language model is a smoothed trigram model.

4   The PoS-Tagging Problem as a MT Problem

As stated above, the tagging process can be viewed as a translation process. Therefore, the probability of obtaining the set of POS tags t for a source language sentence s is

$$t_{best} = \operatorname*{argmax}_t p(t|s) = \operatorname*{argmax}_t p(s|t)p(t) . \tag{3}$$

where $p(t)$ is a tag language model and $p(t|s)$ is a translation/tagging model.

As in the translation process, the source language input sentence is segmented into a sequence of phrases. Each phrase is "translated" into tag phrases. However, tag phrases cannot be reordered because each tag must be aligned with its corresponding word in a sentence.

There are some special features that make phrase-based POS tagging simpler than translation:

1. Reordering is not necessary.
2. Given a source language phrase composed of n words, its corresponding tag phrase has exactly n tags. There are no insertions or deletions, so every n-long source language sentence is *translated* into a n-long tag sentence.

Thus, the reordering probability distribution, $d(a_i - b_{i-1})$, and the word penalty factor, ω, can be removed from the model.

4.1   Phrase Extraction

For the reasons mentioned above, phrase extraction is easier for PoS tagging than for translation. Thus, from the training sentences, we obtained all the sequential parallel phrases that were shorter than a given length l. Then, we obtained the probability of each segment by counting and normalizing.

It is important to note that the size of the translation table increases as l increases. Therefore, only small values for l can be considered. Moreover, the inclusion of long phrases does not provide a significant improvement in quality [11] since the probability of the reapearence of long phrases is very low.

4.2   Treatment of OOV Words

The translation of a word that does not appear in the training set is very difficult in classical machine translation. In the POS tagging problem, the target language vocabulary is a closed, well-defined set of POS tags. Therefore, it is possible to assign a POS tag to OOV words. Of course, it is more difficult to tag a word that has not appeared in the training set because there is no history of assigned tags. For this reason, other information such as context or morphological features should be taken into account. Tagging of OOV words is similar to a classification problem where an OOV word is assigned to a class (POS tag) depending on its context and certain other features.

Thus, we need to obtain phrases to *translate* OOV words. If the training set is large enough, it can be assumed that OOV words are infrequent words. Therefore, OOV words will probably have a behaviour that is similar to the behaviour of infrequent words of the training set. These infrequent words will be used to obtain the OOV word translation phrases.

Hence, we proceeded in the following way: We createe a set V composed by the N most frequent words of the training set. Every word in the training and test sentences that was not in V was replaced by the symbol *unk*. Then, we obtained the probability translation table phrases from the training sentences as we have explained in section 4.1.

When the phrase-based translation software finds an *unk* in a test sentence, it uses the *unk* phrases obtained from the training set. The words of the training set that have been replaced are considered to be OOV words. This is why N must be carefully chosen. If N is too large, there will not be enough *unk phrases* to get a reliable translation. On the other hand, if N is too small, the information from important words will be lost and the system performance will decrease.

5   Experiments

In this section, we present some preliminary experiments with the phrase-based tagger (PBT). The aim of these experiments was to test the system performance and to compare it with the performance of other taggers.

For these experiments, we chose the Penn Treebank corpus [12] to evaluate our phrase-based POS tagging system. This corpus has been automatically tagged and manually checked. Its tagset is composed of 45 different tags. We divided the corpus into three sets: training, tuning and test. Table 1 shows some features of these sets.

Table 1. Corpus and partition features

	Directories	Sentences	Words	Vocabulary	OOV words
Training	00-20	42,075	1,004,073	40,695	-
Tuning	21,22	3,371	80,156	9,942	2,172
Test	23,24	3,762	89,537	10,568	2,045

The phrase-based machine translation software Pharaoh [13] was used in these experiments. Pharaoh implements a beam search decoding for phrase-based statistical machine translation.

We have used a tag trigram model that was smoothed using the Kneser-Ney discount technique with Chen-Goodman modifications as the language model. Perplexity values of tuning and test sets are 8.36 and 8.28, respectively.

All the experiments except the ones in subsection 5.3 used the tuning set for tagging. To avoid an excessively large translation table, we used phrases whose maximum length was 3 in all the experiments. Note that, the larger the translation table, the slower the tagging system.

5.1 OOV Words

An important factor that affects system performance is the treatment of OOV words. As we stated in section 4.2, the size of the vocabulary of OOV words must be chosen carefully. Table 2 shows the results of the system using OOV word treatment with different vocabulary sizes. The accuracy of the basic system, which does not use OOV word treatment, is displayed in the first row.

Table 2. Performance of PBT with OOV word treatment for different vocabulary sizes

Vocabulary Size	OOV Words	Accuracy		
		Known Words	OOV Words	Global
Basic System	2172	96.83	0%	94.2%
10,000	6001	97.12%	60.52%	94.39%
20,000	3778	97.03%	60.43%	95.31%
30,000	3081	96.96%	62.60%	**95.72%**

The performance of the basic system for OOV words was 0%. As stated above, the use of OOV word treatment increases the number of OOV words. In spite of this, the system performance increased because OOV word accuracy improved to 60.52% with a vocabulary of only 10,000 words. With a larger vocabulary of 30,000 words, the OOV word accuracy did not improve but the number of OOV words decreased significantly. This increased the global system accuracy to 95.72%.

OOV word treatment can be improved if some morphological features are taken into account. Following other works, we chose capitalization, hyphenation, suffixes, and prefixes. To use capitalization information, a new OOV word class (with its corresponding replacement word) was created. Infrequent training words and OOV test words were replaced using two different special *unk* symbols depending on their capitalization.

The same strategy was used with hyphenation and suffixes. Only the most significant English suffixes were taken into account. Table 3 shows some of the suffixes that were used. English prefixes usually only provide semantic information. Therefore, if pw is a OOV word and p is a semantic prefix and w is in the training set vocabulary, then pw will be replaced by w. Hence, we used w tag history information to tag pw because p does not modify the POS tag.

Table 3. Frequent significant English suffixes

Suffix	Usual tags
-ed	VBN VBD JJ
-ing	VBG
-er	JJR
-ion	NN
-an	JJ
-ness	NN
-al	JJ
-able	JJ
-est	JJS
-ly	RB
-s	NNS NNPS

Table 4 shows the improvement in tagging obtained by using these features. When all of them were used, the performance of the tagger on OOV words increased to 76.53%. The global system accuracy was 96.54%.

In the experiments described below, the tagger used OOV word treatment with a 30,000-word vocabulary and all the morphological features.

Table 4. Performance of PBT with OOV word treatment for different morphological information. B: Basic system; C: Capitalization; S: Suffixes; H: Hyphenation; P: Prefixes.

	Accuracy		
Information used	Known Words	OOV Words	Global
B	96.96%	61.6%	95.72%
B+C	96.94%	72.92%	96.21%
B+C+S	96.92%	74.47%	96.45%
B+C+S+H+P	96.96%	76.53%	**96.54%**

5.2   Maximum Phrase Length

As we stated in section 4.1, long phrases produce very large translation tables and slow taggers. In addition, long phrases are rarely used in translation systems.

Table 5. Accuracy and number of phrases produced by different maximum phrase length values

Maximum phrase length	Phrases produced	Accuracy
1	35,882	96.22%
2	358,791	**96.57%**
3	973,992	96.54%
4	1,694,364	96.54%
5	2,427,061	96.53%

Therefore, we carried out a serie of experiments to test how the length of the phrases affected the performance of the tagger. Table 5 displays these results.

As the table indicates, the maximum phrase length 2 had the best performance: 96.57%. Learning longer phrases did not yield much improvement. This may be due to the fact that long training phrases rarely appear in test sentences.

5.3   Final Results and Comparison

In this section, we compare the accuracy of PBT with two well-known taggers: the Brill rule-based tagger[2], and the TnT[3] which is a HMM-based tagger. In order to make an adequate comparison we trained three taggers with the same training set and tagged the same test set. The results are shown in Table 6.

As the table indicates, the phrase-based tagger (PBT) performed significantly better than the other taggers.

Table 6. Comparison between PBT and other taggers

Tagger:	TnT	Brill	**PBT**
Tagging accuracy:	96.61%	96.39%	**96.78%**

Experiments reported in other publications used some typical training, tuning and test sets[2]. To compare their results with the results obtained with PBT, we carried out a final experiment using these sets, and we obtained an accuracy of 96.97%.

6   Conclusions

We have presented a new approach to the POS tagging problem using machine translation techniques. The phrase-based translation model has been chosen since the use of phrase information improves tagging. Some special tagging features simplify the translation model by making the word penalty and the reordering model unnecessary. In addition, OOV words can be tagged using context and morphological information.

---

[2] Directories 2-20 for training, 23 for tuning and 24 for test.

The experiments reported here show that phrase-based Part-of-Speech tagging is a viable approach for achieving state-of-the-art accuracy. Moreover, with these techniques it is very easy to obtain taggers for other languages.

Acknowledgements. This work has been partially supported by the *Universitat Politècnica de València* with the ILETA project and by the EC (FEDER) and the Spanish MEC under grant TIN2006-15694-CO2-01.

References

1. Harris, Z.: String analysis of sentence structure. Mouton, The Hague (1962)
2. Brill, E.: A Simple Rule-Based Part-of-speech Tagger. In: Proceedings of the Third Conference on Applied Natural Language Processing. ANLP (1992)
3. Brants, T.: TnT – A Statistical Part-of-Speech Tagger. In: Proceedings of the Sixth Applied Natural Language Processing (ANLP-2000), Seattle, WA (2000)
4. Ratnaparkhi, A.: A Maximum Entropy Part-of.Speech Tagger. In: Proceedings of the 1st Conference on Empirical Methods in Natural Language Processing, EMNLP 1996 (1996)
5. Bender, O., Macherey, K., Och, F., Ney, H.: Comparison of Alignment Templates and Maximum Entropy Models for Natural Language Understanding. In: Proceedings of the 10th Conference of the European Chapter of the Association for Computational Linguistics. EACL 2003 (2003)
6. Zens, R., Och, F., Ney, H.: Improvements in phrase-based statistical machine translation. In: Proceedings of the Human Language Technology Conference, HLT-NAACL'2004 (2004)
7. Klein, S., Simons, F.: A computational approach to grammatical coding of English words. Journal of the Association for Computing Machinery. vol. 10(3) (1963)
8. Greene, B., Rubin, M.: Automatic tagging of English. Technical report, Department of Linguistics. Providence, Rhode Island. 1071 (1962)
9. Weischedel, R., Schwartz, R., Palmucci, J., Meteer, M., Ramsaw, L.: Coping with ambiguity and unknown words trhough probabilistic models. Computational Linguistics. vol. 19(2) (1993)
10. Merialdo, B.: Tagging English text with a probabilistic model. Computational Linguistics. vol. 20(2) (1994)
11. Koehn, P., Och, F., Marcu, D.: Statistical phrase-based translation. In: Proceedings of the Human Language Technology Conference, HLT-NAACL'2003 (2003)
12. Marcus, M., Santorini, B., Marcinkiewicz, M.: Building a large annotated corpus of english: The Penn Treebank. Computational Linguistics, vol. 19(2) (1994)
13. Koehn, P.: Pharaoh: A beam search decoder for phrase-based statistical machine translation models. In: Frederking, R.E., Taylor, K.B. (eds.) AMTA 2004. LNCS (LNAI), vol. 3265, Springer, Heidelberg (2004)

Bilingual Text Classification*

Jorge Civera, Elsa Cubel, and Enrique Vidal

Instituto Tecnológico de Informática
Universidad Politécnica de Valencia
{jorcisai,ecubel,evidal}@iti.upv.es

Abstract. Bilingual documentation has become a common phenomenon in official institutions and private companies. In this scenario, the
categorization of bilingual text is a useful tool. In this paper, different approaches will be proposed to tackle this bilingual classification task. On
the one hand, three finite-state transducer algorithms from the grammatical inference framework will be presented. On the other hand, a naive
combination of smoothed n-gram models will be introduced. To evaluate
the performance of bilingual classifiers, two categorized bilingual corpora
of different complexity were considered. Experiments in a limited-domain
task show that all the models obtain similar results. However, results on
a more open-domain task denote the supremacy of the naive approach.

1 Introduction

Nowadays the proliferation of bilingual documentation is a widely extended phenomenon in our information society. This fact is reflected in a vast number of official institutions (EU parliament, the Canadian Parliament, UN sessions, Catalan
and Basque Parliaments in Spain, etc.) and private companies (user's manuals,
newspapers, books, etc.). In many cases, this textual information needs to be
categorized by hand, entailing a time-consuming and arduous burden.

On the other hand, the categorization of bilingual text can be applied to the
field of machine translation to train specific statistical translation models for particular subdomains, automatically detected in more general bilingual corpus [1].
This strategy can alleviate a typical problem of statistical translation models;
namely, good results are generally obtained only in constrained semantic scopes.
In its monolingual form, text classification has demonstrated reasonably good
performance using a number of well-known techniques such as naive Bayes [2],
Bernoulli mixtures [3], etc. The incorporation of a second language offers an
additional information source that can help reducing classification error rates.

In the present work, four techniques for bilingual text classification will be
presented along with results on two datasets of different complexity. Previous
work reported in [4] has been extended with additional experiments and results
on the dataset used in [4] have been significantly improved through a better
understanding of smoothing in the framework of probabilistic error correcting.

* Work supported by the EC (FEDER) and the Spanish MEC under grant TIN2006-
15694-CO2-01 and the *Consellería d'Empresa, Universitat i Ciència - Generalitat
Valenciana* under contract GV06/252 and the Ministerio de Educación y Ciencia.

J. Martí et al. (Eds.): IbPRIA 2007, Part I, LNCS 4477, pp. 265–273, 2007.
© Springer-Verlag Berlin Heidelberg 2007

2   Bilingual Classification

Bilingual classification can be seen from a probabilistic perspective. Given a bilingual sample (s, t) composed by a pair of sentences (being t a possible translation for s) and a set of classes $1, 2, \ldots, C$, the pair (s, t) will be assigned to class $\hat{c}$ according to the maximum *a posteriori* probability criterion:

$$\hat{c} = \underset{c}{\operatorname{argmax}} P(c \mid (s, t)) = \underset{c}{\operatorname{argmax}} P(c) \, P((s, t) \mid c) \tag{1}$$

This joint class-conditional probability can be modeled in various ways, some of them will be analyzed in the next sections.

3   Transducer Inference and Decoding Algorithm

Stochastic finite-state transducers (SFSTs) are translation models [5,6] that can be learned automatically from bilingual sample pairs. SFSTs are finite-state networks that accept sentences from a given input language and produce sentences of an output language. Optimal maximum likelihood estimates of the transition probabilities can be obtained by computing the relative frequency each edge is used in the parsing of the input-output sample pairs. This results in SFSTs which model the joint probability distribution over bilingual sentence pairs.

3.1   A Subsequential Transducer Inference Algorithm: OSTIA

Given a set of training sentence pairs, OSTIA efficiently learns a subsequential transducer (SST) [7]. Nevertheless, there are *partial* subsequential functions for which OSTIA inference is troublesome. This limitation can be solved by an extension, called OSTIA-DR (OSTIA with Domain and Range constraints) [8] in which the learnt transducers only accept input sentences and only produce output sentences compatible with the input/output language models. Another possibility to overcome the partial-function limitation is to rely on statistical knowledge. This extension of OSTIA-DR is known as OSTIA-P [9].

3.2   Hybrid (Statistical/Finite-State) Inference Algorithms

An inconvenience of finite-state transducer learning techniques like OSTIA is that they require large amounts of training data to produce adequate results. However, some byproducts of statistical translation models [10] can be useful to improve the learning capabilities of finite-state models. Following this reasoning, two hybrid transducer inference algorithms have been introduced.

OMEGA. The OMEGA (for the Spanish OSTIA *Mejorado Empleando Garantías y Alineamientos*) [11] algorithm is an extension of the OSTIA algorithm that incorporates additional information extracted from statistical translation models into the learning process. It allows the use of statistical dictionaries and alignments estimated from the same training pairs that will be employed by

OMEGA. In the present work, these statistical translation models were estimated using the GIZA++ toolkit [12], which implements IBM statistical models [10]. An stochastic extension of OMEGA, called OMEGA-P, can be defined with the same transition and final state probability estimation strategy than OSTIA-P.

GIATI. An algorithm for learning SFSTs is the GIATI technique [13]. Given a finite sample of string pairs, it works in three steps. First, each training pair is transformed into a single string from an extended alphabet to obtain a new sample of strings. Then, a smoothed n-gram language model is inferred from this set of strings. Finally, the transformation of the inferred regular grammar into a transducer is trivial. The symbols associated to the grammar rules are replaced by source/target symbols, thereby converting the grammar inferred in the previous step into a transducer. The transformation of a parallel corpus into a single string corpus is performed using statistical alignments. As in the OMEGA algorithm, these statistical alignments were calculated with the GIZA++ toolkit.

3.3   Probabilistic Error-Correcting Classification

The translation and bilingual classification performance achieved by transducer models tends to be poor if input samples do not strictly comply with the syntactic and structural restrictions imposed by the model. This problem can be approached by means of error-correcting decoding. Under this approach, the sentence, x, is considered to be a *corrupted* version of some sentence, $\hat{x} \in \mathcal{L}$, where $\mathcal{L}$ is the input language associated with the SFST. On the other hand, an error model $\mathcal{E}$ accounts for the transformation from $\hat{x}$ into x.

Formalizing the framework given above, our goal is to calculate the *posterior* probability of observing x given a language model $\mathcal{L}$ and an error model $\mathcal{E}$:

$$P(x \,|\, \mathcal{L}, \mathcal{E}) = \sum_{x' \in \mathcal{L}} P(x, x' \,|\, \mathcal{L}, \mathcal{E}) \approx \max_{x' \in \mathcal{L}} P(x' \,|\, \mathcal{L}) \, P(x \,|\, x', \mathcal{E}) \qquad (2)$$

Two approximations are performed in order to compute $P(x \,|\, \mathcal{L}, \mathcal{E})$. First, only the most probable string in $\mathcal{L}$ under the probabilistic error-correcting framework is considered. This is also known as the Viterbi approximation and aims at reducing the computational effort required to compute $P(x \,|\, \mathcal{L}, \mathcal{E})$. The second approximation makes two reasonable assumptions: The transformation from x' into x only depends on the error model $\mathcal{E}$, while the generation of x' is dictated only by the language model $\mathcal{L}$.

Under the bilingual classification framework, Eq. (2) is integrated in Eq. (1), considering x to be instantiated in (s, t), as follows:

$$\hat{c} = \operatorname*{argmax}_{c} P(c) P((s,t)|c) \approx \operatorname*{argmax}_{c} \max_{(s,t)' \in \mathcal{L}_c} P(c) P((s,t)' | \mathcal{L}_c) P((s,t)|(s,t)', \mathcal{E}_c) \quad (3)$$

where $P((s,t)' \,|\, \mathcal{L}_c)$ and $P((s,t) \,|\, (s,t)', \mathcal{E}_c)$ denote class-dependent error and language models, respectively. The probabilistic error-correcting computation stated in Eq. (3) would require an error-correcting extension of the methods for computing the joint probability in ambiguous SFSTs presented in [5]. In this work, we approximate Eq. (3) by restricting the probabilistic error-correcting parsing to one of the languages involved in the bilingual pair:

$$\hat{c} \approx \underset{c}{\operatorname{argmax}} \max_{x' \in \mathcal{L}_c} P(c) \, P(x' \mid \mathcal{L}_c) \, P(x \mid x', \mathcal{E}_c) \tag{4}$$

where x represents either the input string s or the output string t. Note that while this approximation discards one of the two strings of the test pairs, the models used for the parsing were learned with full bilingual information. It is thus expected that these models have captured contextual restrictions coming from the two languages involved.

Specifically, this probabilistic error-correcting classifier described above, was applied on the input language for OSTIA and OMEGA transducers to calculate $P(s \mid \mathcal{L}, \mathcal{E})$. This is due to the deterministic properties of OSTIA and OMEGA transducers that associate each unique input string to a single output string. Then, only the input string s is used to classify a test bilingual pair (s, t). In the case of GIATI transducers, probabilistic error-correcting was applied to the output language. GIATI transducers are inferred using smoothed n-gram language models on an extended version of the training corpus as described in Section 3.2. This causes GIATI transducers to be non-deterministic and smoothed in the input language, so the classification of a bilingual sample (s, t) needs to be carried out in two steps. First, the source sentence s is parsed over the transducer giving place to a so-called word graph [14]. This word graph contains all possible translations of s found in the transducer. Then, the probabilistic error-correcting classifier parses the output sentence t on the word graph in order to compute $P(t \mid \mathcal{L}, \mathcal{E})$.

On the other hand, the final parameter configuration for the error model was a smoothed version of the 0-1 conventional error-correcting parser. Regarding the language model $P(x' \mid \mathcal{L}_c)$, this term corresponds to the probability distribution inferred for each supervised class by the various grammatical inference algorithms proposed in Section 3.

4   Naive Bayes Bilingual Classification

An alternative approach to the joint class-conditional probability representation (Eq. (1)) is to consider that the random variables s and t included in the model are independent. While this assumption is clearly false in most real-world tasks, it often performs surprisingly well in practice. This way, Eq. (1) can be reformulated as follows:

$$\hat{c} = \underset{c}{\operatorname{argmax}} P((s, t) \mid c) \approx \underset{c}{\operatorname{argmax}} P(s \mid c) \cdot P(t \mid c) \tag{5}$$

The conditional probability $P(s \mid c)$ and $P(t \mid c)$ can be modelled in different manners. In this work, n-gram language models from the statistical language modeling area will be employed. An important argument that supports this decision is the existence of powerful smoothing techniques and its successful application in many language modeling tasks [15]. Different discount strategies can be found in the literature [16]. However, Witten-Bell discount in which non-observed events are modelled as seen for the first time is used in the present work. This discounting technique offered superior classification performance compared to the rest of discounting techniques that were studied.

5   Experimental Results

5.1   Corpora

The first corpus employed in these experiments was developed in the EUTRANS EU project [17]. The general domain in EUTRANS is that of a tourist visiting a foreign country. Specifically, in this work, the domain has been restricted to human-to-human communication in the front-desk of a hotel, which is known as the *Traveler* task. To control task complexity, 16 subdomains were considered together with the pairs of sentences associated to them. The final corpus was generated from the previous "seed corpus" by four persons, A, F, J and P, assigning a subset of subdomains to each one. It should be noted that each person defines a supervised class, so that the task will be to recognize the authorship of a given bilingual pair. However the subdomain coverage of these four classes do overlap and no perfect classification is possible, low error rates would indicate that the models employed are able to deal with the underlying class variability.

On the other hand, the BAF corpus [18] is a compilation of bilingual "institutional" French-English texts ranging from debates of the Canadian parliament (Hansard), court transcripts and UN reports to scientific, technical and literary documents. This dataset is composed of 11 texts that are organized into 4 natural genres (Institutional, Scientific, Technical and Literary) trying to be representative of the types of text that are available in multilingual versions. In our case, we decided to employ each text as an independent supervised class. Thus, some of the classes can be found to be theme related, but devoted to heterogeneous purposes or written by different authors, entailing a challenging classification task. This dataset is far more complex than the *Traveler* task as shown by the statistics of some selected classes presented in Table 1.

5.2   Results

To assess the performance of bilingual classifiers described in previous sections, random training-test partitions in 1/2-1/2 split for the *Traveler* task and 4/5-1/5 for the BAF corpus were made. Table 2 shows the results of classification error rate as a function of the degree of the underlaying n-gram language model employed for the *Traveler* task. The left table introduces a set of monolingual baseline experiments to serve as a reference for bilingual experiments that appear on the right. The Bernoulli results were extracted from [3].

A shallow analysis of the results presented in Table 2 reveals that transducer classifiers perform similarly or even better than monolingual classifier based

Table 1. *Traveler* (left) and BAF (right) corpora statistics, for all classes in the form "Spanish/English" (*Traveller*) and for some selected classes "French/English" (BAF). Abbreviations used: SENTS=sentences; ASL=average sentence length; RKW=running Kilo-words; VOCKW=vocabulary size in Kilo-words; and STS=singletons.

	Traveler dataset					BAF dataset			
CLASS	A	F	J	P	All	ilo	verne	tao3	All
SENTS	2000	2000	2000	2000	8000	4798	2421	154	18509
RKW	19/17	25/23	20/17	21/22	86/80	173/154	56/50	3/3	522/441
VOCKW	.3/.3	.4/.3	.2/.1	.1/.05	.7/.5	8/6	7/6	1/1	20/15
ASL	9/8	12/11	10/8	10/11	10/10	36/32	23/21	26/22	28/23
STS	95/106	78/71	0/0	1/0	47/43	3163/2237	4023/2527	624/540	8084/5281

on Bernoulli mixtures and smoothed n-grams. However, bilingual smoothed n-grams models outperform their monolingual counterparts and finite-state models when the degree of the n-gram goes beyond bigrams.

A more in-depth examination of the results unveils some interesting details of the underlying models. It is noteworthy that transducers outperform n-gram models when using unigrams. This is due to the fact that grammatical inference algorithms capture the sentence-internal structure, although no language model structure is provided. Another possible reason behind this advantageous position of transducer classifiers is their capability to integrate input-to-output mapping information in the model. This phenomenon is observed in the unigram when comparing monolingual n-gram classifiers to OSTIA-P and OMEGA-P transducers, since OSTIA-P and OMEGA-P transducers only make explicit use of its input language model in the classification process due to their determinism. However their results are better than those of monolingual n-gram classifiers.

Table 2. Baseline table corresponds to monolingual results using Bernoulli mixture and smoothed n-gram language models (left). Bilingual classification error (in %) obtained with OSTIA-P, OMEGA-P, GIATI and smoothed n-gram language models in the *Traveler* task (right).

Monolingual		1-gram	2-gram	3-gram
Bernoulli	Es		1.5	
n-gram	Es	3.1	1.1	1.1
	En	4.8	1.4	1.1

Bilingual		1-gram	2-gram	3-gram
OSTIA-P	Es-En	2.8	1.1	1.3
	En-Es	3.1	1.2	1.5
OMEGA-P	Es-En	2.5	1.1	1.3
	En-Es	2.5	1.3	1.5
GIATI	Es-En	2.3	1.1	1.1
	En-Es	1.3	1.0	1.1
Naive (n-gram)		4.1	1.1	0.8

In the case of bigrams, all classifiers obtain similar figures, although OSTIA-P and OMEGA-P use non-smoothed input and output language models. Moreover, the benefits of transducer models stated in the previous paragraph are also applicable here, and indeed, these benefits make transducer performance evolve at the same pace than bilingual n-grams. Beyond bigrams, non-smoothed models like OSTIA-P and OMEGA-P increase its classification error rate, while input smoothed models like GIATI work slightly worse than smoothed n-gram models.

Table 3 shows the classification error rates for the different models in the BAF corpus. The general reading of the results denotes that bilingual n-gram models clearly surpass their monolingual counterparts, and surprisingly, transducer performance is not as good as expected. There were two main reasons that theoretically suggested some superiority of transducer models over simple n-gram language models. On the one hand, transducers are supposed to capture the sentence-internal structure more accurately than n-gram models. On the other hand, transducers model the input-to-output mapping existing across languages, providing a more complex and richer structure than a simplistic naive approach based on n-gram models.

Table 3. Baseline table corresponds to monolingual results using n-gram language models (left). Bilingual classification error (in %) obtained with OSTIA-P, OMEGA-P, GIATI and smoothed n-gram language models in the BAF corpus (right).

Monolingual		1-gram	2-gram	3-gram
n-gram	Fr	9.0	7.7	7.8
	En	7.6	6.1	6.1

Bilingual		1-gram	2-gram	3-gram
OSTIA-P	Fr-En	17.2	10.0	14.4
	En-Fr	12.5	9.3	14.9
OMEGA-P	Fr-En	17.3	10.5	14.3
	En-Fr	15.6	9.4	14.9
GIATI	Fr-En	13.0	11.7	11.3
	En-Fr	14.0	12.9	12.8
Naive (n-gram)		6.2	4.6	4.6

Transducer models aim at learning more sophisticated patterns in the data that, given the scarcity of samples in many of the classes of the BAF corpus (see Table 1), are very difficult to capture. Instead, transducer models seem to be missing some of the essential attributes of the BAF corpus. As observed if we compare the performance of transducer models in the *Traveler* task, a fairly simple synthetic task where sentence-internal structure and input-to-output relationships can be easily learned, to the complex real-world BAF corpus.

6   Conclusions and Future Work

This paper has been devoted to bilingual classification using two possible approaches to attempt this task: stochastic finite-state transducers and smoothed n-gram language models. The idea behind these approximations was the modelization of the joint probability for a given bilingual sample (s, t).

The performance of these models as bilingual classifiers was evaluated on two datasets of different complexity, the *Traveler* task and the BAF corpus. The classification error rates reported in the present work reflect the appropriateness of inference algorithms for controlled limited tasks such as the *Traveler* task. However, the application of these finite-state inference techniques to real-world problems, such as the BAF corpus, do not seem to capture the fundamental task properties that would boost the performance of transducer classifiers.

In contrast, a fairly simple naive Bayes approach like n-gram models, which explicitly aims at the core of this classification problem, has been able to produce better experimental results. On the other hand, the usefulness of the incorporation of an additional information source through a second language in this bilingual classification task has sufficiently proved its importance to further improve the performance of monolingual text classifiers.

Finally, a challenging idea that is left out as a future work consists in the implementation of the probabilistic error-correcting parsing, as presented in Eq. (3), which would take into account the two components of each test pair of sentences. In addition, another appealing idea would be the incorporation of smoothing into transducer models based on n-grams as proposed in [19].

References

1. Civera, J., Juan, A.: Mixtures of IBM Model 2. In: Proc. of EAMT. pp. 159–167 (2006)
2. McCallum, A., Nigam, K.: A comparison of event models for naive bayes text classification. In: AAAI-98 on Learning for Text Categorization. pp. 41–48 (1998)
3. Juan, A., Vidal, E.: On the use of Bernoulli mixture models for text classification. Pattern Recognition 35(12), 2705–2710 (2002)
4. Civera, J., et al.: Different approaches to bilingual text classification based on grammatical inference techniques. In: IbPRIA, Estoril (Portugal) pp. 630–637 (2005)
5. Picó, D., Casacuberta, F.: Some statistical-estimation methods for stochastic finite-state transducers. Machine Learning 44, 121–142 (2001)
6. Knight, K., Al-Onaizan, Y.: Translation with finite-state devices. In: Farwell, D., Gerber, L., Hovy, E. (eds.) AMTA 1998. LNCS (LNAI), vol. 1529, pp. 421–437. Springer, Heidelberg (1998)
7. Oncina, J., García, P., Vidal, E.: Learning subsequential transducers for pattern recognition interpretation tasks. IEEE Transactions on PAMI 15, 448–458 (1993)
8. Oncina, J., Varó, M.: Using domain information during the learning of a subsequential transducer. In: ICGI, Berlin, Germany, pp. 301–312 (1996)
9. Cubel, E.: Aprendizaje de transductores subsecuenciales estocásticos. Technical Report II-DSIC-B-23/01, Universidad Politécnica de Valencia, Spain (2002)
10. Brown, P., et al.: The mathematics of statistical machine translation: Parameter estimation. Computational Linguistics 19(2), 263–312 (1993)
11. Vilar, J.: Improve the learning of subsequential transducers by using alignments and dictionaries. In: Proc. of ICGI'00, pp. 298–311. Springer, Heidelberg (2000)
12. Och, F., Ney, H.: Improved statistical alignment models. In: ACL., pp. 440–447 (2000)
13. Casacuberta, F., et al.: Some approaches to statistical and finite-state speech-to-speech translation. Computer Speech and Language 18, 25–47 (2004)
14. Civera, J., et al.: A syntactic pattern recognition approach to computer assisted translation. In: SSPR. pp. 207–215 (2004)
15. Jelinek, F.: Statistical Methods for Speech Recognition. MIT Press, Cambridge (1998)

16. Chen, S., Goodman, J.: An empirical study of smoothing techniques for language modelling. In: Proc. of ACL'96, San Francisco, USA, pp. 310–318 (1996)
17. Amengual, J., et al.: The EuTrans-I speech translation system. Machine Translation 15, 75–103 (2000)
18. Simard, M.: The BAF: A Corpus of English-French Bitext. In: Proc. of LREC'98. Granada, Spain, vol. 1, pp. 489–494 (1998)
19. Llorens, D., Vilar, J.M., Casacuberta, F.: Finite state language models smoothed using n-grams. IJPRAI 16(3), 275–289 (2002)

Robust Lane Lines Detection and Quantitative Assessment

Antonio López, Joan Serrat, Cristina Cañero, and Felipe Lumbreras

Computer Vision Center & Computer Science Dept.
Edifici O, Universitat Autònoma de Barcelona,
08193 Cerdanyola, Spain

Abstract. Detection of lane markings based on a camera sensor can be a low cost solution to lane departure and curve over speed warning. A number of methods and implementations have been reported in the literature. However, reliable detection is still an issue due to cast shadows, wearied and occluded markings, variable ambient lighting conditions etc. We focus on increasing the reliability of detection in two ways. Firstly, we employ a different image feature other than the commonly used edges: ridges, which we claim is better suited to this problem. Secondly, we have adapted RANSAC, a generic robust estimation method, to fit a parametric model of a pair or lane lines to the image features, based on both ridgeness and ridge orientation. In addition this fitting is performed for the left and right lane lines simultaneously, thus enforcing a consistent result. We have quantitatively assessed it on synthetic but realistic video sequences for which road geometry and vehicle trajectory ground truth are known.

1 Introduction

A present challenge of the automotive industry is to develop low cost advanced driver assistance systems (ADAS) able to increase traffic safety and driving comfort. Since vision is the most used human sense for driving, some ADAS features rely on visual sensors [2]. Specifically, lane departure warning and lateral control can be addressed by detecting the lane markings on the road by means of a forward–facing camera and computer vision techniques. In this paper we focus on this problem, which is one of the first addressed in the field of ADAS. Many papers have been published on it, since it is a difficult and not yet completely solved problem due to shadows, large contrast variations, vehicles occluding the marks, wearied markings, vehicle ego–motion etc. Recent reviews of detection methods can be found in [1,2].

The main contributions of this paper are three. The first one is to employ a different low–level image feature, namely, *ridgeness*, to obtain a more reliable lane marking points detection under poor contrast conditions (section 2). Aside from this practical consideration, conceptually, a ridge describes better than an edge what a lane line is: the medial axis of a thick, brighter line. Secondly, we have adapted RANSAC, a generic robust estimation method, to fit a parametric model

J. Martí et al. (Eds.): IbPRIA 2007, Part I, LNCS 4477, pp. 274–281, 2007.

Fig. 1. Left: road image with a region of interest (ROI) outlined. Right: ROI seen as a landscape, where lane markings resemble mountains and ridges correspond correspond to the center of the lane markings.

to the candidate lane marking points, using as input data both ridgeness and ridge orientation (section 3). Thirdly, we quantitatively assess the method with regard to four quantities derived from the segmented lane markings: vehicle yaw angle and lateral offset, lane curvature and width. This is possible on synthetic sequences, for which we know exactly the value for these parameters since they are provided as input to the program which generates them (section 4). Section 5 draws the main conclusions and comments future work. A previous version of this work was presented in [3]. However, it did not include the validation on synthetic sequences and the pair of lane lines model was different.

2 Lane Markings as Ridges

Ridges of a grey–level image are the center lines of elongated, bright structures. In the case of a lane line is its longitudinal center. This terminology comes from considering an image as a landscape, being the intensity the z axis or height, since then these center lines correspond to the landscape's ridges (figure 1). Accordingly, ridgeness stands for a measure of how much a pixel neighborhood resembles a ridge. Therefore, a ridgeness measure must have high values along the center of the line and decrease as the boundary is approached. A binary ridge image, corresponding to the centerline, can be obtained by simple thresholding, provided we have a well–contrasted and homogeneous ridgeness measure.

This notion of ridge or medial axis is a simpler and, as we will see in short, computationally better characterization of lane lines than that provided by edges. Instead of defining (and trying to find out) a lane line as points between two parallel edge segments with opposite gradient direction, a ridge is the center of the line itself, once a certain amount of smoothing has been performed. And this amount is chosen as the scale at witch ridges are sought.

There are different mathematical characterizations of ridges. In [4] a new one is proposed which compares favorably to others and that we have adapted for the problem at hand. Let $\mathbf{x} = (u, v)$ be the spatial coordinates (u columns, v rows). Then, ridgeness is calculated as the positive values of the divergence of

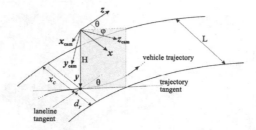

Fig. 2. Image acquisition geometry

the normalized gradient vector field $\tilde{\mathbf{w}}$ of the image:

$$\tilde{\kappa}_{\sigma_\mathrm{d},\sigma_\mathrm{i}}(\mathbf{x}) = -\mathrm{div}(\tilde{\mathbf{w}}_{\sigma_\mathrm{d},\sigma_\mathrm{i}}(\mathbf{x})) \tag{1}$$

The parameter σ_d is the *differentiation scale*, in opposition to σ_i which is the *integration scale*. The former must be tuned to the size of the target structures, while the later determines the size of the neighborhood we want to use in order to compute the dominant orientation.

We only take into account those pixels $\mathbf{x}$ for which $\tilde{\kappa}_{\sigma_\mathrm{d},\sigma_\mathrm{i}}(\mathbf{x}) > 0.25$, a value fixed experimentally but with a large margin before the selected pixels change significantly. Due to perspective, the imaged lane lines width decreases with distance. In order not to miss them, σ_d also decreases with the row number so that upper rows are less smoothed than lower rows.

Interesting properties of $\tilde{\kappa}_{\sigma_\mathrm{d},\sigma_\mathrm{i}}(\mathbf{x})$ are invariance to image translation and rotation, as one would expect, but also to monotonic grey–level transforms. The later greatly helps in lane detection in presence of shadows and low contrast conditions, opposite to gradient–based measures. Shadows cast by vehicles and road infrastructure (like fences, tunnel entries, lamp posts) give rise to long and straight contour lines which can fool edge–based lane detection methods.

3 Lane Model and Fitting

3.1 Lane Lines Model

A number of geometrical models for the projected lane lines have been proposed, from simple straight lines to quadratic, spline and other polynomial curves, with the aim of performing a good image segmentation. However, few are built on a sound geometrical base like in [6]. There it is shown that, under several reasonable assumptions (flat road, constant curvature), a lane line on a planar road is projected onto the image plane as an hyperbola. Admittedly, this is not a new model, but what that work reveals are the relationships among model parameters and meaningful and interesting geometrical entities such as lane width, curvature and the vehicle's lateral position, which we want to compute in order to validate our method, aside of their own evident applicability in ADAS.

As illustrated in figure 2, the camera coordinate system has Y axis coincident with the vehicle's direction and sustains an angle $\theta \ll 1$ rad. with the road tangent line (also referred as yaw angle). It also forms an angle φ with the road plane (pitch angle). The lane has width L and the camera is located at a horizontal distance of d_r meters from the right border and at height H above the ground. Of course, L, d_r, θ and φ may vary over time, but H is supposed constant. Finally, let be E_u and E_v the focal lengths in pixels/meter along the horizontal and vertical camera axes, and the image origin centered in the principal point (intersection of the optical axis with the image plane). Then, the following equation relates (u_r, v_r), the pixel coordinates where the right lane line is imaged, to the road parameters it belongs to [6]:

$$u_r = E_u \left(\frac{\theta}{\cos \varphi} + \frac{d_r \cos \varphi}{HE_v}(v_r + E_v \tan \varphi) + \frac{E_v HC_0/\cos^3 \varphi}{4(v_r + E_v \tan \varphi)} \right) \quad (2)$$

The former equation clearly follows the formulation of a hyperbola with a horizontal asymptote. In order to enforce parallelism of lane borders, we introduce a new variable x_c, which is the signed distance along the X axis between the camera projection on the road plane and the central axis of the left lane line (figure 2). It follows that $d_r = x_c - L$, $d_l = x_c$ and we have the following couple of equations, for points $(u_l, v_l), (u_r, v_r)$ on the left and right border, respectively:

$$u_l = E_u \left(\frac{\theta}{\cos \varphi} + \frac{\cos \varphi}{HE_v}x_c(v_l + E_v \tan \varphi) + \frac{E_v HC_0/\cos^3 \varphi}{4(v_l + E_v \tan \varphi)} \right) \quad (3)$$

$$u_r = E_u \left(\frac{\theta}{\cos \varphi} + \frac{\cos \varphi}{HE_v}(x_c - L)(v_r + E_v \tan \varphi) + \frac{E_v HC_0/\cos^3 \varphi}{4(v_r + E_v \tan \varphi)} \right)$$

Since parameters E_u, E_v, H and φ can be estimated through a camera calibration process [7], equation (4) is linear with respect to the four unknowns θ, x_c, L and C_0. It can be compactly rewritten as

$$\begin{bmatrix} 1 & 0 & v'_l & 1/v'_l \\ 1 & -v'_r & v'_r & 1/v'_r \end{bmatrix} \begin{bmatrix} a_1 \\ a_2 \\ a_3 \\ a_4 \end{bmatrix} = \begin{bmatrix} u_l \\ u_r \end{bmatrix} \quad (4)$$

with $v'_r = v_r/E_v + \tan \varphi, v'_l = v_l/E_v + \tan \varphi$ and

$$\theta = \frac{\cos \varphi}{E_u}a_1, \quad L = \frac{H}{E_u \cos \varphi}a_2, \quad x_c = \frac{H}{E_u \cos \varphi}a_3, \quad C_0 = \frac{4 \cos^3 \varphi}{E_u H}a_4 \quad (5)$$

Note that according to this model, four points, not all on the same line, define a *pair* of hyperbolas sharing the same horizontal asymptote. In addition, they correspond to two parallel curves L meters apart, when back projected to the road plane. This implies that we are going to fit *both left and right* lane lines at the same time and enforcing parallelism, that is, consistency in the solution. Besides, the sparsity of candidates in one lane side due to shadows, occlusions or dashed lane marks can be compensated by those in the other side.

3.2 Model Fitting

A minimum of four points are necessary in order to solve equation (4), provided there is at least one point on each curve. If more points are known, we get an overconstrained system that is solved in the least–squares sense. The problem, of course, is the selection of the right points among all candidates from the previous detection step. We need a robust technique in the sense of, simultaneously, classify candidate points into lane points (inliers) and not lane points (outliers, at least for that side), and perform the fitting only to the former ones. RANSAC, which stands for Random Sample Consensus [9], is a general estimation technique for such purpose based on the principle of hypotheses generation and verification.

An observation must be made concerning the lane model of equation (4). In it we supposed the pitch angle φ known from the calibration process, but actually it suffers variations around its nominal value due to non–planar roads, acceleration, brake actioning etc. To account for this fact, quite influential in the instantiated model because it changes its horizontal asymptote, we test several possible values for φ, taking n_φ equispaced samples within $\varphi \pm \Delta\varphi$.

4 Results

As pointed out in a recent survey on video–based lane departure warning [10], results in the literature are often presented only in the form of several frames, where the reader can check the correspondence between detected lane lines and real lane markings. We also present results in this qualitative way, but just to show examples of challenging situations (see figure 3). However, since our fitted model has a direct relation to geometrically meaningful parameters of interest in the context of ADAS, we base the evaluation on the comparison of these computed values with the actual ones. The construction of digital road maps at lane line resolucion is a research issue in itself. Therefore, we have resorted to build a simulator which generates sequences of synthetic but realistic images of 3D roads of known geometry.

The simulator, implemented in Matlab, models the road geometry, photometry and the camera focal length, trajectory and pose with regard a world coordinate system. Whereas the camera roll angle has been fixed and yaw depends on the trajectory, the pitch angle φ has not, since it is responsible for the horizon line vertical motion, which is not static in real sequences. Besides, it turns out that this parameter is quite influential on the results. Thus, we have randomly varied the pitch angle so as to mimic the effects of 1) uneven road surface and 2) acceleration and brake actioning, both observed in real sequences. Specifically, pitch variation is generated by adding two random noises: the first one of high

Fig. 3. Segmented lane line curves. From left to right and top to bottom : dashed lines, occlusion, tunnel exit, special road marks, shadows, night image with reflections. Complete sequences from which these frames have been extracted can be viewed at `www.cvc.uab.es/adas/projects/lanemarkings/IbPRIA07.html`.

frequency and small amplitude ($\leq 0.2°$) and the second one of low frequency but larger amplitude (between $0.5°$ and $1°$), which account respectively for the two former pitch variation sources.

We have performed several tests on synthetic sequences in order to calculate the error in the estimation of C_0, L, θ, x_c and also φ on a 5 Km long road, one frame per meter. Sudden slope changes introduce large errors, though logically localized in time, whereas almost no error is observed at curvature changes. At frames where the pitch variation has its largests peaks ($t = 380, 720, 1200, 1450$), the error is small for x_c, moderate for L but large for C_0 and θ (figure 4, due to space limitations, we do not include the figures for all the parameters). The reason is that x_c and L are local road measures very close to the camera position and thus not affected by the global lane line shape, specially its shape at a large distance, close to the horizon line. On the contrary, C_0 and θ do depend on the global shape (according to the road model, the curvature is supposed to be constant) which is in turn dependent on the shared lane lines horizontal asymptote. In addition, a small amplitude noise appears elsewhere mainly due to the small amplitude pitch variation.

We have tried to minimize the effect of pitch changes (both large and small) by considering φ another parameter to estimate. The second row of figure 4 shows the result for $n_\varphi = 7$ and $\Delta\varphi = 1°$. Close examination of the estimated pitch angle allows us to conclude that the best pitch search is often able to correctly estimate it (the four largest pitch variations are well detected), but not always. The most prominent errors are localized around the four slope changes, where this simple approach of guessing the best pitch fails. Elsewhere, a sort of impulsive error is observed, caused by a small number of inliers. In spite of it, a causal median filter (median of a number of pitch estimations before the current frame) produces an acceptable result, even for a small n_φ. Finally, figure 5 shows the root–mean square error between computed and ground truth for four different values of n_φ, and also for their median filtered versions. Whereas there is only a slight improvement, or even no improvement at all, when n_φ

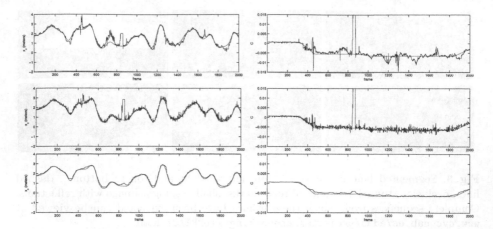

Fig. 4. Ground truth and computed x_c (left) and C (right) for (top to bottom): n_φ=1 and 7 pitch angles around nominal camera pitch, and median filtering of this latter result.

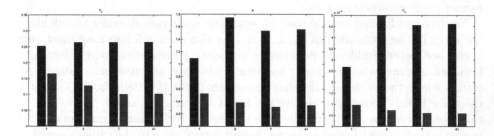

Fig. 5. Root-mean square error of computed x_c, θ and C_0 (angles in degrees) n_φ =1, 3, 7 and 41. In each pair, left bar corresponds to the computed value and right bar to its causal median filtered version.

increases, the error of the filtered parameters clearly decreases. Therefore, it seems that it does not pay to look for the best pitch if no filtering is performed afterwards.

5   Conclusions

We have developed a new method for the extraction of lane lines from video sequences. Robustness is achieved both in the feature detection phase, where we employ an image feature well suited to this problem, and in the model fitting phase, which we have addressed with the RANSAC approach. This method relies just on images, that is, we do not take into account data from other vehicle sensors, like the steering angle or yaw rate. Also, we have avoided any kind of result post processing: each frame is processed independently of the others. The reason is that our aim was to build a 'baseline' system to which add later filtering and data fusion to improve the result. Our lane line extraction method has the advantage of computing four road and vehicle trajectory parameters which are of interest in the context of ADAS. We have compared the computed values with ground truth from a synthetic but realistic road. The present implementation of feature detection, model fitting and parameter computation runs in real–time, at 40 ms/frame on a 2 Ghz Pentium IV, no matter if the image is synthetic or real. From these experiments we conclude that we can compute reasonable estimations of road curvature, width and vehicle lateral position and direction, even in the case where the road does not follow the assumed model of flatness, constant curvature and known camera pitch. However, the weak point of our method is the estimation of the pitch angle, which we expect to predict on the basis of previous frames.

Acknowledgments. This research has been partially funded by Spanish MEC grant TRA2004-06702/AUT.

References

1. Jung, C.R., Kelber, C.R.: Lane following and lane departure using a linear–parabolic model. Image and Vision Computing 23, 1192–1202 (2005)
2. Bertozzi, M., Broggi, A., Fascioli, A.: Vision–based Intelligent Vehicles: State of the Art and Perspectives. Robotics and Autonomous Systems 32, 1–16 (2000)
3. López, A., Cañero, C., Serrat, J., Saludes, J., Lumbreras, F., Graf. T.: Detection of Lane Markings based on Ridgeness and RANSAC, IEEE Conf. on Intelligent Transportation Systems, Vienna pp. 733–738, (2005)
4. López, A., Lloret, D., Serrat, J., Villanueva, J.: Multilocal Creaseness Based on the Level–Set Extrinsic Curvature. Computer Vision and Image Understanding 77, 111–144 (2000)
5. Dickmanns, E.D., Mysliwetz, B.D.: Recursive 3D road and relative ego–state recognition. IEEE Trans. on Pattern Analysis and Machine Intelligence 14, 199–213 (1992)
6. Guiducci, A.: Parametric Model of the Perspective Projection of a Road with Application to Lane Keeping and 3D Road Reconstruction. Computer Vision and Image Understanding, 73, 414–427 (1999)
7. Zhang, Z.: A flexible new technique for camera calibration. IEEE Transactions on Pattern Analysis and Machine Intelligence 22(11), 1330–1334 (2000)
8. Aufrère, R., Chapuis, R., Chausse, F.: A Model–Driven Approach for Real–Time Road Recognition. Machine Vision and Applications 13, 95–107 (2001)
9. Fischler, M.A., Bolles, R.C.: Random Sample Consensus: a Paradigm for Model Fitting with Applications to Image Analysis and Automated Cartography. Commun. ACM, 24, 381–395 (1981)
10. McCall, J.C., Trivedi, M.M.: Video–based lane estimation and tracking for driver assistance: survey, system and evaluation. IEEE Trans. on Intelligent Transportation Systems 7(1), 20–37 (2006)

Matrics, a Car License Plate Recognition System*

Andrés Marzal, Juan Miguel Vilar, David Llorens, Vicente Palazón,
and Javier Martín

Departament de Llenguatges i Sistemes Informàtics
Universitat Jaume I
Castelló, Spain
{amarzal,jvilar,dllorens,palazon}@dlsi.uji.es,
al021533@alumail.uji.es

Abstract. Matrics is a system for recognition of car license plates. It works on standard PC equipment with low-priced capture devices and achieves real-time performance (10 frames per second) with state of the art accuracy: the character error rate is below 1% and the plate error rate is below 3%. The recognition process is divided in two phases: plate localization and plate decoding. The system finds the plate analyzing the connected components of the image after binarization. The decoding algorithm is a Two Level process which uses fast template-based classification techniques in its first stage and optimal segmentation in the second stage. On the whole, the system represents a significant improvement over a previous version which was based on HMM.

1 Introduction

Car License Plate Recognition (CLPR) is an application of Pattern Recognition with high demand in several fields [1,5]: control of highways and borders, traffic monitoring, law enforcement, recovery of stolen cars, etc. When the working conditions can be controlled (light settings, camera position with respect to vehicle, background, etc.), CLPR can be satisfactorily solved with well-known Pattern Recognition techniques [2]. But there is a large number of situations where not all these conditions can be controlled. To meet industry-standard requirements [6], a CLPR must (1) operate in a wide range of illumination conditions (indoors and outdoors); (2) be invariant to size, scale, and font boldness; (3) be robust to broken strokes, printing defects, and other kind of noise; (4) be insensitive to camera-car relative positions within a reasonable distance and angle interval; (5) provide real-time response; and (6) work with different capturing devices (including image repositories). There is a demand for flexible CLPR engines satisfying these requirements and easily integrable in final application programs.

The Matrics system is a CLPR engine that meets these requirements and runs on the .NET 2.0 platform, which allows easy portability (it can run on the

---

* Work partially supported by the *Ministerio de Educación y Ciencia* (TIN2006-12767), the *Generalitat Valenciana* (GV06/302) and *Bancaixa* (P1 1B2006-31).

J. Martí et al. (Eds.): IbPRIA 2007, Part I, LNCS 4477, pp. 282–289, 2007.

Microsoft Windows system and on Linux under the Mono platform). The engine has been designed to ease its integration in application software.

2   The Matrics System Architecture

Typically, CLPR systems proceed in two stages: (1) license plate localization and (2) license character recognition. There are several approaches for plate localization: connected component detection, morphology, texture, etc. Matrics uses a connected component based approach that yields a series of "Regions Of Interest" (ROIs): it finds lined-up connected components on several binarizations of the image. Recognition is performed on each ROI until some stop criterion is met (or all ROIs have been considered). A decoding procedure, consisting of a template-based Two Level algorithm, is executed on each ROI: every segment of the ROI is pre-classified in a first stage and, then, an optimal composition of classified segments compatible with a language model is found by iteratively solving a recursive equation. Decoding more than one ROI provides a great degree of robustness against false plate detections. The stop criterion for this "ROIs on demand" generation is related to the confidence on the quality of the decoding result. Since the number of ROI decoding attempts can be large, the decoding stage must be extremely efficient. This tight integration of coarse localization and fast recognition greatly improves the overall results.

2.1   ROIs Detection Subsystem

The aim of the ROIs detection phase is to find a set of quadrangles that can be considered promising places for containing a plate and nothing else than a plate. A ROI cannot be assumed to have a rectangular shape due to the perspective distortion introduced by the angle of the camera with respect to the car. These ROIs are searched for by analyzing the connected components of binarized images. Connected components of similar height, aspect ratio in some range, and (approximately) distributed along a line are considered probable license characters and, therefore, their minimum inclusion quadrangle is a plate place candidate, i.e, a ROI.

As a single binarization procedure cannot yield the right connected components in all lighting settings, camera distance/angle and blur conditions, Matrics uses up to four different binarizations. All of them are applied to a smoothed image (obtained by applying a Gaussian filter to the original, gray-scale image). This filtered image suffers a mean-minus-C local thresholding that produces a binary image. This thresholding filter has two parameters: n, the window length; and c, the value to be subtracted to the mean gray-level in a pixel neighbourhood before deciding whether the current pixel is black or white.

Three different binarizations result of applying the mean-minus-C filter with parameters $(n = 21, c = 2)$, $(n = 21, c = 6)$, and $(n = 9, c = 6)$. Under hard-light conditions such as direct exposition to sunlight, projected shadows on the plate make it hard for any local thresholding technique to properly binarize the

(a)   (b)   (c)   (d)

Fig. 1. (a) Plate directly exposed to sunlight. (b) A single connected component in the binarized image groups several characters. (c) Edges in the original image. (d) Removal of edges from the binary image: the characters of the plate are separated from one another.

image: the frontier between the shadowed and lighted regions is a high contrast line that usually connects most characters in the plate. A fourth binarization is performed to solve this problem. The (binarized) image resulting from the application of a Canny filter is "subtracted" from the $(n = 9, c = 6)$ binarization. This subtraction of thin edges effectively disconnects the characters (see Fig. 1). Sometimes this subtraction produces connected components smaller than those associated to a character. A post-processing phase heuristically joins connected components of similar width and very closely placed in the vertical axis (thus joining the two connected components split by the shadow border from a single character).

The set of connected components in a binarized image is filtered according to the absolute size and the aspect ratio in order to discard noise and too large items in the image. Connected components along the line joining every pair of surviving connected components are selected as candidates to be part of a ROI. Whenever the number of selected elements is between 3 and 9, the minimum-area quadrangle enclosing all these components becomes a ROI candidate. ROIs whose baseline has an absolute slope of more than 45 degrees are discarded (these parameters can be modified to tune the system for different requirements).

Only ROIs not included in other ROIs and whose four vertices are sufficiently different of those defining other ROIs are effectively generated. Former versions of the system heuristically scored each ROI and yielded ROIs in a picture in decreasing-score order [4]. The score took into account the number of included connected components, baseline angle, percentage of overlapping in components, etc. According to our experiments with the new system, this ROI scoring does not have a significant impact on the recognition accuracy of the whole CLPR system.

Finally, the quadrilateral ROIs are mapped into rectangles by means of a bilinear transform. The rectangle dimensions are chosen as close as possible to the quadrangle side lengths. Since the resulting image is expected to be a plate, i.e., a locally high-contrast region, it is enhanced with an adaptive contrast-stretching filter that takes into account the average gray level on each row and column of pixels. In order to avoid the perspective distortion introduced by the bilinear transform, the enhanced gray-image is slant-corrected before being yield by the ROIs detection subsystem.

2.2 Plates Decoding Subsystem

A gray scale image can be seen as a sequence of frames, each one consisting of a column of pixels. The decoding problem can be formulated as the computation of an optimal segmentation of this sequence of frames: each segment is a sequence of consecutive frames labeled as either a character or a white space, and such that the concatenated string of labels belongs to a given language (the valid license plate codes). This problem can be solved by a Two-Level decoding algorithm consisting of a segments classification stage and a simultaneous optimal segmentation/decoding stage. For the sake of clarity, we describe first the second stage.

Second stage: optimal segmentation and decoding. Let $\langle f_1, f_2, \ldots, f_n \rangle$ be a sequence of frames (in our case, a sequence of pixel columns) and let $A = (\Sigma, Q, q_0, \delta, F)$ be a Finite State Automaton (FSA) where Σ is an alphabet, Q is the set of states, $q_0 \in Q$ is the initial state, $\delta \subseteq Q \times \Sigma \times Q$ is the set of transitions, and $F \subseteq Q$ is the set of final states. Let $d(i, j, a)$ be a dissimilarity measure between the subsequence (segment) $\langle f_i, f_{i+1}, \ldots, f_j \rangle$ and the character $a \in \Sigma$ (we will present its computation in the next subsection).

A segmentation of f into m segments is a sequence of $m + 1$ integers, $\langle s_0, s_1, \ldots, s_m \rangle$, such that $s_0 = 0$, $s_m = n$, and $s_i < s_{i+1}$ for all $i \neq j$. The i-th segment is the subsequence $\langle f_{s_{i-1}}, f_{s_{i-1}+1}, \ldots, f_{s_i} \rangle$.

Given both a sequence of states, $\mathbf{q} = \langle q_0, q_1, \ldots, q_m \rangle$, and a segmentation, $\langle s_0, s_1, \ldots, s_m \rangle$, we define their (normalized) distortion as

$$D_{\mathbf{q}}(\langle s_0, s_1, \ldots, s_m \rangle) = \frac{\sum_{i=1}^{m} \min_{a \in \Sigma : (q_{i-1}, a, q_i) \in \delta} d(s_{i-1}, s_i, a)}{m}. \tag{1}$$

If all sequences of states ending at the same final state, $q \in F$, have the same length, $l(q)$, we can minimize (1) over all state sequences and segmentations computing $\min_{q \in F} \Delta(n, q)/l(q)$, where

$$\Delta(j, q) = \begin{cases} 0, & \text{if } j = 0 \text{ and } q = q_0; \\ +\infty, & \text{if } j = 0 \text{ and } q \neq q_0; \\ \min_{0 \leq i < j} \min_{\substack{q' \in Q, a \in \Sigma : \\ (q', a, q) \in \delta}} \Delta(i, q') + d(i+1, j, a), & \text{if } j > 0. \end{cases} \tag{2}$$

This recursive expression can be evaluated in $O(|Q|^2 n^2)$ time by means of Dynamic Programming [3]. Segment-length constraints can be easily imposed by restricting the range of values of i in the outer minimization of the general term. This reduces the time complexity to $O(|Q|^2 nr)$, where r is the maximum segment length. An appropriate use of backpointers on the Dynamic Programming trellis allows obtaining the optimal (minimum distortion) segmentation and decoding (sequence of symbols along the optimal sequence of states) in $O(|Q|n)$ space.

First stage: segments classification. In principle, the purpose of the first stage is to compute $d(i, j, a)$ for all $\max(0, j - r) \leq i < j \leq n$ and for all $a \in \Sigma$. We use a template-based approach: several images for each symbol in Σ are available in a database. In order to perform a fast comparison of segments and symbol templates, each segment (and symbol) is represented with a 5×9 image (obtained with a smoothly interpolated scaling of the segment or symbol image), which yields a 45 components vector: the segment (or symbol) *signature*. The value of $d(i, j, a)$ is defined as the squared euclidean distance between the signature of the segment $\langle f_i, f_{i+1}, \ldots, f_j \rangle$ and the nearest-neighbour template among all those representing the symbol a.

The obtention of $|\Sigma|$ nearest-neighbors for $O(n^2)$ segments is computationally expensive and it must be speeded-up in order to work in real-time. Different techniques have been applied to achieve this goal. First, not all possible segments are taken into account: only those between pairs of probable character beginning/ending frames are considered candidates to character or white space. A preprocessing phase provides an over-segmentation of the frame sequence, i.e., a segmentation that ideally includes all the marks of the optimal segmentation (and possibly some more). The marks are placed between frames of high variation in the black-to-white pixels proportion, since these are good candidates to begin/end a symbol. This reduces the number of segments from $O(n^2)$ to $O((n')^2)$, where $n' \ll n$, which is a drastic gain (we typically pass from 200–400 possible segment mark locations to 20–40, i.e., a speed-up factor of 100x). On the other hand, the dimensionality of the signatures is significantly reduced by means of a Principal Component Analysis (PCA). As we will show in the experiments section, taking into account only the first 24 components of the transformed PCA vectors provides a good compromise between speed-up and recognition error rate. The nearest-neighbour classification is performed on kd-trees. The search is greatly accelerated without a significant impact on the global accuracy of the distortion measure when only approximate nearest-neighbours are obtained. This is done by relaxing the pruning function in the prototypes elimination steps. Finally, we do not perform an (approximate) nearest-neighbour search for all the characters in Σ, one by one. Symbols are grouped into categories induced by the FSA modeling the valid license codes: for any pair of states $q, q' \in Q$, all the symbols $a \in \Sigma$ such that $(q, a, q') \in \delta$ are grouped into a category (note that categories are not necessarily disjoint). For instance, there is a single kd-tree for all the digits' templates, since all the digits appear in the same state-to-state transitions. Other categories of symbols seem less natural, such as the letters starting province codes. This categorization of symbols simplifies the inner minimization in the general term of equation (2): a single loop on the predecessor states of q provides the optimal value. White spaces are dealt with differently: both recognition accuracy and speed improved when we classified as white space any segment whose black-to-white ratio was under a manually chosen threshold.

2.3   Implementation Details

The plate localization module does not initially compute all ROIs in the image: it preprocesses the image and locates ROIs on demand. This allows for a lazy, data-flow guided implementation. The decoding stages asks for ROIs until some confidence criterion is met: when we are rather sure that the plate has been found and correctly decoded (i.e., a low distortion value is obtained), the ROIs localization module aborts its execution.

Matrics has been implemented in C# and runs on the .NET 2.0 platform. It runs in real-time —at a rate of nearly 10 frames (640×480 images) per second— on low-cost personal computers. Images can be captured with TCP/IP cameras (http-based) and USB cameras.

3   Experiments

We performed experiments on a corpus consisting of 467 images of cars captured in poorly controlled conditions (there are pictures with hard perspective distortions, blurred pictures due to movement, dirty and broken characters and/or plates, pictures taken with flash, etc). This set was randomly split into a training set consisting of 417 images and a test set with the other 50 pictures. Each image was acquired with a digital camera and resized to a resolution of 640×480 pixels.

The system can be tuned by assigning a value to three parameters:

- PCA dimensions: number of dimensions taken into account after the PCA transformation.
- kd-tree approximation parameter: the nearest-neighbour is approximated by relaxing the bounds computation according to this value.
- Stop value for distortion: the ROIs generation procedure is aborted when a ROI with a distortion under this value is found. When this parameter is set to 0, all ROIs are generated and decoded.

We have measured the character error percentage (CEP) and the plate errors percentage (PEP). On the other hand, we have also measured the number of images processed per second (frames per second or FPS) on a PC with a 3 GHz Pentium IV processor and 2 Gb of memory.

When the number of PCA dimensions is set to 20, the kd-tree parameter is set to 1 and the stop value is set to 0, the CEP is 0.8% and the PEP is 3.8% on the training set. On the test set, this produced 0.0% error rates both at the character and plate levels. With these settings, the system processed 9.2 FPS.

We tried to reduce the error rates while keeping or improving the FPS value. First we tried different values of the PCA dimension parameter. Fig. 2 (a) shows the error percentages on the training set and the FPS for different values of this parameter between 5 and 45. A value of 24 seems a good compromise between speed (8.3 FPS) and accuracy (0.7% CEP and 3.4% PEP). We fixed the PCA number of dimensions to 24 and tried with values of the kd-tree approximation

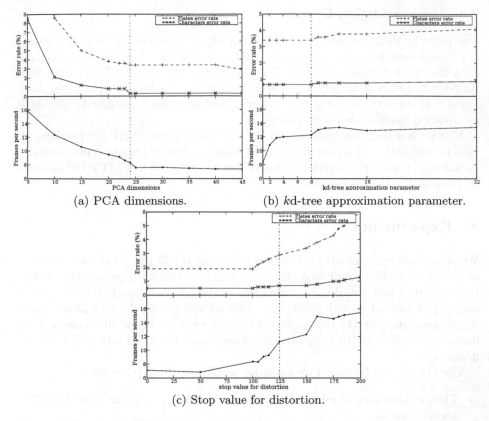

(a) PCA dimensions.   (b) kd-tree approximation parameter.

(c) Stop value for distortion.

Fig. 2. Influence of different parameters on error percentages over the training set (upper part of each graph) and recognition speed in frame per second (lower part of each graph)

parameter comprised between 1 and 32. A value of 8 preserved the same CEP and PEP while raising the number of FPS to 12.3 (see Fig. 2 (b)). After setting this parameter to that value, we changed the stop value in the 0 to 200 range. When the stop value is set to 115, the CEP is reduced to 0.6% and the PEP falls to 2.6% (see Fig. 2 (c)). The number of FPS is 9.5, a slightly better value than the one in the starting point for a lower error rate. With these ultimate settings, the CEP on the test set was 0.3% and the PEP, 2%. This increase in the error rate is due to one character mismatch in a single plate.

For comparison purposes, the results are superior to those presented in [2] and [6], although not comparable as the corpora are different. A more appropriate comparison can be done to our previous system [4]: 1.9% CEP and 6% PEP, for manual detection of the plate. A time comparison is not appropriate since that system was designed in a batch framework and no effort was directed towards increasing the throughput.

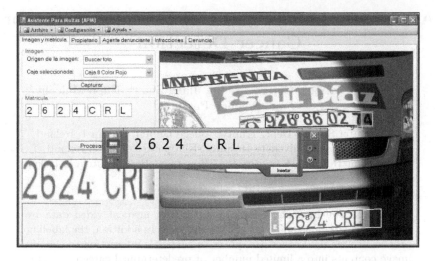

Fig. 3. Interactive application using the Matrics CLPR engine running on a Tablet PC

4   Conclusions and Future Work

We have presented a CLPR system with an "on demand" ROIs generation and a Two-level decoding algorithm whose first stage is based on nearest-neighbour classification. The experimental results show that the system offers state-of-the-art performance and can be used in real applications. The experimental results are much better than those obtained for an HMM-based system developed by the same research group and presented in [4]. We have developed a demonstration system running on a Tablet PC with a low-cost USB webcam that runs in real time (see Fig. 3). In the near future, we plan to introduce threads in the CLPR engine to optimally exploit mid-to-low multi-processor architectures (hyperthreaded and dual-core systems).

References

1. Albiol, A., Mossi, J.M., Albiol, A., Naranjo, V.: Automatic license plate reading using mathematical morphology. In: Proceedings of the The 4th IASTED International Conference on Visualisation, Imaging and Image Processing, Marbella, Spain (September 2004)
2. Chang, S.-L., Chen, L.-S., Chung, Y.-C., Chen, S.-W.: Automatic license plate recognition. IEEE Transactions on Intelligent Transportation Systems 5(1), 42–53 (2004)
3. Cormen, T.H.: Introduction to Algorithms. MIT Press, Cambridge (2001)
4. Llorens, D., Marzal, A., Palazón, V., Vilar, J.M.: Car license plates extraction and recognition based on connected components analysis and hmm decoding. In: Marques, J.S., de la Blanca, N.P., Pina, P. (eds.) IbPRIA 2005. LNCS, vol. 3522, Springer, Heidelberg (2005)
5. Martín, F., García, M., Alba, J.L.: New methods for automatic reading of vlp's (vehicle license plates). In: SSPRA (2004)
6. Shapiro, V., Gluhchev, G., Dimov, D.: Towards a multinational car license plate recognition system. Machine Vision and Applications 17, 173–183 (2006)

Automatic Labeling of Colonoscopy Video for Cancer Detection

Fernando Vilariño[1], Gerard Lacey[1], Jiang Zhou[1], Hugh Mulcahy[2], and Stephen Patchett[3]

[1] Computer Science Dept. Trinity College Dublin, Dublin 1. Ireland
[2] St. Vincent's University Hospital, Elm park, Dublin 4. Ireland
[3] Beaumount Hospital, P.O. Box 1297 Beaumont Road, Dublin 9. Ireland

Abstract. The labeling of large quantities of medical video data by clinicians is a tedious and time consuming task. In addition, the labeling process itself is rigid, since it requires the expert's interaction to classify image contents into a limited number of predetermined categories. This paper describes an architecture to accelerate the labeling step using eye movement tracking data. We report some initial results in training a Support Vector Machine (SVM) to detect cancer polyps in colonoscopy video, and a further analysis of their categories in the feature space using Self Organizing Maps (SOM). Our overall hypothesis is that the clinician's eye will be drawn to the salient features of the image and that sustained fixations will be associated with those features that are associated with disease states.

1 Introduction

In the last years, the increase in minimally invasive approaches to medicine has driven to the fact that clinical decisions are increasingly being made on the basis of both still and moving images. This is particularly the case in cancer screening for endoscopy. Recent publications have drawn attention to the variability in miss rates between endoscopists in the detection of colon cancer [1],[2]. From this perspective, our ultimate objective is to develop a realtime computer aided detection system to support endoscopists achieve low miss rates.

Endoscopy video is characterized by a large amount of data; a typical procedure may generate one million separate images, many of which irrelevant from a clinical point of view. In order to train a classifier such as a Support Vector Machine (SVM) [3] it is necessary to have a labeled training set ideally classified by a number of clinicians so that inter rater reliability can be assessed. Some data reduction can be performed using techniques from video parsing to remove certain irrelevant images [4] but the remaining data is still too large to produce a significant data set labeled in a frame by frame basis. Using small training sets places an upper limit on the number of features that can be used to reliably train a classifier such as a SVM, given the high variability of both cancer and non cancer images this represents a significant challenge to developing a computer aided detection system for colonoscopy.

J. Martí et al. (Eds.): IbPRIA 2007, Part I, LNCS 4477, pp. 290–297, 2007.

Given the difficulty of generating large data sets of labeled training and test data, previous contributions on detecting cancerous lesions in endoscopic video have been constrained to use restricted data sets [5] ,[6] . The large variability in the presentation of both healthy and diseased tissue would indicate that larger training sets will be required to develop a practical classifier.

Models of the human visual system have been used to identify regions of high saliency in images and videos [7], [8] and a number of image processing operators correlate well with this bottom up model of salience. In task specific activities there is a significant top-down element to visual attention [9]. Kienzle et. al. [10] presented preliminary results using eye movement data to learn an interest operator on still images. Their learned operator was compared against the output of a range of interest operators however this was not related to a specific task. Chung et.al.[11] discussed the use of eye tracking to determine which features are salient in colonoscopy video for the specific issue of registering a still 2D endoscopy image to a 3D CT scan of a phantom lung.

This paper presents a preliminary evaluation of a novel architecture that uses eye-tracking data on colonoscopy video rather than still images to train a SVM classifier to recognize polyps. The system uses gaze fixation to identify salient and non salient regions of the image. These regions are used to train a SVM for the automatic detection of polyps. For the analysis of the classification results, we use a Self Organizing Map (SOM) [12] in order to visualize the distribution of the images and perform a further categorization of the data. We deploy this approach through the rest of the paper as follows: Section 2 explains the methodology of our proposal. In Section 3, we provide the preliminary results of our experiments. Finally, we close this paper with the conclusions of our work and the highlighting of the future lines of research in Section 4.

2   Methodology

2.1   General Procedure

We propose and architecture to accelerate the creation of massive data sets of clinical video data using eye tracking data to perform labeling of regions of interest in endoscopy images. The large data sets will be used to train and test machine learning based cancer detection and categorization systems. In addition to this, the eye tracking information can be used to discover the salient features used by experts in detecting cancer in endoscopic images. Figure 1 shows a graphical scheme of this approach.

In order to build up our database, we propose the following strategy: The endoscopy data is visualized by an expert wearing an eye tracking system. While our ultimate objective is to study the patterns of fixation of the experts as they review the data to identify regions of clinical saliency, in this study we ask the experts to press and hold a key to select video sequences containing polyps. The experts are asked to center their attention on the region of interest while the key is pressed. Further implementations of this approach could avoid the keyboard interaction, substituting it by either voice guided sequence selection or

Fig. 1. General scheme of the eye tracker-based methodology of this paper

eye-fixation analysis. These two alternative strategies would require a separate study, which falls outside the scope of this paper but remain the goal of our team. The final region of interest (ROI) segmentation is obtained using the gaze position provided by the eye tracker -see Figure 2 a)-.

The eye tracker consists of an adjustable helmet which carries a pair of cameras pointing the the user's eyes. The eye tracking procedure involves the recording the gaze direction and translating this into the location on the image where the wearer is focusing their attention. Figure 2 b) shows a scheme of the EyeLink II (c) eye tracker which was used for our experiments. The video signal from the cameras is sent to a host PC in which the eye tracker software is installed, and which communicates to the experiment PC in which the visual stimuli are shown.

2.2 Polyp Detection, Polyp Categorization and Saliency Identification

In order to perform the polyp detection within the regions of interest, we apply a SVM classifier to the pre-processed images corresponding to the regions of interest containing polyps and non-polyps. This approach has been investigated in recent works [13], [10], and appears as a simple and effective strategy. The pre-process stage consists of a noise filtering by means of a median filter, followed by an intensity normalization for the whole region of interest, so that it presents a zero mean value. Once the polyp is detected a further categorization step is performed, since different types of polyps have different levels of risk associated

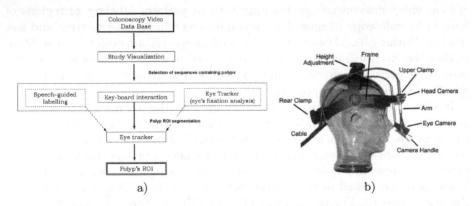

Fig. 2. a) Data acquisition scheme. b) EyeLink II (c) eye tracker device.

to them. We implement the data categorization by means of a SOM, which produce reliable 2D grid representations of multidimensional data. We use the same raw data, namely, the pre-processed ROIs, as in the case of the polyp classification with the SVM.

Saliency identification consists of the process of finding out what the traits driving the expert's attention are. Eye tracking data is specially suitable for this task, since the gaze position is stored for every frame. We perform the study of saliency identification regarding the features in which the experts focus their attention during the visualization of sequences containing polyps.

2.3 Data Set

In order to build up our data set, we analyzed 6 different colonoscopy videos. Each analyzed sequence spanned 2 seconds. The image size varied from 700 to 1000 pixels of width and from 500 to 700 pixels in height depending on the video source, and corresponded with the raw data video format.

All the videos were visualized at the typical live colonoscopy frame rate of 25 fps. For each sequence, the expert was asked to fix the experts attention on the polyp to be shown, and in order to avoid time delays during the first frames, the initial image of the sequence was shown for 2 sec. before the experiment started. For all the videos, the gaze position was recorded each 4 millisec. using the information provided by both eyes. The overall gaze position was calculated as the mean associated with one frame. A re-calibration and drift correction were performed before each experiment in order to re-adjust the device.

Two different types of regions of interest (polyp ROI and non-polyp ROI) of 128 by 128 pixels were defined for each frame in the following way: On the one hand, the polyp center, namely, the center of the 128 by 128 pixels square corresponding to the polyp ROI, was defined using our eye-tracking method previously described. On the other hand, multiple non-polyp ROIs were defined as all possible 128 by 128 pixels square regions in the image, not overlapping the polyp ROI. We defined this regions as a running window, starting from the top left corner of the frame, and stepping 64 pixels in the horizontal and vertical directions. Thus, each non-polyp ROI has 25% or 50% of overlapping region with each neighbor non-polyp ROI. The value of 128 pixels was derived from the typical size of the area of projection from the computer display into the phobia, which is known to be the area of the eye responsible for saliency detection.

3 Results

For each frame in each single video sequence, we labeled the polyp ROIs obtained by eye tracking as the positive class and the non-polyp ROIs as the negative class. We performed the gray level normalization pre-processing by subtracting from every pixel the mean gray level value of the ROI. We resize the image by a quarter using the bilinear approx., obtaining a new 32 by 32 pixels image. These images constitute the data used for the polyp detection experiments.

3.1 Polyp Detection

The polyp detection was performed by means of the SVM classifier. All the ROIs in our data set were normalized in zero mean and unity standard deviation and split into training and test sets, using 80% of the data for training and the remaining 20% for testing. The training set was used to train a SVM classifier, under-sampling the majority class, with a radial basis functions kernel, using $\gamma = 0.0005$. Both the kernel type and the γ value were obtained by exhaustive search, using the area under the ROC curve (AUC) of the resulting classifier as the reference function. We ran 10 experiments with random sampling with replacement, and we averaged the classification performance results. Figure 3 shows the graphical plots for a) the ROC curve and b) the precision-recall (PR) curve.

The ROC curve obtained showed an overall value of $AUC = 0.93$, presenting a feasible working point around 80% sensitivity and 20% of false positive rate (the PR curve provides 80% of precision for this value of sensitivity).

Qualitative Analysis: In order to perform a qualitative analysis of the SVM output we used a SOM so that to visualize the data distribution of the polyp and non-polyp samples. Figure 4 a) shows the 13 by 9 hexagonal grid of the obtained SOM. The geometry of the SOM was calculated automatically, showing a quantization error about 12.4 and a topographic error about 0.02. Those cells associated with polyp clusters are marked with the *Pol* label, while those cells associated with non-polyp clusters are marked with the *o* label -those empty cells which have no samples associated with are left with no label-. The analysis of the cell arrangement depicted in Figure 4 a) shows an underlying distribution in several clusters. In order to investigate the extent to which these clusters are associated with different clinical categories of polyps, we labeled the polyps into three basic categories: *sessile* polyps, *peduncular* polyps and *mixed* polyps.

Figure 4 b) shows both U-matrix -in grey- and the superimposed colored hit histograms for each cell of the SOM. The U-matrix represents the distance between cells which provide information about how the different clusters are

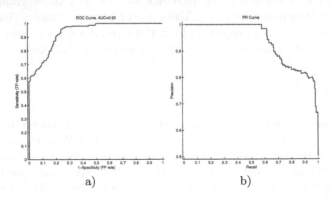

Fig. 3. Global performance. b) ROC curve. c) PR curve.

distributed in the original feature space: the darker the gray level, the closer the cells of the SOM. The colored cells represent hit histograms according to the number of samples falling on each cell. Thus, each color represents the type of polyp falling on each cell -red for *sessile* , green for *peduncular* and yellow for *mixed*-, and the size of each cell is proportional to the number of samples contained in it. The analysis of Figure 4 suggests that an efficient separation of the different classes is achieved. Only the peduncular type shows an outlier cluster (top left corner), which creates two non-connected components for this class. The other two classes show a cluster distribution within one single connected component.

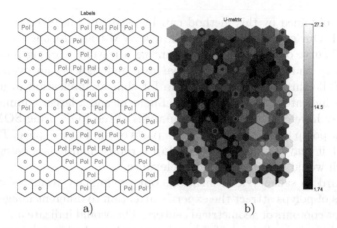

Fig. 4. a) SOM constructed from the output of the SVM. a) U-matrix -in gray- and overlapped hit histograms -colored- for the different types of polyps (red, yellow and green represent sessile , peduncular and mixed polyps, respectively. Blue represents the non-polyp frames.).

Our ultimate objective in this type of analysis is to develop an image categorization strategy which will map images of polyps to the Paris classification of superficial neoplastic lesions [14], that is used by clinicians to guide the selection of appropriate therapies. The outcome shown in Figure 4 suggests the potential suitability of a more sophisticated multi-class approach for this task.

4   Conclusions

In this paper we proposed an architecture which used video eye tracking for both segmenting regions of interest from endoscopy video that contain polyps, and studying the saliency of different image features for the various polyp types. Our objective in this work is to create large databases of labeled video data for training and testing machine learning based systems for computer aided detection in colonoscopy.

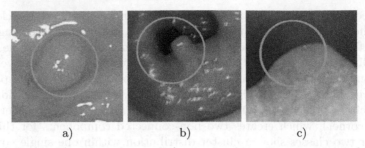

a)   b)   c)

Fig. 5. a) Sessile, b) peduncular, and c) mixed polyps. Gaze position is highlighted -visual angle: 6°-.

The ROIs obtained by this method can be used to train powerful classifiers, such as SVM. Our preliminary results show a SVM trained using this approach had an ROC curve of $AUC = 0.93$, presenting a feasible working point around 80% sensitivity and 20% of false positive rate and showing an overall 80% of precision. While this may not be suitable for clinical application in its present form, it does indicate that with further refinement and a larger training set this approach may have clinical value. Our analysis of the ROIs using SOM showed that different polyp types occupy different parts of the feature space. This would indicate that it may be feasible to develop a robust multi-class categorization system which would have high clinical relevance.

With regard to saliency identification, our preliminary results showed that diverse types of polyps attract the expert's attention to different image features, such as object contours or geometrical centers. This would indicate an interesting field of future study in the area of saliency research applied to colonoscopy video analysis.

Figure 5 a) depicts a sessile polyp together with the expert's gaze position. For this class of abnormalities, the eye tracker data shows that the saliency area is located around the centroid of the polyp. Opposite, for peduncular and mixed polyps, 5 b) and c) respectively, the experts attention is located in the polyp contour, instead of its center.

Our future work will be to build on this research by exploring further the analysis of gaze fixation patterns and voice labeling to create an efficient user interface for clinicians labeling large databases of clinical video. We will also be exploring further how techniques in image processing and video parsing can be applied to the automatic detection and categorization of lesions in endoscopy video.

A final remark must be added regarding the main advantage of the proposed methodology: although complex to set up, eye tracking data has the benefit that the implicit segmentation provided by the expert's gaze position represents the lowest bound in terms of labeling time for large data sets.

Acknowledgments

This research is supported by Enterprise Ireland contracts PC-2006-038 and CFTD-2006-216.

References

1. Bressler, B., Paszat, L.F., et al.: Colonoscopic miss rates for right-sided colon cancer: a population-based analysis. Gastroenterology 127, 452–456 (2004)
2. Atkin, W., Rogers, P., et al.: Inter-endoscopist variation in polyp and neoplasia pick-up rates in flexible sigmoidoscopy screening for colorectal cancer. Gastroenterology 126, 1247–1256 (2004)
3. Vapnik, V.: The Nature of Statistical Learning Theory. Springer, Heidelberg (1995)
4. Hwang, S., Oh, J., et al.: Automatic measurement of quality metrics for colonoscopy videos. In: MM'05, Singapore (2005)
5. Monroy, R., Arroyo-Figueroa, G., Sucar, L.E., Sossa, H.: MICAI 2004. LNCS (LNAI), vol. 2972. Springer, Heidelberg (2004)
6. Magoulas, G., Plagianakos, V., et al.: Tumor detection in colonoscopy using the unsupervised k-windows clustering algorithm and neur. networsks. In: ESBE (2004)
7. Privitera, C., Stark, L.: Algorithms for defining visual regions-of-interest: Comparison with eye fixations. IEEE Trans. on PAMI 22, 970–982 (2000)
8. CHENG, W.H., CHU, W.T., WU, J.-L.: A visual attention based region-of-interest determination framework for video sequences. IEICE Trans Inf. & Syst. E88-D, 1578–1586 (2005)
9. Droll, J., Hayhoe, M., et al.: Task demands control acquisition and storage of visual information. Journal of Experimental Psychology: Human Perception and Performance 31(6), 1416–1438 (2005)
10. Kienzle, W., Wichmann, F., et al.: Learning an interest operator from human eye movements. In: CVPR'o6 Workshop (2006)
11. Chung, A.J., Deligianni, F., et al.: Extraction of visual features with eye tracking for saliency driven 2D/3D registration. Im. and Vision Comp. 23, 999–1008 (2005)
12. Kohonen, T.: Self-Organized Maps. Springer, Heidelberg (1995)
13. Jones, M., Viola, P.: Face recognition using boosted local features (2003)
14. Paris Workshop Participants: The Paris endospcopic classification of superficial neoplastic lesions. Gastrointestinal Endoscopy (Supplement) vol. 58(6), pp. 3–23 (2003)

Functional Pattern Recognition of 3D Laser Scanned Images of Wood-Pulp Chips

Marcos López[1], José M. Matías[2], José A. Vilán[1], and Javier Taboada[3]

[1] Dpt. of Mechanical Engineering
[2] Dpt. of Statistics and Operations Research
[3] Dpt. of Natural Resources, University of Vigo, 36310, Vigo, Spain

Abstract. We evaluate the appropriateness of applying a functional rather than the typical vectorial approach to a pattern recognition problem. The problem to be resolved was to construct an online system for controlling wood-pulp chip granulometry quality for implementation in a wood-pulp factory. A functional linear model and a functional logistic model were used to classify the hourly empirical distributions of wood-chip thicknesses estimated on the basis of images produced by a 3D laser scanner. The results obtained using these functional techniques were compared to the results of their vectorial counterparts and support vector machines, whose input consisted of several statistics of the hourly empirical distribution. We conclude that the empirical distributions have sufficiently rich functional traits so as to permit the pattern recognition process to benefit from the functional representation.

1 Introduction

Wood chips, which are the main raw material in the paper pulp manufacturing process, are obtained using a chipper to cut up tree logs. Uniform chip size directly affects the behaviour of the chips in the cooking process, as variations in chip size cause problems in the cooking operation, and thus ultimately produces poor quality paper pulp [1].

Nonetheless, in most production centres, the functioning of the chipper is not controlled in real time, the typical methods for measuring chips are manual or semi-manual [6] and the quality of these chips is evaluated on the basis of a set of statistics for these measurements, such as the mean, standard deviation, asymmetry, kurtosis, etc. [1].

We have developed a real-time quality control system for wood chips based on a functional pattern recognition model, whose input is the hourly empirical distribution for each chip dimension and whose output is chip quality (good or bad). With a view to selecting the most suitable functional technique for this system, we compared the behaviour of the functional linear model [5] and the functional logistic model [4]. Likewise, with a view to determining the suitability of the functional approach, we compared the results to those obtained for vectorial techniques applied to a vector of statistics of the hourly empirical distribution, namely, linear regression, logistic regression and support vector machines (e.g. [7]).

J. Martí et al. (Eds.): IbPRIA 2007, Part I, LNCS 4477, pp. 298–305, 2007.

Our article is structured as follows: we first briefly describe the functional classification techniques used; we then describe the results obtained after applying the functional techniques to the construction of the chip quality control system, and compare them to the results obtained using vectorial techniques; finally, we describe our conclusions.

2   Functional Pattern Recognition. The Functional General Linear Model

In general, given a sample of data $\{(x_i, y_i)\}_{i=1}^n$ where $x_i \in \mathcal{X}$ and $y_i \in \mathcal{Y}$, $i = 1, ..., n$, $\mathcal{X}$ is the input space and $\mathcal{Y}$ is a set of identification labels for the classes, the pattern recognition problem consists of determining, from the sample data, a classification rule $h : \mathcal{X} \rightarrow \mathcal{Y}$, which can be applied to the classification of a new example x, optimal according to an optimality criterion defined a priori.

If the technique used to resolve the problem provides good estimations $\hat{\mathbb{P}}(Y = s | X = x)$ of the a posteriori probabilities of the classes, usually considered is the plug-in classification rule which emulates the Bayes rule.

In a vectorial pattern recognition problem, the input space verifies $\mathcal{X} \subset \mathbb{R}^d$; in other words, the objects to be classified are determined by means of a d-dimensional vector of variables. In a functional pattern recognition problem, on the other hand, the objects to be classified are determined by functions; in other words, the input space verifies $\mathcal{X} \subset \mathcal{F}$ where $\mathcal{F}$ is a functional space.

2.1   Function Registration

In the functional model, in most of the applications we do not see the functions x_i, $i = 1, ..., n$ but only their values $x_i(t_j)$ in a set of n_p points $t_j \in \mathbb{R}$, $j = 1, ..., n_p$. For the sake of simplicity, we will assume these to be common to all the functions x_i, $i = 1, ..., n$. These observations may, moreover, be subject to noise, and in this case they take the form: $z_{ij} = x_i(t_j) + \varepsilon_{ij}$, where we assume that ε_{ij} is random noise with zero mean, $i = 1, ..., n$, $j = 1, ..., n_p$.

Therefore, the functional focus first requires the sample functions to be registered, and this requires estimation of each function $x_i \in \mathcal{X} \subset \mathcal{F}$, $i = 1, ..., n$. One approach is to assume that $\mathcal{F} = \text{span}\{\phi_1, ..., \phi_{n_b}\}$ with $\{\phi_k\}$ set of basic functions [5]. For our research we chose a family of B-splines as the set of basic functions, given their good local behaviour. If, for the sake of simplicity, we represent as x any of the functions x_i, $i = 1, ..., n$ in the sample, we have:

$$x(t) = \sum_{k=1}^{n_b} c_k \phi_k(t) \tag{1}$$

Hence, the registration problem consists of determining the solution to the following regularization problem:

$$\min_{x \in \mathcal{F}} \sum_{j=1}^{n_p} \{z_j - x(t_j)\}^2 + \lambda \Gamma(x) \tag{2}$$

where $z_j = x(t_j) + \varepsilon_j$ is the result of observing x at the point t_j, Γ is an operator that penalizes the complexity of the solution, and λ is a regularization parameter that regulates the intensity of this penalization. In our case, we have used the operator $\Gamma(x) = \int_{\mathcal{T}} \left\{ D^2 x(t) \right\}^2 dt$ where $\mathcal{T} = [t_{\min}, t_{\max}]$ and D^2 is the second-order differential operator.

Bearing in mind the expansion (1), the above problem (2) may be written as:

$$\min_{\mathbf{c}} \left\{ (\mathbf{z} - \mathbf{\Phi c})^T (\mathbf{z} - \mathbf{\Phi c}) + \lambda \mathbf{c}^T \mathbf{R c} \right\}$$

where $\mathbf{z} = (z_1, ..., z_{n_p})^T$, $\mathbf{c} = (c_1, ..., c_{n_b})^T$, $\mathbf{\Phi}$ is the $n_p \times n_b$ matrix with elements $\mathbf{\Phi}_{jk} = \phi_k(t_j)$ and $\mathbf{R}$ is the $n_b \times n_b$ matrix with elements $R_{kl} = \left\langle D^2 \phi_k, D^2 \phi_l \right\rangle_{L_2(\mathcal{T})}$ $= \int_{\mathcal{T}} D^2 \phi_k(t) D^2 \phi_l(t) dt$.

The solution to this problem is given by $\mathbf{c} = (\mathbf{\Phi}^T \mathbf{\Phi} + \lambda \mathbf{R})^{-1} \mathbf{\Phi}^T \mathbf{z}$, in such a way that the estimated values of x at the observation points are obtained by means of $\mathbf{x} = \mathbf{Sz}$ where $\mathbf{S} = \mathbf{\Phi}(\mathbf{\Phi}^T \mathbf{\Phi} + \lambda \mathbf{R})^{-1} \mathbf{\Phi}^T$, with $\mathbf{x} = (x(t_1), ..., x(t_{n_p}))^T$.

The selection of the λ forms part of the model selection problem and is usually performed using crossed validation.

2.2   Functional Generalized Linear Model

The functional generalized linear model is a functional generalization of the generalized linear model (GLM) [3]. In the GLM it is assumed that the responses follow an exponential family distribution, with the density function as:

$$f(y_i; \theta_i, \phi) = \exp \left\{ \frac{y_i \theta_i - b(\theta_i)}{\phi} + c(y_i, \phi) \right\}$$

where θ_i and ϕ are parameters and where $b(\theta_i)$ and $c(y_i, \phi)$ are known functions. The mean verifies $\mu_i = \mathbb{E}(Y_i; \theta_i, \phi) = b'(\theta_i)$, the derivative of $b(\theta)$. The GLM denomination derives from the consideration of a linear model:

$$\eta_i = \beta_0 + \langle \beta, x_i \rangle \tag{3}$$

for the new general parameter $\eta_i = g(\mu_i)$, $i = 1, ..., n$, where g is the link function, which is chosen according to the type of problem.

The expression (3) suggests an immediate generalization of the GLM to the functional case (FGLM), by substituting the inner product with an inner product of the functional space which is considered to include the functional input space.

The above model includes, as particular cases, the functional linear model and the functional logistic regression model, both of which are used in this research (described below).

Once the functions $x_1, ..., x_n \in \mathcal{X}$ have been registered, a function β can be defined which will be the functional coefficient of the FGLM and which can be expressed as a linear combination of the basic functions already defined:

$$\beta(t) = \sum_{k=1}^{n_b} \beta_k \phi_k(t) \tag{4}$$

Substituing the equations (1) and (4) into the expression (3) with a functional philosophy and denominating, for the sake of simplicity, any of the η_i and x_i as η and x, respectively, $i = 1, ..., n$, we obtain $\eta = \beta_0 + \mathbf{c}^T \mathbf{\Psi} \beta$, where $\mathbf{\Psi}$ is the matrix with elements $\Psi_{kl} = \langle \phi_k, \phi_l \rangle$, with $k, l = 1, ..., n_b$ and $\beta = (\beta_1, ..., \beta_{n_b})^T$.

Hence, grouping the new variables of the sample in a vector $\eta = (\eta_1, ..., \eta_n)^T$ and the row vectors of coefficients of the expansion of each x_i in the $n \times n_b$ matrix $\mathbf{C}$, we obtain: $\eta = \mathbf{C} \mathbf{\Psi} \beta + \mathbf{1} \beta_0$. By defining the extended vector $\bar{\beta} = (\beta_0, \beta^T)^T$ and a new $n \times (n_b + 1)$ matrix $\mathbf{D} = [\mathbf{1} \ \mathbf{C} \mathbf{\Psi}]$ this expression is simplified and results in:

$$\eta = \mathbf{D} \bar{\beta} \tag{5}$$

From this we ultimately obtain $\mu = g^{-1}(\eta)$.

The FGLM is estimated by means of the regularized maximum likelihood. If the observations are independent, the objective function to be minimized is:

$$\ell(\mathbf{y}, \theta(\bar{\beta}), \phi) = - \log f(\mathbf{y}; \theta(\bar{\beta}), \phi) + \lambda \Lambda(\bar{\beta}) \tag{6a}$$

$$= - \sum_{i=1}^{n} \left(\frac{y_i \theta_i(\bar{\beta}) - b(\theta_i(\bar{\beta}))}{\phi} + c(y_i, \phi) \right) + \lambda \bar{\beta}^T \mathbf{Q} \bar{\beta} \tag{6b}$$

where $\mathbf{y} = (y_1, ..., y_n)^T$, $\theta(\bar{\beta})$ reflects the dependence of each θ_i of $\bar{\beta}$ through the link function and through the relationship between θ_i and the mean μ_i, $\Lambda(\bar{\beta}) = \bar{\beta}^T \mathbf{Q} \beta$ is an regularization operator for some squared matrix $\mathbf{Q}$ of dimension $(1 + n_b)$ and λ is the corresponding regularizing parameter.

The expression (6b) is not linear in $\bar{\beta}$, and so we need to use a non-linear optimization algorithm. For example, the application of the Newton-Raphson algorithm gives rise to what is known as the Fisher scoring algorithm in the literature; in each iteration, this algorithm updates the estimation of the vector of parameters by means of:

$$\bar{\beta}^{new} = \bar{\beta}^{old} - \left(\frac{\partial^2 \ell}{\partial \bar{\beta} \partial \bar{\beta}^T} \right)^{-1} \frac{\partial \ell}{\partial \bar{\beta}}$$

Using the equation (5) and applying the chain rule we obtain:

$$\bar{\beta}^{new} = \bar{\beta}^{old} + \left(\mathbf{D}^T \mathbf{W} \mathbf{D} + \bar{\lambda} \mathbf{Q} \right)^{-1} \mathbf{D}^T \mathbf{W} \mathbf{a} \tag{7}$$

where $\mathbf{W} = \phi \partial^2 \ell / \partial \eta \partial \eta^T$, $\mathbf{a}$ is the vector of components $a_i = (y_i - \mu_i) g'(\mu_i)$, $i = 1, ..., n$, and $\bar{\lambda} = \phi \lambda$ has to be selected through cross-validation.

2.3 The Functional Linear Model and Functional Logistic Regression Model as Particular Cases of the Functional GLM

If the observations follow a Gaussian distribution with $b(\theta_i) = \frac{1}{2} \theta_i^2$, $c(y_i, \phi) = -\frac{1}{2} y^2 / \phi - \log \sqrt{2\pi\phi}$ and $\phi = \sigma^2$, adopting the identity as the link function, the functional linear regression model is obtained $\mu_i = \eta_i = \beta_0 + \langle \beta, x_i \rangle$, $i = 1, ..., n$.

In this case, $\mathbf{a} = \mathbf{y} - \mu$ and $\mathbf{W} = \mathbf{I}_{n \times n}$ with $\mathbf{I}_{n \times n}$ as the identity matrix.

This model can be applied to the problem of pattern recognition with two classes, $\mathcal{Y} = \{0, 1\}$, if we consider the predictions $\hat{y}_i$, $i = 1, ..., n$ as estimations of the a posteriori probabilities of the classes $\mathbb{P}\{Y = 1 | X = x\}$. However, it cannot be guaranteed that these estimations are to be found in $[0, 1]$.

In fact, for this pattern recognition problem, the responses y_i, $i = 1, ..., n$ follow a Bernoulli distribution, which also belongs to the exponential family, with $b(\theta_i) = \log\left(1 + e^{\theta_i}\right)$, $\phi = 1$ and $c(y_i, \phi) = 0$. If assuming this distribution we now choose as the link function g the logit function $\eta_i = g(\mu_i) = \log[\mu_i/(1 - \mu_i)]$ the new variables η_i reflect the log odds ratio and coincide with the parameters θ_i given that:

$$\mu_i = b'(\theta_i) = \frac{e^{\theta_i}}{1 + e^{\theta_i}} \Rightarrow \theta_i = \log\frac{\mu_i}{1 - \mu_i} = \eta_i \qquad (8)$$

The modelling of η_i by means of a functional linear model of the type (3) gives rise to the functional version of the logistic model, which provides an estimation of the a posteriori probabilities of the classes by using the first part of the equation (8):

$$\mu_i(x_i) = \frac{1}{1 - e^{-(\beta_0 + \langle \beta, x_i \rangle)}}$$

thus guaranteeing the requirement $\mu_i(x) \in [0, 1]$. This expression coincides with the output of a functional neural network composed of a single neuron with logistic activation function.

3   Application of Functional Pattern Recognition to the Evaluation of the Wood-Pulp Chips Quality

3.1   Problem Framework and Data Sample

A 3D laser scanner system (Fig. 1) following [2] was developed for a paper pulp production process with a view to measuring, in real time, the dimensions of the chips that came out of the chipper. This system is based on laser beam triangulation to estimate the dimensions of the chips that pass through the laser beam. The CMOS-sensor camera, with a resolution of 1024×128 pixels, captures images in the azimuth position, with the size of the chips determined by the distortions in the laser beam. This system provides data on the length, width and thickness of each wood chip, as also on the date and time of measurement. We focus in particular, however, on the thickness variable, as the most important magnitude for Kraft processes. In order to assess chip quality, the hourly empirical distribution for thickness is determined in $[0.85, 2.85]$ (in millimetres) at intervals of 0.1 mm. In order to build the pattern recognition system, a sample representing 8 days of production (randomly selected) was chosen; this consisted of a total of 192 hourly empirical distributions, 144 and 48 of which, respectively, were used for training and testing. According to their impact on chipper output quality, the distributions were catalogued by the production team as apt or not apt.

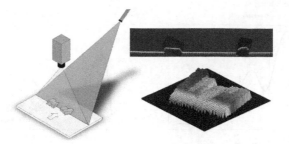

Fig. 1. Depiction of the 3D laser scanner measurement process (left): photographic image (above right) and digitalized chip (below right)

3.2 Functional and Vectorial Models Compared

We evaluated linear functional models and logistic functional models, with each example classified, according to the plug-in rule, in the class with the greatest a posteriori estimated probability. As a reference, we used vectorial models (also applied for the first time in this application area). In this case the input variables were the following hourly empirical distribution statistics: the mean, 5%, 50% and 95% quantiles, variance, skewness and kurtosis. The vectorial models used were a linear regression model and a logistic regression model, as also support vector machines (SVMs), which have been reported as being particularly effective in handling pattern recognition problems.

Ten-fold cross validation was used to select the regularizer λ for the functional and vectorial versions of the linear and logistic models. A Gaussian kernel was used for the SVMs and the kernel parameter and the regularizer were also selected using 10-fold cross validation.

3.3 Function Registration

Hourly empirical distributions were registered in order to apply the functional techniques. Registration was by means of a family of sixth-order B-splines, based on 21 knots in the support for the thickness variable.

The same value for the regularizing parameter λ (Eq. (2)) was used for all the curves, on the basis of the hypothesis that all the curves were subjected to the same level of noise. This value was selected using ten-fold cross validation for the error occurring in all the curves simultaneously. The value $\lambda_{opt} = 10^{-4}$ was obtained as the optimal value. It was observed, however, that the final classifier was not greatly sensitive to the value of this parameter. Figure 2 shows one of these distributions and its registration using B-splines. Bearing in mind that we are working with empirical density functions (discretized), another alternative would be to first estimate the densities using non-parametric techniques and then to perform the registration. However, apart from implying two estimation processes, we are more interested in the functional traits of the input space functions than the requirement that their integral be unity.

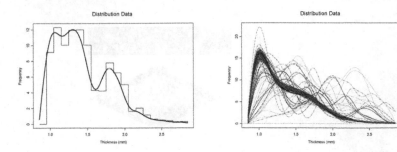

Fig. 2. Left: an hourly empirical distribution for chip distribution and its registration using B-splines. Right: set of functions for the training sample once registered.

3.4 Results

Table 1 shows the classification error rate for the training, test and combined samples for the models compared here. As can be observed, the functional models are superior to the vectorial models. Figure 2 shows an example of functions that the functional model, unlike the vectorial model, classified correctly on the basis of the statistics used.

The two functional models show no difference in the results for the test sample, although the logistic model has an overall error rate lower than half that of the linear model. Furthermore, the estimations of the logistic model are much more accurate than those for the linear model, as it produces estimates of $\mathbb{P}(Y = 1|x)$ that are closer to 0 or 1 when the examples are from Class 0 or 1, respectively.

From the computational point-of-view, functional models do not imply a significantly greater computational load than vectorial models, as they are, in reality, vectorial models for the coefficients of the basic functions. In our problem, and including the necessary registration and cross-validation processes, the CPU time required to construct the classifier was 2.031 seconds for the functional linear model (0.97 seconds for the vectorial linear model) and 3.001 seconds for the functional logistic model (1.649 seconds for the vectorial logistic model).

Table 1. Classification error rate for the training, test and combined samples for the models compared

	% Error		
Model	Train	Test	Total
Functional Linear	2.08	4.17	2.60
Functional Logistic	0.00	4.17	1.04
Vectorial Linear	7.64	16.67	9.90
Vectorial Logistic	2.08	20.83	6.77
SVM	0.00	14.58	3.65

4   Conclusions

We constructed a quality control system, for wood chips produced by a chipper in a Kraft paper pulp production process, using functional pattern recognition techniques that were both linear and logistic. The results obtained clearly demonstrate that, for our particular problem, the functional approach is more satisfactory that the vectorial approach. Of the two functional models, moreover, the logistic model produced more accurate a posteriori probabilities for the classes and so produced a better classification. This method can be easily extended to other chip magnitudes.

The lines of research being pursued to further this work include function registration using non-parametric density estimation techniques, the use of functional non-parametric techniques, and the construction of a multivariant response classification system in order to simultaneously handle various chip magnitudes (thickness, length and width).

Acknowledgments. J. M. Matías's research was supported by the Spanish Ministry of Education and Science, Grant No. MTM2005-00820.

References

1. Broderick, G., Cacchione, E., Héroux, Y.: The importance of distribution statistics in the characterization of chip quality. Tappi Journal 81(2), 131–142 (1998)
2. López, M., Vilán, J.A., Casqueiro, C., Matías, J.M.: 3d laser scanner: A new method for estimating the dimensions of wood pulp chips. Nordic Pulp and Paper Research Journal 21(3), 342–348 (2006)
3. McCullagh, P., Nelder, J.A.: Generalized Linear Models. Chapman & Hal, Sydney, Australia (1989)
4. Müller, H.G.: Functional modelling and classification of longitudinal data. Scandinavian Journal of Statistics 32(2), 223–240 (2005)
5. Ramsay, J.O., Silverman, B.W.: Functional data analysis. Springer, Heidelberg (1997)
6. SCAN-47:92: Wood chips for pulp production - thickness and thickness distribution. Scandinavian Pulp, Paper and Board Testing Committee. Stockholm, Sweden (1992)
7. Scholkopf, B., Smola, A.J.: Learning with Kernels. MIT Press, Cambridge, MA (2002)

Hardware Implementation of Moment Functions in a CMOS Retina: Application to Pattern Recognition

Olivier Aubreton[1], Lew Fock Chong Lew Yan Voon[1],
Matthieu Nongaillard[1], Guy Cathebras[3], Cédric Lemaitre[2],
and Bernard Lamalle[1]

[1] Laboratoire LE2I – UMR CNRS 5158, 12 rue de la fonderie, 71200 Le Creusot, France
[2] Laboratoire LE2I – UMR CNRS 5158, BP 47870, 21078 DIJON Cedex, France
[3] Laboratoire LIRMM - UMR 5506, 161, rue Ada, 34392 Montpellier Cedex 5, France

Abstract. We present in this paper a method for implementing moment functions in a CMOS retina for object localization, and pattern recognition and classification applications. The method is based on the use of binary patterns and it allows the computation of different moment functions such as geometric and Zernike moments of any orders by an adequate choice of the binary patterns. The advantages of the method over other methods described in the literature are that it is particularly suitable for the design of a programmable retina circuit where moment functions of different orders are obtained by simply loading the correct binary patterns into the memory devices implemented on the circuit. The moment values computed by the method are approximate values, but we have verified that in spite of the errors the approximate values are significant enough to be applied to classical shape localization and shape representation and description applications.

1 Introduction

Geometric and Zernike moments are functions that are often used in the field of image analysis and pattern recognition. Their main applications are in position and shape orientation detection for geometric moments, and in pattern recognition for both geometric and Zernike moments [1, 2]. Geometric moment functions have already been implemented in a certain number of retina chips [3, 4, 5, 6] but none of the circuits are capable of computing geometric moment values of different orders. The advantage and novelty of the method that we propose are that it can be implemented as a programmable architecture that allows the computation of not only geometric moment function values but also other moment values such as Zernike moments of different orders by simply uploading the adequate binary patterns into memory devices integrated on the circuit.

In the next section, we will describe the basic principle of binary pattern matching as well as the proposed retina architecture. In section 3, we show how the binary pattern matching method can be used to compute an approximated value of respectively geometric and Zernike moments of different orders before we conclude in section 4.

J. Martí et al. (Eds.): IbPRIA 2007, Part I, LNCS 4477, pp. 306–313, 2007.
© Springer-Verlag Berlin Heidelberg 2007

2 Binary Pattern Matching CMOS Retina

2.1 Binary Pattern Matching

The basic principle of binary pattern matching is to compute two correlation values, denoted by S_1 and S_2, between a gray level image and a binary image (or binary pattern) according to the two following equations:

$$S_1 = \sum_{x=1}^{N} \sum_{y=1}^{M} F(x, y) \times I(x, y) \tag{1}$$

$$S_2 = \sum_{x=1}^{N} \sum_{y=1}^{M} \overline{F(x, y)} \times I(x, y) \tag{2}$$

where M and N are the size of the image, $F(x, y)$ the binary pattern (a binary function that takes the value 0 or 1 according to the x and y coordinates of the pixel), $\overline{F(x, y)}$ the inverse binary pattern and $I(x, y)$ the intensity of the pixel at coordinates (x, y) of the gray level image.

The reason why a binary pattern is used instead of a gray level pattern is due to hardware implementation constraints. The circuit architecture that is proposed uses memory devices to store the binary pattern on the chip and computes the correlation values between the image of the scene under observation and the stored pattern. With binary patterns only a one-bit memory device is necessary to store each pixel of the pattern whereas with gray level patterns several bits are necessary resulting in larger memory devices. Since the latters are integrated at the pixel level, large memory devices will result in low fill factor value (percentage of the pixel devoted to the collection of light) and consequently a less sensitive retina.

2.2 CMOS Retina Architecture

Fig. 1 represents the architecture of the pixel with two one-bit memory devices, $M_0(x, y)$ and $M_1(x, y)$, for the memorization of two binary patterns. The product between the two binary patterns $F_0(x, y)$ and $F_1(x, y)$ (respectively their inverses) and the intensity of the image pixel $I(x, y)$ as expressed in Eq. 1 and Eq. 2 is electronically achieved by switching the photocurrent $I_{ph}(x, y)$ delivered by the photosensitive element to one of the four outputs, o_0, o_1, o_2 and o_3 according to the values of the patterns at coordinates (x, y) stored in the two memory devices $M_0(x, y)$ and $M_1(x, y)$. Note that there is a direct relationship between image intensity $I(x, y)$ and the photocurrent $I_{ph}(x, y)$. For example, if both of the two memory devices contain the logic value 1 then the photocurrent due to the illumination of the photodiode will be switched to the output o_0. The advantage of storing two binary patterns is that it allows us to compute simultaneously four correlation values: two for the first pattern and two for the second pattern.

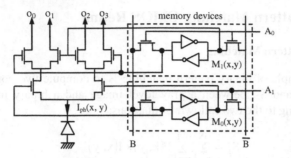

Fig. 1. Architecture of the pixel

The mathematical expressions of the four outputs are:

$$o_0(x, y) = F_0(x, y) \times F_1(x, y) \times I_{ph}(x, y) \qquad o_2(x, y) = \overline{F_0(x, y)} \times \overline{F_1(x, y)} \times I_{ph}(x, y)$$

$$o_1(x, y) = F_0(x, y) \times \overline{F_1(x, y)} \times I_{ph}(x, y) \qquad o_3(x, y) = \overline{F_0(x, y)} \times F_1(x, y) \times I_{ph}(x, y)$$

In the array of pixels, all the outputs with the same index are connected together in order to do current summations that are next converted to voltages using four current to voltage converters. At the output of the retina we obtain thus four signals that can be expressed as:

$$O_0 = K \sum_{x=1}^{N} \sum_{y=1}^{M} F_0(x, y) \times F_1(x, y) \times I_{ph}(x, y) \qquad O_2 = K \sum_{x=1}^{N} \sum_{y=1}^{M} \overline{F_0(x, y)} \times \overline{F_1(x, y)} \times I_{ph}(x, y)$$

$$O_1 = K \sum_{x=1}^{N} \sum_{y=1}^{M} F_0(x, y) \times \overline{F_1(x, y)} \times I_{ph}(x, y) \qquad O_3 = K \sum_{x=1}^{N} \sum_{y=1}^{M} \overline{F_0(x, y)} \times F_1(x, y) \times I_{ph}(x, y)$$

where K is the gain conversion factor of the current to voltage converters. These four outputs can finally be combined in order to obtain simultaneously the following four correlation products:

$$O_0 + O_1 = K \sum_{x=1}^{N} \sum_{y=1}^{M} F_0(x, y) \times I_{ph}(x, y) \qquad O_0 + O_3 = K \sum_{x=1}^{N} \sum_{y=1}^{M} F_1(x, y) \times I_{ph}(x, y)$$

$$O_2 + O_3 = K \sum_{x=1}^{N} \sum_{y=1}^{M} \overline{F_0(x, y)} \times I_{ph}(x, y) \qquad O_1 + O_2 = K \sum_{x=1}^{N} \sum_{y=1}^{M} \overline{F_1(x, y)} \times I_{ph}(x, y)$$

3 Moment Computation

3.1 General Moment Definition

The moment function m_{pq} of order $(p+q)$ of an image is defined by Eq. 3.

$$m_{pq} = K \times \sum_{x=1}^{N} \sum_{y=1}^{M} f_{pq}(x, y) \times Im(x, y) \qquad (3)$$

where K is a constant term, $Im(x, y)$ is the value of the pixel of the image under analysis at coordinates (x, y) and $f_{pq}(x, y)$ a function that depends on the type of the calculated moment. For non-central and central geometric moments, for example, the expression of $f_{pq}(x, y)$ is given by respectively Eq. 4 and Eq. 5.

$$f_{pq}(x, y) = \left(\frac{x}{N}\right)^p \times \left(\frac{y}{M}\right)^q \quad \text{and} \quad K = N^p \times M^q \tag{4}$$

$$f_{pq}(x, y) = \left(\frac{x - x_0}{N}\right)^p \times \left(\frac{y - y_0}{M}\right)^q \quad \text{and} \quad K = N^p \times M^q \tag{5}$$

where (x_0, y_0) is the intensity centroid of the image or the coordinates of the center of mass of the object in the case of a bright object over a uniform dark background. Applications of central moments are in pattern recognition, classification and shape descriptions, and one usually needs to compute moment values of different orders. For example, in the approach proposed by Hu [7] central moments of different orders are combined in order to obtain shape descriptors that are invariant to translation or rotation. Another class of moment functions are orthogonal moments. Among the most powerful orthogonal moments used in pattern recognition are Zernike moments. The Zernike moment of order p of an image inside a circle of unit radius is defined by the following equation [1]:

$$z_{pq} = \frac{(p+1)}{\pi} \int_0^{2\pi} \int_0^1 V_{pq}^*(r, \theta) \times Im(r, \theta) \times r \times dr \times d\theta \tag{6}$$

with $r \leq 1$, p a positive integer and q an integer such that $p - |q|$ is even and $|q| \leq p$. The functions $V_{pq}^*(r, \theta)$ denote the complex conjugate of Zernike polynomials of order p and repetition q, and $Im(r, \theta)$ denotes the image under analysis. For N×N pixels digital images, Eq. 6 can be written in the discrete form [1] as follows:

$$z_{pq} = \frac{(p+1)}{\pi(N-1)^2} \sum_{x=1}^N \sum_{y=1}^N V_{pq}^*(r, \theta) Im(x, y) \tag{7}$$

where $r = \frac{\sqrt{(x^2 + y^2)}}{N}$ and $\theta = \tan^{-1}\left(\frac{y}{x}\right)$.

Expressions of Zernike polynomials can be found in [1] and thus will not be detailed here. The Zernike moment values are thus complex values that can be expressed as the sum of a real part and an imaginary part.

$$z_{pq} = \Re(z_{pq}) + j \times \Im(z_{pq}) \tag{8}$$

where $\quad \mathfrak{R}(z_{pq}) = \dfrac{(p+1)}{\pi (N-1)^2} \sum\sum \mathfrak{R}(V^*_{pq}(x, y)) \times Im(x, y) \quad$ and

$$\mathfrak{I}(z_{pq}) = \dfrac{(p+1)}{\pi (N-1)^2} \sum\sum \mathfrak{I}(V^*_{pq}(x, y)) \times Im(x, y).$$

To conclude, moment values are always obtained by computing correlation products between the image under analysis and one (or two for Zernike moments) 2D function.

3.2 Binary Pattern Matching and Geometric Moment Function

Comparing the expression of geometric moment functions given by Eq. 3 to that of the binary pattern matching correlation expression given by Eq. 1, we notice that they are similar. The differences are in the K constant term and the $f_{pq}(x, y)$ and $F(x, y)$ functions. $f_{pq}(x, y)$ is a real function with values in the interval $]-1, +1]$ and $F(x, y)$ is a binary one. Let

$$f_{pq}(x, y) = K_1 F_{pq}(x, y) + K_2 \overline{F_{pq}}(x, y) + \varepsilon_{pq}(x, y) \tag{9}$$

where $F_{pq}(x, y)$ is the binary function to determine, $\varepsilon_{pq}(x, y)$ an error function, K_1 the maximum value of $f_{pq}(x, y)$ and K_2 a value that depends on the values of the function $f_{pq}(x, y)$. K_2 is equal to 0 if $f_{pq}(x, y)$ is a real and positive function and the minimum value of $f_{pq}(x, y)$ if the latter is a real function with both positive and negative values. K_1 and K_2 are scaling or normalization factors to account for the fact that $f_{pq}(x, y)$ is first normalized to the interval $[0, 1]$ before the binary pattern $F_{pq}(x, y)$ is determined by a dithering operation as we will describe later. Replacing $f_{pq}(x, y)$ by its expression given by Eq. 9 in Eq. 3 yields

$$m_{pq} = N^p \times M^q \times \left[K_1 \sum_{x=1}^{N} \sum_{y=1}^{M} F_{pq}(x, y) \times Im(x, y) + \right.$$
$$\left. K_2 \sum_{x=1}^{N} \sum_{y=1}^{M} \overline{F_{pq}(x, y)} \times Im(x, y) + \sum_{x=1}^{N} \sum_{y=1}^{M} \varepsilon_{pq}(x, y) \times Im(x, y) \right] \tag{10}$$

that can be expressed in terms of the two correlation values S_1 and S_2 given in Eq. 1 and Eq. 2 as follows:

$$m_{pq} = N^p \times M^q \times [K_1 S_1 + K_2 S_2] + err_{pq} = M_{pq} + err_{pq} \tag{11}$$

with M_{pq} the approximated moment value obtained by binary pattern matching and err_{pq} an error term.

$$M_{pq} = N^p \times M^q \times [K_1 S_1 + K_2 S_2] \tag{12}$$

$$\text{err}_{pq} = N^P \times M^q \times \sum_{x=1}^{N} \sum_{y=1}^{M} \varepsilon_{pq}(x, y) \times \text{Im}(x, y) \qquad (13)$$

The problem is to find a binary function $F_{pq}(x, y)$ such that the absolute relative error term given by Eq. 14 is minimal.

$$\text{Re}\,\text{rr}_{pq} = \left| \frac{\text{err}_{pq}}{m_{pq}} \right| \qquad (14)$$

This problem is similar to the problem of rendering gray level images on a printer and one can find in the literature several techniques to achieve this [8, 9]. We have studied some of the techniques and, for all the images of the Columbia COIL object image database [10], computed the absolute relative error given by Eq. 14 for non-central geometric moment values of order less than or equal to 3 using 128×128 pixels images. Among all the dithering algorithms that we have studied, the Floyd-Steinberg error diffusion algorithm [9] is the one that give the best trade off between computation time and error value. Using this algorithm the absolute relative error has been found to be less than 5%.

Fig. 2. Example of binary pattern

Fig.2 is an example of the binary pattern obtained by applying the Floyd-Steinberg dithering algorithm to the function $f_{01}(x, y)$ for calculating non-central geometric moment of order 1. To conclude, binary pattern matching can be used to compute approximate values of geometric moments using Eq. 12. In the case of geometric moments where $f_{pq}(x, y) \in \,]0, 1]$, such as non-central geometric moments, $K_1 = 1$ and $K_2 = 0$, and the equation simplifies to

$$M_{pq} = N^P \times M^q \times K_1\, S_1 = N^P \times M^q \times S_1 \qquad (15)$$

The significance of the approximated geometric moment values have been verified on shape localization applications where the position and orientation of several shapes have been computed using both the exact and the approximated moment values [11]. The error in the position along the x and y coordinates have been found to be less than 1 pixel. Concerning the orientation the error is less than 3 degrees.

3.3 Zernike Moment Computation

The binary pattern matching method can also be used to compute approximate values of Zernike moments that find applications in pattern recognition and image reconstruction [12]. Zernike moments are complex values that can be expressed as the sum of a real part and an imaginary part (see Eq. 8). Comparing the real and imaginary parts with the binary pattern matching correlation equation we notice again that, as for geometric moments, there is a similarity. Thus, the real and imaginary parts can be determined by binary pattern matching in the same way as for geometric moments. The binary patterns here are obtained by applying a dithering operation to the gray level image representation of the real and imaginary parts of the Zernike polynomials. Since our method gives approximate moment values, the influence of the error on the value obtained must be studied with respect to pattern analysis, pattern recognition or image compression applications. This is done in the same way as described in [13] on several images. For each image, the approximate values of the Zernike moments are first computed. Then, images reconstructed using both the approximated and the exact values are compared to the original image and the relative error calculated. The relative error is higher when using approximated Zernike moment values however it is less than 2% above the relative error value obtained using exact Zernike moment values. Details of the experiments and more complete results are reported in [11]. Fig.3 shows an example of the reconstructed images using both the approximated and the exact values.

Original image   Reconstruction using   Reconstruction using
                            exact values   approximated values

Fig. 3. Reconstruction of an image using exact and approximated values of Zernike moments

The influence of the error on the values of the Zernike moments has also been studied in an application of pattern recognition. Objects are recognized using two types of classifiers: Support Vector Machine (SVM) and a geometric classifier based on the use of 20 values of Zernike invariants. For our experiment we have used images excerpted from the COIL-100 image database [10] of four different objects: mugs, cars, boxes and soda cans. The database contains 72 different views of each object, a fraction of which is used to train the classifiers and the remaining used together with the images of other objects as the test set. An example of the percentage classification error (for both exact and approximated Zernike moment values) for a given object among the four types of objects considered is given in Table 1. The classification error due to the use of an approximated value of the Zernike moment is higher but it is less than 1% above the classification error value using exact Zernike moment values.

Table 1. Example of percentage classification error

	Exact values of Zernike invariants	Appoximated values of Zernike invariants
Geometric classifier (Stress polytope)	3,9%	4,5%
SVM	2,7%	3,3%

4 Conclusion

We have presented a binary pattern matching method that allows the design of a programmable CMOS retina capable of computing approximated values of geometric and Zernike moment functions of different orders. To study the influence of the error in the moment value with respect to object localization, and pattern recognition and classification applications, we have conducted several experiments and quantify the localization and classification errors. We have found that the use of approximated moment values results in a higher percentage localization and classification errors with respect to the exact values. However, the increase in the percentage localization and classification errors is not significant and our method is a good hardware implementable solution.

References

1. Mukundan, R., Ramakrishnan, K.R.: Moment functions in image analysis – Theory and applications. World Scientific, Singapore (1998)
2. Zhang, D., Lu, G.: Review of shape representation and description techniques. In: Pattern Recognition, vol. 37, pp. 1–19. Elsevier, North-Holland, Amsterdam (2004)
3. Standley, D.L.: An Object Position and Orientation IC With Embedded Imager. IEEE Journal Of. Solid State Circuits 26(12), 1853–1859 (1991)
4. Yu, N.M., Shibata, T., Ohmi, T., real, A.: time center of mass tracker circuit implemented by neuron MOS technology, IEEE Trans. on Circuits and Systems, vol. 45 (1998)
5. Cummings, R.E., Gruev, V., Abdel, M.G.: VLSI implementation, of motion centroid localization for autonomous navigation, Adv. Neural Inf. Process. Syst., vol. 45 (1998)
6. Deweerth, S.P.: Analog VLSI Circuits For Stimulus Localization and Centroid. International Journal of Computer Vision 8, 191–202 (1992)
7. Hu, M.K.: Visual pattern recognition by moment invariants. IRE Trans. on Inf. Theory 8(1), 179–187 (1962)
8. Pappas, T.N., Allebach, J.P., Neuhoff, D.L.: Model Based Digital Halftonning. IEEE Signal Processing Magazine 20(4), 14–27 (2003)
9. Floyd, R.W., Steinberg, L.: An adaptative algorithm for spatial grey scale. Proc. of Society for Information Display 17(2), 75–77 (1976)
10. Nene, S.A., Nayar, S.K., Murase, H.: Columbia Object Image Library (COIL-100), Technical Report CUCS-006-96, University of Columbia, http://www1.cs.columbia.edu/CAVE/databases/ (1996)
11. Aubreton, O.: Rétines à masques: Utilisation de masques binaires pour l'implantation d'un opérateur de reconnaissance de forme dans une rétine CMOS, Ph.D. thesis, Université de Bourgogne, France (December 2004)
12. Zhang, D., Lu, G.: Review of shape representation and description techniques. Pattern Recognition 37, 1–19 (2004)
13. The C.H.,, Chin, R.T.: On image analysis by the methods of moments. IEEE Trans. Pattern Analysis Machine Intelligence 10(4), 496–513 (1988)

Decimation Estimation and Linear Model-Based Super-Resolution Using Zoomed Observations

Prakash P. Gajjar, Manjunath V. Joshi, Asim Banerjee, and Suman Mitra

Dhirubhai Ambani Institute of Information and Communication Technology,
Gandhinagar, India

Abstract. In this paper we present a model based approach for super-resolving an image from a sequence of zoomed observations. From a set of images taken at different camera zooms, we super-resolve the least zoomed image at the resolution of the most zoomed one. Novelty of our approach is that decimation matrix is estimated from the given observations themselves. We model the most zoomed image as an autoregressive (AR) model, learn the parameters and use in regularization to super-resolve the least zoomed image. The AR model is computationally less intensive as compare to Markov Random Field (MRF) model hence the approach can be employed in real-time applications. Experimental results on real images with integer zoom settings are shown. We also show how the learning of AR parameters in subblocks using Panchromatic (PAN) image gives better results for the multiresolution fusion process in remote sensing applications.

1 Introduction

Physical constraints of the imaging systems limit image resolution quality in many imaging applications. These imaging systems yield aliased and under-sampled images as their detector array is not sufficiently dense. Super-resolution refers to the process of producing a high spatial resolution image from several low-resolution observations. The amount of aliasing differs in the observations captured with different zoom settings. More aliasing is present in an image captured with least zoom setting. This is because the entire area is represented by a very limited number of pixels, i.e., it is sampled with a very low sampling rate. By varying the zoom level, one observes the scene at different levels of aliasing and blurring. Thus, one can use zoom as a cue for generating high-resolution images at the lesser zoomed area of a scene.

The super-resolution idea was first proposed by Tsai and Huang [1] using frequency domain approach and employing motion as a cue. Capel and Zisserman [2] have proposed a technique for automated mosaicing with super-resolution zoom by fusing information from several views of a planar surface in order to estimate its texture. Most of the methods of super-resolution proposed in literature estimate high resolution image using motion as a cue. This requires registration of images with sub-pixel accuracy. It is also possible to extract non-redundant information by using different camera parameters or different lighting

J. Martí et al. (Eds.): IbPRIA 2007, Part I, LNCS 4477, pp. 314–321, 2007.

conditions while capturing the scene. The authors in [3] describe a Maximum a posteriori-MRF (MAP-MRF) based super-resolution technique using blur cue. They recover both the high-resolution scene intensity and the depth fields simultaneously using the defocus cue. For more details on motion free super-resolution refer to [4]. In [5], the authors propose a model-based approach to multiresolution fusion in remotely sensed images. They utilize the spatial correlation of each of the high resolution multispectral channels by using an AR model. However they use known decimation model.

In this paper, we obtain super-resolution by using zoom as a cue. As the decimation depends on the aliasing process, we estimate the decimation from the observations. We assume a linear dependency of a pixel to its neighbors in a high spatial resolution image and represent it with an AR model. In our image formation model, we learn the decimation matrix from the most zoomed observation and use MAP formulation to obtain super-resolved image for least zoomed observation covering entire scene. We also show that learning the AR parameters block by block using PAN image results in better fusion in remotely sense images.

2   Image Formation Model

Let Y_i, $i = 1$ to p, be the p observed images each captured with different integer zoom settings and are of size $M_1 \times M_2$ pixels each. The most zoomed observation Y_p that covers only a part of scene has the highest spatial resolution and least zoomed observation Y_1 covering the entire scene has least spatial resolution. Fig. 1(a) illustrates the relationship between the low-resolution observations of a scene at $p = 3$ different zoom settings and the high-resolution image.

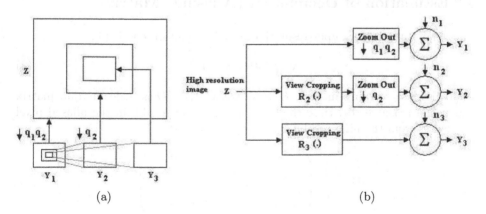

| (a) | (b) |

Fig. 1. (a) Relationship between observations at three different integer zoom levels and the high resolution image z of the scene, Y_1 corresponds to the least zoomed and Y_3 to the most zoomed images, (b) Low-resolution image formation model for three different zoom levels. View cropping block just crops the relevant part of the high resolution image Z as the field of view shrinks with zooming.

Since different zoom settings give rise to different resolutions, the least zoomed image needs to be upsampled to the size of $(q_1 q_2 \ldots q_{p-1}) \times (M_1 \times M_2)$ pixels ($= N_1 \times N_2$ pixels), where $q_1, q_2, \ldots, q_{p-1}$ are the corresponding zoom factors between two successively observed images of the scene $Y_1 Y_2, Y_2 Y_3, \ldots, Y_{p-1} Y_p$ respectively. Given Y_p, the remaining $(p-1)$ observed images are then modeled as decimated and noisy versions of this single high-resolution image of the appropriate region in the scene. The most zoomed observed image will have no decimation. The low resolution image observation model is shown in Fig. 1(b).

Let $\mathbf{y}_m$ represent the lexicographically ordered vector of size $M_1 M_2 \times 1$, which contains the pixels from differently zoomed images Y_m and $\mathbf{z}$ be the super-resolved image. The observed images can be modeled as

$$\mathbf{y}_m = D_m \mathbf{R}_m (\mathbf{z} - z_{\alpha_m}) + \mathbf{n}_m, \qquad m = 1, \cdots, p, \qquad (1)$$

where D is the decimation matrix which takes care of aliasing present while zooming and subscript m in D denotes that the amount of decimation depends on the amount of zoom for m^{th} observation, size of which depends on the zoom factor. For an integer zoom factor of q, the decimation matrix D consists of q^2 non-zero elements along each row at appropriate locations. The procedure for estimating the decimation matrix is described in section 3. $\mathbf{R}_m$ is a cropping operator with $z_{\alpha_m} = z(x - \alpha_{m_x}, y - \alpha_{m_y})$ and $\alpha_m = (\alpha_{m_x}, \alpha_{m_y})$ representing the lateral shift of the optical shift during zooming process for the mth observation. $\mathbf{n}_m$ is an independent and identically distributed (i.i.d) noise vector with zero mean and variance σ_n^2. It is of the size, $M_1 M_2 \times 1$.

Our problem is to estimate $\mathbf{z}$ given $\mathbf{y}_m$s, which is an ill-posed inverse problem. We assume that the observations captured are not blurred.

3   Estimation of Decimation (Aliasing) Matrix

The general model for super-resolution based on motion cue is [6],

$$\mathbf{y} = DHW\mathbf{z} + \mathbf{n}, \qquad (2)$$

where W is a warping matrix, H is a blur matrix, D is a decimation matrix and $\mathbf{n}$ is a noise vector. Here the decimation model to obtain the aliased pixel intensities from the high resolution pixels has the form [7]

$$D = \frac{1}{q^2} \begin{pmatrix} 1\ 1 \ldots 1 & & \mathbf{0} \\ & 1\ 1 \ldots 1 & \\ \mathbf{0} & & 1\ 1 \ldots 1 \end{pmatrix}. \qquad (3)$$

This decimation matrix is constant and doesn't account for aliasing in Eq.(2). All q^2 high resolution intensities are weighted equally by $\frac{1}{q^2}$ ($\frac{1}{4}$ for $q = 2$) to obtain the distorted or aliased pixel. This decimation model simulates the integration of light intensity that falls on the high resolution detector. This assumes that the entire area of a pixel acts as the light sensing area and there is no space in the pixel area for wiring or insulation. However, in practice, the observed intensity at a pixel captured due to low resolution sampling depends on various factors such as camera gain, illumination condition, zoom factor, noise etc. Hence the aliased low resolution pixel intensity of an image point is not always equally weighted sum of the high resolution intensities. Since we capture the images at different resolutions using zoom camera and the most zoomed image is assumed to be alias free, we estimate the weights from the most zoomed region. These weights are obtained by considering the most zoomed image and corresponding portion in the lesser zoomed images. We estimate 4 weights for a zoom factor of 2 and 16 for a zoom factor of 4. The estimated weight vectors are then used in Eq.(1) for forming D matrix to get the observation model. Since the average brightness of each observation varies due to AGC of camera, we use mean correction to maintain average brightness of the captured images approximately the same.

The decimation matrix of the form shown in Eq.(3), can now be modified as,

$$D = \begin{pmatrix} a_1 & a_2 & \dots & a_{q^2} & & & & \mathbf{0} \\ & & & a_1 & a_2 & \dots & a_{q^2} & \\ & \mathbf{0} & & & & a_1 & a_2 & \dots & a_{q^2} \end{pmatrix}, \tag{4}$$

where $|a_i| \leq 1, i = 1, 2, \dots q^2$.

We use Least Squares (LS) estimation approach discussed in [8] to obtain decimation matrices for different zoom factors.

4 Super-Resolving a Scene

MRF model characterizes the mutual influence among context dependent entities. MRF model for priors involves very high computational complexity. This motivates us to use a different prior. We represent the linear dependency of a pixel to its neighbors in a high resolution image using an AR model.

Let $z(s)$ be the gray level value of the image pixel at site $s = (i, j)$ in an $M_1 \times M_2$ lattice, where $i = 1, 2, \cdots M_1$ and $j = 1, 2, \cdots M_2$. The AR model for $z(s)$ can be expressed as [8]:

$$z(s) = \sum_{r \in \mathcal{N}_s} \theta(r)z(s+r) + \sqrt{\rho}n(s), \tag{5}$$

where $\mathcal{N}_s$ is the neighborhood of pixel at s. $\theta(r)$, r being a neighborhood index with $r \in \mathcal{N}_s$, and ρ are unknown parameters, and $n(.)$ is an i.i.d noise sequence with zero mean and unit variance. Here ρ is the variance of the white noise that generates the specified data for the given AR parameters. We use a third order neighborhood that requires a total of 8 parameters $\theta(i, j)$. We estimate the AR model parameters by considering the image as a finite lattice model using the scheme given in [8]. We use,

$$\sum_{s=i,j} \left(z_m(s) - \sum_{r \subset \mathcal{N}_s} \theta(r) z_m(s+r) \right)^2, \tag{6}$$

as a prior term in cost function.

Having defined the AR prior, we use the MAP estimator to restore the high-resolution field $\mathbf{z}$. Given the ensemble of images $\mathbf{y}_i$, $i = 1$ to p, at different resolutions, the MAP estimate $\hat{\mathbf{z}}$, using Bayesian rule, is given by

$$\hat{\mathbf{z}} = \begin{array}{c} \text{argmax} \\ \mathbf{z} \end{array} P(\mathbf{z}|\mathbf{y}_1, \mathbf{y}_2, \cdots, \mathbf{y}_p) = \begin{array}{c} \text{argmax} \\ \mathbf{z} \end{array} P(\mathbf{y}_1, \mathbf{y}_2, \cdots, \mathbf{y}_p|\mathbf{z}) P(\mathbf{z}). \tag{7}$$

From this, the cost function is derived as

$$\hat{\mathbf{z}} = \begin{array}{c} \text{argmin} \\ \mathbf{z} \end{array} [\sum_{m=1}^{p} \frac{\|\mathbf{y}_m - D_m C_m(\mathbf{z} - z_{\alpha_m})\|^2}{2\sigma_n^2} + \sum_{i,j} \left(z_m(s) - \sum_{r \in \mathcal{N}_s} \theta(r) z_m(s+r) \right)^2]. \tag{8}$$

The above cost function is convex and is minimized using the gradient descent technique.

5   Experimental Results

In this section, we present the results of the proposed method of obtaining super-resolution by estimating the decimation and fitting AR model to unknown high resolution image. All the experiments were conducted on real images with known integer zoom factors. It is assumed that the lateral shift during zooming is known. We compare the result with that obtained using successive Bicubic interpolation and that obtained by fitting MRF model without decimation estimation. We use Mean Square Error (MSE) as a quantitative measure. The MSE used here is

$$MSE = \frac{\sum_{i,j} [f(i,j) - \hat{f}(i,j)]^2}{\sum_{i,j} [f(i,j)]^2}, \tag{9}$$

where $f(i,j)$ is the original high resolution image and $\hat{f}(i,j)$ is estimated super-resolution image.

In the first experiment, we considered three low resolution observations of an image 'Divya' shown in Fig. 2(a)-(c). The images were scanned from a film negative using a scanner with different resolution settings. Fig. 2(a) is an image of size 72×96 pixels scanned with resolution of 300 dots/inch (dpi). To obtain second observation shown in Fig. 2(b), the same region was scanned at 600 dpi resolution and cropped the centermost region of the size 72×96. Similarly, the third observation Fig. 2(c) was obtained by scanning the region at 1200 dpi resolution and cropping the centermost region of the size 72×96. Fig. 2 (g) shows 'Divya' image of size 288×384 expanded by successive Bicubic interpolation

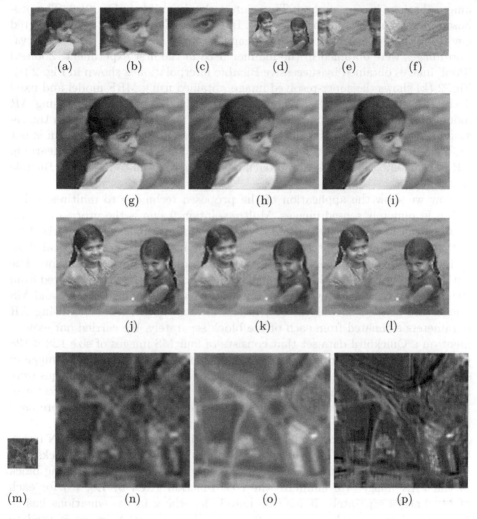

Fig. 2. (a)-(c) Observed 'Divya' images, (d)-(f) Observed 'Pool' images, (g) 'Divya' image expanded using Bicubic interpolation, (h) 'Divya' image super-resolved using MRF model and fixed decimation matrix of the form shown in Eq.(3), (i) 'Divya' image super-resolved by the proposed method, (j) 'Pool' image expanded using Bicubic interpolation, (k)-(l) 'Pool' images super-resolved using MRF model and fixed decimation matrix and using the proposed method, respectively, (m) Observed MS image (Band 2), (n) Zoomed MS (Band 2) image using Bicubic expansion and (o)-(p) Fused MS (Band 2) images using MRF model (and fixed decimation matrix) and the proposed method, respectively.

and Fig. 2(h) shows super-resolved 'Divya' image of same size obtained using MRF model and fixed decimation matrix of the form shown in Eq.(3) and (i) shows super-resolved 'Divya' image obtained by proposed method. The comparison of the images show more clear details in the regions containing edges in the image obtained by our method. The seam is clearly visible in Fig. 2(g). The proposed method has less smoothing effect. In the second experiment, we considered low resolution observations of 'Pool' image shown in Fig. 2(d)-(f). The observation images were obtained in the manner used in the first experiment. Zoomed 'Pool' images obtained by successive Bicubic interpolation is shown in Fig. 2 (j). Fig. 2 (k) shows the super-resolved image obtained using MRF model and fixed decimation matrix and (l) shows the super-resolved image obtained using AR model and estimated decimation matrix. In Fig. 2 (j), seam is visible in the region of head and face of the girl on right, where as in Fig. 2 (l) the seam is not visible. Although the most zoomed image has not enough texture for learning AR parameters, the proposed approach has performed well compared to Bicubic interpolation.

Now we show the application of the proposed technique to multiresolution fusion in remotely sensed images. Multiresolution fusion is the process of combining PAN and multispectral (MS) data to produce images characterized by both high spatial and spectral resolutions. Because of the technological limitations, MS images are generally captured with a lower spatial resolution. The authors in [5], obtain multiresolution fusion using AR parameters estimated from the entire PAN image. However, better results can be obtained if PAN and MS images are divided into blocks and fusion of each block is achieved using AR parameters estimated from each of the block separately. We carried out experiment on a Quickbird data set that consists of four MS images of size 128×128 pixels at a spatial resolution of $2.4m \times 2.4m$ and a coregistered PAN image of size 512×512 pixels with a spatial resolution of $0.6m \times 0.6m$. The images were acquired at the same time over a city. The PAN image decimated by a factor of 4 was used to learn the AR parameters, and the original MS images were used as reference (true) data in order to make a quantitative comparison.

In our experiment, first we learn the decimation matrix from the PAN image for each of MS images and then divide the an MS image into 16 blocks and learn AR parameters for each block of MS image by using corresponding block in the PAN image. We minimize the cost function given by Eq. (8) for each of MS images separately. It may be noted that the z in the equations has to be replaced by z_m, where $m = 1, 2, \ldots, 4$. The same PAN image is used to estimate the aliasing on each of MS images. Available PAN image (in this case, degraded) can be used for estimating aliasing matrices for all the MS images as the aliasing depends on difference in spatial resolution between high resolution and low resolution images.

Due to space limitation, we show results for only one MS image. Fig. 2(m) shows observed MS image (Band 2). The zoomed images obtained by Bicubic expansion and super-resolved images obtained using MRF model (without decimation estimation) and proposed method are shown in Fig. 2(n), (o) and (p) respectively. From the figure it is clear that the fused image obtained by the proposed method has high spatial resolution with negligible spectral distortion as compared to images obtained using the other two methods. Table 1. shows the quantitative comparison of performance of our method with that of the other

Table 1. Comparison of performance of proposed method with Bicubic expansion

	MSE		
Technique	Divya	Pool	MS (Band 2)
Bicubic Expansion	0.003526	0.006508	0.023230
MRF model and Fixed Decimation	0.005277	0.005280	0.192880
Proposed	0.002438	0.005827	0.022506

two methods. It can be seen that MSE of the super-resolved images obtained using our method is considerably lower.

6   Conclusion

We have presented a technique to recover the super-resolution intensity field from a sequence of zoomed observations. The resolution of the entire scene is obtained at the resolution of the most zoomed observed image that consists of only a small portion of the actual scene. Decimation that depends on aliasing process is estimated from the observations themselves. The spatial dependency in the super-resolved images is learnt from the observations by using an AR model. Learning the decimation and AR parameters indeed perform better and also can be employed for real time super-resolution applications.

References

1. Tsai, R.Y., Huang, T.S.: Multiframe image restoration and registration. Advances in Computer Vision and Image Processsing. pp. 317–339 (1984)
2. Capel, D., Zisserman, A.: Automated mosaicing with super-resolution zoom. In: Proc. IEEE Int. Conf. Comput. Vision Pattern Recogn. pp. 885–891 (1998)
3. Rajan, D., Chaudhuri, S.: Generation of super-resolution images from blurred observations using an MRF model. J. Math. Imag. Vision, (16), pp. 5–15 (2002)
4. Chaudhuri, S., Joshi, M.V.: Motion-free Super-resolution. Springer, Heidelberg (2005)
5. Joshi, M.V., Bruzzone, L., Chaudhuri, S.: Model-based approach to multiresolution fusion in remotely sensed images. IEEE Trans. on Geoscience and Remote Sensing 44(9), 2549–2562 (2006)
6. Park, S., Park, M.K., Kang, M.: Super-resolution image reconstruction: A technical overview. IEEE Signal Processing Magazine 20, 21–36 (2003)
7. Schultz, R.R., Stevenson, R.L.: A bayesian approach to image expansion for improved definition. IEEE Trans. Image Process. 3, 233–242 (1994)
8. Kashyap, R., Chellappa, R.: Estimation and choice of neighbors in spatial-interaction models of images. IEEE Trans. Inf. Theory IT-29, 60–72 (1983)

Line Extraction from Mechanically Scanned Imaging Sonar

David Ribas[1], Pere Ridao[1], José Neira[2], and Juan Domingo Tardós[2]

[1] University of Girona
[2] University of Zaragoza

Abstract. The extraction of reliable features is a key issue for autonomous underwater vehicle navigation. Imaging sonars can produce acoustic images of the surroundings of the vehicle. Despite of the noise, the phantoms and reflections, we believe that they are a good source for features since they can work in turbid water where other sensors like vision fail. Moreover, they can cover wide areas incrementing the number of features visible within a scan. This work presents an algorithm to extract linear features from underwater structured environments including as major contributions a novel sonar model sensor and an adapted implementation of the Hough transform.

1 Introduction

Vehicle localization, map building and more recently, the simultaneous localization and mapping (SLAM) are fundamental problems to achieve true autonomous vehicles [1], [2]. One of the key issues on those techniques is to develop reliable systems to extract features from the environment in order to build maps or navigate thorough existing ones. Working in underwater environments is specially challenging because of the reduced sensorial possibilities. Acoustic devices are the most common choice while the use of cameras and laser sensors is limited to applications where the vehicle navigates very near to the seafloor. One of the issues on working on this kind of environments is the difficulty on finding reliable features. There are approaches using clusters of acoustic data as features [3], [4], some merge visual and acoustic information in order to improve the reliability [5], while others simply introduce artificial beacons to deal with complex environments [6]. Most of the previous work using mechanically scanned imaging sonars (MSIS) have focused on the use of point features assuming the robot remains static or moves sufficiently slow. In this work we propose an algorithm to take advantage of structured elements typically present in common underwater scenarios (drilling platforms, harbours, channels, dams,...) in order to extract line features. Moreover, our algorithm removes the "static" assumption. This paper briefly introduces MSISs, presents a novel sonar model which improves the sensor measurements characterization and depicts a modified version of the Hough transform algorithm for detecting line features (cross sections of planar structures present in the environment) in imaging sonar scans. Finally, the results and conclusions are presented.

J. Martí et al. (Eds.): IbPRIA 2007, Part I, LNCS 4477, pp. 322–329, 2007.

2   Extracting Line Features from Acoustic Images

MSISs perform scans in a 2D plane by rotating a sonar beam through a series of small angle steps. For each emitted beam, distance vs. echo-amplitude data is returned. Thus, accumulating this information along a complete 360° sector, an acoustic image of the surroundings can be obtained (Fig. 1). Commonly, these devices have a slow scanning rate (f.i. a Tritech Miniking sonar head needs about 6 seconds to complete a 360° scan). For this reason, the vehicle movement along a complete scan usually induces important distortions in the acoustic image (Fig. 1b). Extracting features from this kind of images produces inaccuracies and yields to poor results. Therefore, the first step of the procedure consists on merging the raw sensor data together with the information from the vehicle's navigation system [7]. Incorporating the displacements and rotations of the sensor into the positional information of each sonar measurement leads to an undistorted acoustic image such the one represented in Fig. 1c.

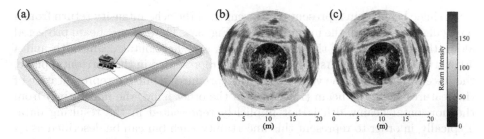

Fig. 1. (a) Schematic representation of the environment where the sonar data were gathered. The highlighted zones represent the expected sonar returns. Images generated from acoustic data, (b) distorted and (c) undistorted image through navigation integration.

2.1   Beam Segmentation

At a given orientation of the transducer head, the sensor gathers an acoustic profile of the surroundings which is represented by a vector of echo amplitude values (called bins) each one corresponding to a particular distance along the emitted beam. Since objects present in the environment appear as high echo-amplitude returns, only part of the information stored in the vector is useful for feature extraction. Therefore, a segmentation process can be done in order to get the more significant information from the acoustic beam and, in addition, reduce the computational cost of the algorithm. In the context of this work several approaches have been tested (Fig. 2):

- *H*ighest intensity: The bin with the maximum value over a threshold is selected.
- *P*eak values: The set of local maxima over the threshold are selected. Moreover, they must accomplish a "minimum distance between them" criterion.

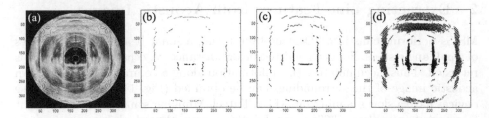

Fig. 2. (a) Acoustic image generated with the complete set of measurements, (b) highest intensity return selection, (c) peak values selection, (d) thresholding

– *Thresholding:* All the bins with values over a threshold are selected. The performance of these approaches is reported in section 3.

2.2 Sonar Modeling

Each single beam's bin represents the strength of the echo intensity return from a particular place within the insonified area (Fig. 3a). The acoustic beam projected along the central axis of the transducer has a 3° horizontal beamwidth and a 40° vertical beamwidth. As the sonar data is represented in the horizontal plane, the uncertainty due to the vertical aperture produces a blurred representation of the features along the beam (Fig. 3a). On the other hand, the uncertainty from the horizontal beamwidth is not implicitly represented in the resulting data. Typically, in order to represent this uncertainty, each bin can be described as an arc showing all the possible locations of tangent surfaces producing compatible sonar returns [8],[9]. While this simple model is well suited for air sonar ranging systems, it is not able to explain the acoustic images gathered with a MSIS. A careful analysis on such images (see Fig. 3b) reveals that their object detection capability is not limited to the arc-tangent surfaces. Even those beams which meet a surface with a considerable incidence angle (for the Miniking, $\beta = 60°$) produce a discernible high intensity profile. For this reason, we have adopted an extended model to describe the imaging sonar. Each bin represents a zone described by an arc which corresponds to the horizontal beamwidth α (in our sensor, $\alpha = 3°$). Given a resolution and the incidence angle β, for each point belonging the arc, its tangent surface as well as the intersecting planes with an incidence angle smaller than $\pm\beta/2$ are visible for the beam's bin (Fig. 4). Hence, the acoustic intensity represented by the bin should correspond to one of those candidate planes.

2.3 The Hough Voting Space

The Hough transform [10] accumulates the information from the sensor data into a voting table which is a parameterized representation of all the possible feature locations. Those features that receive a great number of votes are the ones with a relevant set of compatible sensor measurements and thus the ones

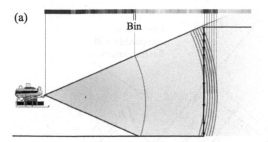 

Fig. 3. (a) Dispersion of the high intensity returns provoked by the vertical aperture of the sonar beam, (b) representation of the horizontal beamwidth as an arc. Note that at the maximum incidence angle the line feature is still distinguishable although the arc is not tangent.

that most likely correspond to a real object in the environment. We have chosen line features to represent the planar objects existing in the scene. These line features are described by two parameters, ρ^B and θ^B (distance and orientation with respect to the base frame B). Hence, the resulting Hough space is a two-dimensional space where the voting process and the search for maxima can be done efficiently. Another key issue is the quantization of the Hough space. In our case, we have observed that tuning the quantization to match the angular and lineal resolutions of our sensor (typically, 0.1 m and 1.8°) works fine.

2.4   Voting

Each time a beam is obtained, the segmented bins vote in the Hough space. The next step is to determine the candidate lines that will receive the votes. As previously introduced in section 2.2, the measurement is modeled as an arc in order to represent the uncertainty that appears due to the horizontal beamwith α (Fig. 4). Hence, θ_{S_j} will take values within an aperture of $\pm\alpha/2$ around the real angle of the transducer head. Then, for each θ_{S_j} value, a set of k candidate lines will be determined. As said before, not only the lines tangent to the arc are candidates, but also the ones inside the maximum incidence angle limits of $\pm\beta/2$. So, for each θ_{S_j} value we can define θ_k^B as:

$$\theta_{S_j} - \frac{\beta}{2} \leq \theta_k^B \leq \theta_{S_j} + \frac{\beta}{2} . \tag{1}$$

Finally, the ρ_k^B value that corresponds to each value of θ_k^B is calculated as:

$$\rho_k^B = x_{S_j} cos(\theta_k^B) + y_{S_j} sin(\theta_k^B) + \rho^{S_j} cos(\theta_k^{S_j}) . \tag{2}$$

In Fig. 5a it is shown how the set of voters corresponding to a single sonar return looks like when assigned to the Hough space. Note that each selected cell of the Hough space only receives one single vote. However, we have tested two different

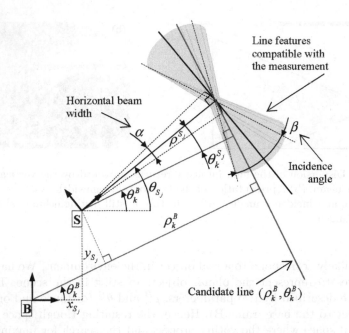

Fig. 4. Model of the sonar sensor for line features. Where B is the base reference frame and S is a reference frame attached to the current beam.

ways to assign values to the votes. The first method assigns to each vote a value of 1, while the second gives to the vote a value related with the echo intensity of its corresponding bin. In this way, we try to give more weight to those sonar returns that more strongly reflect the presence of objects in the environment.

As the sensor constantly produces measurements, the number of votes assigned to the space grows without limit. Moreover, when a 360° scan around the sensor is completed, the new upcoming measurements would correspond to a zone already visited and hence, redundant votes could corrupt the candidate election. To avoid this, we tagged each bin with the angle of its corresponding beam so the oldest voters can easily be identified and discarded. The key issue of this idea is determining which measurements are identified as old voters. A rough option is to consider the voters tagged one 360° scan away from the actual beam orientation. A smarter approach is to determine the minimum scan sector necessary to detect a line feature. In the extreme case, a line can exist in a 180° sector (when the feature is very close to the sonar head so it is placed at the diameter of the scan). Therefore, each time a new measurement is incorporated, a voting process is performed for the measurements corresponding to the most recent 180° sector. Then, a search among the potential candidate lines is done. If a line obtains a sufficient number of votes (this changes depending on many factors such as the chosen beam segmentation procedure or the discretization of the voting space) it is considered as detected and thus, their voters can be eliminated (one bin can only correspond to a single line feature in our

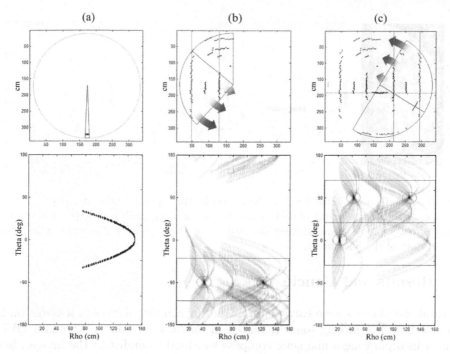

Fig. 5. (a) Votes assigned to the voting space for one single measurement. (b) Aspect of the voting space after a small scan sector. The actual voting scan sector is marked by a red line, the present features are in green, the blue line indicates the features detection zone. (c) Aspect of the voting space after almost one complete scan. Note that the old voters (the ones before the 180° scan) have been removed from the space.

application). If there is no line detected, the votes will be stored and used when new measurements arrive. This solves the problem of continuously dealing with new information provided by the sensor while, at the same time, keeps the number of votes low improving the overall efficiency of the algorithm (Fig. 5b and c).

2.5   Line Extraction

The algorithm looks for winning candidates each time a new beam arrives. However, we have to ensure that the algorithm detects the line when it has received all the possible votes (or what is the same, the line is totally inside the scan sector and the newest sonar beam cannot provide more information to it). Analyzing all line features existing in the sector scan it is possible to determine when they have received all the votes. A simple and robust strategy consist on setting the zone for the line detection 90° away from the last beam measurement, just in the bisector of the 180° scan sector (see the blue lines in Fig. 5b and c). Beyond this point, all the feature lines had been detected and hence, all the votes assigned to this lines had been removed so they cannot interfere with the detection of further features.

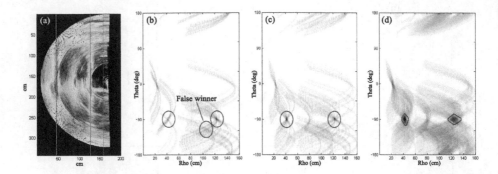

Fig. 6. (a) 180° scan sector used in the example, (b) aspect of the voting space when using only the highest value of each beam, (c) when using peak values, (c) when using a threshold for measurement selection. Note that the shapes of the peaks reflect the uncertainty of the lines in the scan.

3   Results and Conclusions

Several experiments were carried out gathering acoustic images in a water tank with a Tritech Miniking sonar mounted in an AUV. A Sontek Argonaut DVL sensor incorporating a magnetic compass was used to undistort the images. Selecting the parameters (threshold, incidence angle, minimum distance between local maxima, ...) according to the particular characteristics of our sensor and using the extended sonar model proposed in this paper, all the segmentation strategies were able to detect the line features. The proposed voting space (last 180° scan sector) together with the line extraction strategy allows to deal continuously with the sonar beams as provided by the sonar instead of waiting to collect a full scan before detecting the lines. With the proposed strategy, the maximum delay between the time instant in which the last bin of a line has been measured and the detection instant is 1.5 seconds (90° scan time) instead of the 6 seconds needed for mapping a full slam. in the future we will explore alternatives to reduce this delay to zero, looking for the Hough peaks not in linear region but in a nonlinear region.

Fig. 6 shows a representative experiment comparing the different beam segmentation strategies, using votes with a value of one. In our experiments, voting proportionally to the acoustic intensity didn't improve results appreciably. Hereafter we describe the conclusion related to each segmentation strategy:

- *Highest intensity:* This method is the one computationally more efficient because of the small number of votes. After the voting process, the winners appear in the Hough space as identifiable small peak zones. However, the low number of votes make easier the existence of "false winners" (a small but elongated shape can produce a similar number of votes that a line feature with lower intensity measurements, see Fig. 6b).
- *Peak values:* This method seems to be a good compromise between low computational cost and robustness. The higher number of votes gives a better

description of the elements present in the scene. The resulting Hough space is similar to the one obtained with the previous method. However, it seems to be more "contrasted" as winners present a much higher concentration of votes (Fig. 6c).

— *Thresholding:* This is by far the less efficient approach due to the large number of measurements involved in the voting. However, it presents a interesting property that the other methods had not shown: The thickness of the linear features present in the sonar scan seems to be related to the size and shape of the winner peaks in the Hough space (see Fig. 6d). As introduced in section 2.2, the vertical aperture of the fan shaped beam, among other causes, provokes a thickening of the elongated form corresponding to the line feature. This effect leads to uncertainty on the estimate of the real position of the feature and, for some applications, such as robot localization or SLAM, knowing this uncertainty is crucial. We think that, using this method, we can probably not only obtain the parameters of the existing features but also its related uncertainty. Further work will be done on this matter.

References

1. Durrant-Whyte, H., Bailey, T.: Simultaneous Localisation and Mapping (SLAM): Part I The Essential Algorithms. Robotics and Automation Magazine (June 2006)
2. Durrant-Whyte, H., Bailey, T.: Simultaneous Localisation and Mapping (SLAM): Part II State of the Art. Robotics and Automation Magazine (September 2006)
3. Leonard, J.J., Carpenter, R.N., Feder, H.J.S.: Stochastic Mapping Using Forward Look Sonar. Robotica 19, 341 (2001)
4. Tena, I., Petillot, Y., Lane, D.M., Salson, C.: Feature Extraction and Data Association for AUV Concurrent Mapping and Localisation. In: Proc. of the IEEE International Conference on Robotics and Automation, Seoul, Korea (2001)
5. Williams, S., Mahon, I.: Simultaneous Localisation and Mapping on the Great Barrier Reef. In: Proc. of the IEEE International Conference on Robotics and Automation, New Orleans, USA (2004)
6. Newman, P.M., Leonard, J.: Pure range-only sub-sea SLAM. In: Proceedings of the IEEE International Conference on Robotics and Automation, Taipei, Taiwan (2003)
7. Ribas, D., Neira, J., Ridao, P., Tardós, J.D.: SLAM using an Imaging Sonar for Partially Structured Environments. In: Proc. of IEEE/RSJ International Conference on Intelligent Robots and Systems, Beijing, China (2006)
8. Leonard, J.J., Durrant-Whyte, H.F.: Directed Sonar Sensing for Mobile Robot Navigation. Kluwer Academic Pub. London (1992)
9. Tardós, J.D., Neira, J., Newman, P., Leonard, J.: Robust Mapping and Localization in Indoor Environments using Sonar Data. International Journal of Robotics Research 21(4), 311–330 (2002)
10. Illingworth, J., Kittler, J.: A survey of the Hough transform. Computer Vision, Graphics, and Image Processing, Academic Press Professional 44(1), 87–116 (1988)

Road Signs Recognition by the Scale-Space Template Matching in the Log-Polar Domain

Bogusław Cyganek

AGH - University of Science and Technology
Al. Mickiewicza 30, 30-059 Kraków, Poland
cyganek@uci.agh.edu.pl

Abstract. This paper presents a cascaded system for recognition of the circular road-signs. The system consists of two compound detectors-classifiers. Each operates on the Gaussian scale-space and does template matching in the log-polar domain. The first module is responsible for detection of the potential sign areas at the coarsest level of the pyramid. The second one, in turn, refines the already found places at the finest level. Thanks to this composition, as well as to the efficient matching in the log-polar domain, the system is very robust in terms of recognition of the signs with different scales and rotations, as well as under partial occlusions, poor illumination conditions, and noise.

1 Introduction

The problem of automatic recognition of the road signs (RSs) finds still growing attention and significant research effort. The most successful realizations are considered to be built into the driving assisting systems (DAS), mounted on cars, with the main purpose of increasing safety on our roads [9]. A driver's distraction, or even a moment of inattention, very often lead to serious traffic situations. Thus the described system can warn a driver of the passing stop signs, speed limits, etc. to draw his or her attention to the road events. For the recent years, many different RS recognition systems have been proposed. For an overview one can refer to [2-6][10] [13][16] and the references cited therein. Usually the recognition systems are further divided into detection and classification stages. However, some systems join the two tasks under one platform [1]. This is also the case of the presented system.

In this paper we deal with the circular prohibition RSs. The main problem with their recognition is the errorless detection and registration. The difficulties arise mostly due to the small area with the characteristic colour (a red dye on the outer ring), great variations in size of a sign, its scale and rotation, as well as quality of the processed images (occlusions, distortions, etc.). To cope with shape variations one solution is to generate deformable models and perform search in such space [6]. However, if we allow rotation the search space becomes prohibitively large. Thus, the solution in this paper is based on the Gaussian scale-space and the log-polar (LP) transformation which maps scale and rotation into horizontal and vertical translations. Experimental results show good performance of the method on real traffic scenes.

J. Martí et al. (Eds.): IbPRIA 2007, Part I, LNCS 4477, pp. 330–337, 2007.

2 Road Signs Recognition System

In this paper we propose a method of road signs (RSs) recognition. Under 'recognition' we understand simultaneous detection and classification. The problem with recognition of the circular RSs (e.g. the prohibition signs) is that it is very difficult for the detection module to determine their scale and rotation. This problem is less severe for other groups of RSs, e.g. the triangular-shaped information signs "A" or rectangular information signs "D", for which detector finds specific points-corners and then the affine registration allows proper adjustment for subsequent match [4][6]. However, this is not a case for the circular signs. Moreover, their detection based on colour segmentation is frequently not reliable due to relatively small red areas, only at an outer rim of a sign.

The proposed method tries to overcome these and other problems encountered in RS recognition systems, such as partial occlusions, luminance variations or noise. The key techniques that help to solve this task is processing in the Gaussian scale-space and search in the log-polar domain – both are inspired by the biological vision systems [15]. The second technique gained much attention in computer vision, mostly in image registration, as proposed for instance by Zokai & Wolberg [17]. Their work was very influential on the proposed method, as well.

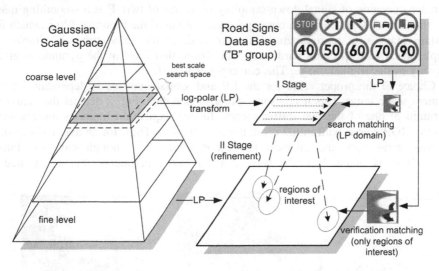

Fig. 1. Architecture of the system for recognition of the circular road signs

Fig. 1 depicts basic structure of the proposed system. The colour image acquisition and filtering modules are responsible for delivering the input image. Here we use the Marlin F-033C camera by Allied Vision Technologies®. From the monochrome version of the input image, the Gaussian scale-space pyramid is built. Its coarsest level is then used for the initial search for templates from the data base (DB) of the RSs. For this research we limited our DB to ten most important signs. A sign from the DB is LP transformed and matched to each LP-transformed area in the coarse image. This way found best matches give us information on the areas of interest, but also on the possible *scale* of an object and its *rotation*. Taking these information, the second classifier is launched. It does the same type of match but taking the finest level of the pyramid and constraining the search only to the already found places of interest.

3   Transformations of the Input Space

In this section we review the two transformations of digital images which were shown to have functional equivalents in biological visual systems [15]: The Gaussian scale-space and the log-polar transform. They show also to be very efficient in machine object recognition [12][17].

3.1   The Gaussian Scale-Space

The process of creation of the Gaussian image pyramid is given by the following recursive formulas [11]:

$$\mathbf{G}^{(i=0)} = \mathbf{I} \tag{1}$$

$$\mathbf{G}^{(i+1)} = \downarrow_2 \mathbf{F}\!\left(\mathbf{G}^{(i)}\right) \tag{2}$$

where I is an input image, $G(i)$ denotes an image at the *i-th* level of the pyramid, $\downarrow_2$ denotes operation of signal down-sampling by factor of two, $\mathbf{F}$ is a smoothing mask i.e. the Gaussian. However, in our experiments we used the binomial filter, which for certain mask size approximates Gaussian and, at the same time, is simpler in implementation (especially hardware). The finest, first level of the pyramid is given directly by the original image; This corresponds to *i=0*.

Choice of the proper scale for the LP and spatial matches is dependant on the camera scene setup. This needs some experimental data. Fig. 2 depicts the Gaussian pyramid of one of the real traffic scenes. In our acquisition modules images were always RGB colour with initial resolution of 640×480. Thus, for an average size of a circular road sign, the coarsest resolution which has enough data for initial recognition is about 160×120 (Fig. 2c). In our experiments this constituted a

Fig. 2. The Gaussian scale space pyramid of a road scene: 640×480 (a), 320×240 (b), 160×120 (c), 80×60 (d). The level (c) is then log-polar transformed for a coarse search.

reasonable compromise between object details and computation time. Alternatively, we search *several scales around the initial one* – the best scale search area in Fig. 1. However, this requires additional computations which slow down the whole process. Thus, for practical applications the latter requires efficient hardware accelerator [8].

3.2 The Log-Polar (LP) Transform

The log-polar transformation is applied to the coarsest level of the scale space and to the searched patterns. The log-polar (LP) transformation at a point $x=(x_1,x_2)$ can be defined as follows [17] (further references on LP can be found in [17], as well):

$$r = \log_B\left(\sqrt{(x_1-c_1)^2+(x_2-c_2)^2}\right), \ \alpha = \arctan\frac{x_2-c_2}{x_1-c_1}, \ \text{for} \ x_1 \neq c_1, \tag{3}$$

where $C=(c_1,c_2)$ is a centre of transformation, B is a base of a logarithm; B can be any value >1.0. In practice it is chosen to fit the value of r_{max} which is the maximal distance from the centre C and points in the area of interest around C, as follows:

$$B = \exp\left[\frac{\ln(d_{max})}{r_{max}}\right], \ d_{max}>1, \ r_{max}>1, \tag{4}$$

where $d_{max}=min\{d_{1max}, d_{2max}\}$ denotes a minimal distance from a chosen centre C and delimiting window, as depicted in Fig. 3a. r_{max} is the maximal number of columns in the LP image. Thus, LP results in a nonlinear and nonuniform sampling of the spatial intensity signal. Nonlinearity is caused by the polar mapping, whereas log operation leads to the nonuniform sampling (3).

In the proposed system the LP space is used at the coarsest level of the image pyramid to search for the 'promising' sign locations. Since our objects are the circular road signs, the search window was set to be rectangle and the centre C of the log-polar is set to be a geometrical centre of each search window (Fig. 3b). Thus, the most important part of a sign, i.e. its centre with a pictogram, will be given most attention.

In the system the inverse warping scheme is used to transform images from the spatial to the LP representation. In this scheme, for a point in the output image, a

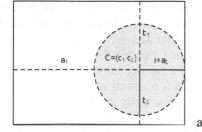
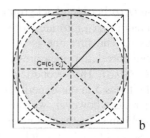

Fig. 3. Selection of the central point $C=(c_1,c_2)$ and d_{max} for the log-polar transformation. In the general case the smallest projected distance is chosen (a). For the geometrical centre in a square search window, d_{max} is a radius of an inscribed circle (b) – the pictogram of a sign gets most attention, the outer ring is at coarse sampling, and the background corners (white) are excluded.

point in the input is computed and its intensity is found by the bilinear interpolation. For the quantized values of r and α the inverse LP transformation is given as follows:

$$x_1 = B^r \cdot \cos(\alpha) + c_1 \quad , \quad x_2 = B^r \cdot \sin(\alpha) + c_2 , \tag{5}$$

assuming $B>1$, and $0 \leq r \leq r_{max}$, $0 \leq \alpha < 2\pi$, where r is a vertical, α horizontal coordinate.

4 Template Matching

The system consists of two cascaded classifiers, each does its own template matching, and each operates in different signal scale. The first template matching is done in the LP domain, computed from the coarse level of the image pyramid (Fig. 1).

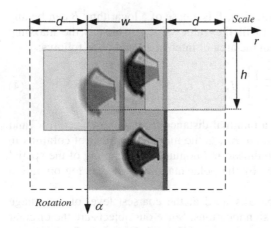

Fig. 4. Search space in the log-polar domain (first sign in Fig. 2). The background pattern $w{\times}h$ is wrapped around to allow proper match of the rotation. Scale search is extended by d.

This search for the best matches in the LP space performs in four dimensions [17]. At first a template is transformed into the LP representation. Then, for each position (x_{1b}, x_{2b}) in the background image, a region is selected of the same size as the template. This region is also LP transformed. Next, the two LP images are matched. This match, however, is done in an extended space, depicted in Fig. 4. The background pattern is *wrapped around to 2h* to allow proper search of the rotation parameter. The scale search span is also *extended by a distance d*, which can be up to the template width w (in practice was set to $0.8w$).

The best match position in this extended LP space corresponds to the scale and rotation (r, α) between background and the template. For the best match(es) the four parameters $(x_{1b}, x_{2b}, r, \alpha)$ are stored. The two techniques of selecting the best matches were used: The first one is to set a fixed threshold and accept only values which produced correlation measures above this threshold. For (6) this threshold was in a range *[0.6-0.8]*. The second technique is to build a priority queue of a fixed length L (usually it was 5 in our experiments), which stores N positions of the best matches. In the latter case, however, we can allow areas which actually are false alarms. This is not a problem since the second classifier can resolve this difficulty.

The second template matching is performed also in the LP domain, however at the fine scale (the bottommost image in the pyramid in Fig. 1). This time, *only* the interest areas, already selected by the previous matching process, are checked. Thus, the purpose of this run is to verify the already found objects. Nevertheless, this matching has to be preceded by registration of the DB stored template to the finest scale. This is done by an affine warping based on the already found scale s from the tuple

$(x_{1b}, x_{2b}, r, \alpha)$ for this area; Additionally we have to adjust for the right scale in the pyramid. The match value is checked and if it is above a threshold (0.9-0.95 in case of (6)) the match is accepted, thus a sign is recognized.

Very important is a choice of the matching measure used in the aforementioned searches. Because of the luminance variations, the only possible solutions here are the correlation measures which can compensate this effect. One of them, also suggested in [17], is the cross correlation ρ (covariance-variance), defined as follows:

$$\rho = \frac{\sum_{(i,j) \in U} \left(I_1(x_1 + i, x_2 + j) - \overline{I_1(x_1, x_2)_U} \right) \cdot \left(I_2(x_1 + i, x_2 + j) - \overline{I_2(x_1, x_2)_U} \right)}{\sqrt{\sum_{(i,j) \in U} \left(I_1(x_1 + i, x_2 + j) - \overline{I_1(x_1, x_2)_U} \right)^2 \cdot \sum_{(i,j) \in U} \left(I_2(x_1 + i, x_2 + j) - \overline{I_2(x_1, x_2)_U} \right)^2}}, \quad (6)$$

where $\overline{I_n(x_1, x_2)_U}$ denotes average intensity in a pixel region U in an n-th image.

The problem with the above is its excessive computation time due to calculation of the mean values in every position, necessary divisions and fractional arithmetic. Although the first obstacle can be tackled to some extent by the integral image technique [14], the better results were obtained with the Census measure E:

$$E(\mathbf{I}, P) = \underset{P' \in U(P, \beta)}{\otimes} e(I, P, P') \text{ where } e(I, P, P') = \begin{cases} 0 & if \quad I(P) \leq I(P') \\ 1 & otherwise \end{cases}, \quad (7)$$

I stands for intensity, P is a central pixel, $\otimes$ denotes bit concatenation, $U(P, \beta)$ is a local neighbourhood around a pixel P with a radius β, P' denotes pixels belonging to U. In practice U is a 3×3 window which results in 8 bits nonparametric representation of U. Details of Census computation can be found in [7]. Both (6) and (7) were used in the experiments. However, for the latter we have to remember that the best match is for $E=0$, while for (6) it is 1.0. Therefore, the thresholds t have to be reversed: $t_8 = 1 - t_7$.

Nevertheless, after profiling it appeared that computations of (6) and (7) are the main bottlenecks of the software. Therefore, although the system was designed to work exclusively in the monochrome images, we augment matching in the LP domain with red colour information from the segmentation module. The rule is simple: a match window is taken into consideration iff it contains at least 5% of red pixels.

5 Experimental Results

The system was implemented in C++ (Visual® C++ 6.0 with Intel® C++ compiler 9.0), then tested on the IBM PC® endowed with Pentium 4 3.4GHz and 2GB RAM.

The experiments were performed in two directions. The first was to assess the flexibility of a method in terms of possible variations in the resolution, sign visibility, scale and rotation. The other experiments were performed on real road scenes (more than hundred from our DB) to determine recognition abilities of the method.

Fig. 5 depicts one road scene from our data base (a), its binary segmentation map of red areas (b) and the recognized road sign (c). For most of the scenes and RSs depicted in Fig. 1 the recognition was almost perfect under broad variations of

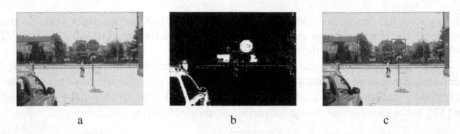

a   b   c

Fig. 5. Exemplary road scene (a). The red segmentation (b). The recognized STOP sign (c).

illumination conditions, scale and rotation - the results contains Table 1. The problems arise with false alarms (decay of the Precision parameter in Table 1), e.g. if a scene does not contain a sign the decision relies on proper choice of the thresholds. On the other hand, too restrictive thresholds lead sometimes to rejection of e.g. slightly occluded or not well visible signs. The second problem is complexity of the method (especially the four dimensional search) – single run takes approximately 100s on our software platform. Thus, the real time implementation would require hardware acceleration, e.g. as described in [8].

Table 1. Accuracy of recognition for the selected prohibition signs (Fig. 1), under different deformations. The data base with real road scene examples was used (total of 100 scenes).

Real road scenes:	Precision	Recall
original image from the data base	0.98	0.99
+ additional rotations ±5°, scaling ±5%	0.93	0.98
+ additional rotations ±15°, scaling ±15%	0.92	0.98

The two distance measures CoVar (6) and Census (7) were also compared. There is no evidence of one being superior. Census performs about 20-25% faster, however.

6   Conclusions

The paper presents the system for recognition of the circular road signs. The main advantage of the proposed method is its great versatility in RS recognition under different scales and rotations, as well as variations of illumination, resolution and noise. This high recognition rate was achieved thanks to the joint operations in the Gaussian scale-space and matching in the log-polar space. The search process is twofold. The first search is done at the coarse level of the Gaussian pyramid and its purpose is to select possible places of RS occurrences. To speed up computations this match process is guided by the areas of the red dye, obtained from the segmentation module. Nevertheless, the method can work with the monochrome images with the same recognition accuracy, what was verified experimentally. The search is done in the LP space and with help of two comparison measures. Thanks to this strategy, the patterns different in scale and rotation can be reliably matched. The purpose of the second search run is to verify the already found potential places of RSs. Although it is done at the finest pyramid level (the highest resolution) it is fast because only the interest places are checked.

Unfortunately, due to four dimensional search space, the software implementation of the presented method does not perform in real time. However, if necessary this can be alleviated with the hardware acceleration (or GPUs). Actually this is our next subject of research.

Acknowledgement

This work was supported from the Polish funds for the scientific research in 2007.

References

1. Amit, Y.: 2D Object Detection and Recognition. MIT Press, Cambridge, MA (2002)
2. Aoyagi, Y., Asakura, T.: A study on traffic sign recognition in scene image using genetic algorithms and neural networks in IEEE Conf. Electronics, Control, pp. 1838–1843 (1996)
3. Chen, X., Yang, J., Zhang, J., Waibel, A.: Automatic Detection and Recognition of Signs From Natural Scenes. IEEE Trans. on Image Proc. 13(1), 87–99 (2004)
4. Cyganek, B.: Soft System for Road Sign Detection. Accepted to the IFSA – Theory and Applications of Fuzzy Logic and Soft Computing, Cancun, Mexico, (June 18-21, 2007)
5. Cyganek, B.: Rotation Invariant Recognition of Road Signs with Ensemble of 1-NN Neural Classifiers. In: Kollias, S., Stafylopatis, A., Duch, W., Oja, E. (eds.) ICANN 2006. LNCS, vol. 4132, pp. 558–567. Springer, Heidelberg (2006)
6. Cyganek, B.: Recognition of Road Signs with Mixture of Neural Networks and Arbitration Modules. In: Wang, J., Yi, Z., Zurada, J.M., Lu, B.-L., Yin, H. (eds.) ISNN 2006. LNCS, vol. 3973, pp. 52–57. Springer, Heidelberg (2006)
7. Cyganek, B.: Matching of the Multi-channel Images with Improved Nonparametric Transformations and Weighted Binary Distance. In: Reulke, R., Eckardt, U., Flach, B., Knauer, U., Polthier, K. (eds.) IWCIA 2006. LNCS, vol. 4040, pp. 74–88. Springer, Heidelberg (2006)
8. Cyganek, B.: Hardware-Software System for Acceleration of Image Processing Operations. Accepted to be published in the Machine Graphics & Vision (2007)
9. DaimlerChrysler, The Thinking Vehicle, http://www.daimlerchrysler.com (2002)
10. Escalera, A., Armingol, J.A.: Visual Sign Information Extraction and Identification by Deformable Models. IEEE Tr. On. Int. Transportation Systems 5(2), 57–68 (2004)
11. Forsyth, D., Ponce, J.: Computer Vision. In: A Modern Approach, Prentice-Hall, Englewood Cliffs (2003)
12. Kara, L.B., Stahovich, T.F.: An image-based, trainable symbol recognizer for hand-drawn sketches. Computers & Graphics 29(4), 501–517 (August 2005)
13. Piccioli, G., Micheli, E.D., Parodi, P., Campani, M.: Robust method for road sign detection and recognition. Image and Vision Computing 14, 209–223 (1996)
14. Porikli, F.: Integral Histogram: A FastWay to Extract Histograms in Cartesian Spaces. TR2005-057, Mitsubishi Electric Research Laboratories, Cambridge, MA, USA (2005)
15. Wandell, B.A.: Foundations of Vision. Sinauer Associates Publishers Inc. (1995)
16. Zheng, Y.J., Ritter, W., Janssen, R.: An adaptive system for traffic sign recognition, In: Proc. IEEE Intelligent Vehicles Symp. pp. 165–170 (1994)
17. Zokai, S., Wolberg, G.: Image Registration Using Log-Polar Mappings for Recovery of Large-Scale Similarity. IEEE Transactions on Image Processing, 14(10) (2005) 1422-1433

The Condition of Kernelizing an Algorithm and an Equivalence Between Kernel Methods

WenAn Chen and Hongbin Zhang

College of Computer Science, Beijing Univesity of Technology, Beijing, 100022, China
wenan.chen@gmail.com, zhanghb@bjut.edu.cn

Abstract. For a learning algorithm, especially a linear algorithm, it can usually be extended to its kernel version endowed with the power of extracting non-linear features. In this paper, we explore two key questions in the kernelization of an algorithm. The first is the existence of the kernel version of an algorithm. We propose a new method to determine whether an algorithm can be kernelized. It has the advantage that it is not limited by the specific form of the algorithm and shows an insight view of kernelization. The second question is how to kernelize an algorithm. We prove a kind of equivalence between two kernelization processes. Related details are also discussed.

Keywords: Kernelization, Kernel PCA, Equivalence Relation.

1 Introduction

Kernel methods are studied intensively in the field of pattern recognition and machine learning in recent years [1] [2] [3]. These kernel methods can be viewed as extensions and applications of kernel mapping on existing linear methods, the essential idea applied in Support Vector Machine(SVM) [4]. In addition to SVM, many originally linear algorithms are extended to their corresponding kernel methods, such as Kernel PCA(KPCA) [5], Kernel Fisher Discriminant Analysis(KFDA) [6] [7]. These kernel methods have already shown their merit in dealing with complex data in real world, for example, dealing with classification problems with nonlinear separating surfaces. In this paper, we explore two key questions in the kernelization of an algorithm. That is, for a learning algorithm, whether this algorithm can be kernelized and how it is kernelized to its kernel version. Although there are already several instances of kernel methods [5] [8] [9], they all require the knowledge of inner processing of the specific algorithms to extend them to corresponding kernel versions. In this paper we tackle these questions in kernelization in a more general way which can be applied to any algorithm. The result is that the kernelization of an algorithm is just a modification of the input of the algorithm, without changing the inner processing.

J. Martí et al. (Eds.): IbPRIA 2007, Part I, LNCS 4477, pp. 338–345, 2007.

2   Related Work

After KPCA is proposed as a nonlinear variant of classical algorithm PCA[5], other variants of classical algorithms are also proposed [6] [7]. In [5], two nonlinear variants of algorithms, ICA and k-means clustering, are also constructed. These nonlinear variants are regarded as kernel methods because of their nonlinear construction through kernel mapping. All these kernelizations of classical algorithms embed kernel functions into the original algorithms utilizing the fact that these algorithms actually require only dot products of input data for computing. Since many algorithms are not expressed explicitly dependent on dot products of input data, determining whether they can be kernelized has to examine the inner processing of algorithms and try to embed kernel functions to explicitly show their solely dependence on inner products in feature space. This kind of determining the capability for kernelization needs many mathematical skills and the way of kernelizing one algorithm can not be extended to other algorithms. In [10], KFDA is implemented in another way by combining KPCA and FDA. This method inspires the new general kernelization process proposed in this paper and it becomes a specific case of our method.

3   Kernelization of Algorithms

First of all, let us explain the concept of kernelization clear here. The kernelization of an algorithm means extending the algorithm to its corresponding kernel version. The process of kernelizing an algorithm is: first, map the data in input space to feature space implicitly through kernel function; second, use original algorithm on the corresponding feature space. Figure 1 shows the processing steps of kernelization. From Figure 1 we can see that the presumption for the algorithm to be kernelized is that it must take the kernel matrix K as input. However, generally the input of an algorithm is usually the processing data in the leftmost part of the figure, which result in modifications of the input interface or inner processing in its kernel version. Besides, this difference of input interface makes it difficult to know whether an algorithm can be expressed in the inner product form showed in Figure 1.

To kernelize an algorithm, the following two questions need to be answered:

– Whether the algorithm can be kernelized.
– How to kernelize the algorithm if it can be kernelized.

4   A New Determining Condition for Kernelization of Algorithms

4.1   Requirements of Kernelization

From the process of kernelization given above, we see that any linear algorithm which can be carried out in terms of dot products can be made nonlinear by substituting a chosen kernel, known as kernel trick[3] [5] [8]. This can be summarized as follows:

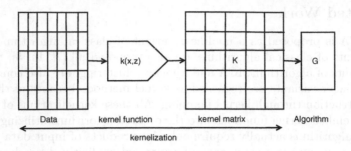

Fig. 1. Kernelization of algorithms

Proposition 1. *Let $x_i, i = 1, \cdots, N$, be inputs of an algorithm, the algorithm can be kernelized if and only if the output of the algorithm depends only on the inner products between inputs $x_i, i = 1, \cdots, N$.*

Proposition 1 is expressed directly according to the process of kernelization described above. Here we give more explanation of its meaning. Let A denote the inner product matrix of input data $x_i, i = 1, \cdots, N$, that is $A_{ij} = \langle x_i, x_j \rangle$. The algorithm with capability to be kernelized does not take $x_i, i = 1, \cdots, N$, but A as input actually. Suppose $\phi(x)$ is the implicit feature mapping function induced by a kernel function $\kappa(x, x')$. Through kernel mapping, input data x_i is mapped to $\phi(x_i)$ implicitly. In the feature space, inner product can be expressed as $K_{ij} = \kappa(x_i, x_j) = \langle \phi(x_i), \phi(x_j) \rangle$. Let G denote the original algorithm capable of being kernelized, G_k denote the algorithm after kernelization. The process of kernelizing an algorithm G is to take the new inner product matrix K in the feature space instead of inner product matrix A in input space as the input of the algorithm G. According to Proposition 1, the input of G is actually the inner product matrix $A = X^T X$ of input data. That is

$$O = G(X^T X), \tag{1}$$

where X is the input matrix with each row as a data point, O denotes the output of the algorithm. The kernelized algorithm G_k and the original algorithm G has the following relation:

$$O_k = G_k(X) = G(K), \tag{2}$$

O_k denotes the output of the algorithm G_k.

Although Proposition 1 can be applied to decide whether an algorithm can be kernelized, it has limitations in practice. It requires that the input of the algorithm is expressed in the explicit form of inner product to show its dependence only on inner products of input data. This is usually not easy to achieve without plenty of mathematical skills.

4.2   Rotation Invariance Is the Condition for Kernelization

The characteristic of the algorithm capable of being kernelized is that its real inputs are inner products of input data. In other words, the output of the algorithm depends only on the inner products of input data. Suppose X is the data matrix stacked by input data with every row as an input data point, then $A = XX^T$ is the inner product matrix for input data. To determine whether an algorithm can be kernelized or not is to find out whether the actual input is A or X. In order to analyze the characteristic of the algorithm that can be kernelized, we consider the different scenario of taking A and X as input respectively.

Denote the eigen-decomposition of A as $A = PDP^T$, where P is the matrix with each column as an eigenvector and D is the diagonal matrix with corresponding eigenvalues. Let $Y = PD^{1/2}$, then Y can be computed from A and it is unique if we fix the order of eigenvalues(it does not loss generality by assuming that eigenvalues are not equal). Since $A = YY^T$, we can think Y is a special input data matrix when actually taking A as input. If for any input data X, we always have $Y = X$, then taking A as input is equivalent to taking X as input, because they can be induced from each other. However it is not true. By studying the relation of Y and X, we find that Y and X are related to each other by a rotation transformation. Specifically, we have the following:

Proposition 2. *Suppose X is a $N \times p$ matrix, N is the number of input data point, p is the dimension of input data. Let $A = XX^T$, the eigen-decomposition of A is $A = PDP^T$ with eigenvalues in descending order in D, and let $Y = PD^{1/2}$. We have:*

If $N \geq p$, then $Y = [XQ, 0]$; If $N \leq p$, then $[Y, 0] = XQ$. Q is an orthogonal matrix satisfying $Q^T Q = I_p$ where I_p is $p \times p$ identity matrix, and 0 represents a zero matrix to fill remaining place to make sure equal dimensions on each side.

This proposition shows that input data X and Y computed from A are basically the same, the difference is a rotation transformation Q, Q is an arbitrary matrix satisfying $Q^T Q = I_p$.[1] This means that for an algorithm with input of matrix A, the implicit original input data can not be determined as a unique input matrix, it is in the set including all of the rotation transformation of Y. Any element in this set can be viewed as an implicit input of the algorithm, because it can result in the same inner product matrix A. In other words, the output of the algorithm capable of being kernelized is rotation invariant. On the other side, when the output of an algorithm is rotation invariant, then the original input X has no difference with input Y computed from A because the output depends on A only, so the outputs are the same and the algorithm can be kernelized. Therefore, we can conclude the requirement of kernelization as follows:

Proposition 3. *An algorithm can be kernelized if and only if the output of the algorithm is invariant on the rotation transformation of the algorithm's input.*

There are some notes we need to make here. The output mentioned in Proposition 3 refers to the final output we are focusing. For example, for Maximum Margin Classifier(MMC), what we are concerned is the final decision values from decision function $f(x) = w^T x + b$, not the inner parameters w, b of the algorithm which may be changed with the rotation transformation of inputs.

---

[1] Mathematically, The orthogonal matrix Q with determinant $detQ = 1$ is a rotation matrix. In this paper, we also include the case $detQ = -1$ as rotation.

4.3   Application of the New Method

In this section, we give several examples to show the effectiveness of the new method. We use the prime form of Maximum Margin Classifier(MMC), whose corresponding kernel method is Support Vector Machine(SVM) [2], to determine whether it can be kernelized directly without transformation to its dual form.

Suppose x_i is transformed to x'_i by a rotation transformation Q, $x'_i = Q^T x, Q^T Q = I$, then the new expression of MMC is:

$$\min_{w',b'} \frac{1}{2} \langle w', w' \rangle, \tag{3}$$
$$s.t. : y_i(w'^T x'_i + b') \geq 1,$$
$$i = 1, \ldots, N.$$

Using $x'_i = Q^T x$, This form is equivalent to the following:

$$\min_{w',b'} \frac{1}{2} \langle w', w' \rangle, \tag{4}$$
$$s.t. : y_i((Qw')^T x_i + b') \geq 1,$$
$$i = 1, \ldots, N.$$

Let $Qw' = w$ and $b' = b$, then we get $w' = Q^T w$, $\langle w', w' \rangle = w^T Q Q^T w = w^T w$. For decision function $f(x) = w^T x + b$ and $f(x') = w'^T x' + b'$, because $x' = Q^T x$, then $f(x') = w^T Q Q^T x + b = w^T x + b$. We get that the two decision function value are the same for the two different inputs. Since the output, here is the decision value, is rotation invariant, applying Proposition 3 we can determine that MMC is able to be kernelized. This kind of rotation invariant makes it easy to determine whether an algorithm can be kernelized, without restrictions on the specific representation form while using Proposition 1.

There are also other examples, such as PCA, LDA. According to Proposition 3, it can be showed that they can be kernelized to Kernel PCA(KPCA) [5], and Kernel Fisher Discriminant Analysis(KFDA)[6] [7] respectively.

5   Kernel Method Can Be Viewed as Original Algorithm Operating on the Nonlinear Principal Components Extracted by Kernel PCA

In this section, we point out an equivalence relation between kernel methods. That is kernel method can be viewed as original algorithm operating on the nonlinear principal components extracted by Kernel PCA. This leads to another kernelization method with the advantage that no modification of the inner processing of the original algorithm is required. First of all, let us review some characteristics of Kernel PCA.

5.1   The Characteristics of Kernel PCA

The objective of Kernel PCA(KPCA) [5] is to perform PCA in the feature space. Because of high-dimension of feature space in most cases, it often requires huge computation cost if we calculate them in feature space directly. For example, there are C_d^{n+d-1} distinct features in feature space for polynomial kernel $\kappa(x, z) = \langle x \cdot z \rangle^d$ corresponding to dimension n in input space. However, through kernel trick, it needs not to compute kernel mapping directly and KPCA can be calculated effectively through kernels. From the calculation of KPCA we can have the following relation:

Proposition 4. *Suppose Y is the nonlinear Principle Components(PCs) with each row as PCs in feature space computed by KPCA from input data matrix X, K is the kernel matrix of input data. Consider all PCs representing the mapped input data in feature space, then the inner product matrix of PCs is K:*

$$Y^T Y = K. \tag{5}$$

5.2   The Equivalence Between the Process of Kernelization of the Algorithm G and the Process of KPCA Plus the Algorithm G

All kernel methods can use the same kernel function to realize implicit feature mapping. This is a common point among kernel methods. Here we show a deeper relation between various kernelization and Kernel PCA, the relation is a kind of equivalence. It can be described as follows:

Theorem 1. *The kernelization of an algorithm G is equivalent to the following process: use KPCA on input data to extract all nonlinear Principal Components(PCs) in feature space, and then let algorithm G take these PCs as input.*

Figure 2 illustrates the computing process of the new process of kernelization. This equivalence establishes a deeper relation between kernel methods, comparing with the obvious relation of kernel methods, say, sharing kernel function and corresponding implicit mapping. The equivalent relation also provides a way to kernelize an algorithm. The advantage of this kind kernelization is that we do

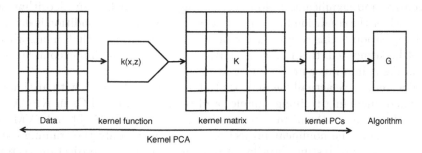

Fig. 2. A new kernelization process

not need to change the original algorithm. The only change is the input of the original algorithm.

Now we prove the equivalence of these two processes. In order to prove the equivalence, we only need to prove the two processes(algorithms) have the same output.

Let G_k denote the kernelization of algorithm G, the process of kernelization is to use the kernel matrix K of input data instead of original inner product matrix A as the real input of algorithm G. The output of this process is displayed in Eq. 2.

Consider the process of KPCA plus algorithm G. After KPCA, the input of algorithm G is the PCs of mapped data in feature space. Because G is able to be kernelized, the output of G depends only on the inner product matrix of input data. So the output of algorithm G taking PCs in feature space as input depends only on the inner product matrix of these PCs. The process can be expressed as follows:

$$Y = KPCA(X) \tag{6}$$

$$O'_k = G(Y^T Y) \tag{7}$$

Here Y is the PCs in feature space. From the relation between PCA and the kernelization of PCA, that is Kernel PCA, we have

$$Y = KPCA(X) = PCA(K). \tag{8}$$

Here K is the kernel matrix of input data matrix X. According to Proposition 4 and Eq. 2, we get:

$$O'_k = G(Y^T Y) = G(K) = O_k. \tag{9}$$

This proved the equivalence between the kernelization of G_k and the process of KPCA+G.

6   Discussion

In this section, we discuss some details and extensions. The new condition proved seems to be naturally derived and easy to understand, however its application is extensive and significant. Before any attempt to kernelize an algorithm, we must consider the condition first. Secondly, although the new condition is derived from Proposition 1, this condition is more convenient to prove that an algorithm can not be kernelized, this is very important when an algorithm is complex and formulating it into inner product format is tricky.

In Theorem 1, we actually assume that all samples to be dealt with are known beforehand, including training samples and testing samples. PCs in KPCA are computed with all of them. In real practice, such as in KPCA [5] and SVM, we usually compute the nonlinear projection vectors using only the training data, and get the PCs of testing data by projecting them to the projection vectors. In this case, similar with the proof given for Theorem 1, we can show that the relation of equivalence is also correct, just needing to show that the inner product matrix of testing data and the training data for the input keeps unchanged.

The key relation of the equivalence stated above can be ascribed to the characteristic of KPCA described in Proposition 4. KPCA forms the new inner product matrix(kernel matrix K), and keep the inner product matrix invariant for the computed PCs in feature space. From the proof of Theorem 1, Y may not be restricted to the matrix of all PCs, it can be arbitrary matrix that satisfies $Y^T Y = K$. The Cholesky factorization of K is probably the fastest one to obtain. One drawback of using this kind of generic kernelization is that they require $O(N^3)$ complexity (both for KPCA and Cholesky), N is the number of training samples[11].

The last to mention is that the algorithm G to be kernelized needs not be linear. It can be nonlinear and the equivalence still holds as long as it depends only on the inner product matrix. This relaxes the constraint of kernel methods which always assumes G a linear algorithm [3].

References

1. Cristianini, N., Shawe-Taylor, J.: An Introduction to Support Vector Machines and Other Kernel-based Learning Methods. Cambridge University Press, Cambridge (2000)
2. Shawe-Taylor, J., Cristianini, N.: Kernel Methods for Pattern Analysis. Cambridge University Press, Cambridge (2004)
3. Schlkopf, B., Smola, A.J.: Learning with Kernels: Support Vector Machines, Regularization, Optimization, and Beyond. The MIT Press, Cambridge (2001)
4. Vapnik, V.N.: The Nature of Statistical Learning Theory, 2nd edn. Springer, Berlin Heidelberg New York (1999)
5. Scholkopf, B., Smola, A., Muller, K.-R.: Nonlinear component analysis as a kernel eigenvalue problem. Neural Computation 10, 1299–1319 (1998)
6. Mika, S., Ratsch, G., Weston, J., Scholkopf, B., Muller, K.: Fisher discriminant analysis with kernels. In: Proceedings of IEEE Neural Networks for Signal Processing Workshop (1999)
7. Baudat, G., Anouar, F.: Generalized discriminant analysis using a kernel approach. Neural Computation 12(10), 2385–2404 (2000)
8. Scholkopf, B., Mika, S.B., Knirsch, C., Miiller, P., Ratsch, K., Smola, G.: Input space vs. feature space in kernel-based methods. IEEE Transactions on Neural Networks 10(5), 1000–1017 (1999)
9. Muller, K.-R., Mika, S., Ratsch, G., Tsuda, K., Scholkopf, B.: An introduction to kernel-based learning algorithms. IEEE Transactions on Neural Networks 12(2), 181–201 (2001)
10. Yang, J., Jin, Z., Yang, J.-Y., Zhang, D., Frangi, A.F.: Essence of kernel fisher discriminant: Kpca plus lda. Pattern Recognition 37(10), 2097–2100 (2004)
11. Personal communication

A Probabilistic Observation Model for Stereo Vision Systems: Application to Particle Filter-Based Mapping and Localization

Francisco Angel Moreno, Jose Luis Blanco, and Javier Gonzalez

System Engineering and Automation Department
University of Malaga, Spain

Abstract. In this paper we propose a probabilistic observation model for stereo vision systems which avoids explicit data association between observations and the map by marginalizing the observation likelihood over all the possible associations. We define observations as sets of landmarks composed of their 3D locations, assumed to be normally distributed, and their SIFT descriptors. Our model has been integrated into a particle filter to test its performance in map building and global localization, as illustrated by experiments with a real robot.

1 Introduction

Due to the rich information cameras provide and their low cost in comparison with traditional robotics sensors, like laser scanners, vision systems have acquired more and more importance in mobile robotics during the last years. In particular, a large number of vision-based localization approaches have been reported in the literature either using single ([2],[3]), stereo ([13],[14]), or omnidirectional [8] cameras. Errors in the formation of the images (e.g. discretization) and in detecting features may lead to large inaccuracies in the robot localization. The resulting uncertainty can be managed by probabilistic Bayesian filters, extensively discussed elsewhere ([12], [16]). The underlying principle of those filters is the Bayes' theorem, which states how to update a prior belief about a variable x given a new observation z and an observation model:

$$\underbrace{p(x|z)}_{\text{posterior}} \propto \underbrace{p(x)}_{\text{prior}} \underbrace{p(z|x)}_{\text{obs. model}}$$

(1)

In mobile robot localization, the filter can be implemented by iteratively executing a prediction and an update step. In the former, the system state (the robot pose) is propagated in time according to an evolution model (the motion model), giving the *prior estimation* of the robot pose. In the second step, the prior is refined according to a given observation model, obtaining the *posterior distribution*.

Two widely extended implementations of Bayesian filters are the Extended Kalman Filter (EKF) [7], and the family of sequential Monte Carlo (SMC) methods (also named *particle filters* (PF)) [1]. EKF has been successfully used in mobile robot localization [4], but it is limited by the assumption of Gaussian models in both, the

J. Martí et al. (Eds.): IbPRIA 2007, Part I, LNCS 4477, pp. 346–353, 2007.

robot pose and the observation model. On the other hand, a PF can cope with complex, even multi-modal distributions, providing a unified method for map building and global localization. Due to these advantages, in this work we focus on observation models for PF. Although an observation model is required in both EKFs and PFs, notice that, in the former, the observation model has a parametrical form whereas in PFs it is necessary only to evaluate it pointwise.

This paper addresses the derivation of a suitable observation model for stereo vision systems. We assume that observations are sets of landmarks defined by their three-dimensional positions and a distinctive feature descriptor. In particular, we use SIFT [9] descriptors due to their invariance to image translation, scaling, and rotation. The main contribution of this work is the avoidance of explicit data association between observations and the map, which is achieved by marginalizing the observation model over all the possible associations. This model has been validated by experiments with a real robot: first a map of the environment has been successfully built applying vision-based SLAM, next, global localization is performed using the so built map.

The rest of this paper is organized as follows. In Section 2, we state the problem and define the involved variables. Section 3 describes our proposal for the observation model, and experimental results are presented in Section 4. Finally, we provide some conclusions and discuss possible future works in Section 5.

2 Problem Statement

2.1 Preliminary Definitions

Let m be the map of the environment, x_t the robot pose, u_t the robot action (which typically consists of odometry readings), and z_t the observation, all of them for the time step t. Then, the recursive Bayesian filter for the robot pose reads [16]:

$$\underbrace{p\left(x_t \mid z_{1:t}, u_{1:t}, m\right)}_{\text{current pose estimation}} \propto \underbrace{p\left(z_t \mid x_t, m\right)}_{\text{observation model}} \int \underbrace{p\left(x_t \mid x_{t-1}, u_t\right)}_{\text{motion model}} \underbrace{p\left(x_{t-1} \mid z_{1:t-1}, u_{1:t-1}, m\right)}_{\text{previous pose estimation}} dx_{t-1} \quad (2)$$

where we have employed the notation $z_{1:t} = \{z_1, \ldots, z_t\}$ for clarity. In this work we define observations z_t and the map m as sets of three-dimensional landmarks:

$$z_t = \left\{z_t^i\right\}_{i=\{1,\ldots,N\}} \quad \text{where } z_t^i = \left\langle \mathbf{X}_t^i, \mathbf{F}_t^i \right\rangle, \quad \mathbf{X}_t^i \sim N\left(\mu_t^i, \Sigma_t^i\right)$$

$$m = \left\{m_j\right\}_{j=\{1,\ldots,M\}} \quad \text{where } m_j = \left\langle \mathbf{X}_m^j, \mathbf{F}_m^j \right\rangle, \quad \mathbf{X}_m^j \sim N\left(\mu_m^j, \Sigma_m^j\right), \quad \mathbf{F}_m^j \sim N\left(\mu_{\mathbf{F}_m^j}, \Sigma_{\mathbf{F}_m^j}\right) \quad (3)$$

Notice that a landmark, either in the map or in an observation, comprises of its 3D location $\mathbf{X}$ (which we assume to be normally distributed), and its associated SIFT descriptor $\mathbf{F}$. For each landmark in the map, the descriptor $\mathbf{F}_m^j$ is also assumed to be normally distributed whereas the descriptor of an observation landmark $\mathbf{F}_t^i$ is just a sample vector. The process for extracting observations from the stereo images is described next.

2.2 Extraction of Reliable Landmarks for Observations

To extract the set of 3D landmarks (i.e. the observation) from a pair of stereo images we need to find feature points in both images, to match them, and to estimate their corresponding 3D locations. Next we describe the whole process in more detail.

Many methods have been proposed in the literature for extracting interest points from images, as the well known detectors of Kitchen & Rosenfeld [8] and Harris [5], based on the first and the second-order derivatives of images, respectively. More recently, the SIFT detector proposed by Lowe [9] deals with the detection process by identifying local extrema in a pyramid of Difference of Gaussians (DoG). It also provides the detected features with a descriptor that exhibits invariance to rotation and scale, and partial invariance to lighting changes and affine distortions. In our work, the detection of interest points in the images is carried out by the method proposed by Shi and Tomasi [15]. In addition, their corresponding SIFT descriptor is also computed to make them sufficiently distinguishable and improve the matching process robustness.

Once a set of keypoints has been detected in each image they are robustly matched according to both the similarity of their descriptors and the restriction imposed by the epipolar geometry. More precisely, in the former restriction, for each keypoint in the left image, it is computed the Euclidean distance between its descriptor and those of the keypoints in the right image. For a pair of keypoints to be considered as a candidate match, the minimum distance must be below a fixed threshold and the second lowest distance must be sufficiently apart from the minimum (see Fig. 1(b)). Moreover, the points must fulfill the epipolar constraint: they have to lay on the conjugate epipolar lines. In a stereo vision system with parallel optical axis as the one shown in Fig. 1(a), epipolar lines are parallel and horizontal, thus, the epipolar constraint reduces to checking that both features are in the same row.

Once matching have been robustly established, it is straightforward to estimate the most likely 3D coordinates of the landmark by using well-known methods [6],[14]. However, we also consider here the uncertainty in the 3D landmark position due to errors in the image quantization and in feature detection methods. Assuming a stereo system with parallel optical axes and a pinhole camera model (see Fig. 1(a)), the 3D coordinates (X, Y, Z) of a landmark can be computed from two matched points in the left and right images as [14]:

$$X = (c - c_0)\,b/\!d \quad Y = (r - r_0)\,b/\!d \quad Z = f\,b/\!d \tag{4}$$

where (r_0, c_0) are the coordinates of the reference image centre, (r, c) are the coordinates of the keypoint in the reference image (say, the left one), b is the baseline, d is the disparity, and f is the focal length of both cameras (please, refer to Fig. 1(a)).

The errors in obtaining the variables r, c, and d, are usually modelled as uncorrelated zero-mean Gaussian random variables [10]. Using a first-order error propagation to approximate the distribution of the variables in (4) as multivariate Gaussians, we obtain the following covariance matrix:

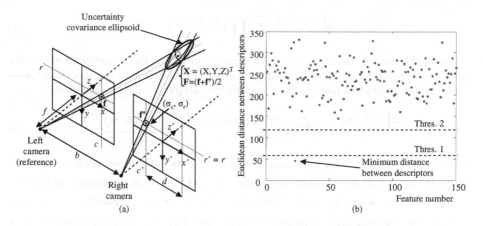

Fig. 1. (a) Configuration of a stereo vision system and schematic representation of uncertainty in the localization of the 3D landmarks. (b) Euclidean distance between the descriptors of a feature in the left image and all the features in the right one.

$$\Sigma = \mathbf{J}\, diag\left(\sigma_c^2, \sigma_r^2, \sigma_d^2\right)\mathbf{J}^{\mathrm{T}} \tag{5}$$

where $\mathbf{J}$ stands for the Jacobian matrix of the functions in (4), and $\sigma_X^2, \sigma_Y^2, \sigma_Z^2, \sigma_c^2, \sigma_r^2$, and σ_d^2 are the variances of the corresponding variables. Expanding (5) we come to the following expression for Σ:

$$\Sigma = \begin{pmatrix} \sigma_X^2 & \sigma_{XY} & \sigma_{XZ} \\ \sigma_{XY} & \sigma_Y^2 & \sigma_{YZ} \\ \sigma_{XZ} & \sigma_{YZ} & \sigma_Z^2 \end{pmatrix} = \begin{pmatrix} \dfrac{b^2\sigma_c^2}{d^2} + \dfrac{b^2(c-c_0)^2\sigma_d^2}{d^4} & \dfrac{(c-c_0)b^2\sigma_d^2(r-r_0)}{d^4} & \dfrac{(c-c_0)b^2\sigma_d^2 f}{d^4} \\ \dfrac{(c-c_0)b^2\sigma_d^2(r-r_0)}{d^4} & \dfrac{b^2\sigma_r^2}{d^2} + \dfrac{b^2(r-r_0)^2\sigma_d^2}{d^4} & \dfrac{(r-r_0)b^2\sigma_d^2 f}{d^4} \\ \dfrac{(c-c_0)b^2\sigma_d^2 f}{d^4} & \dfrac{(r-r_0)b^2\sigma_d^2 f}{d^4} & \dfrac{f^2 b^2\sigma_d^2}{d^4} \end{pmatrix} \tag{6}$$

which approximately models the uncertainty in the coordinates of landmarks computed from the noisy measurements of a stereo system. Finally, each landmark is assigned a SIFT descriptor which is simply computed as the mean value of the descriptors from each image ($\mathbf{F} = (\mathbf{f}+\mathbf{f'})/2$).

3 The Proposed Observation Model for Stereo Vision

In the following we introduce our proposal for the probabilistic observation model $p\left(z_t \mid x_t, m\right)$, which models the likelihood of an observation at time t, given the robot pose (x_t) and a map (m). Firstly, assuming conditional independency between the errors in the detection of the individual landmarks z_t^i, the likelihood function can be factorized as follows:

$$p(z_t|x_t,m) \overset{\text{cond.ind}}{=} \prod_i p(z_t^i|x_t,m) \tag{7}$$

To avoid explicit data association between landmarks in the observation and in the map, we apply next the law of total probability to marginalize out the observation likelihood of individual landmarks by considering all the possible associations:

$$p(z_t^i|x_t,m) = \sum_{j=\{1,\ldots,M,\phi\}} p(z_t^i|x_t,m,c_i=j) \underbrace{P(c_i=j|x_t,m)}_{\eta} \tag{8}$$

where c_i is an unknown discrete variable that represents the correspondence of the i-th observed landmark. Its possible values are $\{1,\ldots,M\}$ for map landmarks, or ϕ for no correspondence with the map. Notice that the *a priori* probability of a given correspondence with the j-th landmark in the map, $P(c_i=j|x_t,m)$, is constant since the actual observation z_t^i is not taken into account. Assuming the same probability for all the possible correspondences, including the null one, we have:

$$p(z_t^i|x_t,m) = \eta \sum_{j=\{1,\ldots,M,\phi\}} p(z_t^i|x_t,m,c_i=j) \tag{9}$$

Next, if we expand the likelihood term conditioned to a given correspondence according to the definitions in (3), we obtain:

$$p(z_t^i|x_t,m_j,c_i=j) = p\left(\underbrace{\mathbf{X}_t^i,\mathbf{F}_t^i}_{z_t^i} \middle| x_t, \underbrace{\mathbf{X}_m^j,\mathbf{F}_m^j}_{m_j}, c_i=j\right)$$
$$\overset{\text{cond.ind}}{=} \underbrace{p(\mathbf{X}_t^i|x_t,\mathbf{X}_m^j,c_i=j)}_{\text{Localization term}} \underbrace{p(\mathbf{F}_t^i|x_t,\mathbf{F}_m^j,c_i=j)}_{\text{Descriptor term}}, \tag{10}$$

Here we have assumed conditional independence between the errors in localization and the descriptor of landmarks, which seems a plausible approximation. The descriptor term is easily computed by evaluating the probability density function associated to $\mathbf{F}_m^j$ at the vector $\mathbf{F}_t^i$. Regarding the localization term, we approximate it by the probability density of the pair of landmarks to coincide in the 3D space:

$$p(\mathbf{X}_t^i|x_t,\mathbf{X}_m^j,c_i=j) = \int_{\mathbf{X}\in\mathbb{R}^3} p_{\mathbf{X}_m^j}(\mathbf{X}) p_{\mathbf{X}_t^i}(\mathbf{X}) d\mathbf{X} \equiv I \tag{11}$$

where $p_{\mathbf{X}_m^j}(\mathbf{X})$ and $p_{\mathbf{X}_t^i}(\mathbf{X})$ are the distributions of the random variables $\mathbf{X}_m^j$ and $\mathbf{X}_t^i$, respectively. Since both distributions are Gaussian their product is also a Gaussian and hence the integral I in (11) has a closed-form solution:

$$I = \left(2\pi|\Sigma_m^j + \Sigma_t^i|\right)^{-\frac{1}{2}} \exp\left\{-\frac{1}{2}\left(\mu_m^j - \mu_t^i\right)^{\mathrm{T}} \left(\Sigma_m^j + \Sigma_t^i\right)^{-1} \left(\mu_m^j - \mu_t^i\right)\right\} \tag{12}$$

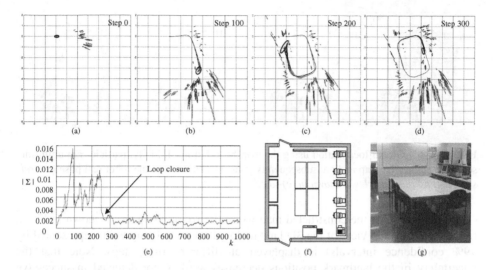

Fig. 2. Map building with a Rao-Blackwellised Particle Filter. (a)-(d) Map representation at different time steps. (e) Value of the covariance matrix determinant through time. (f) Plan and (g) a picture of the environment.

4 Experimental Results

Our proposed observation model has been tested within a particle filter framework for both Simultaneous Localization and Mapping (SLAM) and global localization. In robotics, particle filters represent the distribution of the robot pose by a set of samples which are propagated through the robot motion model and subsequently weighted according to the observation model. In the following experiments we additionally fit the particle set with a Gaussian to easily measure the degree of uncertainty in the robot pose estimation.

For the experiments, our Sancho mobile robot, equipped with a BumbleBee stereo vision system [18] (with a baseline of 11.9 cm and 2 mm of focal length), was manually driven following a circular trajectory of about 40 m inside one of our laboratories while taking images with the stereo camera at 3Hz (up to a grand total of 1000 stereo images). In the feature extraction process, it has been assumed that errors in the variables r, c and d have a variance of 1 pixel. A complete video showing the evolution of both experiments can be downloaded in [17].

4.1 Map Building

The sequence of stereo images is firstly used to build a map of the environment through a Rao-Blackwellised Particle Filter (RBPF). RBPFs are efficient solutions to the SLAM problem where each particle carries a hypothesis of the whole robot path and the associated map [16].

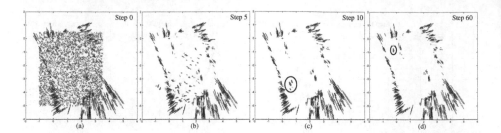

Fig. 3. (a)-(d) Global localization using the map built before. Initially, particles are uniformly scattered across the map and are subsequently concentrated around the robot real pose (*a circle surrounding the particles is shown in (c)-(d)*).

The evolution of the constructed map while the robot navigates is shown in Fig. 2 (a)-(d), where a top view of the 3D landmarks of the map being built (represented by 99% confidence intervals) is displayed at different time steps. Note that the uncertainty in the landmark positions decreases as they are detected in successive observations. Moreover, the covariance of the particles grows during the experiment since only new landmarks are being added to the map, until the point where the robot reaches an already navigated position, which is called the *loop closure*. Then, the estimation of the robot position is improved and particles converge towards the real robot location. This occurs in some point between Fig. 2 (c) and (d), and its effects in the uncertainty can be seen through the evolution of the determinant of the covariance matrix (Fig. 2 (e)). For this experiment, a sample size of 50 particles has been sufficient to yield a correct estimation of the map. The relatively small sample set is the reason of the noisy appearance of the fitted covariance in Fig. 2(e).

4.2 Global Localization

In this experiment we deal with the global localization problem. We take the map associated to the particle with the highest weight from the previous experiment as the map of the environment. Initially, a set of 3000 particles is uniformly distributed over the whole map (see Fig. 3 (a)) and, as the filter processes observations, they tend to converge towards the robot actual location (Fig. 3 (b)-(d)). Notice that in the early iterations particles are scattered over multiple possible positions since the available information is not enough to unambiguously localize the robot.

5 Conclusions

In this paper we have introduced a novel observation model for stereo vision systems suitable for particle filters, which considers observations as sets of landmarks determined by their 3D positions and their SIFT descriptors. As an important contribution, we avoid explicit data association by marginalizing out the observation likelihood over all the possible associations. Matching features in stereo image pairs is robustly solved by checking simple restrictions regarding their descriptors and epipolar geometry. The model takes into account the uncertainty both in the localization of landmarks and in their feature descriptors.

Two experiments have been performed in order to validate our proposal in the context of map building and global localization. The experimental results illustrate its adequate performance when coping with both problems and reveal the proposed observation model as a promising approach for stereo vision in robotics.

References

1. Arulampalam, M.S., Maskell, S., Gordon, N., Clapp, T.: A tutorial on particle filters for online nonlinear/non-Gaussian Bayesian tracking. IEEE Transactions on Signal Processing 50, 174–188 (2002)
2. Davison, A.J.: Real-Time Simultaneous Localisation and Mapping with a Single Camera. In: Proc. International Conference on Computer Vision, vol. 2, pp. 1403–1410 (2003)
3. Davison, A.J., Cid, Y.G., Kita, N.: Real-Time 3D SLAM with Wide-Angle Vision. In: 5th Symposium on Intelligent Autonomous Vehicles. Lisbon Portugal (2004)
4. Dissanayake, M.W.M.G., Newman, P., Clark, S., Durrant-Whyte, H.F., Csorba, M.: A solution to the simultaneous localization and map building (SLAM) problem. IEEE Transactions on Robotics and Automation 17, 229–241 (2001)
5. Harris, C.J., Stephens, M.: A combined edge and corner detector. In: Proceedings of 4th Alvey Vision Conference, Manchester, pp.147–151 (1988)
6. Hartley, R., Zisserman, A.: Multiple View Geometry in Computer Vision, 2nd edn. Cambridge University Press, Cambridge (2003)
7. Julier, S.J., Uhlmann, J.K.: A New Extension of the Kalman Filter to Nonlinear Systems. Int. Symp. Aerospace/Defense Sensing, Simul. and Controls. Orlando (1997)
8. Kitchen, L., Rosenfeld, A.: Gray-level corner detection. Pattern Recognition Letters 1, 95–102 (1982)
9. Lowe, D.G.: Distinctive image features from scale-invariant keypoints. International Journal of Computer Vision 60(2), 91–110 (2004)
10. Matthies, L., Shafer, S.A.: Error modeling in Stereo Navigation. IEEE Journal of Robotics and Automation, vol. RA-3(3) (1987)
11. Menegatti, E., Pretto, A., Scarpa, A., Pagello, E.: Omnidirectional Vision Scan Matching for Robot Localization in Dynamic Environments. IEEE Trans. on Robotics 22(3), 523–535 (2006)
12. Montemerlo, M.: FastSLAM: A Factored Solution to the Simultaneous Localization and Mapping Problem With Unknown Data Association. PhD Thesis (2003)
13. Saeedi, P., Lawrence, P.D., Lowe, D.G.: Vision-Based 3-D Trajectory Tracking for Unknown Environments. IEEE Transactions on Robotics 22(1), 119–136 (2006)
14. Se, S., Lowe, D., Little, J.: Local and Global Localization for Mobile Robots using Visual Landmarks. In: Proc. International Conference on Intelligent Robots and Systems, pp. 414–420 (2001)
15. Shi, J., Tomasi, C.: Good features to track. In: Proc. Computer Vision and Pattern Recognition, pp. 593–600 (1994)
16. Thrun, S., Burgard, W., Fox, D.: Probabilistic Robotics. MIT Press, Cambridge (2006)
17. Website: http://www.isa.uma.es/C6/SLAM/default.aspx
18. Website: http://www.ptgrey.com

New Neighborhood Based Classification Rules for Metric Spaces and Their Use in Ensemble Classification

Jose-Norberto Mazón, Luisa Micó, and Francisco Moreno-Seco

Departamento de Lenguajes y Sistemas Informáticos
Universidad de Alicante
P.O. box 99, E-03080 Alicante, Spain
{jnmazon,mico,paco}@dlsi.ua.es
http://www.dlsi.ua.es

Abstract. The k-nearest-neighbor rule is a well known pattern recognition technique with very good results in a great variety of real classification tasks. Based on the neighborhood concept, several classification rules have been proposed to reduce the error rate of the k-nearest-neighbor rule (or its time requirements). In this work, two new geometrical neighborhoods are defined and the classification rules derived from them are used in several real data classification tasks. Also, some voting ensembles of classifiers based on these new rules have been tested and compared.

1 Introduction

Several scientific fields like pattern recognition, information retrieval, or data mining frequently use the same techniques for different purposes. For example, the k-Nearest Neighbor rule (k-NN) is often used in pattern recognition [1] for classification tasks. Also, the k-NN is used to obtain high performance data mining [2] [3], or efficient similarity retrieval of information [4].

Given a set T of n points that are labelled with J different labels $(\omega_1, \ldots, \omega_J)$, and given an unlabelled sample x, the k-NN rule R assigns to the sample x the most frequent label among the k points closest to x, i.e., if $K_i(x)$ is the number of points that are labelled with ω_i among the k nearest points to x, this rule can be defined as:

$$R(x) = \omega_i \quad \text{if} \quad K_i(x) = \max_{c=1 \ldots J} \{K_c(x)\}$$

From a theoretical point of view, the k-NN rule error rate is low (and bounded by as much as twice the Bayes error), and usually the classification time of a k-NN based classifier is small (by using a fast k-NN search algorithm). However, in real data tasks the behavior of the k-NN rule is not usually as good. In the last years, a number of alternative neighborhood definitions have been proposed in the literature in order to reduce the error rate of the k-NN rule, or to speed up the classification [5,6]. Some of the new alternative rules to reduce the error rate are based on the use of the Gabriel and the Relative Neighborhood graphs [7]. There

J. Martí et al. (Eds.): IbPRIA 2007, Part I, LNCS 4477, pp. 354–361, 2007.

are also some surrounding rules, as the k Nearest Centroid Neighborhood rule, k-NCN, that classifies the sample using the neighbors whose centroid (mean) is closest to the sample. This rule looks for points that are not only close enough but also symmetrically distributed around a sample [5].

The k-NCN rule has been shown to give significantly better results than the classical k-NN approach in many real data tasks. However, this rule cannot be used in the general case, where objects are represented by data structures such as strings. For example, in the k-means clustering algorithm, the median[1] can be used instead of the mean when strings are used and the number of strings belonging to a cluster is high enough [2]. However, in the k-NCN rule the mean is computed for a relatively small number of points (between 1 and k, with $k << n$). In this case, the use of the median instead of the mean is a wrong option.

In this paper some alternatives to the k-NN and k-NCN rules have been defined, compared and tested experimentally with a database where the objects are represented as strings. The edit distance between strings [8] has been used to compare the objects. The proposed classification rules (based on new neighborhood definitions) are suitable for any classification task where a dissimilarity measure is defined. As a complement to this work, some classifier ensembles (some of them based on the rules proposed) have been tested.

In the following section, two different alternatives to the k-NN rule based on the concept of surrounding neighborhood are presented. Section 3 describes the different ensemble schemes for combining classifiers. Next, the results for the proposed classifiers and ensembles are presented and compared in real data tasks. Finally, the conclusions drawn from the results are discussed, pointing the research to further work lines.

2   New Geometrical Neighborhood Definitions for Metric Spaces

The k-NN rule uses the neighborhood defined by the k closest points to an unlabelled sample to classify it. The k-NCN rule defines the neighborhood using the k neighbors whose mean is closest to the sample. Thus, a neighborhood definition has a corresponding classification rule that classifies the sample using the points belonging to the neighborhood. In this section, we propose two alternative neighborhood definitions based on the same type of information used in k-NCN rule: the distances and the geometrical distribution of points. The neighborhood definitions are proposed to overcome the problem of the representation of data in non vectorial spaces (i.e., metric spaces in general), that is, to select the surrounding points without computing the mean.

---

[1] Given a set of n points and a distance function, the median is defined as the point in the set that minimizes the sum of distances to the remaining points in the set.

[2] As the number of points increases, the diference between the median and the mean decreases.

---

1. The first neighbor of x is also its nearest neighbor, q_1.
2. To obtain the $i <= k$ point:
   (a) among the unselected points, the k' nearest neighbors to x are obtained;
   (b) among these k' points, the one whose sum of distances to the previously selected $i - 1$ points is maximum is selected as a new neighbor, q_i
3. return to step 2 (increasing i) until k points are selected

---

Fig. 1. k-MMS neighborhood

Given a set T of points, two different approaches have been defined. Both are incremental methods that use a new parameter (k', with $k' : 1 \dots k$); each new k_i surrounding point to a test sample x is selected in two steps:

1. a set $B \subset T$ with the k' nearest points to x is obtained;
2. k_i is selected among the points belonging to B.

2.1 k-Min Max Sum (k-MMS) Neighborhood

In a neighborhood based classifier, the unlabelled sample x is classified using k neighbors that should be very close to x. However, in a surrounding neighborhood definition, each of the k neighbors should be far away from the previously selected neighbors, while at the same time they should be close to the sample.

The first surrounding neighborhood definition (see figure 1) is based on the incremental selection of the k nearest surrounding points using the ideas mentioned above. This rule is called k-*MinMaxSum* because the points whose sum of distances is maximum among the k' nearest points (minimum distance) to the sample are selected as new candidates to belong to the neighborhood.

2.2 k-Min Ranking Sum (k-MRS) Neighborhood

In the second neighborhood definition, two vectors are used to store the $k' < k$ nearest points to the sample x (see figure 2):

1. K_{min} stores the k' points in increasing value of the distances to the sample x
2. K_{max} stores the points in decreasing value of the sum of distances to the previously selected points.

Then, the prototype whose sum of indexes in both vectors is minimum is selected to be included in the neighborhood. For example, if $K_{min} = \{k_1, k_2, k_3, k_4\}$ and $K_{max} = \{k_3, k_1, k_4, k_2\}$, the first selected point would be k_1, the second k_3, etc.

3   Combining Schemes

In order to increase the performance of single classifiers, a combination may be used instead [9]. In this paper, some known alternatives have been explored based on confidence methods and ranked voting methods using the proposed rules.

1. The first neighbor of x is also its nearest neighbor, q_1.
2. To obtain the $i <= k$ point:
   (a) the k' nearest neighbors to x are selected and ordered by their distances from the test sample (the nearest the first), K_{min};
   (b) the same selected k' points are ordered by the sum of distances to the previously selected $i - 1$ points (the largest the first), K_{max};
   (c) the point whose sum of its indexes in both vectors is the lower, is selected as new neighbor, q_i.
3. return to step 2 (increasing i) until k points are selected

Fig. 2. k-MRS neighborhood

Confidence Voting Approaches. Confidence methods are based on the use of the confidence of classifiers about their preference for a candidate. In this case, a confidence value 1 means the higher preference in the decision. This preference is put into practice by assigning a confidence value to every possible class for each point. A wide range of different confidence methods can be used, based on distances or probabilities.

The confidence methods associated to each class c_i used in k selected points are defined to obtain a value in the range $[0, 1]$. If m_i is the number of neighbors among the selected k that belong to the class c_i ($m_i \leq k$):

$$conf(c_i)_{PROP} = \frac{m_i}{k}$$

$$conf(c_i)_{SD} = \frac{1}{1+\sum_{j=1}^{m_i} d_j/m_i}$$

where $\sum_{j=1}^{m_i} d_j$ is the sum of distances of the m_i neighbors belonging to the class c_i among the k selected neighbors.

Based on these definitions of confidence, three well known ensembles have been used in this work:

1. Pandemonium. Each single classifier gives a confidence value for each class. Then, the class whith the highest confidence value among the single classifiers is returned [10,11].

2. Sum rule. As in the previous method, each classifier assigns a confidence value to each class. All confidence values associated to each class are added, and the class whose sum of confidences is the highest is assigned to the sample [13].

3. Product rule. Unlike the sum rule, in this case confidence values associated to each class are multiplied [13].

Ranked Voting Methods. In these approaches, single classifiers have to give a preference ranking of the class assigned to each point.

4. Borda count. This method was originally developed by Jean-Charles de Borda [12]. It has been adapted to classification problems in [11]. The only prerequisite is that each single classifier must return a complete preference ranking list of the possible classes. Then, the class with minor mean rank among all single classifiers is returned.

4   Experiments

Some experiments have been developed in order to study the performance of the new rules and the performance of the voting schemes presented in the previous section.

4.1   Neighborhood Based Rules

The experiments consist on a human chromosome classification task, where the objects (chromosomes) are represented as strings.

The Chromosome database [14,15,16] used for experiments contains 4400 samples (22 classes with 200 samples per class) coded as strings. The Levenshtein distance [8] has been used to measure the distance between chromosomes. The whole set has been divided into two sets of 2200 samples each, and the experiments have been performed using one of them for training and the other one for test. In a first experiment, the training set has been used to build training sets of different sizes. Table 1 shows the error rates for the proposed rules and the k-NN rule when different training set sizes have been used. This experiment was performed using different values of k, from 1 to 15. Due to the lack of space, only results for $k = 11$ are presented. After some tests, the value of k' used in k-MMS and k-MRS methods was set to 3 for all the experiments.

These experiments show that the k-MMS and k-MRS rules obtain results very similar to those of the k-NN rule. In particular, the k-MMS rule and the k-MRS rules outperform slightly the k-NN rule when the training set is not very small. Though the improvements are not very important, it can be observed that for increasing sizes of the training set, even if the error rate decreases quickly with the size of the training set, the proposed rules reduce the error rate.

In the following experiment, a fixed training set size was used (2200 chromosomes) for different k-values in the classifiers that use the rules (see table 2). As the previous experiment, the proposed rules reduce (slightly) the error rate.

4.2   Ensemble Classification

The combinations tested were:

- two combinations of 2 classifiers: k-NN and k-MMS rules (C1), and k-NN and k-MRS rules (C2)
- two combinations of 6 classifiers: 3 k-NN and 3 k-MMS rules (C3), and 3 k-NN and 3 k-MRS rules (C4) (varying the value of k).

Table 1. Error rates (in %) of the different classification rules with the Chromosome data sets using different training set sizes

Training set size	k-NN	k-MMS	k-MRS
220	37.81	39.18	**37.50**
660	20.40	20.40	**20.13**
1100	11.90	13.09	**11.54**
1540	8.27	8.31	**8.18**
1980	6.77	**6.40**	6.72
2200	6.59	**6.18**	6.27

Table 2. Error rates (in %) of the different classification rules with the Chromosome data sets using different values of k for a fixed training set size of 2200 chromosomes

k	k-NN	k-MMS	k-MRS
1	10.09	10.09	10.09
3	8.23	9.59	**8.13**
5	6.90	7.40	**6.72**
7	6.68	7.40	**6.54**
9	6.77	7.00	**6.54**
11	6.59	**6.18**	6.27
13	6.45	6.09	**6.00**
15	6.68	**6.27**	6.36

Table 3 shows the results of these experiments using the confidence voting approaches $conf(c_i)_{PROP}$ and $conf(c_i)_{SD}$. As the best results were obtained by the C1 and C3 combinations, the experiments with the confidence $conf(c_i)_{SD}$ were only developed for these two combinations.

Finally, an experiment using C1 and C3 (with the sum rule and the confidence method $conf(c_i)_{SD}$) has been performed using different sizes of the training set. The comparison with k-NN is presented in figure 3. This figure shows that better results can be obtained in general for different training set sizes, but the best results are achieved when the training set is small.

Table 3. Error rates (in %) of the different ensembles with the Chromosome data sets using the confidence voting method $conf_{PROP}$ and $conf_{SD}$

	$C1_{PROP}$	$C2_{PROP}$	$C3_{PROP}$	$C4_{PROP}$	$C1_{SD}$	$C3_{SD}$
Pandemonium	6.18	6.31	6.09	6.18	8.13	6.18
Sum rule	5.90	6.27	5.50	5.86	6.68	**5.36**
Product rule	5.95	6.27	8.13	8.45	6.63	8.00
Borda count	6.81	6.45	6.27	6.50	6.82	6.27
k-NN	6.59					

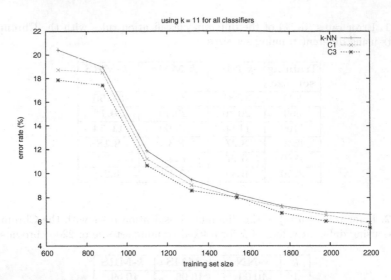

Fig. 3. Error rates (in %) of the different ensembles with the Chromosome data sets using different sizes of the training set and the confidence method $conf_{SD}$.

5 Conclusions

The k-NN rule is often used in classification tasks. However, sometimes the results may be improved if another neighborhood definition is used instead, as for instance the k-NCN rule. The main drawback of this rule is that it requires a vector space representation of data. In this work, two alternative neighborhood definitions that do not require a vector space are presented and the corresponding classification rules are tested in a real data task. The experimental results with the Chromosome database show that the proposed rules outperform the k-NN rule.

Moreover, the experiments with several ensembles of classifiers show that the proposed classification rules may perform adequately in a combination scheme. Future work includes a more exhaustive study of the rules with other real data tasks to know better their possibilities.

Acknowledgements

This work has been supported in part by grants DPI2006-15542-C04-01 and TIN2006-14932-C02 from the Spanish CICYT (Ministerio de Ciencia y Tecnología), GV06/166 from Generalitat Valenciana, and the IST Programme of the European Community, under the Pascal Network of Excellence, IST-2002-506778.

References

1. Duda, R., Hart, P., Stork, D.: Pattern Classification, 2nd edn. Wiley, Chichester (2001)
2. Bohm, C., Krebs, F.: High performance data mining using the nearest neighbor join. Second IEEE International Conference on Data Mining, pp. 43–50 (2002)

3. Dasarathy, B.V.: Data mining tasks and methods: Classification: nearest-neighbor approaches. In: Handbook of data mining and knowledge discovery, pp. 288–298. Oxford University Press, Oxford (2002)
4. Katayama, N., Satoh, S.: Distinctiveness-Sensitive Nearest-Neighbor search for efficient similarity retrieval of multimedia information. In: Proceedings of the 17th International Conference on Data Engineering, pp. 493–502 (2001)
5. Sanchez, J.S., Pla, F., Ferri, F.J.: On the use of neighbourhood-based nonparametric classifiers. Pattern Recognition Letters 18, 1179–1186 (1997)
6. Moreno-Seco, F., Micó, L., Oncina, J.: Extending fast nearest neighbour search algorithms for approximate k-NN classification. In: Perales, F.J., Campilho, A., Pérez, N., Sanfeliu, A. (eds.) IbPRIA 2003. LNCS, vol. 2652, pp. 589–597. Springer, Heidelberg (2003)
7. Jamonczyk, J.W., Toussaint, G.T.: Relative neighbourhood graphs and their relatives. In: Proceedings IEEE, vol. 80, pp. 1502–1517 (1992)
8. Wagner, R.A., Fischer, M.J.: The String-to-String Correction Problem. Journal of the Association for Computing Machinery 21(1), 168–173 (1974)
9. Kuncheva, L.: Combining Pattern Classifiers: Methods and Algorithms. Wiley InterScience, Chichester (2004)
10. Selfridge, O.: Pandemonium: a paradigm for learning in mechanisation of thought processes. In: Proceedings of a Symposium Held at the National Physical Laboratory, pp. 513–526 (1958)
11. Van Erp, M., Vuurpijl, L.G., Schomaker, L.R.B.: An overview and comparison of voting methods for pattern recognition. In: Proceedings of the 8th International Workshop on Frontiers in Handwriting Recognition pp. 195–200 (2002)
12. Borda, J.-C.d.: Memoire sur les Elections au Scrutin. Histoire de l'Academie Royale des Sciences, Paris (1781)
13. Duin, R.: A theoretical study of six classifier fusion strategies. IEEE Transactions on Pattern Analysis and Machine Intelligence 24(2), 281–286 (2002)
14. Lundsteen, C., Phillip, J., Granum, E.: Quantitative analysis of 6985 digitized trypsin G-banded human metaphase chromosomes. Clinical Genetics 18, 355–370 (1980)
15. Granum, E., Thomason, M.G., Gregor, J.: On the use of automatically inferred Markov networks for chromosome analysis. In: Lundsteen, C., Piper, J. (eds.) Automation of Cytogenetics, pp. 233–251. Springer, Heidelberg (1989)
16. Granum, E., Thomason, M.G.: Automatically inferred Markov network models for classification of chromosomal band pattern structures. Cytometry 11, 26–39 (1990)

Classification of Voltage Sags Based on MPCA Models

Abbas Khosravi, Joaquim Melendez, and Joan Colomer

eXit Group, Dept. of Electronics, Informatics & Automatics
Institute of Informatics and Applications, University of Girona
{khosravi,quimmel,colomer@eia.udg.es}

Abstract. In this paper, we introduce a new framework for classification of short duration voltage reductions in the area of Power Quality Monitoring using Multiway Principal Component Analysis (MPCA). Firstly, we recast the sags occurred in High Voltage (HV) and Medium Voltage (MV) lines in a format which is suitable for MPCA. Then, MPCA technique is employed for building statistical models for classification of sags originated in HV and MV networks and recorded in the same substation. Projecting sags registered in different substations to MPCA models of other substations has been also explored to deduce similarities and dissimilarities between different substations according to the sags registered in them.

1 Introduction

Power quality is an important research area dedicated to analyze variations in the nominal values of electric waveforms known as disturbances. The goal is not only to monitor those disturbances but also to characterize them, deduce the causes and location of its origin in order to improve the knowledge related to the power system. Power quality affects any deviation in the voltage, current, or frequency and the importance of them is due to the effects that can produce to customer equipment [1]. Independently, of why (due to external agents, electrical facility operation, the operation of specific loads) and where (HV or MV) those alterations happen, they directly affect the power quality delivered to customers. Often the distribution companies are named responsible for the possible damages to the public/domestic electrical equipments, while the source of sag might be found in transmission network (HV). Based on this scenario, utility companies are highly interested for developing reliable methods which can discriminate between sags originated in the transmission (HV) or in the distribution (MV) system. With such an aim this work has been focused on finding statistical patterns to represent HV and MV sags and exploit them to recognize new sags as member of one or other class.

In the last decades, making a decision about an occurred fault registered in a substation has been done based on sags coordination charts [2]. Recently, great deals of effort were devoted to the utilization of different classifiers used in pattern recognition methods for deciding about the type of the sag. Many promising applications of neural networks, fuzzy inference systems, and wavelet transformation have been reported in the recent years [3] [4] [5] [6] [7]. A common drawback of these methods is the fact that they often try to find to some extent sophisticated and

J. Martí et al. (Eds.): IbPRIA 2007, Part I, LNCS 4477, pp. 362–369, 2007.

sometimes meaningless features from the crude data to use them for classification. Plus this, in some cases, complexity of the method makes its practical implementation restricted.

The purpose of this paper is introducing a new classification framework in the area of power quality which is simple, understandable, and quick. We hire MPCA as a powerful method for classification of electrical sags. The novelty of this research work relies in two parts: Firstly, recasting and modeling the occurred sags, second using MPCA model for discernment between HV and MV sags.

Following the introduction, paper proceeds as follows: Section 2 interprets the problem and research goals. Section 3 concisely clarifies Principal Component Analysis (PCA) and MPCA methods. The proposed method will be elucidated in section 4 which will be the main body of the paper. The capability of the proposed method will be tested using HV and MV sags registered in some substation in section 5. A conclusion and some points about the future works will end the paper.

2 Problem Interpretation and Purposes

A voltage disturbance is registered as *sag* whenever the voltage drops and stays between 90% and 10% of its nominal value for less than 1 sec. Duration of sags directly depends on reaction time of protective system to recover the network to its normal behavior or duration of the transient faults. No matter where the sags happen, in transmission or distribution network, their occurrence is sensed in term of a vigorous or gradual damage to electrical domestic facilities.

The main purpose of this paper is focusing on classification of occurred sags in HV and MV classes based on the information contained in the registered waveforms, of three voltages and currents, in substations after the detection of the sag. Also, as a subordinate objective, we will try to explore and point out principal similarities and dissimilarities between different substations according to the obtained models for each substation. Indeed, different substations are working in different voltage levels and supporting diverse loads. We expect that these differences will be reflected in the built models.

3 Fundamental of PCA and MPCA

3.1 PCA

PCA is an unsupervised, nonparametric approach for finding the most relevant informative features in data. As a promising result of linear algebra, PCA has been diversely used in different forms of data analysis: image processing, biology, meteorology, and so forth. The reason for so much striking applications of PCA relies on the fact that it provides a simple but quite efficient way for reducing the dimension of datasets. Often some variables are highly correlated such that the information contained in one variable is largely a duplication of the information contained in another variable. PCA guarantees that in the dimension reduction procedure the minimum information is lost. After throwing away those redundant variables, it re-express the data in using some new variables named principal components.

Generally, PCA has been developed based on Singular Value Decomposition (SVD) of the covariance matrix of a data set, X. To have a convention about our presentation, let's consider that $X \in R^{m \times n}$ and its rows and columns correspond to samples (time histories) and measurements (variables) respectively. After auto-scaling columns of X (zero mean and unit variance), the sample-covariance matrix is computed as follows [8] [9]

$$C = \frac{X^T X}{m-1}. \tag{1}$$

Then the data are projected to a new space

$$X = \sum_{i=1}^{r} t_i \cdot p_i^t + E \tag{2}$$

where t_i and p_i are named scores and loading vectors respectively. t_i reflects relevant relation amongst samples, while p_i highlights the correlation among variables. p_i vectors are eigenvectors of covariance matrix, C,

$$C p_i = \lambda_i p_i. \tag{3}$$

In (2), $r \leq \min(m, n)$ realizing the concept of dimension reduction. PCA assumes that the eigenvectors with bigger eigenvalues are the best ones for expressing the data upon [8]. According to this condition, we keep those eigenvectors which capture the majority of the variation and throw away others as meaningless variation caused by noise, E (residual matrix) in (2).

The first r principal components build up a new space/model with a lower dimension than the original one. Projection of the data to the i-th axis in this new space can be done using the following linear transformation

$$t_i = X p_i \tag{4}$$

where $i = 1, \cdots, r$.

The lack of model fit can be measured using two statistical criteria named Q-residual and T^2. Multivariate control charts based on T^2 can be plotted as follows:

$$T^2 = \sum_{j=1}^{r} \frac{t_j^2}{S_{t_j}^2} \tag{5}$$

where $S_{t_j}^2$ is the estimated variance of t_j. This control chart will only detect variation in the plane of the first r principal components. When a new type of special event occurs which was not present in the in-control data used to build the PCA model, the new observations will move off the plane. This type of event can be detected by computing the Q-statistic or Squared Prediction Error (SPE) of the residual for new observations. It is defined as:

$$Q_x = \sum_{j=1}^{r} (xj - \hat{x}_{j,new})$$ (6)

where $\hat{x}_{j,new}$ is computed from the reference PCA model. Normally, Q-statistic is much more sensitive than T^2. It's due to the fact that Q is very small and therefore any minor change in the system characteristics will be observable. T^2 has a great variance and therefore requires a great change in the system characteristic for it to be detectable. More information about this can be found in [8] or other references about PCA [9] [10].

3.2 MPCA

As a promising extension of PCA, Multiway PCA (MPCA) not only finds and captures the correlation between variables and their time histories, but also does the same task over the data gathered from different runs of a system/plant [8] [10].

Fig.1 presents a three-dimensional matrix containing information of variables (J) and their time histories (K) for different runs of a system (I). If we decompose this data set as shown in this figure, we obtain a $I \times KJ$ two-dimensional matrix which can be used by PCA.

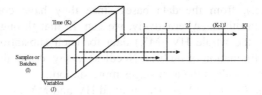

Fig. 1. Unfolding the three-dimensional matrix of data

Like (2), matrix X is projected to a new space as follows

$$X = \sum_{r} t_r \otimes P_r + E$$ (7)

This decomposition optimally separates data into meaningful and noise (residual) parts. The concepts of scores and loading in MPCA are a bit more sophisticated than PCA. Variation in the i-th run with respect to other runs over the entire history of the run is summarized in the i-th element of each score vector. Likewise, the loadings sum up the time variation of the measured variables about their average trajectories (data are auto-scaled) [8]. More points about different methods of decomposition as well as more mathematical discussion can be found in [8].

4 Proposed Method

The proposed method includes two main parts: first preparation of the data, and second building MPCA models and projection of data over them. Next is the explanation of those stages in detail:

- I- *Preprocessing*: rms values for three voltages and three currents are calculated (number of variables J=6) for HV and MV data sets (See Fig.2). FFT (Fast Fourier Transfom) in a one period sliding window is used to estimate the magnitude of nominal frequency (50 Hz) during the sag and from it the rms value has been calculated. Waveforms have been sampled at 6400 Hz resulting 128 samples per period (20 msec.). The number of periods is 39 which gives K=4993 samples.
- II- *Dataset Organization*: A three dimensional matrix is built using HV and MV rms values of each substation ($X_{I \times J \times K}$) where I stands for the number of sags in each substation. The original dataset also contains information about the origin of these sags and have been labeled as MV or HV to identify downstream or upstream origin of disturbances.
- III- *Recasting and Autoscaling*: Three voltages and three currents are put consecutively constituting a waveform which contains all information of a sag. After unfolding the data set like Fig. 1, since the magnitudes of voltages and currents are different (Fig. 2), autoscaling is done in each column.
- IV- *Removing Outliers*: Visual inspection of rms values for different sags suggests that we remove some registers of different disturbances (interruptions, over-voltages, etc.), from the data bases since they have completely different behavior from others. Alternatively, we can do that through building MPCA model using the whole HV (MV) data for each substation and using Q-T^2 criteria for elimination of outliers. Needless to say, doing this stage makes the MPCA models built in the next stages more smooth.
- V- *Training and Test Data Sets*: The cleaned HV and MV data sets are randomly split into two subsets: training (75%) and test (25%) subsets built according to the cross validation methodology and using 4 folds for this purpose. Thus, four test sets (each time 25% of data) and four training sets (the remained data) have been used for building and testing models.
- VI- *Building MPCA Models*: HV (MV) training sets are used for building MPCA models of the respective class.
- VII- *Projection*: HV and MV data sets are projected to HV and MV MPCA models in different substations. Since we have four test data sets in each substation, we do projection four times (cross validation).
- VIII- *Classification*: Classification then is done based on T^2-Q criteria or just based on one of them.

It is possible to add some stages after stage VI in order to obtain a better classification rate or make it more practical.

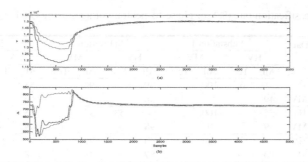

Fig. 2. rms values for three voltages and currents during the occurrence of a HV sag

5 Numerical Results

In this section, we employ the designed method to the real data gathered from three substations in Catalonia in Spain. According to the available information, HV and MV sags have been occurred at different hours of a day or night in different seasons during one year. So, we can conclude that they properly cover different types of faults and well reflect the network behavior after their occurrence.

In the data bases, phase-to-phase and phase-to-neutral voltage waveforms are available. We use both waveforms for building MPCA models and we will compare the results of classification in each method.

A typical HV sag has been presented in Fig. 2. As is shown in this figure, rms value of each phase falls down after occurrence of the fault. Then after a short time, the protective system revitalizes the network and rms values come up to their normal magnitude.

For building MPCA models we first make the data auto-scaled and then use 10 principle components in order to capture a high rate of variation of the sags. After building HV and MV MPCA models, data are projected to these models and Q and T^2 are calculated for each projection to have a measure of fit. The classification rate can be obtained using T^2, Q, or their combination. Our experience showed that classification rates are quite poor using T^2 criterion alone. In contrast, Q and Q-T^2 criteria accomplish this task much better as shown in Tables 1 and 2. Each table shows classification rates for using both Q criterion and Q-T^2 criteria. The vertical axis of tables presents HV and MV MPCA models for each substation, while HV and MV data sets are along the horizontal axis. In the projection stage, if the data type (HV/MV) and model type (HV/MV) of a substation are the same, we just project the test data set; otherwise the whole data set is projected.

As an important point, Table 1 suggests that T^2 is an irrelevant index in classification of electrical sags since the results with or without its contribution are exactly the same. The same scenario can be explored in Table 2 highlighting rightness of this claim.

Also, we can roughly, not exactly, conclude that that phase-to-phase waveforms have better and more discriminating information of HV and MV sags in comparison to phase-to-neutral ones. Higher classification rates in Table 2 endorse this idea.

Table 1. Classification rate (%) for phase-to-neutral voltages using Q and Q-T^2 criteria

MPCA Model	Data	Substation 1				Substation 2				Substation 3			
		HV		MV		HV		MV		HV		MV	
		All	Test	All	Test	All	Test	All	Test	All	Test	All	Test
Substation 1	HV	-	60	100	-	39	-	96	-	53	-	100	-
	MV	49	-	-	48	56	-	0	-	66	-	6	-
Substation 2	HV	34	-	100	-	-	53	97	-	25	-	100	-
	MV	99	-	0	-	98	-	-	17	99	-	0	-
Substation 3	HV	43	-	100	-	33	-	97	-	-	57	100	-
	MV	86	-	1	-	87	-	0	-	78	-	-	29

Table 2. Classification rate (%) for phase-to-phase voltages using Q criterion

MPCA Model	Data	Substation 1				Substation 2				Substation 3			
		HV		MV		HV		MV		HV		MV	
		All	Test	All	Test	All	Test	All	Test	All	Test	All	Test
Substation 1	HV	-	62	99	-	49	-	95	-	58	-	98	-
	MV	50	-	-	65	75	-	60	-	63	-	53	-
Substation 2	HV	29	-	100	-	-	53	99	-	31	-	100	-
	MV	88	-	3	-	90	-	-	41	86	-	5	-
Substation 3	HV	48	-	100	-	37	-	97	-	-	69	100	-
	MV	60	-	12	-	73	-	40	-	57	-	-	61

Apart from the point that we made above, the followings are also noteworthy:

- If the MPCA model is HV and a MV data set is projected to it, no matter which methods we use, the classification rate is approximately perfect.
- The classification rates for test sets are not much satisfactory. We could reason for such a phenomenon based on small number of sags available in data sets. Logically, the higher the number of sags, the more reliable the classification rates. As an endorsing evidence we can observe classification rates for bigger data sets are better (substation 3 has the maximum numbers of HV (64) and MV sags (38)).
- The classification rate for projection of HV (MV) data set of a substation to HV (MV) MPCA models of other substations some times are quite small while we expect that they should be higher. It implicitly points out correlations between HV (MV) waveforms of those substations are negligible. Different loads or measuring standards and equipments stations could cause such a difference.
- More attention on selecting the number of principle components could raise the rates of discrimination. It's true that choosing it higher might lead to a better performance for the opposite data sets, but, regrettably, at the same time it has a negative impression on classification rate of similar data bases to the model type. Trade-off between these opposite objectives can enhance the results for both cases.

In a nutshell, we are exploring the possibility of working with all the information contained in the waveforms without resorting to preprocessing approaches which are computationally expensive. Put in other way, what we are looking for is the benefits of using a reduction technique to manage original waveforms and obtaining a few number of relevant parameters, e.g. 10 instead of 6×4993, without using additional knowledge of the system.

6 Conclusion and Future Works

In this paper we present a method for localization of occurred voltage drops in power networks using MPCA technique. Three voltages and currents were skillfully recast in a format useable by MPCA. It was showed that Q-T^2 criterion partly well separates sags in two classes. Redundancy of T^2 criterion for classification was proven through obtained results. Also, we concluded that phase-to-phase waveforms contain better explanatory information for classification of sags into two HV and MV classes.

As a very interesting research line for improving results, we will move toward using Kernel MPCA to avoid the drawback of MPCA as a linear method. Also, in this paper, we just used traditional criteria for separation between projected data while implementation of other methods such the k-nearest neighbors or Fisher Discriminant Analysis can enhance the results. These two lines will be addressed in future works.

Acknowledgment. This work has been partially supported by the projects Diagnostico de Redes de Distribución Eléctrica Basado en Casos y Modelos -DPI2006-09370- and PTR1995-1020-0P (coparticipated by the utility ENDESA DISTRIBUCION under contract with the University of Girona) from the research and transfer programs, respectively, of the Spanish Government.

References

1. Leon, C., Lopez, A., Montano, J.C., Monedero, I.: Classification of Disturbances in Electrical Signals Using Neural Networks. In: Mira, J.M., Prieto, A.G. (eds.) IWANN 2001. LNCS, vol. 2085, pp. 728–737. Springer, Heidelberg (2001)
2. Bollen, M.H.J.: Understanding Power Quality problems. IEEE Press, New York (2000)
3. Dash, P.K., Salama, M.M.A., Mishra, S.: Classification of power system disturbances using a fuzzy expert system and a Fourier linear combiner. IEEE Trans. Power Delivery 15, 472–477 (2000)
4. Poisson, O., Rional, P., Meunier, M.: Detection and measurement of power quality disturbances using wavelets transform, IEEE Tran. on Power Delivery, vol. 15(3), (2000)
5. Gaing, Z.-L.: Wavelet-based neural network for power quality disturbance recognition and classification, IEEE Tran. on Power Delivery, vol. 19(4) (2004)
6. Zhu, T.X., Tso, S.K., Lo, K.L.: Wavelet-based fuzzy reasoning approach to power-quality disturbance recognition, IEEE Tran. on Power Delivery, vol.19(4) (2004)
7. Silva, K.M., Souza, B.A., Brito, N.S.D.: Fault Detection and Classification in Transmission Lines Based on Wavelet Transform and ANN, IEEE Tran. on Power Delivery, vol. 21(4), pp. 2058–2063 (2006)
8. Wise, B.M., Gallagher, N.B.: The process chemometrics approach to process monitoring and fault detection. J. Proc. Cont. 6(6), 329–348 (1996)
9. Russell, E.L., Chiang, L.H., Braatz, R.D.: Data-Driven Methods for Fault Detection and Diagnosis in Chemical Processes, London. Springer-Verlog, Berlin Heidelberg New York (2000)
10. Yoon, S., MacGregor, J.F.: Statistical and causal model-based approaches to fault detection and isolation. AIChE Journal 46, 1813–1824 (2000)

On-Line Handwriting Recognition System for Tamil Handwritten Characters*

Alejandro H. Toselli[1], Moisés Pastor[2], and Enrique Vidal[2]

[1] Institut Tecnològic d'Informàtica
[2] Departament de Sistemes Informàtics i Computació
Universitat Politècnica de València
Camí de Vera s/n, 46071 - València, Spain
{ahector,moises,evidal}@iti.upv.es

Abstract. We describe the recognition system we used for the "On-Line Tamil Handwritten Character Recognition Competition", hosted by the "International Workshop on Frontiers in Handwriting Recognition". The system is based on continuous density *Hidden Markov Models* and characterized by feature extraction based on time and frequency-domain features. In that contest we have obtained the third best score in character classification accuracy.

1 Introduction

In occasion of the "On-Line Tamil Handwritten Character Recognition Competition[1]" hosted by the "International Workshop on Frontiers in Handwriting Recognition", we implemented and presented an on-line handwriting recognition system, which obtained the third best score in character recognition accuracy.

The objective of the competition was to recognize 156 different classes of handwritten Tamil isolated characters. The competition organizers supplied a corpus of these online characters, each one represented by a finite sequence of points (x_t, y_t) ordered in time. This representative sequence o points is also arranged into a series of consecutive strokes (called pen-down strokes), that is, clumps of point sequences acquired with the digital pen touching the pad surface.

Following the currently most accepted standard approach for on-line handwritten text recognition, our system is based on Hidden Markov Models (HMMs) (see por example [1,2,3]). The 156 Indian character classes are modelled by continuous left-to-right HMMs, representing each character class instance as a sequence of real-valued feature vectors.

In this context, two keys factors were important to increase its classification accuracy. One was the selection of features to represent adequately each character instance. The other was tuning one of the most critical HMM parameters, i.e. setting the appropriate number of states for each HMM character class.

---

* This work has been partially supported by the Spanish project iDoc TIN2006-15694-C02-01 and by *Consellería d'Empresa, Universitat i Ciència - Generalitat Valenciana* under contract GV06/252.

[1] http://algoval.essex.ac.uk:8080/iwfhr2006/index.jsp

J. Martí et al. (Eds.): IbPRIA 2007, Part I, LNCS 4477, pp. 370–377, 2007.
© Springer-Verlag Berlin Heidelberg 2007

In the next two sections preprocessing and feature extraction are described. Section 4 considers the models which the system is based on. Experimental results are presented in section 5 and conclusions are drawn in the final section.

2   Preprocessing

The preprocessing of each sample involves four steps: repeated points elimination, noise reduction, writing speed normalization and size normalization.

Noise in handwritten strokes is due to erratic hand motions and inaccuracy of the digitalization process. In order to reduce it, we employ a smoothing technique consisting on replacing every point (x_t, y_t) in the trajectory by the mean value of its neighbors [4].

The goal of speed normalization is to achieve an independence from the writing speed. This is implicitly carried out by *first derivatives normalization* in the feature extraction phase (see section 3.1), which has probed to lead to better results than using *trace segmentation* technique, that is, making equidistant the points along each stroke [5,6]. Finally size-normalization was performed by re-scaling the points sequence (x_t, y_t) to a fixed range, preserving the original aspect-ratio of the character sample.

It is important to remark that the temporal order of the data points is preserved throughout all preprocessing steps.

3   Feature Extraction

Once the original coordinate sequence of each sample has been preprocessed, it is transformed into new a temporal sequence of 15-dimensional real-valued feature vectors. These features can be classified into two different groups. The seven first are time-domain features; namely, point locations, first and second time derivatives and curvature. The remaining eight features are extracted in the frequency domain. The four lowest frequency Fourier coefficients (each composed by a real and an imaginary part) are computed and included in the feature set. All these features are explained in the following subsections.

3.1   Time-Based Feature Extraction

Normalized Horizontal and Vertical Position: the coordinate pairs of each sample are scaled and translated to obtain new pair values (x_t, y_t), so that y_t is in the range $[0, 100]$, and the original aspect-ratio of the sample is preserved (see figure 1).

Normalized First Derivatives: x'_t and y'_t are calculated using the method given in [7]:

$$x'_t = \frac{1}{||\Delta||} \cdot \frac{\sum_{i=1}^{r} i \cdot (x_{t+i} - x_{t-i})}{2 \cdot \sum_{i=1}^{r} i^2} \qquad y'_t = \frac{1}{||\Delta||} \cdot \frac{\sum_{i=1}^{r} i \cdot (y_{t+i} - y_{t-i})}{2 \cdot \sum_{i=1}^{r} i^2} \qquad (1)$$

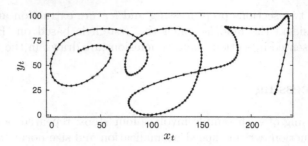

Fig. 1. Size-normalized Tamil character stroke with $y_t \in [0, 100]$

where $||\Delta|| = \sqrt{x_t'^2 + y_t'^2}$ and r defines a window size which determines the number of neighbor points involved in the computation. For our purposes, setting up this range to 2 has provided satisfactory results.

Since these derivatives are normalized (their modules are constant), they do not give any information about the speed at which the strokes were drawn, but they explain the speed of direction change along the character stroke.

Using the normalized first derivatives, is possible to rebuild the point sequence, but only with similar shape as that of the original character strokes. This can be performed by an integration operation (in this case, approximated by a sum) of x_t' and y_t', as shown in the figure 2.

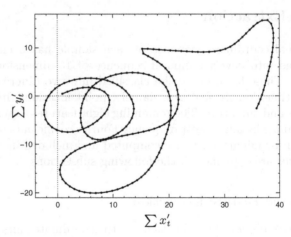

Fig. 2. Approximated Tamil character reconstruction using first derivatives incremental sum

Second derivatives: x_t'' and y_t'' are computed in the same way as the first derivatives, but using x_t' and y_t' instead of x_t and y_t.

These features give information about the acceleration of *curve* strokes tracing. Thanks to the normalization, x_t' and y_t' do not change along the *straight* strokes, so their respective second derivatives are zero.

Curvature: k_t, is the inverse of the radius of the curve in each point. It is calculated as:

$$k_t = \frac{x_t' \cdot y_t'' - x_t'' \cdot y_t'}{\left(x_t'^2 + y_t'^2\right)^{3/2}} \tag{2}$$

Although this feature is directly determined by the other four (first and second derivatives), it provides direct information about shapes and has experimentally proven to help in the recognition process.

3.2   Frequency-Based Feature Extraction

On-line handwriting can also be represented as a function $f_t : t \rightarrow (x_t + iy_t) \in \mathbb{C}$, $t = 0..N-1$. Then, its *Discrete Fourier Transform* (DFT) F_n is given by:

$$F_n = \sum_{t=0}^{N-1} f_t\, e^{-2\pi i \frac{tn}{N}} \tag{3}$$

where N is the total number of points of a generic stroke segment and also the total number of Fourier coefficients associated with f_t.

The eight frequency-domain features we have adopted are computed in a similar way as it is done in speech recognition systems, i.e. using a Hamming sliding-window running along the whole character stroke. This Hamming sliding-window (H) of size ω is defined by:

$$H_t = 0.54 - 0.46 \cdot \cos\left(\frac{\pi \cdot t}{\omega}\right) \tag{4}$$

At each point t, the DFT (3) is computed from the result of modulating the original point sequence by the Hamming window centered at t (this process is generally referred to as *"short-time Fourier Transform"*). Optimal values for the sliding-window size ω and for the number of considered Fourier coefficients were empirically determined: $\omega=40$ and the four lowest frequency Fourier components (excluding F_0). These four Fourier coefficients, each of them involving a real and a imaginary parts (8 values in total), are added to the set of seven former features.

As an illustration of this process, figure 3 shows a set of successively extracted segments (left column) from the Tamil character of the figure 1. The middle column shows the truncated power spectra obtained for each segment (5 coefficients). Using these truncated spectra, the original segments can be approximately reconstructed by means of the inverse DFT.

Figure 4 shows an approximated reconstruction of the whole character stroke through an assembling of the later regenerated parts (F_0 coefficients give the relative positions among them).

4   Recognition Module

The on-line handwritten recognition system used here accepts as input a time ordered sequence of data points and outputs a character class hypothesis. Three

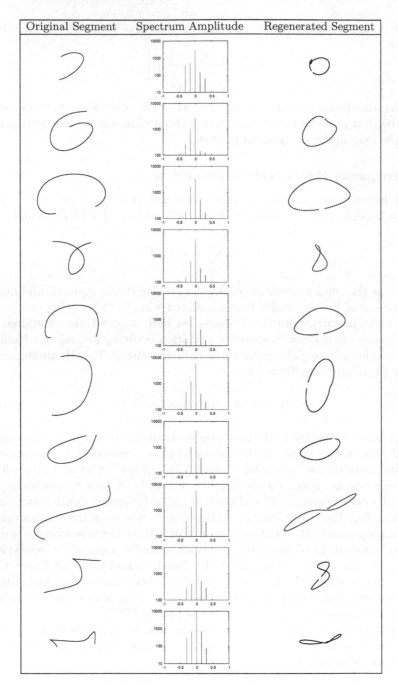

| Original Segment | Spectrum Amplitude | Regenerated Segment |

Fig. 3. Left: Tamil character stroke segments obtained from figure 1, using a rectangular sliding-windows of 40 points of size and a moving-step of 20 points (implying 20 points of overlapping window). **Middle**: power spectrum plots considering the 4 lowest Fourier coefficients (F_0 is also included here). **Right**: constructed stroke segments using the inverse DFT with the 5 considered Fourier coefficients.

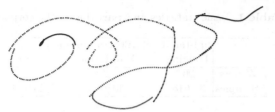

Fig. 4. Regenerated segments assembling taken out (from each of them) the 10 first and last points corresponding to the overlapping window regions

different modules take part in this system: preprocessing, feature extraction and recognizer module. The two first have been explained in the later sections.

The recognition module is based on continuous density Hidden Markov Models (HMMs [1]). A HMM is a stochastic finite-state device used to estimate the probability of a sequence of feature vectors, which characterize the stroke time evolution of a given handwritten character. Thereby each character class is modeled by a continuous left-to-right HMM. It is assumed that each HMM state generates feature vectors following an adequate parametric probabilistic law; typically, a *mixture of Gaussian densities*. The adequate number of densities in the mixture per state, as well as the number of HMM states, need to be tuned empirically and the optimal values may be conditioned by the available amount of training data.

Once an HMM *topology* (number of states, transitions between them and number of densities per state) has been adopted, the model parameters can be easily trained from samples of handwritten characters. This training process is carried out using a well known instance of the EM algorithm called *Baum-Welch re-estimation* [8].

The recognition of an unknown sequence of feature vectors $\mathbf{x}=\{x_0 \ldots x_{N-1}\}$, $x_i \in \mathbb{R}^{15}$ is formulated as the problem of finding a HMM character class $\hat{c}$, that maximizes the class-posterior probability, .i.e.,

$$\hat{c} = \arg\max_{c \in C} p(\mathbf{x}|c, \theta) P(c) \tag{5}$$

Where C is the number of character classes, θ is the trained set of HMM parameters and $P(c)$ is the a-priori probability of the character class c. The optimization problem (5) can be solved using the well known *Viterbi* algorithm [8].

5   Experimental Results

The target of the competition was to recognize 156 different classes of handwritten Tamil characters. The competition organizers had provided two corpora: the labeled "`hpl-tamil-iwfhr06-train-online`" for training/validation purposes and the unlabeled "`hpl-tamil-iwfhr06-test-online`" for the final test[2]. The criterion for evaluation was the highest top-choice accuracy at zero reject rate.

---

[2] It was used only once, to estimate the real error rate of the system.

Table 1. Basic statistics and partition of the corpora

	hpl-tamil-iwfhr06-train-online		Test
	Training	Validation	Test
#Writers	90	27	–
#Samples	39,618	11,065	26,926

The corpora were preprocessed using the preprocessing and feature extraction modules described in sections 2 and 3. The "hpl-tamil-iwfhr06-train-online" corpus was partitioned into a training set with $39,618$ samples and a validation set with $11,065$ samples. Table 1 shows the used partition of the resulting corpora.

As discussed in section 4, there are two basic design parameters characterizing continuous density left-to-right HMMs: the number of (diagonal) Gaussian densities assigned to each state mixture and the number of states for each character HMM. Tested values for the number of densities were $1, 2, 4, 8, 16, 32, 64$. On the other hand, the number of states s_c chosen for each HMM character class M_c ($c = 1, \ldots, 156$) was computed as $s_c = l_c/k$, where l_c is the average length of the sequences of feature vectors used to train M_i, and k is a design parameter measuring the average number of feature vectors modelled per state (*state load*). This rule of setting up s_c tries to balance modelling effort across states and, for our task, has greatly improved the classification accuracy. In the experiments reported here, tested values for k were 15, 13, 10, 7, 6, 5, 4 and 2, obtaining the best classification results for $k = 4$.

Table 2. Classification error rate (%) for different number of Gaussian densities (in the mixture) per HMM state, and different types and combination of feature extractions: TFE (time-based feature extraction) and FFC (Fourier coefficients). The final test classification error rate was obtained by the Tamil competition organizers.

	Validation			Final Test
#Gauss	TFE	FFC	TFE+FFC	TFE+FFC
1	12.7	19.6	12.4	–
2	12.2	15.4	11.1	–
4	12.1	14.2	10.5	–
8	12.0	13.6	10.3	–
16	11.6	13.1	10.0	**9.3**
32	11.6	13.5	10.2	–
64	11.7	13.9	10.4	–

Table 2 gives the best classification results obtained with the validation partition. The best result is 10.0% classification error rate for 16 Gaussian densities. The final test was carried out on the test corpus (hpl-tamil-iwfhr06-test-online) with the optimized parameter values obtained in the validation phase. The final classification error score obtained by the Tamil competition organizers was 9.3%, which corresponds to the third position in the ranked list of competition results.

6 Remarks and Final Conclusions

The on-line handwriting recognition system we have used for the "On-Line Tamil Handwritten Character Recognition Competition" has been presented.

Initially seventeen participant recognition systems took place in the contest. The final rank list of classification error rates [9], ranges from 33.8% (the worst) to 6.5% (the best). As was seen in section 5, the final classification result of our system is around to 9% of error rate, which is ranked in third position. The system which obtained the best classification result scoring (6.5%) was based on neural networks and employed both online and the off-line types of features extraction. Instead the second best (8.8%), was based on a nearest neighbor classifier which employed a Dynamic Time Warping as distance measure (kNN-DTW).

The computational cost of HMM based classification is well known to be typically much less expensive than that based on kNN-DTW. That is because kNN-DTW cost depends, among other things, linearly on the number of prototypes (usually the whole training set), whereas HMMs depend in this way on the overall number of Gaussians, which is typically much smaller. It is difficult to compare these costs with that of the contest winner system, because of the lack of information that was published about that system [9].

References

1. Rabiner, L.: A Tutorial of Hidden Markov Models and Selected Application in Speech Recognition. In: Proc. IEEE. vol. 77, pp. 257–286 (1989)
2. Shu, H.: A On-line Handwriting Recognition Using Hidden Markov Models. Master's thesis, Massachusetts Institute of Technology (1996)
3. Kosmala, A., Rottland, J., Rigoll, G.: Improved On-Line Handwriting Recognition Using Context Dependent Hidden Markov Models. In: Proc. of the 4th International Conference Document Analysis and Recognition (ICDAR '97), Ulm, GERMANY, pp. 641–644 (1997)
4. Jaeger, S., Manke, S., Reichert, J., Waibel, A.: On-Line Handwriting Recognition: The NPen++ Recognizer. International Journal on Document Analysis and Recognition 3(3), 169–181 (2001)
5. Pastor, M., Toselli, A.H., Vidal, E.: Writing Speed Normalization for On-Line Handwritten Text Recognition. In: Proc. of the Eighth International Conference on Document Analysis and Recognition (ICDAR '05), Seoul, Korea, pp. 1131–1135 (2005)
6. Vuori, V., Laaksonen, J., Oja, E., Kangas, J.: Speeding Up On-line Recognition of Handwritten Characters by Pruning the Prototype Set. In: Proc. of the Sixth International Conference on Document Analysis and Recognition (ICDAR '01), Seattle, Washington, pp. 0501–0507 (2001)
7. Young, S., Odell, J., Ollason, D., Valtchev, V., Woodland, P.: The HTK Book: Hidden Markov Models Toolkit vol. 2(1), Cambridge Research Laboratory Ltd (1997)
8. Jelinek, F.: Statistical Methods for Speech Recognition. MIT Press, Cambridge (1998)
9. Madhvanath, S., Lucas, S.M.: IWFHR 2006 Online Tamil Handwritten Character Recognition Competition. In: Suvisoft LTD., (ed.). Proccedings of the Tenth International Workshop on Frontiers in Handwriting Recognition, La Baule (France), pp. 239–242 (2006)

A New Type of Feature – Loose N-Gram Feature in Text Categorization

Xian Zhang[1] and Xiaoyan Zhu[2]

[1] Department of Computer Science and Technology, Tsinghua University
Beijing 100084, China
vivian@tsinghua.org.cn
[2] Department of Computer Science and Technology, Tsinghua University
Beijing 100084, China
zxy-dcs@tsinghua.edu.cn

Abstract. This paper introduces a new type of feature in text categorization. Based on an interesting linguistic observation, Loose N-gram feature, defined as co-occurring words within limited range, is quite different from traditional features, such as words, phrases or n-grams. Not only retaining useful context information, this kind of feature also has considerable classification ability. The features generated by our algorithm have acceptable statistical characteristics, thus can effectively avoid the sparseness problem. Experiment results show that the Loose N-gram feature is helpful and promising in statistical text categorization systems, especially for the categorization tasks which rely on more semantic information. Our new type of feature could also be helpful in Information Retrieval research.

1 Introduction

Text Categorization (TC) is an important task in content-based document management. Many statistical classification methods and machine learning techniques have been applied to text categorization in recent years [9, 13]. Most of current TC approaches are based on Vector Space Model. As one of the key factors of the categorization task, features reflect the category information of documents efficiently [14].

In TC approaches, to which category a document is assigned greatly depends on the statistics of words in the document. Such a model has been proved to be simple and effective for processing some corpora. However, it can hardly work for complex corpra, as reported by many researchers [1, 4]. It is natural that the word feature with no context information has limitations in dealing with TC task which sometimes could only be done under the help of some deep semantic knowledge.

To overcome this problem, in recent years, many researchers have focused on various types of feature that can retain certain amount of context information. N-grams (mainly bi-grams), phrases, and consequent character strings, which intuitively contain more context information than single words, are used to help form the feature set. Aizawa selected appropriate Compound Words as features [1]. Bi-grams features are used in [12] by Tan to improve TC performance. Cohen and Singer used Sparse

J. Martí et al. (Eds.): IbPRIA 2007, Part I, LNCS 4477, pp. 378–385, 2007.

Phrases in their sleeping expert methods, which allowed small holes within limited length of ordered words [4]. Lodhi even tried to use character strings instead of words to build string kernels for an SVM classifier in [6]. Some researcher attempted to use other learning methods to improve TC performance [8]. Many approaches give positive results on various text data sets compared with original "Bag of Words" system.

However, those features still have some problems such as ultra high dimensional vector space, sparseness problem and knowledge redundancy. Many researchers have reported that longer features, other than word features, do more harm than good in TC [2]. The new feature is just the simple combination of single words, thus carries much redundant information with the original word features. This would certainly downgrade the merit of the context information.

In order to solve above problems, a new type of feature, *Loose N-gram feature*, is proposed in this paper. It is a group of unordered words co-occurring within a limited scope to fix in the sparseness problem. A seed-based generation algorithm is designed to effectively control the feature set size. The algorithm guarantees that new feature has good discrimination ability as well as considerable amount of occurrence.

The rest of paper is arranged as follows: section 2 describes our new feature and the generation algorithm in detail. In section 3, some experiments are introduced. Section 4 is the conclusion and discussion.

2   Loose N-Gram Feature

In most of TC systems, words are considered independently. This would certainly lose some useful context information. It is natural that different words from neighboring phrases or sentences express certain semantic information. This linguistic nature suggests that it may be helpful to use such words that are apart from each other by a longer distance as a new type of feature. This is the initial motivation of our Loose N-gram feature: it is an unordered word list, within the scope of neighborhood sentences.

2.1   Characteristics of the Feature

A Loose N-gram feature (*lNgram*) is defined as a group of words $(w_1, w_2, ..., w_n)_R$ ($n>1$), where w_i, ($i=1...n$) can be any word in the corpus. The range within which the words co-occur, denoted by R, could be either a single sentence, or two neighboring sentences, or a number of sequential words. The relative positions of the words are not restricted at all. For instance, within the range of a sentence, the following sentences have a common feature $(ship\ sunk)_{10}$:

✧ *A ship full of coffee sunk in the Pacific yesterday.*
✧ *The ship left. After three days, it sunk in a storm.*

This type of feature is more free-style, more descriptive, and more powerful, in the point of semantic view. However, restriction on the words is so poor that there exists tens of thousands of such groups in the corpus. It is definitely impossible to get all the combinations of all the words and then select the best ones as features, just as many traditional algorithms do to word features or phrase features. Therefore it is necessary to find out a way to select good features directly and easily. To make it simple and clear, in the remainder of this subsection, we assume the word number in one group, $n=2$, and the range in which the words are allowed is within R words.

Firstly, the generation method is *seed-based*. It has been proved that DF is effective to measure the classification ability [14]. A feature with low DF is more likely to be a noise. Therefore, DF values of the component words in the new feature should be big enough considering $df_{lNgram} \leq \min_{w \in lNgram} df_w$. Thus it is natural to select words with high DF values as "seeds", and then make them "grow up" as new features.

In our approach, the Loose N-gram features are selected as the addition to the word features, so we must take care that they should not be highly related to the original features to make redundancy. If word w has great discriminative power, it will not be so necessary to make new features expand from w. The reasons above lead to the criteria of the seeds in the algorithm:

❖ *A seed should have good coverage, that is, a considerable DF value.*
❖ *A seed should not have great discrimination ability, for instance, a low χ^2 value.*

Secondly we will show that the statistical characteristics of our features can be good. When we limit R to 2 and then our features are just unordered bi-grams. Then we expand R to 3, 4 and larger values, we notice that the features can be easily divided to 3 types (see Fig. 3 in section 3.1).

Finally, we will see that there can be enough "good" features. The number of the noise features is the largest among the three types. Fortunately, since the total number of the new features is extremely large, the good features, which are only a small fraction of the whole feature set, are enough to provide very rich context information.

2.2 Feature Generation Algorithm

In order to effectively get those "good" features described above, we apply a top-down strategy to generate features. First, we would like to describe some important concepts and notions useful in our algorithm as following:

❖ A sentence is denoted by ξ as defined in [7].
❖ *lNgram* is a group of words as well as the range R within which the words are allowed to co-occur. Denoted by $(w_1, w_2, ..., w_n)_R$ $n>1$.
❖ A seed can be either a word w or an lNgram feature.
❖ Term Frequency *(TF)* of a term t in a document denotes the number of times the term occurs in the document. To effectively calculate TF(t, doc) for *lNgram t*, we designed a sliding-window algorithm, as shown in Fig. 1.
❖ The χ^2 measure of term tk with respect to class ci is defined as in [14].

In fact, there are still newly selected *lNgram* features that satisfy the criterions of seeds, thus with these features as new seeds, longer *lNgram* features can be generated. As explained in section 2.1, the newly generated features are filtered with a χ^2_{max} threshold. The detailed algorithm is shown in Fig. 2.

```
Input: the word sequence S and the lNgram feature t
Notations and functions:
f, b: front and end positions of sliding window
w: sliding window width
tf: Term frequency value
isFeature(p): judges if the pst word of S is in t
NextPos(p): returns p' after p for isFeature(p')=true
Hits(f,b): the hit count of feature t in the window
Algorithm:
1. b = NextPos(0), f = b
2. Loop
 2a. f = min(p), where p-b > w and isFeature(p)
 2b. tf = tf + hits(b, f-1)
 2c. if there is no more NextPos(f), exit Loop to 3
 2d. b = min(p), where p-b < w and isFeature(p)
 2e. tf = tf - hits(b, f-1)
3. output tf
```

Fig. 1. Sliding window algorithm. For the words can be previously indexed, the function *NextPos*($\cdot$) can be done in const time. Thus the time complexity of this algorithm is $O(\sum n_w)$, where n_w is the number of occurrences of the *lNgram*'s component word w, which is quite small and acceptable in most approaches.

```
Input: Feature set F
Notations:
V: Vocabulary of the corpus
C: Candidate set
S: Seed set
χ²_f: lower χ² limit for features
χ²_s: upper χ² limit for seeds
df_s: lower DF limit for seeds
Algorithm:
```
1. $F = \{w \mid w \in V, \chi^2_{\max} > \chi^2_f\}$, $C = \emptyset$
2. $S = \{s \mid s \in V, DF(s) > df_s, \chi^2_{\max} < \chi^2_s\}$
3. While $S \neq \emptyset$ do a, b and c
3a. $C = \{(w,w') \mid w \in S, \exists \xi, w \in \xi, w' \in \xi, w' \notin F\}$
3b. $F = F \cup \{c \mid c \in C, \chi^2_{\max}(c) > \chi^2_f\}$
3c. $S = \{s \mid s \in C, DF(s) > df_s, \chi^2_{\max} < \chi^2_s\}$
4. Output F

Fig. 2. *lNgram* feature generation algorithm

In our Reuters-21578 experiment, the word "million", who has large *DF* (df=789) and poor χ^2 (χ^2=33.26), is selected as a seed. Then (*million share*), is generated with much larger χ^2 value (df=374, χ^2=384.6). What's more, this feature can expand as a seed to longer features (*million share stake*) with a still larger χ^2 (df=86, χ^2=522.86). This example shows how a "bad" feature is extended to a "good" discriminative feature in this process.

3 Experiments

The experiments are performed on two common datasets. The 10 largest categories of Reuters-21578 corpus, usually called R10, are used in our experiments. The training and test set (9,603 vs. 3,299 docs) are split according to the standard ModApte Split.

The TREC2005 dataset is the common database for the TREC Genomics TC tasks. Alleles task is one of four TREC2005 TC tasks to judge whether a full-text biological article is about Alleles of mutant phenotypes, with 5789 docs for training and 6053 docs for test. This task is quite different from Reuters-21578 task by two means: the average document length is much longer (3236.38 words vs. 72.77 words), and this TC task requires deep semantic information, since all the documents are science papers on genomics, unigram features apparently not enough.

For all the datasets, stop words are removed and a Porter stemmer is applied as preprocessing. We implemented a sentence splitter to divide a document into sentences [7]. The word features are selected with χ^2 measure. We use $logTFIDF$ weighting scheme and perform normalization on feature vectors as defined in [10].

The *libsvm* classifier [3] is adopted in our experiments with the simplest linear kernel, with *no* threshold or *any other special parameters* changed throughout all the training and predicting process. So it is acceptable that our results are a little worse than state-of-the-art results ever reported in Reuters dataset. Classical evaluation measurements of TC: *Recall (Re)*, *Precision (Pr)* and *F*1-measure *(F1)* are used to measure the categorization performance [14].

3.1 Statistics of the Loose N-Gram Feature

In Reuters-21578 experiment, 2014 *lNgram*s are generated in the first iteration of our generation algorithm. On these features, as well as some random selected word pairs for contrast, we do the allowed range varying experiment described in section 2.1, and some of the results are shown in Fig. 3. The distribution of sentences according to the sentence length is plotted in Fig. 4., in which we can see that most sentences consist of about 10~30 words. This is interesting considered together with Fig. 3. There seems to be a summarization that:

If two words often occur together in documents, they will most likely to co-occur within 2 neighboring sentences.

This is very interesting and thus could give a *linguistic base* for the *lNgram* feature.

We trained a decision tree classifier to tell apart the three kinds of curves in Fig. 3. The classification result on 2014 features is: 40 bi-grams or phrases, 1727 *lNgrams*, and 247 noise word-pairs. Most of the features generated actually are clustered to "real" loose features. Actually there should be much more noise features than extracted, however, in our generation procedure, most of such noises are filtered.

3.2 Categorization Results

In our experiments, we select the top 10% word features with χ^2 feature selection method. The χ^2_f and χ^2_s are all set according to the minimum χ^2 value in this selected feature set, and the df_s threshold is also set to the minimum DF value in it.

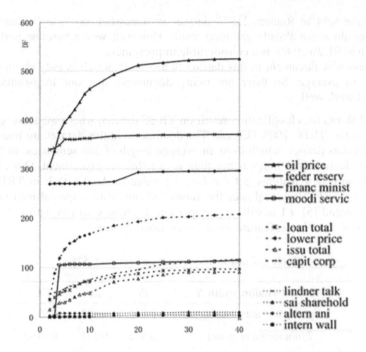

Fig. 3. *DF* curves with respect to allowed range *R*. Every four items in the legend contains a type of features. The curves of the first four reach a high value at the very beginning and change little afterwards. The four curves in the middle increase mildly until the saturation point at about 20~30 words. The last four features are just noises with very small *DF* values.

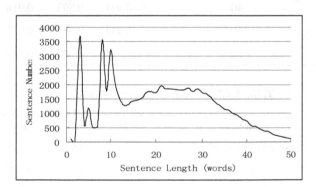

Fig. 4. The distribution of sentences according to the length

Table 1 shows the classification result on Reuters-21578. However, increasing the allowed window width makes only a little improve in both precision and recall. The reason is that we add strict criterion on the new features that their χ^2 value are larger than the "worst" unigram features. Therefore the new features are both informative and discriminative. We think there could be two reasons why performance improvement is not quite notable:

✧ The Apte split in Reuters-21578 dataset is somewhat too "*easy*", that unigram features alone can already get good result. However, with a baseline performance as high as 91.2%, 0.6% is a considerable improvement.

✧ The newswire document in this dataset is too *short*, which is only about 6~7 sentences in average. So there are many documents that our long-range feature doesn't work well.

Table 2 shows the classification result on TREC dataset, where we achieve the *best* F1 result in this TREC 2005 TC task. The documents in this dataset are much longer than the Reuters dataset, which have an average length of 246 sentences. In this case, the *lNgram* feature does much better than in the Reuters experiment. Our classification result with new features got the *best* F1 value in Alleles task in TREC 2005. Although the TREC task evaluates the submitted runs with a special measure which encourages recall [5], F1 is still very important. Compared to run with only the unigram features, the *lNgram* feature shows great improvement.

Table 1. Classification result on Reuters-21578

Allowed window width R	Pr	Re	$F1$
unigram, do feature selection	0.944	0.882	0.912
2 (unordered bi-gram)	0.942	0.891	0.916
10	0.942	0.890	0.915
20	0.943	0.890	0.916
30	0.943	0.892	0.917
40	0.944	0.893	0.918
50	0.943	0.893	0.917
60	0.943	0.892	0.917

Table 2. Classification result on TREC dataset

Runs	Pr	Re	$F1$
2nd submit in TREC submissions[1]	0.467	0.934	0.623
unigram	0.450	0.775	0.570
lNgram	**0.490**	0.900	**0.635**

4   Conclusion and Discussion

Our new *lNgram* feature integrates the context information for TC tasks. This feature is generated from the corpus using seed-based learning algorithm, which guarantees

---

[1] This result is achieved by regression method, with domain specific knowledge adopted.

that the feature is controlled to a relatively low dimension while having good discrimination abilities. Experiment results show the improvements over the traditional features. In fact, the *lNgram* features are more like *Information Retrieval queries* than TC features. There are such queries similar to *lNgram* features which are just words combined by logical operators in *limited length window* in existing text retrieval systems, for example Indri (http://www.lemurproject.org/indri/). In the TREC TC task, the *lNgram* features with high χ^2 values provide *strong* evidence indicating that the sentence with such features is about the knowledge on Alleles of mutant phenotypes. Thus our research is also valuable for current IR researches by automatically extracting patterns to help forming queries.

Acknowledgments. This paper is supported by Natural Science Foundation No.60572084 and No. 60321002.

References

1. Aizawa, A.N.: Linguistic techniques to improve the performance of automatic text categorization. In: NLPRS'01, Tokyo, Japan vol. 11, pp. 307–314 (2001)
2. Moschitti, A., Basili, R.: Complex linguistic features for text classification: a comprehensive study. In: McDonald, S., Tait, J. (eds.) ECIR 2004. LNCS, vol. 2997, pp. 181–196. Springer, Heidelberg (2004)
3. Chang, C.-C., Lin, C.-J.: LIBSVM: A library for support vector machines (2001)
4. Cohen, W.W., Singer, Y.: Context-sensitive learning methods for text categorization. In: Proceedings of ACM SIGIR'96, pp. 307–315. ACM Press, New York (1996)
5. Hersh, W., Cohen, A., Yang, J., Bhupatiraju, R.T., Roberts, P., Hearst, M.: TREC 2005 genomics track overview. http://trec.nist.gov/pubs.html (2005)
6. Lodhi, H., Saunders, C., Shawe-Taylor, J., Cristianini, N., Watkins, C.: Text classification using string kernels. J. Mach. Learn. Res. 2, 419–444 (2002)
7. Mikheev, A.: Tagging sentence boundaries. In: Proceedings of NAACL'00. ACM International Conference Proceeding Series, vol. 4. San Francisco, CA, pp. 264–271
8. Riloff, E., Lorenzen, J.: Extraction-based text categorization: generating domain-specific role relationships automatically. In NLIR. Springer-Verlag, Berlin
9. Sebastiani, F.: Machine learning in automated text categorization. ACM Comput. Surv. 34(1), 1–47 (2002)
10. Singhal, A., Buckley, C., Mitra, M.: Pivoted document length normalization. In: Proceedings of ACM SIGIR '96., pp. 21–29. ACM Press, New York (1996)
11. Smadja, F.A.: From n-grams to collocations: an evaluation of Xtract. In: Proceedings of Annual Meeting of the ACL, ACL, Morristown, NJ, pp. 279–284 (1991)
12. Tan, C., Wang, Y., Lee, C.: The use of bigrams to enhance text categorization. Inf. Process. Manage 38(4), 529–546 (2002)
13. Yang, Y., Liu, X.: A re-examination of text categorization methods. In: Proceedings of ACM SIGIR '99, pp. 42–49. ACM Press, New York (1999)
14. Yang, Y., Pedersen, J.O.: A comparative study on feature selection in text categorization. In: Proceedings of ICML'97. San Francisco, CA, pp. 412–420 (1997)

Variational Deconvolution of Multi-channel Images with Inequality Constraints

Martin Welk[1] and James G. Nagy[2]

[1] Mathematical Image Analysis Group
Faculty of Mathematics and Computer Science, Bldg. E1 1
Saarland University, 66041 Saarbrücken, Germany
welk@mia.uni-saarland.de
http://www.mia.uni-saarland.de
[2] Department of Mathematics and Computer Science
Emory University, 400 Dowman Drive, Suite W401,
Atlanta, Georgia 30322, USA
nagy@mathcs.emory.edu
http://www.mathcs.emory.edu

Abstract. A constrained variational deconvolution approach for multi-channel images is presented. Constraints are enforced through a reparametrisation which allows a differential geometric reinterpretation. This view point is used to show that the deconvolution problem can be formulated as a standard gradient descent problem with an underlying metric that depends on the imposed constraints. Examples are given for bound constrained colour image deblurring, and for diffusion tensor magnetic resonance imaging with positive definiteness constraint. Numerical results illustrate the effectiveness of the methods.

1 Introduction

Blurring occurs in practically every image acquisition process, due to a variety of reasons like camera and object movement, defocussing, atmospheric perturbations, optical aberrations, etc. Removing this blur and restoring undegraded images – *deblurring* – is therefore a crucial task in many application contexts, for which numerous methods have been developed. Often blurring can be described or approximated as convolution of the unknown sharp image with a fixed kernel, the *point-spread function (PSF)*. In this case, deblurring is also called *deconvolution*. A further distinction is between deconvolution with known and unknown PSF, the latter being called *blind* deconvolution.

Variational deconvolution methods aim at reconstructing the sharp image by minimising an energy functional that encodes the convolution relation between the given and sought images together with regularity assumptions on the sought image. Since typical deconvolution problems are ill-posed inverse problems, it is highly desirable to use any additional information that is available to support the sharpening process. One condition that can often be derived e.g. from physical considerations is given by inequality constraints: In a grey-value image whose

J. Martí et al. (Eds.): IbPRIA 2007, Part I, LNCS 4477, pp. 386–393, 2007.
© Springer-Verlag Berlin Heidelberg 2007

values are proportional to radiance, they are bounded from below since radiance cannot take negative values. Sometimes also an upper bound can be derived from the image acquisition parameters.

A similar situation occurs in the context of diffusion tensor magnetic resonance imaging (DTMRI), a recent three-dimentional medical imaging modality that measures, in each voxel, a symmetric 3×3 matrix that encodes the direction-dependent diffusion behaviour of water molecules in tissue. DTMRI data are highly valuable in detecting connectivity within the brain white matter which is very useful in schizophrenia or stroke studies; another potential field of application is given by heart-muscle tissue. The physical nature of the measured diffusion tensors implies that they must be positive (semi-)definite, which is an inequality constraint, too.

In this paper, we present an approach for non-blind variational deconvolution under inequality constraints. Its main component is a reparametrisation of the image range which allows a differential geometric reinterpretation. The reparametrisation principle has been used before in the context of a discrete deconvolution model [9]. We also present the extension of our framework to multi-channel images. The capabilities of the approach are demonstrated by experiments on photographic images with positivity constraints and DTMRI data with the positive definiteness constraint.

Related work. Blind or non-blind variational deconvolution has been studied by many authors, see [4,7,15,1]. Though considered in a slightly different setting in 1995 [16], robust data terms have attracted broader attention recently [1], see also [14] for extensions to spatially variant PSFs and [2] for an explicit formulation with colour images. Reparametrisation has been used to impose a positivity constraint on a discrete deconvolution model in [9]. A differential geometric framework for gradient descent constrained to submanifolds (i.e. equality constraints) has been discussed in [5].

2 Variational Deconvolution with Constraints

Basic Deconvolution Model. We start from a general model for variational deconvolution of grey-value or multi-channel (colour, vector- or matrix-valued) images with spatially invariant point-spread function which is based on minimising the energy functional

$$E[u] = \int_{\Omega} \left(\Phi\Big(\sum_{k \in J} (f_k - u_k * h)^2 \Big) + \alpha \Psi\Big(\sum_{k \in J} |\nabla u_k|^2 \Big) \right) \mathrm{d}x \qquad (1)$$

where $u = (u_k)_{k \in J}$ is the image to be determined, $f = (f_k)_{k \in J}$ is the given blurred image, the index set J enumerates the image channels ($|J| = 1$ for grey-value images), and h is the uniform point-spread function for all channels. Further, Φ and Ψ are monotonically increasing functions from $\mathbb{R}_0^+$ to $\mathbb{R}$. The first summand in the integrand is the *data term* which favours images u with small reconstruction error $f - u * h$. The second summand, the *regulariser*, encourages smoothness of the deblurred image, see also [13] for additional discussion. The *regularisation weight* $\alpha > 0$ balances the influences of both contributions.

If Φ grows slower than $\Phi(s^2) = s^2$, one speaks of a *robust data term* [1] since it reduces the influence of large residual errors (outliers) on $E[u]$ compared to a least-squares term. A typical choice is the regularised L^1-norm $\Phi(s^2) = \sqrt{s^2 + \beta^2}$ with small $\beta > 0$. Robust data terms considerably improve the performance of variational deconvolution approaches in the presence of noise [1] or data that fulfil model assumptions imperfectly, including imprecise PSF estimates [14].

As to the regulariser, non-quadratic choices like (regularised) total variation $\Psi(s^2) = \sqrt{s^2 + \varepsilon^2}$ ($\varepsilon > 0$) [7,4,1] or even the non-convex Perona–Malik term $\Psi(s^2) = \lambda^2 \ln(1 + s^2/\lambda^2)$ [13] are generally favoured in the image processing literature for their edge-preserving or even edge-enhancing capabilities.

Note that in our model the channels u_k are coupled by quadratic summation in the arguments of both Ψ and Φ. While this is well-established in practice in the regulariser [11] the situation in the data term is more delicate and depends on the characteristics of noise and perturbations across the channels. A separate robustification $\sum_k \Phi((f_k - u_k * h)^2)$ as advocated in [2] can be adequate when noise is independent in the different channels, while channel-coupled noise calls for the joint robustification of (1). Due to the image acquisition procedures the latter will often apply to colour images and practically always to diffusion tensor images. Perturbations due to imperfect fulfilment of model assumptions also tend to be channel-coupled. For a discussion of joint versus separate robustification in a different context (optic flow) see also [3, p. 38].

One way to compute a minimiser of (1) is via the gradient descent

$$\partial_t u_k = \alpha \operatorname{div}\left(\Psi'\left(\sum_{l \in J} |\nabla u_l|^2\right)\nabla u_k\right) + \left(\Phi'\left(\sum_{l \in J}(f_l - u_l * h)^2\right)(f_k - u_k * h)\right) * \tilde{h} \quad (2)$$

where $\tilde{h}(x) := h(-x)$ denotes the PSF reflected at the origin. Starting from a suitable initial condition, which will often be the blurred image f itself, the process converges to a minimiser of (1).

We next consider how the model (1) can be modified to incorporate constraints on the solution.

Constraints for Greyvalue Images. Assume for a moment the single channel case, where the pixels represent grey-value intensities. Since negative intensities do not physically make sense, we would like to modify (1) to constrain the grey-values to be nonnegative. One obvious approach is to add a penalty for negative values, with the drawback of not strictly enforcing the inequality. Another approach, which has been shown to be very effective for discrete deconvolution problems [9], reparametrises the greyvalues via $u = \exp(z)$ with a new image function z whose values are unconstrained in $\mathbb{R}$, and calculates the gradient descent for z. Slightly generalising, we substitute $u = \varphi(z)$ with a smooth invertible function $\varphi : \mathbb{R} \to \mathbb{R}$ into (1) and obtain

$$\tilde{E}[z] = \int_\Omega \left(\Phi((f - \varphi(z) * h)^2) + \alpha \Psi\left((\varphi'(z) |\nabla z|)^2\right)\right) dx. \quad (3)$$

The gradient descent is now computed for z, after which z can be eliminated by the inverse function $z = \varphi^{-1}(u)$. This gives the new gradient descent

$$\partial_t u = \varphi'(\varphi^{-1}(u)) \left(\alpha \operatorname{div} \left(\Psi'(\, |\nabla u|^2\,) \, \nabla u \right) + \left(\Phi'((f - u * h)^2)(f - u * h) \right) * \tilde{h} \right) \quad (4)$$

which differs from (2) (with one channel) only by the factor $\varphi'(\varphi^{-1}(u))$ on the right-hand side.

A positivity constraint is imposed by $\varphi(z) = \exp(z)$, thus $\varphi'(\varphi^{-1}(u)) = u$. This can easily be generalised to an interval constraint $a < u < b$ by using a sigmoid function such as $\varphi(z) = \frac{a\exp(-z)+b}{\exp(-z)+1}$, leading to $\varphi'(\varphi^{-1}(u)) = (u - a)$ $(b - u)/(b - a)$.

Constraining Colour Images. Going from a single grey-value to multi-channel images, one notes first that constraints that act separately on the channels can be handled easily. For example, positivity or interval constraints for the channels of colour images are imposed by setting $u_k = \varphi_k(z_k)$ for $k \in J$. The corresponding gradient descent in channel k is given by equation (2) with the right-hand side multiplied by $\varphi'_k(\varphi_k^{-1}(u_k))$.

Geometric Reinterpretation. We now show that it is possible to interpret the reparametrisation approach geometrically, and this leads to a very convenient form in which more general constraints can be easily incorporated into the model. Let us consider once more grey-value images with positivity constraint, i.e. $\varphi'(\varphi^{-1}(u)) = u$. A short calculation then reveals that the right-hand side of (4) expresses the negative (variational) gradient of the *original* energy functional $E[u]$ according to (1) in a function manifold whose metric is constructed from the well-known *hyperbolic* metric $\mathrm{d}_\mathrm{h} u := \mathrm{d}u/u$ on the range of grey-values u, instead of the usual (Euclidean) metric. We can therefore represent our modified gradient descent process as standard gradient descent with a different underlying metric! From this viewpoint, zero and negative greyvalues are avoided simply because the hyperbolic metric puts them at infinite distance from any positive values. A similar reinterpretation is possible in the interval constraint case: Now both interval ends are pushed away to infinite distance.

Positive Definiteness Constraint in Matrix-Valued Images. As a consequence of our geometric reinterpretation, we no longer need to rely on an explicit reparametrisation of our image range to compute a constrained gradient descent. Instead, it is sufficient to calculate the gradient descent of (1) with respect to a suitably chosen metric on the image range.

This observation immediately enables us to formulate a gradient descent for variational deconvolution of matrix-valued images with positive definiteness constraint. To this end, we use the Riemannian metric on the cone of positive definite matrices that is given by $\mathrm{d}_\mathrm{S} A^2 = \left\| A^{-1/2} \, \mathrm{d}A \, A^{-1/2} \right\|_\mathrm{F}^2$ with $\|\cdot\|_\mathrm{F}$ denoting the Frobenius norm, see [12,6]. This metric has recently been investigated intensively in the context of DTMRI data processing, see e.g. [8,10].

Fig. 1. Top left: Paris from Eiffel tower at dusk, colour photograph blurred by camera movement (480 × 480 pixels). *Inserted:* estimated point-spread function (enlarged). **Top right:** Variational deconvolution result with robust data term, Perona–Malik regulariser ($\lambda = 26$), regularisation weight $\alpha = 0.03$, with positivity constraint. **Middle left:** Detail (240 × 90 pixels) of deconvolution with the same regulariser, $\alpha = 0.06$, no constraint. **Middle right:** Same with $\alpha = 0.06$ and positivity constraint. **Bottom left:** $\alpha = 0.03$, no constraint. **Bottom right:** $\alpha = 0.03$, positivity constraint.

Denoting the matrix-valued image by $U = (u_k)_{k \in J}$, $J = \{1, 2, 3\} \times \{1, 2, 3\}$, the gradient descent for (1) with respect to the metric d_S is given by

$$\partial_t U = U^{1/2} \, G \, U^{1/2} \tag{5}$$

where G is the matrix of all the right-hand sides of (2) for channels $k \in J$.

3   Experiments

In our experiments, we consider a deconvolution problem for a colour image using the gradient descent (4) with $\varphi(z) = \exp(z)$, and a deconvolution problem for DTMRI data with gradient descent given by (5). We always use robust L^1

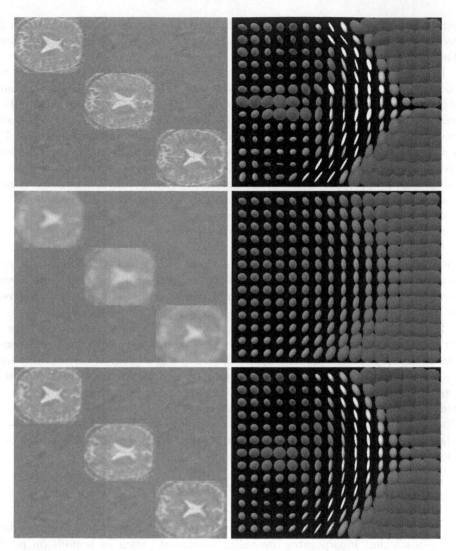

Fig. 2. Top left: One 2D slice from a DTMRI data set of a human brain. The 3×3 tiles represent the matrix components, with middle grey representing 0. **Top right:** Detail from the corpus callosum region visualised by ellipsoids. Directions and lengths of the principal axes correspond to eigenvectors and eigenvalues, resp. **Middle row:** Blurred by iterated box filtering, approximating convolution with a Gaussian of standard deviation 2. **Bottom row:** Variational deconvolution with robust data terms, total variation regulariser, regularisation weight 0.03, and positive definiteness constraint.

data terms. As in the case of the unconstrained gradient descent (2), a straight forward numerical implementation is through an explicit time-stepping scheme which is stopped when the updates fall below some small positive threshold. Some speedup is possible by more sophisticated schemes, but this does not affect the behaviour of the solution, which is the main focus of this paper. Also, we do not focus on experiments with additional noise since the robustness of variational deconvolution with robust data terms under e.g. impulsive noise has already been demonstrated in [1,14].

In our first experiment (Fig. 1), we demonstrate deconvolution of a colour photograph with positivity constraint. Note that the exact PSF is unknown and slightly space-variant while a space-invariant PSF estimated from an impulse response in the image has been used for deconvolution. The ability of the method to cope with these violations of model assumptions underlines its robustness. It is evident that the positivity constraint significantly reduces oscillatory (Gibbs) artifacts along edges. Interestingly, this includes not only undershoots to negative values which are suppressed directly, but also overshoots in the positive range, due to the convolution in the data term that links over- and undershoots. We can therefore reduce the regularisation weight in the constrained deconvolution and thereby achieve reconstruction of finer details.

Our second experiment (Fig. 2) demonstrates deconvolution of matrix-valued data with positive definiteness constraint. One 2D slice of a DTMRI data set consisting of symmetric 3×3 matrices has been synthetically blurred by iterative box filtering approximating a Gaussian of standard deviation 2, and deconvolved by our method, using a Gaussian PSF of the same standard deviation.

It can be seen that many structures in the DTMRI image are nicely reconstructed by the deconvolution process, e.g. the highly anisotropic diffusion tensors of the corpus callosum region, and the sharp edges between corpus callosum and the large isotropic tensors in the adjacent ventricle. A limitation of the current method that can be seen from the figures is that very thin details with a width of only one or two voxels are still smoothed in the deconvolved image. Due to the low resolution this effect is more relevant in DTMRI data than elsewhere, and further work will be devoted to improve reconstruction quality for such details.

4   Conclusion

In this paper, we have proposed an energy minimisation approach to image deconvolution that incorporates inequality constraints, such as bounds on pixel values. Constraints are modelled either by a reparametrisation of the image values, or in a differential geometric way by modifying the metric on the image values in which a gradient descent is carried out. Particularly the second formulation allows to realise fairly general constraints on multi-channel images.

Our experiments on positivity-constrained colour image deconvolution and positive definite deconvolution of DTMRI data demonstrate the broad applicability and performance of the model.

Acknowledgements. Support of the first author by Deutsche Forschungsgemeinschaft under grant We 3563/2-1 is gratefully acknowledged. Research of the second author is supported in part by the U.S. National Science Foundation under grant DMS-05-11454. The first author also thanks Emory University for their hospitality. The DTMRI data set has been provided by Oliver Gruber and Ilona Henseler, Saarland University Hospital, Homburg, Germany.

References

1. Bar, L., Sochen, N., Kiryati, N.: Image deblurring in the presence of salt-and-pepper noise. In: Kimmel, R., Sochen, N., Weickert, J. (eds.) Scale-Space 2005. LNCS, vol. 3459, pp. 107–118. Springer, Heidelberg (2005)
2. Bar, L., Brook, A., Sochen, N., Kiryati, N.: Color image deblurring with impulsive noise. In: Paragios, N., Faugeras, O., Chan, T., Schnörr, C. (eds.) VLSM 2005. LNCS, vol. 3752, pp. 49–60. Springer, Heidelberg (2005)
3. Bruhn, A.: Variational Optic Flow Computation – Accurate Modelling and Efficient Numerics. PhD thesis, Saarland University, Saarbrücken, Germany (2006)
4. Chan, T.F., Wong, C.K.: Total variation blind deconvolution. IEEE Transactions on Image Processing 7, 370–375 (1998)
5. Chefd'Hotel, C.: Méthodes Géométriques en Vision par Ordinateur et Traitement d'Image: Contributions et Applications. PhD Thesis, ENS Cachan, France (2004)
6. Helgason, S.: Differential Geometry, Lie Groups, and Symmetric Spaces. Academic Press, New York (1978)
7. Marquina, A., Osher, S.: A new time dependent model based on level set motion for nonlinear deblurring and noise removal. In: Nielsen, M., Johansen, P., Olsen, O.F., Weickert, J. (eds.) Scale-Space Theories in Computer Vision. LNCS, vol. 1682, pp. 429–434. Springer, Heidelberg (1999)
8. Moakher, M., Batchelor, P.: Symmetric positive-definite matrices: from geometry to applications and visualization. In: Weickert, J., Hagen, H. (eds.). Visualization and Processing of Tensor Fields, Springer, Heidelberg (2006)
9. Nagy, J.G., Strakoš, Z.: Enforcing nonnegativity in image reconstruction algorithms. In: Wilson, D.C., et al. (eds.). Mathematical Modeling, Estimation, and Imaging, vol. 4121, pp. 182–190 (2000)
10. Pennec, X., Fillard, P., Ayache, N.: A Riemannian framework for tensor computing. International Journal of Computer Vision 66(1), 41–66 (2006)
11. Schnörr, C.: Segmentation of visual motion by minimizing convex non-quadratic functionals. In: Pattern Recognition. Proc. Twelfth International Conference, Jerusalem, Israel, October, pp. 661–663. IEEE Computer Society Press, Los Alamitos (1994)
12. Siegel, C.L.: Symplectic Geometry. Academic Press, New York (1964)
13. Welk, M., Theis, D., Brox, T., Weickert, J.: PDE-based deconvolution with forward-backward diffusivities and diffusion tensors. In: Moreno-Diaz, R., Pichler, F. (eds.) EUROCAST 1991. LNCS, vol. 585, pp. 585–597. Springer, Heidelberg (1992)
14. Welk, M., Theis, D., Weickert, J.: Variational deblurring of images with uncertain and spatially variant blurs. In: Kropatsch, W.G., Sablatnig, R., Hanbury, A. (eds.) Pattern Recognition. LNCS, vol. 3663, pp. 485–492. Springer, Heidelberg (2005)
15. You, Y.-L., Kaveh, M.: A regularization approach to joint blur identification and image restoration. IEEE Transactions on Image Processing 5(3), 416–428 (1996)
16. Zervakis, M.E., Katsaggelos, A.K., Kwon, T.M.: A class of robust entropic functionals for image restoration. IEEE Transactions on Image Processing 4(6), 752–773 (1995)

HMM-Based Action Recognition
Using Contour Histograms

M. Ángeles Mendoza and Nicolás Pérez de la Blanca

University of Granada
Department of Computer Science and Artificial Intelligence
{nines,nicolas}@decsai.ugr.es

Abstract. This paper describes an experimental study about a robust contour feature (*shape-context*) for using in action recognition based on continuous hidden Markov models (HMM). We ran different experimental setting using the KTH's database of actions. The image contours are extracted using a standard algorithm. The *shape-context* feature vector is build from of histogram of a set of non-overlapping regions in the image. We show that the combined use of HMM and this feature gives equivalent o better results, in term of action detection, that current approaches in the literature.

1 Introduction

Automatic action recognition is a constantly expanding research area due to the number of applications for surveillance (behaviour analysis), security (pedestrian detection), control (human-computer interfaces), content-based video retrieval, etc. It is, however, a complex and difficult-to-resolve problem because of the enormous differences that exist between individuals, both in the way they move and their physical appearance and the environment where the action is carried out [5]. An increasingly popular approach to this problem is HMM. One action is sequences of events ordered in space and time, and HMM exploits this ordering to capture structural and transitional features and therefore the dynamic of the system. The contour of the subject, and more explicitly how the contour shape succeeds another in the action cycle is a powerful discriminating signal for HMM-based action recognition (available even though there is no texture or colour information) and may be rapidly extracted with simple techniques. This information, however, can be very noisy in cluttered environments and when there are shadows. Some authors choose to use the full silhouette to increase robustness, Kale et al. [4] identify people by their gait based on the width of binary silhouettes; Sundaresa et al [8] using the sum of silhouette pixels; Yamato [9] also uses binary silhouettes to recognize 6 different tennis strokes with discrete HMM using the ratio of black pixels; Ahmad and Lee [1] combine shape information (applying PCA to the silhouettes to reduce dimensionality) and the optical flow in a discrete HMM in multiple views. But by doing so, they are introducing redundancy (the inside of the pedestrian does not give

J. Martí et al. (Eds.): IbPRIA 2007, Part I, LNCS 4477, pp. 394–401, 2007.

additional information), extraction is more expensive, morphological pre-processing is necessary, and in addition, silhouettes are too affected by background and occlusions.

Belongie and Malik [2] introduced *shape contexts* as shape descriptors, and these are basically log-polar histograms of distances and angles of a point to the neighbouring points of the uniformly sampled contour. Since these are based on histograms, they are reasonably tolerant to variations in pose and occlusion. In this paper, we will focus on *shape contexts* to define a feature that extracts contour information for HMM-based action recognition. This feature is robust to occlusions or bad background segmentation, cluttered environments and shadows, and exploits the contours' good qualities (i.e. lower sensibility to lighting changes and to small viewpoint variations than methods based on optical flow or pixel brightness, similarity at different scales, ease and speed of extraction with simple techniques).

The rest of this paper is organized as follows: Section 2 describes the coding of the contour information in our approach. Section gives an overview of our experimentation and results. Finally, conclusions are drawn in Section 3.

2 Feature Vector

Our features use *shape contexts* [2] to describe the shape of the contour of the subjects performing the actions. We don't calculate the *shape contexts* relative to subject's whole shape but we divide the region where the person is into uniform-shaped tiles, and the *shape contexts* will describe the contour that appears in each tile independently. In other words, for each point sampled in a tile, the log-polar histogram of this point's relative positions in relation to the other points in the same tile is calculated. This is because we want to add position information, although contour histograms encode local shape robustly, they do not preserve spatial information about the image, which would increases the discriminant power of feature vector, for example between walking and waving. When an action is performed, movement is mainly carried out by some of the human body's limbs. Movement is going to be characterized by movement of theses specific limbs. In order to introduce this information, the person's area is divided into four vertical sections corresponding approximately to the area of the head-shoulders, trunk-arms, hips-thighs and knees-feet, which enable a wide range of movements to be covered, and two horizontal sections to exploit human symmetry. If smaller tiles are used, it is not possible to capture the characteristic contours of the human figure. This coding is illustrated in Figure 1.

Once the subject's rectangle is extracted, we divided this rectangle in meaningful tiles (see before paragraph). In each tile, we sampled uniformly a set of points on the contour, for every point a log-polar histogram of relative positions and angles of that point to the remaining point is calculated, *shape context*'s mean histogram in each tile generates a feature vector which will be the HMM input The use of log gives to *shape contexts* greater sensibility to nearby points than to far points, more probably affected by noise. Invariance to uniform scale is achieved by normalizing all the radial distances by the mean distance between all the contour-point pairs. We referred the angles to an absolute axis (positive x-axis) because invariance to rotation is not desirable for our problem, but to exploit this information. In order to minimize redundancy and to compress the data, we compare two widely extended techniques; principal component analysis (PCA) and the discrete cosine transform (DCT). We apply PCA on the eight tile's median histograms and obtain eight eigenvectors of dimension 8, in total 64 coefficients (8x8). With DCT, we calculate the 2D discrete cosine transform of median histogram in each tile and took the first eight coefficients, for obtaining a feature vector of 64 coefficients too (8 coefficients DCT x 8 tiles), and to compare PCA and DCT performance, the number of required training samples is increased with feature vector's size.

We employ continuous HMM (CHMM) with mixed Gaussian output probability, simple left to right topology, where a state can only be reached from itself or from the previous state. Since certain actions have a common pose, since allowing higher jumps between states could result in recognition errors.

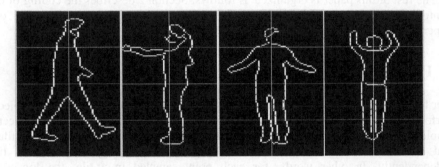

Fig. 1. The eight independent regions in which we split each image. From left to right, walking to the right, boxing to the left, clapping, waving.

3 Experimentation and Results

3.1 Data

We have evaluated our proposal using KTH's database [7] on 10 different types of actions: walking to the right, walking to the left, jogging to the right, jogging to the left, running to the right, running to the left, boxing to the right, boxing to the left, clapping, and waving. These actions were performed outdoors by 25 different people of both sexes with different lighting conditions and shadows. The sequences are made up of grey images with a resolution of 160x120 pixels to 25fps. Figure 2 shows the original images from the database and their corresponding outline images. The outline images are images, which would be obtained, in realistic conditions affected by shadows, people's own clothes, background elements, and bad segmentation. In some sequences of boxing to right there is a continuous zoom during the recording, therefore the subject appears with different size.

Each video was segmented into activity cycles, whereby we defined the boxing cycle as punches with both fists, clapping as the movements corresponding to a single clap, waving to raising the arms above the head and returning to the initial position, the walking and jogging cycle as a step with both legs (as most pedestrian recognition approaches do and so as to increase robustness), but the running cycle only considers one step with either leg since this recorded the most sequences because of the pedestrian's speed. We used a total of 44 samples for walking to the right, 46 for walking to the left, 34 for jogging to the right, 38 for jogging to the left, 51 for running to the right, 54 running to the left, 104 for boxing to the right, 113 for boxing to the left, 164 for clapping, and 119 for waving.

Fig. 2. Top row, original images from KTH's database; bottom row, outline images for the activities (from left to right): walking to the left, jogging to the right, running to the left, boxing to the right, clapping and waving.

3.2 Experimentation

Once the frames representing an activity cycle have been obtained, we extracted a fixed size feature vector for each frame. This vector represents the HMM set of observable. In order to calculate the feature vector proposed in this paper, we first divided the area containing the person performing the action into eight identical tiles, 2 horizontal ones and 4 vertical ones, and we consider 8 main areas of movement: knees-feet, hips-thighs, trunk-arms, shoulders-head (see Section 2.2). In each tile, the shape contexts were calculated. In order to choose the number of sampled contour points and the number of log-polar histogram bins, it is necessary to balance the information we wish to capture with the size of the feature vector, bigger size more training samples are necessary. We have taken 10 contour points in each tile, 4 distance bins (log bin size (d/4), where the diagonal pixels of the tile are represented by d) and 8 angle bins (45 degrees). Finally, we assessed the median histogram of shape contexts in each tile to obtain a 256 D vector (8 tiles x 4 distance bins x 8 angle bins). We referred the angles to an absolute axis (positive x-axis) because invariance to rotation is not desirable but exploitation of this information. In order to reduce the size of the vector to 64 coefficients, we employed PCA or DCT.

The vectors extracted in this way constitute the input to the hidden Markov model toolkit (HTK), which is an integrated environment of software tools for building

HMM, and this facilitates HMM learning for each activity and subsequent recognition. HTK consists of a set of libraries written in ANSI C and a detailed description of its operation can be found in [10].

3.3 Results and Discussion

The proposed coding is validated on two multi-subject open tests, one with PCA and the other with DCT. The samples are divided into three groups, two of which are used for training and the other for testing by cross validation (about 250 samples for testing and 500 for training). For each action, a simple left-right CHMM with mixed Gaussian output probability is learned. New components are incrementally added to the output probability at each stage, one at a time, until 20 Gaussians. HMM were tested with 8, 10 and 12 states since the number of states cannot be higher than the number of frames for the action cycle and for fewer than 8 states, the recognition rate was lower than 60%. Table 1 shows the average accuracy of HMM with 8, 10 and 12 states for PCA and DCT.

Table 1. Accuracy with PCA and DCT: the number of output probability Gaussians with the greatest average accuracy is shown in brackets

	No. states		
	8	10	12
PCA	73.19 (11 Gauss)	81.04 (9 Gauss)	84.06 (4 Gauss)
DCT	88.47 (13 Gauss)	92.35 (8 Gauss)	93.11 (4 Gauss)

The best average accuracy was obtained for an HMM with 12 emitting states and a mixed output probability of 4 Gaussians, 84.06% with PCA and 93.11% with DCT (about 10% higher than PCA). In the literature, the recognition rate of HMM-based actions which use human shape-based features, for example, is 81.3% when only shape features are used and 87.5% when shape and optical flow are combined in [1] for four actions (walking, running, bowing, raising the hand). In [9] the recognition rate is 96% for 6 tennis strokes where training and testing is performed for a single person. Table 2 shows the confusion matrix for the best recognition rate which is obtained with a CHMM of 12 states and an output probability of 4 Gaussians for DCT, where H is the number of correct actions, D the ignored actions (deletion errors), I the erroneously entered actions between two activity cycles (insertion errors), S the wrongly recognized actions (substitution errors), and N the total number of samples, Accuracy=(H-I)/N.

As the actions of walking, jogging and running have similar characteristic and jogging is between the other two, they are often confused. Consequently, walking and running are sometimes confused with jogging, and jogging can be confused with either of the others (as the confusion matrix shows). It is worth mentioning that the two walking actions (to the left and to the right), which are erroneously classified as jogging, correspond to the same person (the 6th person in KTH's database). At times, as the person is centred in the rectangular area, the predominant movement in either jogging or running is the arm movement, and this can be misinterpreted by the system which wrongly classifies it as boxing. Nevertheless, it can be seen that the confusion matrix obtained using our coding is almost diagonal and gives a greater error rate for those actions with a smaller number of samples. We would therefore expect that an increase in the number of samples would be accompanied by an increase in the recognition rate for these actions. Finally, we should mention that

Table 2. Confusion matrix for the best case: for a 12-state HMM and an output probability of 4 Gaussians for DCT

	WORD: %Corr=95.59, Acc=94.71 [H=217, D=0, S=10, I=2, N=227]										
	W A L K I L	W A L K I R	J O G G I L	J O G G I R	R U N N I L	R U N N I R	B O X X I N L	B O X X I N R	C L A P P	W A V I N	Del [%c / %e]
WALKING_L	13	0	1	0	0	0	0	0	0	0	0[92.9/0.4]
WALKING_R	0	13	0	1	0	0	0	0	0	0	0[92.9/0.4]
JOGGING_L	1	0	9	0	1	0	0	0	0	0	0[81.8/0.9]
JOGGING_R	0	0	0	10	0	0	0	1	0	0	0[90.9/0.4]
RUNNING_L	0	0	0	0	9	0	0	0	0	0	0
RUNNING_R	0	0	0	2	0	6	1	0	0	0	0[66.7/1.3]
BOXING_L	0	0	0	0	0	0	33	0	0	0	0
BOXING_R	0	0	0	0	0	0	0	34	0	0	0
CLAPPING	0	0	0	0	0	0	0	0	54	0	0
WAVING	0	0	0	0	0	0	0	0	2	36	0 [94.7/0.9]
Insertions	0	0	0	0	1	0	0	1	0	0	

misclassification could result in two insertions appearing in the matrix (e.g. boxing to the right and running to the left) and in a file with only one activity cycle, the system considers there to be two cycles. In the case of running, for example, this is due to a jogging cycle having been wrongly classified as running, and since a jogging cycle consists of two steps and a running cycle of one, the system considers the second jogging step to be another running cycle, and it therefore appears to have two cycles.

If we examine the outline images, we can see that our recognition system is capable of handling noisy images which are affected by shadows, occlusion and bad background segmentation. In addition, thanks to the locality introduced in our proposal, when we divide the region where the person performs the action into meaningful movement areas, it is possible to distinguish between one direction and another.

In order to study the independence to people, we ran a subject independent test for a system with 12-state HMM for DCT, where the testing's subjects are all different to the training's ones. This was, 11 subjects for training and 3 for testing in walking, 15 for training and 4 for testing in jogging, 18 for training and 4 for testing in running, 9 for training and 2 for testing in clapping, 7 for training and 2 for testing in waving, 6 for training and 2 for testing in boxing to the left, 4 for training and 1 for testing in boxing to the right; with from 2 to 8 sequences by each subject for walking, jogging and running, and from 8 to 15 sequences by subject for clapping, waving and boxing. The accuracy obtained was 81.29% in a 12-state HMM for DCT. The confusion matrix is shown in the table 3.

Table 3. Confusion matrix for the subject independent test with a 12-state HMM and an output probability of 1 Gaussians for DCT

	WA LK IL	WA LK KR	JO GG IL	JO GG GR	RU NN IL	RU NN NR	BO OX IN L	BO OX IN R	CL AP PP	WA AV VI N	Del [%c / %e]
WALKING_L	8	0	0	0	0	0	0	0	0	0	0
WALKING_R	0	6	0	2	0	0	0	0	0	0	0[75.0/1.4]
JOGGING_L	0	0	8	0	0	0	0	0	0	0	0
JOGGING_R	0	0	0	7	0	0	0	0	0	0	0
RUNNING_L	0	0	0	0	9	0	0	0	0	0	0
RUNNING_R	0	0	0	0	0	9	0	0	0	0	0
BOXING_L	0	0	0	0	0	0	26	0	1	0	0[96.3/0.7]
BOXING_R	0	0	0	0	0	0	0	8	0	0	0
CLAPPING	0	0	0	0	0	1	0	2	20	7	0[66.7/7.2]
WAVING	0	0	0	0	0	0	2	0	11	12	0[48.0/9.4]
Insertions	0	0	0	0	0	0	0	0	0	0	

WORD: %Corr=81.29, Acc=81.29 [H=113, D=0, S=26, I=0, N=139]

How can see the matrix is almost diagonal. The confusion is mainly due to waving that is erroneously classified as clapping. But it's worth noting that we only used 7 different subjects for training, too few subjects for building subject independent systems. Even so we obtained promising results, for example, it's obtained 100% of accuracy for boxing to the right, with only 4 training's subjects.

4 Conclusions

Our coding is applied on a rectangular box tracking the subject. How can see in Figure 2, there are body's parts don't detected, shadows and background's noise, by its definition our coding is more robust than other ones based on the subject's exact silhouette. The results show that the use of contour features for HMM-based action recognition can achieve a recognition system capable of operating with low-level features which are easily and rapidly extractable directly from the image, and which can be obtained in realistic training and testing conditions without many *a priori* assumptions.

The proposal coding for incorporating contour information enables us to border the drawbacks suffered by other contour-based coding. (occlusions, shadows, noises resulting from cluttered environments and the subject's own clothes). Allowing us to exploit its advantages: greater robustness to lighting changes and to slight variations in viewpoint than other approaches (such as those based on optical flow or pixel brightness), similarity at different scales (the same approach can therefore be used for different depths in the field of vision), and its speed of extraction.

The speed of feature extraction is also an important issue, since the final aim for most action recognition applications is real-time operation. The recognition speed in HMM-based systems will depend on the number of HMM states, currently there are studies which accelerate the recognition time of the HMM-based system by hardware

[3]. Using features with a computationally efficient calculation and which do not require much pre-processing (as in the case of the contours) will help us achieve our objective.

One possible improvement to our coding would be to use overlapped tiles of sizes (rather than uniformly sized tiles) to divide the area where the subject performs the action using our knowledge of the human body.

Acknowledgments. This research was supported by the Spanish Ministry of Education and Science (TIN2005-01665).

References

1. Ahmad, M., Lee, S.: Human Action Recognition Using Multi-View Image Sequence Features. FGR, pp. 10–12 (2006)
2. Belongie, S., Malik, J.: Matching with Shape Contexts. CBAIVL (2000)
3. Fahmy, A., Cheung, P., Luk, W.: Hardware Acceleration of Hidden Markov Model Decoding for Person Detection. In: Proc. of the Design, Automation and Test in Europe Conference and Exhibition (2005)
4. Kale, A., Rajagopalan, A.N., Cuntoor, N., Krueger, V.: Gait-Based Recognition of Humans Using Continuous HMMS. FGR, pp. 336–341 (2002)
5. Moeslund, T.B., Hilton, A., Krüger, V.: A Survey of Advances in Vision-Based Human Motion Capture and Analysis. CVIU 104, 90–126 (2006)
6. Rabiner, L.: A Tutorial on Hidden Markov Models and Selected Applications in Speech Recognition. In: Proceedings of the IEEE, vol. 2, pp. 257–286 (1989)
7. Schuldt, C., Laptev, I., Caputo, B.: Recognizing Human Actions: a Local SVM Approach. ICPR III, 32–36 (2004)
8. Sundaresan, A., RoyChowdhury, A., Chellappa, R.: A Hidden Markov Model based Framework for Recognition of Humans from Gait Sequences. ICIP, pp. 93–96 (2003)
9. Yamato, J., Ohya, J., Ishii, K.: Recognizing Human Action in Time-Sequential Images Using a Hidden Markov Model. CVPR, pp. 379—385 (1992)
10. Young, S.J.: The HTK Hidden Markov Model Toolkit: Design and Philosophy. In: Technical Report CUED/F-INFENG/TR.152, Department of Engineering, Cambridge University, Cambridge (1994)

Locating and Segmenting 3D Deformable Objects by Using Clusters of Contour Fragments

Manuel J. Marín-Jiménez[1], Nicolás Pérez de la Blanca[1], and José I. Gómez[2]

[1] Dpt. Computer Science and Artificial Intelligence, University of Granada
ETSI Informática y Telecomunicación, Granada, 18071, Spain
[2] Department of Computer Science, University of Jaén
Campus Lagunillas, Jaén, 23071, Spain
mjmarin@decsai.ugr.es, nicolas@ugr.es, nacho@ujaen.es

Abstract. This paper presents a new approach to the problem of simultaneous location and segmentation of object in images. The main emphasis is done on the information provided by the contour fragments present in the image. Clusters of contour fragments are created in order to represent the labels defining the different parts of the object. An unordered probabilistic graph is used to model the objects, where a greedy approach (using dynamic programming) is used to fit the graph model to the labels.

1 Introduction

This paper addresses the problem of simultaneous detection, location and segmentation of 3D objects from contours in images. The contour, as feature, has been recurrently used along the literature to solve location and segmentation problems [11][5], but using it for simultaneously solving both problems we think that represents a new contribution. The contours extracted from an image by the state-of-the-art algorithms, represent a very noisy and deformed estimation of the object boundaries present in it. For this reason, the more relevant advances so far have been given on images of planar objects where an affine deformation on the contours can be assumed. For images of 3D deformable objects, the problem is much more difficult and the current approaches combine textural and contour information for simultaneous location and segmentation [10][13]. In this paper we support the idea that the contour by itself is a feature that allows to extract enough information to locate and to segment a deformable 3D object present in an image. This is the main novelty of this paper.

Elastic graph based algorithms are well-known approaches to detect and to localize 3D objects in general images, [12][10][6][16]. However, most of these approaches need to know some prior information (landmark node) in order to fit the model, Fergus et al. [7] with a star-graph model, or, Crandall and Huttenlocher [4] with the *k-fans* model. Our approach does not need of any prior information since all the required information is extracted from the contour shapes and their relative positions in the image. This point represent the main technical contribution of this paper. Song *et al.* [14], very recently, have proposed a new

J. Martí et al. (Eds.): IbPRIA 2007, Part I, LNCS 4477, pp. 402–409, 2007.

approach to detect 3D objects from motion using a probabilistic graph model. This approach has the main advantage on other graph based approaches of being non-parametric, that means that all relevant information about the graph structure is learnt from the sample data, although the graph is restricted to be a decomposable triangulated graph. Here we assume that this class of graph is rich enough to encode the spatial information provided by the contours present in an image. So, we have adapted this approach to carry out the location and the partial segmentation of the object.

In our method, the learning process follows a semi-supervised approach, where we assume as known the bounding-box of the object, e.g. manually annotated. We start estimating the contours inside the bounding-box and we create a set of clusters from contour fragments of different lengths where each cluster is associated to a label. From the clusters, we generate maps of labels over the image for each different fragment length. These labelled maps are the input to the graph learning algorithm. Geometrical and statistical information on the relative position of the contour present in each cluster has been used to bound the search space and to improve the efficiency of the fitting process. On the fitted graph model, the smallest region in the image containing the graph nodes gives the best object location, and the contours defining each node give a partial object segmentation.

Outline of the Paper. In section 2 we deal with the problem of part learning, where we introduce the representation and distance function of contours fragments, along with the clustering approach. Section 3 presents the structural model used for relating the parts model. In section 4 the experimental results are shown. And finally, the paper concludes with the summary and conclusions.

2   Parts Learning

The first step in our approach is the automatic learning of parts that represent our target object category. This problem is divided in the following subproblems: *(i)* the contour representation and distance measure; *(ii)* clustering of similar fragments; and, *(iii)* relations between clusters of fragments of different lengths.

2.1   Contour Representation and Distance Measure

We consider a contour c as a ordered sequence of n coordinates in the image reference system since we are not interested in full rotation invariance $c = \{(x_1, y_1), (x_2, y_2), (x_3, y_3), ...(x_{n-1}, y_{n-1}), (x_n, y_n)\}$ In order to impose shift invariance we fix the middle point ($\lfloor x_{n/2}, y_{n/2} \rfloor$) of the contour as the $(0, 0)$ of a local reference system. Different measures depending on the representation has been tested for the problem of contour fragment matching [15]. We use the Euclidean distance in a modified way (named SED) since the widely accepted Chamfer matching [2] did not result satisfactory for computing distance in clustering contour fragments.

Soft-Euclidean-Distance (SED). This measure could be understood as a correlation operation, where one contour is fixed and the other is shifted on the first. The curvature of the points lying out of the overlapping region are used to weight this distance. Let C_1 and C_2 be the vectors containing the curvature c_i for each point of the discarded subfragment and d_0 the Euclidean distance of the compared points within the overlapped subfragments. The final distance d is given by the following expression:

$$d = d_0 + f(C_1, m) + f(C_2, m) \tag{1}$$

$$f(C, m) = \begin{cases} \lambda \cdot \beta \cdot max(C, m) & \text{if } max(C, m) \geq \tau \\ 0 & \text{if } max(C, m) < \tau \end{cases} \tag{2}$$

where m is the number of discarded points, $max(C, m)$ is a function that returns the maximum value of the m points of C, λ is a value greater than 1 (to tune), and $\beta = 1 + (m/L)$ with L the full length of the contour (without discarding any piece). This implies that penalization only will be added when the discarded points contain a significative curvature, and, in this case, the penalization will depend on the length of the discarded subfragment (regulated by β) and the value of that maximal curvature.

Before measuring the distance between two contours we remove all possible affine deformations. In order to do this we estimate by least-squares the parameters of an affine transformation between both contours

$$\min_{a_{1..4}, d_1, d_2} \sum_{i=1}^{n} (x_i' - a_1 x_i + a_2 y_i + d_1)^2 + (y_i' - a_3 x_i + a_4 y_i + d_2)^2 \tag{3}$$

where (x_i, y_i) and (x_i', y_i') are the coordinates of each contour points.

Subcontour matching is a core operation in the location and segmentation stage. For each possible position of the shorter contour in the longer, we compute SED. The position of the smallest distance is returned.

2.2   Clustering Contour Fragments

The first step in our approach is to learn the most representative contour fragments defining a specific object. To do this we use a semi-supervised approach, that means, that the bounding-box of the object in the set of learning images is known. We compute the contours present in our region of interest using the Canny's algorithm [3], but any other algorithm could also be used. The detected contours are extracted and split in overlapping fragments of fixed lengths. These fragments will be clustered, attending their shape, in order to discover the object parts. The least populated clusters are discarded.

Since we do not know the number of representative parts defining the shape of an object, our clustering stage is based on a distance based clustering algorithm. In particular we have used the agglomerative clustering proposed by Fred and Leitão's [9]. This is a hierarchical agglomerative clustering based on dissimilarity

Fig. 1. Contour fragments from different categories: (a,b,c) cow, (d,e) horse, (f,g,h) bottle and (i,j,k) swan

between the samples. We tune the parameters α and β described in [9] to generate highly compact clusters, and afterwards we apply the agglomerative clustering proposed in [10] to join some of that clusters (tracking the clusters joint defining equivalencies in matching). We use group-average linkage method.

For recognition purposes, each cluster is represented by a *representative contour*. This is chosen as the sample contour nearest to the medoid contour of the cluster. In fig. 1 some examples of representative contour fragments are shown.

2.3   Fragments Hierarchy

Due to the noise introduced by the current contour detectors, the natural object boundaries appear broken. Hence, we get contour fragments shorter than the fragment models. In order to decide to which cluster to assign each contour fragment, we build a hierarchy and propagate the information throughout it. For learning such hierarchy, we work with the set of the longest medoids S_L. The procedure is as follows: for each predefined length l_i, we split the medoids L_j in S_L into overlapping fragments of length l_i, and put all the fragments of length l_i in a single bag b_i. Them, we compute the SED distance between all the pairs of fragments in bag b_i and perform clustering [9], obtaining k clusters c_i. Since we know where each fragment comes from (L_j), we can set the relations between L_j and the new lower-level clusters c_{ik}. Note that each cluster c_{ik} can have more than one ascendant medoid L_j. In the practice, this hierarchy is employed during recognition in an implicit way, since the detected shorter fragments are submatched over the longest cluster's representative contours.

3   Including Structural Information: DTG

Once we have defined an object as a collection of parts located in fixed relative positions, in this section we tackle the estimation of the spatial structure of the object. Our structural model is based on decomposable triangulated graphs (DTG), used satisfactorily in human action recognition by Song *et al.*[14]. This model allows us to define the spatial structure of a shape as a joint probability distribution on a graph, but with the important property that the conditional independence of model parts can be assumed. Let $S = S_1, S_2, ..., S_M$ be a set of M labels, and X_{Si}, $1 \leq i \leq M$ is the measurement for S_i. If its joint probability density function can be decomposed as a DTG then,

$$P(X_{S_1}, X_{S_2}, ...X_{S_M}) = P_{B_T C_T} \cdot \prod_{t=1}^{T} P_{A_t | B_t C_t} \qquad (4)$$

Fig. 2. Model graphs for categories: cow, horse, swan, bottle and applelogo

where $A_i, B_i, C_i \in S$, $A_1, A_2, ..., A_T, B_T, C_T = S$, $(A_1, B_1, C_1), (A_2, B_2, C_2),...,$ (A_T, B_T, C_T) are the triangles in the graph model, and $(A_1, A_2, ..., A_T)$ gives an order for such vertices. Let $\chi = \{\overline{X}^1, \overline{X}^2, ..., \overline{X}^N\}$ be a set of samples from a probability density function, where $\overline{X}^n = \{X_{S_1}^n, ..., X_{S_M}^n\}$, $1 \leq n \leq N$ are labelled data. Let $P(G|\chi)$ be the probability function to maximize, where G is the best DTG for the observed data χ. Assuming all prior $P(G)$ are equal, by Bayes rule, $P(G|\chi) = P(\chi|G)$ then the goal is to find the graph G that maximize $P(\chi|G)$ where

$$logP(\chi|G) = \sum_{n=1}^{N} logP(\overline{X}^n|G) = \sum_{n=1}^{N}(logP(X_{B_T}^n, X_{C_T}^n) + \sum_{t=1}^{T} logP(X_{A_t}^n|X_{B_t}^n, X_{C_t}^n))$$

(5)

In order to estimate the optimal G we follow the Dynamic Programming approach given in Song [14]. In our case each triangle of the graph (A_t, B_t, C_t) is characterized by a four dimensional Gaussian distribution X defined on the relative positions of triangle vertices:

The most challenging problem in this optimization problem is the size of the configuration space for each image. This size is $O(m^n)$, being m the number of graph nodes and n the number of points. Since each label in the image represents a contour fragment identified by its central point, the statistical and geometrical information about the relative location of the contours can be used to define an heuristic criteria to bound the size of configuration space. We assign a vector of weights (one for each node of the graph) to each observed contour (label). Only the labels whose weight is greater than a threshold will be considered as candidates for such node. The *normalized weight* $\hat{p}$ of a label (contour) c, belonging to a node (cluster) n_i, is defined by:

$$\hat{p}(n_i|c) = \exp(-\gamma * D(c, r_i))$$

(6)

Where γ is a factor which controls the steepness of the function, D is a distance function, and r_i is the representative contour (medoid) of node (cluster) n_i. We adapt the algorithms given in [14] to work with these vectors of weights.

4   Experimental Results

The goal of our experiments is threefold. Firstly, to assert that SED is a suitable way for comparing and matching contours of different lengths, providing a valid

Fig. 3. The top image (5 rows) shows learning samples of the databases. The bottom image shows examples of different stages of our approach. By columns, the images show: 1) original image, 2) detected contours using the Canny's algorithm, 3) points representing the location of the estimated labels, 4) fitted graph, and 5) estimated bounding-box with the contours associated to the fitted nodes, respectively. (Best viewed in color.).

distance for computing robust clusters. Secondly, that DTG is able to encode the spatial information of 3D deformable objects. And, finally, that the proposed framework achieves good enough preliminary results in the task of locating and segmenting objects in real images.

For performing the experiments, we use images from databases with well-defined ground-truth (ETHZ-cows [10], Weizmann-horses[1]), and images from databases with annotated bounding-box (ETHZ Shape Classes [2] [8], i.e. swan, applelogo and bottle).

---

[1] Horses dataset available at: http://www.msri.org/people/members/eranb

[2] Dataset available at: http://www.vision.ee.ethz.ch/~ferrari

In the learning stage, samples are extracted by using the object bounding-box (previously annotated) and resized to a fixed size $[0, 1] \times [0, 1]$. Then we extract all the contour fragments present in the image with a length in $[40, 200]$ pixels in steps of 20, and then we compute the clusters. We have fixed the clustering parameters to values: $\alpha = 0.35, \beta = 0.5$. Taking into account the number of clusters for each length, we decide which length is the most representative and we use the associated clusters as the estimated nodes. In our examples this length has been: 140 (cow), 100 (horse), 120 (bottle), 120 (swan) and 120 (apple). The resulting number of clusters is: 29 (cow), 39 (horse), 29 (bottle), 20 (swan) and 19 (apple). But for efficiency reasons we have selected a smaller but representative set of clusters. In all our experiments we use a graph with four nodes. The graph for each category has been trained with 15 samples. Figure 2 shows the estimated graphs (models) for the selected categories.

In the location stage, we fix the search window's size as the average size of the bounding-box of the training samples. In order to search the best location we carry out a *Sliding window* technique [1]. That is, for each possible window, we compute the matching graph cost C. This cost is weighted by using the information provided by the initial contour matching. So, the weighted cost C_w is given by: $C_w = C / (1 + \sum_i \hat{p}_i)$, where $\hat{p}_i$ is the normalized weight (eq.6) of the i-th point in the graph.

Figure 3 has two parts. The top part shows samples of the databases used in the experiments. The bottom part shows some examples of our approach on the different object classes. The number of nodes of the learnt graphs, for each object class, has been fixed equal to the estimated number of representative clusters. We have use ground-truth contour information to estimate the clusters on two of the databases, cows and horses, and the estimated contours inside the bounding-box for the other three classes. According to these preliminary experiments no difference is appreciated neither in the quality of the estimated clusters nor in the quality of the fitted graph.

Although some of the parameters have been manually fixed, from our experiments we can say that the proposed approach has performed well on the set of images we have used, however much more experimenting is needed, as well as a quantitative comparison with the state-of-the-art approaches. Global affine transformations and local large deformations on the object shape are very well absorbed by the clusters of contours, but strong changes in the point of view remains an important challenge for future research. In the optimization function of the graph fitting process we only have taken into account the relative location of the graph nodes but shape information could also be incorporated.

5   Summary and Conclusions

A new algorithm for simultaneous object location and segmentation from estimated contours has been proposed. This algorithm generalizes the current approach in two different ways. Firstly, it only uses the information provided by the contours present in the image, secondly no landmark or other specific reference is needed in order to locate the object in the image. The core of the approach is twofold. In a first stage, a clustering of contours is carried out in order to extract all information about persistent or relevant shapes present in the contour fragments. In a second stage, a non-parametric approach is used to encode the statistical information provided by the relative positions of the clusters obtained from the learning samples.

The approach is semi-supervised, and therefore it only needs to know the bounding-box of the object during the learning stage. However we think that after improving the clustering stage this constraint could be relaxed. Further experimental work is needed in order to assess the final performance of the approach.

Acknowledgments. Thanks to Dr. Fred, Dr. Santos-Victor and reviewers for their helpful comments. This work was supported by the Spanish Ministry of Education and Science under grant FPU AP2003-2405 and project TIN2005-01665.

References

1. Agarwal, S., Awan, A., Roth, D.: Learning to detect objects in images via a sparse, part-based representation. IEEE PAMI 26(11), 1475–1490 (2004)
2. Borgefors, G.: Hierarchical chamfer matching: a parametric edge matching algorithm. IEEE PAMI 10(6), 849–865 (1988)
3. Canny, J.F.: A computational approach to edge detection. IEEE Transactions on Pattern Analysis and Machine Intelligence 8(6), 679–698 (1986)
4. Crandall, D.J., Huttenlocher, D.P.: Weakly supervised learning of part-based spatial models for visual object recognition. In: ECCV, pp. 16–29 (2006)
5. Cremers, D., Kohlberger, T., Schnorr, C.: Nonlinear shape statistics in Mumford-Shah based segmentation. In: ECCV vol. 1, pp. 93–108 (2002)
6. Fergus, R., Perona, P., Zisserman, A.: Object class recognition by unsupervised scale-invariant learning. In: CVPR, vol. 2, pp. 264–271 (2003)
7. Fergus, R., Perona, P., Zisserman, A.: A sparse object category model for efficient learning and exhaustive recognition. In: CVPR, pp. 380–387 (2005)
8. Ferrari, V., Tuytelaars, T., Van Gool, L.: Object detection by contour segment networks. In: Proc. ECCV (May 2006)
9. Fred, A.L.N., Leitao, J.M.N.: A new cluster isolation criterion based on dissimilarity increments. IEEE Trans. on PAMI 25(8), 1–15 (2003)
10. Leibe, B.: Interleaved Object Categorization and Segmentation. PhD thesis, ETH Zurich (October 2004)
11. Mokhtarian, F., Bober, M.: Curvature Scale Space Representation: Theory, Applications & MPEG-7 Standardisation. Springer, Heidelberg (2003)
12. Opelt, A., Pinz, A., Zisserman, A.: A boundary-fragment-model for object detection. In: Proc of ECCV, vol. 2, pp. 575–588 (2006)
13. Shotton, J., Winn, J., Rother, C., Criminisi, A.: Textonboost: Joint appearance, shape and context modeling for multi-class object recognition and segmentation. In: ECCV (2006)
14. Song, Y., Goncalves, L., Perona, P.: Unsupervised learning of human motion. IEEE Trans. Patt. Anal. and Mach. Intell. 25(7), 1–14 (2003)
15. Veltkamp, R.C.: Shape matching: Similarity measures and algorithms. In: Shape Modelling International, pp. 188–199 (2001)
16. Weber, M., Welling, M., Perona, P.: Unsupervised learning of models for recognition. In: ECCV (2000)

Development of a Cascade Processing Method for Microarray Spot Segmentation

Antonis Daskalakis[1], Dionisis Cavouras[2], Panagiotis Bougioukos[1],
Spiros Kostopoulos[1], Ioannis Kalatzis[2], George C. Kagadis[1], and George Nikiforidis[1]

[1] Department of Medical Physics, School of Medicine, University of Patras, Rio,
GR-26503 Greece
[2] Medical Signal and Image Processing Lab, Department of Medical
Instrumentation Technology,Technological Education Institution of Athens, Ag.
Spyridonos Street, Aigaleo, 122 10, Athens, Greece
daskalakis@med.upatras.gr

Abstract. A new method is proposed for improving microarray spot segmentation for gene quantification. The method introduces a novel combination of three image processing stages, applied locally to each spot image: i/ Fuzzy C-Means unsupervised clustering, for automatic spot background noise estimation, ii/ power spectrum deconvolution filter design, employing background noise information, for spot image restoration, iii/ Gradient-Vector-Flow (GVF-Snake), for spot boundary delineation. Microarray images used in this study comprised a publicly available dataset obtained from the database of the MicroArray Genome Imaging & Clustering Tool website. The proposed method performed better than the GVF-Snake algorithm (Kullback-Liebler metric: 0.0305 bits against 0.0194 bits) and the SPOT commercial software (pairwise mean absolute error between replicates: 0.234 against 0.303). Application of efficient adaptive spot-image restoration on cDNA microarray images improves spot segmentation and subsequent gene quantification.

1 Introduction

Complementary DNA (cDNA) microarray imaging is considered as an important tool for large-scale gene sequence and gene expression analysis [1]. Molecular biologists and bioinformaticians are using microarray technology, not only for identifying a gene in a biological sequence but also for predicting the function of the identified gene within larger systems, such as the human organism. Three basic stages are involved in microarray analysis namely experimental design, image processing, and gene quantification [2].

Initially, the DNA obtained from the genes of interest (targets) is printed on a glass microscope slide by a robotic arrayer, thus, forming circular spots of known diameter. Each spot serves as a highly specific and sensitive detector (probe) of the corresponding gene [3]. In order to create a genome expression profile of a biological system with microarrays, the messenger RNA (mRNA) from a particular sample is isolated, it is labeled using Cy3 (green) and Cy5 (red) fluorescent dyes, and it is

J. Martí et al. (Eds.): IbPRIA 2007, Part I, LNCS 4477, pp. 410–417, 2007.

hybridized on the microarray. Following hybridization, the arrays are scanned by activation using lasers that excite each dye on the appropriate wavelength. The relative fluorescence between each dye on each spot is then recorded using methods contingent upon the nature of the labeling reaction i.e. confocal laser scanners, and Charged Couple Devices.

The output of such systems is two 16-bit TIFF images, one for each fluorescent channel. The relative intensities of each channel represent the relative abundance of the DNA or RNA product in each of the two DNA or RNA samples and are extracted via image analysis techniques, namely griding, spot segmentation, and intensity extraction [2]. Griding is the process of assigning coordinates to each cell; the latter is a square ROI containing the pixels of both the spot and its background. Segmentation, classifies cell-pixels as foreground (spot-pixels) or background. Intensity extraction calculates ratios of red to green fluorescence intensities for the foreground and background respectively.

Finally, molecular biologists translate the extracted expression levels to a biological conclusion (i.e. clustering genes with similar expression level, identifying differentially expressed genes etc.) using data mining techniques.

Extraction of gene expression levels is confounded by a number of technical factors, which operate during the fabrication, target labeling, and hybridization stages. Microarray images are corrupted by spatially inhomogeneous noise and by irregularities in the shape, size, and position of the spot [4]. Another source of degradation is due to noise and characteristics (Modulation Transfer Function) of the confocal laser scanner, employed as "reading" method. These sources of error, lead to inaccurate segmentation of spots (i.e. the boundaries of spots are erroneously estimated), which, as a direct effect, it evokes wrong estimation of the genes expression levels. Consequently, the precision of the extracted microarray intensities is affected causing inaccurate biological inferences [5].

Despite the potential importance of image pre-processing in correcting these error sources, existing software tools pay little attention to pre-processing and focus mainly on spot localization and microarray image segmentation. Additionally, only a few studies [6-10], most using wavelet transform methods, have examined the impact of image pre-processing upon spot enhancement, without however investigating the impact on segmentation. Latest research on general image enhancement has shown that α-rooting based techniques may be of value, since they perform better than wavelet based methods [11, 12]. Nevertheless, image enhancement focuses on modifying selectively the frequency content of images rather than removing the usual sources of spot-image degradation, i.e. biological and electronic noise as well as blurring due to the MTF of the confocal laser scanner. These sources of error may be alleviated by modeling the image degradation functions to design efficient image restoration algorithms that would render the distinction between spot and background more evident, thus, making the segmentation stage more accurate. This has led us to construct a cascade processing segmentation (CPS) method for microarray spot boundary delineation, which incorporates the benefits of image restoration into the spot segmentation procedure. Consequently, the aim of the present study is to propose a new method, which combines 1/the Fuzzy C-means clustering algorithm, for automatically locating spot background area and assessing local noise, 2/the power spectrum filter (PS-filter), designed using background noise information, for enhancing individual cell images, and 3/the GVF-Snake boundary detection algorithm, for spot segmentation and gene quantification.

2   Material and Methods

Material consisted of 7 microarray images downloaded from a publicly available database of the MicroArray Genome Imaging & Clustering Tool (MAGIC) website [13]. Each image contained 6400 spots investigating the diauxic shift of *Saccharomyces cerevisiae*. In the particular dataset the authors [14] used a common reference messenger RNA pool (green, Cy-3) to control for biological variability. Such a design provides an adequate degree of replication, required for the quantitative assessment of image segmentation and subsequent gene quantification.

The proposed CPS method comprised clustering-restoration-segmentation stages that were sequentially applied on each cell image.

2.1   Clustering

Prior to spot segmentation, a griding procedure was applied on the images, following the method proposed in a previous study [15] for locating spot sites (cell images). Following griding, individual spots were segmented from surrounding background by unsupervised segmentation, using the Fuzzy C-Means algorithm [16]. The latter is an iterative clustering algorithm, which finds cluster centers (centroids) that minimize the dissimilarity function

$$J(U, c_1, c_2, ..., c_c) = \sum_{i=1}^{c} J_i = \sum_{i=1}^{c} \sum_{j=1}^{n} u_{ij}^{m} d_{ij}^{2} \tag{1}$$

where c_i is the centroid of cluster i, d_{ij} is the Euclidean distance between i-th centroid (c_i) and j-th data point and $m \in [1, \infty]$ is a weighting exponent. During iteration the algorithm modifies the cluster centers and changes the data memberships (in our case spots or background) until the dissimilarity function is locally minimized. Subsequently, from each segmented cell-image, local noise $(2 \times \sigma^2)$ [17] was assessed from the spot's background. This parameter was used to restore each cell image of the microarray image by employing the power spectrum image deconvolution technique.

2.2   Cell Image Restoration

Power spectrum image deconvolution incorporates both the degradation function and statistical characteristics of noise into the deconvolution process as in (2):

$$\hat{F}(u, v) = \sqrt{\left[\frac{|Fh(u, v)|^2}{|Fh(u, v)|^2 + 2 \times \sigma^2} \right] \frac{G(u, v)}{Fh(u, v)}} \tag{2}$$

where Fh is the Fourier transform of the degradation function, considered constant across the image, and G is the Fourier transform of the degraded cell image. Subsequently, the restored cell image in the spatial domain is obtained by the inverse Fourier transform of (2).

The Fourier transform of the degradation function Fh in (2) was modeled as a low pass Butterworth filter:

$$Fh^{LP}(v) = \left(1 + 0.414\left(\frac{v}{f_{co}}\right)^{2n}\right)^{-1}$$ (3)

where n is the degree of the filter, v is the frequency, and f_{co} the cut-off frequency [17]. The 2-dimensional Fh was then obtained by (4)

$$Fh(u,v) = Fh^{LP}\left(\sqrt{u^2 + v^2}\right), \quad \sqrt{u^2 + v^2} \leq N$$ (4)

where, N is the maximum dimension of the cell-image (which is zero-padded in the case of non-square cell image), and u,v are spatial frequencies.

All algorithms were implemented using Matlab custom-made code.

2.3 Cell Image Segmentation

Following restoration, the GVF-Snake boundary detection algorithm [18] was applied on each cell image. Since intensities in the processed cell images were altered by the deconvolution process, all spot boundary points were referred to the original cell-images. Additionally, the GVF-Snake algorithm was applied on the original images alone and segmentation results, obtained by both methods, were evaluated by applying the Kullback-Liebler (K-L) measure of divergence [19], as described below.

2.4 Benefit Quantification

Foreground (spot) and background intensity values for the common reference channel (green, Cy-3) were extracted. Those values were used to form two density distributions employing a non- parametric kernel density estimation method [20]. The distance between those two distributions was determined employing the Kullback-Liebler (K-L) measure of divergence, shown in (6):

$$KL(P \parallel Q) = \sum_i P(i) \log \frac{P(i)}{Q(i)}$$ (5)

where P and $Q_{,i}$ are the spot and background density distributions respectively.

Higher values of divergence, correspond to well separable distributions of signal and background and, consequently, to more accurate segmentation results [19].

Additionally, in order to quantify the efficiency and robustness of the proposed CPS-Method, we calculated the pairwise mean absolute error (MAE) between the replicates (altogether 21 pairwise MAE values) for the common reference channel. Extracted intensities, for the same series of microarray images, were comparatively evaluated against the intensities obtained from SPOT [21], a publicly available software package, utilizing the Seeded Region Growing segmentation technique.

3 Results

Forty randomly selected cell-images from a microarray image were separately segmented by both the proposed CPS method and the GVF-Snake algorithm. In the CPS method, the image degradation function was optimally designed by a first degree ($n=1$) low-pass Butterworth filter using $f_{co}=0.3xN$, with N being the dimension of the square cell image. Figure 1, shows the result of the cell restoration step.

Fig. 1. Original and image restored sections of microarray images for the optimally designed degradation function

Figure 2 shows the segmentation for five spots (top row) by the GFV-snake algorithm (middle row) and the CPS-method (bottom row).

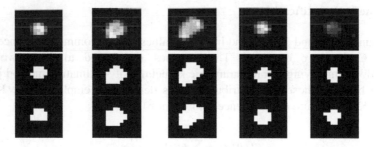

Fig. 2. Segmentation comparison of GVF-Snake algorithm (second row) and the proposed CPS method (third row)

Table 1 shows the Kullback-Liebler (K-L) divergence values obtained by the proposed CPS method and the GVF-Snake algorithm for five different microarray cell images. K-L values were obtained by referring segmented boundary points onto the original cell images.

Table 1. Kullback-Liebler measure of divergence for GVF-Snake and CPS methods: Divergence values (measured in bits) between segmented spot's signal and background intensities, calculated on the original image for both methods

	GVF-Snake	CPS
Spot 1	0.0449	0.0510
Spot 2	0.0182	0.0278
Spot 3	0.0217	0.0270
Spot 4	0.0126	0.0150
Spot 5	0.0194	0.0305

Figure 3 shows the calculated pairwise MAEs between the expression ratios of all possible pairs of the common reference channel for the dataset of the 7 replicated real images.

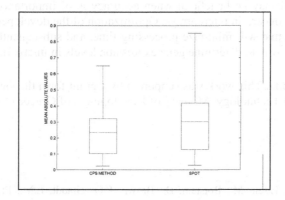

Fig. 3. Boxplots for CPS-Method (Mean Value: 0.234) and SPOT (Mean Value: 0.303)

4 Discussion

In the present study a CPS method was designed that suitably combined 1/the Fuzzy C-means clustering algorithm, for automatically locating spot background area and assessing local noise, 2/the power spectrum filter (PS-filter), designed using background noise information, for enhancing individual cell images, and 3/the GVF-Snake boundary detection algorithm, for spot segmentation and gene quantification.

The success of the proposed CPS method is mostly due to the automatic restoration of the cell image, which took into account background noise information of the cell image. This may be observed in the restored image of Figure 1, where edges appear sharp and with well defined outline. The segmentation results of both methods were evaluated by the Kullback-Liebler divergence metric (Table 1). Accordingly, it was found that the proposed CPS method performed better by increasing the divergence ($K\text{-}L$) between the distributions of signal and background intensity distributions, as compared to the GVF-Snake method. Results were obtained by superimposing boundary points on the original cell images. In this way, higher divergence was attributed to better segmentation of the actual spot image from its surrounding background.

Exploiting the benefits of the provided replication in the real images, we explored the efficiency and robustness of the extracted gene expression levels by measuring the 'sameness' of replicates using their pairwise MAE (totally 21 pairwise MAE values). Figure 3 illustrates the boxplots of MAE as they were calculated for the common reference channel of the 7 replicated microarray images. Lower MAE is indicative of higher segmentation performance and, thus, of more accurate (valid) extraction of gene expression levels. The proposed method achieved better results (0.234) than the publicly available software (0.303). This may be due to the employment by the proposed CPS-method of the automatic local restoration step.

Regarding processing time, it was estimated that it took about half a second for the CPS method to delineate the boundary of a cell spot. This may seem computationally intensive and time consuming as compared to commercial software. However, the proposed method may be beneficial when accuracy is of importance and this is the case of primary concern in microarrays. Optimization of the developed Matlab code is a future concern that will minimize processing time, and subsequently will provide a fast and accurate way to determine gene expression levels in microarray images.

Acknowledgments. This work was supported by a grant form the General Secretariat for Research and Technology, Ministry of Development of Greece (136/PENED03) to B.A.

References

1. Alizadeh, A., Eisen, M., Botstein, D., Brown, P.O.: Staudt, L.M.: Probing lymphocyte biology by genomic-scale gene expression analysis. J. Clin. Immunol. 18, 373–379 (1998)
2. Angulo, J., Serra, J.: Automatic analysis of DNA microarray images using mathematical morphology. Bioinformatics. 19, 553–562 (2003)
3. Schena, M.: Microarray biochip technology. 1st edn. Eaton Publishing Company (2000)
4. Balagurunathan, Y., Wang, N., Dougherty, E.R., Nguyen, D., Chen, Y., Bittner, M.L., Trent, J., Carroll, R.: Noise factor analysis for cdna microarrays. J. Biomed Opt. 9, 663–678 (2004)
5. Ahmed, A.A., Vias, M., Iyer, N.G., Caldas, C., Brenton, J.D.: Microarray segmentation methods significantly influence data precision. Nucleic Acids Res. 32, 50 (2004)
6. Wang, X.H., Istepanian, R.S., Song, Y.H.: Microarray image enhancement by denoising using stationary wavelet transform. IEEE Trans Nanobioscience 2, 184–189 (2003)
7. Lukac, R., K.N., P., B., S., Venetsanopoulos, A.N.: Cdna microarray image processing using fuzzy vector filtering framework. Journal of Fuzzy Sets and Systems: Special Issue on Fuzzy Sets and Systems in Bioinformatics (2005)
8. Mastriani, M., Giraldez, A.E.: Microarrays denoising via smoothing of coefficients in wavelet domain. International Journal of Biomedical Sciences 1, 1306–1316 (2006)
9. Lukac, R., Smolka, B.: Application of the adaptive center-weighted vector median framework for the enhancement of cdna microarray. Int. J. Appl. Math. Comput. Sci. 13, 369–383 (2003)

10. Daskalakis, A., Cavouras, D., Bougioukos, P., Kostopoulos, S., Argyropoulos, C., Nikiforidis, G.C.: Improving microarray spots segmentation by k-means driven adaptive image restoration. In: Proceedings of the ITAB Ioannina, Greece (2006)
11. Arslan, F.T., Grigoryan, A.M.: Alpha-rooting image enhancement by paired splitting-signals. In: Proceedings of the 3rd IEEE International Symposium on Biomedical Imaging: from Macro to Nano,ISBI, Arlington, VA, pp. 968–971 (2006)
12. Arslan, F.T., Moreno, J.M., Grigoryan, A.M.: New methods of image enhancement. In: Proceedings of the SPIE, the International Conference of SPIE Defense and Security Symposium, Orlando, FL, pp. 225–236 (2005)
13. http://www.bio.davidson.edu/projects/MAGIC/MAGIC.html. Available: via the INTERNET. Accessed
14. DeRisi, J.L., Iyer, V.R., Brown, P.O.: Exploring the metabolic and genetic control of gene expression on a genomic scale. Science 278, 680–686 (1997)
15. Blekas, K., Galatsanos, N., Likas, A., Lagaris, I.: Mixture model analysis of DNA microarray images. IEEE Trans. Med. Imaging 24, 901–909 (2005)
16. Bezdec, J.C: Pattern recognition with fuzzy objective function algorithms. ed. Plenum Press, New York (1981)
17. Gonzalez, R.C., Woods, R.E.: Digital image processing 1st edn. (1992)
18. http://iacl.ece.jhu.edu/projects/gvf/. Gradient flow vector active contours. Available: via the INTERNET. Last accessed: 02/02/2007
19. Kullback, S.: Information theory and statistics, 2nd edn. Dover Publications, Mineola, NY (1968)
20. Bowman, A.W., Azzalini, A.: Applied smoothing techniques for data analysis. Oxford University Press, Oxford (1997)
21. Yang, Y.H., Buckley, M., Dudoit, S., Speed, T.: Comparison of methods for image analysis on cdna microarray data. J.Comput.Graph Stat. 11, 108–136 (2002)

Haar Wavelets and Edge Orientation Histograms for On–Board Pedestrian Detection

David Gerónimo, Antonio López, Daniel Ponsa, and Angel D. Sappa

Computer Vision Center, Universitat Autònoma de Barcelona
Edifici O, 08193 Bellaterra, Barcelona, Spain
{dgeronimo,antonio,daniel,asappa}@cvc.uab.es
www.cvc.uab.es/adas

Abstract. On–board pedestrian detection is a key task in advanced driver assistance systems. It involves dealing with aspect–changing objects in cluttered environments, and working in a wide range of distances, and often relies on a classification step that labels image regions of interest as pedestrians or non–pedestrians. The performance of this classifier is a crucial issue since it represents the most important part of the detection system, thus building a good classifier in terms of false alarms, missdetection rate and processing time is decisive. In this paper, a pedestrian classifier based on Haar wavelets and edge orientation histograms (HW+EOH) with AdaBoost is compared with the current state–of–the–art best human–based classifier: support vector machines using histograms of oriented gradients (HOG). The results show that HW+EOH classifier achieves comparable false alarms/missdetections tradeoffs but at much lower processing time than HOG.

1 Introduction

On–board pedestrian detection in the context of advanced driver assistance systems (ADAS) has become an active research field aimed at reducing the number of traffic accidents. The objective is to provide information to the driver and to perform evasive or braking actions on the host vehicle by detecting people in a given range of distances. The most relevant works in the literature [1,2,3] base detection on a classification step that labels regions of interest in the input image as pedestrians or non–pedestrians. The main difficulty of the classification stage comes from dealing with aspect–changing targets like pedestrians, which are subject to a high intra–class variability. In Fig. 1 some pedestrian samples illustrate the variability of this object class for different distances, backgrounds, illuminations, poses or clothes.

In this paper we compare two relevant pedestrian classifiers in the context of ADAS. The first one uses Haar wavelets and edge orientation histograms (HW+EOH) as features and Real AdaBoost as learning machine. This classifier is originally proposed by *Levi and Weiss* to perform face detection in [4]. In this paper we add some slight modifications and use it to classify pedestrian samples. In order to evaluate the performance of the mentioned classifier,

J. Martí et al. (Eds.): IbPRIA 2007, Part I, LNCS 4477, pp. 418–425, 2007.

Fig. 1. Positive samples of the database illustrating the high variability in terms of distance, background, illumination, pose and clothes (contrast enhaced for better visualization). Distance variations are specially relevant in ADAS databases. For instance, in this case the sample size can range from 12×24 to 120×240 pixels.

we make a comparison against the best human–detector in the state–of–the–art literature: support vector machines using histograms of oriented gradients (HOG) by *Dalal and Triggs* [5]. To make a relevant comparison, we first tune the feature parameters for an ADAS pedestrian database, selecting the ones that achieve the best performance, and then we analyse the classifiers in terms of false alarms/missdetection rates and processing time. Experiments show that the HW+EOH based classifier achieves the same detection rates than the HOG based one, but being ten times faster. Moreover, HOG rates are outperformed by increasing the complexity of the HW+EOH classifier, but still requiring half the processing time.

The reminder of the paper is organized as follows. Sect. 2 describes the HW+EOH based classifier and Sect. 3 the HOG based one. Sect. 4 presents the database used, and then evaluates the two classifiers in terms of detection rates and processing time. Finally, Sect. 5 exposes the main conclusions.

2   HW+EOH Based Classifier

Levi and Weiss [4] propose a combination of two sets of features, Haar wavelets (HW) and edge orientation histograms (EOH), to detect faces, outperforming the detection rates of the single sets alone. In this paper, we add some modifications in order to improve the detection results: we use Real AdaBoost [6] instead of the original AdaBoost version, and make some slight modifications when computing the features, as described in this section.

Haar wavelets represent a fast and simple way to calculate region derivatives at different scales by means of computing the average intensities of concrete sub-regions (defined by a set of filters). They are proposed by *Papageorgiou et al.* [3] for object recognition. A feature of this set is defined as the difference of intensity between two defined areas (white and black) in a given position inside a region R:

$$\text{Feature}_{Haar}(x, y, w, h, type, R) = E_{white}(R) - E_{black}(R) \ ,$$

where (x, y) is the bottom–left corner of the filter; w, h are the filter's width and height; and *type* corresponds to the filter's configuration. $E_{white}(R)$ and $E_{black}(R)$ represent the sum of intensities of white and black areas of the template respectively. In order to compute E, the *integral image* (*ii*) representation [7] has been used, where the summed values of a certain region can be efficiently computed by four *ii* accesses.

The original set of filters contains three basic configurations [3] (Fig. 2 (*middle*) (a–c)), that capture changes in intensity along the horizontal, vertical directions and the diagonals. In our case, we use the set proposed by *Viola and Jones* [7], which contains two additional filters (Fig. 2(*middle*)(a–e)). In addition, in this work we have also followed the latter approach [7], where filters are not constrained to a fixed size, as proposed in [3], but can vary in size and aspect ratio.

Due to perspective, different windows framing a pedestrians can have different sizes, so spatial normalization is required to establish an equivalence between the features computed in each window. To achieve that, it is not necessary to

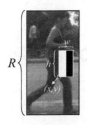
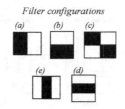
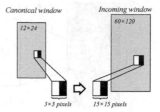

Fig. 2. Computation of Haar wavelet features: (*left*) Haar feature placed in a sample image; (*middle*) some filter configurations; (*right*) filter normalization according to the incoming window size

explicitly resize the windows, but features can be computed in a way that it is equivalent to resizing but more efficient [7]. Our canonical window is 12×24 pixels (Fig. 2(*right*)), which in our acquisition system corresponds to a *standard* pedestrian at about 50m. In addition, we modify the filters to be illumination invariant, in order to obtain responses identical to the ones obtained by previously normalizing the contrast of the processed image region.

Edge orientation histograms[1] are also interesting for our work, since pedestrians often present strong edges in the legs or trunk areas. They rely on the richness of edge information, so they differ from the intensity area differences of HW but maintain invariance properties to global illumination changes.

First, the gradient image is computed by a Sobel mask convolution (contrary to the original paper, no edge–thresholding is applied in our case). Then, gradient pixels are classified into β images corresponding to β orientation ranges (also referred as *bins*, in our case we have tested $\beta = \{4, 6, 9\}$). Therefore, a pixel in bin $k_n \in \beta$ contains its gradient magnitude if its orientation is inside β_n's range, otherwise is null. Integral images are now used to store the accumulation image of each of the edge bins.

At this stage a bin interpolation step has been included in order to distribute the gradient value into adjacent bins. This step is used in SIFT [8] and HOG [5] features, and in our experiments the improvement achieved (using EOH features alone) is 1% Detection Rate (DR) at 0.01 False Positive Rate (FPR).

Finally, the feature value is defined as the relation between two orientations, k_1 and k_2, of region R as:

$$\text{Feature}_{EOH}(x, y, w, h, k_1, k_2, R) = \frac{E_{k_1}(R) + \epsilon}{E_{k_2}(R) + \epsilon} \ .$$

If this value is above a threshold of 1, it can be said that orientation k_1 is dominant to orientation k_2 for R. If the value is lower than 1 it can be said than k_2 is dominant to k_1. The small value ϵ is added for smoothing purposes.

---

[1] In order to respect the author's work, in this paper we maintain the original name. However, since this can lead to confusion with other similar feature names like the *histograms of oriented gradients* (HOG) in [5] (Sect. 3), we think that a more convenient name would be *ratios of gradient orientations*.

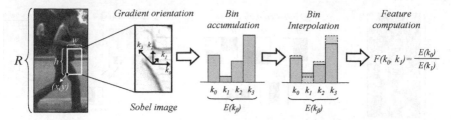

Fig. 3. Computation of edge orientation histograms

In our implementation, we make use of Real AdaBoost [6] as learning machine, rather than the original AdaBoost version used in [4]. The idea is to build a *strong* classifier by combining the response of a set of *weak* classifiers, improving the performance that a complex classifier would have alone. In our case, since both HW and EOH features are represented by a real value, each weak classifier corresponds to a threshold–like rule on each feature value.

In the literature, AdaBoost classifiers are often implemented in a cascade so the number of false positives decreases and hence the overall performance is increased. In this comparison, since we are more interested in the features than in the learning machine, we make use of just one cascade level. However, the multiple–cascade strategy is planned to be implemented in future works.

3   HOG Based Classifier

The current state–of–the–art best classifier is based on histograms of oriented gradients (HOG) as features and support vector machine (SVM) as learning algorithm. It is proposed by *Dalal and Triggs* [5] to perform human detection. HOG are SIFT–inspired features [8] that rely on gradient orientation information. The idea is to divide the image into small regions, named *cells*, that are represented by a 1D histogram of the gradient orientation. Cells are grouped in larger spatial regions called *blocks* so histograms contained in a block are attached and normalized (Fig. 4).

When computing the features, we follow the indications of the authors as strictly as possible. As the authors suggest, no smoothing is aplied to the incoming image, and a simple 1D $[-1, 0, 1]$ mask is used to extract the gradient information. Next, we have tested the best parameters for our database: number of bins ($\beta = \{4, 6, 9\}$ in $0 - 180°$), cell sizes ($\eta = \{1 \times 1, 2 \times 2, 3 \times 3\}$ pixels) and block sizes ($\varsigma = \{1 \times 1, 2 \times 2, 3 \times 3\}$ cells), for our 24×12 canonical windows. Block overlapping is set to the maximum possible, i.e., ς–fold coverage for each cell. Bin interpolation is also used here. As last step, the block histogram is normalized using *L2-Hys*, the best method in the original paper, i.e., L2-normalizing, clipping values above 0.2, and then renormalizing. Finally, the features are fed to a linear SVM (following the authors' indications, SVMLight <http://svmlight.joachims.org> with C=0.01 has been used)[2].

---

[2] Real AdaBoost has also been tested using gradient orientations as weak rules, which results in similar performance rates. Thus, we keep the original formulation.

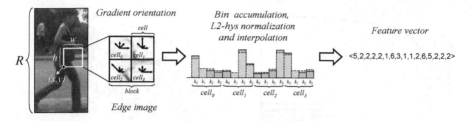

Fig. 4. Computation of histograms of oriented gradients

Although not done in [5], we make use of the integral image representation to store the bins histograms corresponding to each orientation, which dramatically speeds up the features computation. This approach, as previously reported by [9], is incompatible with the Gaussian spatial window applied to the block before constructing the histogram. However, since [9] achieves the same results than [5] without applying the Gaussian spatial window step, we ommit it without danger of significantly decreasing the performance.

4   Experimental Results

In order to illustrate the performance of the classifiers under real driving environments we use our ADAS pedestrian database. Differently to other non ADAS–oriented databases [5], it contains images at different scales from urban scenarios. In our case, color information is discarded as an useful cue, so samples are transformed to grayscale. The complete database consists of $1,000$ positive samples (i.e., pedestrians; Fig. 1) and $5,000$ negative ones (i.e., human–sized windows in regions likely to contain pedestrians). Each experiment randomly selects 700 positive and $4,000$ negative samples (training set) to learn a model, and use the remaining (testing set) to measure the classifier performance. All performance rates and plots are the result of averaging 4 independent experiments.

In order to be rigorous and provide a fair comparison, we have tunned the feature parameters to select the best ones for the database. We have tested $\beta = \{4, 6, 9\}$ for HW+EOH, achieving similar results (Fig. 5($left$)). Hence, we have selected the $\beta = 4$ bins version since it requires less processing time. Regarding to HOG features, the optimum parameters are $\beta = 9$, $\eta = 2 \times 2$ and $\varsigma = 2 \times 2$, which provide a detection rate (DR) of 92.5% at $FPR = 1\%$ (Fig. 5 ($right$)).

Figure 6($right$) presents the comparison between the HW+EOH based classifier and the HOG based one. As can be seen, with 100 features (i.e., Real AdaBoost weak rules) HW+EOH reaches the same performance as HOG. However, the HW+EOH features are at least ten times faster to compute (each window is classified in 0.015 ms). With 500 features the DR improves 4% (at $FPR = 0.01$), and it is computed about two times faster than HOG.

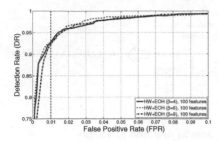
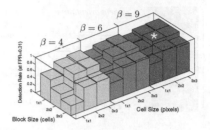

Fig. 5. (*left*) Performance of the proposed classifier using different β for the EOH features. (*right*) Detection rate at FPR=0.01 for all possible configurations of β, η and ς of HOG features (the best one is marked with a star).

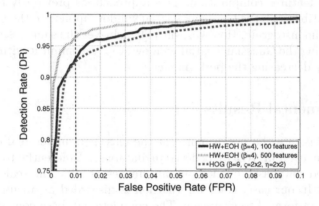

Fig. 6. Comparison between the HW+EOH based classifier and the best HOG based one

Table 1. Number of operations needed for HOG, HW and EOH

	+	×	/	√	>	ii accesses	built ii	edge mask	other
HOG	9,900	3,960	3,960	110	1,980	4,455	9	1D	bin interp.
HW	1,900	400	500	100	–	1,700	2	–	–
EOH	600	–	100			800	4	Sobel	bin interp.

Table 1 provides a summary of the basic operations needed by each feature set to perform the classification. In the case of HOG, 55 blocks are computed to classify each sample, spending in total all the indicated basic operations, building 9 integral images and computing a 1D edge mask for the sample. Next, we have detailed the operations needed supposing that all the features selected by Real AdaBoost are either HW (choosing filter (*c*) in Fig. 2, i.e., the slowest case) or EOH. In both cases, the classifier consists in 100 features, namely weak rules. As can be appreciated, the slowest HW+EOH classifier would consist in a 100 HW features, but it is still much faster than HOG.

5   Conclusions

This paper presents a comparison between two classifiers in an ADAS–oriented pedestrian database: Haar wavelets and edge orientation histograms (HW+EOH) features together with Real AdaBoost as learning algorithm, and the state–of–the–art best human–based classifier, histograms of oriented gradients (HOG) with SVM [5]. We describe the computation of the different features, and then tune their parameters to work with an ADAS pedestrian database. In this way, we provide a fair and accurated comparison in terms of detection rate and processing time (even comparing basic operations), which leads to conclude that HW+EOH based classifier achieves similar performance than HOG based one requiring much less processing time, concretely one order of magnitude faster.

Acknowledgments. This work was supported by the Spanish Ministry of Education and Science under project TRA2004-06702/AUT, BES-2005-8864 grant (first author) and Ramón y Cajal Program (fourth author).

References

1. Gavrila, D., Giebel, J., Munder, S.: Vision–based pedestrian detection: The PROTECTOR system. In: Proc. of the IEEE Intelligent Vehicles Symposium, Parma, Italy (2004)
2. Shashua, A., Gdalyahu, Y., Hayun, G.: Pedestrian detection for driving assistance systems: Single–frame classification and system level performance. In: Proc. of the IEEE Intelligent Vehicles Symposium, Parma, Italy (2004)
3. Papageorgiou, C., Poggio, T.: A trainable system for object detection. IJCV 38(1), 15–33 (2000)
4. Levi, K., Weiss, Y.: Learning object detection from a small number of examples: the importance of good features. In: Proc. of the IEEE Conference on CVPR, Washington, DC, USA. pp. 53–60 (2004)
5. Dalal, N., Triggs, B.: Histograms of oriented gradients for human detection. In: Proc. of the IEEE Conference on CVPR. vol. 2., San Diego, CA, USA. pp. 886–893 (2005)
6. Schapire, R., Singer, Y.: Improved boosting algorithms using confidence–rated predictions. Machine Learning 37(3), 297–336 (1999)
7. Viola, P., Jones, M.: Rapid object detection using a boosted cascade of simple features. In: Proc. of the IEEE Conference on CVPR, Kauai, HI, USA (2001)
8. Lowe, D.: Distinctive image features from scale–invariant keypoints. IJCV 60(2), 91–110 (2004)
9. Zhu, Q., Avidan, S., Yeh, M.C., Cheng, K.T.: Fast human detection using a cascade of histrograms of oriented gradients. In: Proc. of the IEEE Conference on CVPR, New York, NY, USA (2006)

Face Recognition Using Principal Geodesic Analysis and Manifold Learning

Matthew P. Dickens, William A.P. Smith, Jing Wu, and Edwin R. Hancock

Department of Computer Science, The University of York

Abstract. This paper describes how face recognition can be effected using 3D shape information extracted from single 2D image views. We characterise the shape of the field of facial normals using a statistical model based on principal geodesic analysis. The model can be fitted to 2D brightness images of faces to recover a vector of shape parameters. Since it captures variations in a field of surface normals, the dimensionality of the shape vector is twice the number of image pixels. We investigate how to perform face recognition using the output of PGA by applying a number of dimensionality reduction techniques including principal components analysis, locally linear embedding, locality preserving projection and Isomap.

1 Introduction

Face recognition from single image views has attracted considerable interest in the literature. One of the first reported methods was the eigenfaces technique of Turk and Pentland [1] which applies PCA to image long-vectors. This is a purely appearance based method. Several techniques have attempted to additionally incorporate facial shape, including the active appearance model of Cootes et al. [2] and the morphable model approach of Blantz and Vetter [3]. The latter approach uses a statistical model of shape, texture and imaging parameters that is constructed from 3D head scans. Once trained the method can be used for recognition over varying pose, illumination and imaging conditions. Basri and Jacobs [4] focus on the approximation of reflectance functions of Lambertian objects using linear subspaces, and analytically derive a representation based on the spherical harmonic basis. Belhumeur and Kriegman [5] consider the space formed by the set of all images of a Lambertian object and show that this can be built from an orthonormal basis consisting of three images of that object under varying and unknown illumination conditions.

A more direct way of recovering facial shape from a single image is to apply a technique such as shape-from-shading (SFS) and recover either the field of facial surface normals or the facial height function. However, this process is not reliable since there are problems due to concavity/convexity inversion, self-shadowing and albedo variation. In a recent series of papers Smith and Hancock [6,7] have shown how these problems can be overcome using a statistical model that accounts for variations in surface normal direction. This model relies on a representation that is based on the azimuthal equidistant projection of the local

J. Martí et al. (Eds.): IbPRIA 2007, Part I, LNCS 4477, pp. 426–434, 2007.

distribution of surface normals from the unit sphere onto a tangent plane. The statistical model is constructed by applying principal components analysis to the transformed surface normals on the tangent plane.

In this paper we explore a more general way of formulating the statistical model. We treat the surface normals as non-Euclidean data that reside on a manifold. When viewed in this way, the principal geodesic analysis (PGA) [8,9] can be used to analyse variations in facial shape. To do this we draw on the concept of the exponential map for the surface normal data. The exponential map is constructed by projecting the surface normals into the tangent space of the manifold, so as to preserve geodesic distance. Principal geodesic analysis can then be effected by performing PCA in the tangent space, and projecting the result back on to the manifold using the inverse exponential map, i.e. the logarithmic map.

PGA offers the advantage over PCA that it allows the model to be captured in an elegant manner that makes the connection with differential geometry explicit. The aim in this paper is to explore whether the shape-vectors delivered by PGA can be used for face recognition. One of the problems that hinders this endeavour is that of dimensionality, whose length is twice the number of image pixels. Here we explore whether dimensionality can be effected using techniques from manifold learning theory. We explore four methods, namely Locally Linear Embedding (LLE) [13], Locality Preserving Projection (LPP) [14], Isomap [12] and PCA. The former three techniques can all be regarded as extensions of PCA which allow the data to be projected onto a local manifold. The study illustrates that recognition rates in excess of 95% can be achieved with a reduced dimensionality as low as 10.

2   Principle Geodesic Analysis

The surface normal $n \in R^3$ may be considered as a point lying on a spherical manifold $n \in S^2$, therefore, we turn to the intrinsic mean and PGA proposed by Fletcher et al. [9] to analyse the variations of the surface normals.

The Log and Exponential Maps: If $u \in T_n S^2$ is a vector on the tangent plane to S^2 at n and $u \neq 0$, the exponential map, denoted Exp_n, of u is the point, denoted $Exp_n(u)$, on S^2 along the geodesic in the direction of u at distance $\| u \|$ from n. The log map, denoted Log_n is the inverse of the exponential map. The exponential and log maps preserve the geodesic distance between two points, i.e. $d(n_1, n_2) = d(u_1, u_2)$, where $u_1 = Log_n n_1, u_2 = Log_n n_2$.

Spherical Medians: It is more natural to treat the surface normals as points on a unit sphere $n_1, \ldots n_N \in S^2$ than points in Euclidean space. Instead of the Euclidean mean, we compute the intrinsic mean: $\mu = \arg\min_{n \in S^2} \sum_{i=1}^{N} d(n, n_i)$ where $d(n, n_i) = \arccos(n \cdot n_i)$ is the arc length. For a spherical manifold, the intrinsic mean can be found using the gradient descent method of Pennec [8]. Accordingly, the current estimate $\mu^{(t)}$ is updated as follows: $\mu^{(t+1)} = Exp_{\mu^{(t)}}\left(\frac{1}{N} \sum_{i=1}^{N} Log_{\mu^{(t)}}(n_i)\right)$.

PGA of Needle Maps: PGA is analogous to PCA except that each principal axis in PCA is a straight line, while in PGA each principle axis is a geodesic curve. In the spherical case this corresponds to a great circle. Consider a great circle G on the sphere S^2. To project a point $n_1 \in S^2$ onto a point on G, we use the projection operator $\pi_G : S^2 \longrightarrow G$ given by $\pi_G(n_1) = argmin_{n \in G}(n_1, n)^2$. For a geodesic G passing through the intrinsic mean μ, π_G may be approximated linearly in the tangent plane $T_\mu S^2$: $Log_\mu(\pi_G(n_1)) \approx \sum_{i=1}^{K} V^i \cdot Log_\mu(n_1)$, where $V_1, \ldots V_K$ is an orthonormal basis for $T_\mu S^2$.

Suppose there are K training needle-maps each with N pixel locations, and the surface normal at pixel location p for the kth training needle-map is n_p^k. We calculate the intrinsic mean μ_p of the distribution of surface normals $n_p^1, \ldots n_p^K$ at each pixel location p. n_p^k is then represented by its log map position $u_p^k = Log_{\mu_p}(n_p^k)$. $u^k = [u_1^k, \ldots, u_N^k]^T$ is the log-mapped long vector of the kth training needle-map. The K long vectors form the data matrix $U = [u^1| \ldots |u^K]$. The covariance matrix of the data matrix is $L = \frac{1}{K}UU^T$.

We use the numerically efficient snap-shot method of Sirovich [10] to compute the eigenvectors of L. Accordingly, we construct the matrix $\hat{L} = \frac{1}{K}U^T U$, and find the eigenvalues and eigenvectors. The ith eigenvector e_i of L can be computed from the ith eigenvector $\hat{e}_i$ of $\hat{L}$ using $e_i = U\hat{e}_i$. The ith eigenvalue λ_i of L equals the ith eigenvalue $\hat{\lambda}_i$ of $\hat{L}$ when $i \leq K$. When $i > K$, $\lambda_i = 0$. Providing the effects of noise are small, we only need to retain S eigenmodes to retain p percent of the model variance. S is the smallest integer satisfying: $\sum_{i=1}^{S} \lambda_i \geq \frac{p}{100} \sum_{i=1}^{K} \lambda_i$.

Given a long vector $u = [u_1, \ldots, u_N]^T$, we can get the corresponding vector of parameters (feature vector) $b = P^T u$. Given a feature vector $b = [b_1, \ldots b_S]^T$, we can generate a needle-map using: $n_p = Exp_{\mu_p}((Pb)_p)$.

To fit the model to 2D intensity images, an iterative SFS method is used [7]. The field of surface normals can be recovered by iterating between estimation of surface normal direction using the Worthington and Hancock method [11] and projection into the model space. In order to ensure data closeness, the normals from the model are rotated back onto their nearest illumination cone positions using the rotation matrix Θ_p which is constructed from θ_p, defined as the opening angle around the light source direction. This can be computed as $\theta_p = arccos I_p$, where I_p is the normalised image brightness. Where $n_p^{(0)} = \Theta_p \mu_p$ represents the initialisation of the surface normal at the pth pixel location, Θ_p the matrix to rotate the off-cone normals to their on-cone positions, and μ_p the spherical median at location p, the algorithm proceeds as follows:

1. The model parameter vector is computed $b^{(t)} = P^T u^{(t)}$
2. The field of surface normals is then recovered: $n_p^{(t)'} = Exp_{\mu_p}((Pb^{(t)})_p)$
3. The surface normals are rotated back onto the nearest on-cone position: $n_p^{(t+1)} = \Theta_p n_p^{(t)'}$

Convergence occurs when the sum of the angles between the previous and current iteration on-cone normals falls below a predetermined threshold.

3   Dimensionality Reduction and Manifold Learning

Each parameter vector from PGA provides a compact, illumination-invariant representation of facial shape extracted from a single image. By employing dimensionality reduction techniques we aim to discover the intrinsic dimensionality that captures the principal modes of variation in facial shape, whilst simultaneously providing a more manageable pattern space in which to effect classification. This corresponds to discovering the underlying low-dimensional manifold on which the set of faces resides.

We investigate Isomap, LLE and LPP as well as PCA. The former three algorithms aim to preserve the spatial relationships between data in the original high dimensional pattern space so that the recovered embedding provides a useful space in which to perform classification. However, they contrast with classical PCA in that they aim to capture more complex modes of variation in the data using local "manifold" structure. In particular, Isomap and LLE are designed with the goal of recovering non-linear relationships within the input data. LPP is a linear approximation to the non-linear Laplacian eigenmaps technique[15].

4   Results

In this section we provide experimental results. We commence with a brief examination of the embeddings and move on to a description of the algorithm parameters used. Next, the quality of the different embeddings is analysed using a number of quantitative measures, including classification performance, the Rand index and the Davies-Bouldin index. The section is concluded with a summary and discussion of the findings.

We use the Yale B face database and follow the definition of illumination subsets provided in the corresponding paper [16]. In summary, there are 45 images per subject divided into subsets of illumination extremity, for 10 subjects. These subsets are defined as follows: subset 1 uses images 1-7 per subject, with an illumination angle of $12°$, subset 2 uses images 8-19, at $25°$, subset 3 uses images 20-31 at $50°$, and subset 4 uses images 32-45 at $77°$. The experiments that follow state which illumination subset or subsets they operate on.

An example of the outputs of the four algorithms when run on subset 1 (close-to-frontal illumination) is given in Figure 1. Note that only the two most significant dimensions are shown for each algorithm. It is clear that certain subjects in the input data separate themselves, whilst others remain significantly overlapped. Both the non-linear techniques generate broad regions largely corresponding to different subjects with some overlap, whereas LPP produces very tight, well-separated groups for several faces, with some significant overlap for others. PCA produces an embedding that appears to resemble those of LLE and Isomap more than LPP.

Cluster Quality: For cluster quality tests we again use illumination subset 1. We aim to explore how well the different embedding strategies cluster the subject views when applied to the facial shape pattern vectors delivered by PGA,

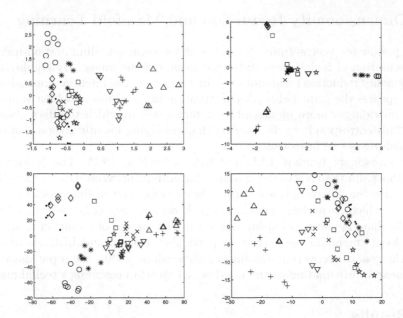

Fig. 1. *(Top)* The embeddings produced by LLE and LPP from left to right. *(Bottom)* Those produced by Isomap and PCA, left to right.

using two common cluster quality measures from the literature. The dimensionality of the pattern vectors was chosen to be thirty dimensions, based on brief empirical tests to determine a reasonable dimensionality to the data. This choice of dimensionality will later be refined.

In Figure 2 we commence our analysis by showing the Rand index for the different embedding methods. The index is defined on the true class assignments C and assignments made by a clustering algorithm K as $R(C, K) = (a+d)/(a+b+c+d)$, where a is the number of pairs of points that share the same label in C and then in K, b represents the number of pairs with the same label in C but

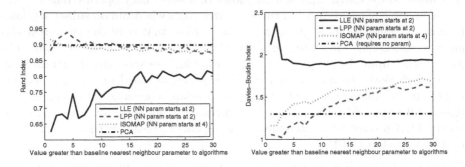

Fig. 2. *(left)* The Rand Index results over the range of parameters shown for each algorithm. *(right)* Davies-Bouldin index over a range of parameters.

different labels in K, c is the number of pairs with different labels in C but the same labels in K and d corresponds to the number of pairs with different labels in C and different labels in K. This measures the agreement between true classes and those assigned by the clustering algorithm. Here we apply k-means in the embedding spaces to cluster the subject views. When the Rand-index is close to unity there is perfect agreement between the true and assigned classes. From the plot it is clear that LPP, Isomap and PCA outperform LLE when combined with k-means clustering. The results are largely insensitive to variations in the number of nearest-neighbours k.

Next we turn our attention to the Davies-Bouldin index, defined as $DB = \frac{1}{K} \sum_{k=1}^{K} max_{j \neq k} \frac{d_{intra}\ (j) + d_{intra}\ (k)}{d_{inter}\ (j,k)}$, where K is the number of clusters present in the data, d_{intra} is the intra-cluster distance and d_{inter} is the inter-cluster distance between any two clusters in the data. This provides a measure of cluster separation and can be computed directly from the embedding, and thus requires no intermediate clustering algorithm. A small index corresponds to tightly grouped, well-separated clusters. LPP, Isomap and PCA again significantly outperform LLE, and the best results overall are obtained with LPP.

Dimensionality: We now investigate the effect of the number of retained dimensions of the embedding on the recognition performance. The test used is a leave-one-out performance measure using a nearest-neighbour classifier on subset 1 of the face vectors. Figure 3 shows the recognition performance as a function of the number of retained dimensions for each of the three embedding methods. In each case the recognition performance reaches a plateaux. Both LLE and LPP reach a plateaux corresponding to a higher recognition rate than Isomap, however it takes LLE and LPP more dimensions to reach their plateaux. PCA surprisingly performs comparatively poorly in this test.

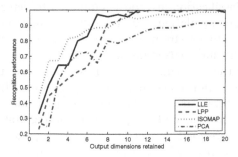

Fig. 3. Recognition performance on a simple recognition task against the dimensionality of the embedding

Cumulative Match Results: Cumulative match has been used both by the FERET program and elsewhere [6] to provide a more detailed analysis of recognition performance than a simple nearest-neighbour classification performance statistic. The method computes the recognition rank, which involves examining

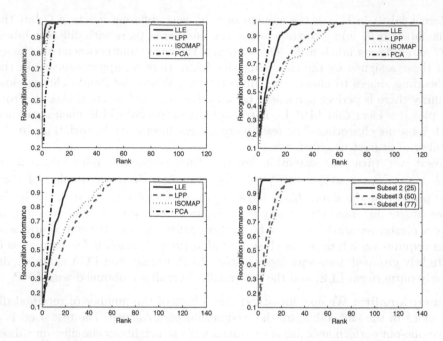

Fig. 4. *(Top left)* Cumulative match characteristic on subset two, *(Top right)* subset three and *(Bottom left)* the most extreme illumination subset, four. *(Bottom right)* The results on different illumination subsets using LLE are given in order to illustrate the difference in the cumulative match score on different subsets.

the nearest-neighbours of each datum in turn until the correct class is discovered. For our experiments the first subset is used for training, and a Euclidean nearest-neighbour classification method is employed to determine neighbours.

Figure 4 shows the cumulative match results for different subsets and there are a number of points to note from the figure. First, and as expected, the performance degrades as the illumination becomes more extreme. On subset two when we exceed rank ten then recognition performance is almost perfect, and even before this point the performance increases rapidly after the first match. This suggests that the test vectors are falling close to their ideal classes, and slight overlap of subjects in the embedding space is hindering first-match recognition. The second subset corresponds to an illumination angle of up to 25°, and LLE performs well on this data, achieving around 85% correct on the first match. By the third subset, performance degrades significantly with an illumination angle of up to 50°, at which point shadowing is significant. Finally, the difference in performance between subsets three and four is relatively small. Considering the performance of the different embedding methods, PCA compares poorly under frontal illumination, but maintains similar performance across illumination subsets, which cannot be said for the other techniques. LLE outperforms both LPP and Isomap under all conditions, which could be attributed to its combination of non-linearity and emphasis on preserving local neighbourhood structure.

Although Isomap and LLE are similar in their goals, with so few subjects in the training set Isomap is likely to generate inaccurate estimations of geodesic distance over a large scale. As for LPP, it provides a linear approximation to a neighbourhood-preserving technique as stated in [15], and therefore underperforms compared to non-linear approaches with the same goal.

5   Conclusions

We have presented a novel approach to face recognition using a variety of manifold learning techniques in conjunction with a shape-based representation of faces. Four algorithms from the literature have been compared using various forms of analysis of the embeddings they produce.

The results have shown recognition performance for near-frontally illuminated images is near-perfect in most cases, with performance not falling drastically over vectors extracted from images with illumination angles of around 25°, and this is encouraging. As for the SFS approach and the statistical model, the resultant vectors have already been shown to encapsulate facial shape very well [6,7].

The application of such methods to a larger image database is desirable, as in the case of Isomap, the resultant embeddings have been proven to be more accurate with a greater number of samples [12]. More subjects in the training data may also place a greater emphasis on the differences between subjects as opposed to subtle characteristics resulting from the variations in the illumination conditions under which the vectors were extracted. Although they are intended to provide an illumination independent representation of facial shape, it is possible that training to illumination may occur in cases of varying shadowing.

References

1. Turk, M., Pentland, A.P.: Eigenfaces for Recognition. Journal of Cognitive Neuroscience 3(1), 71–86 (1991)
2. Cootes, T.F., Edwards, G.J., Taylor, C.J.: Active Appearance Models. ECCV98 2, 484–498 (1998)
3. Blantz, V., Vetter, T.: Face Recognition Based on Fitting a 3D Morphable Model. IEEE PAMI 25(9), 1063–1074 (2003)
4. Basri, R., Jacobs, D.: Lambertian reflectance and linear subspaces. IEEE PAMI 25(2), 218–233 (2003)
5. Belhumeur, P.N., Kriegman, D.J.: What Is the Set of Images of an Object Under All Possible Illumination Conditions? IJCV 28(3), 245–260 (1998)
6. Smith, W., Hancock, E.R.: Recovering Facial Shape using a Statistical Model of Surface Normal Direction. IEEE PAMI 28(12), 1914–1930 (2006)
7. Smith, W., Hancock, E.R.: Face Recognition using 2.5D Shape Information, IEEE CVPR, pp. 1407–1414 (2006)
8. Pennec, X.: Probabilities and statistics of Riemannian manifolds: A geometric approach, Research Report RR-5093, INRIA (2004)
9. Fletcher, P.T., Joshi, S., Lu, C., Pizer, S.M.: Principal geodesic analysis for the study of nonlinear statistics of shape. IEEE Transactions on Medical Imaging 23(8), 995–1005 (2004)

10. Sirovich, L.: Turbulence and the dynamics of coherent structures. Quarterly of Applied Mathematics XLV, 561–590 (1987)
11. Worthington, P.L., Hancock, E.R.: New constraints on data-closeness and needle map consistency for shape-from-shading. IEEE PAMI 21(12), 1250–1267 (1999)
12. Tenenbaum, J.B., de Silva, V., Langford, J.C.: A global geometric framework for nonlinear dimensionality reduction. Science 290, 2319–2323 (2000)
13. Roweis, S.T., Saul, L.K.: Nonlinear dimensionality reduction by locally linear embedding. Science 290, 2323–2326 (2000)
14. He, X., Niyogi, P.: Locality preserving projections, Technical Report TR-2002-09, University of Chicago Computer Science (2002)
15. Belkin, M., Niyogi, P.: Laplacian eigenmaps and spectral techniques for embedding and clustering, In: Dietterich, T.G., Becker, S., Ghahramani, Z. (eds.) Advances in Neural Information Processing Systems, vol. 14 (2001)
16. Georghiades, A.S., Belhumeur, P.N., Kriegman, D.J.: From Few to Many: Illumination Cone Models for Face Recognition under Variable Lighting and Pose. IEEE PAMI 23(6), 642–660 (2001)

Optimized Associative Memories
for Feature Selection

Mario Aldape-Pérez, Cornelio Yáñez-Márquez,
and Amadeo José Argüelles-Cruz

Center for Computing Research, CIC
National Polytechnic Institute, IPN
Mexico City, Mexico
maldapeb05@sagitario.cic.ipn.mx, cyanez@cic.ipn.mx, jamadeo@cic.ipn.mx
http://www.cornelio.org.mx

Abstract. Performance in most pattern classifiers is improved when redundant or irrelevant features are removed, however, this is mainly achieved by high demanding computational methods or successive classifiers construction. This paper shows how Associative Memories can be used to get a mask value which represents a subset of features that clearly identifies irrelevant or redundant information for classification purposes, therefore, classification accuracy is improved while significant computational costs in the learning phase are reduced. An optimal subset of features allows register size optimization, which contributes not only to significant power savings but to a smaller amount of synthesized logic, furthermore, improved hardware architectures are achieved due to functional units size reduction, as a result, it is possible to implement parallel and cascade schemes for pattern classifiers on the same ASIC.

Keywords: Feature Selection, Pattern Classifier, Masking Techniques, Supervised Learning.

1 Introduction

Pattern recognition has existed for many years in a wide range of human activity, however, the general pattern recognition problem can be stated in the following form: Given a collection of objects belonging to a predefined set of classes and a set of measurements on these objects, identify the class of membership of each of these objects by a suitable analysis of the measurements (features). Although features are functions of the measurements performed on a class of objects, most of the times, the initial set of features consists of a large number of potential attributes that constitute an obstacle not only to the accuracy but to the efficiency of algorithms. In countless situations, it is a complicated task to find proper features for all patterns in a class, therefore, many machine learning algorithms have been extensively used as a classification tool. Support vector machines (SVMs) select a small number of critical boundary samples from each class and builds a linear discriminant function that separates them as widely

J. Martí et al. (Eds.): IbPRIA 2007, Part I, LNCS 4477, pp. 435–442, 2007.

as possible, the main reason whereby SVMs are not commonly used for feature selection, results from the fact that SVMs can perform badly in the situation of many irrelevant features [1]. Another approach is to apply different degrees of relevance to information; feature weighting schemes tend to be easier to implement when the obtained subset of "most relevant" features is fed into another algorithm capable of making additive changes to all weights. The main disadvantage of these schemes is that convergence in the learning phase is not assured, moreover, weighting techniques can have difficulties when irrelevant features are present [2]. In order to overcome this limitation, multiclassifier approach arises [3-5], nonetheless, these methodologies lack of criterions that help to ignore redundant information. A remarkable thing to mention about Associative Memories is that they are represented as matrices, generated from an *a priori* finite set of known associations, so convergence in the learning phase is guaranteed, furthermore, the learning capacity is outstanding, not to mention the strong noise tolerance [6].

In this paper an original method for feature selection, whose basic operation rests on a Hybrid Associative Memory is presented. Particularly, a better classifier is obtained when the Learning Phase is done as a Linear Associator [7] and the Classification Phase is done as a Lernmatrix [8]. Each obtained mask value, represents a different subset of features. It is to be said that the best mask value is the one that indicates the smallest subset of features, and hence to permit register size optimization for hardware implementation purposes. From a register transfer level perspective, the smaller the register size is, the better architecture alternative is obtained. In the following two sections, a brief description of Associative Memories foundations and the Feature Selection Procedure are presented. In Section 4, experimental results are shown over several different data sets. The associative memories approach advantages will be discussed in section 5, and a short conclusion follows in Section 6.

2   Associative Memories

An associative memory M is a system that relates input patterns and output patterns as follows: $x \longrightarrow \boxed{\text{M}} \longrightarrow y$ with x and y, respectively, the input and output pattern vectors. Each input vector forms an association with its corresponding output vector. For each k integer and positive, the corresponding association will be denoted as: (x^k, y^k). Associative memory M is represented by a $m \times n$ matrix, $i \in \{1, 2, ..., m\}$ and $j \in \{1, 2, ..., n\}$ so that the ij-th component is m_{ij} [9]. Memory M is generated from an *a priori* finite set of known associations, called the fundamental set of associations. If we consider the fundamental set of patterns $\{(x^\mu, y^\mu) \mid \mu = 1, 2, ..., p\}$ where n and m are the dimensions of the input patterns and output patterns, respectively, it is said that $x^\mu \in A^n$, $A = \{0, 1\}$ and $y^\mu \in A^m$. Then the j-th component of an input pattern is $x_j^\mu \in A$. Analogously, the j-th component of an output pattern is represented as $y_j^\mu \in A$.

Therefore the fundamental input and output patterns are represented as follows:

$$x^{\mu} = \begin{pmatrix} x_1^{\mu} \\ x_2^{\mu} \\ \vdots \\ x_n^{\mu} \end{pmatrix} \in A^n \qquad y^{\mu} = \begin{pmatrix} y_1^{\mu} \\ y_2^{\mu} \\ \vdots \\ y_m^{\mu} \end{pmatrix} \in A^m$$

3   Application to Feature Selection

The task of classification occurs in a wide range of human activity; however satisfactory results depend on the amount of relevant information obtained when coherent features are selected. The main objective of this paper, is to show how Associative Memories can be used to get a mask value which represents a subset of features that allows the elimination of irrelevant or redundant information for classification purposes.

3.1   Learning Phase

In order to keep the information between patterns from the fundamental set of associations, an Associative Memory **M** is calculated in two stages:

1. Consider each one of the p associations $(\mathbf{x}^{\mu}, \mathbf{y}^{\mu})$, so an $m \times n$ matrix is obtained by $\mathbf{y}^{\mu} \cdot (\mathbf{x}^{\mu})^t$

$$\mathbf{y}^{\mu} \cdot (\mathbf{x}^{\mu})^t = \begin{pmatrix} y_1^{\mu} \\ y_2^{\mu} \\ \vdots \\ y_m^{\mu} \end{pmatrix} \cdot (x_1^{\mu}, x_2^{\mu}, ..., x_n^{\mu}) = \begin{pmatrix} y_1^{\mu} x_1^{\mu} & y_1^{\mu} x_2^{\mu} & \cdots & y_1^{\mu} x_j^{\mu} & \cdots & y_1^{\mu} x_n^{\mu} \\ \vdots & \vdots & & \vdots & & \vdots \\ y_i^{\mu} x_1^{\mu} & y_i^{\mu} x_2^{\mu} & \cdots & y_i^{\mu} x_j^{\mu} & \cdots & y_i^{\mu} x_n^{\mu} \\ \vdots & \vdots & & \vdots & & \vdots \\ y_m^{\mu} x_1^{\mu} & y_m^{\mu} x_2^{\mu} & \cdots & y_m^{\mu} x_j^{\mu} & \cdots & y_m^{\mu} x_n^{\mu} \end{pmatrix} \tag{1}$$

2. **M** memory is obtained by adding all the p matrices

$$\mathbf{M} = \sum_{\mu=1}^{p} \mathbf{y}^{\mu} \cdot (\mathbf{x}^{\mu})^t = [m_{ij}]_{m \times n} \tag{2}$$

in this way the ij-th component of **M** memory is expressed as:

$$m_{ij} = \sum_{\mu=1}^{p} y_i^{\mu} x_j^{\mu} \tag{3}$$

3.2   Classification Phase

Consists of finding the class which an input pattern $\mathbf{x}^{\omega} \in A^n$ belongs to. Finding the class means getting $\mathbf{y}^{\omega} \in A^m$ that corresponds to $\mathbf{x}^{\omega}$. Performance of the classification phase is measured in terms of error rate, so, classifier accuracy represents the correct classification rate when unseen patterns are presented. The i-th component of y_i^ω is obtained according to the following rule, where $\vee$ is the *maximum* operator [10].

$$y_i^\omega = \begin{cases} 1 \text{ if } \sum_{j=1}^n m_{ij}.x_j^\omega = \bigvee_{h=1}^m \left[\sum_{j=1}^n m_{hj}.x_j^\omega \right] \\ 0 \text{ otherwise} \end{cases} \tag{4}$$

3.3   Selecting Relevant Features

Before showing how optimal mask is found, it has to be said that the best mask value is the one that indicates the smallest subset of features while classification accuracy is maximal [11].

Definition 1. *Let* **f** *be the number of features from the original set of data.*

Definition 2. *Let* **r** *be an index where* $r \in \{1, 2, ..., (2^f - 1)\}$

Definition 3. *Let* $\mathbf{e}^r$ *be a masking vector of size n represented as:*

$$\mathbf{e}^r = \begin{pmatrix} e_1^r \\ e_2^r \\ \vdots \\ e_n^r \end{pmatrix} \in B^n \tag{5}$$

where $B = \{0, 1\}$ *, and* e_n^r *is the Least Significant Bit (LSB)*

Definition 4. *Let* $\dashv$ *be a new operation called IntToVector which takes* $r \in \{1, 2, ..., (2^f - 1)\}$ *and returns a column vector* $\mathbf{e}^r$ *with r value expressed in its binary form.*

Definition 5. *Let* $\|$ *be a new operation called MagVector which takes a column vector* $\mathbf{e}^r$ *of size n and returns an integer and positive value according to the following rule:*

$$\| \mathbf{e}^r = \sum_{j=1}^n \left(e_j^r \wedge 1 \right) \tag{6}$$

where $\wedge$ *is the logical AND operator.*

Consequently the *Classification Phase* is extended by the following rule:

$$y_i^\mu = \begin{cases} 1 \text{ if } \sum_{j=1}^n m_{ij}. \left(x_j^\mu.e_j^r \right) = \bigvee_{h=1}^m \left[\sum_{j=1}^n m_{hj}. \left(x_j^\mu.e_j^r \right) \right] \\ 0 \text{ otherwise} \end{cases} \tag{7}$$

where $\mu \in \{1, 2, ..., p\}$ *and* $r \in \{1, 2, ..., (2^f - 1)\}$

so each masking vector $\mathbf{e}^r$ of size n masks every input vector x^μ of size n.

Definition 6. *Let* ✠ *be a new operation called DblToInt which takes a floating point number and returns an integer value by eliminating the fractional part.*

3.4   Floating Point Conversion

In order to estimate the original register size requirements, each feature has to be converted from a floating point value to an integer value v, so that $\log_2(v)$ gives the minimum number of bits required to store the original feature value without loss. The floating point to integer coversion is as follows:

1. Let v be the original feature value.
2. Obtain a new value of v, making $v = v \times 10$.
3. Obtain $R = \dfrac{v}{\maltese(v)}$
4. If. $R > 1$ go to step 2
5. Else. (*number of bits*) $= \log_2(v)$

3.5   Feature Selection Procedure

1. Let n be the dimension of each input pattern in the fundamental set, grouped in m different classes.
2. Each one of the input patterns belongs to a k class, $k \in \{1, 2, ..., m\}$, represented by a column vector which components will be assigned by $y_k^\mu = 1$, so $y_j^\mu = 0$ for $j = 1, 2..., k-1, k+1, ...m$.
3. Create a classifier using expression (1), (2) and (3).
4. Use the *IntToVector* operator to get the r-th masking vector as in expression (5).
5. The Classification phase is carried out according to expression (7) so an r-th classification accuracy parameter is obtained.
6. Store both parameters (the r-th classification accuracy parameter and the r-th masking vector) so feature selection can be evaluated in step 8.
7. Compare the r-th classification accuracy parameter with the $(r-1)$-th classification accuracy parameter. The best classification accuracy value is stored thus classification accuracy improvements are achieved with each iteration.
8. The same applies to the r-th masking vector. Feature selection can be evaluated using expression (6). So the smaller this number is, a better mask is obtained.
9. The new subset of features is obtained by a mask value represented by a column vector, where classification accuracy is maximal while the number of selected features is minimal.

4   Experimental Results

Throughout the experimental phase, eight databases taken from the UCI Machine Learning Database Repository (http://www.ics.uci.edu/~mlearn) were included. The main characteristics of these data sets have been summarized in Table 1. The experiments have been carried out as follows: Firstly, the same number of input vectors for each class was randomly taken, which means that a balanced classifier is guaranteed; subsequently we apply the Feature Selection

Table 1. Some characteristics of the data sets used in the experiments

	Iris	Liver	Pima	Breast	CMC	Wine	Heart	Credit
Features	4	6	8	9	9	13	13	14
Classes	3	2	2	2	3	3	2	2
Patterns	150	345	768	699	1473	178	270	690

Table 2. Feature Selection results of the data sets used

	Iris	Liver	Pima	Breast	CMC	Wine	Heart	Credit
Original Set Size	4	6	8	9	9	13	13	14
Optimized Subset Size	2	2	2	4	5	7	4	2
Feature Optimization	50.0%	66.6%	75.0%	55.5%	44.4%	46.1%	69.2%	85.7%

Procedure in order to get the optimal mask value by comparing the two main parameters (classifier accuracy and mask optimality). Afterwards the dataset was broken into k partitions (in our case k=10) in this way, classifier behavior was evaluated using k Fold Cross Validation technique. Efficiency of the developed method was tested by performing the experiments 30 times, each time with different number of randomly taken input vectors.

5   Results Analysis

The results exposed in Table 2, show how associative memories and masking technique constitute a feasible alternative to obtain a reduced set of features. The number of selected features for two of the datasets, used during the experimental phase, was close to 50% which means that almost half of the initial set of features was eliminated. Even better is the number of selected features for the other six datasets, where the optimization rate is between 50% and 85%.

As it is shown in Table 3 and Table 4, classification rate for both cases (original set and optimized set) are presented. A relevant thing to mention is that the classification rate achieved when the optimized set is used, is as good as the classification rate using the initial set of features, which means that the optimized set of features not only maintains but increases classification accuracy.

In Table 5, register size optimization results for each dataset used along this paper, are presented. The original register size is estimated according to the floating point to integer value conversion, detailed in section 3.4. After the feature selection procedure is carried out, a new subset of features is obtained, so register size optimization is evaluated according to the number of features that were selected for classification purposes. Due to the fact that every feature is coded with a fixed number of bits, it is possible to state that exists a direct relation between the number of selected features and the register size optimization, in other words, the fewer the features are selected, the smaller the register size is needed.

Table 3. Classification Rate using Original Set Size

	Iris	Liver	Pima	Breast	CMC	Wine	Heart	Credit
Original Set Size	4	6	8	9	9	13	13	14
Classification Rate	95.6%	52.0%	62.0%	95.2%	55.2%	92.3%	63.0%	52.2%

Table 4. Classification Rate using Optimized Set Size

	Iris	Liver	Pima	Breast	CMC	Wine	Heart	Credit
Optimized Subset Size	2	2	2	4	5	7	4	2
Classification Rate	95.9%	54.0%	69.0%	97.0%	58.0%	95.2%	83.5%	85.5%

Table 5. Optimization Results of the data sets used

	Iris	Liver	Pima	Breast	CMC	Wine	Heart	Credit
Original Set Size	4	6	8	9	9	13	13	14
Optimized Subset Size	2	2	2	4	5	7	4	2
Feature Optimization	50%	66%	75%	55%	44%	46%	69%	85%
Original Rg. Size [bit]	50	105	153	100	130	252	224	360
Optimized Rg. Size [bit]	30	45	51	50	78	144	80	72
Rg. Size Optimization	40%	57%	66%	50%	40%	42%	64%	80%

6   Conclusions

In this paper an original method for feature selection, whose basic operation rests
on associative memories is presented. Experimental results have shown that this
algorithm is an efficient way to get a mask value which represents an optimal
subset of features. While maintaining the discriminatory information necessary
for classifier accuracy improvement, these optimized subsets allow considerable
register size reduction for hardware implementation purposes (summarized in
Table 5). A remarkable thing to mention is that feature selection not only reduces data dimensionality, which represents an important reduction on hardware
resources, it also means significant power savings on ASIC implementations due
to register size reduction.

It is worth pointing out that this method does not have to compute a new classifier in order to estimate classification accuracy, which represents an important
reduction on computational costs.

The learning phase of the process becomes swifter given the associative memories advantages and the reduced number of input vectors considered. One and only
one classifier is used throughout the entire process, which implies simplification
on methodology. Classifier accuracy is not related to the number of input vectors
considered in the learning phase, conversely, classifier accuracy is directly related
to the mask value that allows elimination of redundant or irrelevant information.

Another clear advantage of this method is that the optimal mask search algorithm is applied only to those patterns that were previously considered during

the learning phase, which means that no additional patterns are required to increase classifier accuracy.

This paper represents the initial works on optimized associative memories for Feature Selection.

Acknowledgments. The authors of the present paper would like to thank the following institutions for their support: National Polytechnic Institute, Mexico (CIC, CGPI, PIFI, COFAA) , CONACyT and SNI.

References

[1] Zavaljevski, N., Stevens, F., Reifman, J.: Support vector machines with selective kernel scaling for protein classification and identification of key amino acid positions. Bioinformatics 18(5), 689–696 (2002)

[2] Blum, A.L., Langley, P.: Selection of relevant features and examples in machine learning. Artificial Intelligence 97(1-2), 245–271 (1997)

[3] Valentini, G., Masulli, F.: Ensembles of Learning Machines. In: Marinaro, M., Tagliaferri, R. (eds.) Neural Nets. LNCS, vol. 2486, pp. 3–22. Springer, Heidelberg (2002)

[4] Kittler, J., Hatef, M., Duin, R.P.W., Matas, J.: On combining classifiers. IEEE Transactions on Pattern Analysis and Machine Intelligence 20(3), 226–239 (1998)

[5] Lam, L., Kittler, J., Roli, F.: Classifier combinations: Implementations and theoretical issues. In: Kittler, J., Roli, F. (eds.) MCS 2000. LNCS, vol. 1857, pp. 77–86. Springer, Heidelberg (2000)

[6] Palm, G., Schwenker, F., Sommer, F.: Neural Associative Memories. In: Palm, G., Schwenker, F., Sommer, F. (eds.) Associative Processing and Processors, pp. 307–326. IEEE Computer Society, Los Alamitos (1997)

[7] Kohonen, T.: Correlation Matrix Memories. IEEE Transactions on Computers 21(4), 353–359 (1972)

[8] Steinbuch, K., Frank, H.: Nichtdigitale Lernmatrizen als Perzeptoren. Kybernetik 1(3), 117–124 (1961)

[9] Anderson, J.A., Rosenfeld, E.: Neurocomputing: Fundations of Research. MIT Press, Cambridge (1990)

[10] Steinbuch, K.: Die Lernmatrix. Kybernetik 1(1), 36–45 (1961)

[11] Aldape-Pérez, M., Yáñez-Márquez, C., López-Leyva, L.O.: Feature Selection Using a Hybrid Associative Classifier with Masking Techniques. MICAI 2006, pp. 151–160. IEEE Computer Society, Los Alamitos (2006)

[12] Hassoun, M.H.: Fundamentals of Artificial Neural Networks. MIT Press, Cambridge (1995)

[13] Vasconcelos, N.: Feature selection by maximum marginal diversity: optimality and implications for visual recognition. In: Proceedings IEEE Conference On Computer Vision And Pattern Recognition. vol. 1, pp. 762–769 (2003)

Automatic Construction of Fuzzy Rules for Modelling and Prediction of the Central Nervous System

Fernando Vázquez and Pilar Gómez

UPIICSA. Instituto Politécnico Nacional, Te 950,
Col.Granjas México. C.P.08400, México D.F.
fvazquezt@ipn.mx, pgomez84@hotmail.com

Abstract. The main goal of this work is to study the performance of CARFIR (Automatic Construction of Rules in Fuzzy Inductive Reasoning) methodology for the modelling and prediction of the human central nervous system (CNS). The CNS controls the hemodynamical system by generating the regulating signals for the blood vessels and the heart.CARFIR is able to automatically construct fuzzy rules starting from a set of pattern rules obtained by FIR. The methodology preserves as much as possible the knowledge of the pattern rules in a compact fuzzy rule base. The prediction results obtained by the fuzzy prediction process of CARFIR methodology are compared with those of other inductive methodologies, i.e. FIR, NARMAX and neural networks.

1 Introduction

The Fuzzy Inductive Reasoning (FIR) methodology emerged from the General Systems Problem Solving (GSPS) developed by Klir [1]. FIR is a data driven methodology based on systems behaviour rather than structural knowledge. It is a very useful tool for modelling and simulate those systems from which no previous structural knowledge is available. FIR is composed of four main processes, namely: *fuzzification, qualitative model identification, fuzzy forecasting,* and *defuzzification.*

The fuzzification process converts quantitative data stemming from the system into qualitative data. The model identification process is able to obtain good qualitative relations between the variables that compose the system, building a pattern rule base that guides the fuzzy forecasting process.

The fuzzy forecasting process predicts systems' behaviour. The FIR inference engine is a specialization of the k-nearest neighbour rule, commonly used in the pattern recognition field.

Defuzzification is the inverse process of fuzzification. It makes possible to convert the qualitative predicted output into a quantitative variable that can then be used as input to an external quantitative model. For a deeper insight into FIR methodology the reader is referred to [2,3].

J. Martí et al. (Eds.): IbPRIA 2007, Part I, LNCS 4477, pp. 443–450, 2007.

It has been shown in previous works that FIR methodology is a powerful tool for the identification and prediction of real systems, specially when poor or non structural knowledge is available [4,5,6].

However, FIR methodology has an important drawback. The pattern rule base generated by the qualitative model identification process can be very large if there exists a big amount of data available from the system.

In this paper the methodology of the automatic construction of fuzzy rules (CARFIR) is used to solve the drawback of FIR methodology. CARFIR proposes an alternative for the last two processes of FIR methodology (fuzzy forecasting and deffuzification) that consists on a fuzzy inference system (FIS) that allows to compact the pattern rule base in a classical fuzzy rule base and to define a inference scheme that affords the prediction of the future behaviour of the system.

The extended methodology obtains a fuzzy rule base by means of the *fuzzy rules identification* process that preserve as much information as possible contained in the pattern rule base. Therefore, the former can be considered a generalization of the latter. In other words, the fuzzy rule base is a set of compacted rules that contains the knowledge of the pattern rule base. In this process some precision is lost but the robustness is considerably increased.

The *fuzzy inference* process of CARFIR methodology allows the prediction of systems behaviour by means of two different schemes. The first scheme corresponds to the classical forecasting process of FIR methodology, i.e. *pattern prediction scheme*. The second correspond to purely Sugeno inference system, i.e. *Sugeno prediction scheme*.

In this paper CARFIR performance is studied in the context of a biomedical application, i.e. the human central nervous system. The central nervous system is part of the cardiovascular system and controls the hemodynamical system, by generating the regulating signals for the blood vessels and the heart. These signals are transmitted through bundles of sympathetic and parasympathetic nerves, producing stimuli in the corresponding organs and other body parts.

The CNS control model is composed of five separate controllers: the *heart rate (HR)*, the *peripheric resistance (PR)*, the *myocardiac contractility (MC)*, the *venous tone (VT)*, and the *coronary resistance (CR)*. All of them are single–input/single–output (SISO) models driven by the same input variable, namely the *Carotid Sinus Pressure*. The five output variables of the controller models are not even amenable to a physiological interpretation, except for the *Heart Rate Controller* variable, which is the inverse heart rate, measured in seconds between beats.

The functioning of the central nervous system is of high complexity and not yet fully understood. However, individual differential equation models for each of the hypothesized control mechanisms have been postulated by various authors [7,8]. These models offer a considerably low degree of internal validity. The use of inductive modelling techniques with their reduced explanatory power but enhanced flexibility for properly reflecting the input/output behaviour of a system may offer an attractive alternative to these differential equation models.

In previous works [6,9] the FIR methodology was used to find a qualitative model of the CNS control that accurately represents its input/output behaviour. However, the pattern rule base obtained was quite large, increasing considerably the time needed in the prediction process. It is the aim of this paper to use CARFIR methodology to identify a set of Sugeno rules from the pattern rule base, obtained initially by FIR, preserving as much as possible their prediction capability.

CARFIR methodology is introduced in section 2. In section 3, CARFIR is used to infer a Sugeno rule base for the central nervous system control. CARFIR prediction results (pattern and Sugeno prediction schemes) are presented and discussed from the perspective of the prediction performance and the size of the rule base. CARFIR results are compared with those of other inductive modelling methodologies, i.e. NARMAX and time delay neural networks. Finally, the conclusions of this research are given.

2   The CARFIR Methodology

CARFIR methodology is composed of two parts, a FIR structure and a FIS structure. As mentioned earlier CARFIR is an extension of the FIR methodology. Therefore, the first part of CARFIR consists on the generation of the pattern rule base using FIR methodology. To this end, the next steps are required:

– Specification of the external parameters
– Qualitative model identification

The second part of CARFIR methodology consists on the identification of fuzzy rules and on systems' prediction by means of the fuzzy inference system. To this end, it is necessary to follow the next steps:

– Identification of Sugeno rules starting from pattern rules
– Prediction by means of two different schemes

The first two steps are explained in detail in [2]. Therefore, only the identification of the Sugeno rule base and the CARFIR prediction schemes are described in this paper.

Once the qualitative model identification process has finished, the pattern rule base representing systems' behaviour is already available. The next step is the generation of fuzzy rules starting from the pattern rules by adjusting automatically the parameters of the fuzzy system. Traditionally, the development of a fuzzy system requires the collaboration of a human expert that is the responsible of calibrating and tuning all its parameters manually. It is well known that this is not an easy task and requires a good knowledge of the system.

The CARFIR methodology allows the automatic construction of a fuzzy rule base as a generalization of the previously obtained pattern rule base by means of the *fuzzy rules identification* process. The idea behind the obtaining of fuzzy rules starting from pattern rules is based on the spatial representation of both kind of rules. The pattern rule base can be represented graphically on the input-output space. If the model identified by FIR is of high quality then the pattern rules form a uniform thin surface in the input-output space. However, if the model obtained is not so good the spatial representation looks as a surface where the thickness of some parts is more significant than that of others. The thickness of the surface means that for a given input pattern (i.e. a set of antecedents), the output variable (i.e. consequent) can take different class values, i.e. the pattern rule base is not deterministic.

A good model is obtained when it has a high level of determinism associated in its rules and all the physical behaviour patterns are represented in the model. The spatial representation of such a situation would be a uniform thin surface.

The pattern rule base was constructed using the best model inferred by FIR [6]. The consequent of a Sugeno rule is obtained from the values of the antecedents using equation 1.

$$y = \frac{\sum_{i=1}^{n}(\mu_i \cdot w_i)}{\sum_{i=1}^{n}\mu_i} \tag{1}$$

In equation 1, μ_i is the fire of the ith rule, w_i is the weight of the ith rule and n is the total number of rules of the system. The product is the fuzzy operator used to obtain the fire of each rule. The tuning process consists on adjusting the rules weight, w_i, by iterating through the data set using the gradient descent method [10,11]. The tuning of the ith rule weight is obtained by calculating the derivative of the cost function E with respect to w_i. The cost function is described in equation 2 (quadratic error addition), where ND is the total number of data points, y is the value given by the fuzzy system and y^r is the real value.

$$E = \frac{1}{2}\sum_{k=1}^{ND}(y - y^r)^2 \tag{2}$$

Once the rule base (pattern or fuzzy) is available, system prediction can take place. CARFIR includes the option of using the FIR fuzzy forecasting process that use exclusively the pattern rule base. This option is desirable when the computational resources allow to keep the pattern rule base or when the Sugeno scheme is not able to obtain an accurate representation of the pattern rules. The Sugeno inference system makes use of the fuzzy rules inferred from the pattern rules. The prediction is done by means of the classical Sugeno inference system.

3   CNS Controller Models

In this work the five CNS control models, namely, *heart rate, peripheric resistance, myocardiac contractility, venous tone* and *coronary resistance*, are inferred for a specific patient by means of CARFIR methodology.

As has been mentioned earlier, all the controllers are SISO models driven by the same input variable, the *carotid sinus pressure*. The input and output signals of the CNS controllers were recorded with a sampling rate of 0.12 seconds from simulations of the purely differential equation model. The model had been tuned to represent a specific patient suffering a coronary arterial obstruction, by making the four different physiological variables (right auricular pressure, aortic pressure, coronary blood flow, and heart rate) of the simulation model agree with the measurement data taken from the real patient (neurology section at L'Hospital sant Joan de Déu in Barcelona). However, those simulations obtained from the model match the data taken from the patient. . The five models obtained were validated by using them to forecast six data sets not employed in the training process. Each one of these six test data sets, with a size of about 600 data points each, contains signals representing specific morphologies, allowing the validation of the model for different system behaviours.

In the forecasting process, the normalized mean square error (in percentage) between the predicted output, $\hat{y}(t)$, and the system output, $y(t)$, is used to determine the validity of each of the control models. The error is given in equation 3.

$$MSE = \frac{E[(y(t) - \hat{y}(t))^2]}{y_{\text{var}}} \cdot 100\% \tag{3}$$

where y_{var} denotes the variance of $y(t)$.

The quantitative data obtained from the system is converted into qualitative data by means of the fuzzification process of CARFIR methodology (FIR structure). Several experiments were done with different partitions of the data for the five controllers. Both the input and output variables were discretized into 3, 5, 7 and 9 classes using the equal frequency partition (EFP) method. The identification of the models was carried out using 4200 samples.

Applying the best models obtained to the qualitative data, a pattern rule base with 4198 rules was obtained for each one of the five controllers. Once the pattern rules are available the fuzzy rules identification procedure can take place. From the experiments performed with different number of classes, it was concluded that the best matching between pattern and fuzzy rules is obtained when the input and output variables were discretized into 9 classes. This selection was decided upon an empirical way, but as a further research work the establishment of a clever heuristic will be studied. Therefore, each controller has associated a Sugeno rule base of 81 rules. The reduction of the number of rules is significant (from 4198 to 81). The idea is to maintain a mixed scheme for those regions with more uncertainty, in which the pattern rules are also kept. On the other hand, in those regions with less uncertainty the pattern rules will be thrown away, and a pure fuzzy inference scheme will be used. Therefore, the experimental algorithm allows us to infer that a mayor reduction that the one obtained in this article cannot be possible, and to consider the theoretical basis of this experimental inference as work for the future. The results were handed in to medical experts (at l'Hospital Sant Joan de Déu), who determined that the best forecast was obtained with the discretion of the data base into 9 classes. Therefore, each controller has associated a Sugeno rule base of 81 rules. The reduction of the number of rules is significant (from 4198 to 81).

Once the Sugeno rule base is available for each controller, the Sugeno prediction scheme is performed for each of the 6 test data sets. The MSE errors of the five controller models for each of the test data sets are presented in table 1. The columns of table 1 contain the mean square errors obtained when the 6 test data sets were predicted using each of the five CNS controllers. The last row of the table shows the average prediction error of the 6 tests for each controller.

Table 1. MSE prediction errors of the HR, PR, MC, VT, and CR controller models obtained using the Sugeno prediction scheme of CARFIR methodology

	HRC	PRC	MCC	VTC	CRC
Data Set 1	10.89%	11.00%	5.62%	5.65%	2.13%
Data Set 2	10.81%	9.79%	4.43%	4.45%	2.34%
Data Set 3	9.84%	7.67%	3.76%	3.76%	2.11%
Data Set 4	6.41%	6.66%	1.61%	1.60%	3.09%
Data Set 5	14.38%	9.73%	8.97%	8.96%	2.59%
Data Set 6	13.83%	14.98%	5.64%	5.64%	3.62%
Ave. Error	**11.02%**	**9.97%**	**5.00%**	**5.01%**	**2.64%**

From table 1 it can be seen that the coronary resistance (CR) model captures in a reliably way the behaviour of this controller, achieving an average error of 2.64%. The largest average error is 11.02% obtained with the heart rate controller (HRC) model. Therefore, the HR model is the one that captures less accurately the behaviour of the controller.

The first row of table 2 contains the predictions achieved when the pattern prediction scheme of CARFIR methodology is used for the five controllers. The columns of the table specify the average prediction error of the 6 test sets for each controller. In this case the inference is performed by using exclusively the pattern rule bases. As can be seen, the results obtained are very good, with MSE errors lower than 1.5% for all the controllers [6]. The average error obtained for all the controllers is 1.16% much lower than the 6.72% obtained with the Sugeno prediction scheme. Clearly, the prediction capability of the fuzzy rule base is inferior than that of the pattern rule base. However, the forecasting power of the fuzzy rule base is still acceptable from the medical point of view. It is important to notice that the size of the rule base has been extremely reduced, i.e. from 4198 pattern rules to 81 fuzzy rules. This is a relevant aspect that should be taken into account in the context of the CARFIR methodology.

The second and third rows of table 2 present the prediction results obtained when NARMAX and time delay neural networks are used for the same problem. Both methodologies used the same training and test data sets described previously. The errors obtained for all the controllers using NARMAX models are larger than the ones obtained by the fuzzy prediction scheme of CARFIR methodology (see table 1). The average prediction error for all the controllers is 18.09% in front of the 6.72% accomplished by CARFIR (fuzzy rules). However, NARMAX models are much precise than time delay neural networks. The average prediction error computed by TDNNs for the five controllers is 24.56%, bigger than the 18.09% obtained by NARMAX models. However, it should be

Table 2. MSE prediction errors of the HR, PR, MC, VT, and CR controller models obtained using the pattern prediction scheme of CARFIR (FIR), NARMAX and TDNN methodologies

	HRC	PRC	MCC	VTC	CRC
CARFIR (pattern)	1.37%	1.49%	1.41%	1.47%	0.09%
NARMAX	9.80%	14.89%	17.21%	16.89%	31.69%
TDNN	74.80%	21.10%	12.20%	9.20%	5.50%

noticed that the prediction errors obtained by the TDNN models are comparable and in some cases even better than those of the NARMAX models, except for the heart rate controller. In [6] the results obtained by NARMAX models were considered acceptable from the medical point of view. In extension, also pattern and fuzzy models of CARFIR methodology should be acceptable, due to their higher prediction performance. In reality, a formal analysis of CARFIR methodology was not presented as a result of a lack of space in this paper, but it is considered in the reference as "Clustering Algorithms Developed in the CARFIR Environment Applied to Ozone Concentration Prediction".

4 Conclusions

In this paper CARFIR performance is studied in the context of a biomedical application, i.e. the human central nervous system (CNS). The CNS is composed of five controllers, the *heart rate* , the *peripheric resistance* , the *myocardiac contractility* , the *venous tone*, and the *coronary resistance*. For each one of them a Sugeno rule base has been identified starting form its corresponding pattern rule base. The fuzzy prediction scheme of the CARFIR methodology has been used to predict the 6 test data sets associated to each controller. The results show that the fuzzy models are capable of capturing the dynamic behaviour of the system under study more accurately than NARMAX and NN approaches.

A main result of this research is that although the prediction capability of the fuzzy models is lower than that of the pattern models, the forecasting power of the fuzzy rule base is still acceptable from the medical point of view. Moreover, the size of the rule base has been extremely reduced, i.e. from 4198 pattern rules to 81 fuzzy rules. This is an important goal in the context of the CARFIR methodology.

The next step in CARFIR methodology will be the design of a mixed prediction scheme that will allow to obtain a better compromise between prediction performance and size of the rule base. The mixed scheme should be a combination of the Sugeno rules and a reduced set of pattern rules. The advantage of the pattern rules is that they are more accurate than the fuzzy rules in those areas where a large degree of uncertainty exist.

We believe this methodology has proved to be good and will continue giving the right and more efficient results as far as it is used, studied and related to scientific novelties from other human areas.

Acknowledgments. The authors would like to thank COFAA (Comisión de Operación y Fomento de Acatividades Académicas del Instituto Politécnico Nacional), SIP, and CIC of the Instituto Politécnico Nacional for their economical support to develop this work.

References

1. Klir, G.: Architecture of Systems Problem Solving. Plenum Press, New York (1985)
2. Nebot, A.: Qualitative Modeling and Simulation of Biomedical Systems Using Fuzzy Inductive Reasoning. Ph.d. thesis, Dept. Llenguajtges i Sistemes Informàtics. Universitat Politècnica de Catalunya (1994)
3. Cellier, F., Nebot, A., Mugica, F., de Albornoz, A.: Combined qualitative/quantitative simulation models of continuous-time processes using fuzzy inductive reasoning techniques. Inaternational Journal of General Systems 24, 95–116 (1996)
4. Mugica, F., Cellier, F.: Automated synthesis of a fuzzy controller for cargo ship steering by means of qualitative simulation. In: Proc. ESM'94, European Simulation MultiConference, Barcelona, Spain, pp. 523–528 (1994)
5. Nebot, A., Cellier, F., Linkens, D.: Synthesis of an anaesthetic angent administation system using fuzzy inductive reasoning. Artificial Intelligence in Medicine 8, 147–166 (1996)
6. Nebot, A., Cellier, F., Vallverdú, M.: Mixed quantitative/qualitative modeling and simulation of the cardiovascular system. Computer Methods and Programs in Biomedicine 55, 127–155 (1998)
7. Sagawa, K., Maughan, L., Suga, H., Sunagawa, K.: Cardiac Contraction and the Pressure-Volume Relationship. Oxford University Press, NY (1988)
8. Learning, M., Pullen, H., Carson, E., Finkelstein, L.: Modelling a Complex biological system: the human cardiovascualr system. Trans. Inst. Meas. Control 5, 71–86 (1983)
9. Nebot, A.: Valdés, j., Guiot, M., Alquezar, R., Vallverdú, M.: Fuzzy inductive reasoning approaches to the identification of models of the central nervous system control. In: Proceedings EIS'98, pp. 180–196 (1998)
10. Nomura, H., Hayashi, I., Wakami, N.: A learning method of fuzzy inference rules by descent method. In: IEEE International Conference an Fuzzy Systems, San Diego, CA, pp. 203–210 (1992)
11. Sugeno, M., Yasukawa, T.: A fuzzy=logic=based approach to qualitative modeling. IEEE Transactions on Fuzzy Systems, Man and Cybernetics 1, 7–31 (1993)
12. Mugica, F., Nebot, A.: Carfir A new Methodology for the automatic construction of rules in fuzzy inductive reasoning. In: Proceedings InterSymp'00, Baden Baden, Germany, pp. 322–342 (2000) Mugica, F., Nebot, A., Gómez, P.: Dealing with Uncertainty Inductive Reasoning Methodology. In: Proceedings of the Nineteenth Conference, pp. 427–434. Morgan kaufmann Publishers, San Francisco, California (2003)

A Clustering Technique for Video Copy Detection

N. Guil, J.M. González-Linares, J.R. Cózar, and E.L. Zapata*

Department of Computer Architecture
Complejo Politécnico, Campus de Teatinos, Apdo. 4114, E-29080 Málaga, Spain

Abstract. In this work, a new method for detecting copies of a query video in a videos database is proposed. It includes a new clustering technique that groups frames with similar visual content, maintaining their temporal order. Applying this technique, a keyframe is extracted for each cluster of the query video. Keyframe choice is carried out by selecting the frame in the cluster with maximum similarity to the rest of frames in the cluster. Then, keyframes are compared to target videos frames in order to extract similarity regions in the target video. Relaxed temporal constraints are subsequently applied to the calculated regions in order to identify the copy sequence. The reliability and performance of the method has been tested by using several videos from the MPEG-7 Content Set, encoded with different frame sizes, bit rates and frame rates. Results show that our method obtains a significant improvement with respect to previous approaches in both achieved precision and computation time.

1 Introduction

Video copy detection carries out the comparison of a query video with a target video in order to establish if a copy of the query video is present in the target one. This application is an useful tool for both digital content management and protection of intellectual copyrights (IPR). Thus, on one side, the localization of video copies, e.g. an advertisement, can be used to catalog broadcasted material in a multimedia database, to check whether the material was broadcasted at the suitable time or if its duration was correct. On the other side, the video copy can be compared with original video to check if any violation of IPR has happened. In this sense video copy detection is an alternative to watermarking techniques when no marks can be inserted in the video copies.

Signature selection is a key point to develop a specific approach to video comparison. Spatial and/or temporal information can be used to generate the video signature. In addition, signature content can be determined for every video frame or it can be given for a summary in the form of a set of key frames. We will call to the first and second approach, dense and sparse video comparison methods, respectively. Sparse methods require less computational resources during the comparison process. On the other side, dense approaches are more robust.

* This work was supported in part by the Ministry of Education and Science (CICYT) of Spain under contract TIN2006-01078 and Tedial contract 8.06/29.1821.

J. Martí et al. (Eds.): IbPRIA 2007, Part I, LNCS 4477, pp. 451–458, 2007.

Several dense methods have been developed. Thus, Hampapur et al [1] perform a comparison of video matching techniques using different features extracted from each frame of the reference and test clips: motion direction, ordinal intensity and color histogram. Then, the generated signature is applied to the reference clip by using different types of metrics (convolution for motion direction based signature, L_1 distance for ordinal matching based signature and histogram intersection for color histogram based signature). Kim and Vasudev [2] introduce a method that uses, as features, a combination of spatial and temporal information of the video. Spatial information is calculated from the ordinal intensity of video frames. Temporal information is generated from the evolution of intensity along consecutive frames. Copies are detected when a minimum, less than a predefined threshold, is calculated from a dissimilarity expression that combines both features. In [3] an ordinal measure is used as frame feature. In order to compare videos with different frame rates, original video sequences are resampled at an uniform sampling rate. In addition, two metrics, SSS and RSS, are proposed to measure the similarity between query and target video sequences. These metrics are applied in a two step process. First, SSS is used to obtain results by a coarse search and, then, RSS refines these previous results. In [4] DC and a few AC values from the DCT of each frame are quantized to reduce the size of generated signature. Then, longest common subsequence (LCS) is computed to calculate sequence similarity. Mohan, in [5], also uses ordinal measure of intensity images, called fingerprints, for sequence matching. Also, a variability measure is introduced in order to establish the degree of activity that is present in a video. This measure is used to decide if the ordinal based fingerprints are suitable.

Also, some authors have presented sparse video comparison approaches. Kim and Park [6] implement an approach to video sequence matching by calculating the similarity between sets of key frames. Key frames are extracted using the cumulative directed divergence. Then, the similarity between videos is calculated by employing the modified Hausdorff distance between sets of key frames. Cheung and Zakhor [7,8] propose a measure for video similarity calculation where the percentage of clusters of similar frames shared between two video sequences is obtained. Previously, each video is summarized by selecting frames that are similar to a set of predefined feature vectors common to all video sequences.

In this work, we present a new video comparison approach that can cope with sequences with different resolution, frame rate and bit rate. Our method divides the query video in clusters and extracts a representative key frame for each cluster. Features from these key frames constitute the signature of the video. Then, it performs a dense comparison between the signature of the query video and every frame of the target video using relaxed distance constraints to speed-up the search process.

As shown in the experimental results section, the presented approach obtains a better performance than those from previous dense methods, improving both the achieved precision and the computation time.

This paper is organized as follows. Next section introduces the method for video clustering and the selection of the key frames. Section 3 explains the proposed comparison algorithm, and Section 4 presents the experimental results. Finally, conclusions are pointed out in the last section.

2   Video Clustering and Signature Generation

Video information has a strong temporal redundancy that can be used in a video comparison application to save computational time. This can be carried out by clustering the video and extracting one or several keyframes for each cluster. Thus, the comparison process is restricted to the keyframes instead of the whole video frames.

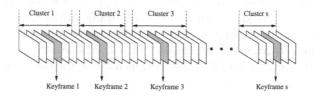

Fig. 1. Video sequence clustering

Following, several approaches which extract keyframes from video clusters are presented. Chen et Chua [9] group the video frames in shots and evaluate the sequence similarity by calculating the number of frames matched between two shots. In [10] keyframes are extracted from shots. Instead of selecting the frames from either predetermined positions [11], or using color/motion based criteria [12], the authors generate a keyframe that represents the probability of occurrence of the pixels at the same position in the frames within a shot. Hanjalic and Zhang [13] find the optimal combination of clusters by applying a cluster-validity analysis.

Our clustering and keyframe selection method is very different to the previous approaches. It does not rely on either a previous temporal segmentation algorithm to extract shots or complex techniques to detect several keyframes from a shot (in case of high variability of the visual content). We argue that in copy video detection application, video clustering techniques can produce a good set of keyframes by performing simple similarity measurements between neighbor frames.

Therefore, our technique divides a video sequence in groups of consecutive frames called clusters as shown in figure 1. Frames in a cluster have the same temporal ordering than in the video sequence and have very similar feature vectors. These feature vectors are finite sets of one or more features, e.g. color histograms or rank matrices, and are compared by a distance function. Thus, distance between frames in the same cluster are below a threshold. In this work a L_1 -distance is used, although any other distance can be considered.

Let $V = \{f_1, f_2, \cdots, f_n\}$ be a video sequence formed by a set of n consecutive frames. Let ϕ_i be the feature vector extracted from frame i and $d(\phi_i, \phi_j)$ be the distance between the feature vectors of frames f_i and f_j. Then, the clustering technique applied to V obtains a signature $S(V) = C^1, C^2, \cdots, C^s$ with the following properties:

1. C^k corresponds to a subset of consecutive frames of V $(f_i, f_{i+1}, \cdots, f_j, i \leq j)$, where i and j indicate starting and ending frame indices of the cluster, respectively.
2. $\forall f_l, f_m \in C^k, d(\phi_l, \phi_m) < \tau$, where τ is a threshold.
3. $C^k \cap C^l = \emptyset, 1 \leq k, l \leq s$

Cluster C^k is represented by its starting and ending frames indices, and the feature vector of its keyframe, that is, $C^k = i, j, \phi_k$. The keyframe feature vector ϕ_k is the feature vector of frame f_l (with $i \leq l \leq j$) and it is selected as the frame in the cluster whose maximum distance to any frame in the cluster is minimum. This keyframe can be located anywhere in the cluster and it is considered the most representative frame of the cluster. This keyframe is a real frame and, as opposed to other works [10], it is not obtained by averaging frames or another combination of frames.

3   Video Sequence Comparison

The objective of this work is to use the signature of the query video, $S(QV)$, to look for a copy sequence in the target video, $TV = \{\phi_1, \phi_2, \cdots, \phi_n\}$. Thus, keyframes of the query video are compared with every frame in the target video.

In a first stage, the query video, QV, is clustered according to the method explained in section 2 in order to generate a query video signature, $S(QV)$. Then, a cluster keyframe, ϕ_i, of the query video is compared with every frame of the target video in order to calculate a vector of distances, D^i (see Figure 2). Finally, a vector of binary values, T^i, is generated by applying a threshold, τ', to D^i. Notice that the lengths of D^i and T^i coincide with the length of the target video.

Regions are extracted from vector T^i by grouping consecutive elements taking a value of 1. As it is shown in Figure 2, several regions can appear for the same T^i along a target video.

The previous region extraction technique is applied to every cluster keyframe of the query video. Thus, one T^i vector is obtained per each cluster keyframe. This is shown in Figure 3 where the query video is assumed to have two clusters.

We propose a method to find the presence of the query video in the target video based on the temporal position occupied by the obtained regions. Two regions generated from different keyframes, R_m^i and R_n^j, (see Figure 3) are candidate to be a copy of the clusters C^i and C^j of the query sequence if the differences between their temporal start and end points, d'_{min} and d'_{max} fulfil the following relaxed conditions:

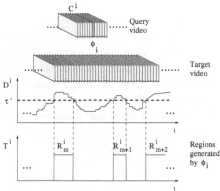

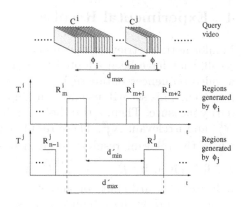

Fig. 2. Regions generation. Distance D^i between keyframe ϕ_i (belonging to cluster C^i) and every frame of video target is calculated. Then, a threshold, τ' is used to generate a binary function, T^i. Regions are formed by grouping consecutive high values of this function.

Fig. 3. Criteria based on distance between regions. Differences among temporal position of the regions R_m^i and R_n^j (d'_{min} and d'_{max}) are calculated and compared with the distance between clusters (d_{min} and d_{max}) to evaluate if they can be part of the copy sequence.

1. The temporal distance between any pair of frames belonging to region R_m^i and R_n^j is lower than the maximum temporal distance (d_{max}) between any pair of frames of the query video belonging to clusters C^i and C^j, respectively. That is $d'_{min} < d_{max}$.

2. The temporal distance between any pair of frames belonging to region R_m^i and R_n^j is higher than the minimum temporal distance (d_{min}) between any pair of frames of the query video belonging to clusters C^i and C^j, respectively. That is $d'_{max} > d_{min}$.

Notice that these temporal distances are signed, that is, they are calculated by subtracting the corresponding temporal region positions.

Then, a complete video copy sequence is detected when previous conditions are satisfied for a set of regions generated for all the query video keyframes. When several sequences in the target video fulfil the previous restrictions, it is necessary to score the quality of the detection by calculating a match value per each detected sequence. This is carried out by calculating a match value equal to the weighted sum of the average distance between the keyframes and the feature vectors of the corresponding regions. Thus, the match value for a solution involving regions R_n^1, R_n^2, $\cdots$, R_n^s is given by $\sum_{l=1}^{s} c_l \cdot L1(\phi^l, R_n^l)$ where s is the number of clusters in the query video, c_l is the length of cluster l normalized with respect to the query video length and $L1(\phi_l, R_n^l)$ is the average L_1 distance between the cluster keyframe and the feature vectors of the frames belonging to the region R_n^l.

4   Experimental Results

In information retrieval two common performance measures exists, precision and recall, that have been adopted for video retrieval performance measure. Given a video sequences database V, a query q is performed and a set of results is retrieved. This set will usually contain an ordered list of results using some similarity measure. Then, a threshold can be used to classify the results in relevant R_q^E, and irrelevant N_q^E. These results can be compared with the ideal response where the relevant results are given by R_q^I and the irrelevant by N_q^I. Finally, recall is given by $R = \frac{\|R_q^E \cap R_q^I\|}{\|R_q^I\|}$ and precision by $P = \frac{\|R_q^E \cap R_q^I\|}{\|R_q^E\|}$ where $\| \cdot \|$ indicates the cardinality of the set.

In this work we have built a video sequences database using several sequences from the MPEG-7 content set ([14], item numbers v3, v7, v16 and v22). These sequences have been joined in a single sequence C of around 160000 frames and encoded with different frame sizes ($384 * 288$ and $192 * 144$), different frame rates (25 fps, 15 fps and 5 fps) and different bit rates (1 Mbps and 128 Kbps). Thus, our database V has 12 versions of the same sequence C summing up around 20 hours of video. For the sake of simplicity, the ideal response of V to a query of one sequence extracted from C is the same sequence and the other 11 versions, with no particular ordering among them. A retrieved result is relevant (true positive) if the intersection between it and the ideal response is not null and it is irrelevant (false positive) if it is null.

We have also recorded several video sequences from digital satellite television, forming a 90 minutes length video, NC. The ideal response of V to queries extracted from NC is none, thus irrelevant solutions (false positives) can be found when any solution is obtained.

Experiments have been conducted over different query sequences lengths: 500, 1000 and 1500 frames (corresponding to 20, 40 and 60 seconds respectively). To test every algorithm, one hundred query sequences have been randomly selected from C and another 25 from NC. Precision and recall values are computed for every query using different thresholds to obtain a precision-recall curve. Then, these curves are averaged to obtain a precision-recall curve for every algorithm.

We have compared our algorithm with a dense one presented in [2], where the feature vectors are rank matrices and their corresponding temporal measures. We have tested 2x2 and 4x4 matrices, and the same feature vectors have been used in our algorithm. To compare the different algorithms, the best pair of precision and recall values have been selected. We consider the best pair is the one with the best precision when recall is at least 95%. In Table 1 is shown the optimum threshold, its corresponding pair of precision and recall values, and the average computation time of a query in seconds. For the algorithm of [2] we show the threshold noted as τ in the paper. In our work there are two threshold values, τ and τ'. We show the value of τ and use $\tau' = 1.3 \cdot \tau$. Computation times don't include feature vectors computation and were obtained in an Intel Core 2 Duo processor, at 1.83GHz, with 1GB of DDR2 SDRAM.

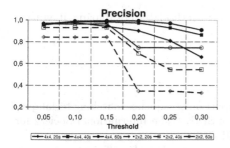
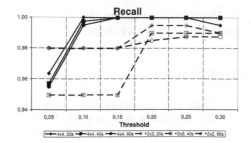

Fig. 4. Precision and recall of our method for different feature vectors and threshold values

Table 1. Experiment results of our method and the one proposed in [2]

Algorithm	20s				40s				60s			
	τ	Precision	Recall	Time	τ	Precision	Recall	Time	τ	Precision	Recall	Time
[2], 2x2	0.05	0.25	0.97	11.44	0.05	0.69	0.98	22.72	0.05	0.84	0.98	33.91
[2], 4x4	0.1	0.71	0.99	32.75	0.1	0.91	0.99	65.33	0.1	0.99	0.99	98.07
Proposed, 2x2	0.1	0.84	0.97	0.33	0.1	0.93	0.94	0.54	0.1	0.96	0.98	0.59
Proposed, 4x4	0.1	0.98	1.0	0.51	0.15	0.99	1.0	0.75	0.15	0.99	1.0	0.87

Our algorithm is consistently better in every experiment, with a much higher precision in short sequences queries. This high precision is due to the fact that our clustering method captures very well the temporal variation of frames in the video sequence, even with short sequences. Regarding the recall value, both the rank feature information and the clusters adapt well to variations produced by different frame rates, bit rates and frame sizes, thus practically all sequences versions are correctly found. It should be noted that both precision and recall are close to 1 for threshold values between 0.05 and 0.2 (see Figure 4), making our algorithm robust to the selection of threshold values.

With respect to computation time, our algorithm is considerably faster because it compares the target sequence with only several keyframes (between 10 and 18 clusters were found in most of the query sequences) instead of the whole query sequence. Our algorithm takes an additional time to compute the relaxed temporal constraints, but this time is almost negligible. Thus, our algorithm is between 30 and 110 times faster.

5   Conclusions

We have presented a novel method for video copy detection that achieves high precision and recall scores keeping low the computational time. It clusters the query video using a similarity criterion and extracts a keyframe per cluster. In opposition to other previous approaches, no previous shot temporal video segmentation is required.

Keyframes are used to find similarity regions in target videos. Then, relaxed temporal distance constraints are applied to the extracted regions in order to detect the copy sequences.

We have also shown the advantages of our method by comparing it with a recent proposed technique.

References

1. Hampapur, A., Hyun, K.H., Bolle, R.: Comparison of sequence matching techniques for video copy detection. In: Proceedings of SPIE - The International Society for Optical Engineering. vol. 4676, pp. 194–201 (2002)
2. Kim, C., Vasudev, B.: Spatiotemporal sequence matching for efficient video copy detection. IEEE Transactions on Circuits and Systems for Video Technology 15(1), 127–132 (2005)
3. Hua, X.S., Chen, X., Zhang, H.J.: Robust video signature based on ordinal measure. In: Proceedings - International Conference on Image Processing, ICIP. vol. 1, pp. 685–688 (2004)
4. Kim, Y., Chua, T.S.: Retrieval of news video using video sequence matching. In: (MMM'05). Proceedings of the 11th International Multimedia Modelling Conference, pp. 68–75. IEEE Computer Society Press, Washington, DC, USA (2005)
5. Mohan, R.: Video sequence matching. In: ICASSP, IEEE International Conference on Acoustics, Speech and Signal Processing. vol. 6. pp. 3697–3700 (1998)
6. Kim, S.H., Park, R.H.: An efficient algorithm for video sequence matching using the modified hausdorff distance and the directed divergence. IEEE Transactions on Circuits and Systems for Video Technology 12(7), 592–596 (2002)
7. Cheung, S.C.S., Zakhor, A.: Efficient video similarity measurement with video signature. IEEE Transactions on Circuits and Systems for Video Technology 13(1), 59–74 (2003)
8. Cheung, S.C.S., Zakhor, A.: Fast similarity search and clustering of video sequences on the world-wide-web. IEEE Transactions on Multimedia 7(3), 524–537 (2005)
9. Chen, L., Chua, T.S.: A match and tiling approach to content-based video retrieval. In: ICME 2001. Proceedings of the 2001 IEEE International Conference on Multimedia and Expo, Tokyo, Japan, August 22-25, IEEE Computer Society, Los Alamitos (2001)
10. Sze, K.W., Lam, K.M., Qiu, G.: A new key frame representation for video segment retrieval. IEEE Transactions on Circuits and Systems for Video Technology 15(9), 1148–1155 (2005)
11. Shahraray, B., Gibbon, D.C.: Automatic generation of pictorial transcripts of video programs. In: Multimedia Computing and Networking 1995. pp. 512–518 (1995)
12. Dufaux, F.: Key frame selection to represent a video. In: IEEE International Conference on Image Processing. vol. 2, pp. 275–278 (2000)
13. Hanjalic, A., Zhang, H.: An integrated scheme for automated video abstraction based on unsupervised cluster-validity analysis. IEEE Transactions on Circuits and Systems for Video Technology 9(8), 1280–1289 (1999)
14. MPEG Requirements Group: Description of mpeg-7 content set. Technical Report Doc ISO/MPEG N2467 (1998)

Invariant Multi-scale Object Categorisation and Recognition

João Rodrigues[1] and J.M. Hans du Buf[2]

[1] University of the Algarve – Escola Superior Tecnologia, Faro, Portugal
[2] University of the Algarve – Vision Laboratory – FCT, Faro, Portugal

Abstract. Object recognition requires that templates with canonical views are stored in memory. Such templates must somehow be normalised. In this paper we present a novel method for obtaining 2D translation, rotation and size invariance. Cortical simple, complex and end-stopped cells provide multi-scale maps of lines, edges and keypoints. These maps are combined such that objects are characterised. Dynamic routing in neighbouring neural layers allows feature maps of input objects and stored templates to converge. We illustrate the construction of group templates and the invariance method for object categorisation and recognition in the context of a cortical architecture, which can be applied in computer vision.

1 Introduction

The visual cortex detects and recognises objects by means of the "what" and "where" subsystems. The "bandwidth" of these systems is limited: only one object can be attended at any time [8]. In a current model [4], the ventral what system receives input from cortical area V1 which proceeds through V2 and V4 to IT cortex. The dorsal where system connects V1 and V2 through MT to area PP. Both systems are controlled, top-down, by attention and short-term memory with object representations in PF cortex, i.e. a what component from ventral PF46v to IT and a where component from dorsal PF46d to PP. The bottom-up (visual input code) and top-down (expected object and position) data streams are necessary for obtaining translation, rotation and size invariance [4].

Object recognition, from the image hitting the retina to feature extractions in V1 and groupings in higher areas, takes time, typically 150–200 ms. Category-specific activation of PF cortex starts after about 100 ms [1]. In addition, IT cortex first receives coarse-scale information and later fine-scale information. This implies that some information propagates rapidly and directly to "attention" in PF cortex in order to pre-select possible object templates, which are then used in the what and where subsystems until recognition is achieved [2].

In [11] it is shown that end-stopped cells in cortical area V1, which combine outputs of complex cells tuned to different orientations, serve to detect line and edge crossings, singularities and points with large curvature. These cells can be used to construct retinotopic keypoint maps at different spatial scales (Level-of-Detail). It was shown that this representation provides very important

J. Martí et al. (Eds.): IbPRIA 2007, Part I, LNCS 4477, pp. 459–466, 2007.

information for object detection and segregation, including the construction of saliency maps for Focus-of-Attention that can be employed for the detection of facial landmarks and faces [11]. In [9] a multi-scale scheme for line and edge detection is presented, also in area V1, based on responses of simple and complex cells. It was shown how object segregation can be achieved with coarse-to-fine-scale groupings, and a two-level object categorisation scenario was tested: pre-categorisation based on coarse scales only, and final categorisation based on coarse plus fine scales.

In the studies mentioned above it was assumed that all input objects and all stored templates are normalised in terms of position, pose and size. This restriction is not realistic in real applications. The invariance problem has been studied in the context of biological vision [3,7,12] and computer vision [6]. In this paper we explore the combination of multi-scale keypoints—by means of saliency maps—and the multi-scale line/edge representation, with feedback data streams from higher cortical areas, for obtaining invariance in the framework of a complete cortical architecture.

2   Methods

Object recognition can be seen as a multi-level categorisation task, for example: (a) an animal, (b) one with four legs, (c) a horse and (d) the brown one with short tail called Tom. By using more features, the categorisation becomes more distinct until final recognition is achieved: a specific object within the class of objects [9]. In this paper we also split the processing into three levels, i.e. pre-categorisation, categorisation and recognition, but we focus on invariant processing.

In our experiments we used the ETH-80 database [5] in which all images are cropped such that they contain only one object, centered, against a 20% background. The views of all objects are also normalised, e.g. all animals with the head to the left (in Fig. 5 marked by white triangle). Images were rescaled to a size of 256×256 pixels. We selected 10 different images in each of 8 groups (dogs, horses, cows, apples, pears, tomatos, cups and cars). The selected images were used at three levels: four types of objects (animals, fruits, cars, cups) for *pre-categorisation*. Two of those were subdivided into three types (animals: horses, cows, dogs; fruits: tomatos, pears, apples) for *categorisation*. Final *recognition* concerns the identification of each individual object (horse number 3) within the corresponding group (horses).

Group templates in memory were created using the normalised objects (see Section 2.3), but in order to test invariance processing a set of additional input images was created by manipulations like translations, rotations and zooms, including deformations (e.g. the head of a horse moved up or down relative to the body). We created 64 additional input images of the most distinct objects: 20 manipulated horse images (horses were used as a special test case for recognition); 6 dogs, 6 cows, 4 tomatos, 4 pears and 4 apples (for categorisation); plus 10 cars and 10 cups (only for pre-categorisation). Typical images are shown in Fig. 5: the bottom line shows the same horse normalised (marked by white triangle) and with the head more down, bigger, rotated, scaled against a white

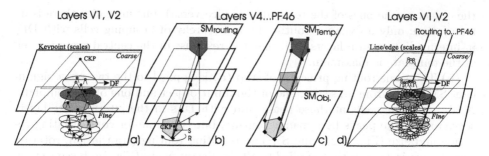

Fig. 1. Dynamic routing scheme (see text)

background, plus an extreme case. The use of this extended database allows to compare our results with invariance processing to previous results obtained with only normalised objects [9]: mean error (standard deviation) of 3.0(1.0)% in the case of pre-categorisation and 9.3(2.1)% in the case of categorisation. These results were obtained by using 8 scales equally spaced on $\lambda = [4, 32]$ (λ refers to the wavelength of simple cells, modelled by Gabor wavelets, given in pixels).

2.1   Invariance by Dynamic Neural Routing

A saliency map (SM) [11] indicates the most important positions to be analysed, because it is constructed on the basis of the multi-scale keypoint representation where keypoints code local image complexity on the basis of end-stopped cells. Activities of all keypoint cells at each position are summed over all scales by grouping cells. At positions where keypoints are stable over many scales, this summation map will show distinct peaks: at centres of objects (coarse scales), at important sub-structures (medium scales) and at contour landmarks (fine scales). The height of the peaks provides information about their relative importance. Such saliency maps are crucial for Focus-of-Attention and are part of the data stream which is data-driven and bottom-up. This data stream can be combined with top-down processing from IT cortex in order to actively probe the presence of objects in the visual field [4]. In our experiments we assume that SMs are also part of object and group templates in memory, and that these are used to project representations of input objects onto representations of templates by dynamic routing in intermediate neural layers (Fig. 1).

In our simulations we explored one possible scenario. Each object template consists partly of significant peaks of the saliency map obtained by non-maximum suppression and thresholding. A grouping cell, with its dendritic field (DF) in the SM, is positioned at the central keypoint that represents the entire object/template at very coarse scales. This central keypoint is located at or close to the object's centroid; see Figs 4 and 6 in [11]. Examples of SMs and significant peaks are shown here in Fig. 2(a,b), in the case of a horse image. The invariant method consists of steps a to f: **(a)** Central keypoints at very coarse scales of an input object and a template are made to coincide (Fig. 1b; T stands for translation). This can be seen as a translation of all keypoints (SM peaks) of the object to the ones of the template (or vice versa), but in reality there is no translation: only a dynamic routing by a hierarchy of grouping cells with DFs in intermediate neural layers such that the response of the central grouping cell of the template is maximum.

(b) The same routing principle of step (a) is applied to the two most significant SM peaks from all scales, one of the input object and one of the template. Again, grouping cells at those peaks and with DFs in the intermediate layers serve to link the peaks by dynamic routing, but this time for compensating rotation and size (Fig. 1b; R and S). The resulting routing (translation, rotation and size projection) is then applied to all significant peaks (Fig. 1c) because they belong to a single object/template.

(c) All other significant SM peaks of the input object and of the template are tested in order to check whether sufficient coinciding pairs exist for a match. To this end another hierarchy of grouping cells is used: from many local ones with a relatively small DF to cover small differences in position due to object deformations etc., to one global one with a DF that covers the entire object/template. Instead of only summing activities in the DFs, these grouping cells can be inhibited if one input (peak amplitude of object, say) is less than half of the other input (in this case of the template).

(d) If the global grouping of corresponding pairs of significant peaks is above a threshold (we used half of the amplitude of the maximum peak), the invariant match is positive. If not, this does not automatically mean that input object and template are different: the dynamic routing established in step (b) may be wrong. Steps (b-c) are then repeated by inhibiting the most significant peak of the object and selecting the next biggest peak.

(e) If no global match can be achieved, this means that the input object does not correspond to the template or that the view of the object (deformation, rotation or size) is not represented by the template. In this case the same processing is applied using all other templates in memory until the ones are found which could match.

(f) Until here, only peaks in saliency maps were used to find possibly matching templates, but mainly for dynamic routing which virtually "superimposes" the input object and the templates. In this step the dynamic routing of SM peaks is also applied to the multi-scale line/edge representation in order to check whether the input object and a template really correspond (Fig. 1d). Again, this is done by many grouping cells with small DFs (local correlation of line/edge events) and one with a big DF (global object/template correlation); see [9]. The use of small DFs can be seen as a relaxation: two events of object and template count for a match if they are at the same position but also if they are very close to each other. The size of the DFs is coupled to the size of complex cells [2].

The template information used in step (f) depends on the level of categorisation. In the case of the first, coarse, pre-categorisation (f.1), only (line/edge) events (Fig. 2d) at 3 coarse scales of the segregated, binary object (Fig. 2c) is used, because (a) segregation must be done before categorisation and (b) coarse-scale information propagates first from V1 to higher cortical areas. Global

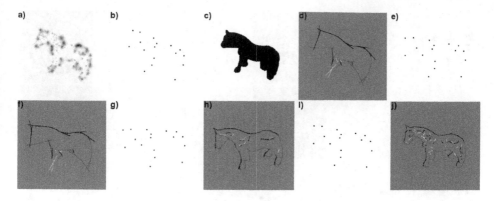

Fig. 2. (a) Saliency map of horse8, (b) SM peaks, (c) segregated image and (d) line/edge coding of segregated image at $\lambda = 24$. (e-f) Corresponding SM peaks and line/edge map in pre-categorisation. (g-h) The same with line/edge map at $\lambda = 8$ in categorisation. (i-j) The same with line/edge map at $\lambda = 4$ in recognition. Input object and matching object are shown in Fig. 5 (marked by a black and white corner triangle).

groupings of events are compared over all possibly matching templates, scale by scale, and then summed over the 3 scales, and the template with the maximum sum is selected [9] (winner-takes-all; Fig. 2f shows a projected and matching line/edge map). In the case of the subsequent finer categorisation **(f.2)**, the process is similar, but now we use (line/edge) events at all 8 scales obtained from the object itself instead of from the binary segregation [9]. Figure 2g and h show projected peaks and the line/edge map used in categorisation. Final recognition **(f.3)** differs from categorisation **(f.2)** in that line and edge events are treated separately: lines must match lines and edges must match edges [10]. This involves three additional layers of grouping cells, two for local co-occurrences of lines and edges and one global. Figure 2i and j show projected peaks and the line/edge map used in recognition.

2.2   Object and Group Templates

Good templates are essential for obtaining correct categorisation and recognition results. Templates for categorisation must be generic enough to represent all possible objects of the group to be tested and no objects of other groups. We assume that templates are composed of saliency maps obtained by combining keypoints detected at many scales and the multi-scale line/edge representation. We also assume that templates are constructed on the basis of normalised views.

Templates must consist of the same information as used in the processing steps described in the previous sections: saliency maps and their significant peaks for obtaining translation, rotation and size invariance, plus line/edge maps at all 8 scales for categorisation and recognition. Group templates for categorisations were created by combining feature maps of all 10 or 30 normalised (not manipulated) images of the selected database. In the case of SMs, all SMs of individual

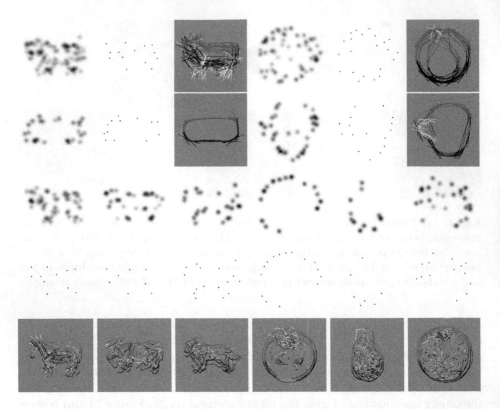

Fig. 3. Top two lines: group templates for pre-categorisation (animal, fruit, car and cup). Bottom three lines: the same for categorisation (horse, cow, dog, tomato, pear and apple). In reality only binary line/edge maps without event types are used.

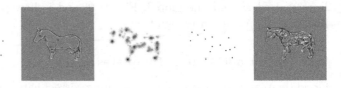

Fig. 4. Templates used for recognition (two different horses)

objects were summed. In the case of line/edge maps, events were combined (OR-ed) in a binary map because only event positions and no event types are used in (pre-)categorisation. Event types are only used in recognition, but this concerns individual object templates and not group templates.

Figure 3 (top two rows) shows group templates for pre-categorisation, i.e., saliency maps, their significant peaks and line/edge maps at $\lambda = 32$ (one of three scales used). The bottom three rows show the same for categorisation (line/edge map at $\lambda = 8$; one of eight scales used). Figure 4 shows two individual object templates used for recognition, i.e. two examples of the ten different horses, with the line/edge representation at $\lambda = 4$ (one of eight scales used).

3   Results and Discussion

Results obtained with the 64 manipulated images were quite good: pre-categorisation (animal, fruit, car, cup) failed in 12 cases. Of the remaining 52 images, categorisation (animal: horse, cow, dog; fruit: tomato, pear, apple) failed in 8 cases. Recognition, which was only tested in the case of horses because of logistic problems due to storage capacity of hard discs (not CPU time!), failed for 2 of all 20 manipulated horse images.

As for previous results obtained with normalised objects [9], categorisation errors occurred mainly for apples and tomatoes, which can be explained by the fact that the shapes are very similar and no colour information has been used. In pre-categorisation there appeared an increased error rate of fruits which were categorised as cups. This mainly concerned pears, and can be explained by the tapered-elliptical shape in combination with size variations such that keypoints and line/edge events of input pears can coincide with those of the cups template.

As expected, problems also occurred with extreme size variations. The scales used ($\lambda = [4, 32]$) are related to the size of the objects and the level of detail that can be represented. Figure 5 (right column, row 1 and 2) shows the smallest objects that can be dealt with by using these scales. The bottom row (right column) shows an extreme example that failed. In this case, the use of finer scales ($\lambda = [4, 11]$) can solve the pre-categorisation problem (the 3 coarsest of 8 scales applied to the segregated, binary object), but categorisation and recognition require scales with $\lambda < 4$ pixels. Gabor wavelets (simple cells) at smaller scales are not well-defined (less samples) and this will lead to problems in the detection of keypoints and lines and edges. It should be emphasised that the method can be applied to images that contain multiple objects. Although our visual system has a limited "bandwidth" and can test only one object at any time [8]), this problem can be solved by sequential processing of all detected and segregated objects (see [11]). However, detection and segregation of objects seen against a cluttered background is also a complex problem, as is the recognition of partially occluded objects.

Finally, it should be mentioned that dynamic routing of keypoints (significant peaks in saliency maps) and line/edge events in intermediate neural layers has consequences for the minimum number of canonical object views in memory, i.e. the number of templates. If a horse template has the head to the left but an input horse has been rotated (2D) 180 degrees such that the head is to the right, dynamic routing will not be possible because there will be a crossing point at some level. In computer vision, this problem can be avoided by applying translation vectors and rotation angles to keypoints and line/edge events. However, recognition in the case of 3D rotation requires separate templates because of asymmetrical patterns of the horse's fell. Extensive experiments with many more object views are required to determine the minimum number of templates, both in human and in computer vision.

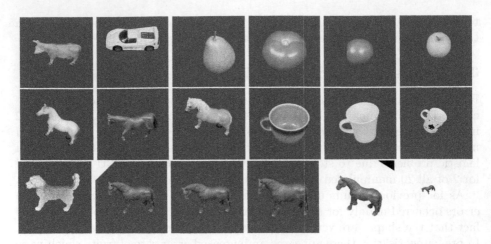

Fig. 5. Examples of objects used for categorisation and recognition

Acknowledgments. This work was partially supported by Fundação para a Ciência e a Tecnologia (ISR/IST plurianual funding) through POS_ Conhecimento Program that includes FEDER funds.

References

1. Bar, M.: Visual objects in context. Nature Reviews: Neuroscience 5, 619–629 (2004)
2. Bar, M., et al.: Top-down facilitation of visual recognition. PNAS 103(2), 449–454 (2006)
3. Cox, D. et al.: "Breaking" position-invariant object recognition. Nat. Neurosci. 8(9), 1145–1147 (2005)
4. Deco, G., Rolls, E.T.: A neurodynamical cortical model of visual attention and invariant object recognition. Vision Res. 44(6), 621–642 (2004)
5. Leibe, B., Schiele, B.: Analyzing appearance and contour based methods for object categorization. In: Proc. IEEE Conf. Comp. Vis. Pat. Recogn. pp. 409–415 (2003)
6. Lowe, D.G.: Distinctive image feature from scale-invariant keypoints. Int. J. Comp. Vis. 2(60), 91–110 (2004)
7. Olshausen, B.A., et al.: A neurobiological model of visual attention and invariant pattern recognition based on dynamic routing of information. J. Neurosc. 13(11), 4700–4719 (1993)
8. Rensink, R.: The dynamic representation of scenes. Visual Cogn. 7(1-3), 17–42 (2000)
9. Rodrigues, J., du Buf, J.M.H.: Cortical object segregation and categorization by multi-scale line and edge coding. In: Proc. Int. Conf. Comp. Vision Theory Applications. vol. 2, pp. 5–12 (2006)
10. Rodrigues, J., du Buf, J.M.H.: Face recognition by cortical multi-scale line and edge representations. In: Campilho, A., Kamel, M. (eds.) ICIAR 2004. LNCS, vol. 3211, pp. 329–340. Springer, Heidelberg (2004)
11. Rodrigues, J., du Buf, J.M.H.: Multi-scale keypoints in V1 and beyond: object segregation, scale selection, saliency maps and face detection. BioSystems 86, 75–90 (2006)
12. Stringer, S., et al.: Learning invariant object recognition in the visual system with continuous transformations. Biol. Cybern. 94, 128–142 (2006)

Combination of N-Grams and Stochastic Context-Free Grammars in an Offline Handwritten Recognition System

Verónica Romero, Vicente Alabau, and Jose Miguel Benedí

Departamento de Sistemas Informáticos y Computación
Universidad Politénica de Valencia
Camino de Vera s/n, 46022 Valencia (Spain)
{vromero,valabau,jbenedi}@dsic.upv.es

Abstract. One area of pattern recognition that is receiving a lot of attention recently is handwritten text recognition. Traditionally, hand-written text recognition systems have been modelled by means of HMM models and n-gram language models. The problem that n-grams present is that they are not able to capture long-term constraints of the sentences. Stochastic context-free grammars (SCFG) can be used to over-come this limitation by rescoring a n-best list generated with the HMM-based recognizer. Howerver, SCFG are known to have problems in the estimation of comlpex real tasks. In this work we propose the use of a combination of n-grams and category-based SCFG together with a word distribution into categories. The category-based approach is thought to simplify the SCFG inference process, while at the same time preserving the description power of the model. The results on the IAM-Database show that this combined scheme outperforms the classical scheme.

1 Introduction

Many documents used every day are handwritten documents, for example, postal addresses, bank cheques, medical prescriptions, etc. In many cases it would be interesting to recognize these documents automatically. The increase in com-puters capacity and the necessity of processing automatically these documents have converted handwritten text recognition in a focus of attention both from industry as well as the research community [1,2]. In the last years a big quantity of different tasks, such as the recognition of postal addresses on envelopes [3] or the recognition of bank cheques [4], have appeared.

Suitable language modelling is an important aspect to consider in large-vocabulary hadwritten recognition systems. The n-gram language models are the most widely-used for a wide range of domains [5]. N-grams are robust and simple models and adequately capture local restrictions between words. More-over, it is well-known how to estimate and integrate the parameters of a n-gram language model in a hanwritten recognition system. However, n-gram language models have a problem: their effectiveness is limited to short distance relation-ships between words.

J. Martí et al. (Eds.): IbPRIA 2007, Part I, LNCS 4477, pp. 467–474, 2007.

On the other hand, Stochastic Context-Free Grammar (SCFG) for language modelling allow modelling long-term relations in a sentence [6]. However, SCFGs work poorly for large-vocabulary, general-purpose tasks, because learning SCFGs and the computation of word transition probabilities present serious problems for complex real tasks. Another problem related with SCFG is that it is difficult to integrate these type of grammars in a hadwritten recognition system.

In this paper, we present a language model defined as a combination of a n-gram, which is used to capture the local relations between words, and a SCFG, which is used to represent the global relation between syntactic structures. In order to solve the problems derived from large-vocabulary complex tasks, the following definition is proposed: a category-based SCFG and a probabilistic model of word distribution in categories [6]. Finally, the integration of both models is made in a sequential coupling way. In first place, a n-best list of candidate sentences for a given input sentence image is obtained, using a recognition system based on n-grams for language modelling. Then the n-best candidates are rescored using a SCFG [7].

The rest of the paper is organized as follows: In Section 2, the methodology used in a handwritten recognition system is described. In Section 3, we explain the combined scheme, while experiments and results are reported in Section 4. Conclusions are shown in the last section.

2   Offline Recognition of Handwritten Sentences

The handwritten text recognition problem can be formulated as the problem of finding the most likely word sequence, $\hat{W} = (w_1 w_2 ... w_n)$, for a given handwritten sentence image represented by a feature vector sequence, $X = (X_1 X_2 ... X_m)$, i. e., $\hat{W} = argmax_W P(W \mid X)$. Using the Bayes' rule we can descompose the probability $P(W \mid X)$ into two probabilities given by optical knowledge $P(X \mid W)$ and linguistic knowledge $P(W)$. So the problem consists in finding the word sequence $\hat{W}$ that maximizes the score $\varphi(W)$.

$$\hat{W} = arg_W max \; \varphi(W) \,, \tag{1}$$

$$\varphi(W) = log \; P(X \mid W) + log \; P(W) \,. \tag{2}$$

$P(X \mid W)$ can be estimated using a recognizer based on the Hidden Markov Model (HMM) technique [8]. Each character considered is modelled using a continuous density HMM with a linear topology . On the other hand, the statistical language model $P(W)$ is approximated with a word bigram language model.

In practice, the simple multiplication of $P(X \mid W)$ and $P(W)$ needs to be modified in order to balance the absolute values of both probabilities. The most common modification is to use a language weight α, which weights the influence of the bigram model on the recognition result, and an insertion penalty β, which helps to control the word insertion rate of the recognizer [9]. So, the score $\varphi(W)$ is:

$$\varphi(W) = log \; P_{HMM}(X \mid W) + \alpha \; log \; P_{BG}(W) + n\beta \,, \tag{3}$$

where n is the word length of the sequence W.

The handwritten recognition system used in this paper follows the classical architecture. It is composed by three modules: preprocess, feature extraction and recognition [10].

The preprocess consists of skew correction [11], slant correction [12,10] and size normalization [13]. Each preprocessed text sentence image is represented as a sequence of feature vectors. In order to do this, the feature extraction module applies a grid to divide the image into $N \times M$ squared cells. In this work, $N = 20$ is adopted. This value has been empirically chosen after tuning the system. For each cell, three features are calculated: normalized gray level, horizontal gray level derivative and vertical gray level derivative. At the end of this process, a sequence of M vectors, each one with 60 dimensions (20 normalized gray level, 20 horizontal derivatives and 20 vertical derivatives), is obtained.

The first term of the expresion (3), $P(X \mid W)$, can be estimated using Hidden markov Models. Each character is a continuous density left-to-right Hidden Markov Models, 6 states per model, each one with a 64 Gaussian densities mixture. The number of Gaussian densities and the number of states were empirically chosen after tuning the system. The character models are trained using a well-known instance of the EM algorithm called forward-backward or Baum-Welch re-estimation while the Viterbi algorithm was used for decoding.

Each word is modelled by a stochastic finite-state automaton (SFSA), which represents all possible concatenations of the individual characters which compose the word.

The statistical language model used to estimate the second term of the expresion 3, $P(W)$, is a back-off bi-gram. It models the concatenation of words of each sentence, using the previous word to predict the current one. N-grams can be learned using the maximum-likelihood criterion from a training (text) corpus, by simply counting relative frequencies of n-word sequences in the corpus.

The result of the recognition process described above consists in a list of n-best candidate sentences for a given input sentence image, with the corresponding recognition scores. Then, those n-best candidates will be rescored using a SCFG and the best candidate after rescoring will be the output of our system. In this way, we try to overcome the shortcoming of the n-grams, related with long-term constraints of the sentences.

3   Combination of N-grams and SCFGs for Language Modelling

In this section, a language model defined as a combination between a n-gram, which is used to capture local relations between words, and a SCFG, which is used to represent global relations between syntactic structures is presented.

3.1   Stochastic Context-Free Grammar

A context-free grammar G can be defined as a four-tuple, $G = (N, \Sigma, S, P)$, where N is a finite set of non-terminals. Σ is a finite set of terminals, $(N \cap \Sigma = \emptyset)$.

S ,which is an element of N, is the starting non-terminal. And finally, P is a finite set of production rules of the form: $A \longrightarrow \alpha, A \in N, \alpha \in (N \cup \Sigma)^+$. A grammar in *Chomsky normal form* is a grammar in which the production rules are of the form $A \longrightarrow BC$ or $A \longrightarrow a$ where $(A, B, C \in N$ and $a \in \Sigma)$.

A stochastic context-free grammar (SCFG) is a context-free grammar in which each production is augmented with a probability. The probability of a derivation (parse) is then the product of the production probabilities used in that derivation; thus some derivations are more consistent with the stochastic grammar than others.

In order to capture long-term relations between syntactic structures and to solve the main problems derived from large-vocabulary, complex tasks, we propose a stochastic grammatical model defined as a combiantion of two different stochastic models: a category-based SCFG (G_c) and a stochastic model of word distribution into categories (C_w). This combiantion of G_c and C_w can be seen as a SCFG which generates word strings.

The probability of generating a string, given G_c and C_w, can be calculated making an easy modification of the well-known algorithm Inside [6]. This probability is based in the definition:

$$Pr(A < i, j >) = Pr_{G_c, C_w}(A \overset{*}{\Longrightarrow} w_i...w_j) , \qquad (4)$$

where $Pr(A < i, j >)$ is the probability that the substring $w_i...w_j$ will be generated from A, given G_c and G_w. This computation is carried out by using the following dynamic programming scheme:

$$Pr(A < i, i >) = \sum_c p(A \longrightarrow c)Pr(w_i \mid c) , \qquad (5)$$

$$Pr(A < i, j >) = \sum_{B,C \in N} \sum_{l=i}^{j-1} p(A \longrightarrow BC)Pr(B < i, l >)Pr(C < l+1, j >) . \qquad (6)$$

In this way, the probability of generating a string $(w_1...w_n)$ is $Pr(S < 1, n >)$.

As we can see in (5), the combination of G_c and C_w is carried out in the value $Pr(A < i, i >)$.

The parameters of the models G_c and C_w are estimated from a set of sentences of a training sample. We work with a treebank corpus, which contains parse trees in the form of bracketed sentences. The probabilities of C_w are estimated from the observed frequencies of the tagged words provided in the samples, whereas the probabilites of G_c are computed as the relative frequence of the production being observed in the treebank.

3.2   Combination Scheme

As we have explained in Section 2, the result of the handwritten recognition system is a list of the n-best candidate sentences for a given input sentence image. For each of these sentences, their probability $Pr_{G_c, C_w}(w_1...w_n)$ is computed and then they are rescored.

This proposed combination can be defined as a modification of the score $\varphi(W)$ adding an additional weighted component, and its results is the extended sentece score $\psi(W)$:

$$\psi(W) = log\ P_{HMM}(X \mid W) + \alpha\ log\ P_{BG}(W) + n\beta + \gamma\ log\ P_{G_c,C_w}(W) \quad (7)$$

The parameter γ weights the influence of the Stochastic Context-Free Grammar in the extended score $\psi(W)$. If $\gamma = 0$, the probability supplied by the SCFG does not affect to the score $\psi(W)$. Therefore (3) and (7) will become identical. If $\gamma > 0$, the probability influences in $\psi(W)$ and the n-best candidate sentences can be reordered. In the same way that the parameters α and β, the parameter γ needs to be optimized experimentally.

4 Experiments

In this section, different experiments carried out to evaluate the combination scheme proposed are presented. Firstly, the corpora used are introduced and then the experimental setup is explained and the obtained results are presented.

4.1 Corpora

Two different corpora have been used in the experiments carried out: a handwritten corpus and a linguistic corpus. The handwritten corpus used is the IAM-Database. This corpus was compiled by the Research Group on Computer Vision and Artificial Intelligence (FKI) at Institute of Computer Science an Applied Mathematics (IAM). The database is described in [14]. It is composed of 1,539 scanned text pages, handwritten by 657 different writers. Of this set of pages, 5,685 sentences have been isolated and labeled, with a total of 13,353 lines and 115,320 words. No restriction was imposed related to the writing style or with respect to the pen used. In Figure 1 we can see an example of a handwritten sentence image from the IAM-Database.

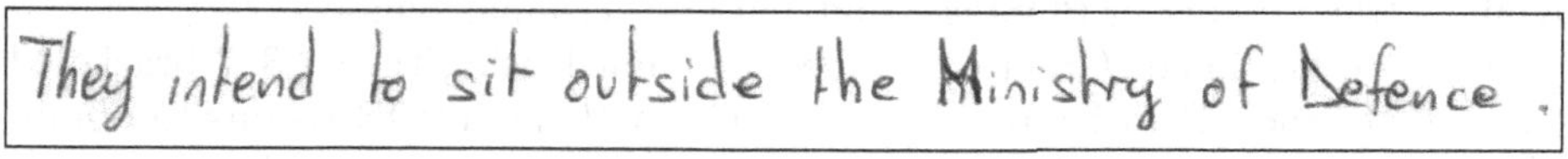

They intend to sit outside the Ministry of Defence .

Fig. 1. A sample sentence from the IAM Database

Since the handwritten sentences in the IAM-Database are based on texts from the Lancaster-Oslo/Bergen Corpus (LOB) [15], the latter has been used as linguistic resource. The LOB corpus contains 500 printed texts of about 2,000 words each, and about a million running words in all. In order to train the different models: n-gram, SCFG (G_c) and word into categories (C_w), we use the Tagged LOB (TLOB) [16] and the Lancaster Parsed Corpus (LPC) [17]. The TLOB represents the same sentences as the LOB, but in this case each word has its grammatical tag attached. The LPC is a subset of the LOB where each sentence has undergone a syntactic analysis in the form of a pharse marker or labelled bracketing. The LPC corpus contains 11,827 sentences compose by 134,740 words. In the next text we can see the bracketed sentence corresponding to the image in Figure 1.

```
[S[Na they_PP3AS Na] [V intend_VB V] [Ti[Vi to_TO sit_VB Vi] [P outside_IN
[N the_ATI ministry_NN [Po of_INO [N defence_NN N]Po]N]P]Ti] ._. S]
```

Several differences have been detected between the IAM-database and the TLOB and the LPC. These differences are related with the surface form of the words as we can see in the previous example (They and they). Other differences related with the simbols have been detected as well, for example the symbol "" is coded as "*@" in the TLOB and in the LPC, while it is coded as "" in the IAM-database.

To carry out the experiments, we used the handwritten text corpus composed by three subcorpus: train, validation and test. The training subcorpus is composed by 5,799 text lines handwritten by 448 different writters, which add up to 2,124 sentences. The validation subcorpus is composed by 200 sentences written by 100 writers and it is used to find optimal values of system parameters. The test subcorpus is composed by 200 sentences written by 100 writers as well and it is used to evaluate the system performance.

4.2   Experimental Results

Several experiments have been carried out to test the combined scheme presented in the previous sections. In order to reduce the number of parameters only the 20,000 most frequent words of the TLOB corpus have been used, whereas the remaining words have been assigned to the UNKNOWN words. Two grammars, which were estimated in different ways, have been used in the experiments.

The first one (Gram. 1) has been obtained parsing the sentences of the TLOB corpus automatically, using the software tool described in [18]. Then, using this bracketed sentences, G_c and C_w have been obtained as it is explained at Section 3. The underlying grammar contains 8998 rules, composed from 46 terminal symbols (the number of POStags) and 339 non-terminal symbols.

On the other hand, Gram. 2 has been obtained using the 11,827 bracketed sentences of the LPC corpus to calculate G_c, and the TLOB corpus to obtain C_w. As in Gram. 1, G_c and C_w have been obtained as it is explained at Section 3. This grammar is composed by 5074 rules, with 41 terminal symbols (the initial number of 130 terminal has been reduced) and 410 non-terminal symbols.

The bigram used in the handwritten recognition system has been estimated with the TLOB corpus. The smoothing technique used is Chen and Goodman's modified Kneser-Ney discounting, interpolated with lower-order estimates.

Note that in order to provide a realistic scenario for the experimental setup, the sentences included in the test set have been excluded from all linguistic resources used for the parameter extraction of G_c, C_w, and the bigram language model.

The results have been assessed using the *word error rate* (WER) measure, which is calculated as:

$$WER = 100 \frac{N_i + N_s + N_d}{N_s + N_d + N_c} \, , \tag{8}$$

where N_i, N_s, N_d and N_c are the number of insertions, substitutions, deletions and correct words, respectively.

In Table 1 we can see the result obtained with the different grammars. The column 1 shows the result obtained with the HMM-based recognizer (baseline). The column 2 and 3 show the results before rescoring the n-best list with the two different grammars explained above. The integration of the word bigram language model and the SCFG (γ) have been optimized on the validation set. The optimum values for γ are 18 and 11, respectively.

Table 1. Word Error Rate without rescore the n-best list (column 1) and rescoring the n-best list with different grammars (column 2 and 3)

Baseline	Gram.1	Gram. 2
31.1	30.7	30.6

Although the results are not conclusive, they show a small improvement using the combination scheme presented in this work (1.2 % in Gram. 1, and 1.6 % in Gram. 2) with resptect to the classical scheme. Moreover, these results outperform results in previous works [7], although we have obtained a worse baseline.

5   Conclusions

This paper has presented a combination of n-grams and SCFG for language modelling in an offline handwritten recognition system. We have shown that the combination scheme may improve the recognition performance. Althought it does not affect the results radically, it outperforms previous results. The fact that SCFGs are difficult to estimate points out the small improvement achieved. However, the use of a category-based SCFG, and a probabilistic model of word distribution in categories reduces the number of parameters to estimate, and hence the grammar estimates are more accurate. This fact may explain the improvement respect to other works.

Future work might include the inference of the SCFG using the other inference algorithms explained in [6], which allow to obtain the grammar in a non-supervised way. Addicional experiments could explore the integration of the n-gram and SCFG using a word-graph from the HMM model.

Acknowledgments. Work supported by the EC (FEDER) and the Spanish MEC under grant TIN2006-15694-CO2-01, by *Consellería d'Empresa, Universitat i Ciència - Generalitat Valenciana* under contract GV06/252 and by the *Programa para la formación de personal investigador (F.P.I.)* of the U.P.V.

References

1. Bozinovic, R.M., Srihari, S.N.: Off-line cursive script word recognition. IEEE Trans. Pattern Anal. Mach. Intell. 11(1), 68–83 (1989)
2. González, J., Salvador, I., Toselli, A.H., Juan, A., Vidal, E., Casacuberta, F.: Off-line Recognition of Syntax-Constrained Cursive Handwritten Text. In: Proc. of the S+SSPR 2000, Alicante (Spain), pp. 143–153 (2000)
3. Yacoubi, A.E., Bertille, J.M., Gilloux, M.: Conjoined location and recognition of street names within a postal address delivery line. In: ICDAR '95. Proceedings of the Third International Conference on Document Analysis and Recognition, vol. 2, p. 1024. IEEE Computer Society, Washington, DC, USA (1995)
4. Dimauro, G., Impedovo, S.P, Salzo, G.: Automatic banckcheck processing: A new engineered system. International Journal of Pattern Recognition and Artificial Intelligence 11(4), 467–504 (1997)
5. Bahl, L.R., Jelinek, F., Mercer, R.L.: A maximum likelihood approach to continuous speech recognition. Readings in speech recognition, pp. 308–319 (1990)
6. Benedí, J., Sánchez, J.: Estimation of stochastic context-free grammars and their use as language models. Computer Speech and Language 19(3), 249–274 (2005)
7. Zimmermann, M., Chappelier, J.C.: Offline grammar-based recognition of handwritten sentences. IEEE Trans. Pattern Anal. Mach. Intell. Member-Horst Bunke 28(5), 818–821 (2006)
8. Bose, C.B., Kuo, S.S.: Connected and degraded text recognition using hidden markov model. Pattern Recognition 27(10), 1345–1363 (1994)
9. Ogawa, A., Takeda, K., Itakura, F.: Balancing acoustic and linguistic probabilities. In: icassp, vol. 1, pp. 181–184 (1998)
10. Toselli, A.H., Juan, A., Keysers, D., González, J., Salvador, I., Ney, H., Vidal, E., Casacuberta, F.: Integrated Handwriting Recognition and Interpretation using Finite-State Models. Int. Journal of Pattern Recognition and Artificial Intelligence 18(4), 519–539 (2004)
11. Gatos, B., Papamarkos, N., Chamzas, C.: Skew detection and text line position determination in digitized documents. Pattern Recognition 30(9), 1505–1519 (1997)
12. Pastor, M., Toselli, A.H., Romero, V., Vidal, E.: Improving handwritten off-line text slant correction. In: Procc. of The Sixth IASTED international Conference on Visualization, Imaging, and Image Processing (VIIP 06), Palma de Mallorca, Spain (2006)
13. Romero, V., Pastor, M., Toselli, A.H., Vidal, E.: Criteria for handwritten off-line text size normalization. In: Procc. of The Sixth IASTED international Conference on Visualization, Imaging, and Image Processing (VIIP 06), Palma de Mallorca, Spain (2006)
14. Marti, U.V., Bunke, H.: The iam-database: an english sentence database for off-line handwriting recognition. Int. Journal on Document Analysis and Recognition 5, 39–46 (2002)
15. Johansson, S., L, G., Goodluck, H.: Manual of Information to Accompany the Lancadster-Oslo/bergen Corpus of British English, for Use with Digital Computers. Dept. of Englis, Univ. of Oslo, Norway (1978)
16. Johansson, S., Atwell, E., G, R., Leech, G.: The Tagged LOB Corpus, User's Manual. Bergen, Norway: Norwegian Computing Center for the Humanities (1986)
17. Garsid, R., L, G., Váradi, T.: Manual of Information for the Lancaster Parsed Corpus. Bergen, Norway: Norwegian Computing Center for the Humanities (1995)
18. Charniak, E.: www.cs.brown.edu/people/ec/

Phrase-Based Statistical Machine Translation Using Approximate Matching

Jesús Tomás[1], Jaime Lloret[2], and Francisco Casacuberta[2]

[1] Instituto Tecnolgico de Informtica,
[2] Departamento de Comunicaciones,
Universidad Politcnica de Valencia, 46071 Valencia, Spain

Abstract. Phrase-based statistical models constitute one of the most competitive pattern-recognition approaches to machine translation. In this case, the source sentence is fragmented into phrases, then, each phrase is translated by using a stochastic dictionary. One shortcoming of this phrase-based model is that it does not have an adequate generalization capability. If a sequence of words has not been seen in training, it cannot be translated as a whole phrase. In this paper we try to overcome this drawback. The basic idea is that if a source phrase is not in our dictionary (has not been seen in training), we look for the most similar in our dictionary and try to adapt its translation to the source phrase. We are using the well known edit distance as a measure of similarity. We present results from an English-Spanish task (XRCE).

1 Introduction

The development of a classical *machine translation* (MT) system requires great human effort. *Statistical machine translation* (SMT) has proven to be an interesting pattern-recognition framework for (quasi) automatically building MT systems if adequate parallel corpora are available [1].

The earlier approaches to SMT were *single-word-based* models [2]. The basic assumption of these models is that each source word is generated by only one target word. This does not correspond to the nature of natural language; in some cases, it is necessary to know the context of the word to be translated.

To upgrade this assumption, the so-called *alignment-template* approach was proposed [3]. A template establishes the alignment (possibly through reordering) between a source sequence of word classes and a target sequence of word classes. The lexical model inside the templates is still based on word-to-word correspondences.

A simple alternative to this model has been introduced in recent works: The *phrase-based* (PB) approach [1,4,5]. This type of model deals also with the probability that a sequence of contiguous words (*source phrase*) in a source sentence is a translation of another sequence of contiguous words (*target phrase*) in the target sentence. However, in this case, the statistical dictionaries of single-word pairs are substituted by statistical dictionaries of *bilingual phrases*.

J. Martí et al. (Eds.): IbPRIA 2007, Part I, LNCS 4477, pp. 475–482, 2007.

Despite its simplicity, the PB approach is one of the most competitive in the present state of the art in SMT [5]. One shortcoming of the PB model is that it does not have an adequate generalization capability. If a sequence of words has not been seen in the training corpus, it cannot be translated as a whole phrase. For example, suppose that the system has in the phrase-dictionary the translation of the English-Spanish bilingual phrase:

"network services user guide" ⇒ *"guia del usuario de servicios de red"* (a)

If a source phrase matches exactly with the left side of (a), the system does not have any problem in obtaining the translation. However, if the source phrase is slightly different,

"network utilities user guide"(b),

the system does not find it in the dictionary, thus the only possibility is translating it using smaller phrases. For example:

"network utilities" ⇒ *"utilidades de red"*
"user guide" ⇒ *"guia del usuario"* or *"guia del usuario de"*.

To obtain the correct translation *"guia del usuario de utilidades de red"* is possible if the system uses the second translation of *"user guide"* and decides to reorder both phrases. However, the correct target phrase has not been seen in training, thus the language model does not have predilection with this output, and the most likely outcome is that the system prefers not to reorder, obtaining the incorrect output *"utilidades de red guia del usuario"*.

Several approaches have been proposed that can overcome the drawback presented by the PB models. In the AT approach, word classes are used. These word classes are learned using an unsupervised method from a bilingual corpus. Another possibility is to use a part-of-speech tagger to determine the word classes [6]. The use of word classes in the AT approach can present a problem of overgeneralization.

Another related work, within the framework of synchronous context-free grammar, is the hierarchical PB model [7]. This model makes it possible to learn a long distance phrase-based reordering. Our goal is different as we focus our attention on a short distance reordering. This kind of reordering is the biggest source of error in English to Spanish machine translation.

In this work, we are interested in obtaining a smooth generalization of the PB approach. For example, if we have the input phrase (b) and we know the translation of a similar source phrase (a), we are interested in using this information to translate (b). The basic idea is that if a source phrase is not in our dictionary (has not been seen in training), we look for the most similar one in our dictionary, and try to adapt its translation to the new source phrase. We use the well known edit distance as a measure of similarity [8].

2   Statistical Machine Translation

The goal of SMT is to translate a given source language sentence $s_1^J = s_1...s_J$ into a target sentence $t_1^I = t_1...t_I$. The methodology used [2] is based on the definition of a function $Pr(t_1^I|s_1^J)$ that returns the probability that t_1^I is a translation of a given s_1^J. Following the log-linear approach [9], this function can be expressed as a combination of a series of feature functions, $h_m(t_1^I, s_1^J)$, that are calibrated by scaling factors, λ_m:

$$\hat{t}_1^{\hat{I}} = \underset{t_1^I}{\operatorname{argmax}} Pr(t_1^I|s_1^J) = \underset{t_1^I}{\operatorname{argmax}} \sum_{m=1}^{M} \lambda_m h_m(t_1^I, s_1^J) \tag{1}$$

This framework allows us a simple integration of several models in the translation system. Moreover, scaling factors allow us to adjust the relative importance of each model. For this objective, Och and Ney propose a minimum error rate criterion [9].

2.1 Phrase-Based Models

In many state of the art SMT systems, the most important feature function in equation 1 is the PB model. The main characteristic of this model is that it attempts to calculate the translation probabilities of word sequences (phrases) rather than only single words. These methods explicitly estimate the probability of a sequence of words in a source sentence ($\tilde{s}$) being translated as another sequence of words in the target sentence ($\tilde{t}$).

To define the PB model, we segment the source sentence s_1^J into K phrases ($\tilde{s}_1^K$) and the target sentence t_1^I into K phrases ($\tilde{t}_1^K$). A uniform probability distribution over every possible segmentation is assumed. If we assume a monotone alignment, that is, the target phrase in position k is produced only by the source phrase in the same position we get:

$$Pr(t_1^I|s_1^J) \propto \max_{K,\tilde{t}_1^K,\tilde{s}_1^K} \prod_{k=1}^{K} p(\tilde{t}_k|\tilde{s}_k) \tag{2}$$

where the parameter $p(\tilde{t}|\tilde{s})$ estimates the probability of translating the phrase $\tilde{s}$ into the phrase $\tilde{t}$. A phrase can be comprised of a single word (but empty phrases are not allowed). Thus, the conventional word to word statistical dictionary is included. If we permit the reordering of the target phrases, a hidden phrase level alignment variable, α_1^K, is introduced. In this case, we assume that the target phrase in position k is produced only by the source phrase in position α_k.

$$Pr(t_1^I|s_1^J) \propto \max_{K,\tilde{t}_1^K,\tilde{s}_1^K,\alpha_1^K} p(\alpha_1^K) \prod_{k=1}^{K} p(\tilde{t}_k|\tilde{s}_{\alpha_k}) \tag{3}$$

where the distortion model $p(\alpha_1^K)$ establishes the probability of a phrase alignment. Usually a first order model is used, assuming that the phrase-based alignment depends only on the distance of a phrase to the previous one [3].

3 Phrase-Based SMT Using Approximate Matching

As section 1 comments, the main weakness of the PB models is the generalization capability. Only phrases that have been seen in a training bilingual corpus can be used in the bilingual dictionary. To deal with this problem, we propose searching the unseen phrases in the bilingual dictionary using approximate matching.

Edit distance (or Levenshtein distance) [10] has proven to be a powerful error-tolerance similarity measure. Moreover, as a subproduct we can determine the minimum edit operations (substitutions, insertions and deletions of words) needed to convert the input phrase into the reference phrase.

The proposed method is used when a source phrase $\tilde{s}$ is not in the dictionary. In this case, we look for bilingual phrases in the dictionary, $(\tilde{s}', \tilde{t}')$, whose source part is very similar to $\tilde{s}$. We consider this case when the edit distance between $\tilde{s}$ and $\tilde{s}'$ is less than a given threshold (typically 1 or 2).

One important issue is to know which words are different in $\tilde{s}$ and $\tilde{s}'$. The difference can be represented as a sequence of edit operations (substitutions, insertions and deletions of words). In many cases there are several minimum edit sequences. For our algorithm, the same result is achieved.

Another important matter is to know which word is the translation of each word in the bilingual phrase that we are generalizing $(\tilde{s}', \tilde{t}')$. For this purpose, we use the most probable word alignment according to the IBM model 1. Word alignments are represented by a, where, $a_{j'}=i'$ indicates that the source word $\tilde{s}'_{j'}$ has been aligned with the target word $\tilde{t}'_{i'}$

Using the minimum edit sequence and the word alignments, we are interested in obtaining $\tilde{t}$, the translation of $\tilde{s}$, based on the known bilingual phrase $(\tilde{s}', \tilde{t}')$, as follows: $\tilde{t}'$ is modified according to the differences found between $\tilde{s}$ and $\tilde{s}'$, These differences are represented in the edit sequence. If a *substitution* operation is found associated to a source word $\tilde{s}_j$, we look for the most probable translation of this word (the translation can be a word or a phrase). Then, the target word, $\tilde{t}_i$, is replaced by this word/phrase. The target position, i, is determined using the word alignment, $i=a_j$. Similar procedures are followed for the *insertion* and the *deletion* operations. A detailed description of the algorithm is presented in figure 2 and an example is shown in figure 1.

The probability of a new bilingual phase, $p(\tilde{t}|\tilde{s})$, is calculated multiplying the probability of the generalized phrase, $p(\tilde{t}'|\tilde{s}')$, by the probability of each word inserted or substituted, $p(\tilde{t}_i|\tilde{s}_j)$, by a special probability to penalize each deletion operation, p_{del}. These bilingual phrase probabilities are introduced in equation 1 as a new feature function.

3.1   Algorithm Implementation

The application of the proposed method should be carried out using three restrictions/modifications. The first obvious restriction is to use this approach only

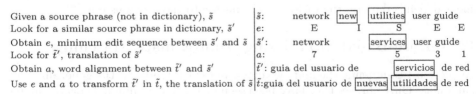

Fig. 1. Algorithm and example of phrase generalization using approximate matching

INPUT:	bilingual phrase dictionary: $p(\tilde{t}'	\tilde{s}')$
	source phrases in test: $\tilde{S}$
OUTPUT:	bilingual phrase dictionary: $p(\tilde{t}	\tilde{s})$
PARAMETERS:	minimum probability of a bilingual phrase for generalizing : p_{min}
	maximum edit distance between source phrases for generalizing: e_{max}
	probability to penalize deletion operation: p_{del}

$\forall \tilde{s} \in \tilde{S} \ / \ \forall \tilde{t} \ p(\tilde{t}|\tilde{s}) = 0$
    $\forall (\tilde{s}', \tilde{t}') \ / \ p(\tilde{t}'|\tilde{s}') \geq p_{min} \wedge EditDistance(\tilde{s}', \tilde{s}) \leq e_{max}$
       Let be e a minimum edit sequence between $\tilde{s}'$ and $\tilde{s}$ ($e_k \in \{E,S,I,D\}$)
       Let be a the more probable IBM1 word alignment between $\tilde{t}'$ and $\tilde{s}'$
       $\tilde{t} = \tilde{t}'; \quad p = p(\tilde{t}'|\tilde{s}'); \quad j=1; \quad j'=1$
       For $k = 1$ to $|e|$
         Case e_k
          E: j++; j'++
          S: $\tilde{t}_{a_{j'}} = \text{argmax}_t \, p(t|\tilde{s}_j); \quad p = p \cdot max_t p(t|\tilde{s}_j); \quad j$++; j'++
          I: $t = \text{argmax}_t \, p(t|\tilde{s}_j);$ insert t at left of $\tilde{t}_{a_{j'}}; \quad p = p \cdot max_t p(t|\tilde{s}_j); \quad j$++
          D: $\tilde{t}_{a_{j'}} = \varnothing; \quad p = p \cdot p_{del}; \quad j'$++
       Insert new bilingual phrase: $p(\tilde{t}|\tilde{s})=p$

Fig. 2. Detailed algorithm used for generalizing bilingual phrases based on approximate matching. $EditDistance(\tilde{s}', \tilde{s})$ is the minimum number of substitution, insertion, and deletion operations needed to convert $\tilde{s}'$ into $\tilde{s}$. This minimum edit sequence is represented as e, using the symbols: E-*equal*, S-*substitution*, I-*insertion*, and D-*deletion*. $|e|$ is the number of symbols in e.

when a very similar phrase is found in the phrasal dictionary. That is, only when the edit distance between both phrases is one ($e_{max}=1$).

The second restriction is motivated by the following argument: In many cases, the unseen phrase can be correctly translated as a monotone concatenation of two phrases in the dictionary. When this occurs, it is not a good idea to use the proposed algorithm. If there are no other alignments that cross it, we consider this phrase can be monotonely generalized, thus, we do not apply the algorithm to this phrase. Figure 3 (a) shows an example.

The third restriction is due to the observation that the replacement of a single word in a phrase produces many concordance errors. As observed in figure 3 (b), when the Spanish word "escaner" is replaced by "impresora" the indefinite article "un" must be replaced by "una" for a correct gender concordance.

In order to solve this kind of error we proceeded as follows: If the previous word of a given word is aligned with a previous word in the target phrase, and we know the translation of this bigram, then we replace the two aligned words with this translation in the target phrase. Figure 3 (c) shows an example. This procedure is also tried using a group of three words: previous word, word to be replaced, and next word. Also using a group of two words: word to be replaced and next word.

3.2 Search

The generalization procedure proposed in this work has been incorporated into a search engine previously developed for the PB models. In our implementation

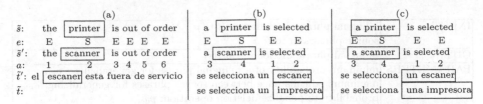

Fig. 3. Examples of several phrase generalizations: (a) The generalization is rejected. (b) Gender concordance error. "un impresora" must be replaced by "una impresora". (c) Error of b is corrected by replacing in $\tilde{t}'$, "un escaner" by the more probable translation of "a printer", that is "una impresora."

we use a simple solution: When phrases in the source sentence are searching in the bilingual dictionary, if a phrase is not found, we use the proposed procedure to obtain a set of possible translations of this phrase.

Given a source phrase, the algorithm described in figure 2 must find all the phrases in the dictionary with edit distance less than a certain threshold, which can be an expensive computational problem.

In a preliminary implementation we have used a serial search. Although the number of phrases can be very high, serial search can be performed in a reasonable time using several restrictions when edit distance threshold is set to one. For example, in the reported experiments, a test of more than a thousand sentences is translated in less than one hour (with a dictionary of two million of phrases).

More efficient search algorithms for this problem are described in [11]. Some of these algorithms can achieve a computational cost of square root of the number of phrases in the dictionary.

4 Experimental Results

In order to validate the approach described in this paper, a series of experiments was carried out using the XRCE corpus [12]. They involve the translation of technical Xerox manuals from English to Spanish [1].

As evaluation criteria we use *Word Error Rate* (WER) [13] and *BiLingual Evaluation Understudy* (BLEU) [14]. Statistical significance of the results is calculated using paired bootstrap [13]. In table 1, we highlight the statistical significance as follows. A result labelled with a "▲" ("△") means that the system is better than the baseline with a confidence of 99% (95%). A "−" means no significant differences.

In the experiments, following log-linear model combination is used:

$$\hat{t}_1^{\hat{I}} = \underset{t_1^I, \tilde{t}_1^K, \tilde{s}_1^K}{\operatorname{argmax}} \sum_{i=1}^{I} \left[c_1 + \lambda_1 \log p(t_i | t_{i-2}^{i-1}) + \lambda_2 \log \sum_{j=1}^{J} p(t_i | s_j) + \lambda_3 \log \sum_{j=1}^{J} p(s_j | t_i) \right] +$$

$$\sum_{k=1}^{K} \left[c_2 + \lambda_4 \log p(\tilde{t}_k | \tilde{s}_k) + \lambda_5 \log p_{am}(\tilde{t}_k | \tilde{s}_k) \right]$$

---

[1] Train (English/Spanish): 56 K sentences, 665/753 K words, 26/30 K vocabulary.

Table 1. Results using several tuning algorithm in English-Spanish XRCE task

	WER	BLEU
baseline	24.7	64.9
+ approximate matching	24.5⁻	65.1⁻
+ excluding monotone	24.1▲	65.5△
+ replace contiguous words	23.9▲	65.7▲

This integrates the following knowledge sources: Target language model (trigram model) $p(t_i|t_{i-2}^{i-1})$. Single word translation models (IBM model 1), both direct $(p(t_i|s_j))$ and inverse $(p(s_j|t_i))$. Conventional phrase based translation model $(p(\tilde{t}|\tilde{s}))$. Phrase based translation model using approximate matching $(p_{am}(\tilde{t}|\tilde{s}))$. Two penalties, c_1 and c_2, are included to control I and K values.

Default parameters in the experiments were: maximum phrase length, which was 14 words; parameter estimation, which was the relative frequency and the search, which was monotone (equation 2). Results with non-monotone search were similar to the results with monotone search.

Several experiments were carried out to assess the approach presented. Table 1 compares the results obtained using the baseline PB model with the approximate matching algorithm. Several modifications of this algorithm have been proposed in section 3.1. Table 1 also shows the improvements obtained with these modifications, which are essential to obtain good results.

In a second experiment, we analyze how often approximate matching is used and how often the results are improved: 64% of the test sentences contain almost one generalized phrase. Many of the generalized phrases are not used in the final output. In the experiment, only 10% of the sentences had different output after adding the new phrases. When the output is different, we compare it with the base-line output in terms of WER obtaining better results in 6% of the sentences and worse results in 2% of the sentences. The WER decreases 0.8 points.

5   Conclusions and Further Work

This work investigates how to deal with the sparsity problem within the PB model. In order to overcome the generalization capability in this model, a new method to adapt the bilingual phrases in the dictionary to unseen phrases has been proposed. The method uses an approximate matching based on the well-known edit distance. In the experimental phase, we have demonstrated that we can significantly statistically reduce the translation errors in the XRCE task.

In the future, we plan to validate this approach with other corpora and language pairs. A more efficient search algorithm must be used. In [15], edit distance is generalized using the permutation operation. We are interested in incorporating this new operation in the algorithm.

Acknowledgments

This work has been partially supported by the Spanish project TIC2003-08681-C02-02 and the IST Programme of the European Union IST-2001-32091.

References

1. Tomás, J., Casacuberta, F.: Monotone statistical translation using word groups. In: Procs. of the Machine Translation Summit VIII, Santiago, Spain, pp. 357–361 (2001)
2. Brown, P.F., Della Pietra, S.A., Della Pietra, V.J., Mercer, R.L.: The mathematics of statistical machine translation: Parameter estimation. Computational Linguistics 19, 263–311 (1993)
3. Och, F., Ney, H.: The alignment template approach to statistical machine translation. Computational Linguistics 30(4), 417–450 (2004)
4. Zens, R., Och, F.J., Ney, H.: Phrase-based statistical machine translation. In: Jarke, M., Koehler, J., Lakemeyer, G. (eds.) KI 2002. LNCS (LNAI), vol. 2479, pp. 18–32. Springer, Heidelberg (2002)
5. Koehn, P., Och, F.J., Marcu, D.: Statistical phrase-based translation. In: Human Language Technology and North American Association for Computational Linguistics Conference (HLT/NAACL), Edmonton, Canada, pp. 48–54 (2003)
6. Tomás, J., Casacuberta, F.: Combining phrase-based and template-based models in statistical machine translation. In: Perales, F.J., Campilho, A., Pérez, N., Sanfeliu, A. (eds.) IbPRIA 2003. LNCS, vol. 2652, pp. 1021–1031. Springer, Heidelberg (2003)
7. Chiang, D.: A hierarchical phrase-based model for statistical machine translation. In: Proc. of ACL 2005, Michigan, USA. pp. 263–270 (2005)
8. Mandreoli, F., Martoglia, R., Tiberio, P.: Searching similar (sub)sentences for example-based machine translation. In: Proc. Atti del Decimo Convegno Nazionale su Sistemi Evoluti per Basi di Dati, Isola d'Elba, Italy (2002)
9. Och, F.J., Ney, H.: Discriminative training and maximum entropy models for statistical machine translation. In: Proc. of the 40th Annual Meeting of the Association for Computational Linguistics (ACL), Philadelphia, PA (2002)
10. Levenstein, V.: Binary codes capable of correcting deletions, insertions, and reversals. Cybernetics and Control Theory 10(8), 707–710 (1965)
11. Hall, P.A.V., Dowling, G.R.: Approximate string matching. ACM Comput. Surv. 12(4), 381–402 (1980)
12. SchlumbergerSema, S.A.: Inst. Tec. de Informática, R.W.T.H. Aachen, University of Montreal, Celer Soluciones, Société Gamma, Xerox Research Centre Europe: TT2. TransType2 - computer assisted translation. Project technical annex. (2001)
13. Bisani, M., Ney, H.: Bootstrap estimates for confidence intervals in asr performance evaluation. In: IEEE International Conference on Acoustics, Speech, and Signal Processing. vol. 1, Montreal, Canada, pp. 409–412 (2004)
14. Papineni, K.A., Roukos, S., Ward, T., Zhu, W.J.: Bleu: a method for automatic evaluation of machine translation. Technical Report RC22176, IBM Research Division, Thomas J. Watson Research Center, Yorktown Heights, NY (2001)
15. Leusch, G., Ueffing, N., Ney, H.: A novel string-to-string distance measure with applications to machine translation evaluation. In: Proc. of Machine Translation Summit IX, New Orleans, USA. pp. 240–247 (2003)

Motion Segmentation from Feature Trajectories with Missing Data

Carme Julià, Angel Sappa, Felipe Lumbreras, Joan Serrat, and Antonio López

Computer Vision Center and Computer Science Department,
Universitat Autònoma de Barcelona,
08193 Bellaterra, Spain
{cjulia,asappa,felipe,joans,antonio}@cvc.uab.es

Abstract. This paper presents a novel approach for motion segmentation from feature trajectories with missing data. It consists of two stages. In the first stage, missing data are filled in by applying a factorization technique to the matrix of trajectories. Since the number of objects in the scene is not given and the rank of this matrix can not be directly computed, a simple technique for matrix rank estimation, based on a frequency spectra representation, is proposed. In the second stage, motion segmentation is obtained by using a clustering approach based on the normalized cuts criterion. Finally, the shape S and motion M of each of the obtained clusters (i.e., single objects) are recovered by applying classical SFM techniques. Experiments with synthetic and real data are provided in order to demonstrate the viability of the proposed approach.

1 Introduction

Several techniques have been proposed for the motion segmentation problem by feature trajectory grouping. Some of these approaches are formulated under the framework of factorization methods (e.g., [1,2,3], to mention a few). Features are tracked over time and their coordinates are stacked into a matrix $W_{2f \times p}$, where f and p are the numbers of frames and feature points respectively—referred to as matrix of trajectories hereinafter W. The key point is that under affine camera model, feature trajectories corresponding to the same object lie in the same linear subspace. Therefore the aim of the different proposed approaches is to find each of these linear subspaces in order to reduce W to a form that allows an easy identification of them.

The aforementioned problem becomes more difficult when the matrix of trajectories contains missing data; that is, when not all the feature point trajectories are visible during the whole sequence (e.g., due to object occlusions, features missed by the tracker or new detected features) and no information of the objects in the scene nor the rank of W are given. In this case two different problems should be faced up. Firstly, the unknown entries in the matrix of trajectories must be filled in. Secondly, once W has been filled in, feature trajectories corresponding to the same object should be clustered together without previous

J. Martí et al. (Eds.): IbPRIA 2007, Part I, LNCS 4477, pp. 483–490, 2007.

Table 1. Summary of relevant features in previous techniques

method	data	rank value of W
Boult, Brown [1]	full	estimated(singular values)
Costeira, Kanade [2]	full	estimated (interaction matrix)
Han, Kanade [3]	full	estimated (maximum 6)
Kanatani [4]	full	estimated (model selection)
Zelnik-Manor, Irani [5]	full	estimated (singular values)
Yan, Pollefeys [6]	full	estimated (model selection[4])
Vidal, Hartley [7]	missing	5

knowledge of the number of objects. Although some approaches have been proposed for this second problem (e.g. [1,2,3,4,5,6]), as far as we know, the missing data case is only tackled in [7] by imposing a rank five for W. Table 1 summarizes the most relevant features of previous works, related to our current proposal.

The current work is focused on motion segmentation from feature trajectories that contain missing data. A robust approach to deal with the two problems mentioned above is presented. On a first stage, a strategy to fill in the matrix of trajectories is introduced. It uses a factorization technique by firstly estimating *the best* rank of W, when no prior information about the scene is given. Rank estimation is based on a novel *goodness* measurement, which considers not only the initial entries of W but also the recovered missing ones. The hypothesis of the proposed goodness measurement is that the *frequency spectra* of the input matrix W should be similar after recovering missing entries. On a second stage, an approach similar to the one presented in [6] is used to obtain the feature trajectory clusters. Once the segmentation is obtained, the shape S and motion M of each of the clusters can be recovered by using any SFM technique (e.g., [8]).

The paper is organized as follows. Section 2 presents the proposed approach for estimating the rank of the matrix W and filling in its missing entries. Section 3 summarizes the procedure used for motion segmentation once the given matrix W has been filled. Experimental results with synthetic and real sequences, testing different percentages of missing data and without a prior knowledge of the scene, are presented in section 4. Conclusions and future work are given in section 5.

2   Fill in Process

The main objective at this stage is to fill in the matrix W in order to proceed with its corresponding segmentation. Factorization techniques have been widely used to tackle this problem in the single object case. The central idea is to express a matrix W as the product of two unknown matrices: $W = AB$. Hence, our motivation is to extend to the multiple object case this factorization-based strategy for filling in the matrix W—concretely, we will use as factorization the *Alternation* technique [9], which deals with missing data in W. In the case of a single rigid moving object, the rank of W is at most four. Therefore, in general W is filled, assuming that its rank is $r = 4$, by minimizing $\|W_{2f \times p} - A_{2f \times r} B_{r \times p}\|_F^2$, where $\|.\|_F$ is the Frobenius norm [10]. Unfortunately, with multiple objects the rank is neither bounded nor easy to estimate, since information about the number of objects or about their motions is not given. Our strategy consists in applying the *Alternation* by assuming different rank values r_0^k for W, obtaining, thus, a *filled* matrix W_{fill}^k for each case. Then, the goodness of these filled matrices is studied and *the best* one is taken for the next stage.

Although different goodness measurements could be defined, it could be noticed that both known and missing entries of W should be equally considered in order to obtain a fair value. For instance, selecting the rank that corresponds to the filled matrix with the minimum rms^1 could be wrong, since as it is pointed out in [11], no goodness measurement of recovered data is used. In this context we propose a novel goodness measurement detailed below.

The philosophy of the proposed approach consists in studying the *frequency spectra* of the input matrix W. The hypothesis of the goodness measurement is that, since feature point trajectories belong to surfaces of rigid objects, the behaviour of the missing data should be similar to the visible one. This similar behaviour is identified with the fact that the computed matrices W_{fill}^k and the input one W have a similar *frequency* content. In order to do that, the *Fast Fourier Transform* (FFT) is applied to each of the columns of the matrices W_{fill}^k and also to the columns of W (adding zeros to its missing entries) for comparing their modulus. Since the idea is to group features according to their motion, the columns of the matrices are taken instead of considering the rows or the two dimensions at the same time. In summary, the strategy is the following:

1. Take different rank values for W: r_0^k, where $k = [5, ..., 15]$ in our experiments.
2. For each r_0^k, apply the *Alternation* technique to fill in the matrix of trajectories, obtaining a W_{fill}^k for each one.
3. Apply the FFT to W and to each W_{fill}^k and compute their modulus:
   $F_0 = |FFT(W)|$, $F_k = |FFT(W_{fill}^k)|$
4. Choose the W_{fill}^k (referred to as W_{fill} hereinafter) for which the following expression is minimum: $\|F_0 - F_k\|_F = \sqrt{\sum_{i,j} ((F_0)_{ij} - (F_k)_{ij})^2}$

3   Motion Segmentation

In this second stage, a similar approach to the one proposed in [6] is used to segment the trajectories. It consists in estimating a local subspace for each feature trajectory, and then compute an affinity matrix based on principal angles between each pair of these estimated subspaces. Finally, the segmentation of the feature trajectories is obtained by applying spectral clustering [12] to this affinity matrix, using the *normalized cut criterion* [13]. The steps of the algorithm are briefly described below.

Rank detection. In the first step of the algorithm, the rank of the filled matrix W_{fill} is computed. In general, in presence of noise all singular values are nonzero.

---

[1] $rms^k = \|W - W_{fill}^k\|_F / \sqrt{\frac{q}{2}}$, where q is the number of known entries in W.

Therefore, the smallest ones must be truncated in order to estimate the rank. However, it is difficult to set an appropriate threshold. In [14], authors propose the *model selection* for rank detection. Based on that, the following expression is used to estimate the rank in presence of noise:

$$r_m = argmin_r \frac{\lambda_{r+1}^2}{\sum_{j=1}^r \lambda_j^2} + \mu r, \tag{1}$$

where λ_i corresponds to the i-th singular value of the matrix, and μ is a parameter that depends on the amount of noise. The higher the noise level is, the larger μ should be (in our experiments, $\mu = 10^{-7}$). Therefore, the r that minimizes this expression is considered as the rank of W_{fill}. Notice that it does not have to coincide with the rank value used in the previous stage to fill in the matrix of trajectories, r_0^k. In most of the cases, error is added to the entries of W in the previous stage, hence its rank could vary.

Data transformation. If W_{fill} is a $2f \times p$ matrix, the idea is to consider each of its p columns as a vector in $\mathbf{R}^{2f}$ and to project them onto the unit sphere in $\mathbf{R}^r$, being r the estimated rank value in the previous step. The SVD decomposes the matrix of trajectories as $W_{fill} = U_{2f \times 2f} S_{2f \times p} V_{p \times p}^t$. In order to project the trajectories onto $\mathbf{R}^r$, only the first r rows of V^t are considered: $V_{r \times p}^t$. Finally, the p columns of this matrix are normalized to project them onto the unit sphere.

Subspace estimation. For each point α in the transformed space, its local subspace is computed, formed by itself and its n closest neighbours: $[\alpha, \alpha_1, \cdots, \alpha_n]$, being $n + 1 = d$; where d is the highest dimension of the linear subspaces generated by each cluster (e.g., 4 for the rigid object case). The closest neighbours are selected using the Euclidean distance between the transformed points.

Affinity matrix. Instead of computing a distance between points, the distance between the local subspaces estimated in the previous step is used, which is measured by principal angles [10]. The affinity A of two points α and β is defined as the distance between their estimated local subspaces $S(\alpha)$ and $S(\beta)$:

$$A(\alpha, \beta) = e^{-\sum_{i=1}^M sin(\theta_i)^2}, \tag{2}$$

where θ_i is the i-th principal angle between the subspaces $S(\alpha)$ and $S(\beta)$ and M the minimum of their dimensions.

Spectral clustering. Finally, the motion segmentation is obtained by applying spectral clustering [12] to the affinity matrix computed in the previous step. Concretely, the *normalized cut criterion*, presented in [13], is used to segment the data. This criterion measures both the total dissimilarity between the different clusters as well as the total similarity within the clusters and it can be optimized by using a technique based on a generalized eigenvalue problem.

4   Evaluation Study

In this section, the performance of the proposed approach is studied by using synthetic and real data. Actually, only the 2–objects case is studied in this paper.

Considering different percentages of missing data, 25 attempts are repeated and the percentage of bad-clustered features over the total of features in W is computed. This gives a measure of error in the clustering. Finally, the mean and median of errors in all the attempts are presented.

Given a full matrix, the missing data are generated by automatically removing parts of random columns in order to simulate the behaviour of tracked features. Non-filled columns correspond to features missed by the tracker or to new features detected after the first frame.

4.1   Synthetic Data

Two different objects are used. The first one is generated by randomly distributing 3D feature points over the surface of a cylinder, see Fig 1 (left). The second object is generated from a set of 3D points, which correspond to a Beethoven sculptured surface represented by a triangular mesh, see Fig 1 (middle).

Taking these two 3D objects, different sequences are obtained by performing rotations and translations over both of them. At the same time, the camera also rotates and translates. Although self-occlusions are produced, all the points are stacked into the matrix of trajectories, since this is a synthetic experiment. The full obtained trajectories of a sequence with a cylinder and a Beethoven are shown in Fig 1 (right). This sequence is defined by 50 frames containing 451 features (185 from the cylinder and 266 from the Beethoven sculpture).

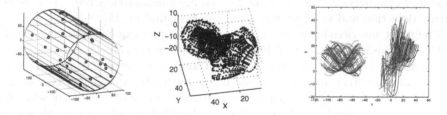

Fig. 1. Synthetic objects: (left) Cylinder. (middle) Beethoven. (right) Full feature trajectories of the second sequence in table 2, plotted in the image plane.

Table 2 presents the mean and median of the error obtained in the 25 attempts for each sequence and each percentage of missing data. In the first two sequences the objects move independently, while in the last one the rotation of both objects is identical and consequently the motion is dependent. Independently of the object motion's dependency, good results are obtained as long as the percentage of missing data is below 50%.

Although out of the scope of this work, since our main target is motion segmentation, Fig 2 shows an illustration of the shape and motion of each object recovered by applying the *Alternation* to the results of the proposed technique. These results correspond to the second sequence in Table 2, 20% of missing data.

Table 2. Synthetic experiments

sequence	2 cyl., $W_{180 \times 145}$				cyl., Beet., $W_{100 \times 451}$				2 cyl., $W_{180 \times 160}$			
missing data	20%	30%	40%	50%	20%	30%	40%	50%	20%	30%	40%	50%
mean error	0.02	0	0.57	15.14	0.07	0.41	0.66	4.98	0.25	0.32	0.20	15.90
median error	0	0	0	2.75	0	0	0	0.66	0	0	0	10.62

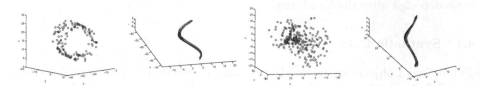

Fig. 2. Recovered 3D shape and motion: (left) Cylinder. (right) Beethoven.

4.2 Real Data

The same procedure applied to the synthetic data is now used with real data. The two objects studied for these real data experiments are shown in Fig 3 (left) and (middle), respectively. For each object, a real video sequence with a resolution of 640×480 pixels is used. A single rotation around a vertical axis is performed to each of the objects. Feature points are selected by means of a corner detector algorithm and only points distributed over the squared-surfaces (box and cylinders) visible in all the frames are considered. More details about corner detection and tracking algorithm can be found in [15].

The input matrices of trajectories corresponding to sequences of multiple objects are generated by merging different matrices of trajectories (corresponding or not to the same object) after having interchanged the x and y coordinates. Overlapping between objects is avoided for clarity by applying a translation. The first studied sequence is generated by using the first object twice, while the second sequence uses both objects. The obtained full trajectories in this second case are plotted in Fig 3 (right). This sequence is defined by 61 frames and 275 features (87 from the first object and 188 from the second one).

Table 3 summarizes the obtained results. It can be seen that the error in the clustering is higher than in the synthetic case, even working with smaller percentages of missing data. The main reason is that, working with real noisy

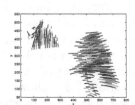

Fig. 3. Real objects: (left) First object. (middle) Second object. (right) Full feature trajectories plotted in the image plane, second sequence in table 3.

Table 3. Real experiments

sequence	First sequence, $W_{202 \times 174}$					Second sequence, $W_{122 \times 275}$				
missing data	10%	20%	30%	40%	50%	10%	20%	30%	40%	50%
mean error	5.19	8.00	14.52	15.10	24.06	11.95	8.21	16.49	23.52	43.02
median error	1.72	3.44	5.74	5.17	20.68	3.63	4.00	7.63	29.09	46.54

data, the *Alternation* propagates the noise to the filled matrices in the filling in process. Consequently, the error in the clustering is higher than working with synthetic free of noise data.

Finally, Fig 4 shows an example of the recovered shape and motion obtained by applying *Alternation* to the trajectories corresponding to the two objects of the second sequence in Table 3, 20% of missing data.

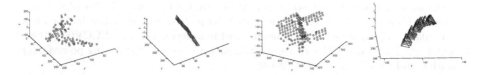

Fig. 4. Recovered shape and motion: (left) First object. (right) Second object.

5   Conclusions and Future Work

In this paper, an approach for motion segmentation from feature trajectories with missing data is presented. It consists of two stages. In the first stage, the missing data in the feature trajectories are filled in. Since working with missing data and with no prior knowledge of the number of objects in the scene, the rank of the matrix of trajectories can not be directly computed, a novel technique to estimate it is proposed. It is based on a *frequency spectra* study of W and motivated by the fact that feature point trajectories belong to surfaces of rigid objects. Therefore the filled matrices should contain a *frequency spectra* similar to the one of the input matrix. In the second stage, motion segmentation is obtained by using a clustering technique based on the *normalized cut criterion*.

Although we focus our work on the study of the error in the clustering, it should be mentioned that, in the first stage, the rank of the input matrix W is properly estimated in most of the cases by using the proposed goodness measurement (it can be checked, since the full initial matrices are known).

Experiments with independent and dependent motions are presented and it is shown that, although the approach performs well in both cases, better results are obtained when the motion subspaces are independent. In the experiments with real data, the error in the clustering is higher than in the synthetic ones. This is due to the added error in the feature trajectories during the first stage.

Further work will include a study of robustness of the proposed approach to noisy data.

490   C. Julià et al.

Acknowledgments. This work has been supported by the Government of Spain under the MEC project TRA2004 - 06702/AUT. The second author has been supported by The Ramón y Cajal Program.

References

1. Boult, T., Brown, L.: Factorization-based segmentation of motions. In: IEEE Workshop on Motion Understanding. pp. 179–186 (1991)
2. Costeira, J., Kanade, T.: A multibody factorization method for independently moving objects. International Journal of Computer Vision pp. 159–179 (1998)
3. Han, M., Kanade, T.: Reconstruction of a scene with multiple linearly moving objects. International Journal of Computer Vision 53, 285–300 (2000)
4. Kanatani, K.: Motion segmentation by subspace separation and model selection. In: CVPR. vol. 2, pp. 586–591 (2001)
5. Zelnik-Manor, L., Irani, M.: Degeneracies, dependencies and their implications in multi-body and multi-sequence factorization. In: CVPR. pp. 287–293 (2003)
6. Yan, J., Pollefeys, M.: A general framework for motion segmentation: independent, articulated, rigid, non-rigid, degenerate and non-degenerate. In: ECCV06 (2006)
7. Vidal, R., Hartley, R.: Motion segmentation with missing data using powerfactorization and GPCA. In: CVPR (2004)
8. Tomasi, C., Kanade, T.: Shape and motion from image streams: a factorization method. Full report on the orthographic case (1992)
9. Buchanan, A., Fitzgibbon, A.: Damped newton algorithms for matrix factorization with missing data. IEEE Computer Society Conference on Computer Vision and Pattern Recognition (CVPR) 2, 316–322 (2005)
10. Golub, G., Van Loan, C. (eds.): Matrix Computations. The Johns Hopkins Univ. Press, Baltimore, MD (1989)
11. Chen, P., Suter, D.: Recovering the missing components in a large noisy low-rank matrix: Application to SFM. IEEE Transactions on PAMI vol. 26 (2004)
12. Weiss, Y.: Segmentation using eigenvectors: a unifying view. In: International Conference on Computer Vision (1999)
13. Shi, J., Malik, J.: Normalized cuts and image segmentation. IEEE Transactions on PAMI (2000)
14. Kanatani, K.: Statistical optimization and geometric inference in computer vision. Philosophical transactions: Mathematical, physical and engineering sciences 356, 1303–1320 (1998)
15. Ma, Y., Soatto, J., Kosecká, J., Sastry, S.: An invitation to 3D vision: From images to geometric models. Springer, Heidelberg (2004)

Segmentation of Rigid Motion from Non-rigid 2D Trajectories

Alessio Del Bue[1], Xavier Lladó[2], and Lourdes Agapito[3]

[1] Instituto de Sistemas e Robótica, Instituo Superior Técnico, Lisboa, Portugal
[2] Dept. of Electronics, Computer Eng. and Automatics, Universtiy of Girona, Spain
[3] Department of Computer Science, Queen Mary, University of London, UK

Abstract. In this paper we evaluate an automatic segmentation algorithm able to identify the set of rigidly moving points within a deformable object given the 2D measurements acquired by a perspective camera. The method is based on a RANSAC algorithm with guided sampling and an estimation of the fundamental matrices from pairwise frames in the sequence. Once the segmentation of rigid and non-rigid points is available, the set of rigid points could be used to estimate the internal camera calibration parameters, the overall rigid motion and the non-rigid 3D structure.

1 Introduction

In this paper we evaluate a method that performs the automatic segmentation of a set of rigidly moving points within a deformable object given a set of 2D image measurements. Several works have previously proposed the use of the dimensionality of the subspace in which the image trajectories lie to perform motion segmentation [1,2,3,4]. However, all these methods focus either on the segmentation of independently moving objects or on the segmentation of objects of different nature (rigid, articulated or non-rigid), but none of them can deal efficiently with the segmentation of rigid and non-rigid points on a single deformable object. Moreover, most of these methods assume an affine camera model but in this paper we are interested in the full perspective camera case. To our knowledge, the work of Del Bue et al. [5] is the first attempt to obtain a reliable segmentation of rigid points from non-rigid bodies, however, the method is restricted to affine camera models.

Our segmentation approach in the perspective case is based on a RANSAC [6] algorithm with guided sampling, similarly to the one proposed by Tordoff and Murray [7]. The RANSAC algorithm is used to estimate the fundamental matrices from pairwise frames in the sequence and to segment the scene into rigid and non-rigid points. We perform experiments of the segmentation algorithm on synthetic and real data which show the validity of our proposed method. The result of the segmentation algorithm could then be used to recover the 3D non-rigid structure and motion using the method described in [8,9].

The paper is organised as follows. Section 2 introduces the general idea of the segmentation algorithm, while sections 3−4 describe in detail the different steps

J. Martí et al. (Eds.): IbPRIA 2007, Part I, LNCS 4477, pp. 491–498, 2007.
© Springer-Verlag Berlin Heidelberg 2007

of the approach. In section 5 we show segmentation results on different synthetic and real data sets.

2 Segmentation of Rigid and Non-rigid Motion Under Perspective Viewing

The approach is based on the fact that rigid points satisfy the epipolar geometry while the non-rigid points will give a high residual in the estimation of the fundamental matrix between pairs of views. We use a RANSAC algorithm [6] to estimate the fundamental matrices from pairwise frames in the sequence and to segment the scene into rigid and non-rigid points. Therefore, in this case we consider the dominant motion to be the rigid one and the non-rigid points to be the outliers.

However, a well known drawback of random sampling and consensus techniques is the computational cost required to obtain a valid set of points when the percentage of outliers is high, due to the large number of samples needed to be drawn from the data. Unfortunately, this is the most likely scenario in non-rigid structure from motion where we normally deal with a small proportion of completely rigid points. Here we exploit a measure of the degree of non-rigidity of a point to infer a prior distribution of the probability of a trajectory being rigid or non-rigid given that measure. These distributions are then used as priors to perform guided sampling over the set of trajectories in a similar approach to the one proposed by Tordoff and Murray [7] for the stereo matching problem.

2.1 Degree of Non-rigidity

In order to increase the likelihood of selecting rigidly moving points in the sampling stage, we associate a measure of non-rigidity to each trajectory. Recently, Kim and Hong [10] introduced the notion of Degree of Non-rigidity (DoN) of a point viewed by an orthographic camera as an effective measure of the deviation of the point from the average shape. If the average 3D shape of a time varying shape $X_i = [\mathbf{X}_{i1} \dots \mathbf{X}_{iP}]$ (in non-homogeneous coordinates) is given by $\check{X} = [\check{\mathbf{X}}_1 \dots \check{\mathbf{X}}_P]$ the Degree of Non-rigidity for point j is defined as:

$$DoN_j = \sum_{i=1}^{F}(\mathbf{X}_{ij} - \check{\mathbf{X}}_j)(\mathbf{X}_{ij} - \check{\mathbf{X}}_j)^T \qquad (1)$$

The 2D projection C_j of the DoN will be thus given by:

$$\mathsf{C}_j = \sum_{i=1}^{F} \mathsf{R}_i(\mathbf{X}_{ij} - \check{\mathbf{X}}_j)(\mathbf{X}_{ij} - \check{\mathbf{X}}_j)^T \mathsf{R}_i^T = \sum_{i=1}^{F}(\mathbf{w}_{ij} - \check{\mathbf{w}}_{ij})(\mathbf{w}_{ij} - \check{\mathbf{w}}_{ij})^T \qquad (2)$$

where R_i are the 2×3 orthographic camera for F frames, $\mathbf{w}_{ij}$ are the non-homogeneous image coordinates of point j in frame i and $\check{\mathbf{w}}_{ij}$ are the coordinates of its projected mean 3D value over the F frames in the sequence. While the *DoN* cannot be computed without an estimation of the mean 3D shape (and this implies finding a 3D deformable reconstruction), the value of its projection can be estimated directly from image measurements.

An approximate estimate of the average projected shape $\check{\mathbf{w}}_{ij}$ can be given simply by the rank-3 approximation of the measurement matrix $\mathtt{W}$ (the matrix that contains the 2D coordinates $\mathbf{w}_{ij}$ of all P points viewed in all F frames) computed using singular value decomposition and given by $SVD_3(\mathtt{W}) = \check{\mathtt{M}}\check{\mathtt{S}}$. The projected deviation from the mean for all the points would then be defined by $\{\mathbf{w}_{ij} - \check{\mathbf{w}}_{ij}\} = \mathtt{W} - \check{\mathtt{M}}\check{\mathtt{S}}$. Kim and Hong computed a more sophisticated estimate of the average shape, but for simplicity we have used the above description which has shown to give a reasonable measure of the degree of deformability.

Notice that the previous definitions all assume affine viewing conditions. However, our trajectories reside in a projective space so a redefinition of the measure of non-rigidity is required. First, the original measurement matrix must be re-scaled by the estimated projective weights λ_{ij}. We calculate the projective weights λ_{ij} using subspace constraints [11] and express the rescaled measurement matrix (in homogeneous coordinates) as $\bar{\mathtt{W}} = \{\lambda_{ij} \ [\mathbf{w}_{ij}^T \ 1]^T\}$. Then, we estimate the mean shape as the rank-4 approximation of the rescaled measurement matrix computed using singular value decomposition and given by $SVD_4(\bar{\mathtt{W}}) = \check{\mathtt{M}}\check{\mathtt{S}}$. The projected deviation from the mean would then be defined similarly as before but computing the mean projected shape $\check{\mathbf{w}}_j$ using the normalized non-homogenous coordinates. Therefefore, the projection of the *DoN* can finally be computed as:

$$C_j = \sum_{i=1}^{F} (\mathbf{w}_{ij} - \check{\mathbf{w}}_{ij})(\mathbf{w}_{ij} - \check{\mathbf{w}}_{ij})^T \tag{3}$$

in the form of a 2×2 covariance matrix. Instead of using the full information of C_j, we approximate the score s as the sum of the diagonal values of C_j.

3   Computation of the Prior

Tordoff and Murray [7] showed that guided sampling based on knowledge extracted from the images can greatly improve the performance of a random sampling method, especially in the presence of noise or high number of outliers. In these cases standard RANSAC becomes computationally prohibitive given the large number of random samples that must be drawn from the data. Here we use the 2D projection of the *DoN* defined in the previous section to provide the score s for each point trajectory which in turn will be used to build a prior distribution of the conditional probability of each point in the object being rigid or non-rigid given this score.

We have inferred the conditional probability density functions for the score s given that a point is rigid $p(s|r)$ (see figure 1(a)) or non-rigid $p(s|\bar{r})$ (see

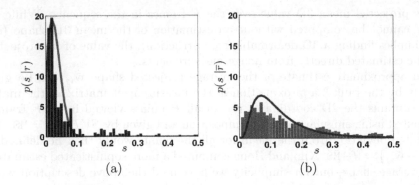

(a)   (b)

Fig. 1. Conditional densities for the score given: (a) that a point is rigid $p(s|r)$ or (b) non-rigid $p(s|\bar{r})$ approximated from the normalised frequency histograms for different synthetic and real sequences with different degrees of perspective distortion, deformation and ratio of rigid/non-rigid points

figure 1(b)) by computing the normalised frequency histograms over many experimental trials with synthetic and real sequences with different perspective distortions, degrees of deformation and ratios of rigid/non-rigid points. We have then approximated the histograms by fitting appropriate analytical functions (a Gamma distribution for $p(s|r)$ and a Lognormal for $p(s|\bar{r})$).

To derive the prior conditional density function of a point being rigid given the non-rigidity score, $p(r|s)$, we use Bayes theorem:

$$p(r|s) = \frac{p(s|r)p(r)}{p(s)} \propto \frac{p(s|r)}{p(s|r) + p(s|\bar{r})} \tag{4}$$

Figure 2 shows an example of a prior obtained from our experiments. Note that, although the computation of the score is specific to each method, the derivation of the prior given the distribution of the score is general.

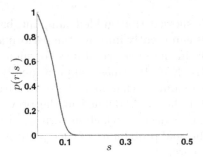

Fig. 2. Estimated prior given by the estimated densities $p(s|r)$ and $p(s|\bar{r})$

4   Guided RANSAC

We use guided RANSAC to estimate the fundamental matrices between pairs of consecutive views for all the F frames composing the sequence. This process will be used to provide a segmentation of the image trajectories into rigid and non-rigid ones since the non-rigid trajectories will not satisfy the epipolar geometry and will therefore give a high residual in the computation of the pairwise fundamental matrices. In order to speed up the process, we use the prior derived in the previous section to draw the point samples: points with the highest conditional probability of being rigid will be chosen more frequently. The RANSAC with priors procedure is outlined as follows:

Algorithm 1. RANSAC with priors

1. Compute the score s for each trajectory in $\bar{W}$.
2. Sample b trajectories given the prior $p(r)$ and the score s.
3. For each sample, estimate $(F-1)$ fundamental matrices from each pair of consecutive frames.
4. Calculate the distance of the points from the $F-1$ instantiated models and find the trajectories that are within a threshold t.
5. Repeat N times and determine the largest consensus given a set of trajectories.

The method employed to estimate the fundamental matrix is the standard 8-point algorithm [12]. The distance threshold t which decides whether a point is an inlier or an outlier (rigid or non-rigid in this case) was set empirically to be $t = 4.12$. It was fixed by taking into account the sum of the residuals given by the estimation of $F-1$ fundamental matrices using normalised coordinates. Notice that we do not consider outliers in the point matching from frame to frame. We show results of the guided sampling RANSAC algorithm applied to the segmentation of rigid and non-rigid points in the experimental section.

Once the scene has been segmented into the rigid and non-rigid point sets we may compute metric non-rigid shape in two further steps as described in [8,9]. First the rigid points are used to estimate the intrinsic parameters of the camera – which provide the necessary information to upgrade the structure to metric – and the overall rotations and translations. Secondly, the estimation of metric non-rigid shape is formulated as a global non-linear minimization with shape priors over the rigid trajectories.

5   Experimental Results

This experimental section validates the rigid/non-rigid segmentation with synthetic and real experiments. The synthetic tests are designed in such a way as to verify the performance of the method in case of different ratios of rigid/non-rigid points and with two different setups of perspective distortions.

5.1   Synthetic Data

The 3D data consists of a set of random points sampled inside a cube of size $100 \times 100 \times 100$ units. Several sequences were generated using different ratios of rigid/non-rigid points. In particular, we used a fixed set of 10 rigid points while using 10 and 50 non-rigid points. The deformations for the non-rigid points were generated using random basis shapes as well as random deformation weights. The first basis shape had the largest weight equal to 1. We also created different sequences varying the number of basis shapes ($D = 3$ and $D = 5$) for both ratios of rigid/non-rigid points. Finally, in order to evaluate different levels of perspective distortion we used 2 different camera setups in which we varied the distance of the object to the camera and the focal length (Setup 1: z=250, f=900; Setup 2: z=200, f=600). The 3D data was then projected onto 50 images applying random rotations and translations over all the axes. Gaussian noise of increasing levels of variance was added to the image coordinates.

Table 1. Mean error of number of non-rigid points being classified as rigid over 100 trials. Results for different levels of Gaussian noise with variance $\sigma = 0.5, 1, 1.5, 2$ pixels and different experimental setups.

Experiments	Noise				
	0	0.5	1	1.5	2
Exp1: $D = 5$, 10/10, setup 1	0.28	0.48	0.55	0.72	0.77
Exp2: $D = 5$, 10/50, setup 1	0.31	0.38	0.46	0.55	0.72
Exp3: $D = 3$, 10/10, setup 1	0.95	1.36	1.53	1.60	1.54
Exp4: $D = 3$, 10/50, setup 1	2.19	2.38	2.33	2.78	2.51
Exp5: $D = 5$, 10/10, setup 2	0.24	0.27	0.32	0.48	0.62
Exp6: $D = 5$, 10/50, setup 2	0.3	0.34	0.39	0.51	0.58
Exp7: $D = 3$, 10/10, setup 2	0.65	0.94	1.27	1.42	1.45
Exp8: $D = 3$, 10/50, setup 2	2.09	2.37	2.28	2.31	2.27

The RANSAC procedure was tested over 100 trials for each setup and for each level of noise. The number of samples randomly chosen over the prior distribution was fixed to 2500. At each new trial the motion components (rotation and translation) of the objects are randomly generated obtaining a 50 frames long sequence. The results in table 1 show the mean error (over the 100 trials) of the number of non-rigid points being classified as rigid for the different setups. Better performances are obtained for more complex deformations (i.e., more basis shapes, $D = 5$) and for stronger perspective effects (Setup 2) since the effects of perspective distortions and deformations are less ambiguous in such cases (Experiments 5 and 6). Experiments 4 and 8 obtain the worse results achieving a mean error of more than 2 points given the smaller deformations occuring in these data and the higher number of non-rigid points (50).

(a)   (b)

Fig. 3. (a) The image frame show the position of the markers used to capture the face deformations. (b) The image shows an example of the setup used for the box and pillow experiment. The segmented rigid points are highlighted with a red star.

5.2   Real Experiments

We tested our segmentation algorithm over two sequences with real deforming objects. The 3D structure was obtained using a VICON motion capture system and was then projected synthetically onto the image plane using a perspective camera model. Gaussian noise of 0.5 pixels was finally added to the image coordinates. The first experiment captured a human face undergoing rigid motion while performing different facial expressions. The subject was wearing 37 markers on the face. Figure 3 (a) shows two frames with the positions of the markers and the selected rigid points. The segmented points mostly belong to the temple and nose areas which udergo a predominantly rigid motion in the sequence. Applying the non-rigid structure from motion algorithm proposed in [9] we obtained a 2D reprojection error (root mean squared) of 0.62 pixels, a 3D error relative to the scene size of 1.81 units (the size of the face model was $168 \times 193 \times 101$ units) and a rotation error of 0.27 degrees.

The second scene consisted of a set of 12 rigid points (9 on two boxes and 3 over a chair) and a set of 20 deformable points situated on a pillow which was deforming during the sequence (see Figure 3 (b)). The segmentation algorithm provided 13 rigid points, including one non-rigid trajectory corresponding to one of the pillow points. However, the inclusion of this non-rigid point did not affect the 3D reconstruction results. We obtained a 2D reprojection error of 0.9 pixels, a 3D relative error of 1.49 units (the size of the scene was $61 \times 82 \times 53$) and a rotation error of 2.82 degrees.

6   Conclusions

We have presented an approach to segment rigid trajectories embedded in a non-rigidly moving shape. The extracted rigid trajectories may be used to obtain prior-based 3D reconstructions as in [9] or to aid non-rigid shape registration tasks. The segmentation stage obtains reasonable results for the configuration of basis, cameras and points tested. However we noticed a higher misclassification ratio with weak perspective effects and higher proportion of non-rigid points. Also, points that are rigid only for a part of the sequence may appear undetected since they only conform with the epipolar geometry for a subset of frames.

Acknowledgments. This work was partly funded by EPSRC grant GR/S61539/ 01. ADB is supported by Fundação para a Ciência e a Tecnologia (ISR/IST funding) through the POS_Conhecimento Program that includes FEDER funds.

References

1. Costeira, J.P., Kanade, T.: A multibody factorization method for independently moving objects. International Journal of Computer Vision 29(3), 159–179 (1998)
2. Kanatani, K.: Motion segmentation by subspace separation: Model selection and reliability evaluation. International Journal of Image and Graphics 2(2), 179–197 (2002)
3. Vidal, R., Hartley, R.I.: Motion segmentation with missing data using powerfactorization and gpca. In: Proc. IEEE Conference on Computer Vision and Pattern Recognition, San Diego, California. vol. 2, pp. 310–316 (2004)
4. Yan, J., Pollefeys, M.: A general framework for motion segmentation: Independent, articulated, rigid, non-rigid, degenerate and non-degenerate. In: Proc. 9th European Conference on Computer Vision, Graz, Austria. vol. 4. pp. 94–106 (2006)
5. Del Bue, A., Lladó, X., Agapito, L.: Non-rigid face modelling using shape priors. In: Zhao, W., Gong, S., Tang, X. (eds.) AMFG 2005. LNCS, vol. 3723, pp. 96–107. Springer, Heidelberg (2005)
6. Fischler, M.A., Bolles, R.C.: Random sample consensus: A paradigm for model fitting with applications to image analysis and automated cartography. In: Fischler, M.A., Firschein, O. (eds.) Readings in Computer Vision: Issues, Problems, Principles, and Paradigms, Los Altos, CA. pp. 726–740 (1987)
7. Tordoff, B.J., Murray, D.W.: Guided-MLESAC: Faster image transform estimation by using matching priors. IEEE Transactions on Pattern Analysis and Machine Intelligence 27(10), 1523–1535 (2005)
8. Del Bue, A., Lladó, X., Agapito, L.: Non-rigid metric shape and motion recovery from uncalibrated images using priors. In: Proc. IEEE Conference on Computer Vision and Pattern Recognition, New York, NY (2006)
9. Lladó, X., Del Bue, A., Agapito, L.: Euclidean reconstruction of deformable structure using a perspective camera with varying intrinsic parameters. In: Proc. International Conference on Pattern Recognition, Hong Kong (2006)
10. Kim, T., Hong, K.S.: Estimating approximate average shape and motion of deforming objects with a monocular view. International Journal of Pattern Recognition and Artificial Intelligence 19(4), 585–601 (2005)
11. Xiao, J., Kanade, T.: Uncalibrated perspective reconstruction of deformable structures. In: Proc. 10th International Conference on Computer Vision, Beijing, China (2005)
12. Hartley, R.I.: In defense of the eight-point algorithm. In: Proc. IEEE Conference on Computer Vision and Pattern Recognition, Puerto Rico vol. 19(6), pp. 580–593 (1997)

Hierarchical Eyelid and Face Tracking

J. Orozco[1], J. Gonzàlez[2], I. Rius[1], and F.X. Roca[1]

[1] Computer Vision Center and Dept. de Ciències de la Computació,
Edifici O, Campus UAB, 08193 Bellaterra, Spain
[2] Institut de Robòtica i Informàtica Industrial (UPC – CSIC),
C. Llorens i Artigas 4-6, 08028, Barcelona, Spain

Abstract. Most applications on Human Computer Interaction (HCI) require to extract the movements of user faces, while avoiding high memory and time expenses. Moreover, HCI systems usually use low-cost cameras, while current face tracking techniques strongly depend on the image resolution. In this paper, we tackle the problem of eyelid tracking by using Appearance-Based Models, thus achieving accurate estimations of the movements of the eyelids, while avoiding cues, which require high-resolution faces, such as edge detectors or colour information. Consequently, we can track the fast and spontaneous movements of the eyelids, a very hard task due to the small resolution of the eye regions. Subsequently, we combine the results of eyelid tracking with the estimations of other facial features, such as the eyebrows and the lips. As a result, a hierarchical tracking framework is obtained: we demonstrate that combining two appearance-based trackers allows to get accurate estimates for the eyelid, eyebrows, lips and also the 3D head pose by using low-cost video cameras and in real-time. Therefore, our approach is shown suitable to be used for further facial-expression analysis.

1 Introduction

Face tracking is focused on the estimation of the head pose position and predefined facial actions, usually eyebrow and lip movements. Current tracking techniques do not address eyelid tracking due to its requirements of accuracy while face tracking demands robustness. Eye states are highly involved in facial expression while determining the degree of sincerity. Once a proper description of the eyelid movement is obtained, it is possible to apply facial expressions analysis for HCI, and emotion evaluation. We need to achieve an accurate eyelid tracking in real time, and eyebrow, lip and head pose estimation. They require a robust and accurate technique for extracting facial actions, which involve a great challenge, especially for gazes and eye blinks.

In order to achieve this goal, current face tracking approaches are based on feature extraction, edge detection or image segmentation, deformable template matching [8,9,5]. However, these techniques do not allow to include eyelid tracking in real time. 3D head and face tracking can be also handled by feature-based trackers with active appearance models [1]. These provide high accuracy but require high memory/time consumptions and depend on image quality, which hinder the development of real-time applications.

J. Martí et al. (Eds.): IbPRIA 2007, Part I, LNCS 4477, pp. 499–506, 2007.

Alternatively, Appearance-Based Models (ABM) have been proposed as a powerful tool for analyzing facial images [2]. Deterministic and statistical appearance-based tracking methods have been proposed and used by some researchers. They handle successfully image variability and drifting problems, since they consider an input image through reduced version in order to apply estimation models, adopting deterministic velocity and registration techniques or statistics tools [6].

In order to track eyelid movements in real time, we improve the ABM framework in three directions. Firstly, we use ABM to track eyelid motions by on-line texture learning. Thus, our proposed approach infers the state of eyes without detecting eye features, such as irises and eye corners. Secondly, we show that by adopting a no self-occluded reference facial texture, it is possible to track eyelid motions. We prove that there is a dependency between the eye region and the rest of face, in order to obtain more accurate and stable 3D head pose estimations. Thirdly, by applying the two aforementioned contributions, we build a hierarchical tracker able to register eyelid movements by reducing estimation errors and adaptation rates.

The paper is organized as follows: in section 2, the deformable 3D facial model is described. In section 3, we will explain the background of adaptive appearance models. In section 4, we explain eyelid and face tracking, the relationship between face and eye region, and the structure of the hierarchical tracking. In section 5, experimental results on hierarchical adaptive appearance-based tracker are presented, which involve tracking in real-time of the 3D head pose and some facial actions, including eyelid movements. Finally, we conclude in Section 6.

2   Tracking with Adaptive Appearance Models

We use the 3D face Candide Model [3]. The Candide provides a simple process to construct an appearance model and a single parameterization to extract facial features. The shape can be described by the matrix $\mathbf{V}$:

$$\mathbf{V}_n = V_0 + \mathbf{D}\vartheta + \mathbf{A}\gamma, \tag{1}$$

where V_0 is the standard shape, $\mathbf{D}\vartheta$ determines the biometry for each person, and $\mathbf{A}\gamma$ distorts the mesh depending on the facial actions. Thus, we encode the tracking parameters by the vector $\mathbf{q}$, which contains two variables; α denotes the head angles and position, and γ the facial actions considered for tracking:

$$\mathbf{q} = [\alpha_i, \gamma_j]^t, \ for \ i = 0, ..., 5 \ and \ j = 0, ..., 6. \tag{2}$$

A shape-free texture represents a facial texture which is obtained by applying an image warping technique, $\chi(\mathbf{q}) = \Psi(\mathbf{I}, \mathbf{q})$, in order to project an input image I_t onto the reference texture, where $\chi(\mathbf{q})$ is the ABM of the image, see Fig. 1.

Face tracking consists of the estimation of the 3D head pose and several facial actions encoded by the vector $\mathbf{q}_t$, Eq. (2). In order to estimate the corresponding vector $\mathbf{q}_t$ at each frame, we obtain the ABM associated with the animation

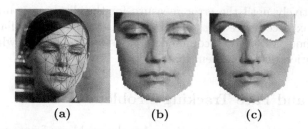

Fig. 1. (a)Input Image. (b) Texture with Eyes. (c) Texture without Eyes.

parameters γ_t through an appearance registration process. We represent as $\hat{\chi}_t$ the tracked parameters and the estimated textures. We suppose each appearance following a Gaussian distribution with mean μ_i and variance σ_i^2, which are vectors of n pixels. The probability for each observation is given by:

$$p(\mathbf{I}_t|\mathbf{q}_t) = p(\chi_t|\mathbf{q}_t) = \prod_{i=0}^{n} N(\chi_i; \mu_i, \sigma_i) \tag{3}$$

When the appearance is tracked for the current image, μ_i and σ_i^2 are updated for the next frame by applying this technique, where ω is the updating factor:

$$\mu_{t+1} = \omega\mu_t + (1-\omega)\hat{\chi}_t, \ and \ \sigma_{t+1}^2 = \omega\sigma_t^2 + (1-\omega)(\hat{\chi}_t - \mu_t)^2, \tag{4}$$

where μ_i and σ_i are initialized with the first patch χ.

In order to estimate the vector $\mathbf{q}_t$ for the next frame, an adaptive velocity model is adopted, where the adaptive motion velocity is predicted using a fixed function to estimate the transition state from the previous frame:

$$\mathbf{q}_t = \hat{\mathbf{q}}_{t-1} + \Delta\mathbf{q}_t \tag{5}$$

where $\Delta\mathbf{q}_t$ is the shift of geometric parameters. The current input image $\mathbf{I}_t$ is registered with the current appearance model by minimizing the Mahalanobis distance between the warped texture and the current average of appearance. Here, the appearance parameters μ and σ are known, and the distance is minimized by an iterative first-order linear approximation. As a result, given Eq. (5), the warped texture will be the closest to the average of appearance,

$$\Psi(\mathbf{I}_t, \mathbf{q}_t) \ \approx \ \mu_t \tag{6}$$

Approximating Eq. (6) via a first-order Taylor series expansion around $\hat{q}_t$ and using the Vanilla gradient descent method [7], we have:

$$\Psi(\mathbf{I}_t, \mathbf{q}_t) \ \approx \Psi(\mathbf{I}_t, \hat{\mathbf{q}}_{t-1}) + \frac{\partial(\chi_t, \mathbf{q}_t)}{\mathbf{q}_t}(\mathbf{q}_t - \hat{\mathbf{q}}_{t-1}) \tag{7}$$

Thus, the increment of vector $\mathbf{q}_t$ is related to the change of the previous adapted shape, and the current average appearance. The solution for this vector is found iteratively until the error measure for the distance is minimum. The gradient matrix is computed by partial differences and the Vanilla gradient descendent method is able to accommodate appearance changes while achieving precise estimation of the gradient matrix.

3   Eyelid and Face Tracking Problem

As said before on the introduction, we solve the problems from previous works, by registering eyelid tracking over time for any kind of blinking, different speed, open, intermediate and closed states. In order to avoid high memory and time consumptions, we do not use low image processes like contours detectors, colour information and so on. We adopt a generic Candide model, to learn the textures on-line, and deal with eyelid facial action [1]. We improve the gradient descent method while hierarchically combining two appearance models. Illumination changes, occlusions and fast movements are considered as outliers by constraining the gradient descent for each component of $\Delta\mathbf{q}$ with the Huber's function. The Huber's function, $\hat{\xi}$ function is defined as:

$$\eta(y) = \frac{1}{y}\frac{d\hat{\xi}(y)}{dy} = \begin{cases} 1 & \textbf{if}|y| \leq c \\ \frac{c}{|y|} & \textbf{if}|y| > c \end{cases} \tag{8}$$

where y is the value of a pixel in the patch χ_t normalized by the mean μ_i and the variance σ_i^2 of the appearance at the same pixel. The constant c is set $3 * \sigma$. This restriction controls the registration of the χ_t, on the probabilistic model.

We have proven the influence of the eyes on head pose estimations, using a reference texture with size of 84 x 80 pixels. There are 5447 pixels by each shape-free texture, and the eye region is represented by only 380 pixels in the warped version of the image (7% of the patch with size 22x14 pixels) [4].

In order to achieve a robust and stable eyelid tracking we construct two different trackers. On the one hand, the first one for adapting head, eyebrows, lips and eyelids. These have thirteen parameters and a texture model with eyelid region but without sclera and iris pixels. On the other hand, the second one is a reference texture without eye region to correct head pose estimations of the first tracker. Therefore, the first tracker has one additional parameter, γ^6. The description of both trackers is detailed next, see Fig. 2.

3.1   Characteristics of Both Facial Trackers

Tracker 1: in order to estimate head, lips, eyebrows and eyelids we consider the 13 parameters of vector $\mathbf{q}$, the Eq. (2).

1. Given an input image $\mathbf{I}_t$, we obtain the warped version of the image, $\chi = \Psi(\mathbf{I}_t, \mathbf{q})$. This is the ABM for this tracker. We obtain μ_t and σ_t^2 of the face from previous adapted frames by applying the recursive filtering technique, Eq. (4). The ω updating factor incorporates new information depending on the velocity of facial movements.

2. The gradient matrix is computed for $[\alpha_i, \gamma_0, ..., \gamma_5]$ by partial differences, considering an increment step δ and a small perturbation range,. On the other hand, the gradient matrix component for eyelids, γ_6 is estimated out using a biggest descent step, $k * \delta$, and a perturbation range which covers the overall FAP, since it is necessary to search the minimum error in the complete range, due to the velocity of the blinking.
3. Given the previous adaptation, $\hat{\chi}_t$, we look for the best estimation in the face space, where the reference texture includes the eye region, comparing the average and likelihood shapes through Mahalanobis distance. We include a backward-forward searching factor for γ_6, exploitation rather than exploration. The convergence is quickly achieved for all parameters of $\mathbf{q} = [\alpha_i, \gamma_0, ..., \gamma_5, \gamma_6]^t$, while avoiding local minimums.

Tracker 2: In order to correct the head pose estimation of the *tracker 1*, we exclude the eye regions.

1. We obtain a warped image, $\chi' = \Psi(\mathbf{I}_t, \mathbf{q})$ with a different reference texture, which excludes the eyes. We have kept more information about previous frames than *tracker 1* by using the recursive filtering with an updating factor $\beta < \omega$, learning lately the texture model, which has skill to handle outliers.
2. The gradient matrix is estimated for $[\alpha_i, \gamma_0, ..., \gamma_5]^t$.
3. Given the previous estimation from *tracker 1*, χ', we measure the distance between the observation likelihood and the current average shape. The best adaptation without the pixels of the eye region is achieved with the convergence by using the same exploration range for all parameters.

3.2   Combination of Eyelid and Face Tracking

Both trackers were tested without any a priori information, thus obtaining inaccurate results because the first tracker needs the uncertainty of the eye region, which the second tracker avoids. Consequently, the first tracker generates rough estimations while the second tracker further refines them. In order to keep the best estimations and to avoid the additional errors, we combine the trackers as follows.

We first begin estimating $[\alpha_i, \gamma_0, ..., \gamma_5, \gamma_6]^t$ with of the *tracker 1* by obtaining a rough estimation for the current image, $p(\chi_t|\mathbf{q}_t)$. Subsequently, the *tracker 2* estimates the vector $[\alpha_i, \gamma_0, ..., \gamma_5]^t$ for the current image, while correcting the previous adaptation from the *tracker 1*, $p(\chi'_t|\mathbf{q}_t)$. Therefore, *Tracker 1* is able to estimate the eyelid tracking and the second one is able to correct the head pose estimations. We constraint the second tracker to modify the vector $\mathbf{q}$ only if the previous estimations are improved. Consequently, *tracker 2* estimation is made according to $p(\chi'|\mathbf{q}_t, M)$, where M is the minimum Mahalanobis distance of the *tracker 1*. The geometrical vector $\mathbf{q}$ is modified only if the Mahalanobis distance is lower for the *tracker 2*.

The result from this hierarchical tracking is a robust and accurate estimation for vector $\mathbf{q}_t$. The minimum distance for both of trackers reduces the adaptation

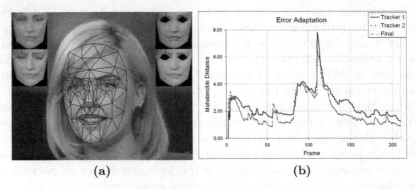

(a)   (b)

Fig. 2. Input image of a sequence composed of 210 frames tested with both ground textures (84x80 and 42x40 pixels, corresponding to 21x5 and 11x4 pixels on eye region). (a) Left and right top on the image are the two trackers, the estimated and current textures. (b) The error adaptation for two Trackers.

error for all parameters and improves the eyelid adaptation. We do not only detect opened and closed eye states, also continuous eyelid movements with a correct adaptation.

4   Experimental Results

The tracking experiments were run in a 3.2 GHz Pentium PC, without optimized C code. It had a performance of 500 MB as RAM memory consumption and 21 average fps for each tracker, using a big mask (84x80). The real time is achieved using a small mask (42x40) with 200 MB and 67 fps for memory and time consumption.

The following experimental results were obtained by using the FGnet[1] database for face and expression recognition, as well as low-resolution video clips. There are videos modified by image compressors or published in web format, so that the hard task of the trackers is to deal with low image resolution, lack of continuity, and illumination changes. In these movie videos, the face and eyelid movements are natural and spontaneous, with large angle variations. In fact, scale variations are found related to in-depth movements or camera zooming.

In the first sequence the size of the input image is 320x240 pixels, the face size is 100x130 pixels Fig 3. It begins from closed eye position describing a simple face expression with two eye blinks at 22nd and 151st frames. We show how our method is robust with standard databases, movies, video clips, etc. See Fig. 3. We show an image sequence where the camera is static and in frontal position, Fig. 4. It has 585 images; the face size is 200x220 pixels. There is in-depth motion of head and several zoom effects.

As a result, a robust and accurate learning is achieved, see Fig. 5. On the one hand, Tracker 1 learns faster and therefore includes quickly early eye blinks into

---

[1] ©FGnet - IST-2000-26434. http://www-prima.inrialpes.fr/FGnet/

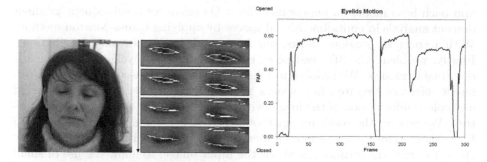

Fig. 3. Eyelid Trackin performance with images of FGnet database

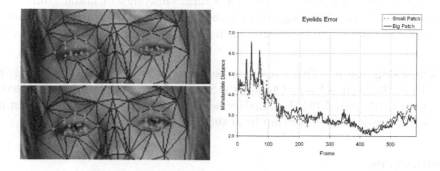

Fig. 4. Eyelid motion comparison between small and big textures

Fig. 5. 111 frame being occludes onto eyes region

appearance model. On the other hand, Tracker 2 learns slowly, in order to keep the previous adaptation whenever occlusions are occurring. In this paper, every sequence has been tested with both of the reference textures and the results are quite similar.

5   Conclusions

Our framework extends the application of ABMs to obtain continuous eyelid tracking, thereby proving the capability for estimating accurately and in real-time the 3D head pose, eyebrows, lips and eyelids. The assumption of this approach is to model an appearance like a Gaussian for a subsequent gradient descent analysis in multidimensional spaces by applying Gauss-Newton method. With respect to previous works, our framework has important contributions. Firstly, we blend the 3D head pose, eyebrows, lips and eyelid tracking, using deformable models. We propose to join two appearance-based trackers with different reference textures, face spaces and learning process. Secondly, we avoid any colour information of the image with respect to colour spaces or edge detectors. We recover the mesh parameters using statistics and estimation tools on finite series. Thirdly, we propose a hierarchical tracking with its respective face space to refine the estimations about the input image, to allow the use of small and big reference textures, in order to reduce memory and time consumption.

We are now working on automatic initialization of tracking system, by implementing a face and feature detector for a future inference of initial geometrical parameters. We are also going to track the iris motion for gaze analysis, that is the first step toward real facial expression and sincerity analysis on human faces.

Acknowledgement. This work has been supported by the EC grant IST-027110 for the Hermes Project and by the Spanish MEC under projects TIN2006-14606 and DPI-2004-5414. J. Gonzàlez acknowledges the support of a Juan de la Cierva Postdoctoral fellowship from the Spanish MEC.

References

1. Ahlberg, J.: An active model for facial feature tracking. EURASIP Journal on Applied Signal Processing 2002(6), 566–571 (2002)
2. Cootes, T.F., Taylor, C.J., Cooper, D.H., Graham, J.: Active shape models - their training and application. Computer Vision and Image Understanding 61(1), 39–59 (1995)
3. Dornaika, F., Ahlberg, J.: Face model adaptation for tracking and active appearance model training. British Machine Vision Conference (2003)
4. Dornaika, F., Orozco, J., González, J.: Combined Head, Lips, Eyebrows,and Eyelids Tracking using Adaptive Appearance Models. In: Perales, F.J., Fisher, R.B. (eds.) AMDO 2006, LNCS, vol. 4069, pp. 110–119, Springer, Heidelberg (2006)
5. Zhang, Y., Tan, H.: Detecting eye blink states by tracking iris and eyelids. Pattern Recognition Letters, 2005 (2005)
6. Sclaroff, S., Cascia, M.L., Athitsos, V.: Fast, reliable head tracking under varying illumination: An approach based on registration of texture-mapped 3d models. IEEE Transactions on Pattern Analysis and Machine Intelligence 22(4), 322–336 (2000)
7. Nocedal, J., Wright, S.: Numerical optimization. Springer, Heidelberg (1999)
8. Cohn, J.F., Tian, Y., Kanade, T.: Dual-state parametric eye tracking. In: International Conference on Automatic Face and Gesture Recognition (2000)
9. Liu, H., Wu, Y., Zha, H.: A new method of detecting human eyelids based on deformable templates. Systems, Man and Cybernetics, 2004 IEEE International Conference, vol. 1, pp. 604–609 (2004)

Automatic Learning of Conceptual Knowledge in Image Sequences for Human Behavior Interpretation

Pau Baiget[1], Carles Fernández[1], Xavier Roca[1], and Jordi Gonzàlez[2]

[1] Computer Vision Center & Dept. de Ciències de la Computació, Edifici O, Campus UAB, 08193 Bellaterra, Spain
[2] Institut de Robòtica i Informàtica Industrial (UPC – CSIC), Llorens i Artigas 4-6, 08028, Barcelona, Spain

Abstract. This work describes an approach for the interpretation and explanation of human behavior in image sequences, within the context of a *Cognitive Vision System*. The information source is the geometrical data obtained by applying tracking algorithms to an image sequence, which is used to generate conceptual data. The spatial characteristics of the scene are automatically extracted from the resuling tracking trajectories obtained during a training period. Interpretation is achieved by means of a rule-based inference engine called *Fuzzy Metric Temporal Horn Logic* and a behavior modeling tool called *Situation Graph Tree*. These tools are used to generate conceptual descriptions which semantically describe observed behaviors.

1 Introduction

A classical problem in computer vision is the analysis of human behavior in observed scenes, where *behavior* refers to human agent trajectories which acquire a meaning in an specific scene. Results obtained in this research may benefit in the human-computer interaction and the video-surveillance domains.

Current motion understanding systems rely on numerical knowledge based on (i) the quantitative data obtained from tracking procedures and (ii) the geometrical properties of the scene[1],[7]. Therefore, this process is usually scene-dependent, and a-priori information of the spatial structure of the scene is required. The questions about the *what* and *why* can be answered by reasoning about the tracking data and transforming it to semantic predicates which relates each tracked agent with its environment. Common problems are the *semantic gap* which refers to the conceptual ambiguity between the image sequence and its possible interpretations, and *uncertainty*, which raises due to the impossibility of modeling all possible human behaviors.

In order to cope with the uncertainty aspects, integration can be learnt using a probabilistic framework: PCA and Mixtures of Gaussians [8], Belief Networks [6,10] and Hidden Markov Models [3] provide examples. However, probabilistic approaches do not provide semantic explanation for observed agent behaviors.

J. Martí et al. (Eds.): IbPRIA 2007, Part I, LNCS 4477, pp. 507–514, 2007.

Alternatively, Fuzzy Metric Temporal Horn Logic (FMTHL) also copes with the temporal and uncertainty aspects of integration in a goal-oriented manner [12]. This predicate logic language treats dynamic occurrences, uncertainties of the state estimation process, and intrinsic vagueness of conceptual terms in a unified manner. FMTHL uses three different strategies to accomplish such an abstraction process, according to the source of knowledge which is exploited to generate the qualitative description [12]. The main advantage of FMTHL over the previously referred algorithms relies on the promise to support not only the interpretation, but in addition diagnosis during the continuous development and test of the so-called *Cognitive Vision Systems* [9]. Further, Situation Graph Trees (SGTs) constitute a suitable behavior model which explicitly represents and combines the specialization, temporal, and semantic relationships of the constituent conceptual predicates in FMTHL. [4].

This contribution is structured as follows: next section describes the quantitative knowledge obtained from tracking. Next, we automatically build a conceptual scene model from the trajectories obtained from tracking during a training period. Consequently, contrary to other approaches, the geometrical properties of the scene are not provided beforehand, but automatically learnt from tracking instead. In Section 4 we show the conceptual description of human behaviors observed in a pedestrian crossing scene. Finally, Section 5 concludes the paper and shows future lines of research.

2   Numerical Knowledge for Motion Understanding

This section presents our procedure which converts the geometrical information obtained from tracking processes into a list of conceptual predicates which semantically describes motion events.

2.1   Information About the Agent

Semantic interpretation is based on the numerical *state vector of the agent*. The state vector is determined by the nature of the parameters used for tracking, which may refer to dynamical, positional and postural properties of the human agent. For example, motion verbs, such as accelerating could be instantiated by evaluating the history of the spatial and velocity parameters of the agent state. In our case, numerical knowledge obtained from tracking is comprised in the following attribute scheme:

$$has\_status(Agent, pos, or, vel, aLabel),$$

which embeds the 2-D spatial position *pos* of the agent *Agent* in the floor plane, in addition to the velocity *vel* and the orientation *or*. These three parameters are called the *spatial status* of the agent. The parameter *aLabel* refers to the action, which obtained with respect to the velocity *vel*: we differentiate between *walking*, *standing* or *running*.

(a)   (b)

Fig. 1. Example of human agent tracking in the pedestrian crossing scene

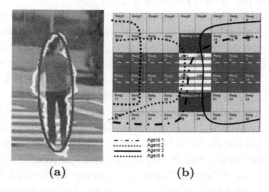

(a)   (b)

Fig. 2. Information of the scene. (a) The area occupied by an agent in a frame step is given by the envolving ellipse obtained in the segmentation process. (b) The roadway scene model and the agents' trajectories.

In our experiments, the quantitative description of the state of the agent is obtained through a segmentation process based on Horprasert algorithm [5] and on a subsequently state estimation method [11] for each time step, see Fig. 1.

2.2 Information About the Scene

Behavior analysis requires an explicit reference to a spatial context, i.e., a conceptual model of the scene. Such a model allows to infer the relationship of the agent with respect to (predefined) static objects of the scene, and to associate *facts* to specific locations within the scene. All this information is expressed as a set of logical predicates in FMTHL. The conceptual scene model is divided into polygonally bounded segments, which describe the possible positions in which an agent can be found.

Here we present a learning procedure for the conceptual scene model, which is based on the work of Fernyhough et al. [2]. We consider that the area (A) occupied by an agent at each frame step is provided by the segmentation process,

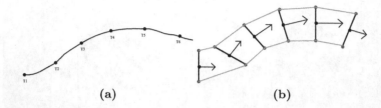

Fig. 3. Creation of trajectory segments. (a) Obtaining the temporal points of the trajectory. (b) Drawing lines perpendicular to the orientation of the agent for each temporal point, Connecting points at distance v from the corresponding temporal point, thus obtaining the trajectory segments.

see Figure 2.(a). In our case, the trajectories of the agents were obtained from the pedestrian crossing scene shown in Figure 2.(b).

Initially, we obtain a set of temporal points of the trajectory (T_i), each one separated from the next by a fixed quantity of time, see Fig. 3.(a). Considering the orientation of the agent at each point T_i, a perpendicular line is drawn and the intersection $(T_{i_r}$ and $T_{i_l})$ is found at distance A to the point T_i, see Figure 3.(b). Then, the T_{i_r} is joined with T_{i+1_r}, and T_{i_l} with T_{i+1_l}. Consequently, the four points $T_{i_r}, T_{i+1_r}, T_{i_l}, T_{i+1_l}$ define a *trajectory segment*.

We build a matrix with the same height and width than the ground plane section of the scene. We traverse the matrix, assigning to each position (i, j) the number of trajectories for which one of their segments are drawn at the position (i, j) of the scene. For example, if three trajectories pass through the same point of the scene, this point's correspondence in the matrix will have value 3, see Fig. 4, where the brighter values represent the most accessed segments by the agents. Then, a threshold value is assigned depending on the number of trajectories analyzed and only those positions of the matrix whose value is equal to or exceeds this threshold are considered. Finally, all adjacent positions are considered to constitute a segment of the new scene, see Fig. 3.(c).

As a result of the learning process of the scene model, this is divided into polygonally bounded *roadway_segments*, which describe the positions in which an agent has been found. Each *roadway_segment*, has a label which determines the conceptual description associated with such a segment. At present, we manually distinguish (at least) four different types of segments, namely: *sideway_segment*, *waiting_line*, *roadway_segment*, and *crosswalk*. Consequently, we can build predicates which relate the spatial position of the agent with respect to these segments.

3   Working with Semantic Concepts

We next describe the use of FMTHL for generation of conceptual predicates from the state vector. Subsequently, we present a SGT for behavior modeling which is used for the organization of plausible predicates into a temporal and conceptual hierarchy.

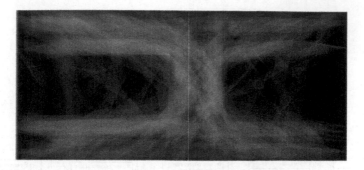

Fig. 4. Representation of the accumulation matrix used to obtain the segments of the new scene. Results match with the precomputed *roadway* scene.

3.1   Generation of Conceptual Predicates

We use a system based on the Horn-Logic Fragment of *Fuzzy Metric Temporal Logic* (FMTHL)[12] which provides a suitable mechanism for processing fuzzy and temporal data. By means of a set of inference rules, FMTHL allows to transform quantitative data into qualitative data, expressed as logic predicates.

First, quantitative state parameters are associated to concepts like *moving*, *small*, *left*, or *briefly* with a fuzzy degree of validity characterizing how good a concept matches the numerical quantity. For example, the speed and orientation parameters of the state vector is associated to fuzzy attributes, thus allowing the instantiation of logic predicates such as *has_speed(Agent, Value)* or *has_direction(Agent, Value)*.

Secondly, spatial relations are derived by considering the positions of the agents and other static objects in the scene. In this case, a conceptual scene model is required to describe the spatial coordinates of the agent with respect to static objects, other agents, and specific locations within the scene. This description is implemented by applying a distance function between the positions of different agents/objects in the scene. Subsequently, a discretization of the resulting distance value is obtained by using Fuzzy Logic, for example *is_alone(Agent, Proximity)* or *has_distance(Agent, Patiens, Value)*.

Lastly, an action label is associated depending on the agent velocity. Thus, we can distinguish between three different actions, namely *running*, *walking* or *standing* by defining predicates such as *is_performing(Agent, aLabel)*.

3.2   Situation Graph Trees

In this paper, predicate evaluation is performed in a goal-oriented manner: we use SGTs to recognize those situations which can be instantiated for an observed agent by applying the so-called *graph traversal* [4]. The goal is to determine the most specialized situation which can be instantiated by considering the state vectors of the agents at each frame step. This traversal of the SGT is applied by

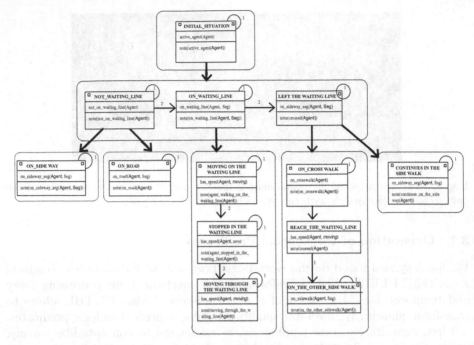

Fig. 5. Situation Graph Tree for behavior interpretation of human agents crossing a roadway

considering the knowledge encoded in the form of prediction and specialization edges: on the one hand, given a situation, only its successors in temporal order will be evaluated at the next time step. On the other hand, each situation can be described in a conceptually more detailed way, thus allowing certain level of abstraction and specificity.

Fig. 5 depicts a simplified version of an SGT which allows to infer the behavior of agents of the roadway scene, as detailed next. The root graph comprises only one situation scheme, in which the predicate states that an agent is presently active, *active(Agent)*. The first possible specialization is the fact that the agent is not currently walking on the walking line. Then, only two situations can be instantiated: the agent is on the road or is on the sidewalk. Because in this scene there are only two kinds of segments where an agent can appear, this situation would repeat until the agent reaches the waiting line or it leaves the scene. When the agent arrives at the waiting line (*ON_WAITING_LINE*) the agent might stop for checking that there is no car on the road. This case is also modeled in the specialization of this situation scheme. After leaving the waiting line, the agent can walk on the pedestrian crossing (*ON_CROSSWALK*) or continue walking on the sideway. Once an agent has reached the sidewalk on the other side of the road, he or she is expected to continue walking on the sidewalk until leaving the scene.

Start	End	Situation
1	26	on_sideway_seg(**agent_1**, sseg24)
27	76	on_sideway_seg(**agent_1**, sseg25)
77	126	on_sideway_seg(**agent_1**, sseg26)
127	179	on_sideway_seg(**agent_1**, sseg27)
180	184	on_sideway_seg(**agent_1**, sseg28)
185	225	agent_walking on_waiting_line(**agent_1**)
226	321	on_crosswalk(**agent_1**)
322	371	crossed(**agent_1**)
372	26	on_the_other_sidewalk(**agent_1**)

Start	End	Situation
523	571	on_sideway_seg(**agent_4**, sseg17)
572	595	on_sideway_seg(**agent_4**, sseg18)
596	635	on_road(**agent_4**, rseg9)
636	680	on_road(**agent_4**, rseg2)
681	740	on_the_other_sidewalk(**agent_4**)

(a)   (b)

Fig. 6. Sequence of conceptual descriptions generated for : (a) *agent_1* (b)*agent_4*

4 Experimental Results

In this section we show the resulting process of predicate generation in order to obtain conceptual descriptions from image sequences recorded at a pedestrian crossing scenario.

The image sequence used for this purpose comprised 4 human behaviors, as summarized next:

- *Agent 1* walks on the sideway towards the waiting line and crosses the pedestrian crossing without stopping to see whether a car is approaching.
- *Agent 2* and *Agent 3* behave initially like *Agent 1*, but they stop on the waiting line for a few seconds before crossing the crosswalk.
- *Agent 4* crosses the road without going to the pedestrian crossing.

Figure 6 show the resulting conceptual descriptions generated for *agent_1* and *agent_4* using the SGT of the previous section. The resulting conceptual information establishes a behavioral layer in a cognitive vision system, which lets knowing what the agent is doing at each frame step and predict what the agent will probably do in the future frames. The first fact helps to generate natural language descriptions about the video sequence. The second allows the vision system to recover from segmentation errors e.g. predictable agent occlusions.

5 Conclusions

We have used a deterministic model suitable for modeling human behaviors. Our information source has been an image sequence previously processed with pattern recognition algorithms, thus extracting quantitative data of the paths followed by human agents. Interpretation of human behavior has been achieved by means of a rule-based inference engine called FMTHL, and a human behavior modelling tool called Situation Graph Tree. This model has been tested for a street scene, and conceptual descriptions have been generated which semantically describe observed behavior.

At present, the SGT described here has not learning capabilities, so the accuracy of the modelled behavior will depend on the accuracy of the a-priory knowledge used. We also need to provide machine learning capabilites to improve reasoning through the sets of training examples. This will allow to confront sociological theories about observed human behavior, whose quantitative base is at present being computed from statistics and not from semantic concepts.

Acknowledgments. This work has been supported by the EC grant IST-027110 for the HERMES project and by the Spanish MEC under projects TIN2006-14606 and and DPI-2004-541. J. Gonzàlez acknowledges the support of a Juan de la Cierva postdoctoral fellowship from the Spanish MEC.

References

1. Buxton, H.: Learning and understanding dynamic scene activity: A review. Image and Vision Computing 21(1), 125–136 (2002)
2. Fernyhough, J., Cohn, A., Hogg, D.: Constructing qualitative event models automatically from video input. Image and Vision Computing 18, 81–103 (2000)
3. Galata, A., Johnson, N., Hogg, D.: Learning variable-length markov models of behavior. Computer Vision and Image Understanding 81(3), 398–413 (2001)
4. Haag, M., Nagel, H.-H.: Incremental recognition of traffic situations from video image sequences. Image and Vision Computing 18(2), 137–153 (2000)
5. Horprasert, T., Harwood, D., Davis, L.: A Robust Background Subtraction and Shadow Detection. In: 4th ACCV, Taipei, Taiwan, vol. 1, pp. 983–988 (2000)
6. Intille, S.S., Bobick, A.F.: Recognized planned, multiperson action. International Journal of Computer Vision 81(3), 414–445 (2001)
7. Kojima, A., Tamura, T., Fukunaga, K.: Natural language description of human activities from video images based on concept hierarchy of actions. International Journal of Computer Vision 50(2), 171–184 (2002)
8. Morris, R.J., Hogg, D.C.: Statistical models of object interaction. International Journal of Computer Vision 37(2), 209–215 (2000)
9. Nagel, H.-H.: From image sequences towards conceptual descriptions. Image and Vision Computing 6(2), 59–74 (1988)
10. Remagnino, P., Tan, T., Baker, K.: Agent oriented annotation in model based visual surveillance. In: Proceedings of International Conference on Computer Vision (ICCV'98), pp. 857–862, Mumbai, India (1998)
11. Rowe, D., Rius, I., Gonzàlez, J., Villanueva, J.J.: Improving tracking by handling occlusions. In: Singh, S., Singh, M., Apte, C., Perner, P. (eds.) ICAPR 2005. LNCS, vol. 3687, Springer, Heidelberg (2005)
12. Schäfer, K.: Fuzzy spatio-temporal logic programming. In: Brzoska, C.(ed.) Proceedings of 7th Workshop in Temporal and Non-Classical Logics – IJCAI'97, pp. 23–28, Nagoya, Japan (1997)

A Comparative Study of Local Descriptors for Object Category Recognition: SIFT vs HMAX

Plinio Moreno[1], Manuel J. Marín-Jiménez[2], Alexandre Bernardino[1],
José Santos-Victor[1], and Nicolás Pérez de la Blanca[2]

[1] Instituto Superior Técnico & Instituto de Sistemas e Robótica
1049-001 Lisboa - Portugal
[2] Dpt. Computer Science and Artificial Intelligence, University of Granada, ETSI
Informática y Telecomunicación, Granada, 18071, Spain
plinio@isr.ist.utl.pt, mjmarin@decsai.ugr.es, alex@isr.ist.utl.pt,
jasv@isr.ist.utl.pt, nicolas@ugr.es

Abstract. In this paper we evaluate the performance of the two most successful state-of-the-art descriptors, applied to the task of visual object detection and localization in images. In the first experiment we use these descriptors, combined with binary classifiers, to test the presence/absence of object in a target image. In the second experiment, we try to locate faces in images, by using a structural model. The results show that HMAX performs slightly better than SIFT in these tasks.

1 Introduction

A key issue in visual object recognition is the choice of an adequate local descriptor. Recently Mikolajczyk *et al.* [1] presented a framework to compare local descriptor performance in image region matching. However, their conclusions are not guaranteed to be valid in object category recognition. Thus, in this work we perform a comparative study of two of the most successful state-of-the-art local descriptors (SIFT and HMAX), applied to object category detection and localization in images. We aim to use the same experimental set-up, to evaluate the actual impact of local descriptor choice.

Scale Invariant Feature Transform (SIFT) [2] is a location-histogram-based descriptor, very successful in single object recognition. Among the several extensions to SIFT descriptor, SIFT-Gabor [3] improves SIFT matching properties, and is also used in this work. On the other side, the biologically inspired descriptor HMAX [4] which combines the information of several filters and max operators, has shown excellent performance in object category recognition.

We perform experiments with two kinds of object models: (i) appearance only, and (ii) shape and appearance. In the first group of experiments we model objects by a bunch of local descriptors. In this model we disregard descriptor's location information, so we are able to decide object presence/absence in new images, but is not possible to estimate object position in the image. We detect nine different object categories, considering each category recognition as a two-class problem

J. Martí et al. (Eds.): IbPRIA 2007, Part I, LNCS 4477, pp. 515–522, 2007.

(object samples and background samples). In order to estimate class models, we use AdaBoost and SVM learning algorithms.

In the second group of experiments, we model objects using local descriptors as appearance and pictorial structure as shape model. This shape model represents an object as a star-like graph. The graph nodes correspond to image region local descriptors (appearances), and edges connect pairs of nodes whose relative location can be modelled by a two dimensional Gaussian (object shape). With this model we are able to decide object presence/absence and location in new images. This model allows object translations, and is robust to small scalings, but it is not fully invariant to object rotations and scalings.

This paper is organized as follows: in Section 2, SIFT and HMAX descriptors are briefly introduced. Then, in Section 3, we describe the object shape model. Afterwards, the experiments and results are presented in Sections 4 and 5. And, finally, we conclude the paper with the summary and conclusions.

2   Appearance Models

In order to compute region appearance models, we compute three descriptors: SIFT, SIFT-Gabor modification and HMAX.

2.1   SIFT Descriptor

In the original formulation of the SIFT descriptor [2], a scale-normalized image region is represented with the concatenation of gradient orientation histograms relative to several rectangular subregions. Firstly, the derivatives I_x and I_y of the image I are computed with pixel differences. Then the image gradient magnitude and orientation is computed for every pixel in the scale-normalized image region:

$$M(x,y) = \sqrt{I_x(x,y)^2 + I_y(x,y)^2}; \quad \Theta(x,y) = \tan^{-1}(I_y(x,y)/I_x(x,y)). \quad (1)$$

The interest region is then subdivided in subregions in a rectangular grid. The next step is to compute the histogram of gradient orientation, weighted by gradient magnitude, for each subregion. Orientation is divided into B bins and each bin is set with the sum of the windowed orientation difference to the bin center, weighted by the gradient magnitude:

$$h_{r_{(l,m)}}(k) = \sum_{x,y \in r_{(l,m)}} M(x,y)(1 - |\Theta(x,y) - c_k|/\Delta_k), \quad (2)$$

where c_k is the orientation bin center, Δ_k is the orientation bin width, and (x,y) are pixel coordinates in subregion $r_{(l,m)}$. The SIFT local descriptor is the concatenation of the several gradient orientation histograms for all subregions:

$$u = (h_{r_{(1,1)}}, \ldots, h_{r_{(l,m)}}, \ldots, h_{r_{(4,4)}}) \quad (3)$$

With 16 subregions and $B = 8$ orientations bins, u size is 128. The final step is to normalize the descriptor in Eq.(3) to unit norm, in order to reduce the effects of uniform illumination changes.

SIFT-Gabor Descriptor. Using the framework provided by Mikolajcyzik *et al.* [1], we improve SIFT distinctiveness for image region matching. We propose an alternative way to compute first order image derivatives using odd Gabor filters, instead of pixel differences [3]. We rely on filter energy, to select the most appropriate Gabor filter width especially suited to represent scale-normalized image regions. Image derivatives are computed as

$$I_x(x,y) = (I * g^{odd}_{0,6,4\sqrt{2}/3})(x,y); \quad I_y(x,y) = (I * g^{odd}_{\pi/2,6,4\sqrt{2}/3})(x,y). \quad (4)$$

where $g^{odd}_{\theta,\gamma,\sigma}(x,y)$ is the 2D odd Gabor function with orientation θ, scale invariant wave number γ, and width σ. Once the image derivatives are computed, we do as original SIFT histogram computation.

2.2 HMAX Model

The biologically inspired HMAX model was firstly proposed by Riesenhuber and Poggio [4], and lately revised by Serre et al. [5], who introduced a learning step based on the extraction of lots of random patches. On the latter version, Marín-Jiménez and Pérez de la Blanca [6] have proposed some changes that we have adopted for this work, in particular, the use of Gaussian derivatives functions (i.e. second order) instead of Gabor functions.

We include a brief description of the steps of the HMAX model to generate C2 features (see [5] for details):

1. Compute S1 maps: the target image is convolved with a bank of oriented filters with various scales.
2. Compute C1 maps: pairs of S1 maps (of different scales) are subsampled and combined, by using the max operator, to generate *bands*.
3. Only during training: extract *patches* P_i of various sizes $n_i \times n_i$ and all orientations from C1 maps, at random positions.
4. Compute S2 maps: for each C1 map, compute the correlation Y with the patches P_i: $Y = \exp(-\gamma \|X - P_i\|^2)$, where X are all the possible windows in C1 with the same size as P_i, γ is a tunable parameter.
5. Compute C2 features: compute the max over all positions and bands for each S2$_i$ map, obtaining a single value C2$_i$ for each patch P_i.

3   Object Shape Model

The objects are composed by a set of P parts, and modelled by the relative locations between parts and appearance of every part. The locations between parts is a star-like graph, where the star's reference point (landmark) must be present in the image in order to detect an object. The pictorial model is parametrized by the graph $G = (V, E)$. $V = \{v_1, \ldots, v_p, \ldots, v_P\}$ is the set of vertices and v_1 is the landmark point. $E = \{e_{12}, \ldots, e_{1p}, \ldots, e_{1P}\}$ is the set of edges between connected parts, where e_{1p} denotes the edge connecting part 1 and part p. We model the edge parameters as Gaussian distributions of the

x and y coordinates referenced to the landmark location. The edge model is $e_{1p} = (\mu_{x_p - x_1}, \sigma^2_{x_p - x_1}, \mu_{y_p - y_1}, \sigma^2_{y_p - y_1}), p = 2, \ldots, P; e_{1p} \in E$, where the mean$(\mu)$ and variance(σ^2) are estimated in the training set. Additionally to edge parameters, the set of appearance models related to vertices is $u = \{u_1, \ldots, u_p, \ldots, u_P\}$.

The statistical framework proposed in [7], computes the probability of an object configuration $L = \{l_1, \ldots, l_p, \ldots, l_P\}, l_i = (x_p, y_p)$, given an image[1] I and a model $\theta = (u, E)$ as

$$p(L|I, \theta) \propto p(I|L, \theta)p(L|\theta). \tag{5}$$

Assuming non-overlapping parts in the object, the likelihood of I given the configuration L and model θ can be approximated by the product of probabilities of each part, so $p(I|L, \theta) = p(I|L, u) \propto \prod_{p=1}^{P} p(I|l_p, u_p)$. The prior $p(L|\theta)$ is captured by the Markov random field with edge set E. Following the reasoning proposed in [7], the prior is approximated by $p(L|\theta) = \prod_{e_{1p} \in E} p(x_1, x_p|\theta)p(y_1, y_p|\theta)$. Thus replacing the likelihood and prior in Eq. (5), and computing the negative logarithm, the best object configuration is

$$L^* = \arg\min_{L} - \sum_{p=1}^{P} \log p(I|l_p, u_p) - \sum_{(e_{1p} \in E)} \log p(x_1, x_p|c_p) - \sum_{(e_{1p} \in E)} \log p(y_1, y_p|c_p). \tag{6}$$

The Eq.(6) computes in a new image I the most probable configuration L^*, after learning the model $\theta = (u, E)$.

4   Object Detection Experiment

In this group of experiments we model an object category by a set of local descriptors (SIFT/HMAX). We select N points from training set images of object class c, and compute local descriptor u_i^c at selected point i. With SIFT descriptors, u is the gradient histogram vector in Eq. (3) and, with HMAX descriptor u is the patch P_i described in Section 2.2. During training, for all cases, we select points searching for local maxima of Difference of Gaussians (DoG), but in original HMAX points are selected at random.

In order to detect an instance of the category modelled in a new image we:

1. Select J interest point locations by applying DoG operator. But in original HMAX, all the image points are candidates (see section 2.2).
2. Compute local descriptors in the new image $u_j, j = 1, \ldots, J$ at interest point locations.
3. Create class-similarity feature vector $v = [v_1, \ldots, v_i, \ldots, v_N]$ by matching each class model point descriptor u_i^c against all image descriptors u_j. In the case of SIFT descriptor $v_i = \min_j \|u_i^c - u_j\|^2$, and in the case of HMAX descriptor $v_i = \max_j \exp(-\gamma\|P_i - u_j\|^2)$.
4. Classify v as object or background image, with a binary classifier.

---

[1] Set of intensity values that represents visually the object.

Fig. 1. Typical images from selected databases

The experiments are performed over a set of classes provided by Caltech[2]: *airplanes side, cars side, cars rear, camels, faces, guitars, leaves, leopards* and *motorbikes side*, plus *Google things* dataset [8]. We use category *Google things* as negative samples. Each positive training set is comprised of 100 images drawn at random, and 100 images drawn at random from the unseen samples for testing. Figure 1 shows some sample images from each category. For all experiments, images have a fixed size (height 140 pixels), keeping the original image aspect ratio and converted to gray-scale format. We vary the number of local descriptors that represent an object category, $N = \{5, 10, 25, 50, 100, 250, 500\}$. In order to evaluate the influence of the learning algorithm, we utilize two classifiers: SVM [9] with linear kernel[3], and AdaBoost [11] with decision stumps.

The experimental set-up for each kind of local descriptor is: (i) original HMAX, (ii) HMAX computed at DoG, (iii) SIFT non-rotation-invariant (NRI), (iv) original SIFT, (v) SIFT-Gabor, and (vi) SIFT-Gabor NRI.

Results and Discussion. In Table 1, we show the mean results of detection for 10 repetitions at equilibrium point (i.e. when the false positive rate = miss rate), along with confidence interval (at 95%). We only show results for 10 and 500 features. In Fig. 2 we see performance evolution as a function of the number of features, in the case of rigid (*airplanes*) and articulated (*leopards*) objects.

Local descriptors can be clustered in three groups using the average performance: HMAX-based descriptors, SIFT-NRI descriptors, and SIFT descriptors. HMAX-based descriptors have the best performance, followed by SIFT-NRI descriptors and SIFT descriptors. The separation between the groups depends on the learning algorithm, in the case of SVM the distance between groups is large. In the case of AdaBoost groups are closer to each other, and for some categories (*motorbikes, airplanes* and *leopards*) all descriptors have practically the same performance. We see that in average, results provided by SVM are better than the AdaBoost ones.

Although in [3] is concluded that SIFT-Gabor descriptor improves SIFT distinctiveness on average for image region matching, we cannot apply this conclusion to object category recognition. In the case of AdaBoost algorithm SIFT and SIFT-Gabor have practically the same performance, while in the case of SVM SIFT performs slightly better than SIFT-Gabor.

---

[2] Datasets are available at: http://www.robots.ox.ac.uk/~vgg/data3.html
[3] Implementation provided by *libsvm*[10].

Table 1. Results for all the categories. (TF: type of feature. NF: number of features). On average over all the categories and using SVM, HMAX-Rand gets 84.2%, versus the 73.9% of regular SIFT. For each experiment, the best result is in bold face.

Support Vector Machines								
	Airplane		Camel		Car-side		Car-rear	
TF/NF	10	500	10	500	10	500	10	500
H-Rand	**87.3, 2.2**	**95.9, 1.0**	**70.4, 3.1**	**84.3, 2.2**	87.9, 4.0	98.1, 1.5	**93.0, 1.1**	**97.7, 0.8**
H-DoG	80.3, 2.6	94.9, 0.8	70.2, 3.9	83.9, 1.4	**88.9, 3.8**	**99.5, 0.9**	86.6, 1.8	97.0, 0.7
Sift	74.6, 1.8	89.1, 1.0	63.9, 2.4	76.1, 1.7	72.9, 3.4	87.9, 3.7	73.7, 2.7	88.4, 2.1
G-Sift	69.7, 2.9	88.6, 1.5	57.3, 1.8	77.2, 2.2	69.1, 5.6	87.0, 2.0	67.2, 2.1	85.8, 1.7
SiftNRI	78.0, 3.2	92.4, 1.3	63.1, 3.8	77.8, 1.9	79.2, 3.4	90.8, 2.2	86.9, 1.8	93.1, 1.2
G-SiftNRI	74.8, 2.6	92.8, 1.5	62.1, 3.4	75.9, 1.9	72.5, 4.9	87.4, 2.2	80.2, 1.9	90.7, 1.2
Faces		Guitar		Leaves		Leopard		Motorbike
10	500	10	500	10	500	10	500	10	500
79.8, 3.4	**96.6, 0.7**	**87.1, 4.0**	**96.7, 1.1**	**88.6, 3.1**	**98.3, 0.6**	81.4, 3.4	**95.7, 0.9**	**81.9, 3.4**	93.7, 0.9
82.7, 1.8	96.0, 0.6	82.9, 4.0	95.9, 0.8	84.6, 2.0	98.3, 0.9	70.9, 3.9	94.2, 1.3	81.6, 2.3	**94.7, 0.7**
74.8, 3.3	88.4, 1.8	66.4, 3.0	81.1, 1.5	81.5, 3.5	92.6, 1.1	**81.7, 2.5**	87.8, 1.1	75.2, 2.3	87.9, 1.4
73.6, 2.9	85.2, 1.9	70.1, 1.9	82.3, 1.1	81.0, 3.3	92.4, 1.0	78.0, 3.0	89.6, 1.3	69.0, 2.6	86.9, 1.4
84.4, 3.4	92.8, 1.2	65.2, 3.3	85.4, 1.0	79.1, 2.8	92.6, 0.9	81.6, 1.7	92.4, 1.2	75.4, 2.4	90.9, 1.7
84.6, 3.3	91.8, 1.2	69.0, 3.8	86.1, 1.6	79.1, 3.3	91.7, 1.3	76.9, 3.2	91.8, 1.4	72.0, 2.9	89.6, 0.7

AdaBoost								
	Airplane		Camel		Car-side		Car-rear	
TF/NF	10	500	10	500	10	500	10	500
H-Rand	**81.0, 0.7**	**94.3, 1.1**	**67.7, 3.3**	**83.1, 1.0**	84.1, 2.8	94.2, 2.0	**90.1, 5.1**	**98.3, 0.7**
H-DoG	77.8, 3.6	93.2, 1.3	63.9, 4.5	79.1, 1.8	**85.5, 5.5**	**96.6, 1.3**	74.1, 15.7	96.4, 1.3
Sift	75.3, 3.3	90.6, 1.5	65.1, 1.9	73.8, 1.6	74.9, 4.0	88.9, 2.1	76.3, 2.6	89.8, 1.6
G-Sift	73.0, 4.1	90.2, 1.2	60.6, 2.4	77.3, 2.0	70.5, 4.7	87.0, 3.5	69.7, 1.5	87.2, 2.0
SiftNRI	79.8, 3.2	93.1, 1.1	65.0, 3.4	78.1, 1.5	81.6, 4.9	90.8, 2.2	89.6, 0.7	94.9, 1.2
G-SiftNRI	77.9, 2.4	94.2, 1.2	62.2, 2.9	74.8, 2.3	78.3, 3.8	89.9, 2.0	83.8, 1.3	92.3, 0.9
Faces		Guitar		Leaves		Leopard		Motorbike
10	500	10	500	10	500	10	500	10	500
77.1, 4.7	94.9, 1.1	**83.7, 7.1**	**96.6, 1.0**	83.1, 6.2	**97.7, 0.7**	76.8, 2.8	85.6, 1.1	74.7, 4.8	92.0, 1.7
74.4, 6.1	**95.7, 1.2**	78.0, 6.9	92.7, 1.5	76.0, 4.6	97.0, 0.9	70.2, 5.5	83.1, 2.0	75.2, 3.7	93.4, 0.9
78.3, 3.1	90.8, 1.2	66.0, 3.4	79.9, 1.1	**84.2, 3.2**	92.6, 1.1	83.6, 2.2	87.0, 1.2	77.9, 1.7	90.7, 1.4
75.3, 3.3	87.4, 1.7	71.6, 2.6	83.4, 2.6	81.1, 4.3	92.9, 1.3	81.2, 1.8	89.7, 2.2	70.8, 2.9	88.9, 1.2
87.6, 2.7	94.3, 0.8	67.2, 2.8	86.4, 1.4	81.0, 3.6	92.9, 1.5	**84.4, 1.5**	**92.8, 1.2**	**80.4, 2.6**	**93.7, 1.1**
86.1, 2.8	92.6, 1.3	69.9, 4.3	87.4, 1.0	81.7, 3.8	92.2, 1.9	78.1, 1.9	91.7, 1.0	75.4, 2.3	92.3, 1.2

HMAX is able to discriminate categories, attaining rates over 80% in most of the cases with a small number of features, e.g. 10. It shows that a discriminative descriptor can detect objects in categories with very high visual difficult images, like *leopards* and *camels*, using an appearance model. Other remarkable data is that HMAX-DoG works better with *car-side* and *motorbikes*, since DoG operator is able to locate the most representative parts, e.g. the wheels.

5   Face Detection and Localization Experiment

The aim of this experiment is to detect and locate faces in images using appearance models (SIFT and HMAX) and shape model (pictorial structure). We use a subset of the Caltech faces (100 images), background (100 images) database images, and the software provided at the "ICCV'05 Short Course" [12]. Here it is important to remark that background images do not model a negative class, but

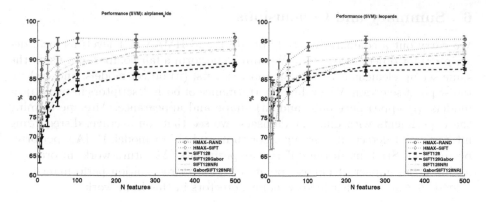

Fig. 2. Comparison of performance depending on the type and number of features representing the images. The used classifier is SVM.

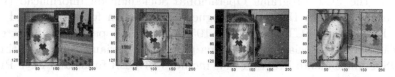

Fig. 3. Face detection samples: 3 hits and 1 miss (right)

they are utilized only to test the object model in images without faces. We select 10% of the face images to learn the local descriptor model $(\mu_{u_p}, \Sigma_{u_p})$, and the pictorial structure model $(\mu_{x_p-x_1}, \sigma^2_{x_p-x_1}, \mu_{y_p-y_1}, \sigma^2_{y_p-y_1})$, with $P = 5$ parts. We recognize faces in the remaining 90% of face image set and background images.

Results and Discussion. Evaluation criterion comprises object detection and location. In the case of object detection we compute the Receiver Operator Characteristic (ROC) curve, varying the threshold in L^* from Eq. (6). In the case of object location we compute precision *vs.* recall curve (RPC), varying the ratio between the intersection and union of ground truth and detected bounding boxes. From ROC we compute area (A-ROC) and equal error rate point (EEP), and, from RPC we compute equal error rate (RPC-eq) presented in Table 2. The results show that HMAX's C1-level based descriptors are suitable to represent object parts, achieving better results than SIFT descriptors. Figure 3 shows three correct detections and one wrong detection, when using five parts for the model and HMAX as part descriptor.

Table 2. Results for face detection and localization using the structural model

Feature	Nparts	A-ROC	EEP	RPC-eq
HMAX	5	94.8	89.0	84.9
SIFT	5	93.4	86.3	80.3
SIFT-Gabor	5	94.9	85.3	81.7

6   Summary and Conclusions

We carry out a comparative study of SIFT and HMAX (C1 level) as local descriptors for object recognition. We aim to perform a fair comparison, using the same set-up elements: (i) training and test sets, (ii) object models, and (iii) interest point selection. We evaluate performance of both descriptors in two object models: (i) appearance only, and (ii) shape and appearance. After performing the experiments with different datasets, we see that, on average, disregarding interest point detection, learning algorithm, and object model, HMAX performs better than SIFT in all the different experiments. As future work, in order to evaluate the impact of interest point selection in recognition performance, we intend to evaluate other interest point detectors in this framework.

Acknowledgments. This work was partially supported by the Spanish Ministry of Education and Science, grant FPU AP2003-2405 and project TIN2005-01665, by the FCT Programa Operacional Sociedade de Informação (POSI) in the frame of QCA III, and Portuguese Foundation for Science and Technology PhD Grant FCT SFRH\BD\10573\2002 and partially supported by Fundação para a Ciência e a Tecnologia (ISR/IST plurianual funding) through the POS_Conhecimento Program that includes FEDER funds and FCT Project GestInteract.

References

1. Mikolajczyk, K., Schmid, C.: A performance evaluation of local descriptors. IEEE PAMI 27(10), 1615–1630 (2005)
2. Lowe, D.G.: Distinctive image features from scale-invariant keypoints. International Journal of Computer Vision 2(60), 91–110 (2004)
3. Moreno, P., Bernardino, A., Santos-Victor, J.: Improving the sift descriptor with gabor filters. Submitted to Pattern Recognition Letters (2006)
4. Riesenhuber, M., Poggio, T.: Hierarchical models of object recognition in cortex. Nature Neuroscience 2(11), 1019–1025 (1999)
5. Serre, T., Wolf, L., Poggio, T.: Object recognition with features inspired by visual cortex. In: IEEE CSC on CVPR (June 2005)
6. Marín-Jiménez, M.J., de la Blanca, N.P.: Empirical study of multi-scale filter banks for object categorization. In: Proc. ICPR, August 2006, IEEE CS, Washington (2006)
7. Felzenszwalb, P.F., Huttenlocher, D.P.: Pictorial structures for object recognition. Intl. J. Computer Vision 1(61), 55–79 (2005)
8. Fergus, R., Perona, P., Zisserman, A.: A sparse object category model for efficient learning and exhaustive recognition. In: CVPR, pp. 380–387 (2005)
9. Osuna, E., Freund, R., Girosi, F.: Support Vector Machines: training and applications. In: Technical Report AI-Memo 1602, MIT, Cambridge, MA (March 1997)
10. Chang, C., Lin, C.: LIBSVM: a library for support vector machines (April 2005)
11. Friedman, J., Hastie, T., Tibshirani, R.: Additive logistic regression: a statistical view of boosting. Technical report, Dept. of Statistics. Stanford University (1998)
12. Fei-Fei, L., Fergus, R., Torralba, A.:
    http://people.csail.mit.edu/torralba/iccv2005/

Moment-Based Pattern Representation Using Shape and Grayscale Features*

Mikhail Lange, Sergey Ganebnykh, and Andrey Lange

Computing Centre RAS

Abstract. A moment-based approach is developed to constructing tree-structured descriptions of patterns given by region-based shapes with grayscale attributes. The proposed representation is approximately invariant with respect to the pattern rotation, translation, scale, and level of brightness. The tree-like structure of the pattern representations provides their independent encoding into prefix code words. Due to this fact, a pattern recognition procedure amounts to decoding a code word of the pattern by the nearest code word from a tree of the code words of selected templates. Efficient application of the pattern representation technique is illustrated by experimental results on signature and hand gesture recognition.

1 Introduction

Pattern representation is one of the basic problems in pattern recognition. In many cases, this problem is solved by constructing invariant descriptions of patterns with respect to their similarity transformations. In addition, it is necessary to construct the structured pattern descriptions that permit to decrease a computational complexity of a recognition procedure against a full search for a decision. Our goal consists in developing a technique of constructing the invariant tree-structured representations for a wide class of patterns given by 2D solid shapes with grayscale features.

A survey of known approaches to 2D shape representation is given in [5]. Among the developed shape descriptors a significant part refers to moment-based techniques [6] and the techniques based on shape decomposition into geometric primitives [2], [3]. A problem of appropriate fitting the objects by primitives of a given shape is considered in [9]. Of particular interest is a recursive decomposition approach providing tree-structured descriptions of shapes. The representations based on such approach are suggested in papers [1] and [4]. However, in many applications, the patterns are given by both shape and grayscale features. The examples are signatures, hand gestures, handwritten sings, and trade marks with nonuniform brightness. Thus, a demand arises for developing a pattern representation technique that combines the shape and grayscale features, and provides a similarity transformation invariance and a tree-like structure of

* This work is supported by the Russian Foundation for Basic Research, project 06-01-00524.

J. Martí et al. (Eds.): IbPRIA 2007, Part I, LNCS 4477, pp. 523–530, 2007.

the pattern description. This kind of pattern representations is convenient for their fast matching in pattern recognition. For these representations, the problem of pattern matching amounts to compare the representing trees by using a tree distance similar to metrics proposed in [7].

In this paper, we propose a technique of constructing tree-structured pattern representation on the basis of a recursive scheme of pattern partitioning and an approximation of the pattern parts (segments) by elliptic primitives using central and axial moments of inertia. The invariance of the representation is achieved by calculating the primitives in principal axis of the segments and by normalizing parameters of the primitives. A new dissimilarity measure is suggested in a space of the pattern representations. Also, an efficient application of the pattern representation technique is demonstrated by experimental results of signature and gesture recognition.

2   Statement of the Problem

Given grayscale image in the Cartesian coordinates X and Y, let a pattern be defined by a set of N pixels

$$P = \left\{ \, p_k = \{(x,y,z) : z(x,y) = z_k, |x-x_k| \leq \frac{\Delta}{2}, |y-y_k| \leq \frac{\Delta}{2}\}, k = \overline{1,N} \, \right\} \quad (1)$$

where $z(x,y)$ is a darkness function; Δ is a linear size of the pixel p_k; (x_k, y_k) are the coordinates of the center and $0 < z_k \leq q$ is the darkness integer value of p_k. The zero darkness is assigned to background pixels. Let U and V be the Cartesian coordinates connected with the coordinates X and Y by a transformation

$$\begin{pmatrix} u \\ v \end{pmatrix} = \begin{pmatrix} c_{ux} & c_{uy} \\ c_{vx} & c_{vy} \end{pmatrix} \begin{pmatrix} x - x^* \\ y - y^* \end{pmatrix} \quad (2)$$

where (x^*, y^*) is a translation point and $\mathbf{c}_u = (c_{ux}, c_{uy})$ and $\mathbf{c}_v = (c_{vx}, c_{vy})$ are unit direction vectors of the coordinate axes U and V relative to the axes X and Y, respectively. In the coordinates U and V, we define an elliptic primitive by a set of points

$$Q = \left\{ (u,v,z^*) : z^*(u,v) = z^*, \, \frac{u^2}{r_u^2} + \frac{v^2}{r_v^2} \leq 1 \right\} \quad (3)$$

where $z^*(u,v) = z^* > 0$ is a uniform darkness function and $r_u > 0$ and $r_v > 0$ are the radii along the appropriate axes U and V. According to (2) and (3), the primitive is determined by the following parameters

$$(x^*, y^*, z^*), (\mathbf{c}_u, \mathbf{c}_v), (r_u, r_v) . \quad (4)$$

An error of approximation of the object P by the primitive Q is defined by

$$E(P,Q) = \frac{1}{\|P \cup Q\|} \sum_{P \cup Q} \frac{|z - z^*|}{\max(z, z^*)}$$

where the sum is taken over all pixels which centers belong to the union $P \cup Q$ and $\|P \cup Q\|$ is the number of these pixels. It is assumed that z and z^* possess the zero values in all points outside P and Q, respectively. If $0 \le \delta < 1$ is a given admissible approximation error, then the criterion of approximation is

$$E(P, Q) \le \delta . \tag{5}$$

A scheme of the approximation of the total pattern P by a set of Q-primitives is based on partitioning the pattern into a set of segments and fitting the segments by the primitives satisfying (5). In what follows, we describe the technique of pattern representation (section 3), the scheme of pattern recognition based on the representation technique (section 4), and the results of experiments on signature and gesture recognition (section 5).

3   Recursive Moment-Based Pattern Representation

Due to recursiveness of the proposed pattern representation, it is enough to describe the moment-based approximation of any segment of the pattern and then to formalize the scheme of pattern partitioning. The approximation is based on calculating the extreme moments of inertia for both the object P (segment or total pattern) and the primitive Q given by (1) and (3), respectively. For the object P, the central moment of inertia relative to a point (x^*, y^*) is

$$J_c(P) = \sum_{k=1}^{N} \int_{p_k \in P} \left[(x - x^*)^2 + (y - y^*)^2 \right] w_z(x, y) \, dx dy \tag{6}$$

and the axial moment of inertia relative to an axis determined by the point (x^*, y^*) and the unit vector $\mathbf{c} = (c_x, c_y)$ is defined by

$$J_a(P) = \sum_{k=1}^{N} \int_{p_k \in P} \left[c_x(y - y^*) - c_y(x - x^*) \right]^2 w_z(x, y) \, dx dy \tag{7}$$

where $w_z(x, y) = z(x, y) \Big/ \sum_{k=1}^{N} \int_{p_k \in P} z(x, y) \, dx dy$ is the darkness distribution function for the object P.

Minimization of the moment (6) over the variables x^* and y^* yields the optimum point $(x^* = \sum_{k=1}^{N} x_k \tilde{w}_k,\ y^* = \sum_{k=1}^{N} y_k \tilde{w}_k)$ with the weights $\tilde{w}_k = z_k \Big/ \sum_{i=1}^{N} z_i,\ k = \overline{1, N}$. The minimum and maximum values of the moment (7) correspond to a pair of orthogonal axes (U, V) with the origin (x^*, y^*) and the unit direction vectors $\mathbf{c}_u = (c_{ux}, c_{uy})$ and $\mathbf{c}_v = (c_{vx}, c_{vy})$. These vectors are determined by a matrix of the second order central moments

$$\mathbf{G} = \begin{pmatrix} g_{yy} & -g_{xy} \\ -g_{yx} & g_{xx} \end{pmatrix}$$

with the elements $g_{xx} = \sum_{k=1}^{N} (x_k - x^*)^2 \tilde{w}_k + \frac{\Delta^2}{12}$, $g_{yy} = \sum_{k=1}^{N} (y_k - y^*)^2 \tilde{w}_k + \frac{\Delta^2}{12}$, and $g_{xy} = g_{yx} = \sum_{k=1}^{N} (x_k - x^*)(y_k - y^*) \tilde{w}_k$.

The eigenvalues are equal to $\lambda_{u,v} = \frac{1}{2}(g_{xx} + g_{yy}) \mp \frac{1}{2}\sqrt{(g_{xx} - g_{yy})^2 + 4g_{xy}g_{yx}}$ and real due to symmetry of the matrix $\mathbf{G}$. Since $\mathbf{G}$ is positive definite (det $\mathbf{G} > 0$), therefore $\lambda_v \geq \lambda_u > 0$. If $\lambda_v > \lambda_u$, then the corresponding eigenvectors $\mathbf{c}_u$ and $\mathbf{c}_v$ determine the directions of the unique axes U and V. Notice that there are four different pairs $(\mathbf{c}_u, \mathbf{c}_v)$ for the given pair (λ_u, λ_v). We choose the decision $(\mathbf{c}_u, \mathbf{c}_v)$ corresponding to the minimum right rotation in the transformation (2). The found point (x^*, y^*) and eigenvectors $\mathbf{c}_u$ and $\mathbf{c}_v$ provide the following extreme moments of inertia

$$J_u(P) = \lambda_u, \qquad J_v(P) = \lambda_v, \quad J_c(P) = \lambda_u + \lambda_v \ . \tag{8}$$

For the primitive Q of the form (3), the moments of inertia relative to the found principal axes U and V are determined by the weighted mean values

$$J_u(Q) = \int_Q v^2 w_z^*(u, v)\, dudv = \frac{r_v^2}{4}, \quad J_v(Q) = \int_Q u^2 w_z^*(u, v)\, dudv = \frac{r_u^2}{4} \tag{9}$$

with the darkness density $w_z^*(u, v) = z^*(u, v) \big/ \int_Q z^*(u, v)\, dudv$ that is equal to $1 \big/ \int_Q dudv$ for the uniform function $z^*(u, v) = z^*$ of the primitive Q. The parameters (x^*, y^*) and $(\mathbf{c}_u, \mathbf{c}_v)$ of the primitive Q are determined by the principal axes U and V of the object P. The radii (r_u, r_v) follow from conditions of a moment-based equivalency of P and Q : $J_u(Q) = J_u(P)$; $J_v(Q) = J_v(P)$ and, using (8) and (9), these radii are equal to $r_u = 2\sqrt{\lambda_v}$ and $r_v = 2\sqrt{\lambda_u}$. The darkness value z^* of the primitive Q is found by the mean value $z^* = \sum_{k=1}^{N} z_k / N$ that yields a minimum mean square deviation of the darkness values for all pixels of the object P.

The pattern representation is constructed by the following recursive scheme. At the zero level ($l = 0$), the total pattern P is regarded as the object P_0 with the number $n = 0$. The object P_0 is approximated by the finest matched primitive Q_0 as described above. Given admissible error δ, if the pair (P_0, Q_0) satisfies the criterion (5) or P_0 consists of a single pixel, the primitive Q_0 is marked as "end" node. Otherwise, the object P_0 is partitioned into two segments by the principal axis V that moment of inertia $\lambda_v > \lambda_u$. The obtained segments are regarded as the new objects P_1 and P_2 of the first level $l = 1$. The described procedure is repeated for the objects P_1 and P_2 and for the new objects of the next levels. In general case, the object P_n of the l-th level produces two new objects P_{2n+1} and P_{2n+2} of the $(l + 1)$-th level. The maximum level of partitioning is upper bounded by a given L and all primitives of the L-th level are marked as "end nodes". Note that if $\lambda_u = \lambda_v$ for some object, then the pair (λ_u, λ_v) does not give the unique pair of eigenvectors $(\mathbf{c}_u, \mathbf{c}_v)$. For this object, the pair of axes (U, V) is assigned by the principal axes of the total pattern. The last notice limits a class of admissible patterns which matrices $\mathbf{G}$ have different eigenvalues.

Given pattern P, the described recursive scheme produces the pattern representation R in a form of a complete binary tree of the primitives (nodes)

$$R = \{Q_n : 0 \leq n \leq n_{\max}\} \tag{10}$$

where n is the node number of the level $l_n = \lfloor \log_2(n+1) \rfloor \le L$. Each node Q_n in the tree (10) is described by the parameters (4) that are recalculated into the principal coordinates $(U = U_0, V = V_0)$ of the root node Q_0 by using the transformation (2). The recalculated centers (u^*, v^*), radii (r_u, r_v), and darkness values z^* of the primitives are normalized for providing scale and brightness invariance of the representation (10).

Two examples of the representations are shown in Fig. 1 for signature and hand gesture. The left pictures correspond to real images, the middle pictures show the extracted patterns ($q = 255$ for signature and $q = 120$ for gesture), and the right pictures illustrate the pattern representations by the grayscale elliptic primitives ($\delta = 0.05$, $L = 7$). Increasing L provides more detailed representation.

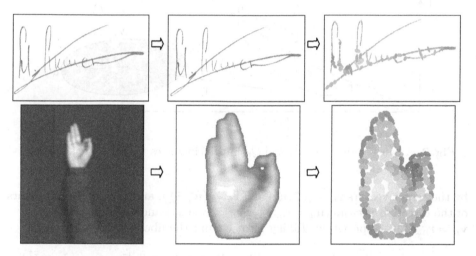

Fig. 1. Examples of the representations for grayscale signature and hand gesture

4   Application for Pattern Recognition

Pattern recognition by the nearest template requires a dissimilarity measure for any pair of the pattern representations. This measure is based on defining both a correspondence between the nodes of a pair of trees and an intersection of the trees. For the trees $(R, \hat{R})$ of the form (10), the nodes $Q_n \in R$ and $\hat{Q}_n \in \hat{R}$ are regarded corresponding to each other if these nodes have the same numbers. A set of the corresponding nodes gives the intersection $R \cap \hat{R}$.

Let $\rho(Q_n, \hat{Q}_n) \ge 0$ be a dissimilarity function of the corresponding nodes Q_n and $\hat{Q}_n$ for the pairs $(Q_n, \hat{Q}_n) \in (R \cap \hat{R})$. Using this function, we define a loss function

$$d(Q_n, \hat{Q}_n) = \begin{cases} \rho(Q_n, \hat{Q}_n), & \text{if } Q_n \text{ and/or } \hat{Q}_n \text{ are "end" nodes,} \\ 0, & \text{otherwise.} \end{cases} \quad (11)$$

Then, the dissimilarity measure of the trees $(R, \hat{R})$ is defined by

$$D(R, \hat{R}) = \sum_{R \cap \hat{R}} d(Q_n, \hat{Q}_n) w(Q_n, \hat{Q}_n) \tag{12}$$

where $w(Q_n, \hat{Q}_n) = 2^{-l_n}$ and the sum is taken over all pairs $(Q_n, \hat{Q}_n) \in (R \cap \hat{R})$. The measure (12) requires a definition of the function $\rho(Q_n, \hat{Q}_n)$ for the ellipses Q_n and $\hat{Q}_n$ given in the same principal coordinate axes U and V of the root nodes Q_0 and $\hat{Q}_0$. A pair of recalculated and normalized primitives Q_n : $((u_n^*, v_n^*, z_n^*), (\mathbf{c}_{nu}, \mathbf{c}_{nv}), (r_{nu}, r_{nv}))$ and $\hat{Q}_n$: $((\hat{u}_n^*, \hat{v}_n^*, \hat{z}_n^*), (\hat{\mathbf{c}}_{nu}, \hat{\mathbf{c}}_{nv}), (\hat{r}_{nu}, \hat{r}_{nv}))$ is shown in Fig. 2. According to Fig. 2, the ellipses Q_n and $\hat{Q}_n$ are determined

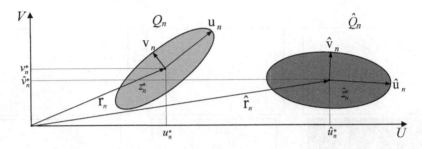

Fig. 2. A pair of primitives Q_n and $\hat{Q}_n$ in principal axes U and V of the pattern

by the center vectors $\mathbf{r}_n = (u_n^*, v_n^*)$ and $\hat{\mathbf{r}}_n = (\hat{u}_n^*, \hat{v}_n^*)$, and the appropriate pairs of the direction vectors $(\mathbf{u}_n = r_{nu}\mathbf{c}_{nu}, \mathbf{v}_n = r_{nv}\mathbf{c}_{nv})$ and $(\hat{\mathbf{u}}_n = \hat{r}_{nu}\hat{\mathbf{c}}_{nu}, \hat{\mathbf{v}}_n = \hat{r}_{nv}\hat{\mathbf{c}}_{nv})$, respectively. Taking into account the above vectors, we choose

$$\rho^2(Q_n, \hat{Q}_n) = \frac{|\mathbf{r}_n - \hat{\mathbf{r}}_n|^2}{\max^2(|\mathbf{r}_n|, |\hat{\mathbf{r}}_n|)} + \frac{|\mathbf{u}_n - \hat{\mathbf{u}}_n|^2 + |\mathbf{v}_n - \hat{\mathbf{v}}_n|^2}{\max(|\mathbf{u}_n|^2 + |\mathbf{v}_n|^2, |\hat{\mathbf{u}}_n|^2 + |\hat{\mathbf{v}}_n|^2)} + \frac{(z_n^* - \hat{z}_n^*)^2}{\max^2(z_n^*, \hat{z}_n^*)}$$

that coupled with (11) completely defines the measure (12).

Selection of the templates is performed at the stage of training the classifier. For this goal, we use a training set $\mathbf{R}_0$ that contains a fixed number of semantic groups of patterns with a given number of the pattern representations in each group. Processing of the semantic groups in $\mathbf{R}_0$ is performed independently and produces a fixed number m of the selected representations in each group. In the result, a set of the templates $\mathbf{R}^m \subset \mathbf{R}_0$ is constructed by combining the templates selected in each semantic group. In case of $m = 1$, the single template $\hat{R}$ in the given group of $\mathbf{R}_0$ yields $\sum_i D(R_i, \hat{R}) = \min_j \sum_i D(R_i, R_j)$, where the sums are taken over all pattern representations of the given semantic group. The template $\hat{R}$ provides the smallest dissipation $\sigma = \sum_i D(R_i, \hat{R}) / \sum_i 1$ per one sample of the group in $\mathbf{R}_0$. In case of $m > 1$, the selected templates $\hat{R}_1, \hat{R}_2, \ldots, \hat{R}_m$ in each semantic group of $\mathbf{R}_0$ yield the conditional maximum $\sum_{i=1}^{m} \sum_{j=i+1}^{m} D(\hat{R}_i, \hat{R}_j) = \max \sum_{i=1}^{m} \sum_{j=i+1}^{m} D(R_i, R_j)$ over all possible sequences $R_1, R_2, \ldots, R_m$ satisfying the inequality $\sum_{i=1}^{m} D(R_i, \hat{R}) \leq m\sigma$.

Given $\mathbf{R}^m$, the recognition decision about a pattern P via the pattern representation R is made by the nearest template $\hat{R}^* \in \mathbf{R}^m$ providing $D(R, \hat{R}^*) = \min_{\hat{R} \in \mathbf{R}^m} D(R, \hat{R})$. The recognition efficiency is determined by a probability $P_{\text{true}} = \Pr\{\text{"true decision"}\}$ that is a ratio of a number of true decisions to a total number of patterns being under recognition.

Any representing tree R of the form (10) can be written as a code word which length of the code word is proportional to the number of the nodes in R. Due to completeness of the representing trees, a given finite set of the code words satisfies the Kraft inequality [8]. This property yields the set $\mathbf{R}^m$ in a form of a tree $T(\mathbf{R}^m)$, in which the search for the nearest template can be performed by a modification of the Viterbi sequential decoding algorithm [8]. This step by step algorithm processes a limited number of subpaths in $T(\mathbf{R}^m)$ at each step. If the length of the subpaths is equal to $K = \gamma \log N$, where $\gamma > 0$ and $N = 2^{L+1}$ is the upper estimation of the code word length, then the computational complexity of the search algorithm is upper bounded by $O(N^{\gamma+1})$.

5   Experimental Results

The utility of the developed pattern representation technique was confirmed by experiments on recognition of signatures and hand gestures given by real grayscale images. The signatures were kindly submitted by our students and the gestures were the letters of American Sign Language (ASL) taken from the website http://www.vision.auc.dk/~tbm/Gestures/database.html.

The training set $\mathbf{R}_0$ of the signatures consisted of 32 (number of persons) semantic groups with 4 signatures of one person in each group. The test set of signatures submitted for recognition contained the same 32 semantic groups with 4 other samples of signatures in each group. In the case of hand gestures, the number of semantic groups was determined by the size of the downloaded ASL alphabet and it was equal to 25 signs. Each semantic group in the gesture training set $\mathbf{R}_0$ was given by 8 samples and the test set of gestures contained the same 25 signs per 8 other samples in each group. In both cases, the sets of the templates $\mathbf{R}^2 \subset \mathbf{R}_0$ ($m = 2$) were used. For $\delta = 0.05$ and different values L, the results in terms of P_{true} are given by table in Fig. 3. As shown in the table, the pattern representations based on shape and grayscale features ($q > 1$) provide a profit relative to the representations using only shape features ($q = 1$). As a whole, the recognition efficiency grows when L increases and, for fixed L, it can be improved by increasing the parameter m.

$\delta=0.05$	Gestures		Signatures	
	grayscale ($q=120$)	binary ($q=1$)	grayscale ($q=255$)	binary ($q=1$)
$L=6$	0.980	0.975	0.977	0.969
$L=7$	0.990	0.980	0.992	0.969
$L=8$	0,995	0.980	0.992	0.977
$L=9$	0,995	0.985	0.992	0.992

Fig. 3. Experimental results of gesture and signature recognition

6   Conclusion

In this paper, we proposed the new technique for constructing the tree-structured representations of region-based grayscale patterns. The basis of the technique consists of the recursive pattern decomposition and moment-based approximation of the pattern segments by elliptic primitives taken in principal axis of the segments. The last property provides the rotation and translation invariance of the pattern representation. The scale and brightness invariance is achieved by appropriate normalization of the primitives. As compared with classical descriptors using Zernike moments or Fourier expansions, our technique is based on zero, first, and second geometric moments and it is meant for structured recognition algorithms. The tree-like structure of the pattern representations permits to construct any set of templates as a tree of code words and to search for the decision templates by a scheme of sequential decoding. The search algorithm has a polynomial computational complexity of the length of the code words. Moreover, a multiresolution property of the proposed representation gives a chance to accelerate the recognition procedure using a scheme of successive refinement. The experiments on recognition of real signatures and ASL gestures showed the probability of true decisions within $0.98 - 0.99$. We plan to develop our technique with other primitives and measures as well as to make experiments on handwritten sign recognition. Also, an accelerated recognition algorithm based on the multiresolution property of the pattern representations will be researched.

References

1. Berretti, S., Del Bimbo, A.: Multiresolution spatial partitioning for shape representation. IEEE Proceedings of ICPR 2, 775–778 (2004)
2. Jagadish, H.V., Bruckstein, A.M.: On sequential shape descriptions. Pattern Recognition 25, 165–172 (1992)
3. Kim, H., Park, K., Kim, M.: Shape decomposition by collinearity. Pattern Recognition Letters 6, 335–340 (1987)
4. Lange, M.M., Ganebnykh, S.N.: Tree-like Data Structures for Effective Recognition of 2-D Solids. IEEE Proceedings of ICPR 1, 592–595 (2004)
5. Loncaric, S.: A survey of shape analysis techniques. Pattern Recognition 34(8), 983–1001 (1998)
6. Prokop, R.J., Reeves, A.P.: A survey of moment-based techniques for unoccluded object representation and recognition. CVGIP: Graphical Models and Image Processing 54, 438–460 (1992)
7. Torsello, A., Hodovic, D., Pelillo, M.: Four metrics for efficiently comparing attributed trees. IEEE Proceedings of ICPR 2, 467–470 (2004)
8. Viterbi, A.J., Omura, J.K.: Principles of Digital Communication and Coding. McGraw-Hill, New York (1979)
9. Voss, K., Suesse, H.: Invariant fitting of planar objects by primitives. IEEE Proceedings of ICPR, pp. 508–512 (1996)

Parsimonious Kernel Fisher Discrimination

Kitsuchart Pasupa[1], Robert F. Harrison[1], and Peter Willett[2]

[1] Department of Automatic Control & Systems Engineering,
[2] Department of Information Studies,
The University of Sheffield, UK

Abstract. By applying recent results in optimization transfer, a new algorithm for kernel Fisher Discriminant Analysis is provided that makes use of a non-smooth penalty on the coefficients to provide a parsimonious solution. The algorithm is simple, easily programmed and is shown to perform as well as or better than a number of leading machine learning algorithms on a substantial benchmark. It is then applied to a set of extreme small-sample-size problems in virtual screening where it is found to be less accurate than a currently leading approach but is still comparable in a number of cases.

1 Introduction

Fisher discriminant analysis has a central role in pattern recognition. It seeks a linear projection that maximizes the separation between data belonging to two classes while minimizing the separation between those of the same class. Its properties are well-documented and under certain circumstances prove optimal [1]. However, the linearity of the approach is frequently insufficient to allow the required level of performance in practical applications. While explicit expansion of data in basis functions can resolve this for problems of low dimension, the combinatorial increase in the number of coefficients to be estimated may make this impractical. Recent focus on kernel machines in the machine learning community seeks to address this problem via the so-called "kernel trick" [2] and a number solutions have been provided e.g. [3] that can be thought of generically as kernel Fisher discriminant analysis (kFDA). While kernels lend the required degree of flexibility to the discrimination task, they bring their own challenges, the foremost being a potential to overspecialize to the sample data (over-fitting) and a computational complexity dominated by sample size which, in some problems, may be large. Complexity control is therefore essential for a good outcome yet it has not been widely explored in the context of kFDA. In [3] complexity is controlled through explicit regularization – placing an appropriate penalty on the coefficients of the estimator, while [4] exploits the connection between FDA and an associated least-squares (LS) problem where an orthogonalization technique is used for forward selection. In benchmarks, the latter technique is seen to be competitive with a number of leading machine-learning classifiers including kFDA while providing more parsimonious estimators.

The motivation for our work lies in the field of chemoinformatics, in particular in virtual screening. Virtual screening (VS) describes a set of computational

J. Martí et al. (Eds.): IbPRIA 2007, Part I, LNCS 4477, pp. 531–538, 2007.

methods that provide a fast and cheap alternative to biological screening which involves the selection, synthesis and testing of molecules to ascertain their biological activity in a particular domain, e.g. pain relief, reduction of inflammation. This is important because reducing the cost and crucially time in the early stages of compound development can have a disproportionate benefit in profitability in a cycle that has a short patent lifetime. The aim of VS is to score, rank and/or filter a set of chemical structures to ensure that those molecules with the highest likelihood of activity are assayed first in a "lead discovery programme"[5].

The use of machine learning methods for VS has been widely studied. Techniques such as artificial neural networks and support vector machines in addition to more conventional approaches such as similarity matching and nearest neighbour analysis have all been explored while little attention has been paid to the use of FDA or its variants. An important recent development is the technique of binary kernel discrimination (BKD) which produces scores based on the estimated likelihood ratio of active to inactive compounds that are then ranked. The likelihoods are estimated through a Parzen Windows approach using the binomial distribution function (to accomodate binary descriptor or "fingerprint" vectors representing the presence, or not, of certain substructural arrangements of atoms) in place of the usual Gaussian choice [6]. This choice of kernel function uses Hamming distance but by substituting the Jaccard/Tanimoto distance instead, additional active compounds can be retrieved [7]. We will use results from BKD and its variant for comparison.

Virtual screening suffers strongly from the so-called small-sample-size problem where the number of covariates is comparable to or exceeds the number of samples. Typically a task in VS comprises a sample of size $\mathcal{O}\left(10^2\right)$ of known descriptors but with fingerprints of dimension $\mathcal{O}\left(10^3\right)$. Clearly some form of complexity control is therefore necessary.

In this paper we again exploit the association of FDA with LS but control complexity by penalizing the likelihood function. It is well-known that penalty functions that induce sparsity lead to non-smooth formulations and these are traditionally solved via mathematical programming techniques [8]. In a departure, we apply a minorize-maximize (MM) technique to overcome this technical problem leading to a very simple iterative algorithm that is guaranteed to converge to the (penalized) maximum likelihood solution. In [9] a general MM framework is presented for variable selection via penalized maximum likelihood but there only a small LS problem in conjunction with the SCAD penalty is examined.

The paper is organized as follows. Section 2 briefly states the well-known link between FDA and LS [1], presents the kernel-based formulation and motivates the use of penalized maximum likelihood. The following section introduces the MM principle and sketches a derivation of the iterative algorithm. Section 4 presents a performance comparison with other leading machine learning methods on a well-studied set of benchmarks and the results of applying the proposed method to VS are given in section 5.

2   Fisher Discriminant Analysis and its Variants

The relationship between FDA and LS is well known [1]. Consider the matrix of m-dimensional sample vectors $U = [u_1, u_2, \ldots, u_N]$ comprising two groups, $\mathcal{G}_i$, of size, n_i, $i = 1, 2$ represented by the partition, $[U_1 \, U_2]$. Membership of $\mathcal{G}_1$ is denoted by $\hat{y} = +n/n_1$ and of $\mathcal{G}_2$ by $\hat{y} = -n/n_2$ then it is straightforward to verify that the solution, $\boldsymbol{\omega} = [b \, \boldsymbol{w}]^{\mathsf{T}}$, to the following LS problem lies in the same direction as the solution for the Fisher discriminant [1].

$$\arg\min_{(b, \boldsymbol{w})} \left\| \begin{bmatrix} \frac{n}{n_1} \mathbf{1}_{n_1} \\ -\frac{n}{n_2} \mathbf{1}_{n_2} \end{bmatrix} - \begin{bmatrix} \mathbf{1}_{n_1} & U_1 \\ \mathbf{1}_{n_2} & U_2 \end{bmatrix} \begin{bmatrix} b \\ \boldsymbol{w} \end{bmatrix} \right\|_2^2 \tag{1}$$

where $\mathbf{1}_p$ denotes a p-vector of ones.

To accommodate more complex discriminants, data can be mapped into a new feature space, $\mathcal{F}$, via some function, ϕ, say. However, vectors in $\mathcal{F}$ will typically be of very high dimension precluding any practical manipulation. The "kernel trick" recognizes that the coefficients, $\boldsymbol{w}$, in the linear model implicit in (1) can themselves be written as a linear combination of the mapped data, leading to a formulation entirely based on inner products that can be computed through the agency of a suitable kernel. These ideas have been explored thoroughly elsewhere e.g. so we omit further exposition and simply present the kernelized version of the LS problem (see e.g. [4] for details).

Let K denote the Gram matrix associated with the kernel, $k(.,.)$, i.e. $k_{ij} = k(u_i, u_j)$, $i, j = 1, 2, \ldots, N$ then the solution, $\boldsymbol{\omega} = [b \, \boldsymbol{\alpha}]^{\mathsf{T}}$, to the following LS problem provides the coefficients of a linear discriminant in the feature space associated with $k(.,.)$ hence non-linear discrimination in the data space.

$$\arg\min_{(b, \boldsymbol{\alpha})} \left\| \begin{bmatrix} \frac{n}{n_1} \mathbf{1}_{n_1} \\ -\frac{n}{n_2} \mathbf{1}_{n_2} \end{bmatrix} - \begin{bmatrix} \mathbf{1}_{n_1} & K_1 \\ \mathbf{1}_{n_2} & K_2 \end{bmatrix} \begin{bmatrix} b \\ \boldsymbol{\alpha} \end{bmatrix} \right\|_2^2 \tag{2}$$

It is common to introduce a quadratic penalty into LS regression and this can be interpreted in the Bayesian framework as placing a Gaussian prior on the values of the coefficients. The quadratic penalty improves numerical condition when data are strongly correlated, militates against over-fitting and also suggests a method for selecting variables – those with relatively small coefficient magnitudes can be discarded. Essentially, large deviations from zero are strongly penalized while small values are only very lightly affected. Instead of using a Gaussian penalty, a prior distribution with a sharp peak has the effect of penalizing non-zero coefficients much more strongly so that the pay-off for setting small coefficients exactly to zero is relatively much greater. A log-likelihood penalty of the form $\|\boldsymbol{\omega}\|_q^q$ $0 < q \leq 1$ has precisely this property. The "sparsity-inducing" property of this penalty is well-known [2]. Introducing this penalty leads to a difficulty in gradient-based optimization owing to its discontinuous first derivative. Mathematical programming is the usually adopted to address this but here we exploit the MM principle to provide a simple, iterative algorithm.

3 Algorithm Development Via the MM Principle

The MM principle seeks to replace a difficult optimization problem, in our case, non-smooth, with a simpler (smooth) one having the same solution. In the case of maximization, the idea is to find a non-unique *surrogate* function that *minorizes* the objective function of interest and then to maximize this. Here we are able to replace the non-smooth element of the likelihood function with a quadratic function and then iterate toward the solution.

Let $\boldsymbol{\omega}(n)$ denote the nth step in an iterative procedure, then a function, $S(\boldsymbol{\omega}|\boldsymbol{\omega}(n))$, is said to minorize the function, $\ell(\boldsymbol{\omega})$, if it is everywhere less than ℓ and is tangent to it at $\boldsymbol{\omega}(n)$ e.g. [10]. Such a function that minorizes a concave objective function can itself be maximized, often analytically, and this fact can be exploited. The minorizing function, $S(.,.)$, acts as a surrogate for the original objective function. The *ascent* property e.g. [10] guarantees that the value of $\ell(\boldsymbol{\omega})$ never decreases. The iteration will therefore converge to the global maximum for a concave objective function. Minorization is closed under the operations of addition and multiplication.

We outline the derivation of a very simple, Newton-like algorithm for the penalized maximum likelihood estimation of the kFDA coefficients, c.f. [9]. The log-likelihood function, $\ell(\boldsymbol{\omega})$, is written as the sum of two functions, $\ell_e(\boldsymbol{\omega}) = -\frac{1}{2}\|\hat{\boldsymbol{y}} - \tilde{K}\boldsymbol{\omega}\|_2^2$, and $\ell_p(\boldsymbol{\omega}) = -\rho N\|\boldsymbol{\omega}\|_q^q$, where $\hat{\boldsymbol{y}} = \begin{bmatrix} \frac{n}{n_1}\mathbf{1}_{n_1} \\ -\frac{n}{n_2}\mathbf{1}_{n_2} \end{bmatrix} \in \mathbb{R}^N$ and $\tilde{K} = \begin{bmatrix} \mathbf{1}_N \ K \end{bmatrix} \in \mathbb{R}^{N\times(N+1)}$, giving:

$$\ell(\boldsymbol{\omega}) = -\frac{1}{2}\|\hat{\boldsymbol{y}} - \tilde{K}\boldsymbol{\omega}\|_2^2 - \rho N\|\boldsymbol{\omega}\|_q^q \tag{3}$$

It is clear that in the case of interest, $0 < q \leq 1$, no closed-form solution exists for the maximization of (3), however, by exploiting the fact that $-|\omega|^q$ is convex on $\mathbb{R}_+$ and $-|\omega|^q = -\left(\omega^2\right)^{\frac{q}{2}}$ it can be shown that $\ell_p(\boldsymbol{\omega})$ is minorized at every point, $\boldsymbol{\omega}(n)$, by a quadratic function thus:

$$\ell_p(\boldsymbol{\omega}) = -\rho N\|\boldsymbol{\omega}\|_q^q \geq -\frac{\rho}{2}N\sum_{i=1}^{i=d}\left(\frac{q\omega_i^2}{|\omega_i(n)|^{2-q}} + (2-q)|\omega_i(n)|^q\right) \tag{4}$$

$$= -\frac{\rho}{2}N\left(q\boldsymbol{\omega}^{\mathsf{T}}B\left(\boldsymbol{\omega}(n)\right)\boldsymbol{\omega} + (2-q)\|\boldsymbol{\omega}(n)\|_q^q\right)$$

with $B\left(\boldsymbol{\omega}(n)\right) = \operatorname{diag}\left\{|\omega_i(n)|^{q-2}\right\}$. The result arises from the relationship $g(x) \geq g(y) + dg(y)(x-y)\forall x, y$ e.g. [10] and is ascribed to [11]. The function, $\ell(\boldsymbol{\omega})$, in equation (3) is therefore minorized when the RHS is replaced by the upper bound given in (4) giving a quadratic surrogate having the ascent property:

$$S(\boldsymbol{\omega}|\boldsymbol{\omega}(n)) = \boldsymbol{\omega}^{\mathsf{T}}\tilde{K}^{\mathsf{T}}\hat{\boldsymbol{y}} - \frac{1}{2}\boldsymbol{\omega}^{\mathsf{T}}\left(\tilde{K}^{\mathsf{T}}\tilde{K} + \rho Nq B\left(\boldsymbol{\omega}(n)\right)\right)\boldsymbol{\omega}$$

(omitting constant terms), which can be maximized analytically w.r.t $\boldsymbol{\omega}$. Identifying $\boldsymbol{\omega}(n+1)$ with $\boldsymbol{\omega}$ and assuming $\boldsymbol{\omega}(0) \neq \mathbf{0}$ gives the following iteration

$$\boldsymbol{\omega}(n+1) = \left(\tilde{K}^{\mathsf{T}}\tilde{K} + \rho N q B\left(\boldsymbol{\omega}(n)\right)\right)^{-1} \tilde{K}^{\mathsf{T}}\hat{\boldsymbol{y}} \tag{5}$$

A potential problem arises when the elements of $\boldsymbol{\omega}(n)$ approach zero, as expected when a sparse solution arises and $S\left(\boldsymbol{\omega}|\boldsymbol{\omega}(n)\right)$ is no longer defined. Hunter and Li [9] deal with this formally but here we avoid the difficulty by re-writing $B\left(\boldsymbol{\omega}(n)\right) = \Psi_n^{-2}$ with $\Psi_n = \mathrm{diag}\left\{|\omega_i(n)|^{\frac{2-q}{2}}\right\}$ [12] leading to

$$\boldsymbol{\omega}(n+1) = \Psi_n \left(\Psi_n \tilde{K}^{\mathsf{T}}\tilde{K}\Psi_n + \rho N q I_N\right)^{-1} \Psi_n \tilde{K}^{\mathsf{T}}\hat{\boldsymbol{y}}; \boldsymbol{\omega}(0) \neq \mathbf{0} \tag{6}$$

Convergence is declared when the relative change in the norm of the coefficient vectors is less than some threshold, ϵ, and a coefficient is deemed to equal zero if its magnitude, relative to the largest, is less than η. We denote the resulting classifiers kFDA_q.

4   Performance Comparison with Previous Methods

To evaluate the performance of kFDA_q extensive experimentation has been carried out on 13 datasets (http://ida.first.fraunhofer.de/projects/bench/) that have been used to benchmark numerous machine learning techniques [3,4,13]. The methodology outlined in [4] was followed to allow direct comparisons with [3,4,13]. We examine two situations: classifiers are selected based on minimum misclassification rate (MCR) and on number of retained samples (NS) from amongst the first five realizations. Each is then applied to all 100 test partitions.

Table 1 shows percentage mean MCR and number of retained samples (below) calculated for the test sets for each of the 13 domains. We report kFDA_q for $q \in \{1, 0.5\}$, the better of the two methods proposed in [4] referred to as $\mathrm{kFDA}_{\mathrm{OLS}}$, and the current best results in [3,13]. From Table 1, the kFDA_1 classifier (selected on MCR) is more accurate than $\mathrm{kFDA}_{\mathrm{OLS}}$ and the best other reported technique across all 13 domains. However, its sparseness is relatively poor in 10 out of 13 cases. Choosing the kFDA_1 classifier for sparseness gives best MCR in 7 out of 13 cases and outperforms $\mathrm{kFDA}_{\mathrm{OLS}}$ in 9 out of 13. This gives comparable sparseness to $\mathrm{kFDA}_{\mathrm{OLS}}$ in many cases but is much worse in a few.

To encourage further sparseness, q is reduced to 0.5. Selecting on MCR, $\mathrm{kFDA}_{0.5}$ now exhibits highest accuracy in 8 out of 13 cases while achieving comparable sparseness with $\mathrm{kFDA}_{\mathrm{OLS}}$ (excepting "Splice"). In the other five cases performance is comparable with $\mathrm{kFDA}_{\mathrm{OLS}}$ but with greater levels of sparsity. Selecting for sparsity even simpler models are frequently found with no substantial loss of performance. Performance on "Splice" is now comparable, for instance.

While differences are not great, it is fair to say that kFDA_q offers convincingly competitive performance across a range of classification tasks.

Table 1. Comparison of mean misclassification rate and sparsity for the proposed algorithm, kFDA$_q$, kFDA$_{OLS}$ (★) [4], and the best algorithm from[3,13]: Support Vector Machine (▲), Regularized AdaBoost (▼), conventional kFDA (■), Sparse kFDA (□) and Sparse kFDA with Linear Loss (◇). Bold – best, italic – sample size.

Database	Published	kFDA$_{OLS}$	kFDA$_1$		kFDA$_{0.5}$	
	Best (%)	(%)	MCR (%)	NS (%)	MCR (%)	NS (%)
Banana	10.6±0.4	10.7±0.5	**9.74±0.00**	13.05±0.15	10.48±0.12	11.60±0.12
400	8.00 ◇	7.25	14.25	5.75	5.75	**2.25**
B. Cancer	25.2±4.4	25.3±4.1	21.21±3.71	25.55±4.05	**20.81±3.73**	25.35±4.02
200	12.00 □	3.50	11.00	2.00	4.00	**1.00**
Diabetes	23.1±1.8	23.1±1.8	**22.93±1.68**	24.04±1.71	23.96±1.69	25.50±1.89
468	2.14 ★	2.14	2.14	1.28	0.85	**0.43**
German	23.6±2.3	24.0±2.1	**19.38±1.87**	23.43±2.04	24.55±2.13	24.08±2.00
700	2.00 □	1.14	11.86	4.00	0.57	**0.43**
Heart	15.8±3.4	15.8±3.4	**14.63±3.36**	**14.63±3.36**	15.46±3.22	15.46±3.22
170	1.76 ★	1.76	4.71	4.71	**1.76**	**1.76**
Image	2.7±0.6	2.8±0.6	**1.10±0.56**	2.19±0.58	1.95±0.44	1.95±0.44
1300	100.00 ▼	21.54	46.15	22.46	**16.69**	**16.69**
Ringnorm	1.5±0.1	1.6±0.1	**1.41±0.03**	1.52±0.03	1.70±0.04	1.70±0.04
400	6.00 ◇	1.75	9.00	3.75	**1.00**	**1.00**
S. Flare	32.4±1.8	33.5±1.6	31.90±1.90	32.69±1.96	**31.07±1.88**	32.60±1.82
660	91.00 ▲	1.36	56.21	44.09	4.85	**2.27**
Splice	9.5±0.7	11.7±0.6	**7.03±0.79**	7.46±0.80	7.32±0.75	8.22±0.91
1000	100.00 ▼	33.00	78.20	64.40	72.90	34.70
Thyroid	4.2±2.1	4.5±2.4	2.88±1.59	3.72±1.54	**1.53±1.16**	3.83±1.77
140	100.00 ■	16.43	10.00	9.29	8.57	**1.43**
Titanic	22.4±1.0	22.4±1.0	**21.10±0.23**	22.09±0.24	**21.10±0.23**	22.72±0.26
150	7.33 ★	7.33	40.67	34.00	6.00	**1.33**
Twonorm	2.6±0.2	2.7±0.2	**2.32±0.00**	**2.32±0.00**	2.87±0.04	2.87±0.04
400	100.00 ■	2.50	3.75	3.75	**1.25**	**1.25**
Waveform	9.8±0.8	10.0±0.4	**9.46±0.13**	10.01±0.13	10.10±0.15	12.23±0.13
400	100.00 ▼	3.50	7.75	5.00	1.50	**0.75**

5 Application to Virtual Screening

Here 11 different activity classes – domains in which molecules have been assayed for activity – from the MDL Drug Data Report (MDDR) database are used [14]. The MDDR database contains 1,024-dimensional fingerprints representing 102,514 known drugs and biologically relevant molecules collected from patent literature, journals, meetings and congresses. The classes used here were selected to reflect typical drug discovery projects for pharmaceutical companies.

A "binomial" kernel is used, $k_{ij} = k\left(\boldsymbol{u}_i, \boldsymbol{u}_j\right) = \lambda^{m-d(\boldsymbol{u}_i,\boldsymbol{u}_j)} \left(1 - \lambda\right)^{d(\boldsymbol{u}_i,\boldsymbol{u}_j)}$ where $\lambda \in [0.5, 1.0]$ denotes the kernel "width" and $m = 1024$. $d\left(\boldsymbol{u}_i, \boldsymbol{u}_j\right)$ is a measure of the degree of dis-similarity between molecules i and j. In [7] the Jaccard/Tanimoto (J/T) distance was found to offer substantial gains over the conventional Hamming distance (HD) when used in BKD. Experiments show that this is also the case for kFDA$_q$ so only results using this function are reported. The experiment was run five times with different random data splits. λ is identified by five-fold cross validation on the basis of *sum of active rank position*, e.g. if all n_1 active compounds are ranked in the first n_1 positions, the rank sum is maximal.

Table 2. Comparison of maximum percentage actives retrieved in top 5% of sample

Index	Activity Class	Self-Similarity		BKD		kFDA$_1$	kFDA$_{0.5}$
		Mean	S.D.	HD (%)	J/T (%)	J/T (%)	J/T (%)
1	5HT3 Antagonists	0.351	0.116	90.19	**93.88**	91.32	90.61
	150					76.00	**57.87**
2	5HT1A Agonists	0.343	0.104	86.77	**88.28**	83.98	82.10
	166					66.87	**51.21**
3	5HTReuptake Inhibitors	0.345	0.122	69.47	**73.62**	64.89	65.08
	72					81.39	**71.67**
4	D2 Antagonists	0.345	0.103	74.25	**77.97**	70.25	68.34
	80					78.50	**59.00**
5	Renin Inhibitors	0.573	0.106	98.84	99.10	**99.25**	99.23
	226					53.63	**28.14**
6	Angiotensin II AT1 Antagonists	0.403	0.101	98.77	97.43	**99.27**	99.22
	190					55.16	**30.11**
7	Thrombin Inhibitors	0.419	0.127	**94.04**	94.02	93.77	92.74
	162					59.63	**41.11**
8	Substance P Antagonists	0.399	0.106	91.86	**93.70**	90.74	90.38
	250					62.16	**54.32**
9	HIV Protease Inhibitors	0.446	0.122	94.37	**94.70**	92.89	93.45
	150					54.53	**45.47**
10	Cyclo-oxygenase Inhibitors	0.268	0.093	68.43	**76.26**	65.52	63.11
	128					86.25	**71.09**
11	Protein Kinase C Inhibitors	0.323	0.142	78.92	**81.23**	71.16	62.95
	92					84.57	**39.57**

In table 2, the mean self-similarity provides a measure of the homogeneity of each of the activity classes and is a useful way to compare design spreads and coverage. It is usual in chemoinformatics applications to report the percentage of the maximum possible number of active compounds ranked in the top 5% of the ranked database. These are shown in Table 2 along with the percentage of retained features (below). Results from kFDA$_q$ and from BKD are presented. It is clear that BKD$_{J/T}$ is the leading contender in eight out of 11 cases but delivers no sparsity, while BKD$_{HD}$ is most accurate in one. As before, we see that kFDA$_1$ is generally more accurate (9/11) than kFDA$_{0.5}$ but is less sparse, as expected. However, kFDA$_q$ only displays best accuracy in two cases but is comparable ($< \pm 3\%$) to BKD$_{J/T}$ in four others. It is worth noting that kFDA$_q$ delivers its best accuracy in the classes that are most homogeneous.

6   Conclusion

We have introduced an algorithm for the solution of the kFDA problem through the application of the MM principle. We have demonstrated that it performs as well as or better than a number of leading machine learning algorithms in a substantial benchmark. We have then applied the method to a problem in chemoinformatics but found that performance is generally worse than an important recent development in this field, BKD. However, operationally, a sparse solution may still be of value since many commercial databases contain $\mathcal{O}\left(10^6\right)$ samples and speed of recall can be an issue. Given that, ultimately, both techniques rely on optimally chosen linear combinations of kernel functions, this failure seems puzzling. Qualitatively, there is a significant difference between the benchmark and the molecular data – the fingerprint samples suffer extremely from the small-sample-size problem and this fact may account for the drop in performance. This issue is to be addressed in the future.

Acknowledgments. Many thanks to thank Jerôme Hert for providing the self-similarity information and David Wood for preparing the MDDR data.

References

1. Duda, R.O., Hart, P.E.: Pattern Classification and Scene Analysis. John Wiley & Sons, New York (1973)
2. Schölkopf, B., Smola, A.: Learning with Kernels. MIT Press, Cambridge (2002)
3. Mika, S., Rätsch, G., Weston, J., Schölkopf, B., Smola, A., Müller, K.-R.: Constructing descriptive and discriminative nonlinear features: Rayleigh Coefficients in kernel feature spaces. IEEE T. Pattern Anal, vol. 25 (2003)
4. Billings, S.A., Lee, K.L.: Nonlinear fisher discriminant analysis using a minimum squared error cost function and the orthogonal least squares algorithm. Neural Networks 15, 263–270 (2002)
5. Leach, A., Gillet, V.: An Introduction to Chemoinformatics. Kluwer Academic Publishers, Dordrecht (2003)
6. Harper, G., Bradshaw, J., Gittins, J.C., Green, D., Leach, A.R.: Prediction of biological activity for high-throughput screening using binary kernel discrimination. J. Chem. Inf. Comp. Sci. 41, 1295–1300 (2001)
7. Chen, B., Harrison, R.F., Pasupa, K., Willett, P., Wilton, D.J., Wood, D.J., Lewell, X.Q.: Virtual screening using binary kernel discrimination: Effect of noisy training data and the optimization of performance. J. Chem. Inf. Mod. 46, 478–486 (2006)
8. Kiwiel, K.C.: An exact penalty function algorithm for non-smooth convex constrained minimization problems. IMA J. Numer. Anal. 5, 111–119 (1985)
9. Hunter, D.R., Li, R.: Variable selection using MM algorithms. Ann. Stat. 33, 1617–1642 (2005)
10. Lange, K., Hunter, D.R., Yang, I.: Optimization transfer using surrogate objective functions. J. Comput. Graph. Stat. 9, 1–59 (2000)
11. Dutter, R., Huber, P.J.: Numerical methods for the nonlinear robust regression problem. J. Stat. Comput. Sim. 13, 79–113 (1981)
12. Krishnapuram, B., Carin, L., Figueiredo, M.A., Hartemink, A.J.: Sparse multinomial logistic regression: fast algorithms and generalization bounds. IEEE T. Pattern Anal. 27, 957–968 (2005)
13. Rätsch, G., Onoda, T., Müller, K.-R.: Soft margins for AdaBoost. Mach. Learn. 42, 287–320 (2001)
14. MDL Information Systems Inc. The MDL Drug Data Report Database. http://www.mdli.com

Explicit Modelling of Invariances in Bernoulli Mixtures for Binary Images

Verónica Romero, Adrià Giménez, and Alfons Juan

Departament de Sistemes Informàtics i Computació
Universitat Politècnica de València
Camí de Vera s/n, 46022 València (Spain)
{vromero,agimenez,ajuan}@dsic.upv.es

Abstract. Bernoulli mixture models have been recently proposed as simple yet powerful probabilistic models for binary images in which each image pattern is modelled by a different Bernoulli prototype (component). A possible limitation of these models, however, is that usual geometric transformations of image patterns are not explicitly modelled and, therefore, each natural transformation of an image pattern has to be *independently* modelled using a different, *rigid* prototype. In this work, we propose a simple technique to make these rigid prototypes more flexible by explicit modelling of invariances to translation, scaling and rotation. Results are reported on a task of handwritten Indian digits recognition.

1 Introduction

Mixture modelling is a common approach for density estimation in pattern classification [1]. On the one hand, maximum likelihood estimation of mixture parameters can be reliably accomplished by the well-known *Expectation-Maximisation (EM)* algorithm [2]. On the other hand, mixtures are flexible enough for finding an appropriate tradeoff between model complexity an the amount of training data available. Usually, model complexity is controlled by varying the number of mixture components while keeping the same parametric form for all components.

Bernoulli mixture models are finite mixtures in which each component has a multivariate Bernoulli probability function. Although they are known for long time in pattern recognition [3], it has not been until recently that they have been proposed as simple yet powerful probabilistic models for many pattern recognition tasks. The only requirement for their application is to have data that can be adequately represented in binary form, such as words [4], text sentences [5] or binary images [6].

Here we will focus on the application of Bernoulli mixtures to binary images. This application is particularly interesting since Bernoulli prototypes can be visually analysed as grey images in which each grey represents the probability of the corresponding pixel to be white. Thus, after EM-based maximum likelihood estimation of a Bernoulli mixture from a collection of unlabelled samples, we may visually analyse each prototype learnt and check whether or not it corresponds

J. Martí et al. (Eds.): IbPRIA 2007, Part I, LNCS 4477, pp. 539–546, 2007.

to a different image pattern found in the data. This is exactly what we have recently done, class-by-class, in a task of handwritten Indian digits recognition [6]. After analysis of the results, we checked that many prototypes correspond to significantly different image patterns, but we also found that many prototypes are simply slightly distorted versions of other prototypes. In our view, this is a limitation of Bernoulli mixtures for binary images. That is, without explicit modelling of simple geometric distortions, each slightly distorted image pattern has to be *independently* modelled using a different, *rigid* prototype; the mixture model does not inform us about obvious dependencies between prototypes and the learning process becomes more difficult since each distorted image pattern has to be learnt from similarly distorted training samples.

In this work, we propose a simple technique to make Bernoulli prototypes more flexible by explicit modelling of invariances to translation, scaling and rotation. This is done on the basis of the usual EM-based maximum likelihood fitting of Bernoulli mixtures from binary data, which is reviewed in the next section. Then our proposed technique can be easily described, in section 3. In section 4, empirical results are reported on handwritten Indian digits recognition.

2   Bernoulli Mixtures for Binary Images

Finite mixtures are probability (density) functions of the form:

$$p_{\Theta}(\boldsymbol{x}) = \sum_{i=1}^{I} p_i \, p_{\Theta'}(\boldsymbol{x} \mid i) \,, \tag{1}$$

where I is the *number of mixture components* and, for each component i, p_i is its *prior or coefficient* and $p_{\Theta'}(\boldsymbol{x} \mid i)$ is its *component-conditional probability (density) function*. The mixture is governed by parameter vector Θ comprising the mixture coefficients and a parameter vector governing the components, Θ'. It can be seen as a generative model that first selects the ith component with probability p_i and then generates $\boldsymbol{x}$ in accordance with $p_{\Theta'}(\boldsymbol{x} \mid i)$.

A Bernoulli mixture model is a particular case of (1) in which each component i has a D-dimensional Bernoulli probability function governed by its own vector of parameters or *prototype* $\boldsymbol{p}_i = (p_{i1}, \ldots, p_{iD})^t \in [0,1]^D$,

$$p_{\Theta'}(\boldsymbol{x} \mid i) = \prod_{d=1}^{D} p_{id}^{x_d} \, (1 - p_{id})^{1-x_d} \,. \tag{2}$$

Note that this equation is just the product of independent, unidimensional Bernoulli probability functions. Therefore, for a fixed i, it can not capture any kind of dependencies or correlations between individual bits. Nevertheless, this drawback is overcome when several Bernoulli components are adequately mixed.

2.1   Bernoulli Mixture-Based Classifiers

As with other types of finite mixtures, Bernoulli mixtures can be used as class-conditional models in supervised classification tasks. Let C denote the number of supervised classes. Assume that, for each supervised class c, we know its prior $p(c)$ and its class-conditional probability function $p(\boldsymbol{x} \mid c)$, which is a mixture of I_c Bernoulli components,

$$p_{\boldsymbol{\Theta}_c}(\boldsymbol{x} \mid c) = \sum_{i=1}^{I_c} p_{ci}\, p_{\boldsymbol{\Theta}'_c}(\boldsymbol{x} \mid c, i)\,, \tag{3}$$

where $\boldsymbol{\Theta}_c = (p_{c1}, \ldots, p_{cI_c}; \boldsymbol{\Theta}'_c)$. Then, the optimal Bayes decision rule is to assign each pattern vector $\boldsymbol{x}$ to a class giving maximum a posteriori probability or, equivalently,

$$c_{\boldsymbol{\vartheta}}(\boldsymbol{x}) = \arg\max_c \ \log p(c) + \log p_{\boldsymbol{\Theta}_c}(\boldsymbol{x} \mid c) \tag{4}$$

$$= \arg\max_c \ \log p(c) + \log \sum_{i=1}^{I_c} p_{ci}\, p_{\boldsymbol{\Theta}'_c}(\boldsymbol{x} \mid c, i)\,, \tag{5}$$

where $\boldsymbol{\vartheta} = (p(1), \ldots, p(C); \boldsymbol{\Theta}_1, \ldots, \boldsymbol{\Theta}_C)$.

Figure 1 (left) shows a simple example of binary image classification task. Two classes of boats are considered which only differ in the relative position of their two masts of different lengths. While boats of class 1 have the tall mast in the stern area, those of class 2 have it towards the bow.

Since boats can appear in both ahead or astern directions, when the boat silhouette images are seen as raw collections of binary pixels, only subtle pixel correlations can help distinguish both classes. For class 1, if black pixels are found in the image zone A (Figure 1, right), zone B should also be black and zones C and D should be white, while if black pixels are found in zone D, then zone C should be black and both zones A and B should be white. Similar, but opposite, pixel correlations hold for images of class 2. Although these subtle dependencies can by no means be captured by a single multivariate Bernoulli model for each class, they can be properly modelled by a two-component mixture per class which, in this simple case, is enough for perfect classification.

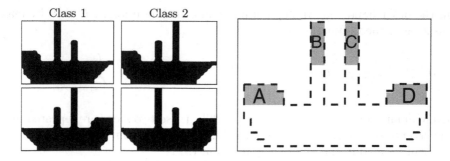

Fig. 1. Left: Samples of boats from two classes. Right: Image zones of interest.

2.2 EM-Based Maximum Likelihood Estimation

Let $(\boldsymbol{x}_1, c_1), \ldots, (\boldsymbol{x}_N, c_N)$ be a collection of samples randomly drawn from class-conditional Bernoulli mixtures of known number of components but unknown coefficients and prototypes. Assuming that class priors are also unknown, let $\boldsymbol{\vartheta} = (p(1), \ldots, p(C); \boldsymbol{\Theta}_1, \ldots, \boldsymbol{\Theta}_C)$ denote the vector of unknown parameters. The likelihood of $\boldsymbol{\vartheta}$ with respect to the data is

$$L(\boldsymbol{\vartheta}) = \prod_{n=1}^{N} \left[p(c_n) \sum_{i=1}^{I_{c_n}} p_{c_n i}\, p_{\boldsymbol{\Theta}'_{c_n}}(\boldsymbol{x}_n \mid c_n, i) \right], \qquad (6)$$

which can be rewritten as

$$L(\boldsymbol{\vartheta}) = \sum_{\boldsymbol{z}_1, \ldots, \boldsymbol{z}_N} \mathcal{L}(\boldsymbol{\vartheta}), \qquad (7)$$

where $\boldsymbol{z}_n \in \{0, 1\}^{I_{c_n}}$ is a *missing label* that has 1 in the position corresponding to the component generating $\boldsymbol{x}_n$ and zeros elsewhere, $n = 1, \ldots, N$; and

$$\mathcal{L}(\boldsymbol{\vartheta}) = \prod_{n=1}^{N} \left[p(c_n) \prod_{i=1}^{I_{c_n}} \left(p_{c_n i}\, p_{\boldsymbol{\Theta}'_{c_n}}(\boldsymbol{x}_n \mid c_n, i) \right)^{z_{ni}} \right], \qquad (8)$$

which is commonly referred to as the *complete* likelihood since it includes both, the observed (incomplete) and missing data.

The EM algorithm maximises (6) iteratively, through the application of two basic steps in each iteration: the E(xpectation) step and the M(aximisation) step. On the one hand, the E step computes, for all $\boldsymbol{\vartheta}$, the expectation of the logarithm of the complete likelihood, conditional to the incomplete data and a current estimation of the parameters, $\boldsymbol{\vartheta}^{(k)}$; i.e., the so-called Q function,

$$Q(\boldsymbol{\vartheta} \mid \boldsymbol{\vartheta}^{(k)}) = E[\log \mathcal{L}(\boldsymbol{\vartheta}) \mid (\boldsymbol{x}_1, c_1), \ldots, (\boldsymbol{x}_N, c_N), \boldsymbol{\vartheta}^{(k)}]. \qquad (9)$$

On the other hand, the M step obtains a new estimate for $\boldsymbol{\vartheta}$, $\boldsymbol{\vartheta}^{(k+1)}$, by maximisation of the Q function,

$$\boldsymbol{\vartheta}^{(k+1)} = \arg\max_{\boldsymbol{\vartheta}} Q(\boldsymbol{\vartheta} \mid \boldsymbol{\vartheta}^{(k)}) \ \text{s.t.} \ \sum_{c} p(c) = 1 \ \text{and,} \ \forall c, \ \sum_{i=1}^{I_c} p_{ci} = 1. \qquad (10)$$

Given an initial value of the parameters, $\boldsymbol{\vartheta}^{(0)}$, these two steps are repeated until convergence to a local maximum of the likelihood function.

It can be readily checked that Q function (9) is

$$Q(\boldsymbol{\vartheta} \mid \boldsymbol{\vartheta}^{(k)}) = \sum_{n} \log p(c_n) + \sum_{i=1}^{I_{c_n}} z_{ni}^{(k)} (\log(p_{c_n i} + \log p_{\boldsymbol{\Theta}'_{c_n}}(\boldsymbol{x}_n \mid c_n, i)), \qquad (11)$$

where $z_{ni}^{(k)}$ is the posterior probability of $\boldsymbol{x}_n$ being actually generated by the ith component of the c_nth mixture,

$$z_{ni}^{(k)} = \frac{p_{c_n i}^{(k)} P_{\Theta_{c_n}'^{(k)}}(\boldsymbol{x}_n \mid c_n, i)}{\displaystyle\sum_{i'=1}^{I_{c_n}} p_{c_n i'}^{(k)} P_{\Theta_{c_n}'^{(k)}}(\boldsymbol{x}_n \mid c_n, i')} . \tag{12}$$

Maximisation of (11), as indicated in (10), leads to the following re-estimates for each class c $(c = 1, \ldots, C)$ and each component i $(i = 1, \ldots, I_c)$,

$$p(c)^{(k+1)} = \hat{p}(c) = \frac{N_c}{N} , \tag{13}$$

$$p_{ci}^{(k+1)} = \frac{1}{N_c} \sum_{n:c_n=c} z_{ni}^{(k)} , \tag{14}$$

$$\boldsymbol{p}_{ci}^{(k+1)} = \frac{\displaystyle\sum_{n:c_n=c} z_{ni}^{(k)} \boldsymbol{x}_n}{\displaystyle\sum_{n:c_n=c} z_{ni}^{(k)}} , \tag{15}$$

where N_c is the number of samples from class c. Note that coefficients and prototypes of each mixture are computed from data of its own class exclusively; $p_{ci}^{(k+1)}$ is the average posterior probability for a sample from class c to have been generated from component i of the cth mixture, while $\boldsymbol{p}_{ci}^{(k+1)}$ is a posterior probability-weighted average over data from class c.

3   Explicit Modelling of Invariances

As discussed in the introduction, the lack of explicit modelling of invariances in Bernoulli mixtures is a limitation we try to overcome. To begin with, in this work we only propose a minor variation on the conventional model described in the previous section. The basic idea is to distort each prototype with as many transformations as desired, and include a new prototype for each transformation which will be linked bit-by-bit to its source prototype. This bit-by-bit link makes distorted prototypes *virtual*, as opposed to source, *real* prototypes, in the sense that they do not add extra parameters to the model. Moreover, as will be seen shortly, this simple one-to-one (bit-by-bit) parameter dependency leads to parameter re-estimation equations that are similar to those of the conventional model. In terms of number of parameters, the only difference is that we need an extra mixture coefficient for each virtual prototype.

Formally, most of what we said about the conventional model in the preceding section is still valid. It suffices to replace each prototype index i by a pair it, to denote the tth transformation applied to the ith prototype. As source prototypes themselves can be considered as distorted by the identity transformation, we use $t = 0$ (the identity transformation) to refer to them. Let T_{ci} denote the total number of transformations applied to the ith prototype from mixture c; thus, given c and i, $t = 0, 1, \ldots, T_{ci}$. Then, the bit-by-bit link between the the ith source prototype and its tth transformation is assumed to be given as a *linking indicator variable*

$$l_{citdd'} = \begin{cases} 1 & \text{if } p_{citd} = p_{ci0d'} \\ 0 & \text{otherwise} \end{cases}, \tag{16}$$

where p_{citd} is the bit number d of the ith prototype from the cth mixture, distorted by the tth transformation; thus, $l_{citdd'}$ says whether or not this bit is linked to bit d' of its corresponding prototype. Obviously, for $t = 0$, $l_{citdd'} = 1$ if $d = d'$; 0 otherwise. Figure 2 shows an example of linking.

$t = 0$
1 2 3 4 5
6 7 8 9 10
11 12 13 14 15
16 17 18 19 20
21 22 23 24 25

$t = 1$
6 7 2
16 12 7 8 4
17 17 13 9 9
22 18 19 14 10
24 19 20

$t = 2$
7 8 8 9 9
12 13 13 14 14
12 13 13 14 14
17 18 18 19 19
17 18 18 19 19

$t = 3$
2 3 4 5
7 8 9 10
12 13 14 15
17 18 19 20
22 23 24 25

$t = 4$
7 7 8 8
13 13 9 9
13 13 9 9
19 19 13 13
19 19 13 13

Fig. 2. Example of linking for a given mixture and prototype, showing 5 transformations of a 25-dimensional, 5×5 source image prototype. Image pixels are read from the top-left ($d = 1$) to the bottom-right ($d = 25$) corners; each number refers to the source pixel number d' to which it is linked (non-numbered image pixels have no link and are assumed to be white). From left to right: $t = 0$) identity, $t = 1$) 45° rotation, $t = 2$) 200% scaling, $t = 3$) (-1,0) translation, and $t = 4$) all of them together.

The EM algorithm for invariant Bernoulli mixtures is very similar to that of the conventional case. The E step is a t-dependent version of (12),

$$z_{nit}^{(k)} = \frac{p_{c_n it}^{(k)} \, P_{\Theta_{c_n}^{'(k)}}(\boldsymbol{x}_n \mid c_n, it)}{\displaystyle\sum_{i'=1}^{I_{c_n}} \sum_{t'=0}^{T_{c_n i'}} p_{c_n i't'}^{(k)} \, P_{\Theta_{c_n}^{'(k)}}(\boldsymbol{x}_n \mid c_n, i't')}. \tag{17}$$

The M step includes (13), the following t-dependent version of (14),

$$p_{cit}^{(k+1)} = \frac{1}{N_c} \sum_{n:c_n=c} z_{nit}^{(k)}, \tag{18}$$

and the following re-estimate for bit d' of the ith prototype from mixture c:

$$p_{ci0d'}^{(k+1)} = \frac{\displaystyle\sum_{n:c_n=c} \sum_{t=0}^{T_{ci}} z_{nit}^{(k)} \sum_{d} l_{citdd'} \, x_{nd}}{\displaystyle\sum_{n:c_n=c} \sum_{t=0}^{T_{ci}} z_{nit}^{(k)} \sum_{d} l_{citdd'}}, \tag{19}$$

which takes into account each transformation t and bit d linked to source bit d'. It reduces to (a bit d' version of) (15) when only $t = 0$ is considered.

The time complexity of the invariant algorithm equals that of the conventional algorithm applied to a mixture of all real and virtual prototypes.

4   Experiments

In the experiments carried out we consider an OCR task consisting in the recognition of Indian digits, extracted from *courtesy amounts* of real bank drafts. We have used the 10425 samples included in the non-touching part of the *Indian digits database* recently provided by CENPARMI [7].

Original digit samples are given as binary images of different sizes (minimal bounding boxes). Since a Bernoulli classifier for binary images requires the images to be represented as binary bit vectors of fixed dimension, a normalisation process was carried out. First, each digit image was pasted onto a square background whose centre was aligned with the digit centre of mass. This square background was a white image large enough (64×64) to accommodate most samples though, in some cases, larger background images were required. Second, given a size S, each digit image was subsampled into $S \times S$ pixels, from which its corresponding binary vector of dimension $D = S^2$ was built. In Figure 3 we can see examples of each Indian digit for $S = 30$.

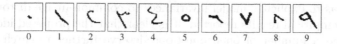

Fig. 3. 30×30 examples of each Indian digit

The standard experimental procedure for classification error rate estimation in the CENPARMI Indian digits task is a simple partition with 7390 samples for training and 3035 for testing (excluding the extra classes delimiter and comma). Figure 4 shows the average error of the I-component Bernoulli mixture, with explicit modelling of invariances, tested on the data subsampled at 20×20,

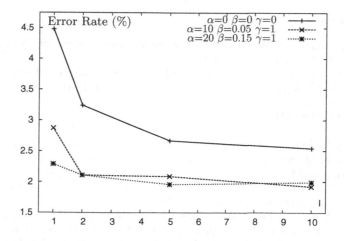

Fig. 4. Classification error rate as a function of the number of mixture components in each class (I), for several different sets of transformations

for $I \in 1, 2, 5, 10$ and several transformations. The transformations taken into account have been rotation, scaling and translation. The set of rotation angles is defined by the parameter α as $\{-\alpha + i \cdot \triangle\alpha : 0 \leq i \leq \frac{2}{\triangle\alpha}\alpha\}$ with $\triangle\alpha = 5$. The set of scale percentages is defined by the parameter β as $\{1 - \beta + i \cdot \triangle\beta : 0 \leq i \leq \frac{2}{\triangle\beta}\beta\}$ with $\triangle\beta = 0.05$. The set of translations is defined by the parameter γ as $\{(-\gamma + i, -\gamma + j) : 0 \leq i \leq 2\gamma, 0 \leq j \leq 2\gamma\}$. For simplicity, we did not use classifiers with class-conditional mixtures of different number of components, i.e. an I-component classifier means that a mixture of $I_c = I$ Bernoulli components was trained for each digit c. In the same way the number of transformations considered is the same in all mixture components.

From the results in Figure 4, it becomes clear that explicit modelling of invariances outperforms the conventional model (α=0 β=0 γ=0). Note also that, in the range of tested values for I, the error rate curves decrease as I increases.

5   Conclusions and Future Work

In this work, a simple variation on Bernoulli mixtures for binary images has been proposed so as to explicitly model invariances to common image distortions.

From the empirical results reported, it is clear that the proposed idea is very promising and a number of open questions deserve further research work. In particular, a very important issue is model selection. Apart from deciding on the number of components, now we also have to decide on which transformations to apply and in which order. Other issues are: other data sets, better evaluation methods (leaving-one-out), other image distortions, fast implementations, etc.

Acknowledgements. Work supported by the EC (FEDER), the Spanish MEC (TIN2006-15694-CO2-01 and AP2005-1840 grants), the Valencian Conselleria d'EUiC (GV06/252 grant) and the Polytech. Univ. of Valencia (FPI grant).

References

1. Jain, A.K., Duin, R.P.W., Mao, J.: Statistical Pattern Recognition: A Review. IEEE Trans. on PAMI 22(1), 4–37 (2000)
2. Dempster, A.P., Laird, N.M., Rubin, D.B.: Maximum likelihood from incomplete data via the EM algorithm (with discussion). Journal of the Royal Statistical Society B. 39, 1–38 (1977)
3. Duda, R.O., Hart, P.E.: Pattern Classification and Scene Analysis. Wiley, Chichester (1973)
4. González, J., Juan, A., Dupont, P., Vidal, E., Casacuberta, F.: A Bernoulli mixture model for word categorisation. In: Proc. of the IX Spanish Symposium on Pattern Recognition and Image Analysis. vol. I, Benicàssim (Spain), pp. 165–170 (2001)
5. Juan, A., Vidal, E.: On the use of Bernoulli mixture models for text classification. Pattern Recognition 35(12), 2705–2710 (2002)
6. Juan, A., Vidal, E.: Bernoulli mixture models for binary images. In: Proc. of the 17th Int. Conf. on Pattern Recognition (ICPR 2004), Cambridge (UK) (2004)
7. Al-Ohali, Y., Cheriet, M., Suen, C.: Databases for recognition of handwritten Arabic cheques. Pattern Recognition 36, 111–121 (2003)

Computer Vision Approaches to Pedestrian Detection: Visible Spectrum Survey

David Gerónimo, Antonio López, and Angel D. Sappa

Computer Vision Center, Universitat Autònoma de Barcelona
Edifici O, 08193 Bellaterra, Barcelona, Spain
{dgeronimo,antonio,asappa}@cvc.uab.es
www.cvc.uab.es/adas

Abstract. Pedestrian detection from images of the visible spectrum is a high relevant area of research given its potential impact in the design of pedestrian protection systems. There are many proposals in the literature but they lack a comparative viewpoint. According to this, in this paper we first propose a common framework where we fit the different approaches, and second we use this framework to provide a comparative point of view of the details of such different approaches, pointing out also the main challenges to be solved in the future. In summary, we expect this survey to be useful for both novel and experienced researchers in the field. In the first case, as a clarifying snapshot of the state of the art; in the second, as a way to unveil trends and to take conclusions from the comparative study.

1 Introduction

Pedestrian accidents are the second source of traffic injuries and fatalities in the European Union. In this sense, advanced driver assistance systems (ADAS), and specifically pedestrian protection systems (PPS), have become an important field of research to improve traffic safety. Of course, in order to avoid collisions with pedestrians they must be detected, being camera sensors key due to the rich amount of cues and high resolution they provide.

Currently there are two main lines of work, one based on images of the visible spectrum, and the other, mainly motivated by nighttime, based on thermal infrared. The former has accumulated more literature because the easier availability of either CCD or CMOS sensors working in the visible spectrum, their cheaper price, better signal–to–noise ratio and resolution, and because most of the accidents happen at daytime. Therefore, we restrict the discussion presented in this paper to works based on images of the visible spectrum.

In this context, difficulties of the pedestrian detection task for PPS arise both from working with a mobile platform in an outdoor scenario, recurrent challenge in all ADAS applications, and from dealing with a so aspect–changing class like pedestrians. Difficulties can be summarized in the followings: *(a)* targets have a very high intra–class variability; *(b)* background can be cluttered and changes in milliseconds; *(c)* targets and camera usually follow different unknown

J. Martí et al. (Eds.): IbPRIA 2007, Part I, LNCS 4477, pp. 547–554, 2007.

movements; and *(d)* fast system reaction together with a very robust response is required.

The high social relevance of PPS and the above mentioned difficulties have given rise to a number of works. However, due to the lack of common datasets for validation and the complexity of the different proposals, most of the papers present their own approach without comparison with others. Thus, a *comparative review* is of high relevance both for novel and experienced researchers in the field. In this paper, a survey of works with images of the visible spectrum is presented.

Addressing such a review just by summarizing the most relevant papers one by one in isolation would make difficult the comparative viewpoint. Thus, we propose first (Sect. 2) a common framework (i.e., a system architecture) in which the main works of the literature are fitted. This framework is based on the main subtasks of the pedestrian detection for PPS, then we will use it also for providing a critical overview of the described techniques together with the main challenges for the future (Sect. 3). Finally, conclusions are presented in Sect. 4.

2   Proposed Architecture and Literature Review

Figure 1 presents an architecture of modules used in the sequel as common framework to review the literature. This architecture–based review is summarized in Table 1 from the viewpoint of each individual work, while Table 2 provides some relevant details of the previous systems. Although the PPS architecture has six modules here we focus only on the most active ones due to the lack of space: Foreground Segmentation, Object Classification, Verification/Refinement and Tracking. Refer to Fig. 1 to see each module's responsibility.

2.1   Foreground Segmentation

Binocular Stereo. The use of stereo in this module aims to provide 2D ROIs corresponding to 3D vertical objects fitting some pedestrian size constraints (PSC). *Gavrila et al.* [1] scan the depth map with PSC–sized ROIs laying in the assumed ground plane. A ROI is accepted if its depth distribution agrees with the expected. *Zhao et al.* [2] apply thresholding, morphological operations and blob analysis to the depth map, selecting remaining PSC–sized blob bounding boxes. *Broggi et al.* [3] use the v–disparity [4] to distinguish between ground, background and vertical objects in the scene.

Rough Appearance. These are 2D approaches. In several works [5,3] by *Broggi et al.* vertical symmetry, derived from grey level and vertical gradient magnitude, is used to select PSC–sized ROIs around each relevant symmetry axis. *Shashua et al.* [6] select PSC–sized ROIs with an expected texture.

2.2   Object Classification

All found approaches fitting object classification are purely 2D, thus they only use the 2D information of the ROIs provided by the foreground segmentation.

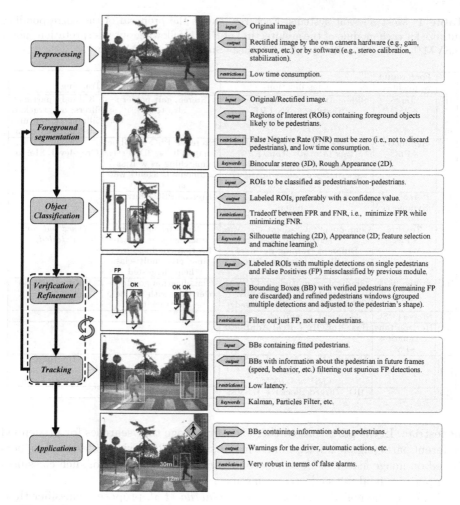

Fig. 1. Proposed module–based architecture and responsibility of each module

Silhouette Matching. In [5] a ROI is considered as containing a pedestrian if there is a good matching with a head–shoulders like binary pattern. A more sophisticated technique is the *Chamfer system* [1,7] by *Gavrila et al.*, where a distance transform of the ROI is calculated and used for a coarse–to–fine template matching in a space of pedestrian shapes hierarchically organized.

Appearance. The methods included here start by defining a space of image features, and then learning a classifier by using ROIs containing examples (pedestrians) and counter–examples (non–pedestrians). A common detail is to normalize the size and aspect ratio of the incoming ROIs, as well as discarding color information (because the variability of clothes).

Two approaches can be found: holistic or parts–based. In the holistic approach a classifier uses different image features to determine if a ROI contains a full

Table 1. Most relevant systems. Each row shows the proposal of the corresponding authors for each module of the architecture of Fig. 1, following our interpretation (note: Q.SVM/L.SVM states for Quadratic/Linear Support Vector Machine).

	Foreground Segmentat.	Object Classification	Verification/ Refinement	Tracking
[1] [7] [8] [9]	Stereo +PSC	Silhouette + Chamfer System Texture + NN-LRF	Stereo, gait pattern also tested	Kalman; particle filters; α-β tracker. Silhouette, texture, stereo, CAN data
[10]	Symmetry +PSC	(here another possibility was to think about PSC as segmentation and symmetry as classification)	Stereo + PSC + adhoc image filters, 3D curves matching as well as autonomous agents were also tested	Kalman. Grey-level, Stereo.
[5] [3]	Stereo (v-d) Symmetry +PSC	Silhouette of head and shoulders	Stereo+PSC+entropy	
[6]	Texture +PSC	Components: Gradient Or.*Mag + RR-AdaBoost Different training per pose and illumination conditions	Multi frame after tracking: gait, classi- fication goodness over time, etc., multi-class help suggested	(used but not detailed)
[11]	Stereo (v-d)	Gradient magnitude + Q.SVM Different training per pose (Front/Rear or Side viewed)	Classification goodness over time with the help of tracking	Kalman. Stereo
[2]	Stereo+PSC	Gradient magnitude + NN		
[12]	Horizon Line estimation +PSC	Haar + EOH + Real AdaBoost		
[13] [14]		Holistic: Basic Haar + Q.SVM Parts–based: Basic Haar + Q.SVM-L.SVM		Heuristic integration through time
[15]		HOG/Fixed Blocks + L.SVM		

pedestrian. In the parts–based, there is a first stage that searches for predefined different parts (e.g., head, legs and arms) inside of a ROI using different classifiers based on image features. Next, a second stage uses the output of such classifiers as input of a final full pedestrian classifier.

Following the holistic approach, in [1] *Gavrila et al.* propose a classifier that, for the ROIs preclassified as pedestrian for the Chamfer System, uses texture as feature and learning with a Neural Network of Local Receptive Fields (NNLRF, further study in [8]). In [2], the feature used by *Zhao et al.* is gradient magnitude, and a three–layer Feed Forward Neural Network (FFNN) is the learning machine. In [13] a preestablished set of Haar wavelets is used by *Papageorgiou et al.* as features to learn a classifier for front/rear viewed pedestrians with a quadratic Support Vector Machine (SVM). *Dalal and Triggs* [15] present a human classification algorithm that uses Histograms of Oriented Gradients (HOG) as features and a linear SVM as learning method. In order to obtain a classifier for front, rear and side viewed pedestrians *Gerónimo et al.* [12] use a Real AdaBoost learning method to select the best features among a set of Haar wavelets and Edge Orientation Histograms (EOH) that cover all possible scales of a ROI.

Haar wavelets are also used by *Mohan et al.* in a parts–based classification [14]. In this case, each ROI is divided in four parts (head, legs, right and left arms), and for each part a classifier is learned using a quadratic SVM. Then, the final

Table 2. Details of the most relevant classifier based approaches. (DR: Detection Rate, FPR: False Positive Rate, FPPW: False Positives Per Window, n/a: information not available/applicable). Note that training and testing sets are different in each system.

	Learning ROI size	Classifier Train Set	Classifier Test Set	Classifier Performance	System Test Set	System Performance	Detection Range
[1] [7] [8] [9]	(Chamfer) 70–102 pix wide (NN-LRF) 18 × 36	(Chamfer) 1,250pos (NN-LRF) 14,400 pos 15,000 neg	(Chamfer) 900 images (NN-LRF) 9,600 pos 10,000 neg	(Chamfer) 60–90% DR n/a FPR (NN-LRF) 90% DR 10% FPR	24 min driving	(all) 52–76% DR 30% precision (risky) 80–90% DR 75% precision	5–25m
[6]	12 × 36	25,000 pos 25,000 neg	15,244 in total	93.5% DR 8% FPR	5hr driving	(inward moving) 96%DR, 1FPPW (statio. inpath) 93%DR, 3FPPW (statio. outpath) 85%DR,102FPPW	3–25m
[11]	–	1,500 pos 20,000 neg	150 pos 2,000 neg	75% DR 2% FPR	2,500frame (14 pedest.)	83.5% DR 0.4% FPR	up to 30m
[2]	30 × 65	1,012 pos 4,306 neg	254 pos 363 neg	85.4% DR 0.05 % FPR	FGS ROIs	85.2% DR 3.1% FPPW	n/a
[12]	no downscale	700 pos 4,000 neg	300 pos 1,000 neg	90% DR 1% FPR	n/a	n/a	5–50m
[13]	64 × 128	1,848 pos 11,361 neg	123 images scan	(color) 93% DR 0.1% FPPW (grayscale) 83% DR 0.1% FPPW	n/a	n/a	n/a
[14]	64 × 128	889 pos 3,106 neg	12 images scan	96% DR 10^{-4}% FPPW	n/a	n/a	n/a
[15]	64 × 128	2,478 pos 12,180 neg	images scan	85% DR 10^{-4}% FPPW	n/a	n/a	n/a

ROI classification combines the parts–classifiers responses by using a linear SVM. In [6] *Shashua et al.* use thirteen overlapping parts described by SIFT inspired features and ridge regression (RR) to learn the classifier of each part. Moreover, to deal with the high intra–class variability, the training set is divided in nine clusters according to pose and illumination conditions, thus getting $9 \times 13 = 117$ classifiers. The outputs of the 117 classifiers are fed as *weak rules* to an AdaBoost machine that sets the final classification rule.

2.3   Verification/Refinement

In many systems, the methods used in this module take advantage of previously exploited techniques. For instance, in [1], a cross–correlation using the left image and the isolated silhouette computed by the Chamfer System in the right image is used to refine the location of the pedestrian. In [9], the authors suggest to analyse the gait pattern for pedestrians crossing perpendicular to the camera. In this case, the target must be tracked before applying this method, thus verification/refinement and tracking modules are interchanged (Fig. 1). In [5], the head and shoulders silhouette matched during classification is taken as reference to refine the detection until the feet by making use of the vertical edges computed for the symmetry detection. Additionally, since no stereo reasoning is done in the segmentation module, refinement can be improved by this cue.

In [6], *Shashua et al.* propose a *multi–frame approval process*, which consists in validating the pedestrian–classified ROIs by collecting information from several frames: gait pattern, inward motion, confidence of the single–frame classification, etc. In this case, verification comes after tracking too.

2.4   Tracking

Kalman filter is the most used technique for tracking. Two examples are [10], where a Kalman–filter tracker is used to reject spurious detections as well as computing the trajectory of the pedestrian. In [11], Kalman filters are used to maintain pedestrian estimates and Bayesian probability to provide an estimate of pedestrian classification certainty over time and a targets' trajectory and speed.

3   Discussion

In spite of the high number of works in the field and the clear progress achieved, pedestrian detection is still an open area of research. The difficulties this problem carries are so wide that the methods exploited in each module must still improve their robustness before expecting convincing results for the complete system. Next, some discussion is made at each stage of the proposed architecture in order to emphasize the strengths and weaknesses of the described techniques.

Foreground segmentation based on stereo has several advantages: 1) robustness to illumination changes; 2) the provided distances are useful to determine ROIs at the foreground segmentation itself, for tracking and as associated information of the detected pedestrians; 3) stereo information can be shared by different ADAS applications. The main drawbacks come from the high computation time needed to extract depth (considerable improvements are being achieved in this matter [16]) and the problems of the technique when uniform areas appear. Despite these problems, stereo is a very reliable technique. Rough–appearance is not so promising. [6] claims to select just 75 ROIs per frame, but details about the technique are not provided. Moreover, works exploiting vertical symmetry [5,3] tend to be supported by stereo information, so we guess that symmetry alone is not sufficient.

Referring to object classification, it seems clear that silhouette matching methods are not applicable in a stand–alone fashion. Even the very elaborated Chamfer System needs an extra step that follows the appearance–based classification idea. On the other hand, appearance–based seem to be a promising line of research, nowadays still being explored in computer vision. However, despite the improvements in generalization achieved with SVM or AdaBoost, and the more and more faster–to–extract and meaningful features presented in recent years (e.g., Haar, HOG, EOH, etc.), there is still much work to do.

Next we illustrate this with a simple example inspired by [17]. Let us assume 10,000 ROIs per image by using PSC to be classified by the best classifier in the

PPS literature, i.e., a 95% Detection Rate at 0.1% FPR [6] (a full scan would imply at least one million of ROIs for a 640 × 480 image). This means that if 95% of pedestrians have to be detected, then in the worse scenario we could have about 1,000 FP per image, i.e., 25,000 FP per second at 25 fps. Thanks to additional procedures like foreground segmentation or detection clustering, we can assume that this number can be reduced to only 75 ROIs to check *per* frame as suggested in [6], but still this would represent 187.5 FP/s. A tracking module could filter out spurious and not coherent detections to reduce the final number to, say, 1 FP/s. Anyway, even 1 FP/s (i.e., 60 FP/minute) is still useless for a PPS. From this example we see the importance of improving all the system modules, specially the classification rate.

As can be noticed, state–of–the–art classifiers like the HOG–based [15] still need a verification and refinement step. Two points can be highlighted from the this module. First, stereo information tends to be used as long as the classification has been based on the 2D image. However, it is unclear for us why some works do not exploit this 3D information during the foreground segmentation. Second, using verification after tracking seems to be an interesting approach since common movement–based techniques (e.g., gait pattern analysis) used in surveillance could be applied. This

Up to now, the tracking module in PPS has not received as much attention as other modules like segmentation or classification. Each paper has its own proposal and no comparisons have been made. It is clear that tracking could provide useful information for other modules (e.g., trajectory information for applications, potential ROIs for segmentation, etc.).

4   Conclusions

We have presented a review of on–board pedestrian detection works based on images of the visible spectrum. A general module–based architecture is proposed so the reviewed techniques can be fitted and compared according to their objectives and responsibilities in the system, thus providing an comparative snapshot the state of the art. Regarding the future trends, it can be said that object classification is subject to the most active and fruitful research. However, as can be appreciated, the absence of comparisons with common benchmarks and the constant improvement of learning algorithms and features make it hard to state which is the best approach. Finally, it is worth to say in order to achieve commercial performance (e.g., detection rates and timings), the other modules must also be further developed. In this sense, sensors fusion (e.g., visible spectrum cameras with radar) seem to be a promising approach.

Acknowledgments. This work was supported by the Spanish Ministry of Education and Science under project TRA2004-06702/AUT, BES-2005-8864 grant (first author) and Ramón y Cajal Program (third author).

References

1. Gavrila, D., Giebel, J., Munder, S.: Vision–based pedestrian detection: The PRO-TECTOR system. In: IV, Parma, Italy (2004)
2. Zhao, L., Thorpe, C.: Stereo and neural network–based pedestrian detection. TITS 1(3), 148–154 (2000)
3. Broggi, A., Fascioli, A., Fedriga, I., Tibaldi, A., Del Rose, M.: Stereo–based pre-processing for human shape localization in unstructured environments. In: IV, Columbus, OH, USA, pp. 410–415 (2003)
4. Labayrade, R., Aubert, D., Tarel, J.: Real time obstacle detection in stereovision on non flat road geometry through v–disparity representation. In: IV, Versailles, France (2002)
5. Broggi, A., Bertozzi, M., Fascioli, A., Sechi, M.: Shape–based pedestrian detection. In: IV, Dearborn, MI, USA (2000)
6. Shashua, A., Gdalyahu, Y., Hayun, G.: Pedestrian detection for driving assistance systems: single–frame classification and system level performance. In: IV, Parma, Italy (2004)
7. Gavrila, D.: Pedestrian detection from a moving vehicle. In: ECCV. vol. 2. Dublin, Ireland, pp. 37–49 (2000)
8. Munder, S., Gavrila, D.: An experimental study on pedestrian classification. TPAMI 21(11), 1863–1868 (2006)
9. Franke, U., Gavrila, D.: Autonomous driving goes downtown. IS 13(6), 40–48 (1999)
10. Bertozzi, M., Broggi, A., Fascioli, A., Tibaldi, A., Chapuis, R., Chausse, A.: Pedestrian localization and tracking system with Kalman filtering. In: IV, Parma, Italy, pp. 584–589 (2004)
11. Grubb, G., Zelinsky, A., Nilsson, L., Rilbe, M.: 3D vision sensing for improved pedestrian safety. In: IV, Parma, Italy (2004)
12. Gerónimo, D., Sappa, A., López, A., Ponsa, D.: Pedestrian detection using Ad-aBoost learning of features and vehicle pitch estimation. In: Proc. of the International Conference on Visualization, Imaging and Image Processing, Palma de Mallorca, Spain, pp. 400–405 (2006)
13. Papageorgiou, C., Poggio, T.: A trainable system for object detection. IJCV 38(1), 15–33 (2000)
14. Mohan, A., Papageorgiou, C., Poggio, T.: Example–based object detection in images by components. TPAMI 23(4), 349–361 (2001)
15. Dalal, N., Triggs, B.: Histograms of oriented gradients for human detection. In: CVPR. vol. 2, San Diego, CA, USA, pp. 886–893 (2005)
16. van der Mark, W., Gavrila, D.: Real–time dense stereo for intelligent vehicles. TITS 7(1), 38–50 (2006)
17. Gavrila, D.: Sensor–based pedestrian protection. IS 16(6), 77–81 (2001)

A Decision-Tree-Based Online Speaker Clustering

Wei Wang, Ping Lv, QingWei Zhao, and YongHong Yan

ThinkIT Speech Lab, Institute of Acoustics, Chinese Academy of Sciences

Abstract. When performing online speaker clustering, it is common to make clustering decision as soon as an audio segment is received. When the wrong decision is made, the error can propagate the posterior clustering. This paper describes a decision-tree-based online speaker clustering algorithm. Unlike typical online clustering approaches, the proposed method constructs a decision tree when an audio segment is received. A pruning strategy for candidate-elimination is also applied. Experiments indicate that the algorithm achieves good performance on both precision and speed. Finally, we discuss the relation between the performance and the width of the decision tree beam.

1 Introduction

The goal of speaker clustering is to associate all segments from the same speaker together in an audio stream and assign them a unique label. Speaker clustering procedure has many applications, including improving the performance of speech recognition systems by supporting unsupervised adaptation, aiding speaker diarisation task, and enabling speakers to be tracked, conversations to be followed, audio data to be indexed, browsed or searched by speaker.

Hierarchical clustering(HC) is a widely used clustering method[1][2]. In this method, different numbers of clusters are hypothesized based on local distance measure. A global criterion is used to find the best number of clusters. But for some applications, it is important to produce speaker labels immediately without collecting all of the potential data from a particular scenario. This constraint prevents the standard HC technique being used, and instead requires the clustering to be performed online. Online speaker clustering method takes the segments in turn and decides if they match any of the existing speaker clusters using thresholds on distance metrics and a penalized within-cluster dispersion. If a match is found, the statistics of the matched cluster are updated using the new segment information, whereas if no match is found, the segment starts a new speaker cluster. This process is much faster than the conventional hierarchical approach. But this online clustering method seems a little slapdash. In case of online clustering, initial error can propagate the posterior clustering, causing an increase in error rate of clustering. Several alternative methods, such as soft-decision in the procedure of clustering, could be employed to redeem this deficiency. A new online speaker clustering algorithm is proposed in this paper which introduces a decision tree in the decision procedure. Each node in decision tree corresponds to a possible cluster result. To

J. Martí et al. (Eds.): IbPRIA 2007, Part I, LNCS 4477, pp. 555–562, 2007.

acquire the final result of clustering, one starts at the root node of the tree and apply sequentially a global within-cluster criterion to select the appropriate successor. Finally a unique terminal node is reached and the clusters stored there are assigned to result, and the path from the top node to the terminal node correspond the process of the clustering. Pruning strategy is also applied to speed up the clustering by cutting unnecessary nodes.

The paper is organized as follows. First, we brief overview the theory of HC and online speaker clustering. Second, we describe the details of the decision-tree-based online speaker clustering algorithm. Third, the experiment results are provided to show the effectiveness of this algorithm. Finally, the conclusion is given.

2 HC and Online Clustering

2.1 Hierarchical Clustering

Consider a collection of audio segments $X = \{x_1, x_2, \cdots, x_N\}$, and each x_n represents a sequence of spectral feature vectors. HC can be described as follows[2][3][4]:

```
1) Initialize the number of clusters c :  c ← N
2) Compute pair-wise distances between each cluster
3) Find the nearest pair in the c clusters:  x_i and x_j
4) Merge x_i and x_j as a new cluster
5) Update distances of clusters to new cluster
6) Calculate global criterion: G(c),  c ← c−1
7) Iterate steps 3)−6) until c = 1
8) Find speaker number:  c ← arg min G(c) and c clusters
                                  c
```

where c is the hypothesized number of clusters and $G(c)$ is the global criterion to be minimized. The global criterion used here is within-cluster dispersion penalized by number of cluster[2][3][5], which is expressed as follows:

$$G(c) = \left| \sum_{j=1}^{c} N_j \Sigma_j \right| \sqrt{c} . \tag{1}$$

where N_j is the number of feature vectors in cluster j, and Σ_j is the covariance matrix of cluster j, $|\cdot|$ denotes the determinant.

2.2 Online Clustering

D.Liu, et al, presents a delicate approach called hybrid speaker clustering(HSC)[6], which is described as follows:

1) Initialize the upper and lower thresholds θ_u, θ_l, the first cluster: $\mathbf{D}_1 \leftarrow \mathbf{x}$, the num of clusters c: $c \leftarrow 1$
2) Accept new segment $\mathbf{x}$
3) Calculate the nearest distance between new segment and clusters: $d_j \leftarrow \min_j \mathrm{GLR}(\mathbf{X}, \mathbf{D}_j)$ $j \in [1, c]$

4) If $d_j < \theta_l$, update $\mathbf{D}_j$ with $\mathbf{x}$, go step 10)

5) If $d_j > \theta_u$, add new $\mathbf{D}_{c+1} \leftarrow \mathbf{x}$, $c \leftarrow c+1$, go step 10)

6) Calculate G1 if $\mathbf{x}$ merged with $\mathbf{D}_j$: $\mathrm{G1} \leftarrow \mathrm{G}(\mathbf{D}_j\{\mathbf{x}\}, \mathbf{D})$
7) Calculate G2 if $\mathbf{x}$ is made a new cluster: $\mathrm{G2} \leftarrow \mathrm{G}(\mathbf{x}, \mathbf{D})$
8) If $\mathrm{G1} < \mathrm{G2}$, update $\mathbf{D}_j$ with $\mathbf{x}$, go step 10)

9) If $\mathrm{G1} > \mathrm{G2}$, add new $\mathbf{D}_{c+1} \leftarrow \mathbf{x}$, $c \leftarrow c+1$
10) Iterate steps 2)-9) until no more new segment
11) Return $\mathbf{D}_1, \mathbf{D}_2, \cdots \mathbf{D}_c$

The upper and lower thresholds θ_u and θ_l is used to speed up the clustering[6]. When $\theta_l \rightarrow -\infty$ and $\theta_u \rightarrow \infty$, HSC becomes a dispersion-based speaker clustering(DSC)[4].

3 Decison-Tree-Based Online Speaker Clustering Algorithm

In this paper, the distance metric used between clusters is the generalized likelihood ratio(GLR)[7]. Consider two audio segments are denoted as $\mathbf{x}$ and $\mathbf{y}$. Assume that $\mathrm{L}(\mathbf{x}; \boldsymbol{\mu}_\mathbf{x}, \boldsymbol{\Sigma}_\mathbf{x})$ and $\mathrm{L}(\mathbf{y}; \boldsymbol{\mu}_\mathbf{y}, \boldsymbol{\Sigma}_\mathbf{y})$ denote the likelihood of $\mathbf{x}$ for Gaussian model $\mathrm{N}(\boldsymbol{\mu}_\mathbf{x}, \boldsymbol{\Sigma}_\mathbf{x})$ and $\mathbf{y}$ for Gaussian model $\mathrm{N}(\boldsymbol{\mu}_\mathbf{y}, \boldsymbol{\Sigma}_\mathbf{y})$. The likelihood of attribute the segments from the same speaker is given by $\mathrm{L}(\mathbf{z}; \boldsymbol{\mu}_\mathbf{z}, \boldsymbol{\Sigma}_\mathbf{z})$, where $\mathbf{z}$ is the union of the $\mathbf{x}$ and $\mathbf{y}$ segments. The generalized likelihood ratio is defined by:

$$
\begin{aligned}
\mathrm{GLR}(\mathbf{x}, \mathbf{y}) &= -\log\left[\frac{\mathrm{L}(\mathbf{z}; \boldsymbol{\mu}_\mathbf{z}, \boldsymbol{\Sigma}_\mathbf{z})}{\mathrm{L}(\mathbf{x}; \boldsymbol{\mu}_\mathbf{x}, \boldsymbol{\Sigma}_\mathbf{x}) \mathrm{L}(\mathbf{y}; \boldsymbol{\mu}_\mathbf{y}, \boldsymbol{\Sigma}_\mathbf{y})}\right] \\
&= -\log\left[\frac{|\boldsymbol{\Sigma}_\mathbf{x}|^\alpha |\boldsymbol{\Sigma}_\mathbf{y}|^{1-\alpha}}{|W|}\right]^{\frac{N}{2}} - \log\left[1 + \frac{N_\mathbf{x} N_\mathbf{y}}{N^2}(\boldsymbol{\mu}_\mathbf{x} - \boldsymbol{\mu}_\mathbf{y})' W^{-1}(\boldsymbol{\mu}_\mathbf{x} - \boldsymbol{\mu}_\mathbf{y})\right]^{-\frac{N}{2}}
\end{aligned}
\tag{2}
$$

where $N_\mathbf{x}$ and $N_\mathbf{y}$ is the frame numbers of $\mathbf{x}$ and $\mathbf{y}$ respectively, $N = N_\mathbf{x} + N_\mathbf{y}$, $\alpha = N_\mathbf{x} / N$, and W is their frequency weighted average: $W = (N_\mathbf{x} \boldsymbol{\Sigma}_\mathbf{x} + N_\mathbf{y} \boldsymbol{\Sigma}_\mathbf{y}) / N$.

The GLR distance and dispersion criterion have been found successful in the HC clustering and online clustering framework[2][6][8]. This paper also examines the usefulness of the GLR distance and dispersion criterion for decision-tree-based clustering(DTC). The DTC is comprised of decision tree and pruning strategy.

3.1 Decision Tree

In order to improve the clustering performance on precision, a decision tree is built to record the possible cluster results in the clustering procedure. The decision tree can be presented as follows:

1) Initialize the number N

2) Initialize the root node (0,1) with the cluster $\mathbf{D}_1 \leftarrow \mathbf{x}$

3) Accept new segment $\mathbf{x}$

4) Fetch the node i which corresponds to a set of the clusters $\{\mathbf{D}_1^i, \mathbf{D}_2^i, \cdots \mathbf{D}_c^i\}$

5) Calculate distances between new segment and clusters: $d_j^i \leftarrow \mathrm{GLR}(\mathbf{x}, \mathbf{D}_j^i)\ j \in [1, c]$

6) Find N-nearest distances $d_{j1}^i, d_{j2}^i, \cdots d_{jN}^i$ ($d_{j1}^i < d_{j2}^i < \cdots < d_{jN}^i$) and build a nodes stack $(1, i), (2, i), \cdots, (N, i)$

7) Calculate J2[i] (assuming $\mathbf{x}$ is made a new cluster: J2[i] $\leftarrow$ J($\{\mathbf{x}, \mathbf{D}^i\}$)) form the node (0,$i$)

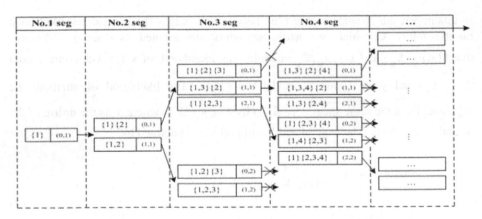

Fig. 1. A construction procedure of the decision tree. The horizontal axis in above shows the incoming audio segments in time sequence. The first segment is initialized as the first cluster {1} and builds the root node(0,1). The second segment merges with the first cluster{1,2} or starts a new cluster{1}{2} and form the leaf nodes(1,1) and(0,1) respectively. Five new leaves come into being in the same means along with the third segment's coming. A proper pruning cut which according the dispersion criterion only leave N (N=2) nodes for the posterior clustering.

8) Fetch the next node until no more nodes
9) Apply the Pruning strategy for candidate-elimination and remain N nodes(describe in the section3.2 in detail)
10) Iterate steps 3)-9) until no more new segment
11) Retrieve the terminal node in the N nodes and return the final result $\mathbf{D}_1, \mathbf{D}_2, \cdots \mathbf{D}_c$

where N is the number of nodes at each tree level. J 2[i] is the array of within-cluster dispersion value when x is made a new cluster. When a new segment comes, N node stacks are built to record the possible result. After applying the pruning strategy, only N nodes which correspond to N most possible clustering result leave. It is obvious that the computational complexity for this clustering algorithm increase with value of N. When N = 1, DTC becomes the DSC algorithm. Section.4 discusses the relations between the value of N and the performance of the clustering in detail.

3.2 Pruning Strategy

The pruning strategy proposed here is used to save N nodes for clustering of next stage when new segment comes. An outline of the pruning procedure is as follows:

1) Initialize a J value array with $J2[i]$, $i \in [1, N]$, index $\leftarrow 1$
2) Sort the array: $J2[i1] < J2[i2] < \cdots J2[iN]$

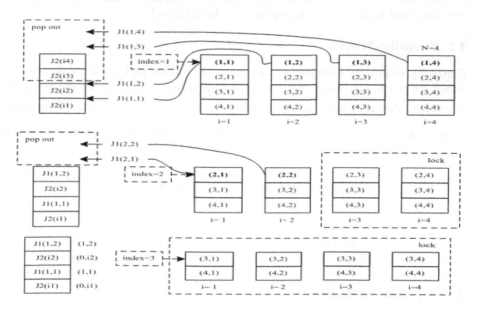

Fig. 2. This procedure is illustrated in Fig2. The N (N=4) node stacks which are built in the section 3.1 are shown in the right part of the figure, and the J value array is appear in the left. N nodes leaved are (1,2),(0,i2),(1,1),(0,i1).

3) Insert J1[*index,i*] values into the array, $i \in [1,N]$
4) Sort the decision queue, leave the N lowest values in the array and pop out the rest values
5) Lock the stacks whose J1 value be popped from array
6) Set *index* ← *index* +1
7) Iterate steps 3)-6) until no more stacks available

Where J1[*i, j*] is the within-cluster dispersion of the result node (i, j).

4 Experiment Results and Evaluation

4.1 Data Used for Evaluation

To evaluate the performance of the proposed algorithm, experiments are conducted on the 1997 Mandarin Broadcast News Speech Corpus(Hub4-NE) data, which are recorded broadcasts from CCTV, KAZN and VOA. The main content of this data are news reports and interviews. There are short segments in conversation of less than 1 second and long reports of more than 30 seconds. Each file in this database is approximately 30 minutes long, and contains more than 10 speaker's voices. The environment in this database is close to real life. There are background noises, short time noises, and even background occasional music. We use the five half-hour broadcast-news episodes, named as voa1, kean1, kean2, cctv1, cctv2 as our development data to optimize the algorithm. The evaluation data is taken from the next three half-hour episodes, named as voa2, kean3, cctv3.

4.2 Evaluation Metrics

Clustering results are evaluated in two facts: the cluster purity and speaker purity, which are commonly used to suggest the performance of speaker clustering. Consider n speakers that are clustered into c groups, where n_{ij} is the number of segments from speaker j that are labeled with cluster i. Assume that n_{ij} has N_{ij} speech frames.

$$\text{Cluster purity} = \sum_{i=1}^{c} \max_{j \in [1,n]} (N_{ij}) / \sum_{i=1}^{c} \sum_{j=1}^{n} N_{ij} . \tag{3}$$

$$\text{Speaker purity} = \sum_{j=1}^{n} \max_{i \in [1,c]} (N_{ij}) / \sum_{i=1}^{c} \sum_{j=1}^{n} N_{ij} . \tag{4}$$

4.3 Experimental Results

Table1 shows the clustering performance of different algorithms using the two evaluation metrics described in 4.2. In general, DSC performs the worst in both measures, suggesting that within-cluster dispersion measure alone might not be a good choice for online speaker clustering. By define θ_u and θ_l in high confidence regions, HSC yield better performance compared to DSC. Even though HSC perform superior on some development files than HC, HC perform more robust than HSC on the evaluation files. When N > 2 DTC work consistently well on most data set.

Table 1. Error analysis of speaker clustering

	Speaker purity (%)						Cluster purity (%)					
	HC	HSC	DSC	DTC(N=)			HC	HSC	DSC	DTC(N=)		
				2	3	4				2	3	4
voa1	90.3	86.8	83.7	87.5	87.5	87.5	90.2	87.8	84.6	87.2	88.3	88.3
kean1	96.0	97.5	91.5	93.7	93.7	94.8	95.3	95.5	93.5	94.4	94.4	94.4
kean2	82.3	88.7	87.8	92.7	94.1	94.1	81.4	90.6	89.8	90.6	90.6	90.6
cctv1	82.9	73.6	66.4	72.5	78.9	80.6	85.0	71.7	69.9	75.5	80.7	82.9
cctv2	84.4	85.6	79.9	87.3	90.4	92.4	82.9	86.7	80.0	90.3	92.4	93.4
voa2	89.5	84.1	84.7	86.0	86.1	86.1	88.4	84.2	84.6	86.1	86.3	86.3
kean3	95.8	91.2	89.5	95.2	95.9	96.1	94.5	91.6	89.1	94.3	94.7	94.8
cctv3	83.4	72.1	69.4	73.5	78.2	80.1	82.0	72.5	69.4	70.0	75.3	77.8
avg	*88.0*	*84.9*	*81.6*	*86.0*	*88.1*	*88.9*	*87.4*	*85.0*	*82.6*	*86.0*	*87.8*	*88.5*

Fig. 3 provides the computational complexity of the speaker cluster. We run the test on a series of data sets which contain from 50 to 800 segments. The cost of DTC is smaller than the HC algorithm.

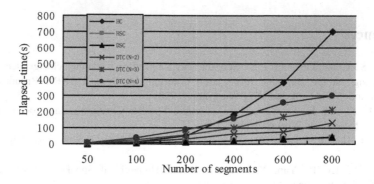

Fig. 3. The computational complexity for HC algorithm increases exponentially with number of audio segments. The time consuming for all online speaker clustering algorithms is linear to the number of input audio segments. Also, the complexity of the DTC algorithm increases with N .

Fig. 4. show the relation between performance of DTC and the value of the N . From the figure we can come to the conclusion that the computational complexity increase linear with the value of N . But the accuracy improvement of the algorithm is degressive according to the increase of N .

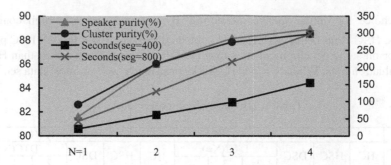

Fig. 4. The vertical axis in left represents the purity of cluster and speaker in percent. The vertical axis in right means the elapsed-time in second. Two curves of time consuming in seconds are drawn under the condition when number of segments is 400 and 800 respectively.

5   Conclusion

We propose a new online speaker clustering algorithm. Different from conventional online speaker clustering algorithm DSC and HSC, we use decision tree and decision queue to cluster the segments. Experiments show that it achieves good performance on both precision and speed. Experiments also show that within-cluster dispersion measure alone might not be a good choice for online speaker clustering. So more criterions such as criterions based on hypothesis test or BIC can be tested in this online clustering algorithm in our future work.

References

1. Chen, S., Gopalakrishnan, P.S.: Speaker, environment and channel change detection and clustering via the Bayesian information criterion. In: Proc. DARPA Broadcast News Transcription and Understanding Workshop (1998)
2. Jin, H., Kubala, F., Schwartz, R.: Automatic Speaker Clustering. In: Proc. of DARPA. Speech Recognition Workshop (1997)
3. Duda, R., Hart, P.: Pattern Classification, 2nd edn. John Wiley & Sons, Inc, New York, NY (2001)
4. Wang, W., Lv, P., Yan, Y.H.: An Improved Hierarchical Speaker Clustering. ACTA ACUSTICA (In Chinese) (To appear) (2006)
5. Everitt, B.: Cluster Analysis. Halsted Press, New York (1980)
6. Liu, D., Kubala, F.: Online Speaker Clustering, ICASSP (2004)
7. Gish, H., Siu, M., Rohicek, R.: Segregation of Speaker for Speech Recognition and Speaker Identification. ICASSP (1991)
8. Liu, D., Kiecza, D., Srivastava, A., Kubala, F.: Online speaker adaptation and tracking for real-time speech recognition. In: Proc. Eur. Conf. Speech Commun. Technol. Lisbon, Portugal (2005)

Classification of Continuous Heart Sound Signals Using the Ergodic Hidden Markov Model

Yong-Joo Chung

Department of Electronics, Keimyung University
Daegu, S. Korea

Abstract. Recently, hidden Markov models (HMMs) have been found to be very effective in classifying heart sound signals. For the classification based on the HMM, the continuous cyclic heart sound signal needs to be manually segmented to obtain isolated cycles of the signal. However, the manual segmentation will be practically inadequate in real environments. Although, there have been some research efforts for the automatic segmentation, the segmentation errors seem to be inevitable and will result in performance degradation in the classification. To solve the problem of the segmentation, we propose to use the ergodic HMM for the classification of the continuous heart sound signal. In the classification experiments, the proposed method performed successfully with an accuracy of about 99(%) requiring no segmentation information.

1 Introduction

Heart auscultation is important in the diagnosis of heart diseases. Although there are some advanced techniques such as the echocardiography and the MRI, it is still widely used in the diagnosis of the heart disease because of its relatively low cost and easy accessibility. However, detecting symptoms and making diagnosis from hearing the heart sound require a skill that takes years of experience in the field.

A machine-aided diagnosis system for the heart sound signal would be very useful for assisting the clinicians to make better diagnosis of the heart disease. With the recent developments of the digital signal processing techniques, artificial neural networks (ANNs) have been widely used as the automatic classification method for the heart sound signals [1-5]. Recently, the HMM has also shown to be very effective in modeling the heart sound signal [6-7]. The highly dynamic and non-stationary nature of the heart sound signal makes it appropriate to model the signal with the HMM. In a recent study [8], they found that the HMM performed much better than the ANN in classifying the heart sound signals corresponding to 10 different kinds of classes (heart conditions). The superior performance of the HMM may come from its proven excellence to model non-stationary time-sequential input patterns compared with the ANN. In the classification method using the HMM, they used each isolated cycle from the continuous heart sound signal as the input to the classifier and manual segmentation is required for the reliable classification performance[8]. The segmented one cycle from the continuous heart sound signal is considered as a pattern in both the

J. Martí et al. (Eds.): IbPRIA 2007, Part I, LNCS 4477, pp. 563–570, 2007.

training and testing of the classifier based on the HMM. But, in real situations where the classifier is operating on-line, the continuous heart sound signal will be directly input to the classifier and it will be impractical to apply the manual segmentation in real time. Although, there have been some research efforts for the automatic segmentation of the continuous heart sound signals, the segmentation errors seem to be inevitable and will result in performance degradation in the classification. To solve the problem of the segmentation, we propose to use the ergodic HMM for the classification of the continuous heart sound signal. Because of its fully connected structure, the ergodic HMM will be quite suitable for modeling the continuous heart sound signal without any segmentation information.

In the next section, we explain in detail methods how to model the continuous heart sound signal using the ergodic HMM and the experimental results are shown in section 3 and finally conclusions are given in section 4.

2 Methods

2.1 Ergodic Hidden Markov Model

The HMM has proven to be efficient in recognizing non-stationary time sequential patterns like speech. As the heart sound signal is similar to the speech in that its statistical characteristic is non-stationary, the modeling of the heart sound signal with the HMM will be feasible. The types of the HMM depend on its structure. In the speech recognition, the speech signal is usually modeled by the left-right HMM in which the state transitions are allowed only from left to right including self-transitions. This is quite reasonable because the left-right HMM can model signals whose properties change with time in a sequential manner. In this viewpoint, we think that the heart sound signal may be modeled by the left-right HMM. A four state left-right HMM for a cycle of the heart sound signal is shown in Fig. 1 in line with the four components of the heart sound signal, namely S1, systole, S2 and diastole [7][8]. The number of states in the HMM is usually determined based on the nature of the signal being modeled. Each state of the HMM in Fig.1 is assigned to a component of the heart sound signal because the signal characteristics in each component may be thought to be homogeneous.

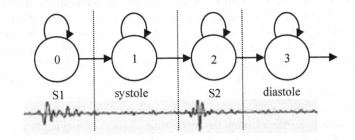

Fig. 1. An HMM for a cycle of the heart sound signal

In [8], they found that the 4-state left-right HMM was sufficient to model a cycle of the heart sound signal. The spectral variability in each state is modeled using multiple mixtures of multivariate Gaussian distributions. Given the observation $\mathbf{y}(t)$, the output probability distribution in the state j is given by

$$b_j(\mathbf{y}(t)) = \sum_{m=1}^{M} c_{jm} N(\mathbf{y}(t); \mathbf{\mu}_{jm}, \mathbf{\Sigma}_{jm}) \qquad (1)$$

where $N(\mathbf{y}(t); \mathbf{\mu}_{jm}, \mathbf{\Sigma}_{jm})$ is a multivariate Gaussian distribution, with mean vector $\mathbf{\mu}_{jm}$ and covariance matrix $\mathbf{\Sigma}_{jm}$, each mixture component having an associated weight c_{jm}. From the segmentation results from the Viterbi decoding, we determined the number of mixture components in each state to be 10 [8]. Also, the transition from the state i to j is controlled by the transition probability as follows.

$$a_{ij} = P(j \mid i) \qquad (2)$$

We note that it is difficult to model the continuous heart sound signal using the left-right HMM in Fig. 1. The left-right HMM assumes that the first component in the heart sound signal is S1, so we should segment the continuous heart sound signal into isolated cycles to use them as the input to the left-right HMM. Although, this approach may be feasible in the off-line training of the HMM, it will be impractical in the on-line conditions where manual segmentation is inappropriate. Although some

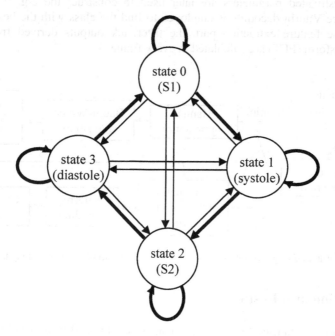

Fig. 2. The ergodic HMM used in the classification of the continuous heart sound signal

methods have been used to automatically segment the continuous heart sound signal, they are prone to segmentation errors which lead to performance degradation in the classification.

In this paper, we used the ergodic HMM shown in Fig. 2 to model the continuous heart sound signal without using any segmentation information. It is basically fully connected between the states but we allowed only those transitions marked in boldfaced arrows by taking into account the time sequence information between the components of the heart sound signal. The distinctive merit of the ergodic HMM compared with the left-right HMM is that the initial and final state of the ergodic HMM can be any one among the 4 possible states. This feature of the ergodic HMM makes it possible to model directly the continuous heart sound signal irrespective of the duration and the initial/final component of the signal. For example, if the signal starts with the component S2 and ends in S1, the state sequence with the initial and final states corresponding to those components will dominate in the Viterbi decoding for finding the best likelihood state sequence.

2.2 Classification Using HMMs

In Fig. 3, we show the procedure of classifying the continuous heart sound signal. Contrary to testing, the manually segmented isolated cycles of the continuous heart sound signal will be used in the training to model the left-right HMM by using the Baum-Welch algorithm where the HMM parameters μ_{jm}, Σ_{jm}, c_{jm} and a_{ij} in Eq. (1) and (2) are estimated based on the maximum likelihood estimation (MLE) criterion [11]. The estimated parameters are later used to construct the ergodic HMM for testing where Viterbi decoding is employed to find the class with the best likelihood score. In the feature extraction part, the filterbank outputs derived from the fast Fourier transform (FFT) are calculated in every frame.

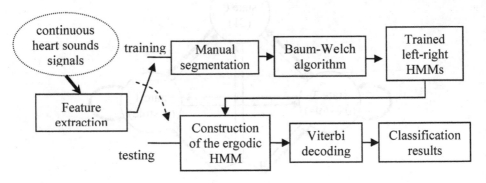

Fig. 3. The procedure of classifying the continuous heart sound signal

3 Experimental Results

The heart sound data used for the experiments were obtained from the clinical training audio CDs for the physicians [10]. The original data were down sampled to 16 KHz and stored in a 16 bit resolution. The heart sound signal was already diagnosed and labeled as a specific heart condition. The classification experiments were done using 159 heart sound examples corresponding to 10 different heart conditions: NM(normal sound), IM(innocent murmur), AR (Aortic Regurgitation), AS (Aortic Stenosis), CA (Coarctation of the Aorta), MR (Mitral Regurgitation), MS (Mitral Stenosis), MVP (Mitral Valve Prolapse), TR (Tricuspid Regurgitation) and VSD (Ventricular Septal Defect). An ergodic HMM was constructed for each type of the heart condition using the corresponding data. To overcome the problem of small amount of data collected, the classification test was done by the Jack-Knifing method. In the process, the HMM is trained with all the available examples except the one which is used for the testing. This process is repeated so that all the examples can be used for the testing. The test results are then averaged to give the final classification accuracy rate.

The heart sound signal is processed on a frame by frame basis in the HMM. The length of a cycle in the signal ranges from 500 ms to 1000 ms and we set the frame rate and length to be 2.5 ms and 7.5 ms, respectively.

As a preliminary work, we have done classification experiments on the isolated cycle of the heart sound signal using the conventional left-right HMM. Based on the spectral analysis of the heart sound signal [8], the frequency ranges were determined as 0~900 Hz, 0~210 Hz, 200~900 Hz and 200~300 Hz. The detailed classification results for each type of heart conditions are shown in Table 1 where separate results are shown depending on the frequency ranges in the filterbank outputs. The 0~900 Hz and 200~900Hz ranges performed better than others although there were not significant differences in the classification accuracy. Larger width in the frequency ranges seems to help increase the classification accuracy.

Table 1. The classification results on the isolated cycle of the continuous heart sound signal using the left-right HMM

	0~900[Hz]		0~210[Hz]		200~900[Hz]		200-300[Hz]	
	Accur-acy(%)	Correct/Total	Accur-acy(%)	Correct/Total	Accur-acy(%)	Correct/Total	Accur-acy(%)	Correct/Total
NM	100	15/15	93.33	14/15	100	15/15	93.33	14/15
IM	100	14/14	100	13/14	100	14/14	92.86	13/14
AR	100	14/14	100	14/14	100	14/14	100	14/14
AS	100	18/18	100	18/18	100	18/18	100	18/18
CA	95	19/20	95	19/20	95	19/20	95	19/20
MR	100	21/21	100	21/21	100	21/21	100	21/21
MS	100	14/14	100	14/14	100	14/14	100	14/14
MVP	100	13/13	92.31	12/13	100	13/13	92.31	12/13
TR	100	20/20	100	20/20	100	20/20	100	20/20
VSD	100	10/10	100	10/10	100	10/10	100	10/10
Average	99.37	158/159	98.74	157/159	99.37	158/159	97.48	155/159

This may come from fact the effective frequency range in the spectrum of the heart sound signal is usually between 0 and 500 Hz as shown in our previous work [8]. In Table 2, the results are shown when the classification experiments have been done on the continuous heart sound signal itself using the left-right HMM. We added the

0~420 [Hz] in the frequency range for more detailed investigation. As the classification experiments were done off-line, we generated the continuous heart sound signal from the isolated cycles used in Table 1 by two methods. First, the segmented one cycle was duplicated to make it a 3 cycle signal. Then, we generated 8 continuous heart sound signals from the 3cycle signal differing in their staring points by 100 ms. To make their length equal, the original samples in the 3 cycle signal before the starting point were appended to the end of the continuous heart sound signal. In the second method, 15 continuous heart sound signals were generated from the 3 cycle signal similarly as in the first method. But, their starting points were randomly selected. For the notational convenience, we call the continuous heart sound data from the first method as set A and the continuous heart sound data from the second method as set B.

Table 2. The classification results on the continuous heart sound signalusing the left-right HMM

Frequency range(Hz)	set A		set B	
	Accuracy(%)	Correct / Total	Accuracy(%)	Correct / Total
0 - 900	75.47	960/1272	73.75	1759/2385
0 - 210	64.15	816/1272	61.25	1461/2385
200 - 900	73.11	930/1272	72.99	1741/2385
200 - 300	49.05	624/1272	43.27	1032/2385
0 - 420	64.77	824/1272	60.04	1432/2385

As we can see in Table 2, the classification accuracy for the continuous heart signal using the left-right HMM is very poor. We could confirm from the results that the left-right HMM is inadequate to the continuous heart sound signal because it fixes the initial and final state of the HMM.

Table 3. The classification results on the continuous heart sound signal using the ergodic HMM

Frequency range(Hz)	set A		set B	
	Accuracy(%)	Correct / Total	Accuracy(%)	Correct / Total
0 - 900	99.37	1264/1272	99.28	2368/2385
0 - 210	95.59	1216/1272	94.67	2258/2385
200 - 900	98.74	1256/1272	98.57	2351/2385
200 - 300	93.23	1186/1272	92.87	2215/2385
0 - 420	100	1272/1272	99.07	2363/2385

In Table 3, we show the classification results on the continuous heart sound signal using the ergodic HMM. The results are shown as the frequency range in the filterbank outputs varies. The classification accuracy is a little more sensitive to the frequency range compared with the results on the isolated cycles in Table 1. When the frequency range is small (0-210Hz, 200-300Hz), we can clearly observe the degraded performance in Table 3. There may be more mismatches in the ergodic HMM between the heart sound signal components and the HMM states because the state transitions are less restricted than the left-right HMM. We think that the wider frequency range in the filterbank outputs contributes to make the ergodic HMM more robust against the mismatches. Given sufficient frequency range (0~900Hz, 0~420Hz, 200~900Hz) in the filterbank outputs, the classification accuracy is similar to the results on the isolated cycle in Table 1.

From Table 3, we can see that there is not much difference in accuracies between the test set A and set B.

In Fig. 4, we show the matching between the state sequence from the Viterbi decoding in the ergodic HMM and the corresponding continuous heart sound signal in the normal condition. There are some alternations in the state occupancy during the period of the component in the heart sound signal due to the less restricted state transitions in the ergodic HMM. However, we can see that the matching is quite accurate during the period of S1 and S2. There is some confusion in the period of the systole and diastole between them. This may be due to the fact that the spectral characteristic of the systole and diastole is quite similar in the normal heart sound signal.

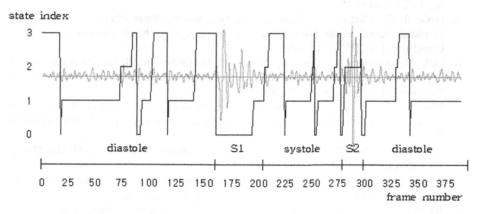

Fig. 4. The matching between the state sequence and the corresponding continuous heart sound signal in normal condition

4 Conclusion

In this paper, we proposed a method to classify the continuous heart sound signal using the ergodic HMM. Although the conventional left-right HMM performed very well on the isolated cycle of the heart sound signal, its performance dropped severely when the continuous heart sound signal is input without any segmentation information. The ergodic HMM alleviated this problem by incorporating the segmentation into the HMM structure. By employing sufficient frequency ranges in the filterbank outputs, the performance of the ergodic HMM on the continuous heart sound signal have shown little difference with the results on the isolated cycle of the signal.

Acknowledgments. This work has been supported by The Advanced Medical Technology Cluster for Diagnosis and Prediction at KNU, which carries out one of the R&D Projects sponsored by the Korea Ministry Of Commerce, Industry and Energy.

References

1. Leung, T.S., White, P.R., Collis, W.B., Brown, E., Salmon, A.P.: Acoustic diagnosis of heart diseases. In: Proceedings of the 3rd international conference on acoustical and vibratory surveillance methods and diagnostic techniques, Senlis, France, pp. 389–398 (1998)
2. Cathers, I.: Neural Network Assisted Cardiac Asculation. Artif. Intell. Med. 7, 53–66 (1995)
3. Bhatikar, S.R., DeGroff, C., Mahajan, R.L.: A Classifier Based on Artificial Neural Network Approach for Cardiac Auscultation in Pediatrics. Artif. Intell. Med. 33, 251–260 (2005)
4. Lippmann, R.P.: An Introduction to Computing with Neural Nets, IEEE ASSP Magazine, pp. 4–22 (April 1987)
5. DeGroff, C., Bhatikar, S., Hertzberg, J., Shandas, R., Valdes-Cruz, L., Mahajan, R.: Artificial neural network-based method of screening heart murmur in children. Circulation 103, 2711–2716 (2001)
6. Gill, D., Intrator, N., Gavriely, N.: A Probabilistic Model for Phonocardiograms Segmentation Based on Homomorphic Filtering, 18-th Biennial International EURASIP Conference Biosignal, pp. 87–89 (2006)
7. Ricke, A.D., Povinelli, R.J., Johnson, M.T.: Automatic segmentation of heart sound signals using hidden Markov models, Computers in Cardiology, pp. 953–956 (September 2005)
8. Chung, Y.: A Classification Approach for the Heart Sound Signals Using Hidden Markov Models, SSPR/SPR, pp. 375–383 (2006)
9. Rabiner, L.R., Wilpon, J.G., Juang, B. H.: A segmental k-means training procedure for speech recognition, IEEE Trans. ASSP, pp. 2033–2045 (December 1990)
10. Rabiner, L. R.: A Tutorial on Hidden Markov Models and Selected Applications in Speech Recognition. In: Proceedings of the IEEE, vol. 77 (February 1989)
11. Mason D.: Listening to the Heart, Hahnemann University (2000). In: Baum, L. E., Petrie, T., Soules, G., Weiss, N.: A Maximization Technique Occurring in the Statistical Analysis of Probabilistic Functions of Markov Chains, Annals of Mathematical Statistics, vol. 41 pp. 164–171 (1970)
12. Lee, K.F.: Automatic Speech Recognition. Kluwer Academic Publishers, Boston (1989)

A Protocol to Cipher Digital Images Based on Cat Maps and Cellular Automata

A. Martín del Rey[1], G. Rodríguez Sánchez[2], and A. de la Villa Cuenca[3]

[1] Department of Applied Mathematics, E.P.S., Universidad de Salamanca
C/Hornos Caleros 50, 05003-Ávila, Spain
delrey@usal.es

[2] Department of Applied Mathematics, E.P.S., Universidad de Salamanca
Avda. Cardenal Cisneros 34, 49022-Zamora, Spain
gerardo@usal.es

[3] Department of Applied Mathematics and Computation, E.T.S.I. (ICAI)
Universidad Pontificia Comillas
C/Alberto Aguilera 23, 28015-Madrid, Spain
avilla@upco.es

Abstract. In this paper a novel symmetric protocol to cipher digital images is introduced. The protocol proposed in this work is based on the paradigm stated by J. Fridrich at 1998. Consequently, there are two iterative stages in the algorithm: The confusion stage permutes the pixels in the image using the Cat map, whereas in the diffusion stage, the pixel values (the color of each pixel) are modified sequentially such that a small change in the color of only one pixel is spread out to many pixels. This second phase is carryied out by means of a reversible cellular automaton. The proposed protocol is shown to be secure against the more important cryptanalytic attacks.

1 Introduction

The advent of personal computers and the Internet has made it possible for anyone to distribute worldwide digital information easily and economically. In this new environment, there are several security problems associated with the processing and transmission of digital images over an open network: It is necessary to assure the confidentiality, the integrity and the authenticity of the digital image transmitted. To meet these challenges, a wide variety of cryptographic protocols have been appeared in the scientific literature (see, for example [1,2]). Traditional data cryptosystems exhibits some drawbacks and weakness in the encryption of digital images (for example, low-level efficiency when the image is large); consequently, they are not suitable for image encryption. In this respect two-dimensional chaotic maps are naturally employed as each digital image can be represented as a two-dimensional array of pixels ([4,5,6,10]). Moreover, chaos-based and dynamical systems-based algorithms have shown their superior performance: They have many important properties such as the sensitive dependence on initial conditions and system parameters, pseudorandom

J. Martí et al. (Eds.): IbPRIA 2007, Part I, LNCS 4477, pp. 571–578, 2007.

properties, ergodicity, nonperiodicity and topological transitivity. Most properties meet some requirements such as sensitive to keys, diffusion and mixing in the sense of cryptography.

In [4], J. Fridrich suggested that image encryption protocols based on chaotic maps should compose of two iterative stages: Chaotic confusion stage and pixel diffusion stage. The confusion stage permutes the pixels of the image without changing its value (the color of the pixel) by using an adequate two-dimensional chaotic map such as Baker map, Cat map or the Standard chaotic map. In this phase, the parameters of the chaotic map serve as the confusion key. In the diffusion stage, the pixel values are modified sequentially such that a small change in the value of only one pixel is spread out to many pixels (avalanche effect). The initial value or the control parameter of the diffusion function serves as the diffusion key. To decorrelate the relationship between adjacent pixels, there must be $n \geq 1$ permutation rounds in the confusion stage. The whole confusion-diffusion round repeats for a number of times to achieve a satisfactory level of security.

Fridrich also proposed in [4] two diffusion methods: In the first one, the image is divided into a regular tessellation of 2×2 squares such that the new value of each pixel depends on the four values of the pixels belonging to the group. In the second one, the diffusion is obtained by scanning the image by rows and changing the value of the pixels according to the following formula: $p_i = q_i + G(p_{i-1}) \pmod{L}$, where p_i and q_i are the value of the ciphertext pixel and the plain-text pixel, respectively, L is the number of grey levels, and G is some arbitrary function.

The main goal of this paper is to introduce a new symmetric image encryption protocol following the paradigm stated by Fridrich at 1998. In this work, the confusion stage is carryied out by using the Cat map which exhibits good cryptographic properties (see [7]), and in the diffusion stage the use of a suitable reversible cellular automata with appropiate diffusion properties is proposed.

The rest of the paper is organized as follows: In section 2, the basic definitions and results about the Cat map and cellular automata are introduced; the encryption scheme is presented in section 3 and its security analysis is shown in section 4. Finally, the conclusions are introduced in section 5.

2 Mathematical Background

Arnold's Cat map is a simple discrete dynamical system that stretches and "folds" the trajectories in phase space which is a typical feature of chaotic processes. Specifically, the Cat map is the best known example of Anosov diffeomorphism; it is a two-dimensional invertible chaotic map given by the following transformation (see, for example [3]):

$$\begin{pmatrix} x_{n+1} \\ y_{n+1} \end{pmatrix} = \begin{pmatrix} 1 & a \\ b & ab+1 \end{pmatrix} \cdot \begin{pmatrix} x_n \\ y_n \end{pmatrix} \pmod{1}, \qquad (1)$$

where a, b are control parameters, and the notation $x \pmod 1$ stands for the fractional parts of a real number x by subtracting or adding an appropiate integer number. The Cat map is non-Hamiltonian, nonanalytic and mixing. As the determinant of its linear transformation matrix is equal to 1, it is also area-preserving. Moreover, its Lyapunov characteristic exponents are $\sigma_1 = 2.61803 > 1$ and $\sigma_2 = 0.381966 < 1$, and as the leading Lyapunov characteristic exponent is strictly larger than 1, then the Cat map is chaotic.

Cellular automata (CA for short) are a particular type of discrete dynamical system (see [9]) defined as a 4-uplet $\mathcal{A} = (C, S, V, f)$, where C is the cellular space formed by a linear array of cells which are denoted by $\langle i \rangle$, $1 \leq i \leq n$. The state set $S = \mathbb{Z}_2$ is the finite set of all possible values of the cells. The neighborhood of every cell $\langle i \rangle \in C$ is given by the set $V = \{-r, \ldots, -1, 0, 1, \ldots, r\}$, such that for every cell $\langle i \rangle \in C$ its neighborhood is: $V_i = \{\langle i - r \rangle, \langle i \rangle, \langle i + r \rangle\}$. Moreover, the local transition function $f: \mathbb{Z}_2^{2r+1} \rightarrow \mathbb{Z}_2$ is the function determining the evolution of the CA throughout the time, i.e., the changes of the states of every cell taking the states of its neighbors into account. Hence, if $s_i^t \in \mathbb{Z}_2$ stands for the state of the i-th cell at time t, the next state of the i-th cell is given by the formula $s_i^{t+1} = f(s_{i-r}^t, \ldots, s_i^t, \ldots, s_{i+r}^t)$. As the cellular space is finite, periodic boundary conditions must be established in order to assure that the evolution of the cellular automata is well-defined.

Note that the state of each cell at a particular time step t depends only on the states of its neighbor cells at the previous time step $t - 1$. Nevertheless, when this dependence is extended to the states of neighbor cells at time $t - 2$, the CA is called memory CA. Moreover, a CA is called reversible when there exists another cellular automaton which produces the inverse evolution ([8]).

The set of states of all cells at time t is called the configuration at time t and it is represented by the vector $C^{(t)} = (s_1^t, s_2^t, \ldots, s_n^t) \in \mathbb{Z}_2 \times .^n. \times \mathbb{Z}_2$. In particular, C^1 is the initial configuration and the evolution of the CA is the sequence $\left(C^{(1)}, C^{(2)}, C^{(3)}, \ldots \right)$.

If we denote by $\mathcal{C}$ the set of all possible configurations of a CA, the global function of the cellular automata is a transformation that yields the configuration at the next time step during the evolution of the CA. That is $\Phi: \mathcal{C} \rightarrow \mathcal{C}, C^{t-1} \mapsto C^t = \Phi\left(C^{t-1}\right)$, or $\Phi: \mathcal{C} \times \mathcal{C} \rightarrow \mathcal{C}, C^t = \Phi\left(C^{t-1}, C^{t-2}\right)$ for memory CA.

3   The Encryption Scheme

Let's consider a digital image defined by $N \times N$ pixels (N even) and by a palette of 2^c colors such that p_{ij} stands for the numeric value of the color of the (i, j)-th pixel. Set $I = (p_{ij})$ the matrix defining the digital image. As is mentioned in the Introduction, the cryptographic algorithm introduced in this work follows the traditional paradigm for image encryption protocols stated in [4]. Consequently, two iterative stages are given: the confusion and the diffusion phases.

The confusion phase is carried out using the Cat map and the number of iterations of this state is T_0. In the diffusion phase a reversible memory CA is used and their evolutions of order T_1 are computed. The whole confusion-diffusion round repeats for $T_2 = 6$ times.

The Confusion Phase. In this phase, the pixels of the image will be permuted using the discretized Cat map over the image lattice:

$$\begin{pmatrix} x_{n+1} \\ y_{n+1} \end{pmatrix} = \begin{pmatrix} 1 & a \\ b & ab+1 \end{pmatrix} \cdot \begin{pmatrix} x_n \\ y_n \end{pmatrix} \pmod{N}. \tag{2}$$

The confusion key is formed by the control parameters a and b, and the number of iterations T_0. The matrix associated to the permuted image is P_I.

The Diffusion Phase. In this phase, the value of the pixels of the permuted image will be changed according to a reversible memory cellular automata $C^t = \Phi\left(C^{t-1}, C^{t-2}\right)$ with the following local transition function:

$$s_i^t = \sum_{-8 \leq \alpha \leq 8, \alpha \neq 0} k_\alpha s_{i+\alpha}^{t-1} + s_i^{t-2} \pmod{2}, \tag{3}$$

where $k_\alpha \in \mathbb{Z}_2$ for every α.

Let $P_I = (q_{ij})$ be the $N \times N$ matrix obtained from the confusion phase with $q_{ij} \in \mathbb{Z}_{2^c}$. Each row is interpreted as a configuration of a CA with $c \cdot N$ cells where each value q_{ij} is defined by c bits; then the i-th row is denoted as C^i. Now, if we consider the ordered pairs of configurations: $\{C^1, C^2\}, \{C^3, C^4\}, \ldots, \{C^{N-1}, C^N\}$, and we use the memory CA defined by (3) to compute the corresponding evolutions of order T_1 (starting from each pair of configurations respectively), it yields: $\{\bar{C}^1, \bar{C}^2\}, \{\bar{C}^3, \bar{C}^4\}, \ldots, \{\bar{C}^{N-1}, \bar{C}^N\}$. As a consequence, the matrix associated to the diffused image is $\bar{P}_I$ whose rows are $\{\bar{C}^1, \ldots, \bar{C}^N\}$. The diffusion key is formed by T_1 and $K = \{k_{-8}, \ldots, k_{-1}, k_1, \ldots, k_8\}$.

As is mentioned above, the whole confusion-diffusion phase is repeated for T_2 rounds. In each round, a different key K is used and the corresponding key for the i-th round is denoted by K_i. Then, the secret key of the cryptosystem is given by the parameters $a, b, T_0, T_1, K_1, \ldots, K_6$. As a consequence the secret key is of bit-length 128. Finally note that the number of bit operations involved in the diffusion phase is given by $68N^3T_1$.

4   The Security Analysis

In this section the security of the protocol introduced in the last section is analyzed. Specifically, some cryptanalytic attacks are studied: statistical attacks, sensitivity to initial conditions, differential attack and chosen-plainimage attack.

4.1   Brutte-Force Attacks and Statistical Analysis

As the secret key is of bit-length 128, its key space size is $2^{128} \approx 3.4028 \cdot 10^{38}$. Then, it is large enough to prevent exhaustive searching.

We have also performed a statistical analysis in order to prove the confusion and diffusion properties of the proposed protocol, which allows it to strongly resists statistical attacks. Specifically the histrograms of original image the and cipher image are checked and the correlation coefficients are computed.

Let us consider the 256 grey-scale image of size 128×128 given in Figure 1-(a). Its histogram is shown in Figure 1-(c). If we compute the cipher image by means of the proposed protocol with the following parameters:

$$a = 1, b = 2, T_0 = 32, T_1 = 10, K = \texttt{f80dfa19f240a988f034ea45}, \qquad (4)$$

(that is, the secret key is $\texttt{102200af80dfa19f240a988f034ea45}$) the encrypted image obtained is shown in Figure 1-(b). Moreover, its histogram is shown in Figure 1-(d). From the figure one can see that the histogram of the ciphered image is fairly uniform and it is significantly different from that of the original image. It demonstrates that the encryption algorithm has covered up all the characters of the plain image and shows good performance of balanced 0-1 ratio and zero correlation.

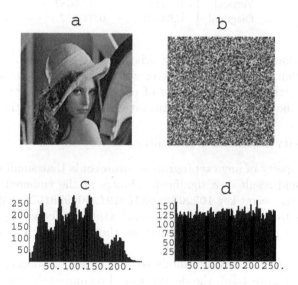

Fig. 1. (a) Lena's picture defined by 128×128 pixels and 256 grey levels; (b) Cipher image of Lena's picture; (c) Histogram of original picture; (d) Histogram of cipher image

The following procedure will be carryied out to test the correlation between two adjacent pixels in the original and the cipher image: First of all randomly select 1.000 pairs of two adjacent pixels from the image, and then, calculate the correlation coefficient of each pair by using the following formula:

$$r_{xy} = \frac{cov\,(x,y)}{\sqrt{D\,(x)}\sqrt{D\,(y)}}, \qquad (5)$$

where x and y are the grey-scale values of the two adjacent pixels in the image and:

$$cov\,(x,y) = \frac{1}{N} \sum_{i=1}^{N} (x_i - E\,(x))\,(y_i - E\,(y)),$$

$$E\,(x) = \frac{1}{N} \sum_{i=1}^{N} x_i, \quad D\,(x) = \frac{1}{N} \sum_{i=1}^{N} (x_i - E\,(x))^2. \tag{6}$$

As a consequence, the results obtained are shown in Table 1.

Table 1. Correlation coefficients of two adjacent pixels

	Lena picture	Cipher image
Horizontal	0.941845	0.017490
Vertical	0.851011	−0.055082
Diagonal	0.844094	0.033057

The correlations coefficients of the original image and cipher image are far appart (note that the correlation coefficients of Lena's picture are close to 1, whereas the corresponding coefficients of the cipher image are very close to 0). Consequently, the encryption algorithm satisfy zero co-correlation.

4.2   Sensitivity to Initial Conditions

A desirable property of any cryptographic protocol is that small changes in the secret key should result in a significant change in the ciphered image. In our case, if we use the secret key `1022009f80dfa19f240a988f034ea45` which differs in only one bit from the secret key given in (4), the difference between the two ciphered images is the 99.6094 % (that is, the percentage of different bits is 49.9115%).

Moreover, if the last trivially modified key is used to decrypt the ciphered image given in Figure 1-(b), the decryption also completely fails as it is shown in Figure 2. As a consequence, it can be concluded that the encryption protocol is sensitive to key, a small change of the key yields a different deciphered image and no information about the original one is obtained.

4.3   Differential Attack

To test the influence of one-pixel change on the whole ciphered image, two usual measures are used: the number of pixels change rate, $NPCR$, which measures the percentage of different pixel numbers between two images; and the unified average changing intensity, $UACI$, which measures the average intensity of differences between two images.

Suppose that $\bar{I}_1$ and $\bar{I}_2$ are two ciphered images whose corresponding plain-images differ in only one-pixel. Moreover, set $\bar{P}_{I^1} = \left(\bar{p}_{ij}^1\right)$ and $\bar{P}_{I^2} = \left(\bar{p}_{ij}^2\right)$ their

Fig. 2. Deciphered image with the modified key 1022009f80dfa19f240a988f034ea45

associated matrices, and define a bipolar array of size $N \times N$, $D = (d_{ij})$, such that $d_{ij} = 0$ if $\bar{p}^1_{ij} = \bar{p}^2_{ij}$, and $d_{ij} = 1$ otherwise. The $NPCR$ and $UACI$ are defined as follows:

$$NPCR = \frac{\sum_{i,j=1}^{N} d_{ij}}{N^2} \times 100\%, \ UACI = \frac{1}{N^2} \left(\sum_{i,j=1}^{N} \frac{|\ p^1_{ij} - p^2_{ij}\ |}{255} \right) \times 100\%, \quad (7)$$

Some tests have been performed on the proposed scheme about the influence of only one-pixel change on the 256 grey scale image of size 128×128 given in Figure 1. If we change the $(64, 64)$-th pixel of the original image and its value passes from 29 to 30, the $NPCR$ is 82.8308, whereas the $UACI$ coefficient is 5.60744. These results are better than those obtained in other works (see [7]).

4.4 Other Cryptanalytic Attacks

Finally, we will study the robustness of the protocol against cipherimage-only attack, known-plainimage attack and chosen-plainimage attack. In the cipherimage-only attack, an opponent must determine the secret key solely from an intercepted cipherimage $\bar{I}$. In the known-plainimage attack, the opponent must deduce the secret key starting from several pairs of plainimages and corresponding ciphered images and, finally, in the chosen-plainimage, the cryptanalist is able to chose the plainimages and obtain the corresponding cipherimages. If the encryption protocol is secure against the chosen-plainimage attack, it is also secure against cipherimage-only attack and known-plainimage attack. Suppose the opponent choses a plainimage I, whose pixels are all of the same color, for example $p_{i,j} = 0$, for every i, j, the ciphered image obtained, $\bar{I}$, is defined by $\bar{P}_I = (0)$ and no information about the secret key is obtained. Moreover, suppose the chosen plainimage is defined by the matrix P_I whose coefficients are all 0 except for only one, whose value is 1. Then, the encrypted image yields a system of $8 \times N \times N$ non-lineal equations with $8 \times N \times N + 128$ variables. Moreover, there are $8 \times N \times N$ variables secretly permuted. As a consequence, no information about the key can be obtained.

5   Conclusions and Further Work

In this paper, a new symmetric encryption protocol for digital images is introduced. It is based on the well-known paradigm stated by Fridrich, that is, the proposed protocol consists of two stages: The confusion stage and the diffusion stage, which repeats for a number of times to achieve a satisfactory level of security. The confusion stage is given by means of the Cat map whereas in the diffusion stage some evolutions of a particular reversible memory cellular automata are computed. The algorithm shows to be secure against the most important cryptanalytic attacks.

Further work aimed at designing similar encryption protocols involving cellular automata in the confusion stage. Moreover, it is also very interesting the study and classification of the more suitable cellular automata for their use in both stages.

Acknowledgments. This work has been partially supported by Junta de Castilla y León (Spain) under grant SA110A06, and by Ministerio de Educación y Ciencia (Spain) under grant SEG2004-02418.

References

1. Álvarez Marañón, G., Hernández Encinas, L., del Rey, A.M.: A New Secret Sharing Scheme for Images Based on Additive 2-Dimensional Cellular Automata. In: Marques, J.S., de la Blanca, N.P., Pina, P. (eds.) Pattern Recognition and Image Analysis. IbPRIA 2005. LNCS, vol. 3522, pp. 411–417. Springer-Verlag, Heidelberg (2005)
2. Chang, Ch.-Ch., Hwang, M.-S., Chen, T.-S.: A new encryption algorithm for image cryptosystems. J. Sist. Software, vol. 58, pp. 83–91 (2001)
3. Chen, G., Dong, X.: From chaos to order: methodologies, perspectives and applications. World Scientific, Singapore (1998)
4. Fridrich, J.: Symmetric ciphers based on two-dimensional chaotic maps. Int. J. Bifucar. Chaos 8, 1259–1284 (1998)
5. Gao, H., Zhang, Y., Liang, S., Li, D.: A new chaotic algorithm for image encryption. Chaos Soliton Frac. 29, 393–399 (2006)
6. Guan, Z.H., Huang, F.J., Guan, W.J.: Chaos-based image encryption algorithm. Phys. Lett. A. 346, 153–157 (2005)
7. Lian, S.G., Sun, J., Wang, Z.: A block cipher based on a suitable use of chaotic standard map. Chaos Soliton Frac. 26, 117–129 (2005)
8. Toffoli, T., Margolus, N.: Invertible cellular automata: A review. Physica D. 45, 229–253 (1990)
9. Wolfram, S.: A New Kind of Science. Wolfram Media, Champaign, Illinois (2002)
10. Zhang, L.H., Liao, X.F., Wang, X.B.: An image encryption approach based on chaotic maps. Chaos Soliton Frac. 24, 759–765 (2005)

Perceptually-Based Functions for Coarseness Textural Feature Representation

J. Chamorro-Martínez[1], E. Galán-Perales[1], B. Prados-Suárez[2], and J.M. Soto-Hidalgo[1,*]

[1] Department of Computer Science and Artificial Intelligence, University of Granada
C/ Periodista Daniel Saucedo Aranda s/n, 18071 Granada, Spain
{jesus,elena,soto}@decsai.ugr.es
[2] Department of Computer Science, University of Jaén
C/ Alfonso X el Sabio s/n, 23700 Linares, Jaén, Spain
belenps@ujaen.es

Abstract. Coarseness is a very important textural concept that has been widely analyzed in computer vision for years. However, a model which allows to represent different perception degrees of this textural concept in the same way that humans perceive texture is needed. In this paper we propose a model that associates computational measures to human perception by learning an appropriate function. To do it, different measures representative of coarseness are chosen and subjects assessments are collected and aggregated. Finally, a function that relates these data is fitted.

Keywords: Image features, textural features, human perception, visual coarseness.

1 Introduction

Texture is being increasingly recognized as an important cue for the analysis of natural imagery. Great research efforts are devoted to analyze this visual feature mainly due to the imprecission relative to its concept. In fact, different definitions of texture are found over the literature being described by some authors as local changes in the intensity patterns while others consider texture as a set of basic items or texels set out in conformity with some rules. Moreover, texture is also described by humans according to some concepts like coarseness, regularity, orientation [1].

Different approaches for texture characterization have been developed over the years. Haralick [2] proposed a classification of such approaches in two main groups: *statistical methods* (which analyze gray tone spatial distribution by computing some statistics on pixels intensity) and *structural methods* (which characterize texture by means of *texels* arranged in a certain way that is given by a set of rules). The author used statistics of *Gray Level Coocurrence Matrices* as

---

* This work has been supported by the MEC under the TEC2006-13845 project.

J. Martí et al. (Eds.): IbPRIA 2007, Part I, LNCS 4477, pp. 579–586, 2007.

Fig. 1. Some examples of images with different degrees of fineness

measures of texture but such statistical values do not consider the way humans perceive texture. One of the first papers where textural measures are used taking into account human perception of texture was presented by Tamura [3]. However, in Tamura's paper the relationship between the computational measures and the human perception of the different textural features is not learnt, just a rank correlation value is given. This value is calculated from the ordering results obtained from humans and from the computational measures of a small set of images. More recent approaches perform experiments with humans in order to model human perception but it is frequently found that the results given by such models can just compare two images and give a measure of their similarity [4,5] or they just analyze the presence or not of texture [6] but the presence degree of texture for a given image is not obtained.

In this paper we focus our study on coarseness, one of the textural properties most used in the literature which allows to distinguish between fine and coarse textures. In fact, the concept of texture is usually associated to the presence of fineness. A *fine* texture can be considered as small texture primitives with big gray tone differences between neighbour primitives (e.g. the image in figure 1(A)). On the contrary, if texture primitives are bigger and formed by several pixels, it is a *coarse* texture (e.g. the image in figure 1(I)).

In our approach we propose to model fineness by learning a function that captures human perception. To do this, two questions will be faced: what data should be used as independent variable, and how to obtain the related function. To solve the first question, a set of measures will be automatically computed from the texture image. To answer the second question, functional relationship between a certain measure and the presence degree of a textural concept related to it will be learnt.

The rest of the paper is organized as follows. In section 2 we introduce our methodology to obtain the functions that model the fineness textural concept. In section 3 we show the results of applying the models and the main conclusions and future work are summarized in section 4.

2   Obtaining Functions for Fineness Representation

There are different measures over the literature that, given an image, capture the fineness (or coarseness) presence in the sense that the greater the value given by the measure, the greater the perception of texture. However two main drawbacks are found: on the one hand, there is no perceptual relationship between that value and the degree that humans perceive the texture; on the other hand, there are no thresholds that, given a certain measure, allow to decide whether there is fine texture, coarse texture or something intermediate (i.e. there are no intervals on the measure domain allowing for textural interpretation).

In this paper, we face these questions by proposing a function of fineness perception defined on the domain of a given measure. Concretely, we propose to model the fineness perception by means of a function

$$\mathcal{T} : \mathbb{R} \to [0,1] \tag{1}$$

defined as[1]

$$\mathcal{T}(x; a_n \dots a_0, \alpha, \beta) = \begin{cases} 0 & x < \alpha, \\ poly^n(x; a_n \dots a_0) & \alpha \le x \le \beta, \\ 1 & x > \beta \end{cases} \tag{2}$$

with $poly^n(x; a_n \dots a_0)$ being a polynomial function of the form:

$$poly^n(x; a_n \dots a_0) = a_n x^n + a_{n-1} x^{n-1} + \dots + a_1 x^1 + a_0 \tag{3}$$

The value given by the function $\mathcal{T}$ will indicate how fine or coarse is the texture present in an image. Thus, a value of 1 will mean fineness presence while a value of 0 will mean no fineness presence (i.e. coarseness presence). Moreover, the parameters α and β will split the domain of the measure in three intervals: $(-\infty, \alpha)$ corresponding to values related to coarse textures, (β, ∞) corresponding to values related to fine textures, and $[\alpha, \beta]$ corresponding to intermediate values. For values in the interval $[\alpha, \beta]$, the function defined in equation 2 will obtain a value between 0 and 1 representing the degree of how fine the image is perceived (the closer the value to 1, the greater the perception of fineness).

In this paper, we propose to obtain the parameters that define the function given in equation 2 by "learning" a functional relationship between a certain measure and the perception degree of fineness. To learn this relationship, we will use a set $\mathcal{I} = \{I_1, \dots, I_N\}$ of N images that fully represent the perception of fineness. Also, a set of measures $\mathcal{P} = \{P_1, \dots, P_K\}$ will be considered, with $P_k \in \mathcal{P}$ being a measure of the perception of fineness in an image (e.g. $\mathcal{P} = \{EdgeDensity, Variance, Entropy\}$). Thus, for each image $I_i \in \mathcal{I}$, we will have (a) a value obtained applying the measure $P_k \in \mathcal{P}$ to the image I_i, noted as m_k^i, and (b) an assessment v^i of the perception degree of fineness. To get

---

[1] Note that this function is defined for measures that increases according to the perception of fineness but for those that decreases, the function needs to be changed appropriately.

this assessment, a poll will be performed (section 2.1). Thus, for a given measure $P_k \in \mathcal{P}$, the multiset $\Psi_k = \{(m_k^1, v^1), \ldots, (m_k^N, v^N)\}$ is obtained and the function $\mathcal{T}$ is estimated by carrying out a Least of Squares Fitting (section 2.2).

2.1   Assessment Collection

In this section, the way to obtain a vector $\Gamma = [v^1, \ldots, v^N]$ of the assessments of the perception degree of fineness from the image set $\mathcal{I} = \{I_1, \ldots, I_N\}$ will be described. Thus, firstly a criterion for choosing the image set $\mathcal{I}$ is needed. After that, a poll which allows to get assessments of the perception degree of fineness will be designed. These assessments will be obtained for each image in $\mathcal{I}$, so an aggregation of the different assessments will be performed.

The Texture Image Set. A set $\mathcal{I} = \{I_1, \ldots, I_N\}$ of $N = 80$ images representative of the concept of *fineness* has been selected. Figure 1 shows some images extracted from the set $\mathcal{I}$. The selection was done to cover the different perception degrees of fineness with a representative number of images. Furthermore, the images have been chosen so that as far as possible, just one perception degree of fineness is perceived.

The Poll. Given the image set $\mathcal{I}$, the next step is to obtain assessments about the perception of fineness from a set of subjects. From now on we shall denote $\Theta^i = [o_1^i, \ldots, o_L^i]$ the vector of assessments obtained from L subjects for image I_i. To get Θ^i, subjects will be asked to assign images to classes, so that each class has associated a perception degree of texture. In particular, 20 subjects have participated in the poll and 9 classes have been considered. The first nine images in figure 1 show the nine representative images for each class used in this poll. It should be noticed that the images are decreasingly ordered according to the perception degree of fineness.

Assessment Aggregation. Our aim at this point is to obtain, for each image $I_i \in \mathcal{I}$, one assessment v^i that summarizes the vector of assessments Θ^i given by the different subjects about the perception degree of fineness. To aggregate opinions we have used an OWA operator guided by the quantifier "the most" [7] which allows to represent the opinion of majority of the polled subjects.

2.2   Fitting the Function

At this point, the aim is to obtain the function $\mathcal{T}$ (equation 2) from the multiset Ψ_k corresponding to each measure $P_k \in \mathcal{P}$. In this paper, this function is calculated by carrying out a Least Squares Fitting taking into account the restriction of obtaining a monotonic function and considering n=1,2,3 (i.e. linear, cuadratic and cubic functions) to define the polynomial function. In this paper, we have selected as P a wide variety of measures, up to 18 shown in the first column of table 1 (that includes classical statistical measures well known in the literature, measures in the frequency domain, etc.).

Table 1. Fitting RMSE and parameter values that define the function related to each measure

Measures	RMSE	Parameter values				Knots	
		a_3	a_2	a_1	a_0	α	β
Tamura [3]	0.2240	-	-0.247	0.822	0.421	3.77	2.31
Fractal dimension [8]	0.2243	-	-	1.05	-2.36	2.25	3.2
Edge density [9]	0.2483	562	-536	175	-19	0.25	0.387
Amadasun [10]	0.2546	-0.0007	0.0282	-0.376	2.22	20.3	4.66
Correlation [2]	0.2555	-	-	-1.15	1.12	0.978	0.106
Local Homogeneity [2]	0.3022	-953	395	-54.7	2.9	0.211	0.0514
SNE [11]	0.3065	51.5	-110	77.8	-18	0.511	0.935
Weszka [12]	0.3159	106	-42.7	9.87	-0.132	0.0142	0.203
Newsam [13]	0.3179	0.0306	-1.71	31.9	-198	16.2	21.3
Wu [14]	0.3186	$6 \cdot 10^{-6}$	-0.0006	0.0422	-0.119	2.95	42.7
Short Run Emphasis [15]	0.3349	17900	-52000	50300	-16200	0.94	1
Contrast [2]	0.3459	$9 \cdot 10^{-13}$	$-3 \cdot 10^{-8}$	0.0003	-0.024	70.6	5420
Entropy [2]	0.3622	1.22	-31.6	273	-785	8.02	9.44
Uniformity[2]	0.3802	$-5 \cdot 10^{10}$	$5 \cdot 10^7$	-17900	2.19	0.0005	$9 \cdot 10^{-5}$
Variance[2]	0.3987	-	-	$5 \cdot 10^{-5}$	-0.267	5880	27800
DGD [16]	0.4073	0.0001	-0.0104	0.205	-0.194	1	14.1
FMPS [17]	0.4127	0.005	-0.081	-1.62	27.2	18.2	19.9
Abbadeni [1]	0.4928	-	-	98.5	-49.4	0.502	0.512

Table 1 shows for each measure $P_k \in \mathcal{P}$ the least RMSE fitting error obtained, the corresponding parameters $(a_3, \ldots, a_0)$ and the knot values α and β necessary to define the spline function. Note that the fitting error can be viewed as a goodness measure of the ability of the measure to represent the perception of fineness. Table 1 has been sorted in increasing order of the errors and it can be noticed that the five first measures obtain a similar RMSE which difference is as much of 0.03 what implies that these measures will give similar results when employed. Furthermore, the last measures appearing in table 1 have associated a high RMSE very distant from the above mentioned measures which implies that little representativeness of the perception of fineness is found for those measures.

3   Results

The function $\mathcal{T}$ obtained for each measure (defined by the parameter values shown in table 1) has been applied to different real images. Table 2 shows three real images with different perception degree of fineness. For each image and each measure, this table shows the value obtained by the related function and the error obtained when comparing this value with the assessment value given by subjects (by computing the difference between both of them). It can be noticed by looking the results shown in this table that our model allows to represent appropriately the perception of fineness. Note that the values given by the different functions are similar to the corresponding assessment degree for most of the obtained functions.

Table 2. Estimated and error values obtained by applying the proposed model to three real images

Measure	Assessment Value=0		Assessment Value=0.5		Assessment Value=1	
	Value	Error	Value	Error	Value	Error
Tamura	0	0	0.545	0.045	0.966	0.034
Fractal dimension	0	0	0.594	0.094	1	0
Edge density	0	0	0.488	0.012	1	0
Amadasun	0	0	0.489	0.011	0.854	0.146
Correlation	0.012	0.012	0.475	0.025	1	0
Local Homogeneity	0	0	0.459	0.041	0.735	0.265
SNE	0	0	0.421	0.079	0.843	0.157
Weszka	0.085	0.085	0.572	0.072	0.741	0.259
Newsam	0	0	0.435	0.065	0.605	0.395
Wu	0.076	0.076	0.607	0.107	0.774	0.226
Short Run Emphasis	0	0	0.548	0.048	0.709	0.291
Contrast	0.028	0.028	0.634	0.134	0.604	0.396
Entropy	0.285	0.285	0.687	0.187	0.484	0.516
Uniformity	0.115	0.115	0.820	0.320	0.663	0.337
Variance	0.271	0.271	0.640	0.140	0.743	0.257
DGD	0	0	0.331	0.169	1	0
FMPS	0.360	0.360	0.717	0.217	0.803	0.197
Abbadeni	0.396	0.396	0.396	0.104	0.396	0.604

Let's consider figure 2(A) corresponding to a mosaic made by several images, each one with a different increasing perception degree of fineness. The perception degree of fineness for each subimage has been calculated using the Tamura measure (the one with least fitting error according to table 1) and the results are shown in figure 2(B) where a white grey level means maximum perception of fineness, while a black one corresponds to no perception of fineness (the numeric value is also shown on each subimage). It can be noticed that our model captures the evolution of the perception degrees of fineness.

Table 3 shows a comparative between our model and the assessments obtained from subjects for the images in figure 2. The second column shows the assessments given by humans for the different images. The third column shows the perception degree of fineness obtained by applying our model, the fourth column shows the difference between the computed degree and the human assessment. In the case of the fifth column we calculate the differences between the assessment given by each subject and the computed degree, and we obtain

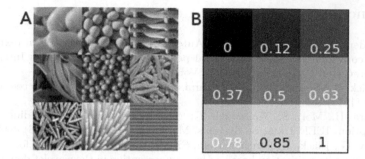

Fig. 2. Results for a mosaic image: (A) original mosaic image (B) presence degree of fineness textural concept obtained with the proposed model for the Tamura measure

Table 3. Errors obtained from mosaic image of figure 2 for the Tamura measure

Image	Human Assessment(H)	Estimated Value (V)	Error #1 ($|H - V|$)	Error #2
1	0	0	0	0
2	0.125	0.125	0	0.021
3	0.250	0.250	0	0.010
4	0.375	0.375	0	0.094
5	0.500	0.500	0	0.010
6	0.625	0.625	0	0.052
7	0.750	0.780	0.030	0.010
8	0.875	0.852	0.023	0.010
9	0.960	1	0.040	0.052
			Avg: 0.011	Avg: 0.029

as error measure the mean from these 20 differences. Finally, the average errors shown in the last row with values of 0.011 and 0.029 show the goodness of our approach to represent the subjectivity found in fineness perception.

4   Conclusions and Future Works

In this paper, functions of fineness perception have been defined on the domain of certain measures. To define such functions, the relationship between a given measure (automatically computed over the image) and the perception degree of fineness has been achieved. In order to obtain the perception degree of fineness, a group of human subjects have been polled. The functions presented in this paper allow to decide whether there is fine, coarse or intermediate texture, splitting the domain into three perceptual meaningful intervals. The results given by our approach show a high level of connection with the assessments given by subjects.

As future work, we will extend the proposed approach to obtain functions on $\mathbb{R}^n$, i.e. functions on vectors of measures. Furthermore, the performance of the fineness functions will be analyzed in applications like textural classification or segmentation.

References

1. Abbadeni, N., Ziou, N., Wang, D.: Autocovariance-based perceptual textural features corresponding to human visual perception. In: Proc. of 15th International Conference on Pattern Recognition. Volume 3. (2000) 901–904
2. Haralick, R.: Statistical and structural approaches to texture. Proceedings IEEE **67**(5) (1979) 786–804
3. Tamura, H., Mori, S., Yamawaki, T.: Textural features corresponding to visual perception. IEEE Trans. on Systems, Man and Cybernetics **8** (1978) 460–473
4. Fahmy, G., Black, J., Panchanathan, S.: Texture characterization for joint compression and classification based on human perception in the wavelet domain. IEEE Transactions on Image Processing (2006)
5. Manian, V., Vasquez, R.: Texture discrimination based on neural dynamics of visual perception. In: Proc. International Joint Conference on Neural Networks. Volume 1. (2003) 113–118
6. Chen, J., Pappas, T., Mojsilovic, A., Rogowitz, B.: Adaptive perceptual color-texture image segmentation. IEEE Transactions on Image Processing (2005)
7. Yager, R.: On ordered weighted averaging aggregation operators in multicriteria decisionmaking. IEEE Trans. on SMC **18**(1) (1988) 183–190
8. Peleg, S., Naor, J., Hartley, R., Avnir, D.: Multiple resolution texture analysis and classification. IEEE Transactions on Pattern Analysis and Machine Intelligence (4) (1984) 518–523
9. Canny, J.: A computational approach to edge detection. IEEE Transactions on Pattern Analysis and Machine Intelligence **8**(6) (1986) 679–698
10. Amadasun, M., King, R.: Textural features corresponding to textural properties. IEEE Transactions on Systems, Man and Cybernetics **19**(5) (1989) 1264–1274
11. Sun, C., Wee, W.: Neighboring gray level dependence matrix for texture classification. Computer Vision, Graphics and Image Processing **23** (1983) 341–352
12. Weszka, J., Dyer, C., Rosenfeld, A.: A comparative study of texture measures for terrain classification. IEEE Trans. on SMC **6** (1976) 269–285
13. Newsam, S., Kammath, C.: Retrieval using texture features in high resolution multi-spectral satellite imagery. In: Data Mining and Knowledge Discovery: Theory, Tools, and Technology VI, SPIE Defense and Security. (2004)
14. Wu, C., Chen, Y.: Statistical feature matrix for texture analysis. CVGIP: Graphical Models and Image Processing **54**(5) (1992) 407–419
15. Galloway, M.: Texture analysis using gray level run lengths. Computer Graphics and Image Processing **4** (1975) 172–179
16. Kim, S., Choi, K., Lee, D.: Texture classification using run difference matrix. In: Proc. of IEEE 1991 Ultrasonics Symposium. Volume 2. (1991) 1097–1100
17. Yoshida, H., Casalino, D., Keserci, B., Coskun, A., Ozturk, O., Savranlar, A.: Wavelet-packet-based texture analysis for differentiation between benign and malignant liver tumours in ultrasound images. Physics in Medicine and Biology **48** (2003) 3735–3753

Vehicle Trajectory Estimation Based on Monocular Vision

Daniel Ponsa and Antonio López

Centre de Visió per Computador, Universitat Autònoma de Barcelona
Edifici O, 08193 Bellaterra, Barcelona, Spain
{daniel,antonio}@cvc.uab.es
www.cvc.uab.es/adas

Abstract. This paper proposes a system to estimate the 3D position
and velocity of vehicles, from images acquired with a monocular camera.
Given image regions where vehicles are detected, Gaussian distributions
are estimated detailing the most probable 3D road regions where vehicles
lay. This is done by combining an assumed image formation model with
the Unscented Transform mechanism. These distributions are then fed
into a Multiple Hypothesis Tracking algorithm, which constructs trajectories coherent with an assumed model of dynamics. This algorithm not
only characterizes the dynamics of detected vehicles, but also discards
false detections, as they do not find spatio-temporal support. The proposals is tested in synthetic sequences, evaluating how noisy observations
and miss-detections affect the accuracy of recovered trajectories.

1 Introduction

The research in Computer Vision applied to intelligent transportation systems is
mainly devoted to provide them with situational awareness, either to ascertain
the state of their driver and passengers or to characterize its external surroundings. Some of the applications required by the automobile industry [1] (automatic
cruise control, autonomous stop & go driving, lane change assistance, etc.), rely
on determining accurately the position and velocity of other vehicles on the road
ahead. First approaches to this problem have been based on active sensors as
radar or lidar. However, the research on camera–based solutions has gained popularity, as vision sensors (CCD/CMOS) are passive and cheaper, and provide a
richer description of the acquired environment. Different vision-based methods
have been proposed to detect vehicles [2], some of them identifying their frontal
or rear view on images acquired by a single camera [3,4,5]. These proposals detect vehicles in a frame-by-frame basis, inferring in some cases their position on
the road from the 2D image regions where they are detected. From the point of
view of a real application, besides the 3D vehicle location, it is very important
to estimate its 3D velocity. This allows to predict the location of vehicles in
the future, and in that way warning about problematic situations in advance.
Thus, the topic of this paper is a method to provide this required dynamics information, based on properly integrating vehicle detections along time. The task

J. Martí et al. (Eds.): IbPRIA 2007, Part I, LNCS 4477, pp. 587–594, 2007.

performed corresponds to the target state initialization that precedes a target tracking process (figure 1). Given detections provided by the vehicle detection module, the objective is to check their spatio-temporal coherence and estimate the vehicle initial state (road position and velocity). Once this state is computed, then it can be efficiently updated along time by a target tracking module, which thanks to assumed system and observation models, localizes vehicles in frames more precisely and efficiently than the target detector can do.

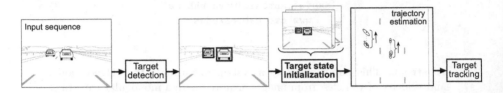

Fig. 1. The method proposed fills the gap between vehicle detection and tracking

The paper proposes a method to construct trajectories from detections, which is useful also to reject spurious false alarms. Indeed, most of false detections are caused by image regions whose appearance is momentarily similar to the one of vehicles. When due to the own vehicle movement the scene is captured from a different viewpoint, these regions are no longer identified as vehicles. In these cases is not possible to construct a coherent trajectory from them (according to expected vehicle dynamics), and this is used to discard them.

The structure of this paper is as follows. Next section details a new proposal to infer 3D vehicle coordinates from the 2D image regions where they are detected. Provided that some assumptions hold, the method combines projective geometry equations with the Unscented Transform to estimate with a Gaussian distribution the road region more likely to contain the detected vehicle. Section 3 describes an algorithm to integrate along time these estimated distributions, building trajectories that corroborate the presence of vehicles and estimate their dynamics. Section 4 evaluates the proposal using synthetic sequences, checking its performance against noisy vehicle detections, and miss-detections. Finally, the paper ends drawing some conclusions.

2   From 2D Detection to 3D Location Hypothesis

Algorithms to detect objects on single frames consist usually on evaluating a similarity criterion at different rectangular image regions, looking for the object of interest. These regions can be established by a deterministic scanning procedure [5], or by a rough preprocessing step that selects a set of candidate regions to be evaluated [4]. Commonly, real targets are detected in several overlapping regions. In order to provide a single detection per target, a clustering process groups neighboring detections, and returns a list of final detections. Each detection is specified by the parameters of a 2D region: its bottom-left corner

(x^r, y^r), and its width and height (w^r, h^r). Each of these parameters have some uncertainty, due to the inaccuracy of the detection/clustering process, which is commonly modeled as a Gaussian perturbation. Thus, for each detection a Gaussian distribution $\mathcal{N}(\mu^r, \Sigma^r)$ is given, where μ^r details the 2D region parameters, and Σ^r their uncertainty. To extract the 3D vehicle location from this observation, $\mathcal{N}(\mu^r, \Sigma^r)$ has to be retroprojected onto the 3D road coordinates. In general, this retroprojection can not be solved, but by assuming that the road conforms to a flat surface (which is realistic for highways and A roads), and that the camera position with respect to it is known, this is feasible.

2.1   Camera Model

The projective geometry of the acquisition system has been modeled in the following way. Image formation is represented using a pin–hole camera model with zero-skew [6], with effective focals (f^x, f^y) and center of projection (x^0, y^0). This camera is mounted on a *host* vehicle, facing the road ahead at a given height h over the ground, inclined slightly a pitch angle θ (figure 2). Using this model, 3D road points $(x, 0, z)$ are related with their image projection (x^r, y^r) by

$$x = \frac{f^y h \left(x^0 - x^r\right)}{f^x \left((y^0 - y^r) \cos(\theta) + f^y \sin(\theta)\right)}, \tag{1}$$

$$z = - \left(\frac{h \left(f^y \cos(\theta) - (y^0 - y^r) \sin(\theta)\right)}{(y^0 - y^r) \cos(\theta) + f^y \sin(\theta)} \right). \tag{2}$$

These expressions require knowing the camera extrinsic parameters (h, θ), which unfortunately can vary in every frame due to the action of the host vehicle suspension system. The variation of h can be ignored, as provokes a negligible error on x and z estimations, but a correct θ value is essential to estimate them accurately. θ could be estimated if the width w of the observed vehicle and its rotation φ relative to the Y–axe (Yaw angle) were known. At ground level, $w' = w \cos(\varphi)$ with commonly $\varphi \approx 0$, and w' projects onto w^r image pixels

$$w^r \sim \frac{f^x w'}{z \cos(\theta) - h \sin(\theta)}. \tag{3}$$

Combining properly equations (2) and (3), it is found that

$$\theta = 2 \arctan \left(\left(1 - \sqrt{1 + \left(\frac{y^0 - y^r}{f^y}\right)^2 - \left(\frac{w^r h}{w' f^x}\right)^2} \right) \Big/ \left(\frac{y^0 - y^r}{f^y} - \frac{w^r h}{w' f^x} \right) \right),$$

and this makes feasible using equations (1) and (2) to hypothesize the 3D vehicle location. Unfortunately, to estimate θ the values of w and φ of observed vehicles are required, which are unknown a priori. However, relatively to the initial problem of unknowing θ, now there are some advantages. φ has a narrow range of feasible values, and its value is very close to zero in most of the situations. The range of feasible w values can also be very narrow, if for instance the vehicle detection process identifies the type of vehicle (bus, lorry, sedan, etc.). Thus, estimations more accurate than just by guessing directly θ can be obtained.

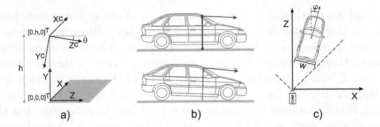

Fig. 2. a) Camera coordinate system relative to the road coordinate system. b) Extrinsic camera parameters vary when the vehicle suspension system actuates. c) Top view of the road coordinate system, detailing the vehicle orientation angle φ.

2.2 Retroprojecting a Gaussian Distribution

The vehicle detection procedure generates as result not simple 2D regions, but normal distributions $\mathcal{N}(\mu^r, \Sigma^r)$ of region parameters (x^r, y^r, w^r) (h^r is discarded because is irrelevant in the proposed retroprojection scheme). Estimating the distribution of 3D road points corresponding to a detection is not straightforward, basically because the retroprojection equations (1) and (2) are non–linear. This paper proposes computing a Gaussian approximation of this distribution by applying the Unscented Transform [7]. Given a Gaussian distribution to be transformed, a set of samples (sigma–points) are deterministically chosen which jointly match its mean and covariance. These samples are propagated using the non–linear equations, generating a cloud of transformed points. Computing the sample mean and covariance of these points (properly weighted) the Gaussian distribution fitting the transformed distribution is characterized (figure 3). The uncertainty of the final vehicle location distribution depends on the particular uncertainty in each detection parameter, being w^r the one who affects 3D locations the most.

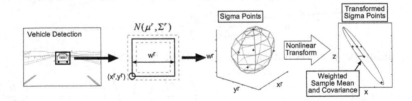

Fig. 3. Process of transforming 2D detections into 3D road coordinates

3   Detection Confirmation and Tracking

The procedure described up to this point analyses sequences in a frame-by-frame basis, and it can not provide information about the dynamics of detected vehicles. It performs like a sensor that perceives an image, and provides as output a noisy list of 3D location distributions where vehicles may lay. These distributions may correspond to real vehicles or not, so the burden is also sort out false alarms from genuine detections. One possibility to deal with this problem is using Multiple Hypothesis Tracking (MHT) methods [8]. The idea is to connect consecutive detections along time, constructing trajectories or *tracks*. As new observations are collected, they may be integrated in existent trajectories, as well as start new ones. Trajectory construction is not always a trivial task, as several detections can verify a same trajectory at a given instant. One way to deal with this *data association problem* is considering all the feasible hypothesis, constructing a tree of trajectories along time. Trajectories started from false detections are commonly discarded in a few frames, since they will not receive more detections in the future. Trajectories coherent with a given number of observations confirm the presence of real vehicles, and then their dynamics can be estimated.

There exist many different MHT algorithms in the literature, which differ basically in how they deal with the data association problem. In general, the tree of trajectories can grow exponentially with the observations. If occasional miss-detections have also to be considered, the growth in the number of hypothesis is even more severe. So in order to fulfill computational requirements, *suboptimal* algorithms propose different strategies to consider only a (presumably good) subset of all possible trajectories. In the studied application, each observation can be generated only by a single vehicle, what reduces significantly the trajectories to be spreaded. Another important characteristics of vehicle detection is that 3D coordinates of observed vehicles are significantlly apart (they are at least separated by the width of one vehicle). These facts allow to pose a MHT with one of the simplest association methods: the Global Nearest Neighbor (GNN) criterion. It finds the best (most likely) assignment of input observations to existing trajectories, under the constrain that an observation can be associated with at most one track. For observations that remain unassigned, new trajectories are initiated. Due to paper size restrictions, is not possible to detail the algorithm implemented, based on the multiple target Kalman tracker in [9].

3.1   Trajectory Characterization

Trajectories managed in the MHT algorithm collect measurements until a given number N of them is reached. This task is done by a Kalman Filter (KF), estimating the state distribution of the vehicle at each instant t (i.e. $\mathbf{x}_t$, mantaining the vehicle coordinates on the road), using observations available up to t ($\mathbf{y}_{1:t}$). In formal terms, the MHT characterises $p(\mathbf{x}_t|\mathbf{y}_{1:t})$. A maximal use of the N collected observations can be done, by using all of them to estimate the vehicle state at each instant t. Formally, this corresponds to estimate $p(\mathbf{x}_t|\mathbf{y}_{1:N})$ where $N \geq t$. In estimation theory terms, this procedure corresponds to the *smoothing* of the trajectory. The Kalman Smoother (KS) scheme implemented in this paper is based on the Rauch–Tung–Striebel fixed–interval optimal smoother [10]. This algorithm estimates a smoothed trajectory, from where the forward velocity v_t and orientation φ_t of the vehicle are computed. Figure 4 sketches the procedure carried out. The value of φ_t is constrained in the range $[-\pi/2, \pi/2]$, forcing in that way to maintain the vehicle movement direction in the sign of v_t.

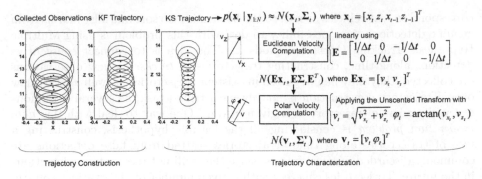

Fig. 4. Process to estimate the vehicle 3D velocity

4   Performance Evaluation

The proposal presented shows qualitatively a very good performance on real sequences, specially in discarding false vehicle detections. However, a quantitatively analysis of its operation is necessary to validate it objectively. Due to the lack of ground truth information in the available real sequences (i.e, knowledge about the real 3D location and velocity of vehicles), the system has been evaluated using synthetic data. Its accuracy depends on many factors (the 3D position of vehicles, their velocities, the noise perturbing detections, inaccurate assumptions, etc.). In this paper, an experiment has been designed to evaluate the system performance when assumptions hold, but vehicles are noisely detected and occasionaly missdetected. Synthetic vehicle trajectories have been simulated, and the parameters of their corresponding 2D image regions computed. An artificial variance has been given to these parameters, emulating the one of real detections. Three different situations have been analyzed, showing a vehicle at three different starting points, with a velocity relative to the host of 6 Km/h. The vehicle detection parameters (x^r, y^r, w^r) have been randomly distorted by different amounts of noise, corresponding to disturbances of the real vehicle position and width between $[-0.15, 0.15]$ meters. Missdetection events with probabilities between 0 and 40% have been considered. For each considered noisy situation, 100 different random sequences have been generated and processed, computing the disparity between the real and recovered trajectory, forward velocity, and orientation. The performance criterion used is the average of the Mean Square Error (MSE) in the 100 experiments. The presence of vehicles is confirmed, when their corresponding trajectories collect 12 observations. Figure 5 shows results obtained.

With respect to recover the vehicle trajectory, the system performs similarly wherever the trajectory starts. Accuracy depends critically on the presence of miss-detections along the trajectory. In the estimation of the vehicle velocity $[v, \varphi]^T$, better results are obtained for closer vehicles, as the uncertainty in the 3D road locations composing the trajectory is smaller. Concerning the x position of vehicles, centered ones provide a more accurate estimation of φ, while the

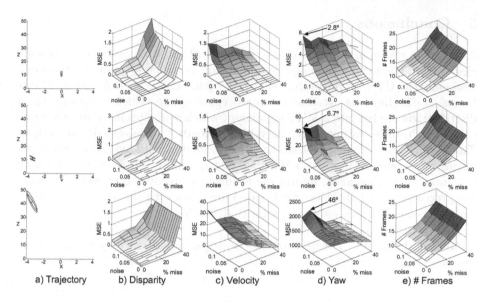

a) Trajectory   b) Disparity   c) Velocity   d) Yaw   e) # Frames

Fig. 5. a) Extremes of the trajectories considered. b–d) Respectively, MSE between real and recovered 3D trajectory locations, forward velocities (v), and orientations (φ). e) Average number of frames required to confirm a vehicle detection.

estimation of v is a little bit more imprecise. Note that the factor that affects more critically the estimation of vehicle dynamics is the noise perturbing observations, while surprisingly, miss-detections clearly favour its better estimation. This results from the fact that due to miss-detections, it takes a longer time to obtain the N observations that compose a *complete* trajectory, and this favours having observations more distant (in spatial terms) between each other. This attenuates the effect of the uncertainty of 3D locations in the velocity estimation (figure 6). The presence of false positives in the observations has also been evaluated. In each frame, false detections has been added, distributed randomly on the acquired road following a uniform distribution. Results obtained are extremely similar to the ones in figure 5, showing the great capacity of the proposal to discard uncorrelated false detections.

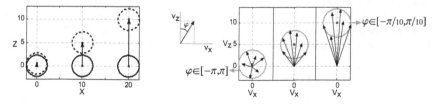

Fig. 6. Left) Consecutive observations of three trajectories. Right) Distribution of their corresponding velocity. The more distant observations are, the less uncertain φ is.

5   Conclusions

A system has been proposed to characterize the 3D position and velocity of vehicles, from 2D detections in images obtained from a camera on a mobile platform. Combinig the UT with projective geometry, vehicle detections are converted into Gaussian distributions detailing the road region where vehicles may lay. These distributions are fed into a MHT algorithm, which evaluates its spatio-temporal coherence in order estimate the 3D vehicle velocity and reject false detections. The performance of the proposal has been evaluated with synthetic sequences, in order to compare results obtained against ground truth data. Results show that miss-detections affect mostly the accuracy of recovered trajectories, while the precision on the 3D velocity estimated degrades with the noise in the observations. False detections are satisfactorily discarded.

Acknowledgments. This research has been partially funded by Spanish MEC project TRA2004-06702/AUT.

References

1. Dickmanns, E.: The development of machine vision for road vehicles in the last decade. In: Int. Symp. on Intelligent Vehicles, Versailles (2002)
2. Sun, Z., Bebis, G., Miller, R.: On-road vehicle detection: A review. IEEE Trans. on Pattern Analysis and Machine Intelligence 28(5), 694–711 (2006)
3. Betke, M., Haritaoglu, E., Davis, L.: Realtime multiple vehicle detection and tracking from a moving vehicle. Machine Vision & Applications, (12), pp. 69–83 (2000)
4. Khammari, A., Lacroix, E., Nashashibi, F., Laurgeau, C.: Vehicle detection combining gradient analysis and adaboost classification. In: IEEE Conf. on Intelligent Transportation Systems, pp. 1084–1089 (2005)
5. Ponsa, D., López, A., Lumbreras, F., Serrat, J., Graf, T.: 3D vehicle sensor based on monocular vision. In: IEEE Conf. on Intelligent Transportation Systems, pp. 1096–1101 (2005)
6. Hartley, R.I., Zisserman, A.: Multiple View Geometry in Computer Vision, 2nd edn. Cambridge University Press, Cambridge, ISBN: 0521540518 (2004)
7. Julier, S.J.: The spherical simplex unscented transformation. In: Proceedings of the American Control Conference, Denver, Colorado, pp. 2430–2434 (2003)
8. Blackman, S.B.: Multiple hypothesis tracking for multiple target tracking. IEEE Aerospace and Electronic Systems Magazine 19(1), 5–18 (2004)
9. Davies, D., Palmer, P., Mirmehdi, M.: Detection and tracking of very small low constrast objects. In: British Machine Vision Conference, pp. 599–608 (1998)
10. Gelb, A., et al.: Applied Optimal Estimation. The MIT Press, Cambridge (1974)

A Neural Network Model for Image Change Detection Based on Fuzzy Cognitive Maps

Gonzalo Pajares[1], Alfonso Sánchez-Beato[2], Jesús M. Cruz[3], and José J. Ruz[3]

[1] Dpt. Ingeniería del Software e Inteligencia Artificial, Facultad Informática, Universidad Complutense, 28040 Madrid, Spain
pajares@dacya.ucm.es
[2] Dpt. Informática y Automática, E.T.S. Informática UNED, 28040 Madrid, Spain
alfonsosanchezbeato@yahoo.es
[3] Dpt. Arquitectura Computadores y Automática, Facultad Informática, Universidad Complutense, 28040 Madrid, Spain
{jmcruz,jjruz}@dacya.ucm.es

Abstract. This paper outlines a neural network model based on the Fuzzy Cognitive Maps (FCM) framework for solving the automatic image change detection problem. Each pixel in the reference image is assumed to be a node in the network. Each node has associated a fuzzy value, which determines the magnitude of the change. Each fuzzy value is updated by a trade-off between the influences received from the fuzzy values from other neurons and its own fuzzy value. Classical approaches in the literature have been designed assuming that the mutual influences between two nodes are symmetric. The main finding of this paper is the assumption that mutual influences could not be symmetric. This non symmetric relationship can be embedded by the FCM paradigm. The performance of the proposed method is illustrated by comparative analysis against some recent image change detection methods.

1 Introduction

A major portion of the research efforts of the computer vision community has been directed towards the study of automatic image change detection methods [1]. In [2] we have proposed a Hopfield Neural Network (HNN) model, where the comparative analysis against some existing strategies has been proven favorably. In HNN, given a reference image we build a network of nodes where each pixel in the reference image is a node in the network. The goal is to determine if a pixel has changed based on the corresponding node's value. Each node value is updated iteratively through a trade-off between two kinds of relations: *binary* and *unary*. Binary relations establish the degree of influence that a neuron exercises over other neuron during the iterative process. Unary relations determine the self-influence of each neuron during such process. Binary relations have been used in some well-tested strategies [3,4]. The binary relations in HNN are mapped as symmetric weights, as required by the Hopfield neural network paradigm. This symmetry is also used in [3,4] where an energy function is to be minimized. The minimization is carried out by taking into account

J. Martí et al. (Eds.): IbPRIA 2007, Part I, LNCS 4477, pp. 595–602, 2007.

only the previous system configuration (state) without to resort to historic states. This implies that these approaches follow the Markov Random Fields framework.

The main finding of this paper is the assumption that mutual influences could not be symmetric, based on the hypothesis that different nodes could have different levels of relevance. So, assuming that the node i is more relevant than the node j, the influence of i over j should be greater than the influence of j over i. The relevance is a concept introduced in this work based on the assumption that the value of a relevant node should remain unchanged during the iterative process. The neurofuzzy FCM paradigm is a suitable strategy to deal with non-symmetric influences under binary relations and also to embed the self-influence under unary relations.

This paper is organized as follows. Section 2 contains the customized FCM approach, where the mapping of mutual influences is obtained. Also the mapping of the relevance associated to each node is computed. The performance of the method is illustrated in section 3, where a comparative analysis against other existing image change detection strategies is carried out. Finally, in section 4, there is a discussion of some related topics.

2 Fuzzy Cognitive Maps for Image Change Detection

2.1 The FCM Framework for Image Change Detection

FCMs are networks used to create models as collections of concepts and the various causal relations that exist between these concepts [5-11]. The concepts are represented by nodes and the causal relationships by directed arcs between the nodes. Each arc is accompanied by a causal weight that defines the type of causal binary relation between the two nodes. The causal weights w_{ij} take values in the fuzzy causal interval [−1, +1]; $w_{ij} = 0$ indicates no causality. Positive causal relation ($w_{ij} > 0$) between two concepts C_i and C_j indicates causal increase: C_i increases as C_j increases and C_i decreases as C_j decreases. Negative causal relation ($w_{ij} < 0$) indicates causal decrease or negative causality: decreases as C_j increases and C_i increases as C_j decreases. In FCMs no feedback from a node to itself is allowed, so $w_{ii} = 0$.

The image change detection problem is formulated as follows: given two registered images $I_1(x,y)$, $I_2(x,y)$ of size MxN of the same area in the scene, taken at different times, the goal is to detect if a pixel, located at (x,y), has changed and the magnitude of the change. With such purpose, we build a network of $n = MxN$ nodes, where each node i represents a pixel location (x,y). We create the $n \times n$ weight matrix W, assuming that it can be non-symmetric. At each iteration k, the node i in the network has the activation level A_i^k ranging in [−1, +1]. This implies that every node is positively or negatively activated to a certain degree that determines the magnitude of the change at each pixel location, i.e. $A_i^k = +1$ maximum degree of change and $A_i^k = -1$ without change.

In Bruzzone and Prieto [3] and Aach and Kaup [4] an iterative scheme determines if a change has occurred at a given pixel location based on the mapping of data and contextual consistencies between such pixel location and the pixels in its neighbourhood. The contextual consistencies only take into account the previous state without to resort to historic states. This implies that they follow the Markov Random Field (MRF) framework. In Pajares [2], the contribution of the neighbours is also mapped as data and contextual consistencies; but unlike in [3,4], an explicit self-contribution is incorporated. So, the degree of change for each pixel is achieved through a trade-off between the consistencies provided by the neighbours and its own contribution. This scheme, based on the HNN approach, requires that the binary relations between nodes i and j are symmetric ($w_{ij} = w_{ji}$), i.e. W must be symmetric. Although, this method performs favourably, we have verified that the mapping of the contextual consistencies can be still improved. Indeed, we assume that different nodes could have different levels of relevance. In this paper, the relevance is determined as a measure of the strength that a node shows, during the iterative process, against the variations on its activation level. The mutual relevance is embedded in the mapping of the contextual information. This implies that W could not be symmetric; hence the HNN paradigm cannot be applied. Nevertheless, the FCM scheme with certainty neurons, Tsardias and Margaritis [5,6], has the ability to assume this non-symmetry. Additionally, it can embed the unary relations. Indeed, a certainty neuron i has memory capabilities and its activation level at iteration $k + 1$ is computed as,

$$A_i^{k+1} = f\left(A_i^k, S_i^k\right) = f\left(A_i^k, \sum_{j=1}^{n} w_{ji} A_j^k\right) - d_i A_i^k \tag{1}$$

where A_i^k is the activation of certainty neuron i at iteration k, S_i^k is the sum of the weighted influence that certainty neuron i receives at the iteration k from all other neurons, $d_i \in [0,1]$ is the decay factor of certainty neuron i. This factor determines the fraction of the current activation level that will be subtracted from the new activation level as a result of the neuron's natural intention to get closer to activation level zero. The bigger the decay factor the stronger the decay mechanism. Following Tsadiras and Margaritis [5] the function f is that used in the MYCIN expert system for the aggregation of the certainty factors, defined as follows,

$$f(x, y) = \begin{cases} x + y(1-x) & \text{if } x, y \geq 0, \\ x + y(1+x) & \text{if } x, y < 0, \\ (x+y)/(1-\min(|x|,|y|)) & \text{else} \end{cases} \tag{2}$$

where $|x|, |y| \leq 1$. A_i^k is always in that interval, but this does not apply for S_i^k, as a concept can be influenced by many concepts and perhaps the sum $\sum_{j=1}^{n} w_{ji} A_j^k$ can take a value outside the interval $[-1, +1]$. In order to keep S_i^k within that interval it is passed through the sigmoid function, i.e. $S_i^k = tanh\left(S_i^k\right)$, as suggested by Tsadiras and Margaritis [5]. So, under the FCM framework the binary influences are mapped in S_i^k as data and contextual consistencies, assuming that they could be non-symmetric; the self-influence is embedded in the A_i^k memory term. From equation (1), the goal is to compute: a) the w_{ij} in order to build the weight matrix W and b) the decay factor.

2.2 Data and Contextual Consistencies

The data and contextual consistencies are computed following the model described in Pajares [2] and related references. From the images $I_1(x,y)$, $I_2(x,y)$ we compute the difference image $D(x,y) = I_1(x,y) - I_2(x,y)$ assuming that each pixel of D is either with the hypothesis H_0 (no change) or the hypothesis H_1 (change). We build a Bayesian model so that each pixel (x,y) in the difference image $D(x,y)$ should be associated to the hypothesis that maximizes the posterior conditional probability, i.e.

$$H_s = \arg \max_{H_s \in \{H_0, H_1\}} \{P(H_s/D(x,y))\} = \arg \max_{H_s \in \{H_0, H_1\}} \{P(H_s)p(D(x,y)/H_s)\} \quad (3)$$

From (3) we build a *data map* with the same size as the difference image and identical (x,y) locations that those of the pixels in D and nodes in the network. Each node i at location (x,y) is loaded with the data information $r(i)$ according to the following criterion,

$$r(i) = (-1)^{s+1} P(H_s/D(x,y)); \quad s = \{0,1\} \quad (4)$$

The data consistency between nodes i, j is measured through the data compatibility coefficient d_{ij} as follows,

$$d_{ij} = \begin{cases} 1 - 0.5|r(i) - r(j)| & j \in N_i^8 \\ 0 & j \notin N_i^8 \end{cases} \quad (5)$$

N_i^8 is the 8-connected neighborhood of the node i. From (5) we can see that d_{ij} ranges in $[0,1]$ where the lower/higher limit means minimum/maximum data consistency respectively.

The mapping of contextual consistencies is computed through the equation (6) taking into account mutual influences.

$$c_{ij} = \begin{cases} p_{ij}\left(1 - |A_i^k - A_j^k|\right) & j \in N_i^8 \\ 0 & j \notin N_i^8 \end{cases} \quad (6)$$

where p_{ij} is a coefficient that measures the influence of the node i over node j taking into account the relevance of each node. The relevance is a concept introduced in this paper in order to measure the strength of each node against changes in its activation level. We build an accumulator of cells of size $n = MxN$, where the each cell i is associated to the node of identical name. Each cell i contains the number of times, p_i, that the node i has changed significantly its activation level. Initially, all p_i are set to zero and then $p_i = p_i + 1$ if $\left| A_i^k - A_i^{k-1} \right| > \varepsilon$, where ε is set to 0.05 in this paper. Now, p_{ij} is computed as follows,

$$p_{ij} = \begin{cases} p_j / (p_i + p_j) & (p_i + p_j) \geq 2 \\ 1 & \text{else} \end{cases} \tag{7}$$

The equation (7) measures the fraction of changes accumulated for the node j against the node i; p_{ji} measures the reverse influence of j over i. This equation is interpreted as follows, if $p_i < p_j$ the node i has accumulated less number of changes than the node j, i.e. the node i has a higher relevance than the node j and vice versa. This implies that p_{ij} could be different from p_{ji}. From (6) we can see that c_{ij} varies with the iteration and ranges in $[0,1]$ where the lower/higher limit means minimum/maximum contextual consistency respectively. One can see that c_{ij} could be different from c_{ji} (non symmetry).

Now the goal is to combine appropriately d_{ij} and c_{ij} in order to derive the causal weights required by the equation (1). Making use of the fuzzy set theory, we consider the fuzzy sets A and B, where their elements are pairs of nodes (i,j) and the degrees of compatibility (membership functions) are given by d_{ij} and c_{ij} respectively. According to the dissertations of Zimmermann [10] we propose the Hamacher's union operator because of its performance,

$$W_{ij} = \frac{(\gamma - 1)d_{ij}c_{ij} + d_{ij} + c_{ij}}{1 + \gamma c_{ij}d_{ij}} \tag{8}$$

where $\gamma \geq -1$; by setting $\gamma = -1$ the Hamacher's union operator matches with the Hamacher sum. Hence, in our experiments the best results are obtained with this value.

Once we have computed W_{ij} according to equation (8) a rescaling from the range $[0,+1]$ to the range $[-1,+1]$ allows us to compute the causal weight between nodes i and j as required by the equation (1),

$$w_{ij} = 2W_{ij} - 1 \tag{9}$$

In Tsadiras and Margaritis [5,6] is reported after the experimentation that the decay factor must range in $[0,0.4]$ trying to avoid that the system collapses to zero. This factor subtracts a fraction to the current activation level. Hence, we assume that if a node i is relevant as compared to its neighbors, the fraction to be subtracted must be as minimum as possible and the number of iterations k must be embedded as follows,

$$d_i = \begin{cases} \dfrac{\bar{p}_j}{(\bar{p}_j + p_i)k} & k \geq 4 \\ 0 & \text{else} \end{cases} \tag{10}$$

where p_i is the cell's accumulator value for the node i and $\bar{p}_j$ is the average value accumulated by the nodes $j \in N_i^8$.

The network is initialized from the histogram of the difference image $D(x,y)$ according to the method described in Bruzzone and Prieto [3] and reproduced in Pajares [2]. The iterative process ends if all nodes in the network fulfill the following criterion: $\left| A_i^k - A_i^{k-1} \right| > \varepsilon$ or a number of iterations, k_{max} is reached. The final values A_i^k determine the magnitude of the change.

3 Performance Analysis

This paper introduces the relevance criterion when mapping the contextual consistencies, which could introduce a non symmetric influence between two nodes. This implies a modification with respect the HNN approach described in Pajares [2]. So, for comparative purposes we use the same four data sets described in [2]: 1) 40 pairs of real video sequences of outdoor environments of size 1392 x 1040; 2) 36 pairs of real video sequences of indoor environments of size 840 x 760; 3) 10 pairs of real remote sensing images of size of size 400 x 400; and 4) 60 pairs of synthetic sensing images of size of size 400 x 400. All results are verified against a *ground truth map* which is previously determined. Figure 1 (*a, b*) shows a representative pair of the outdoor environment with the changes detected by the FCM process in (*c*).

The HNN method of Pajares [2] was compared against six existing image change detection strategies including the approach of Bruzzone and Fernández-Prieto [3] (BRU), which follows the MRF framwork. The best performances were obtained by HNN followed by BRU. This paper compares the performance of the proposed FCM approach against the iterative HNN and BRU methods. FCM, HNN and BRU use the same initialization process and a neighborhood region of size 3x3. We use a set of seven experiments, a brief description of the experiments is the following: **E1**: 30 outdoor pairs of images from the same sequence; **E2**: 10 outdoor pairs of images from different sequences of the same scene; **E3**: 12 indoor pairs of images from the same sequence without changes in the illumination levels; **E4**: 12 indoor pairs of images from the same sequence, during the full capture process the illumination levels are on-line changed, i.e. the images have different intensity levels; **E5**: 12 indoor pairs of images from the same sequence, an image is obtained without changes in the illumination during its capture and the other, as before, by varying on-line the illumination; **E6**: 10 pairs of remote sensing images of the same scene; **E7**: 30 pairs of synthetic remote sensing images of the same scene corrupted with Gaussian noise of zero-mean.

The results obtained for each method are compared against the ground truth, based on the *PCC* magnitude described in Rosin and Ioannidis [11], also used in Pajares [2]: $PCC = (TP + TN)/(TP + FP + TN + FN)$, where TP: number of change pixels correctly detected; FP: number of no-change pixels incorrectly labelled as change; TN: number of no-change pixels correctly detected; FN: number of change pixels incorrectly labelled as no-change.

Fig. 1. Outdoor environment; (*a*) and (*b*) two images of the same sequence; (*c*) changes detected with the FCM approach

Table I shows the results in terms of the correct classification for the seven experiments. The final result for each experiment is averaged by the number of pairs of images processed. The number of iterations used in our FCM (k_{max}) is set to the number of iterations where HNN gained the convergence for each set of experiments, i.e. E1, E3 = 4, E2, E5 = 8, E4 = 10 and E6, E7 = 5.

Table 1. Averaged PCC scores for each method against the set of experiments

$x10^{-3}$	**E1**	**E2**	**E3**	**E4**	**E5**	**E6**	**E7**
BRU	921	821	945	653	698	819	615
HNN	987	943	991	789	876	901	847
FCM	944	954	956	823	901	848	844

From the results in Table I, one can see that FCM improves the performance of HNN for experiments E2, E4 and E5 where the number of iterations is higher than the used for the other experiments. This means that the FCM approach is suitable for images where the number of iterations is high.

The above behavior appears when the pair of images displays high variability due to different illumination conditions or other causes as in the experiments E2, E4 and E5. This means that the FCM should be applied in image sequences captured under such illumination conditions where it is foreseeable that the number of iterations could become high.

The best performance achieved by the FCM approach can be interpreted in the light of the mutual influence between two nodes based on the relevance's values. Indeed, as the number of iterations increases, the relevance of each node achieves higher stability (less number of changes in the activation level). This is reflected in the equation (6). FCM and HNN achieve a similar performance for E7 (with noise).

4   Conclusions

In this paper we have developed a new automatic strategy for image change detection based on the well-founded FCM paradigm, which allows the computation of a non-symmetric weight matrix based on binary relations between the nodes in the network thanks to the introduction of the relevance concept. The FCM paradigm also includes unary relations as in HNN. The FCM has proven its performance against some existing strategies. As all iterative approaches this method is computational intensive. The execution time is similar to the obtained by HNN. So, for real-time requirements under surveillance tasks it should be implemented under parallel architectures.

Acknowledgments. This research was sponsored under project no. 143/2004 Fundación General UCM and the Spanish Council for Science and Technology (CICYT) under grant DPI2006-15661-C02-01.

References

1. Radke, R.J., Andra, S., Al-Kofahi, O., Roysam, B.: Image Change Detection Algorithms: A Systematic Survey. IEEE Trans. Image Processing 14(3), 294–307 (2005)
2. Pajares, G.: A Hopfield Neural Network for Image Change Detection. IEEE Trans. Neural Networks 17(5), 1250–1264 (2006)
3. Bruzzone, L., Fernández-Prieto, D.: Automatic Analysis of the difference Image for unsupervised change detection. IEEE Trans. Geoscience Remote Sensing 38(3), 1171–1182 (2000)
4. Aach, T., Kaup, A.: Bayesian algorithms for adaptive change detection in image sequences using Markov Random fields. Signal Processing: Image Communication 7, 147–160 (1995)
5. Tsardias, A.K., Margaritis, K.G.: An experimental study of the dynamics of the certainty neuron fuzzy cognitive maps. Neurocomputing 24, 95–116 (1999)
6. Tsardias, A.K., Margaritis, K.G.: Cognitive Mapping and Certainty Neuron Fuzzy Cognitive Maps. Information Sciences 101, 109–130 (1997)
7. Kosko, B.: Fuzzy Cognitive Maps. Int. J. Man. Machine Studies 24, 65–75 (1986)
8. Kosko, B.: Neural Networks and Fuzzy Systems: a dynamical systems approach to machine intelligence. Prentice-Hall, NJ (1992)
9. Miao, Y., Liu, Z.Q.: On Causal Inference in Fuzzy Cognitive Maps. IEEE Trans. Fuzzy Systems 8(1), 107–119 (2000)
10. Zimmermann, H.J.: Fuzzy Set Theory and its applications. Kluwer Academic Publishers, Dordrecht (1991)
11. Rosin, P.L., Ioannidis, E.: Evaluation of global image thresholding for change detection. Pattern Recognition Letters 24, 2345–2356 (2003)

Semiring Lattice Parsing Applied to CYK*

Salvador España Boquera[1], Jorge Gorbe Moya[1], and
Francisco Zamora Martínez[2]

[1] DSIC, Universidad Politécnica de Valencia, Valencia (Spain)
[2] LSI, Universitat Jaume I, Castellón (Spain)
{sespana,jgorbe}@dsic.upv.es, fzamora@guest.uji.es

Abstract. Context-Free Grammars play an important role in the pattern recognition research community. Word graphs provide a compact representation of the ambiguous alternatives generated during many pattern recognition, machine translation and other NLP tasks. This paper generalizes the framework for string parsing based on semirings and hypergraphs to the case of lattice parsing. This framework is the basis for the implementation of a parsing interface in a dataflow software architecture where modules send and receive word graphs in a serialized form using a protocol which allows the easy generation, filtering and parsing of word graphs. An implementation of the CYK algorithm is presented as an example. Experimental results are reported to demonstrate the proposed method.

1 Introduction

Context-Free Grammars (CFG) play an important role in the pattern recognition research community [3,4,5,6]. Stochastic grammars are used to model the fact that some structures are more preferable than others and CFGs can represent more longer-term and more complex structural dependencies than regular models.

Several efforts have been made in order to specify parsing algorithms for these grammars in a general framework. These works show that a single algorithm description can deal with the computation of several quantities [1], that parsing algorithms can be specified in a modular way [7] (i.e., as a combination of sub-algorithms) or that parsing can be viewed as particular cases of more general algorithms [2]. Most of these formalisms consider only the parsing of strings.

Word graphs provide a compact and useful representation of a finite set of sentences with associated values which has many applications [8]. To cite one of them, they can be used to represent the ambiguous alternatives generated during speech recognition, machine translation and other natural language processing (NLP) tasks. In a sequential-coupling approach, a set of n-best hypotheses is produced by one module and is rescored by other module. This is the reason why several algorithms for parsing word graphs have been proposed. Bottom-up chart parsing, through various forms of extensions to the CYK algorithm [9,10,11], has

---

* This work has been partially supported by the Spanish Government under contract TIN2006-12767 and by the Generalitat Valenciana under contract GVA06/302.

J. Martí et al. (Eds.): IbPRIA 2007, Part I, LNCS 4477, pp. 603–610, 2007.

been applied to word graphs [12,13,14]. Earley parser has also been extended [15]. Previous work on parsing word graphs with CFGs is usually considered a straightforward extension of the sentence counterpart. For instance, in [16] Section *"Parsing a lattice as a chart"* we do not find much more detail that: *"we parse the lattice using the standard mapping of frame numbers to chart edges"*.

One of the aims of this paper is to formally describe the search space of word graph parsing in such a way that weights associated to the word graph edges are also taken into account. This formalization is not only of theoretical importance since, as it is shown in an example, the search space of some previous lattice parsing algorithms [13] is larger than necessary.

The second goal of this paper is the description of a general lattice parsing algorithm interface so that a parser can be implemented by specifying the actions to be taken when each message is received. This implementation can be used in a dataflow software architecture where lattices or word graphs can be sent from one module to another by means of a serialization protocol. This protocol allows the easy computation of the desired quantities by the parser, and the generation and filtering of word graphs by other modules. An example of CYK lattice parsing is described for the proposed approach and experimental results are reported.

2   Context-Free Parsing of Lattices

We follow the work of Goodman [1] to describe weighted CFG parsing based on complete semirings [17], but we generalize this work in order to take into account the weights associated to the input data.

A CFG is a tuple $G = \langle N, \Sigma, R, S \rangle$ where N and Σ are disjoint sets. N is the set of nonterminals including the start symbol S, Σ is the set of terminal symbols, and R is the set of rules, each of the form $A \to \gamma$ for $A \in N$ and $\gamma \in (N \cup \Sigma)^\star$. Given the string $\alpha A \beta$ and a grammar rule $A \to \gamma \in R$, we write $\alpha A \beta \Rightarrow \alpha \gamma \beta$ to indicate that the first string produces the second string by substituting γ for A. The symbol $\overset{\star}{\Rightarrow}$ denotes the reflexive, transitive closure of $\Rightarrow$. The language generated by the grammar is $L(G) = \{s \in \Sigma^\star | S \overset{\star}{\Rightarrow} s\}$. G is null-free if $\gamma \in (N \cup \Sigma)^+$ for all rules $A \to \gamma \in R$. Our work is restricted to CFGs which are both null-free and also allow an ordering of their nonterminals $A_1 < A_2 < \cdots < A_{|N|}$ such that if $A_i \to A_j \in R$ then $i < j$, which is not the general case.

A complete semiring [17] is a tuple $\langle \mathbb{A}, \oplus, \otimes, 0, 1 \rangle$ where $\mathbb{A}$ is a set of values over which a multiplicative operator $\otimes$ and a commutative additive operator $\oplus$ have been defined, and for which infinite summations are defined.

A weighted context free grammar is simply a CFG where every rule $A \to \alpha$ is associated a weight $W(A \to \alpha) \in \mathbb{A}$. The boolean semiring $\langle \{0, 1\}, \vee, \wedge, 0, 1 \rangle$, when used in parsing provides *acceptance* information. Other semirings compute values like the number of parse trees, the inside probability, etc. The derivation forest semiring [1] and others are noncommutative. Since word graphs are, in essence, acyclic weighted finite state automata, the result of parsing for the general case of noncommutative semirings cannot be reduced to the parsing of the sentences the word graph represents. The reason is that weights from the word graph and those from the grammar rules are, in general, interleaved. In order to define how weights from input edges and grammar rules are combined, we must define the parsing of a weighted CFG by means of *weighted deriva-tion trees* (WDT). A WDT is a child-ordered tree with nodes from $N \cup \Sigma \cup \mathbb{A}$. The start symbol S is a WDT. Given a WDT w with a leave $A \in N$, and a grammar rule $A \to \alpha$, $\alpha = \alpha_1 \alpha_2 \dots \alpha_n$, the replacement of A in w by the tree $W(A \to \alpha)(\alpha_1, \dots, \alpha_n)$ is also a WDT.

Given a sentence $s = a_1 \dots a_n$, we denote WDT(s) as the set of WDT whose concatenation of leaves in postorder traversal is s. Since word graph edges are weighted, sentence symbols have associated a weight $s' = \langle a_1, x_1 \rangle \dots \langle a_n, x_n \rangle \in (\Sigma \times \mathbb{A})^*$, and the value of s' in G is defined by means of WDT(s) by replacing a_i with x_i, and then by multiplying the nodes in postorder traversal. The value associated to the word graph is the sum of values associated to word graph paths.

Now, as shown in [18], hypergraphs can be used to represent the search space of most parsers (just as trellises can represent the search space of finite-state models). A parser just needs to compute the traversal of an hypergraph.

An hypergraph H is a tuple $\langle V, E \rangle$, where V is a finite set of vertices, E is a finite set of hyperarcs. Each hyperarc $e \in E$ has a head $h(e) \in V$ and a vector of *tail* nodes $T(e) \in V^*$. H is weighted if every hyperarc e is associated a weight $W(e) \in \mathbb{A}$. The backward-star $BS(v)$ of a vertex v is the set of incoming hyperarcs $BS(v) = \{e \in E | h(e) = v\}$.

The graph projection of an hypergraph $H = \langle V, E \rangle$ is a directed graph $G = \langle V, E' \rangle$, $E' = \{(u, v) | \exists e \in BS(v), u$ contained in vector $T(e)\}$. H is said to be *acyclic* if its graph projection G is a directed acyclic graph (DAG).

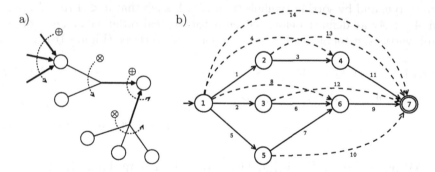

Fig. 1. a) Hypergraph traversal. b) Transitive closure and topological order of vertices and edges.

Given a directed weighted hypergraph, the value at each vertex v can be de-fined as $Val(v) = \bigoplus_{e \in BS(v)} Val(e)$ where $Val(e) = (\bigotimes_{v \in T(e)} Val(v)) \otimes W(e)$. This hypergraph traversal (Figure 1a) can be computed efficiently by dynamic pro-gramming using a topological order of hyperarc vertices. Further improvements can be taken into consideration when the semiring satisfies some properties [19] so that the traversal is analogous to the shortest path computation.

Now, the hypergraph representing the search space for parsing a given word graph will be defined. Hypergraph vertices correspond to chart items of chart parsers like CYK. A word graph is a directed acyclic (multi)graph $WG(V, E)$ where $from : E \mapsto V$, $to : E \mapsto V$, $W : E \mapsto \mathbb{A}$ and $L : E \mapsto \Sigma$ denote the initial and final vertex, the weight and the label associated to each edge respectively, and $initial : V \mapsto \mathbb{A}$ and $final : V \mapsto \mathbb{A}$ denote the initial and final weight of vertices. Given a directed acyclic (multi)graph $G = (V, E)$ the transitive closure of G is a directed acyclic graph $TC(G) = (V, \{(u, v) \in V \times V | \exists \text{path from } u \text{ to } v \text{ in graph } G\})$. Each $(u, v) \in TC(G)$ represents the set of spans (contiguous substrings) that lie between u and v.

Given the word graph WG, the vertices of the search space hypergraph is $edges(TC(WG)) \times (\Sigma \cup N)$, where $edges(TC(WG)) \times \Sigma$ is used for input data and the others for the value of each nonterminal at the associated span. The set of hyperarcs is defined as follows:

- for every word graph edge e, there exists an hyperarc e' with $W(e') = W(e)$, $h(e') = \langle (from(e), to(e)), L(e) \rangle$ and an empty $T(e')$,
- given an hypergraph vertex $v = \langle (u, v), A \rangle$, a grammar rule $A \to \alpha$ with $\alpha = \alpha_1 \ldots \alpha_n$, and a path in $TC(WG)$ from u to v which traverses n edges $e_1, \ldots, e_n$, there exist an hyperarc with head node $\langle (u, v), A \rangle$, weight $W(A \to \alpha)$ and tail nodes $\langle e_i, \alpha_i \rangle$, $i = 1, \ldots, n$.

This hypergraph is directed and acyclic because tail nodes have been derived from edges from a path whose span is the head node. Thus, hypergraph vertices can be topologically sorted and this order corresponds to sorting the edges of $TC(G)$ in such a way that an edge (u, v) is greater than edges contained in a path from u to v, and by sorting symbols from $N \cup \Sigma$ such that $a < A \, \forall a \in \Sigma, A \in N$ and $A_i < A_j$ as defined before. Given a topological order $v_1, \ldots, v_{|V|}$ of word graph vertices, a topological order of hypergraph vertices (Figure 1b) is:

$$\langle (u, v), x \rangle < \langle (r, s), y \rangle \text{ iff } (v < s) \vee (v = s \wedge u > r) \vee (v = s \wedge u = r \wedge x < y)$$

The result of parsing the word graph WG is:

$$\bigoplus_{\langle e, S \rangle \in edges(TC(WG)) \times \{S\}} initial(from(e)) \otimes Val(e) \otimes final(to(e)) \qquad (1)$$

3   Word Graph Serialization and Parsing Interface

A dataflow software architecture allows the easy construction of pattern recognition systems where some modules can be replaced easily. In the proposed implementation, word graphs can be sent from one module to another by means of a serialization protocol using the following messages (see Figure 2):

- the beginning and ending of the word graph must be notified with `begin_dag` and `end_dag` messages respectively,
- vertices are sent in a topological order with a `vertex` message, the last vertex sent is known as *current vertex*,

– all edges with the same destination vertex are sent together with one edge
  message for each edge, with no particular order among them. These edges
  can only be transmitted when their destination vertex is the current vertex,
– the current vertex may be qualified as initial or final with is_initial and
  is_final messages,
– the message no_more_in_edges is sent when current vertex has no more
  incoming edges.
– the message no_more_out_edges is sent when a vertex has no more outgoing
  edges. The receiver can use it to free resources associated to the vertex.

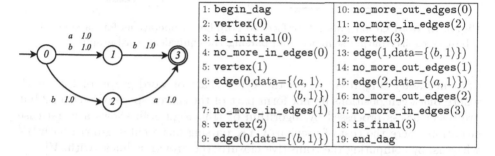

1: begin_dag	10: no_more_out_edges(0)
2: vertex(0)	11: no_more_in_edges(2)
3: is_initial(0)	12: vertex(3)
4: no_more_in_edges(0)	13: edge(1,data=$\{\langle b, 1\rangle\}$)
5: vertex(1)	14: no_more_out_edges(1)
6: edge(0,data=$\{\langle a, 1\rangle,$	15: edge(2,data=$\{\langle a, 1\rangle\}$)
$\langle b, 1\rangle\}$)	16: no_more_out_edges(2)
7: no_more_in_edges(1)	17: no_more_in_edges(3)
8: vertex(2)	18: is_final(3)
9: edge(0,data=$\{\langle b, 1\rangle\}$)	19: end_dag

Fig. 2. Message sequence generated for the graph following our incidence protocol

A general lattice parsing algorithm interface has been defined in C++ as
shown in Figure 3a, so that a parser can be implemented by specifying the actions
to be taken every time a message is received. Any parser which implements this
interface can be used by a dataflow process responsible of invoking the parser
methods, which return a boolean value to indicate the absence (or presence) of
errors in order to act accordingly.

4   CYK Parsing Algorithm for Serialized Word Graphs

CYK algorithm uses a grammar in Chomsky Normal Form (CNF), where there
are only *unary* $(A \rightarrow a)$ and *binary* $(A \rightarrow BC)$ grammar rules. Previous work
on lattice parsing [13] considers that parsing a word graph only changes the
initialisation step:

> *As far as parsing algorithm is concerned, not much needs to be changed but the
> initialisation step: rather than initializing the chart with POS tags only in the
> first row of the table as it is usually the case, initialization now occurs in all
> the cells corresponding to an arc in the lattice. [. . .]. The rest of the parsing
> algorithm remains unchanged.*

The traditional CYK chart table is equivalent to the adjacency matrix representation of the transitive closure of the input string (a linear graph). When
the input is no longer linear, this approach might explore a bigger search space

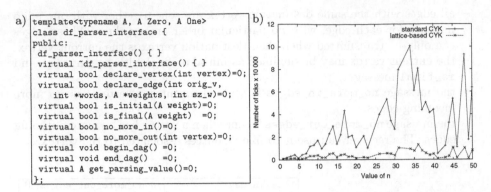

a)
```
template<typename A, A Zero, A One>
class df_parser_interface {
public:
  df_parser_interface() { }
  virtual ~df_parser_interface() { }
  virtual bool declare_vertex(int vertex)=0;
  virtual bool declare_edge(int orig_v,
      int *words, A *weights, int sz_w)=0;
  virtual bool is_initial(A weight)=0;
  virtual bool is_final(A weight)  =0;
  virtual bool no_more_in()=0;
  virtual bool no_more_out(int vertex)=0;
  virtual void begin_dag() =0;
  virtual void end_dag()   =0;
  virtual A get_parsing_value()=0;
};
```

Fig. 3. a) Word Graph Parser Interface. b) Number of operations for parsing sets of n-best recognizer output sentences and parsing the equivalent word graphs.

than necessary. Figure 4c shows the CYK chart of word graph of Figure 1b where black cell positions do not form part of the search space of Section 2 but are nevertheless processed by algorithm of [13]. Figure 4b shows a worst-case situation where the cost of previous CYK parsing has a cubic growth with $|V|$ whereas, by computing the transitive closure, the growth is linear with $|V|$.

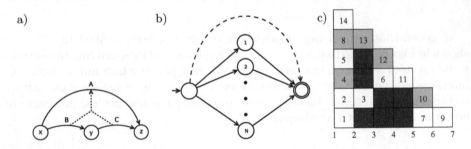

Fig. 4. a) Hyperarc of a binary production (dotted lines.) b) Worst-case situation for a traditional CYK lattice parser. c) CYK chart of Figure 1b.

The proposed parsing algorithm maintains the transitive closure of the input graph which is represented with incidence lists (each vertex has a list of incoming edges). Each edge e stores a mapping $chart(e) : N \mapsto \mathbb{A}$ from nonterminals to semiring values. Since the input graph is received serialized, the algorithm is described as the actions to be taken when each message is received:

- `begin_dag` and `no_more_out_edges` are ignored, other parsers can use them.
- when `vertex` is received, a new vertex is added to the graph with an empty list of incoming edges, and it is marked as the *current* vertex.
- when a `is_initial` or `is_final` is received, the default value 0 of being initial or being final is changed in the current vertex.

- when **edge** is received, the new edge e is added to the incidence list of the current vertex, along with possibly other edges belonging to the transitive closure. Edge e contain a set of terminal symbols with an associated weight. For every pair $\langle a, x \rangle \in \Sigma \times A$ and every grammar rule $A \rightarrow a$ we update $chart(e)(A) := chart(e)(A) \oplus (x \otimes W(A \rightarrow a))$.
- when **no_more_in_edges** is received, all the incoming edges (including those ones in the transitive closure) are reverse-ordered by their origin vertices (whose numbering is a topological order). Then, for each incoming edge $e_1 = (x, z)$ and for each rule $A \rightarrow BC$ we look for edges $e_2 = (x, y)$ and $e_3 = (y, z)$ (Figure 4a) and update the value accordingly:

$$chart(e_1)(A) := chart(e_1)(A) \oplus (chart(e_2)(B) \otimes chart(e_3)(C) \otimes W(A \rightarrow BC))$$

- when **end_dag** is received, the result is computed according to Equation 1.

The cost of searching an edge during the algorithm is $O(1)$, since the destination vertex is always the current vertex and a vector with timestamps is used. A worst case cost of the **edge** operation is $O(|V|)$. A worst case cost of the **no_more_in_edges** operation is $O(|V|^2)$ and is applied $|V|$ times. Therefore, the cost of this bottom-up CYK algorithm is $O(|V|^3)$. A more adjusted bound is the summation, over all edges (u, v) from the transitive closure, of "1 plus the number of vertices that lie between u and v", which explains why parsing the word graph of Figure 4b has only a cost linear with $|V|$.

5   Experimentation

A categorized CNF grammar with 35 nonterminal symbols, 45 categories (corresponding to 10 000 terminal symbols), 1 414 binary productions and 260 679 unary productions, as described in [20] is used. The corpus consists of 213 sets of n_i-best sentences generated by a recognizer ($i = 1, \ldots, 213$). A minimal word graph is constructed for every set using the algorithm of [21] and is parsed with our CYK algorithm. Figure 3b shows the mean number of basic operations for parsing word graphs constructed with n sentences, varying n, along with the mean number of operations needed to parse the strings separately.

6   Conclusions

A generalization of a framework based on semirings and hypergraphs for context-free string parsing to the case of lattices has been proposed. Unlike previous work, the proposed lattice parsing takes into account the weights associated to the word graph edges in a possibly noncommutative semiring.

An implementation of CYK is presented to show how the search space can be reduced with respect to previous CYK lattice parsers and to show the feasibility of a dataflow architecture where modules send and receive serialized word graphs.

References

1. Goodman, J.: Semiring parsing. Comput. Linguist. 25(4), 573–605 (1999)
2. Gallo, G., Longo, G., Pallottino, S.: Directed hypergraphs and applications. Discrete Applied Mathematics 42(2), 177–201 (1993)
3. Gonzalez, R., Thomason, M.: Syntactic pattern recognition – An introduction. Addison-Wesley, Reading, MA (1978)
4. Sakakibara, et al.: Stochastic context-free grammars for tRNA modeling. Nucleic Acids Research 22, 5112–5120 (1994)
5. Jelinek, F., Lafferty, J.D., Mercer, R.L.: Basic methods of probabilistic context free grammars. In: Laface, P., Mori, R.D. (eds.) Speech Recognition and Understanding. Recent Advances, Trends, and Applications. Proceedings of the NATO ASI, vol. F75, pp. 345–360. Springer, Heidelberg (1992)
6. Ney, H.: Dynamic programming parsing for context-free grammars in continuous speech recognition. IEEE Transactions on Signal Processing 39(2), 336–340 (1991)
7. Nederhof, M.J.: Weighted deductive parsing and knuth's algorithm. Comput. Linguist. 29(1), 135–143 (2003)
8. Oerder, M., Ney, H.: Word Graphs: An Efficient Interface Between Continuous Speech Recognition And Language Understanding. In: Proc. ICASSP'93 vol. 2, pp. 119–122 (1993)
9. Cocke, J., Schwartz, J.: Programming languages and their compilers: Preliminary notes. Tech. report, Courant Inst. of Mathematical Sciences, NY University (1970)
10. Younger, D.H.: Recognition and parsing of context-free languages in time n^3. Information and Control 10(2), 189–208 (1967)
11. Kasami, T.: An efficient recognition and syntax analysis algorithm for context-free languages. Tech. report, Air Force Cambridge Research Laboratory (1965)
12. Hall, K., Johnson, M.: Language modeling using efficient best-first bottom-up parsing. In: Proc. ASRU'03, pp. 507–512 (2003)
13. Chappelier, J., Rajman, M., Aragues, R., Rozenknop, A.: Lattice parsing for speech recognition (1999)
14. Jelinek, F., Chelba, C.: Structured language modeling for speech recognition. Computer Speech and Language 14(4), 283–332 (2000)
15. Paeseler, A.: Modification of earley's algorithm for speech recognition. In: Proc. of the NATO Advanced Study Institute on Recent advances in speech understanding and dialog systems, pp. 465–472. Springer, New York (1988)
16. Weber, H., Spilker, J., Gorz, G.: Parsing n best trees from a word lattice. In: KI - Kunstliche Intelligenz, pp. 279–288 (1997)
17. Kuich, W.: Semirings and formal power series: their relevance to formal languages and automata. Springer, Berlin Heidelberg New York (1997)
18. Klein, D., Manning, C.D.: Parsing and hypergraphs. In: The Seventh Internation Workshop on Parsing Technologies (2001)
19. Mohri, M.: Semiring frameworks and algorithms for shortest-distance problems (2002)
20. Benedí, J., Sánchez, J.: Estimation of stochastic context-free grammars and their use as language models. Computer Speech and Language 19(3), 249–274 (2005)
21. Carrasco, R.C., Forcada, M.L.: Incremental construction and maintenance of minimal finite-state automata. Computational Linguistics 28(2), 207–216 (2002)

Constrained Monocular Obstacle Perception with Just One Frame

Lluís Pacheco, Xavier Cufí, and Javi Cobos

Computer Vision and Robotics Group
Institute of Informatics and Applications, University of Girona
Av. Lluís Santaló sn, 17071 Girona, Spain
{lluispa,xcuf}@eia.udg.es

Abstract. This paper presents a monocular perception system tested on wheeled mobile robots. Its significant contribution is the use of a single image to obtain depth information (one bit) when robots detect obstacles. The constraints refer to the environment. Flat and homogeneous floor radiance is assumed. Results emerge from using a set of multi-resolution focus measurement thresholds to avoid obstacle collision. The algorithm's simplicity and the robustness achieved can be considered the key points of this work. On-robot experimental results are reported and a broad range of indoor applications is possible. However, false obstacle detection occurs when the constraints fail. Thus, proposals to overcome it are explained.

1 Introduction

Obstacle detection is a requirement of WMRs (wheeled mobile robots) to devise proper navigation strategies. In this regard, the research community has developed multiple perception systems that result in feasible navigation strategies and machine vision systems can provide information that is meaningful for the required environmental understanding. The various methods proposed by scientists can be compared, taking into consideration different aspects, such as active or passive methods, number of cameras used, processing frames needed, computational effort, robustness, reliability, accuracy, etc. Hence, the methodology and algorithms implemented are closely related with the final application requirements.

Various techniques can be used to achieve visual obstacle perception. For instance, SVS (Stereo Vision Systems), OFM (Optical Flow Methods) or DFF (Depth from Focus) are all methods that permit 3D scene recovery. Stereo vision seems to provide the easiest way to acquire 3D understanding [1]. However, when compared with other methods, it has both advantages and drawbacks. Studies comparing SVS and DFF methods are reported in [2]. The results show that while SVS has greater resolution and sensitivity, DFF has better robustness, requires less computational effort and can deal properly with correspondence and occlusion problems. However, the need for several images of the same scene, acquired with different optical setups, may be considered an important drawback to using DFF methods in major WMR applications. On the other hand, when the number of cameras is taken into consideration, only DFF and OFM allow monocular systems. The use of an image sequence,

J. Martí et al. (Eds.): IbPRIA 2007, Part I, LNCS 4477, pp. 611–619, 2007.

where the differences between frames are used to extract 3D information, has attracted researchers to the WMR applications of OFM [3]. However, OFM are not exempt from problems. For instance, efficient segmentation is required to find matches between frames and the aperture problem is another inconvenience OFM cannot minimize. The use of DFF in mobile robotics has been reported in [4], where Nourbakhsh used three cameras with almost the same scene, achieving robust and efficient obstacle detection. In this context, this work analyses the performance of DFF methods applied to WMRs when there is only one frame. The research shows that, using one image, obstacle positions can be achieved when homogeneous radiance and flat floor constraints are present. Thus, bit depth can be obtained using DFF methodology and a set of multi-resolution focus measure thresholds. The experimental results, and the algorithms implemented, are reported. The research concludes that obstacle detection is robust, even when significant lightness changes occur, but that a lack of floor constraints results in false obstacle detection.

This paper is organized as follows. In Section 1, the main ideas and research objectives are presented. Section 2 describes the state of the art of basic DFF used in this research. Section 3 depicts the monocular perception algorithms that have been successfully implemented and tested. In Section 4, the mobile robot platform used is briefly presented, and special attention is paid to the description of the perception system. Section 5 shows the experimental results obtained even when an unconstrained floor is present. Finally, the concluding remarks are presented in Section 6.

2 A Short Depth from Focus Survey

DFF has been used in interesting applications such as 3D scene maps and passive autofocus consumer camera systems. DFF techniques acquire 3D scene information through an image sequence based on an optical setup. These methods use a collection of images of the same scene, but acquired at different focus positions. The PSF (point spread function) of a camera system for unfocused objects produces blurred image points. The OTF (optical transfer function) emerges in a first order Bessel function, where its main lobe volume can determine the FM (focus measure) expressed as:

$$M_0 = \iint |I_i(\omega, \nu)| d\omega d\nu. \tag{1}$$

where I_i denotes the image considered, and ω and ν represent the frequency components. Efficient energy image measures have been proposed as focus measure operators. The maximum value is obtained at the best-focused image [5]. A set of focus operators such as the energy of the grey variance level, the gradient, or the Laplacian of the grey level image has been proposed in the literature [6]. Nayar has proposed a modified Laplacian use that improves results in some textures [7]. Studies have also been carried out on the confidence of the measures and the optimal interval selection during the parameter space search [8] [9]. Recovering the 3D information from DFF methods is known as SFF (shape from focus) [7]. The SFF method decomposes the image in different windows. For each image, the best-focused window is searched for. Thus, a better focus position is found for each window and knowledge of the distance is obtained. The curved window approximation, using nine control points, has also been proposed as a way to improve the results [10].

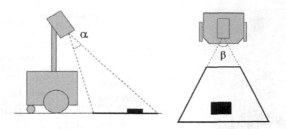

Fig. 1. On-robot monocular camera configuration, where α and β are the vertical and horizontal field of view, respectively

The large number of images, typically between 10 and 30, needed to build an accurate and dense depth map has led to the development of other interesting techniques, known as DFD (depth from defocus) methods, which normally use only two images, acquired with different optical settings [11]. The 3D scene structure is obtained using relative defocus, which is considered as an ill-posed problem known as inverse filtering. From an analysis of the relevant DFD research, the defocus operator kernel has been modeled on Gaussian models, spatial domain, frequency domain, moment filters, frequency invariant filters, shift-variant kernels, Markov random fields, etc. [12] [13] [14]. Despite these efforts, a real-time DFD range sensor has only been implemented over small scene areas, or active illumination has been used to constrain the frequency spectrum [15]. Even nowadays, using DFD in robotics could be computationally expensive.

3   The Monocular Perception Algorithms

The implemented algorithms of the machine vision system are based on important assumptions that are generally obtained in normal indoor scenarios, but also in many outdoor scenarios. These constraints are flat and homogenous energy radiance of the floor surface and experimental knowledge of the focus measurement threshold values. Two important aspects, image window size and camera pose, should be considered. The size of windows should be big enough to get energy information. For example, in the work of Surya, images of 150x150 pixels were used, and the focus measures were computed in 15x15 pixel regions in the images [16]. The camera pose will set the scenario perspective and consequently the floor position coordinates that should be used in the WMR navigation strategy. Fig. 1 shows the corresponding on-robot camera configuration used in this work. The relative robot coordinates corresponding to each pixel can be computed using trigonometric relationships and the corresponding knowledge of the camera configuration [3]. Scale-space representations can reduce the search space, increasing the computation performance [17]. The algorithms used are explained in the remainder of this section. Multigrid representation using low-pass filtering processes can improve the surface radiance homogeneity. Therefore, a Gaussian filter is applied to the frames acquired in PAL format, at 768x576 pixels. Three decreasing resolution levels have been used with picture sizes of 384x288, 192x144 and 96x72 [18]. The average image brightness is also computed. In order to achieve better robustness against changes in lightness, brightness normalization is performed by dividing each image's pixel brightness by the mean value [16].

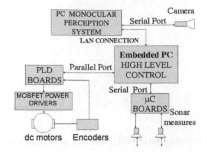

Fig. 2. The WMR PRIM 1   **Fig. 3.** The hardware architecture

The image energy is computed over 3x3 windows at the top level of the pyramid, using the DFF modified Laplacian method [7]:

$$ML(x,y) = |2i(x,y) - i(x-1,y) - i(x+1)| + |2i(x,y) - i(x,y-1) - i(x,y+1)| \qquad (2)$$

The 96x72 modified Laplacian energy measures obtained are divided into 9x7 windows of 10x10 pixel regions. The energy mean value is computed over each 10x10 pixel window and these computed values should be compared with the expected ones, when none obstacle is found. Obstacle detection occurs when energy discrepancies are met. It should be pointed out that the methodology presented is similar to the DFF methods in that the different windows, corresponding to an image sequence of the same scene acquired with different focus set ups, are compared and the one with more energy provides the window depth. In order to increase the floor information, the energy standard deviation is also considered, so that the homogeneity of the floor energy values is related. Thus, a 9x7x2 array is obtained, where each cell represents the mean Laplacian value and the corresponding standard deviation mean, computed over 10x10 pixel windows at the 96x72 space resolution level. The 9x7x2 array is explored, from bottom to top; floor segmentation is performed, using both energy and standard deviation thresholds. Then, the binary results, consisting of a 9x7 local visual perception, are transmitted to the control unit and a new frame is acquired. A LUT (look up table) with the calibrated real floor coordinates, corresponding to the 9x7 windows, has been previously computed. An obstacle map is provided, and the WMR navigation strategy can be properly implemented.

4   The Mobile Robot Hardware Description

The PRIM-1 mobile robot used in this work, shown in Fig. 2, has been designed for indoor navigation. Considered an open platform, it can be used in research and teaching activities [19]. The robot's meaningful hardware is shown in Fig. 3. The dc motor power drivers are based on a MOSFET bridge controlling the energy supplied to the actuators. A set of PCBs (printed circuits boards) based on PLD (programmable logic devices) act as an interface between the PC system, the encoders and the dc motors. A μc processor board controls the 8 sonar sensors. An embedded PC is the core of the basic control system, and that is where the high level decisions are taken. The position and orientation of the WMR are obtained by the odometer system. The

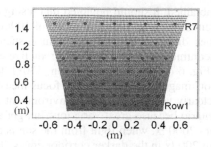

Fig. 4. Typical indoor scenario

Fig. 5. Local perception grid coordinates relative to the robot position, at the 96x72 and 9x7 size level. At the 9x7 size level it is possible to distinguish 7 different rows (Row 1 being the closest to the robot).

software of the PC is implemented in C language and is run under the LINUX operating system. The machine vision system is connected through a LAN.

The machine vision system employs the VISCA RS232C control protocol to control a Sony EVI-D70P-PAL color camera, with motorized pan, tilt, zoom, focus, iris and shutter. The machine vision system computer unit is composed of a PC desktop, where a Meteor-II frame grabber is used together with the MIL libraries. This work is configured using a horizontal field of view of 48° and a vertical one of 37°. The camera pose is set to 109cm from the floor with a tilt angle of 58°. The obstacle perception information is transmitted to the control unit connecting the USB port to the LAN.

5   Experimental Results

In this section the results from the computation of the homogeneous floor radiance thresholds to detect obstacles in the robot trajectory are presented. These values are validated using previously acquired test images. Once thresholds are calculated, the perception algorithms are tested during robot navigation experiences. False obstacle detection analysis can be carried out using obstacle image test files acquired during navigation. Another interesting parameter that has been analyzed is the processing time for each image. The experimental results report robust and effective obstacle detection in typical indoor environments, such as the one shown in Fig. 4. The visual position grid where paths should be planned to avoid obstacle collisions is shown in Fig. 5. It is in the neighborhood of those points where the information about radiance

Fig. 6. Fragments of high resolution floor images, 768x576 pixels, under different light conditions corresponding to 200, 800, 1400, and 2000 lx, respectively

is obtained. It should be noted that, using the odometer system, the robot position and orientation are available at a rate of 100ms. Hence, the robot navigation can be tested under different control algorithms, such as heuristic rules, path following under discontinuous control laws, or predictive control techniques [20].

Fig. 6 depicts high resolution, 130x130 pixel windows, corresponding to different floor images used to compute focus measurement thresholds, where the floor texture is clearly visible. This robot environment can be considered a good indoor benchmark scenario because great variations in light are produced. Light illumination can change from 2000 lx, when light from the sun is clearly present through the windows, to less than 200 lx in the darker corridor zones. The energy floor radiance measures obtained for each 9x7 visual perception row are shown in Table 1. They were computed in a wide range of different light conditions. For each light condition, five samples were used, and the averaged mean results and standard deviation are depicted. The image perspective emerges from a set of multi-resolution thresholds as a function of the camera distances. Note that the table shows larger values at closer 9x7 row positions (row 1 is closest to the robot).

Table 1. Modified Laplacian and standard deviation for each 9x7 image row

Row		200 lx	400 lx	800 lx	1400 lx	1800 lx	2000 lx
1	Mod. Lapl.	4.5×10^{-2}	3.6×10^{-2}	3.5×10^{-2}	4×10^{-2}	3.6×10^{-2}	3.8×10^{-2}
	Std. dev.	3.1×10^{-3}	2.5×10^{-3}	2.4×10^{-3}	2.7×10^{-3}	2.4×10^{-3}	2.7×10^{-3}
2	Mod. Lapl.	4.6×10^{-2}	3.5×10^{-2}	3.5×10^{-2}	3.9×10^{-2}	3.3×10^{-2}	3.7×10^{-2}
	Std. dev	3.1×10^{-3}	2.3×10^{-3}	2.4×10^{-3}	2.6×10^{-3}	2.2×10^{-3}	2.6×10^{-3}
3	Mod. Lapl.	4.6×10^{-2}	3.4×10^{-2}	3.4×10^{-2}	3.8×10^{-2}	3.4×10^{-2}	3.5×10^{-2}
	Std. dev	3×10^{-3}	2.4×10^{-3}	2.3×10^{-3}	2.6×10^{-3}	2.3×10^{-3}	2.3×10^{-3}
4	Mod. Lapl.	4×10^{-2}	3.2×10^{-2}	3.2×10^{-2}	3.6×10^{-2}	3.2×10^{-2}	3.3×10^{-2}
	Std. dev	2.8×10^{-3}	2.2×10^{-3}	2.2×10^{-3}	2.5×10^{-3}	2×10^{-3}	2.1×10^{-3}
5	Mod. Lapl.	3.6×10^{-2}	3×10^{-2}	3×10^{-2}	3.4×10^{-2}	2.8×10^{-2}	3.1×10^{-2}
	Std. dev	2.5×10^{-3}	2×10^{-3}	2×10^{-3}	2.3×10^{-3}	1.9×10^{-3}	2.1×10^{-3}
6	Mod. Lapl.	3.4×10^{-2}	3×10^{-2}	2.9×10^{-2}	3×10^{-2}	2.6×10^{-2}	2.9×10^{-2}
	Std. dev	2.4×10^{-3}	2×10^{-3}	1.9×10^{-3}	2×10^{-3}	1.7×10^{-3}	1.9×10^{-3}
7	Mod. Lapl.	3.3×10^{-2}	2.5×10^{-2}	2.6×10^{-2}	2.9×10^{-2}	2.3×10^{-2}	2.6×10^{-2}
	Std. dev	2.2×10^{-3}	1.7×10^{-3}	1.8×10^{-3}	1.9×10^{-3}	1.6×10^{-3}	1.8×10^{-3}

The setup reported in Table 1 results from scenarios without obstacles. However, greater measures of focus filters are expected when obstacles appear in the scene. Experimentally good results can be achieved using different row thresholds consisting of the maximum modified Laplacian value plus 3 times the maximum standard deviation.

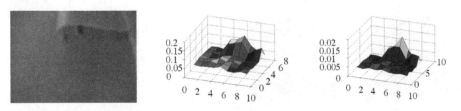

Fig. 7. Obstacle acquired at 180 lx, represented in a 96x72 image size, averaged 9x7 modified Laplacian, and standard deviation values

Using the acquired images of the obstacles, a more in-depth analysis can be performed during the navigation tests. Fig. 7 presents the modified Laplacian energy and standard deviation values, when typical indoor obstacles are present. However, it should be pointed out that false obstacles are detected by the methodology presented. Figs. 8 and 9 show that flat shape lines placed on the floor or light reflections, respectively, can be considered as obstacles (false positives). These false obstacles emerge when constraints fail, and that can be considered the main drawback of the method. Research nowadays, including OFM, is more focused on improving results. For example, OFM can allow for scene structure analysis and, consequently, avoid false obstacle detection.

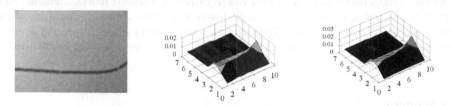

Fig. 8. False obstacle caused by a flat shape acquired at 1400 lx, represented in a 96x72 image size, averaged 9x7 modified Laplacian, and standard deviation values

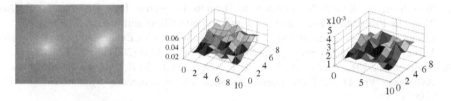

Fig. 9. False obstacle caused by light reflection acquired at 200 lx, represented in a 96x72 image size, averaged 9x7 modified Laplacian and standard deviation values

The processing speed of the machine vision system can be increased. Using a 2.7 GHz desktop, the total frame processing time to compute the three levels of the Gaussian pyramid compression is close to 2s. The use of down-sampling techniques in the first two compression levels, instead of the Gaussian pyramidal resolution method, allows a reduction of computational effort, and the system processes between 2 and 3 frames each second [18].

6 Concluding Remarks

The work presented on this issue has shown that feasible obstacle avoidance can be achieved using a set of previously computed multi-resolution thresholds, based on DFF filters. The methodology can be easily transferable to WMRs. Algorithm robustness, simplicity and fast computation are other interesting features of this work. The method constraints are provided by a large range of indoor and outdoor environments. The experimental results report robust and effective obstacle detection in typical indoor environments. False obstacle detection, when constraints fail, can be considered the weak point of this work. In order to solve this limitation, cooperative DFF and OFM techniques using sensor fusion information will be used. DFF can detect relative obstacle positions, speeding up OFM matches between frames, and OFM can use a frame sequence of the same obstacles in order to obtain qualitative structure information. Robot position and orientation, established using the odometer system, are interesting data that can help detect the floor obstacle contact coordinates from frame to frame. Analysis of the discrepancies can provide qualitative structure knowledge. The actual research is aimed at solving false obstacle detection by obtaining the obstacle structure. Testing the algorithms presented here in other very different homogeneous floor scenarios where different standard indoor elements can appear (stairs, etc.), as well as the use of lower resolution cameras, could be other interesting short term objectives. The navigation and control strategies should also be important issues. Thus, the more accurate the navigation strategies will be, the better the perception algorithm results should be.

References

1. Horn B.K.P.: Robot Vision, McGraw-Hill Book Company, MIT Press Edition, 12th printing (1998)
2. Schechner, Y., Kiryati, N.: Depth from Defocus vs. Stereo: How Different Really Are They? In: Proceedings Fourteenth Int. Conf. on Pattern Recognition, vol. 2 (1998)
3. Campbell, J., Sukthankar, R., Noubakhsh, L.: Techniques for Evaluating Optical Flow for Visual Odometry in Extreme Terrain. In: Proc. of IROS 2004 (2004)
4. Nourbakhsh, I.R., Andre, D., Tomasi, C., Genesereth, M.R.: Mobile Robot Obstacle Avoidance Via Depth From Focus. Robotics and Autonomous Systems 22, 151–158 (1997)
5. Krotkov, E.: Focusing. In: MS-CIS-86-22. Grasp Lab 63. Dept. of Computer and Information Science. University of Pennsylvania (1986)
6. Subbarao, M., Choi, T., Nikzad, A.: Focusing Techniques. Tech. Report 92.09.04, Stony Brook, New York (1992)
7. Nayar, S.K., Nakagawa, Y.: Shape from Focus. IEEE Trans. PAMI, vol. 16(8) (1994)
8. Subbarao, M., Tyan, J.K.: Selecting the Optimal Focus Measure for Autofocusing and Depth-from-Focus. IEEE Trans. PAMI, vol. 20(8) (1998)
9. Subbarao, M., Tyan, J.K.: Root-Mean Square Error in Passive Autofocusing and 3D Shape Recovery. In: Proc. of SPIE's International Symposium, on Three- Dimensional Imaging and Laser-Based Systems for Metrology and Inspection II, vol. 2909, pp. 162–177 (1996)
10. Choi, T., Yun, J.: Accurate 3-D Shape Recovery using Curved Window Focus Measure. In: Proc. of ICIP, vol. 3, pp. 910–914 (1999)
11. Pentland, A.P.: A New Sense for Depth of Field. IEEE Trans. Pattern Anal. Machine Intelligence PAMI-9, 523–531 (1987)
12. Subbarao, M., Surya, G.: Depth from Defocus: A Spatial Domain Approach. International Journal of Computer Vision 13(3), 271–294 (1994)
13. Xiong, Y., Shafer, S.A.: Moment Filters for High Precision Computation of Focus and Stereo, IEEE/RSJ Inter. Conf. on Intel. Robots and Systems, pp. 108–113 (1995)
14. Rajagopalan, A.N., Chaudhuri, S.: Identification of Shift-Variant Point Spread Function For a Class of Imaging Systems, Speech and Image Technologies for Computing and Telecommunications. In: Proc. of IEEE vol. 1, pp. 275–278 (1997)

15. Nayar, S.K., Watanabe, M., Noguchi, M.: Real-Time Focus Range sensor, IEEE Trans. on PAMI, vol. 18(12) (1996)
16. Surya, G.: Three Dimensional Scene Recovery from Image Defocus, PHD thesis, Stony Brook, New York (1994)
17. Wang, Y., Bahrami, S., Zhu, S.: Perceptual Scale Space and Its Apliccations. In: Proc. of IEEE Conf. on Computer Vision, ICCV0 vol. 5 1, pp. 58–65 (2005)
18. Gonzalez, R.C., Woods, R.E.: Digital Image Processing, 2nd edn. Prentice Hall Int. Ed, Englewood Cliffs (2002)
19. Pacheco, L., Batlle, J., Cufí, X., Arbusé, R.: PRIM an Open Mobile Robot Platform, Present and Future Trends. In: Proc. of IEEE-TTTC, AQTR 2006 (2006)
20. Pacheco, L., Ningsu, L., Arbusé, R.: Experimental Modelling and Control Strategies on an Open Robot Platform PRIM. In: Proc. of IEEE-TTTC AQTR 2006 (2006)

Author Index

Agís, R.   137
Agapito, Lourdes   491
Alabau, Vicente   467
Aldape-Pérez, Mario   435
Antón-Canalís, Luis   97
Antequera, T.   145
Ardovini, Alessandro   225
Argüelles-Cruz, Amadeo José   435
Aubreton, Olivier   306
Ávila, M.M.   145

Baiget, Pau   507
Baldrich, Ramon   55
Bandeira, Lourenço P.C.   177, 193
Banerjee, Asim   314
Benedí, José-Miguel   80
Benedí, Jose Miguel   467
Bernardino, Alexandre   515
Binefa, X.   121
Bioucas-Dias, José M.   22
Borges, Janete S.   22
Blanca, Nicolás Pérez de la   72, 394, 402, 515
Blanco, Jose Luis   346
Boquera, Salvador España   603
Borges, Janete S.   22
Bougioukos, Panagiotis   410
Brun, Luc   185
Bue, Alessio Del   491
Buf, J.M. Hans du   459

Cózar, J.R.   451
Cañero, Cristina   274
Carrillo, R.   137
Casacuberta, Francisco   241, 475
Cathebras, Guy   306
Cavouras, Dionisis   410
Chamorro-Martínez, J.   579
Chen, WenAn   338
Chung, Yong-Joo   563
Cinque, Luigi   225
Civera, Jorge   265
Colomer, Joan   362
Cruz, Jesús M.   595
Cubel, Elsa   265

Cuenca, A. de la Villa   571
Cyganek, Bogusław   330

Díaz, J.   137
Daskalakis, Antonis   410
Davison, Andrew J.   9
Dickens, Matthew P.   426
Durán, M.L.   145
Dzemyda, Gintautas   209

Escalera, Sergio   13

Fernández, Carles   507
Ferraz, L.   121
Ferreiro-Armán, Marcos   177
Fornés, Alicia   13
Fraile, Roberto   169
Fuertes, José Manuel   72

Gómez, José I.   402
Gómez, Pilar   443
Gajjar, Prakash P.   314
Galán-Perales, E.   579
Ganebnykh, Sergey   523
Garamendi, J.F.   161
García-Sevilla, Pedro   30
Gerónimo, David   418, 547
Giménez, Adrià   539
González, Jordi   113
González-Linares, J.M.   451
Gonzàlez, J.   499
Gonzàlez, Jordi   507
Gonzalez, Javier   346
Guijarrubia, Víctor G.   233
Guil, N.   451

Hancock, E.R.   39
Hancock, Edwin R.   169, 426
Harrison, Robert F.   531
Hernández-Tejera, Mario   97
Huerta, Ivan   113

Irani, Michal   7

Joshi, Manjunath V.   314

Juan, Alfons 539
Juliá, Carme 483
Justo, Raquel 249

Kagadis, George C. 410
Kalatzis, Ioannis 410
Khosravi, Abbas 362
Kostopoulos, Spiros 410
Kurasova, Olga 209

López, Antonio 47, 274, 418, 483, 547, 587
López, Marcos 298
Lacey, Gerard 290
Lamalle, Bernard 306
Lange, Andrey 523
Lange, Mikhail 523
Lebossé, Jérôme 185
Lemaitre, Cédric 306
Lillo, Antonella Di 89
Lladó, Xavier 491
LLadós, Josep 13
Llorens, David 282
Lloret, Jaime 475
Lucena, Manuel J. 72
Lumbreras, Felipe 274, 483
Luquero, M. 145
Lv, Ping 555

Malpica, N. 161
Marín-Jiménez, Manuel J. 402, 515
Marçal, André R.S. 22
Martí, Joan 129
Martí, Robert 129
Martín, Javier 282
Martín-Herrero, Julio 177
Martínez, B. 121
Martínez, Francisco Zamora 603
Martínez-del-Rincón, Jesús 63, 201
Martínez-Usó, Adolfo 30
Martel, J. 161
Marzal, Andrés 282
Matías, José M. 298
Mazón, Jose-Norberto 354
Melendez, Joaquim 362
Mendoza, M. Ángeles 394
Micó, Luisa 354
Mitra, Suman 314
Mora, Guillem Gascó i 257
Moreno, Francisco Angel 346

Moreno, Plinio 515
Moreno-Seco, Francisco 354
Mota, S. 137
Motta, Giovanni 89
Moya, Jorge Gorbe 603
Mulcahy, Hugh 290

Nagy, James G. 386
Neira, José 322
Nikiforidis, George 410
Nongaillard, Matthieu 306

Orozco, J. 499
Orrite, Carlos 63
Orrite-Uruñuela, Carlos 201

Pérez, A. 121
Pailles, Jean-Claude 185
Pajares, Gonzalo 595
Palacios, R. 145
Palazón, Vicente 282
Paredes, Roberto 217
Pastor, Moisés 370
Pasupa, Kitsuchart 531
Patchett, Stephen 290
Peiró, Joan Andreu Sánchez 257
Peracaula, Marta 129
Pina, Pedro 177, 193
Pla, Filiberto 30
Ponsa, Daniel 47, 418, 587
Prados-Suárez, B. 579
Pujol, Oriol 13

Quinn, John A. 1

Raba, David 129
Radeva, Petia 13
Rey, A. Martín del 571
Ribas, David 322
Ridao, Pere 322
Rius, I. 499
Roca, F.X. 499
Roca, Xavier 507
Rocca, Francesca Della 225
Rodríguez, Luis 241
Rodrigues, João 459
Rodriguez, R. 137
Rogez, Grégory 63, 201
Romero, Verónica 467, 539
Ros, E. 137

Rowe, Daniel   113
Ruz, José J.   595

Sánchez, G. Rodríguez   571
Sánchez, Gemma   13
Sánchez, J.S.   105
Sánchez, Joan-Andreu   80
Sánchez-Beato, Alfonso   595
Sánchez-Nielsen, Elena   97
Sangineto, Enver   225
Santos-Victor, José   515
Sappa, Angel   483
Sappa, Angel D.   418, 547
Saraiva, José   193
Schiavi, E.   161
Serrat, Joan   274, 483
Smith, W.A.P.   39
Smith, William A.P.   426
Soto-Hidalgo, J.M.   579
Sotoca, Jose M.   30
Storer, James A.   89
submission, Anonymous IbPRIA   153

Taboada, Javier   298
Tardós, Juan Domingo   322
Tomás, Jesús   475
Torres, M. Inés   233, 249
Toselli, Alejandro H.   370

Vázquez, Fernando   443
Vainoras, Alfonsas   209
Valdovinos, R.M.   105
Vanrell, Maria   55
Vazquez, Eduard   55
Vazquez, Javier   55
Vidal, Enrique   241, 265, 370
Vilán, José A.   298
Vilar, Juan Miguel   282
Vilariño, Fernando   290
Villanueva, Juan J.   113
Villegas, Mauricio   217
Voon, Lew Fock Chong Lew Yan   306

Wang, Wei   555
Welk, Martin   386
Willett, Peter   531
Williams, Christopher K.I.   1
Wu, Jing   39, 426

Yáñez-Márquez, Cornelio   435
Yan, YongHong   555

Zapata, E.L.   451
Zhang, Hongbin   338
Zhang, Xian   378
Zhao, QingWei   555
Zhou, Jiang   290
Zhu, Xiaoyan   378

Lecture Notes in Computer Science

For information about Vols. 1–4403

please contact your bookseller or Springer

Vol. 4534: I. Tomkos, F. Neri, J. Solé Pareta, X. Masip Bruin, S. Sánchez Lopez (Eds.), Optical Network Design and Modeling. XI, 460 pages. 2007.

Vol. 4526: M. Malek, M. Reitenspieß, A.P.A. van Moorsel (Eds.), Service Availability. X, 155 pages. 2007.

Vol. 4523: Y.-H. Lee, H.-N. Kim, J. Kim, Y. Park, L.T. Yang, S.W. Kim (Eds.), Embedded Software and Systems. XIX, 829 pages. 2007.

Vol. 4521: J. Katz, M. Yung (Eds.), Applied Cryptography and Network Security. XIII, 498 pages. 2007.

Vol. 4519: E. Franconi, M. Kifer, W. May (Eds.), The Semantic Web: Research and Applications. XVIII, 830 pages. 2007.

Vol. 4517: F. Boavida, E. Monteiro, S. Mascolo, Y. Koucheryavy (Eds.), Wired/Wireless Internet Communications. XIV, 382 pages. 2007.

Vol. 4515: M. Naor (Ed.), Advances in Cryptology - EUROCRYPT 2007. XIII, 591 pages. 2007.

Vol. 4514: S.N. Artemov, A. Nerode (Eds.), Logical Foundations of Computer Science. XI, 513 pages. 2007.

Vol. 4510: P. Van Hentenryck, L. Wolsey (Eds.), Integration of AI and OR Techniques in Constraint Programming for Combinatorial Optimization Problems. X, 391 pages. 2007.

Vol. 4509: Z. Kobti, D. Wu (Eds.), Advances in Artificial Intelligence. XII, 552 pages. 2007. (Sublibrary LNAI).

Vol. 4506: D. Zeng, I. Gotham, K. Komatsu, C. Lynch, M. Thurmond, D. Madigan, B. Lober, J. Kvach, H. Chen (Eds.), Intelligence and Security Informatics: Biosurveillance. XI, 234 pages. 2007.

Vol. 4504: J. Huang, R. Kowalczyk, Z. Maamar, D. Martin, I. Müller, S. Stoutenburg, K.P. Sycara (Eds.), Service-Oriented Computing: Agents, Semantics, and Engineering. X, 175 pages. 2007.

Vol. 4501: J. Marques-Silva, K.A. Sakallah (Eds.), Theory and Applications of Satisfiability Testing - SAT 2007. XI, 384 pages. 2007.

Vol. 4500: N. Streitz, A. Kameas, I. Mavrommati (Eds.), The Disappearing Computer. XVIII, 307 pages. 2007.

Vol. 4496: N.T. Nguyen, A. Grzech, R.J. Howlett, L.C. Jain (Eds.), Agent and Multi-Agent Systems: Technologies and Applications. XXI, 1046 pages. 2007. (Sublibrary LNAI).

Vol. 4493: D. Liu, S. Fei, Z. Hou, H. Zhang, C. Sun (Eds.), Advances in Neural Networks – ISNN 2007, Part III. XXVI, 1215 pages. 2007.

Vol. 4492: D. Liu, S. Fei, Z. Hou, H. Zhang, C. Sun (Eds.), Advances in Neural Networks – ISNN 2007, Part II. XXVII, 1321 pages. 2007.

Vol. 4491: D. Liu, S. Fei, Z.-G. Hou, H. Zhang, C. Sun (Eds.), Advances in Neural Networks – ISNN 2007, Part I. LIV, 1365 pages. 2007.

Vol. 4490: Y. Shi, G.D. van Albada, J. Dongarra, P.M.A. Sloot (Eds.), Computational Science – ICCS 2007, Part IV. XXXVII, 1211 pages. 2007.

Vol. 4489: Y. Shi, G.D. van Albada, J. Dongarra, P.M.A. Sloot (Eds.), Computational Science – ICCS 2007, Part III. XXXVII, 1257 pages. 2007.

Vol. 4488: Y. Shi, G.D. van Albada, J. Dongarra, P.M.A. Sloot (Eds.), Computational Science – ICCS 2007, Part II. XXXV, 1251 pages. 2007.

Vol. 4487: Y. Shi, G.D. van Albada, J. Dongarra, P.M.A. Sloot (Eds.), Computational Science – ICCS 2007, Part I. LXXXI, 1275 pages. 2007.

Vol. 4486: M. Bernardo, J. Hillston (Eds.), Formal Methods for Performance Evaluation. VII, 469 pages. 2007.

Vol. 4485: F. Sgallari, A. Murli, N. Paragios (Eds.), Scale Space Methods and Variational Methods in Computer Vision. XV, 931 pages. 2007.

Vol. 4484: J.-Y. Cai, S.B. Cooper, H. Zhu (Eds.), Theory and Applications of Models of Computation. XIII, 772 pages. 2007.

Vol. 4483: C. Baral, G. Brewka, J. Schlipf (Eds.), Logic Programming and Nonmonotonic Reasoning. IX, 327 pages. 2007. (Sublibrary LNAI).

Vol. 4482: A. An, J. Stefanowski, S. Ramanna, C.J. Butz, W. Pedrycz, G. Wang (Eds.), Rough Sets, Fuzzy Sets, Data Mining and Granular Computing. XIV, 585 pages. 2007. (Sublibrary LNAI).

Vol. 4481: J. Yao, P. Lingras, W.-Z. Wu, M. Szczuka, N.J. Cercone, D. Ślęzak (Eds.), Rough Sets and Knowledge Technology. XIV, 576 pages. 2007. (Sublibrary LNAI).

Vol. 4480: A. LaMarca, M. Langheinrich, K.N. Truong (Eds.), Pervasive Computing. XIII, 369 pages. 2007.

Vol. 4479: I.F. Akyildiz, R. Sivakumar, E. Ekici, J.C.d. Oliveira, J. McNair (Eds.), NETWORKING 2007. Ad Hoc and Sensor Networks, Wireless Networks, Next Generation Internet. XXVII, 1252 pages. 2007.

Vol. 4478: J. Martí, J.M. Benedí, A.M. Mendonça, J. Serrat (Eds.), Pattern Recognition and Image Analysis, Part II. XXVII, 657 pages. 2007.

Vol. 4477: J. Martí, J.M. Benedí, A.M. Mendonça, J. Serrat (Eds.), Pattern Recognition and Image Analysis, Part I. XXVII, 625 pages. 2007.

Vol. 4472: M. Haindl, J. Kittler, F. Roli (Eds.), Multiple Classifier Systems. XI, 524 pages. 2007.

Vol. 4471: P. Cesar, K. Chorianopoulos, J.F. Jensen (Eds.), Interactive TV: a Shared Experience. XIII, 236 pages. 2007.

Vol. 4470: Q. Wang, D. Pfahl, D.M. Raffo (Eds.), Software Process Dynamics and Agility. XI, 346 pages. 2007.

Vol. 4465: T. Chahed, B. Tuffin (Eds.), Network Control and Optimization. XIII, 305 pages. 2007.

Vol. 4464: E. Dawson, D.S. Wong (Eds.), Information Security Practice and Experience. XIII, 361 pages. 2007.

Vol. 4463: I. Măndoiu, A. Zelikovsky (Eds.), Bioinformatics Research and Applications. XV, 653 pages. 2007. (Sublibrary LNBI).

Vol. 4462: D. Sauveron, K. Markantonakis, A. Bilas, J.-J. Quisquater (Eds.), Information Security Theory and Practices. XII, 255 pages. 2007.

Vol. 4459: C. Cérin, K.-C. Li (Eds.), Advances in Grid and Pervasive Computing. XVI, 759 pages. 2007.

Vol. 4453: T. Speed, H. Huang (Eds.), Research in Computational Molecular Biology. XVI, 550 pages. 2007. (Sublibrary LNBI).

Vol. 4452: M. Fasli, O. Shehory (Eds.), Agent-Mediated Electronic Commerce. VIII, 249 pages. 2007. (Sublibrary LNAI).

Vol. 4451: T.S. Huang, A. Nijholt, M. Pantic, A. Pentland (Eds.), Artifical Intelligence for Human Computing. XVI, 359 pages. 2007. (Sublibrary LNAI).

Vol. 4450: T. Okamoto, X. Wang (Eds.), Public Key Cryptography – PKC 2007. XIII, 491 pages. 2007.

Vol. 4448: M. Giacobini et al. (Ed.), Applications of Evolutionary Computing. XXIII, 755 pages. 2007.

Vol. 4447: E. Marchiori, J.H. Moore, J.C. Rajapakse (Eds.), Evolutionary Computation,Machine Learning and Data Mining in Bioinformatics. XI, 302 pages. 2007.

Vol. 4446: C. Cotta, J. van Hemert (Eds.), Evolutionary Computation in Combinatorial Optimization. XII, 241 pages. 2007.

Vol. 4445: M. Ebner, M. O'Neill, A. Ekárt, L. Vanneschi, A.I. Esparcia-Alcázar (Eds.), Genetic Programming. XI, 382 pages. 2007.

Vol. 4444: T. Reps, M. Sagiv, J. Bauer (Eds.), Program Analysis and Compilation, Theory and Practice. X, 361 pages. 2007.

Vol. 4443: R. Kotagiri, P.R. Krishna, M. Mohania, E. Nantjeewarawat (Eds.), Advances in Databases: Concepts, Systems and Applications. XXI, 1126 pages. 2007.

Vol. 4440: B. Liblit, Cooperative Bug Isolation. XV, 101 pages. 2007.

Vol. 4439: W. Abramowicz (Ed.), Business Information Systems. XV, 654 pages. 2007.

Vol. 4438: L. Maicher, A. Sigel, L.M. Garshol (Eds.), Leveraging the Semantics of Topic Maps. X, 257 pages. 2007. (Sublibrary LNAI).

Vol. 4433: E. Şahin, W.M. Spears, A.F.T. Winfield (Eds.), Swarm Robotics. XII, 221 pages. 2007.

Vol. 4432: B. Beliczynski, A. Dzielinski, M. Iwanowski, B. Ribeiro (Eds.), Adaptive and Natural Computing Algorithms, Part II. XXVI, 761 pages. 2007.

Vol. 4431: B. Beliczynski, A. Dzielinski, M. Iwanowski, B. Ribeiro (Eds.), Adaptive and Natural Computing Algorithms, Part I. XXV, 851 pages. 2007.

Vol. 4430: C.C. Yang, D. Zeng, M. Chau, K. Chang, Q. Yang, X. Cheng, J. Wang, F.-Y. Wang, H. Chen (Eds.), Intelligence and Security Informatics. XII, 330 pages. 2007.

Vol. 4429: R. Lu, J.H. Siekmann, C. Ullrich (Eds.), Cognitive Systems. X, 161 pages. 2007. (Sublibrary LNAI).

Vol. 4427: S. Uhlig, K. Papagiannaki, O. Bonaventure (Eds.), Passive and Active Network Measurement. XI, 274 pages. 2007.

Vol. 4426: Z.-H. Zhou, H. Li, Q. Yang (Eds.), Advances in Knowledge Discovery and Data Mining. XXV, 1161 pages. 2007. (Sublibrary LNAI).

Vol. 4425: G. Amati, C. Carpineto, G. Romano (Eds.), Advances in Information Retrieval. XIX, 759 pages. 2007.

Vol. 4424: O. Grumberg, M. Huth (Eds.), Tools and Algorithms for the Construction and Analysis of Systems. XX, 738 pages. 2007.

Vol. 4423: H. Seidl (Ed.), Foundations of Software Science and Computational Structures. XVI, 379 pages. 2007.

Vol. 4422: M.B. Dwyer, A. Lopes (Eds.), Fundamental Approaches to Software Engineering. XV, 440 pages. 2007.

Vol. 4421: R. De Nicola (Ed.), Programming Languages and Systems. XVII, 538 pages. 2007.

Vol. 4420: S. Krishnamurthi, M. Odersky (Eds.), Compiler Construction. XIV, 233 pages. 2007.

Vol. 4419: P.C. Diniz, E. Marques, K. Bertels, M.M. Fernandes, J.M.P. Cardoso (Eds.), Reconfigurable Computing: Architectures, Tools and Applications. XIV, 391 pages. 2007.

Vol. 4418: A. Gagalowicz, W. Philips (Eds.), Computer Vision/Computer Graphics Collaboration Techniques. XV, 620 pages. 2007.

Vol. 4416: A. Bemporad, A. Bicchi, G. Buttazzo (Eds.), Hybrid Systems: Computation and Control. XVII, 797 pages. 2007.

Vol. 4415: P. Lukowicz, L. Thiele, G. Tröster (Eds.), Architecture of Computing Systems - ARCS 2007. X, 297 pages. 2007.

Vol. 4414: S. Hochreiter, R. Wagner (Eds.), Bioinformatics Research and Development. XVI, 482 pages. 2007. (Sublibrary LNBI).

Vol. 4412: F. Stajano, H.J. Kim, J.-S. Chae, S.-D. Kim (Eds.), Ubiquitous Convergence Technology. XI, 302 pages. 2007.

Vol. 4411: R.H. Bordini, M. Dastani, J. Dix, A.E.F. Seghrouchni (Eds.), Programming Multi-Agent Systems. XIV, 249 pages. 2007. (Sublibrary LNAI).

Vol. 4410: A. Branco (Ed.), Anaphora: Analysis, Algorithms and Applications. X, 191 pages. 2007. (Sublibrary LNAI).

Vol. 4409: J.L. Fiadeiro, P.-Y. Schobbens (Eds.), Recent Trends in Algebraic Development Techniques. VII, 171 pages. 2007.

Vol. 4407: G. Puebla (Ed.), Logic-Based Program Synthesis and Transformation. VIII, 237 pages. 2007.

Vol. 4406: W. De Meuter (Ed.), Advances in Smalltalk. VII, 157 pages. 2007.

Vol. 4405: L. Padgham, F. Zambonelli (Eds.), Agent-Oriented Software Engineering VII. XII, 225 pages. 2007.